THE OPTION PLAYER'S
ADVANCED
GUIDEBOOK

TURNING THE TABLES
ON THE OPTIONS MARKETS

Kenneth R. Trester

Illustrations by Timothy Sheppard

InvesTrek★
Publishing
Costa Mesa, California

ALSO BY KENNETH R. TRESTER

THE COMPLEAT OPTION PLAYER

Library of Congress Catalog Number: 80-83175
ISBN 0-9604914-1-4

To Merle and Olivia, who provided the magic touches to the manuscript

To my father and mother, Clifford and Violet, who gave me the spirit and substance

. . . and, finally, to the computer, whose innovation and technology made this book possible before its time . . .

Contents

Sit back and enjoy an exciting investment journey into the future

Chapter I

A Journey Into The Future

Wouldn't it be great if you could look into a crystal ball and discover the future that an investment holds? Wouldn't it be wonderful to know before you purchased an option what its value would be the day that it expired? Wouldn't it be fantastic if you could enter a spread or a combination or a straddle and know when you enter that position whether or not it would be profitable? The fantasies that we have just mentioned have been converted into reality in this text.

The objective of this book is to provide the option player with information and tools that go far beyond what is available in the options community today.

USING THE SCIENCE OF *COMPUTER SIMULATION*, WE ARE ABLE TO PEEK INTO THE FUTURE AND VIEW WHAT THE FUTURE HOLDS FOR ALL TYPES OF OPTIONS INVESTMENTS.

The tools and information in this book are in the form of easy-to-read tables that can be referenced in a few seconds. These are not ordinary tables; they are the tables of the *future*. You will be able to determine before you buy or write an option what the long term intrinsic value of that option will be when it expires. You will be able to do the same with a straddle or a combination. You will be able to determine within a few seconds whether or not a calendar spread that you are studying will have profit potential when the strategy expires.

These tables will stack the odds in your favor in the options game. Each table, combined with the other unique information in this book, will insure that you enter inherently profitable strategies every time. Each time you enter a strategy, *the odds of winning will be in your favor.*

But we are not finished yet; our time machine will whisk you into the future to determine what the *high price* of a put or a call will likely be in the future. Our time machine will also journey into the future to develop tools for one of the most popular sports in the options arena, covered option writing. Our visit to view the future of covered option writing strategies will expose some shocking and revealing information.

To unlock these many treasures, you must carefully read and digest the concepts presented in the first series of chapters. The concepts of *future value* and *inherent profitability* (Chapter 3) must be understood before you can properly use the tables in this text.

In the process of opening the door to the future, you must not only absorb the unique information that is provided, but you must also develop the intangible qualities that separate the winner from the loser. We could place all the tools and information that you need to win decisively in the options game on a silver platter, but even then, the majority of option players would be losers. As in any game, in order to win, you must have the proper attitude, the proper temperament, and the necessary professionalism to gain that winning edge. Several segments of this book are dedicated to providing you with the winning philosophy and viewpoint necessary to fully use and optimize the tools and strategies that are presented.

THE OPTION PLAYER'S ADVANCED GUIDEBOOK has been designed for the option player who has some options experience. The terminology and concepts presented are an extension of my previous book, THE COMPLEAT OPTION PLAYER. Rather than emphasize advance mechanics of the options markets, THE ADVANCED GUIDEBOOK provides the investor with a rare and unique look into the future of his options investment.

So, snap on your seat belt and prepare for a very exciting and rewarding journey into the future!

Chapter 2

Play Them As They Lay

Since their first opening in 1973, the listed stock options markets have undergone numerous changes — not in basics, but in behavior. Some strategies that were successful in 1973 and 1974 are *not* successful today. Widely publicized *covered option writing* has moved at times from being profitable to unprofitable and back again to a profitable mode of investment. The environment keeps changing; one moment one strategy is successful, and then another variable enters the picture, and former strategies begin to generate losses. The challenge for the sophisticated professional is to identify the proper strategy and to implement it correctly in today's dynamic market.

The Outside Influences

The profitability of specific option strategies is under the influence of many external factors. The two most important factors that have had tremendous bearing upon the profitability of different types of option investment modes have been:

1. The Institutions
2. Interest Rates

Institutional investors have begun to enter the options markets with far greater frequency. Their presence has at times depressed option premiums, especially on those common stocks that are excellent candidates for covered option writing. However, a counter influence has also unexpectedly entered the options market, and that influence is *interest rates*. Interest rates moved up dramatically in 1979 and 1980, and the result was extremely high prices for both put and call options. Option premiums rose far above their average historical prices. The average six month at-the-money call option on the Chicago Board Options Exchange (CBOE) rose above 14% of the value of the underlying stock.

This rollercoaster activity in the options markets made it almost impossible for the static one-strategy option player to survive. At one moment one option investment mode was highly profitable, while at other times another option investment mode became highly profitable. These outside factors and their significant impact on the options markets demonstrate the importance of flexibility and the ability to *play them as they lay*.

Maintaining Flexibility In Changing Markets

In order to prosper — that is to generate long-term profitability — the option player must play the strategies that are out-of-line. For instance:

The times when the *writing* (selling) of options, either covered or naked, becomes the winning strategy is WHEN OPTION PREMIUMS ARE EXTREMELY *HIGH* due to high interest rates or tremendous activity in the market.

The times when the *buying* of options and option buying strategies are the way to profit is WHEN OPTION PRICES ARE *HIGHLY DEPRESSED* due to the influence of institutional covered writing, a nomad market, or a bear market.

13

In the next chapter through the introduction of the concept of "inherent profitability," you will learn how to identify options or option strategies that are substantially out-of-line.

Play them as they lay and you will score with options

Chapter 3

Scoring With Options

What are the keys to success in the options game? Trading ability, good technical analysis, good intuitive ability, and patience — all are key factors in being successful. But they are not the total answer.

The Hidden Key To Success

In the options game the *hidden* key to success is the ability to select options and option strategies that contain *inherent profitability*. What does "inherent profitability" mean? The term refers to the *quality* of the option vehicle:*

> An option strategy has INHERENT PROFITABILITY when it would be PROFITABLE in the LONG RUN assuming RANDOM STOCK PRICE ACTION.†

---

*The term option vehicle refers to an option strategy that is designed to take advantage of potential underlying stock price action.

†In reference to random stock price action — throughout this text we assume that the underlying common stock price approaches randomness. This assumption is made in order to provide a basis for comparison and to provide a well documented premise for the design and selection of option strategies. The question of whether or not stock prices are random has been debated for decades. The academic studies in favor of random prices are quite convincing. In addition there is sufficient evidence to indicate that a large majority of investors are unable to correctly predict stock price action; even professionals have trouble predicting stock prices, at least in the short run. You may know where the stock price will move in the future, but assuming a random market when selecting option vehicles provides insurance just in case you are wrong.

15

When we refer to "profitable in the long run," we refer to a positive average return per position if the identical strategy were entered thousands of times. Even though *long run* may seem somewhat obscure, the *average return* for each individual strategy is like the house odds in a casino. If an options strategy has inherent profitability, the *average return* is positive, and the option player who enters such strategies takes on the role of the casino that will eventually win all of the chips after many plays. The player who selects strategies that lack inherent profitability (that would show a negative long run *average return*) is playing the fool and bucking the house odds.

How To Measure The Inherent Profitability Of An Option

An option normally is inherently profitable (showing a positive average return) when it is either overpriced or underpriced according to its *future value*.

> **FUTURE VALUE: THE INTRINSIC VALUE THAT AN OPTION WILL HOLD WHEN IT EXPIRES**

For example, if an IBM July 60 call option has the following market price and *future value*, an option buying strategy would have inherent profitability:

```
IBM call
Future Value at expiration..........................$300
Market price........................................ − 200
The inherent profitability of buying the option is........$100
```

Current Means Of Option Price Evaluation

Presently the most popular means of determining whether an option is over or underpriced is through the use of evaluation models such as the Black and Scholes model. In my previous book, THE COMPLEAT OPTION PLAYER, an extensive number of Normal Pricing Charts are provided, giving you a weekly evaluation of what an option price should be. These prices were generated by studies of what actually occurred in the market in the past. Normal prices are prices that exist in the market place. They are a measure of where the market will set the price; however, they do not tell you whether or not the option price reflects the *future* price when the option expires.

The Future Value *Must* Be Uncovered

Normal does not mean *profitable*; it only means that the market should value that option at that price under prevailing market conditions. What is needed is a clear picture of the *future value (not the market value)* of an option or option strategy. That *future value* will then display whether the prevailing market price of an option will really be profitable in the long run for the buyer or for the writer.

How To Measure The Future Value Of An Option

The "Any Horse in a Barn" Approach
The amateur in the options game usually ignores the quality of the option vehicle. He takes the "any horse in a barn will do" approach to selecting an option or an option strategy. His major concern is with the underlying stock price.

For example — we have seen this many times — an investor gets very excited about the potential action of a stock price, such as a gold mining common stock when gold is zooming upwards into the stratosphere. He is so excited about this common stock that he blindly grabs any call option that is available to him, regardless of the option price. He totally ignores other dimensions of the strategy and blindly dives into the position, hoping to take further advantage of the stock price action. Sometimes he gets lucky, but most of the time he pays the consequences.

The Intuitive Approach
Many professionals are able to determine what the *future value* of an option will be intuitively. They select option strategies and option vehicles that through their own experience

17

The novice investor blindly takes the "any horse in a barn will do" approach to selecting option strategies.

are good percentage bets to be profitable. Maybe not this time, but over ten, fifteen or twenty positions, they know the end result will be profitable. Surprisingly they are far more concerned with the price of the option or the option strategy than with the anticipated future price action of the underlying common stock.

The Scientific Approach

A much more scientific and accurate method of measuring an option's *future value* is to use *computer simulation* (see Chapter 5). The computer is able to peek into the future and to ignore factors that mislead the option investor.

IN THE SECOND PART OF THIS BOOK, YOU ARE PROVIDED WITH MORE THAN 130 COMPUTER GENERATED TABLES THAT WILL ENABLE YOU TO SELECT THE *OPTIMUM* OPTION VEHICLE BY DISPLAYING THE *FUTURE VALUE* OF THESE OPTION STRATEGIES.

THESE TABLES WILL TELL YOU WHETHER THE OP-
TION STRATEGIES YOU ARE CONSIDERING HAVE *IN-
HERENT PROFITABILITY.*

The Role Of Stock Price Action

One of the major errors made by most option players is to attach far too much weight to the underlying common stock price action with far too little consideration given to the selection of the option vehicle. The potential underlying stock price action may be an important consideration to the selection of an option strategy, but once you have identified a *playable stock*, you must find a *playable option.*

To score in the options game, the option vehicles that are selected must be priced to pay off more frequently than would normally occur and should not require optimum stock price action (when the stock price does exactly what you want it to) in order to do so. The option professional who is frequently in the winner's circle is one who always selects option strategies that hold inherent profitability up and *beyond* the potential price action of the underlying common stock. Using this tactic you will be able to score decisively with options.

The next chapter evaluates the efficiency of the options markets today. A close look at that chapter will show that there are always plenty of option strategies available which have *inherent profitability.*

20

Chapter 4

There's Gold In Them Thar Hills!

There *is* gold in the hills and valleys of the options exchanges, gold in the form of highly overpriced and highly underpriced option strategies. Your major task is to uncover the bargains that lie in those hills and valleys.

> *The tools and tables in this book will uncover these hidden golden option opportunities by displaying the FUTURE VALUE of all types of option strategies.*

The Question of Market Efficiency

In order to do this, we must dismiss some of the fallacies that so called experts are circulating through the options community, the major one being that the options markets are efficient. Many critics and observers consider the options markets to be quite efficient, efficient in that few option prices are out-of-line. They say that when option prices do become over or underpriced, immediate adjustments are made so that the average investor can rarely take advantage, and only the market makers or specialists can profit.

The Truth — What Is!

Some observations should make it clear that the options markets are *not* efficient; many option prices are out of line *much of the time.* Most option price adjustments are made according to mathematical models that do not measure the *future value* of an option. They only measure what the market has set prices at in the past under prevailing conditions.

Evidence: The Factors That Don't Count

Let's look at a few facts that will demonstrate that the presently accepted studies on the true market value of an option do not indicate the real long term *future value* of an option. The *future value* of an option is dependent upon a single factor:

The price action of the underlying common stock within the set period of time that option lives.

Most mathematical models use other factors that tell you the market value of the option. For example, in determining the price that the option should be set at, they may include interest rates. Yet, although they could strongly influence the market price of the option, interest rates should have little or no influence on the *future value* of an option.

Evidence: The High Interest Rate Distortion

An interesting development that occurred in 1979 and 1980 was very *high* interest rates. These interest rates created very high time values* for options, in fact, time values that were higher than expected from the prevailing models that are used to evaluate options. These interest rates drove up the price of call options, yet the options' *future values* still were unchanged. The only way that the *future value* could change would be if these high interest rates stimulated a much larger increase in the price of the underlying stock prices, but evidence of such price increases does not exist. Not only did these high premiums occur in calls, but also in puts due to conversion activities on the exchange floors.

---

*Time Value is what the market thinks the intrinsic value will be at some time in the future before the option expires. Time value is determined by subtracting the intrinsic value from the option price. The intrinsic value is the real value of an option if it is exercised. Refer to Chapter 4 of THE COMPLEAT OPTION PLAYER.

Evidence: A Fluctuating Market

The familiar comment that the market is efficient and prices options at the right price can be further invalidated by looking at the CBOE TIME VALUE INDEX of ninety-five underlying common stocks for six month at-the-money call options shown in Table I. This Index began in 1977, and for the three years from 1977 to 1980, this Time Value Index fluctuated from a low

Table 1
The CBOE Time Value Index
Versus
The Dow Jones Industrial Average

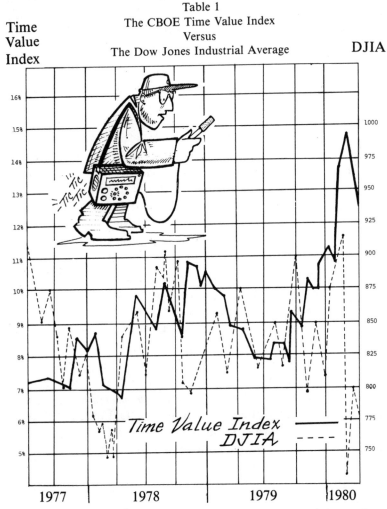

The CBOE Time Value Index is a percentage measure of the market time value of 95 hypothetical 6 month at-the-money calls to the underlying stocks.

23

of 6.7% in 1977 to a high of over 14% in 1980. How can an options market be efficient when its prices are so varied from month to month and from year to year? How can options premiums that have a 6.7% time value at one point in time and over 14% in time value at another time be properly priced?

The only way this could be possible is if option values predicted the future price action of the underlying common stock. If you look closely at this period of time, you will notice that fluctuations in the time value have no correlation at all to the future price action of the underlying common stock.

The Question: To Be Or Not To Be Out-Of-Line

So if we gather all the facts, we discover that option prices in the market are determined by many factors. Interest rates, the psychology of the people in the market, and the movements in the market all have an important influence on the prevailing market price of an option. BUT, and this is a very big *but*, they may not influence the *future value* of the option. Only the future price action of the underlying stock will determine the *future value* of the option. Therefore, option prices in the market may *not* be out-of-line with the mathematical models that determine that they should be at those price levels. However, they could be *way* out-of-line with their *future value*. Consequently, the professional player must know what the *future value* of an option is, and much of this book is dedicated to accomplishing that task.

Now don't throw away your Normal Value Option Tables (See THE COMPLEAT OPTION PLAYER) or whatever other technique you use to determine the *market value* of options. They are excellent guideposts that are crucial in the mapping out of strategies and in the measuring of potential profits and losses if the common stock price moves accordingly. They may not depict the *future value* of an option, but they do depict the prevailing market prices, and the profits for many strategies are dependent upon these prices.

On the other hand, some other method of valuing options is necessary in order to tell you before you enter an option strategy the long run future profitability of that strategy. We want to know the *future value* of an option, not a value based on external market conditions. Once the *future value* is determined, you will be able to find the *gold in them thar hills*.

Computer simulation discloses the future intrinsic value of an option

Chapter 5

The Miracle Of The Computer

The Magic Of Computer Simulation

How do you look into a crystal ball and pull out the *future value* of an option or an option strategy? Of course, you use a computer. In order to measure the *future value* of an option, you must know where the stock price will end up when the option expires. To do this, we made use of the art and science of *computer simulation*. Computer simulation is a method of acting out the future in advance. With the speed of the computer, thousands of years of time can be simulated in a matter of hours. Our landing on the moon was made possible by computer simulation. Now computer simulation is providing breakthroughs in other areas of decision making, for by simulating thousands of years of time in a brief span, we can make far more intelligent decisions. We are able to literally look into the future and see what is going to occur.

In the process of designing our option market simulations, we were required to make some assumptions.

27

Assumptions

A Random Market

The major assumption is that common stock prices move in a random fashion. There is much controversy regarding this subject, but several studies indicate common stock prices do approach randomness at least in the short term, and when we are working with options, we are definitely working in the *short* term. Also due to the sophistication of the market system, the majority of investors should treat the market as a random animal. A little knowledge is far more dangerous than none at all.

With extensive experience the scene changes. The highly experienced and talented stock market trader alters the random aspect of the stock market into one that can be predicted with proper homework. Even then, the stock price action may not be totally predictable. The assumption that the market moves randomly provides a starting point to develop trading tools that can be used by all players.

Therefore, we simulated stock prices at different levels of volatility assuming a random market for thousands of years of time. The model was designed to determine the *future value* of options at each stage of their life cycle and at each stock price. Models were also developed for other option strategies, including the calendar spread, the straddle, the combination (naked spread), and covered option writing. Several other tools were developed through the simulations and will be presented in future chapters.

Most of these results and tools are laid out in table form for your convenience and quick reference. The author finds tables the easiest and fastest way to find and display information. In fact in many cases, when you consider the number of manual (typing action) steps required to call for data from a computer information system, tables can be referred to faster than a computer can return its information to the user.

Hold Until Expiration

The second assumption used in most of the simulations was that the option or option strategy would be held until it expired. The whole premise of most of the simulations was to measure the *future intrinsic value* of options or option strategies when their life was over, rather than merely gauging the present market value as offered in existing evaluation models. Through these simulations, then, we could discover critical information presently unknown in the options community

Mind-Boggling Results

The results of our simulations are quite mind-boggling. They will give you a totally new look at the true value of an option or an option strategy and provide you with new insight into the options game. These revelations will furnish you with unique information and tools available *only* to the readers of this text! You will receive a tremendous edge in this game, one that will separate you from the rest of the crowd. Your challenge now is to develop the skill to understand and utilize the tools and tables provided in the second part of this book. Before you can accomplish that task, you must uncover the secret of the *future value* of an option strategy. That secret is disclosed in the next chapter.

Chapter 6

The Name Of The Game Is Volatility

The Secret Of Future Value

In the process of simulating stock price action and the resulting behavior in the options markets, we discovered some fascinating facts; the major one is that volatility plays a far more important role than was previously indicated. The future profitability of an option is strongly related to the true *volatility* of its underlying common stock price. The ability to estimate that volatility will enable you to come close to measuring the *future value* of a specific stock option or option strategy.

The Different Levels

As you gaze over the many tables that are represented in this book, you will notice the tremendous difference between option prices at different levels of volatility. We have broken down common stock price volatility into three specific levels:

```
THE LEVELS OF VOLATILITY
LOW VOLATILITY
AVERAGE VOLATILITY
HIGH VOLATILITY
```

Therefore, your ability to target in on common stocks that you are playing in one of these categories will optimize the use of the tools we have provided. Volatility is far more important to an option player than to an investor in the stock market. The big trick is not to measure *present* volatility, but to project *future* volatility. However, we can approach that task by measuring the volatility of stock prices in the past.

Some Measuring Devices

In the measurement process there are several tools that you can look at, including the "Beta Factor." The Beta Factor, a method of evaluating the stock price movement of a specific stock as compared to the whole market, is probably one of the most well known of all the volatility measurement devices. However, because the option player needs a more concrete, well defined way of measuring volatility, the Beta Factor has limited value. In my book, THE COMPLEAT OPTION PLAYER, we provide a simple formula that gives you a concrete stock price volatility measure. For your convenience it is repeated in Figure I.

To make things even easier, we have developed a special aid, the Volatility Measurement Table, Page 32, which will enable you to determine the volatility of a common stock in a few seconds without going through the formula or working out some other elaborate means of measuring volatility. This particular table will be invaluable as you use the other tables in this book to determine the profitability of option vehicles, prices, and strategies.

Figure 1

$$\text{VOLATILITY} = \frac{\text{12 MONTH STOCK PRICE RANGE}}{\text{Average 12 Month Stock Price}}$$

or, in algebraic terms:

$$\text{VOLATILITY} = \frac{\text{STOCK HIGH} - \text{STOCK LOW}}{(\text{Stock High} + \text{Stock Low})/2}$$

Table 2
The Volatility Measurement Table

		The Common Stock's High Price																	
		$5	10	15	20	25	30	35	40	45	50	55	60	65	70	75	80	85	90	95
	$5	0%	66%	99%	99%	99%	99%	99%	99%	99%	99%	99%	99%	99%	99%	99%	99%	99%	99%	99%
	10		0%	40%	66%	85%	99%	99%	99%	99%	99%	99%	99%	99%	99%	99%	99%	99%	99%	99%
	15			0%	28%	50%	66%	80%	90%	99%	99%	99%	99%	99%	99%	99%	99%	99%	99%	99%
	20				0%	22%	40%	54%	66%	76%	85%	93%	99%	99%	99%	99%	99%	99%	99%	99%
	25					0%	18%	33%	46%	57%	66%	75%	82%	88%	94%	99%	99%	99%	99%	99%
	30						0%	15%	28%	40%	50%	58%	66%	73%	80%	85%	90%	95%	99%	99%
The	35							0%	13%	25%	35%	44%	52%	60%	66%	72%	78%	83%	88%	92%
Common	40								0%	11%	22%	31%	40%	47%	54%	60%	66%	72%	76%	81%
Stock's	45									0%	10%	20%	28%	36%	43%	50%	56%	61%	66%	71%
Low	50										0%	9. %	18%	26%	33%	40%	46%	51%	57%	62%
Price	55											0%	8. %	16%	24%	30%	37%	42%	48%	53%
	60												0%	8%	15%	22%	28%	34%	40%	45%
	65													0%	7. %	14%	20%	26%	32%	37%
	70														0%	6. %	13%	19%	25%	30%
	75															0%	6. %	12%	18%	23%
	80																0%	6. %	11%	17%
	85																	0%	5. %	11%
	90																		0%	5. %
	95																			0%

Volatility levels which show 99%, represent volatility levels which are over 100%. Refer to Figure I to determine the exact volatility percentage.

32

Watch For The Percentage Move

In the process of measuring volatility, we are concerned with the potential percentage move that the stock will make above its average price for the year, and the percentage move below its average price for the year. For example, let's theoretically say that last year Ford's common stock price was at a high of $50 a share and at a low of $30 a share. By looking quickly at the Volatility Measurement Table, Page   32, we will find that the percentage of volatility as measured by our formula is 50%. Now, the 50% figure is determined by plugging in the high and low for the year to the formula in Figure 1, or see Table 2. 50% volatility means that the Ford common stock price moved 25% *above* its average price and 25% *below* its average price.

(Average price = ((High Price + Low Price)/2))

So the volatility we are looking for is a measurement of the range of the stock price from its high price to its low price.

Once you have determined the past volatility percentage for the year, you must look to the future. The many sets of pricing tables in this book are based on *future* volatility. So now your task is not to measure past volatility, but to come up with the magic figure that will indicate the volatility of that stock price for the next year.

Predicting Future Volatility

Predicting the volatility of a common stock price is just like predicting stock price action; the same types of procedures and approaches should be taken. Let's discuss then some of the methods you can use for predicting stock price volatility for the coming year. They will be the volatility figures you will need if you are going to get a really clear picture of the profitability of your option strategies. Those already skilled in the task of projecting the future stock price action can move on to the next section, although a good review never hurts.

33

The Naive Approach

The naive approach, believe it or not, is probably the best approach for the individual who is not a skilled technician or doesn't want to get into the complexities of the predicting game. The naive approach means that if it rains today, it will rain tomorrow. In other words, whatever happened today will happen tomorrow. This technique may not be the most scientific method for predicting the future, but, believe it or not, the volatility of common stock prices usually is quite consistent over the years. If the volatility of Xerox was in the range of 30% last year, the odds are it will approach the 30% range this year. Look at the volatility for last year, and you will probably target in on the volatility range of a common stock price for the next year.

Following the Trend

In determining future volatility, a more scientific approach is to evaluate the trend of volatility for the common stock price. In some cases the common stock price will become more and more volatile or less and less volatile as the years go by. For example, some of the aggressive growth stocks of the '60's have turned into slow performing Blue Chip stocks in the '70's, while energy and the basic industry stocks became quite volatile in the '70's, when their previous history showed little volatility. To identify these changes, you might want to map out the percentage volatility for a common stock price over a set number of years. An easy approach is to use Table 2 and develop a graph to track the trends developing in the volatility of specific stocks.

Average Volatility

Another simple method to predict future volatility is to look at the yearly volatility of the stock price for the past several years, and then determine the *average* volatility over those years and use that figure to project future volatility. Although averages can be an effective way to estimate future volatility, they can mask violent changes in volatility from year to year and should be used with caution.

Other Insights on Stock Price Volatility

Another method of measuring future volatility is to look not at the stocks themselves, but at the stock markets and to make some estimates of what you project the specific volatility of these markets to be in the future. Also, different industries have different volatility tendencies. Some industries create far more news events which generate more stock price action.

Finally in measuring the potential volatility of a stock price, you should determine if there are any new events or changes, such as structural changes in an organization. This includes any changes in the company's fortunes or any radical changes in the way investors view a company. For example, today energy and gold stocks are looked at far more differently than they were ten or fifteen years ago, and consequently, their volatility pictures have changed dramatically.

The Importance of Predicting Future Volatility

Why go through all this trouble to measure volatility? Is it really worth all the effort to sit down and carry out these projection techniques to find out what the future volatility of a stock will be?

Your time spent will generate big dividends. The value of the options you purchase, the options you write, or the option strategies that you enter are highly dependent upon the volatility of the underlying common stock prices. In many cases it is far more important to project the volatility of a common stock price than to project the specific common stock price action, although they are very much intertwined. If you catch on to a common stock price that is going to make some big fluctuations in the next few months, your accuracy in pinpointing where it will go is far less important than predicting its volatility, for one leap in the right direction could make you some fantastic profits. At other times, when your strategy is dependent upon a stock price that hardly moves at all, mis-estimating its volatility could be highly damaging to the strategies you enter.

The art of projecting future volatility is largely ignored or taken for granted in the options market. Investors disregard this factor when they should be sitting down and doing a little extra homework to really key in on the true *future* volatility of their underlying stock prices.

Now this task is made easier, since with the tables in this text you only need to predict the volatility of an underlying stock price in one of three categories (high, average and low volatility). With a little practice and using the techniques we have presented in this chapter, you will come close to nailing down the future volatility of a stock price. In this way you will make the best use of the many tools and tactics in this book.

Volatility unlocks the treasures of the computer allowing the option player to travel into the future to view the intrinsic value of his option strategies.

Chapter 7

Unlocking The Treasures Of The Computer

The time has come to unlock and use the treasures of the computer. The Call and Put Pricing Tables, which begin on Page T2, will reveal the *future value* of put and call options. They will indicate what an option is truly worth in the long run if it is held to expiration.

The Key To Unlocking The Treasures

As revealed in Chapter 6, volatility is critical in determining the *future value* of an option. Therefore, your first task is to determine the volatility of the underlying common stock price that you are considering before you hit our tables. The previous chapter does an excellent job of providing guidelines in determining the future volatility. If you are not quite clear regarding the concepts presented in the previous chapter, reread it. Practice making volatility determinations; attempt to target in on the future volatility of specific common stocks.

Volatility Classifications

Now the intriguing part of using these treasures will be encountered, and that is — how do you read the tables? How do you properly evaluate the *future value* of an option? First look over the tables that begin on Page T1. You will notice that each exercise price for each put and call option has three potential volatility levels:

- *HIGH* volatility in these tables is the classification for underlying common stocks whose prices are targeted for a 40% to a 60% volatility range over the next year.
- *AVERAGE* volatility is the category for common stocks that are projected to hold a volatility rating of 23% to 39% over the next year.
- *LOW* volatility prices are designed for common stocks whose prices will fluctuate within a 5% to a 22% range over the next year.

To summarize the three volatility categories:

High Volatility   =   40% to 60%
Average Volatility =   23% to 39%
Low Volatility   =   5% to 22%

The volatility percentage is derived from the formula in Figure I, Page 31 or by projecting the stock price high and low for the year and going to Table 2 (Chapter 6).

Using The Options Tables

The best way to demonstrate the use of the tables is to take a few theoretical examples, and use the tables to identify the *future value* of each of the options.

Example I:

Consider the example of the Xerox July 50 call option. The following information has been generated by your own homework on this common stock:

Option Exercise Price.................................50
Projected Volatility of Underlying Stock Price...........30%
Price of Xerox Common Stock.........................48

Current Month.....................................April
Option Expiration Month............................July
Time Remaining in Option's Life.................3 months

The Xerox stock volatility of 30% indicates that we use the "Average" volatility portion of our tables. The table on Page T11 shows the call option prices when the exercise price is 50. Checking the tables where the stock price is 48, with average volatility and three months left before expiration, shows that the *future value* of the call option is 0.8.

```
CALL PRICING TABLE
Exercise Price is 50
Average Volatility
```

Stock Price	Number of Months Before the Options Expire								
	1	2	3	4	5	6	7	8	9
48	0.2	0.6	0.8	1.1	1.3	1.4	1.5	1.7	1.8

The price of 0.8 is $80 per option, or close to 13/16 in the market. If the market price is significantly over 13/16, the option would be a candidate for option writing. A price below 13/16 might be considered for option buying strategies. Remember, these values are the *future value* in the long run — based on the random movement of the stock price. Your technical and fundamental analysis of the underlying stock prices should color the manner in which you view these *future values*.

Example II:

Now let's use the tables to measure the *future value* of a put option. Look at the theoretical data for the Exxon January 70 put.

Option Exercise Price................................70
Projected Volatility of Underlying Stock Price..........45%
Price of Exxon Common Stock........................73
Current Month.................................August
Option Expiration Month........................January
Time Remaining in Option's Life.................5 months

The Exxon stock price volatility of 45% places the stock in the "High" volatility category. Referring to Page T35, you find the future value of the Exxon January 70 put is 4.4 or close to 4½.

PUT PRICING TABLE
Exercise Price is 70
High Volatility

Stock Price	Number of Months before the Options Expire								
	1	2	3	4	5	6	7	8	9
73	1.2	2.3	3.1	3.9	4.4	4.7	5.1	5.6	6.2

In dollar and cents terms, a January 70 put has a future long-term value of $440.

Some additional examples are provided for those who are still having difficulty reading the tables. After a little practice, reading these tables can be accomplished with great ease.

Example III:

Let's evaluate the Houston Oil April 25 call option, using the Future Value Call Pricing Tables.

Option Exercise Price..................................25
Projected Volatility of Underlying Stock Price...........45%
Price of Houston Oil Common Stock.....................20
Current Month......................................October
Option Expiration Month...........................April
Time Remaining in Option's life..................6 months

Page T6 shows the *future value* of the Houston Oil April 25 call at the "High" volatility level. The *future value* is .6, or very close to ⅝. In other words, a Houston Oil April 25 call for 100 shares has a *future value* of $60.

Example IV:
Finally, let's look at an in-the-money put using the General Motors June 50 put and the Future Value Put Pricing Tables:

40

Option Exercise Price................................50
Projected Volatility of Underlying Stock Price...........18%
Price of General Motors Common Stock.................49
Current Month....................................April
Option Expiration Month..........................June
Time Remaining in Option's Life.................2 months

Page T31 shows the *future value* of the General Motors June 50 put is 1.4, or about 1-7/16 — in dollar terms, $140 per option.

Additional Hints And Suggestions For Using the Future Value Tables

• When buying or writing an option, the Put and Call Pricing Tables provide the *breakeven point* in the purchase or writing decision. Therefore, to purchase or write options at the price in the tables will only result in *breaking even* before commissions. Consequently,

ALL *PURCHASES* SHOULD BE MADE *BELOW* THE PRICE INDICATED;

ALL WRITERS SHOULD *SELL* OPTIONS *ABOVE* THE PRICE INDICATED.

• Commissions are not included in any of the tables in this book because they will vary dramatically depending on which broker you use and the size of your order. However, even though commissions are not included, they *must* be incorporated in the decision making process.

• The tables in this book measure the *future value* of options and option strategies, *not* the *market* value. The market value is an important measure in determining bail-out points or target profits and returns. Use the Normal Value Option Tables (as

41

provided in THE COMPLEAT OPTION PLAYER) along with these Future Value Tables to properly select, design and implement your strategies.

• All of the computer generated tables in this book assume a random market. Therefore, your own analysis of stock price action is an important input to the way that you view the Future Value Tables.

• The Future Value Option Tables in this book are based on runs of thousands of years of simulated time. The results in the tables are then based on the *long run*. Short term results could be dramatically different. Therefore, your patience and homework are important keys to success.

• The *future value* of options as measured in the many tables in this book is the *intrinsic* value of the options when they *expire*. The option buyer can purchase options above these *future values* and still profit if he takes profits (when available) before the options expire. The High Price Tables discussed in the next chapter and the Appendix will help you to measure the risks and rewards of such an approach. However, when you buy options above their *future value* or write options below their *future value*, the odds are that they lack inherent profitability.

• Finally, a very important point to remember — the simulated Future Value Tables should only be used as **guideposts**; they should not disable your flexibility.

Option Price Adjustments

Although the tables provided in this book are quite comprehensive, there will be occasions when a specific option or strategy price is not available. For example, tables are provided for options with exercise prices up to 100. Any options with exercise prices over 100 can easily be determined by dividing the option exercise price by 2, going to the appropriate table in the book, determining the *future value*, and then multiplying by 2.

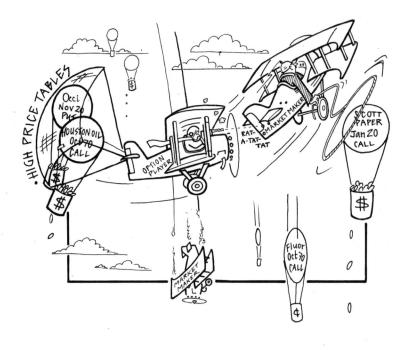

New Weapons for the Wall Street Wars

Chapter 8

New Weapons For The Wall Street Wars

The High Price Tables

Once you have digested the usefulness of the Put and Call Pricing Tables, you will discover a rare new investment tool — *The High Price Tables*. The High Price Tables were again created by computer simulation for the use of option buyers and naked option writers. These tables are special tactical tools that will aid you in:

- Measuring much more accurately the potential *risk* and *return* from a strategy.
- Designing a game plan to determine the optimum point in time to take profits.
- Designing safeguards for naked writing strategies such as setting bail-out points.
- Providing a better picture of the future behavior of the option price.

These are just a few of the ways the High Price Tables can be used in the options game. You will discover many others as you use the tables.

How To Use The High Price Tables

The High Price Tables provide two valuable pieces of information on each option, both puts and calls. First, through our computer simulations they disclose the *average high price* that an option will reach before it expires.

> AVERAGE HIGH PRICE is determined by simulating the stock and corresponding option price action thousands of times. Then from each trial simulation, the high option price reached during the life of the option is included in determining the *average high price* for all the simulated trials. Each individual strategy may not reach the *average high price* because it is an *average*. The chances of reaching that high price are presented just below the average high price figure in the tables.

Second, the tables display the percentage probability that the option price will reach or move above that average high price before it expires.

Somewhat confused? Let's look at an example. Refer back to Example I in Chapter 7, Page 38. There we found that the Xerox July 50 call option, three months before expiration, had a *future value* of $80. Using the High Price Call Tables — Exercise Price 50, on Page T51, we can find the *average high price* that the option is likely to reach in the next three months before it expires.

HIGH PRICE CALL TABLE
Exercise Price is 50
Average Volatility

Stock Price	Number of Months Before the Options Expire								
	1	2	3	4	5	6	7	8	9
48	1.1	2.1	2.9	3.6	4.2	4.6	5.0	5.5	6.0
48	40%	39%	40%	38%	37%	37%	38%	39%	39%

PHIL CARSONE, FICF

FIELD REPRESENTATIVE
201 MILLBROOKE DRIVE
HOPKINSVILLE, KENTUCKY 42241-0215
(502) 885-4123 / 886-3150

93	S	M	T	W	T	F	S
JAN						1	2
	3	4	5	6	7	8	9
	10	11	12	13	14	15	16
	17	18	19	20	21	22	23
	24	25	26	27	28	29	30
	31						
FEB		1	2	3	4	5	6
	7	8	9	10	11	12	13
	14	15	16	17	18	19	20
	21	22	23	24	25	26	27
	28						
MAR		1	2	3	4	5	6
	7	8	9	10	11	12	13
	14	15	16	17	18	19	20
	21	22	23	24	25	26	27
	28	29	30	31			
APR					1	2	3
	4	5	6	7	8	9	10
	11	12	13	14	15	16	17
	18	19	20	21	22	23	24
	25	26	27	28	29	30	
MAY							1
	2	3	4	5	6	7	8
	9	10	11	12	13	14	15
	16	17	18	19	20	21	22
	23	24	25	26	27	28	29
	30	31					
JUN			1	2	3	4	5
	6	7	8	9	10	11	12
	13	14	15	16	17	18	19
	20	21	22	23	24	25	26
	27	28	29	30			

93	S	M	T	W	T	F	S
JUL					1	2	3
	4	5	6	7	8	9	10
	11	12	13	14	15	16	17
	18	19	20	21	22	23	24
	25	26	27	28	29	30	31
AUG	1	2	3	4	5	6	7
	8	9	10	11	12	13	14
	15	16	17	18	19	20	21
	22	23	24	25	26	27	28
	29	30	31				
SEP				1	2	3	4
	5	6	7	8	9	10	11
	12	13	14	15	16	17	18
	19	20	21	22	23	24	25
	26	27	28	29	30		
OCT						1	2
	3	4	5	6	7	8	9
	10	11	12	13	14	15	16
	17	18	19	20	21	22	23
	24	25	26	27	28	29	30
	31						
NOV		1	2	3	4	5	6
	7	8	9	10	11	12	13
	14	15	16	17	18	19	20
	21	22	23	24	25	26	27
	28	29	30				
DEC				1	2	3	4
	5	6	7	8	9	10	11
	12	13	14	15	16	17	18
	19	20	21	22	23	24	25
	26	27	28	29	30	31	

WOODMEN OF THE WORLD
LIFE INSURANCE SOCIETY

THE FAMILY FRATERNITY · SERVICE · PROTECTION

PHIL CARSONE, FICF
FIELD REPRESENTATIVE

WOODMEN OF THE WORLD
LIFE INSURANCE SOCIETY
OMAHA, NEBRASKA

201 MILLBROOKE DRIVE
HOPKINSVILLE, KENTUCKY 42241-0215
(502) 885-4123
886-3150

Looking under the "Average" volatility category, we find the average high price based on our computer simulations is 2.9 when the Xerox common stock price is 48.

Just below the average high price of 2.9, we find a percentage figure. That figure indicates the percentage chance that the option price will actually reach or go beyond the high price. In the example the Xerox July 50 call has a 40% chance of reaching or surpassing the price of 2.9 before it expires.

You will notice that there are only two volatility categories for the High Price Tables, and these two categories require the following future yearly volatility levels for the underlying common stock price:

Average volatility = 23% to 39%
High volatility = 40% to 60%

Interpolation is required to determine the high price of options with underlying common stocks that have different projected volatilities than those listed above.

For those who are still confused, let us look at another example using the High Price Tables.

High Price Table Example:

Mr. James purchases a Tandy October 60 put option at 3. Using the High Price Tables, he is attempting to set a target price where he can take profits. What target price should he set and what are his chances of reaching that target given the following data for the option?

Option Exercise Price. 60
Projected Volatility of Underlying Stock Price. 50%
Price of Tandy Common Stock. 64
Current Month. . . . . .May
Option Expiration Month. . . . . .October
Time Remaining on Option's Life. . . . . .5 months

```
┌─────────────────────────────────────────────────────────────┐
│                  HIGH PRICE PUT TABLE                        │
│                   Exercise Price is 60                       │
│                     High Volatility                          │
│  Stock                                                       │
│  Price    Number of Months Before the Options Expire         │
│        1    2    3    4    5    6    7    8    9              │
│  64   1.8  3.6  4.8  6.3 │7.1│ 7.9  8.6  9.0  9.9             │
│  64   36%  35%  38%  38% │37%│ 37%  38%  40%  41%             │
└─────────────────────────────────────────────────────────────┘
```

The "High" volatility portion of the High Price Table on Page T67 shows that the target price should be 7.1. Mr. James' chance of reaching that target price is 37% which is given directly below the high price for the option.

Tactical Use Of The High Price Tables

These High Price Tables can be an invaluable tool when put to use. For the option buyer, they provide a target price to shoot at, plus a method to more accurately measure the true risk and reward of a position.

A key to success in option buying is to take profits on intraday abberations in the option prices and take advantage of the investor's edge over the market makers on the floors of the options exchanges. (See Chapter 18.) The High Price Tables provide a guide for setting the limit prices to take advantage of these intraday abberations.

To the option writer, the High Price Tables can provide the parameters for naked writing strategies. For example, they can provide the bail-out point for a strategy, plus indicate the percentage chance that you will be bounced out of the strategy. You will notice by reviewing the High Price Tables for both puts and calls that the further the options are out-of-the-money, the smaller the probability that the average high price will be reached. This observation documents the value of writing naked options that are far out-of-the-money.

For the mathematically inclined, the High Price Tables will provide hard data for the Magic Decision Rule (Refer to the Appendix).

Other uses of these tables are limited only by your imagination. Your job is to learn to use these tables quickly and comfortably. If you do, they will enable you to maximize your profits in the options game.

Chapter 9

Professional Option Buying Tactics

The buying of options challenges the professional more than any other options strategy. More players have been burned by buying options than by any other approach to the options market. After experiencing the agony of defeat when option purchases have gone astray, swarms of investors have left the options markets.

Option Buying: For Suckers Only?

The familiar comment by journalists and regulators is that option buying is a "sucker's game," and they document their statements with a large stream of losers, usually widows and orphans, who have been decimated by buying options. Some have even referred to option buying as the one-armed bandit of the stock market. For the inexperienced option player, buying options *can* be a sucker's game. Like slot machines they pay off infrequently. To the professional, these payoffs are big and turn more frequent small losses into a handsome, overall profit. To the amateur, payoffs are small and the overall losses significant.

Why is option buying considered a sucker's game? The main reason is the fact that the majority of out-of-the money options expire worthless. In other words, the payoffs are few and far between. Yet there is some surprising evidence that option buying in the long run can be quite a profitable sport. This evidence comes from some of the leading scholars in the options field.

A Winner In The Long Run

These leading scholars include Professor Myron Scholes of the University of Chicago, Professor Robert Merton of MIT, and Matthew Gladstein of Donaldson, Lufkin and Jenrette. They carried out an interesting theoretical study. This study involved the purchasing of six month call options on the Dow Jones Industrial Average, at-the-money (at the exercise price), for six month periods from mid-1963 through 1975. The study employed a version of the now famous Black and Scholes model to value options at the start of each six month period when the purchases were made.

This process of buying options resulted in a surprising and shocking 21.7% return for each six month period. This means that by buying options from 1963 to 1975, the return for each year of that period would approach 50%.*

Furthermore, the Scholes, Merton, and Gladstein study indicates the reason that options are considered dangerous at times. The variability of returns over the twelve year period of buying options was seven times as great as the variability of owning a portfolio of Dow Jones Industrial stocks.† In other words, there was seven times as much risk during that period in buying options than in buying common stock. This is the reason why there are so many shell-shocked former option buyers. Yet the long term return from option buying looks very positive.

The Option Buyers Clinic

Our computer simulations have unearthed some valuable discoveries that will provide for far more intelligent buying decisions. However, successful option buying requires more than

*A.F. Ehrbar, "The Mythology of the Option Market," *Fortune* (October, 1976); 117-120.

†*Ibid.*, p 120.

just good guidance and effective tools. Option buying, unlike more conservative option strategies, requires some special skills. We covered some of these skills and attributes in THE COMPLEAT OPTION PLAYER, but their importance warrants additional comment and attention.

This section is designed not only for those who are having trouble with their option buying, but also for those who have been quite successful. Because option buying is the toughest game, even those of you who have been successful in the past will have times when option buying will test your temperament and your professionalism. On the other hand, the rewards are greater than most other option strategies. To get those rewards, the trials and tribulations you go through will test your will and your confidence in the options game.

The Ten Classic Errors Of Option Buying

1. **Paying Too Much For Options**

2. **Lack of Timing**

3. **Falling Into The Commission Trap**

4. **Inability To Handle Losses**

5. **Lack Of A Game Plan**

6. **Lack of Diversification**

7. **Using Money You Cannot Afford To Lose**

8. **Improper Temperment For The Game**

9. **The Love Syndrome**

10. **Lack of Patience**

In my book, THE COMPLEAT OPTION PLAYER, we went into the *Ten Commandments of Option Buying*. Based on the number of people who have been blown out of the options markets by buying options, we can assume that many have not been following those Ten Commandments. Now is the time to look at these classic errors and try to correct some of the improper behavior and bad habits that have developed in option buying.

1. Paying Too Much For Options

This is probably the most frequent and the most glaring error made by the option buyer. Many novice option buyers move into the market and buy options that hold far more risk than potential reward, options that will never pay off or require far too large a move in the common stock to provide any kind of reasonable return. The many tables in this book are designed to avoid that problem and to make sure that you are buying options that provide true long term profitability.

2. Lack Of Timing

Timing in the options market is like timing in the stock market. Proper timing is difficult, mind bending and very frustrating. Even the best professionals have trouble with timing. When buying options, timing is extremely critical because of the short life of an option and the fact that many options will expire worthless.

The amateur in the options buying game normally fails to consider his timing. He normally takes profits too early, or when the trends have gone against him for a period of time, he sits in a position until it expires. His timing in entering option positions is also probably faulty and is more controlled by his emotions than by some of the more rational considerations in the options markets. Remember, when you enter or exit an option position, timing is all important.

3. Falling Into The Commission Trap

In the options game commissions sneak up on you and nickel and dime you to death. The commission take in the options market is greater than in most other investment markets due to the vigorous activity required in an options portfolio. To win in the options buying game, you must avoid the commission trap. To avoid that trap, you must watch for the following pitfalls:

a. strategies that lead to excess activity
b. lack of a game plan, which can result in numerous premature transactions
c. strategies that inherently contain a lot of option activity over a set period of time.

To avoid the commission trap, always develop a carefully mapped out game plan that realistically anticipates and measures future commissions. Take every action possible to shave commission costs, such as getting discounts on commissions. Keep a watchful eye on commission costs at all times, or you will fall into the commission trap.

4. Inability To Handle Losses

If you are going to buy options, you are going to lose on many occasions. Anybody who tells you that they win 80% of the time when they buy options is either extremely lucky or a liar. Even if you do everything right, options normally will not pay off more than 40% of the time. Even though buying options provided tremendous returns in the study carried out by Scholes, Merton and Gladstein, there were times when the options portfolio was ravaged by the actions of the market. At one time the portfolio was down over 90% in value.‡

It takes a true professional to handle those losses and not lose confidence or lose his cool. There are few who can handle losses gracefully, but to win in the options buying game, you must develop the ability to handle losses in a rational and professional manner.

5. Lack Of A Game Plan

In our previous book, THE COMPLEAT OPTION PLAYER, we heavily emphasized the importance of developing a solid game plan which sets bail-out points, sets targets, and

---

‡*Ibid.*, p 120.

takes profits when those targets have been reached. Because of the importance of timing, this kind of discipline is critical in the option buying market. If profits are not taken at proper times, options can so easily expire worthless. Without a game plan you are allowing your emotions to control your actions in the options market, and when it comes to option buying, you cannot allow that to occur. When buying options, emotions can destroy performance.

6. Lack of Diversification

Based on the fact that the majority of your positions will be losers, you will need some big winners. In order to get big winners, you need a wide variety of option positions. If you are to provide a profitable return in the short to intermediate term, diversification is critical. In the long term if you have the patience to handle the losses, diversification is not necessary, for in the long term you will have gained that diversification by the fact that you will have entered many option positions. In the short term diversification will help to even some of those losses that might devastate your performance.

7. Using Money You Cannot Afford To Lose

The classic error of the small investor who enters the option buying market is that he brings along money that he can ill afford to lose. Just as in the gambling world, never use money you need for other purposes, for such hot money will force you to make major errors in judgement. You will jump out of positions too early, lack the proper patience, and enter bad positions to try to make up for losses. If you put yourself under pressure by using money that is needed elsewhere in your financial picture, your emotions will take over. As a result, your losses will be much greater than normal, and rarely will you take a profit. If you are using money you cannot afford to lose, all the other classic errors of option buying will come into play.

8. Improper Temperament For The Game

Again I emphasize the fact that when you buy options, you are going to lose quite frequently, and to be successful, you must be able to handle those losses. You must have the temperament of a professional gambler who knows that in the long run after hundreds of plays, he will come out with a good profit. Therefore, he is able to absorb the losses that occur. Because this temperament is counter to our own personalities, it is rare and needs development. It is a quality that separates the men from the boys in the options markets. Either you develop this temperament, or you don't get into this game.

9. The Love Syndrome

When we analyze specific common stocks, it is difficult to avoid generating strong feelings regarding their possible price action. The *Love Syndrome* occurs when you get turned on to a common stock; you get hot on the possible price action of a common stock. As a result, you rush into the options market and buy any options available on that stock. Option buying requires more than a hot stock or a stock that is ready for a big move. This game requires the proper option vehicle. A proper option vehicle is one that is *priced right*. The tendency to get too locked into playing a common stock causes even the professional to make unwise option purchases. These unwise purchases of options will not appreciate enough to compensate for the risk of that position.

As mentioned in our previous book, *all systems must be go* before you make an option purchase. Unfortunately the majority of option purchases are not based on the suitability of the option vehicle, but rather they are made strictly on what the common stock price is likely to do in the future. This is a common pitfall, and it is one of the major errors made by the option buyer.

10. Lack Of Patience

Patience is the most important attribute of the option buyer, and in general the option player; you need patience to wait for the best opportunities, to strike when there are real bargains out there and to pass up potential common stock price moves until the appropriate option vehicle develops. Many an option buyer could turn defeat into victory by just adding this feature to his behavioral repertoire.

If you look closely at the CBOE TIME VALUE INDEX, which is published each week in BARRON'S, and watch the fluctuations in the time values, you will see that there are days, weeks, and months when option buying is inappropriate because time values are too high. Remember, time values in the past have not predicted future stock price behavior, and when time values are high, the option buyer should be out of the option buying game. When time values are low, that is the time to strike because that is when opportunities are there. Unfortunately most option buyers do not have this patience. They have an insatiable desire for action and cannot sit and wait.

One key attribute of the true professional in the option buying market is his ability to forego potential opportunities. Many option buyers are more concerned with losing the chance to make some money than with entering a losing position. Don't worry about opportunities lost. Our concern here is not with opportunities, but only the patience to cut out many of the losers that are normally in your portfolio.

So sit back right now and decide whether you can train yourself to be patient. If not, maybe you should change your game. Lack of patience has been listed as the tenth pitfall, but it probably is the first and foremost pitfall of the option buyer.

Chapter 10

The Naked Edge

The naked edge refers to the advantages of naked writing. Naked option writing (writing options without the cover of the common stock) is one of the most controversial and lucrative option strategies. In this age of higher interest rates, naked writing has many advantages.

Looking At The Statistics

As you gaze over the Future Value Put and Call Pricing Tables, you will notice that the option *future values* are significantly lower than the prevailing option prices from 1977 to 1980. Making a comparison between the *future values* of options as indicated in the tables and the actual values during the period from 1977 to 1980, we discover a definite discrepancy.

Using as a point of reference the six month call option with an exercise price of 50 — and using the CBOE TIME VALUE INDEX, Table I, Page 23, we find that option values ranged from 6.7% of the value of the stock to almost 15% of the value of the common stock price from 1977 to 1980. Going to our Future Value Call Option Pricing Tables, we discover that the *future value* of a six month at-the-money call option with an exercise price of 50 and average volatility is only 4.4% of the value of the underlying stock.

58

What conclusions can we draw from these statistics? Option prices from 1977 to 1980 in general were overpriced according to their *future value*. The most important influence in creating this discrepancy, of course, was interest rates, which attracted many to the option buying game rather than placing ten times as much money in common stock for the same action.

The Naked Advantage

Herein lies the naked edge or the naked advantage. Naked option writing during this period of time, if carried out under a carefully designed and disciplined plan, could have been quite lucrative, and indeed, since the inception of the Chicago Board Options Exchange in 1973, there have been many periods when naked option writing has been quite a fruitful investment strategy.

The beauty of naked writing is that there are a large number of payoffs. Seventy to eighty percent of all out-of-the-money option writing strategies end up in the profitable category. The reason for this advantage is the probability that out-of-the-money options will expire worthless, and, of course, those who write those options are the ones who will profit from worthless options.

Add The Advantage Of Treasury Bills

In this age of high interest rates, there is another major advantage of naked option writing that should be emphasized. When you are writing naked options, you can use *Treasury Bills* to margin those options, and the Treasury Bills are treated exactly like cash. You can be earning the interest return from the Treasury Bills and at the same time writing options against them. This provides double power to the profitability of naked option writing strategies.

During the years 1979 and early 1980, the true return on Treasury Bills ran as high as 15%. Add to that the return from naked writing, which can go over 50% per year, and you have a

59

powerful strategy. What other strategy pays off 70% to 80% of the time, requires only that Treasury Bills be put up to back those bets, and frequently encounters overpriced options in the options markets? Could any strategy be much better?

Don't Throw Caution To The Wind

Although there are many plusses to naked writing, the risks can be quite high. The high returns from naked writing result in investors taking far more risks than are warranted. The game looks so lucrative, so attractive, almost 100% foolproof, that the investor overextends himself in his naked option writing portfolio. As a result, significant losses have occurred through naked writing.

Naked writing is highly successful in the short run, but in the long run the returns are far more ambiguous. As opposed to buying puts and calls, where only once in a while do you make a big killing, the case for naked writing is just reversed. Once in a while you can take a real bloodbath. The true professional never puts himself in the position to take such a bath. However, many who enter the naked writing game have delusions of grandeur, lose perspective of the dangers of their naked writing strategies, and suffer devastating losses. Even market makers lose perspective of the game and highly over extend themselves in naked writing. Many have lost tremendous amounts of money. One market maker lost $5 million in a few days through naked option writing strategies.

However, if you sit down and look closely at these tremendous losses that have occurred in naked writing strategies, you will discover that they could have been prevented by utilizing the proper safeguards. The problem, again, is that once you get into this game, it looks as if you will never lose, and once you think you will never lose, that big one comes along and blows you off the map. Therefore, although rewards can be outstanding, you must be cautious, highly conservative, and well disciplined, or you are doomed, not only to failure, but to possible financial collapse. That is why naked writing is only for the brave of heart, those who have the discipline to develop and implement the proper safeguards.

The Safeguards In Naked Writing

The Strategy: Selectivity and Bail-out Points

In THE COMPLEAT OPTION PLAYER we strongly emphasized the importance of strategy design in writing naked options. You must be highly selective in entering naked positions, and you must set points where you will dump out of the strategy when things go astray. We like to refer to these junctures as "bail-out" points. (See Chapter 16 of THE COMPLEAT OPTION PLAYER.)

Volatility

In selecting naked option writing strategies, you must also closely evaluate the volatility of the underlying common stocks for which you will be writing options, whether puts or calls. We have a full chapter in this book on volatility (Chapter 6). Read and reread it, as volatility can destroy your portfolio. Pinpoint the volatility of the underlying common stocks for which you plan to write options. You must select options with underlying common stock prices that will not fluctuate violently in the future. We don't care about today or yesterday; we care about the *future*.

Liquidity and Capitalization

Another important consideration in naked strategy design is the selection of options of underlying common stocks that have tremendous liquidity and capitalization. Why? So that the stock price cannot double overnight or make a large percentage move in a short period of time (such as gapping open 5 to 10 points). When common stocks have many shares outstanding a big percentage move is quite difficult in a short period of time. We must have the ability to get out of losing strategies with enough time to spare when they reach our bail-out points. Stocks such as Bally Manufacturing and other high flyers that have limited capitalization and liquidity are stocks you should not be playing. When you play with common stocks with little capitalization and liquidity, you are playing with fire. They can make gigantic moves in a short period of time. Such moves will give the naked writer nightmares and may prevent him from bailing out of his strategy at the right time.

Far Out and Fat

When you write options, you try to eliminate as much risk as possible by writing options that are far out-of-the-money and are extremely fat with time value. Our Future Value Pricing Tables and our High Price Tables will enable you to select these prime candidates.

Risk Management

To summarize, we can put what we have discussed in this chapter under one important heading: PROPER RISK MANAGEMENT. With high interest rates the rewards of naked writing can be outstanding. But don't you dare enter the game unless you know how to properly manage the unlimited risk.

Following is a review of the guidelines that should be followed to properly manage the risks of naked writing:

1. Develop a concrete game plan.

2. Determine your bail-out points and use them.

3. Write naked options on underlying common stocks that are not prone to high price volatility and that have a lot of liquidity and capitalization.

4. Write options that are highly overpriced based on our Future Value Option Tables. (Refer to Chapter 7.)

5. Use the High Price Tables to determine your bail-out points and to compare your potential profits against your potential risk. (Refer to Chapter 8.)

6. Discipline yourself! The most important ingredient of successful naked writing is *discipline*. Follow your game plan, follow the strategy you have designed, and bail-out every time that strategy tells you to bail out. If you do this, you will be highly successful in this game.

Chapter 11

The Time Advantage

Far From the Madding Crowd

The buying of options or the writing of naked options are straightforward strategies. Once you get into the options game, you discover that there are more exotic multi-purpose type strategies that do not attract the crowd and, therefore, can provide some unique opportunities. Many of these strategies are classed under the category of *SPREADS*. Spreading is probably the technique most frequently used by market makers to take advantage of out-of-line situations and to hedge against high risk strategies.

A Strategy for Slow Markets

One of the most interesting and successful strategies is the time spread, better known as the *calendar spread*. The calendar spread is designed to make time work for you. Most calendar spreads are designed to take advantage of sloppy, nomad markets that generate a dull, slow moving performance for stock prices. However, there are *bull calendar spreads* and *bear calendar spreads* that can take advantage of limited bullish or bearish moves in specific common stock prices.

A Calendar Spread Defined

What is a calendar spread? A calendar spread can be implemented with either puts or calls. In order to get a good idea of how a calendar spread is designed, let's look at a *call* calendar spread.

The call calendar spread involves the purchase of a call option and the simultaneous sale of a call option with a shorter maturity. Both calls will have the same exercise price and the same underlying common stock.

The reasoning behind this particular strategy is that time will erode the value of the shorter term option at a faster rate than the longer term option. If this faster erosion occurs, the difference between the two calls widens, and a profit will result.

The perfect conclusion of this strategy is if the shorter term option expires when the stock price is at the exercise price of that option. If this event occurs, the option that has been written will expire, and the longer term option that the spreader holds will still have three months of time to run and will be at the exercise price, retaining the maximum time value possible. At this point in time, the spreader can sell the option and take his profits or hold on to the option for further appreciation. Therefore, we try to enter calendar spread strategies where at the conclusion of the strategy, the underlying common stock price will end up at the exercise price at the same time that the shorter term option expires.

Example of a Calendar Spread

Let's take a simple example of a call calendar spread that will illustrate this strategy, using the following theoretical prices as of the middle of May:

Xerox Price = 45

The Xerox Aug. 45 call is 2

The Xerox Nov. 45 call is 3

If you sell the Xerox Aug 45 at 2 and buy the Nov 45 at 3, the spread differential is 3 minus 2, or 1 point. Your investment in this spread, if you were to enter just one position, would be $100 plus commissions. This type of strategy goes into a margin account.

Suppose that three months from now, at the time that the August option expires, Xerox was unchanged at 45. Then a new set of prices would exist for the options presented above.

Xerox Price = 45

Xerox Aug 45 call is 0

Xerox Nov 45 call is 2

The spread, or difference between the Xerox August 45 and the Xerox November 45, is now increased to 2 points (2 − 0 = 2). Therefore, the investor has made a one point profit on his investment ($100 less commissions). He has generated a 100% return on investment because he invested $100, and he made a profit of $100.

When to Use a Calendar Spread

Normally a calendar spread is implemented when the option player determines that the underlying common stock price will only move within a very narrow range. Even a bull calendar spread or a bear calendar spread will normally generate the best profits if the stock only moves up or down a limited percentage.

The risk in a calendar spread occurs when the stock moves too far up or too far down, moving out of that profitable narrow range that is close to the exercise price of both options. If the stock price moves too far up or too far down, the spread narrows and consequently, your profits narrow. As the stock price moves-into-the-money or far out-of-the-money, this type of a spread will narrow.

65

The beauty of the calendar spread is that your investment and therefore, risk are only the difference between the option you have written and the option you have purchased. The smaller that difference when you enter the strategy, the higher your profit potential.

The Advantage of Calendar Spreads

Why should you consider the calendar spread? Because believe it or not, stock prices rarely make big moves. Normally they fluctuate within a narrow range, and the calendar spread takes advantage of this characteristic of common stock prices. Stocks that move nowhere most of the time are ideal candidates and should be considered for calendar spreads.

Selection of Calendar Spreads

As in any other activity in the options game, the selection process is critical in calendar spreading, because in order to profit the shorter term option must expire and waste away faster than the longer term option. If the market were efficient as many feel it is, there would be very few opportunities for calendar spreading. In other words, the shorter term and the longer term option would be priced properly for the amount of time left in each option. If this were the case, there would be no advantage to calendar spreading, and in the long term the only result to your portfolio would be heavy damage from commission costs. Therefore, the best way to capitalize in the spreading game is to find spreads that are really out-of-line, whereby the shorter term option is much fatter per the amount of time that is left in that option than the longer term option.

Mapping Out Strategies — Not the Whole Answer

In THE COMPLEAT OPTION PLAYER, Chapter 19, we demonstrated how to map out a calendar spread and to look at what would occur to that strategy based on changes in the underlying stock price. Mapping out spreads and other types of exotic option strategies takes time. Most professionals and players do not have the time or the patience to go through that tedious process. Up to this point in time, professionals and option players who do an extensive amount of calendar spreading have had few guidelines to use in evaluating the effectiveness of calendar spreads. Their only way of taking a look at the future was to map it out and look at the profit-loss picture at each price level of the underlying common stock.

Mapping out the strategy is great if you know where the common stock is going to go, but it does not depict the *future value* of a spread. In other words, if the spread between the Xerox Aug 45 and Nov 45 is 1, in the long run what is the *future value* of that spread? What is the expected profit or loss in three months if we enter that spread at 1 today and the stock price moves randomly in the future?

The Future Value Calendar Spread Tables — An Indispensable Aid In Spreading

As we did with our Future Value Put and Call Option Pricing Tables, we have done with calendar spreads. We designed a model that simulated the movement of the underlying stock price, comparing it to calendar spreads for each month in the life of each option. Our purpose was to determine what is the *future value* of a spread.

Through our simulations we have developed one of the most valuable tools the calendar spreader will ever put to use. We have devised tables that will provide fingertip accuracy in measuring the *future value* of a spread. By going to the table at the present price level of the underlying common stock and keeping under consideration the time left in both the shorter and longer term options of the calendar spread, the option player will immediately be able to determine the *future value* of the spread. By comparing the *future value* to the actual spread, he will be able to determine whether or not the spread under consideration has any profit potential.

These tables assume random movements in the common stock price. Most calendar spreaders make the same assumption because they are hoping for a nomad, random, slow moving underlying common stock price. Therefore, these tables are a *must* if you plan to do calendar spreading. Not only will they eliminate the tedious amount of time and effort put into mapping out strategies, but they will provide you with a very fast and easy method of eliminating many of the calendar spreads that initially look attractive.

This is the first time that this type of treatment has been made available to the option player. Now, rather than using only his intuition to pick and choose among the many hundreds of calendar spreads available, he can quickly, much faster than with a computer, evaluate whether or not a calendar spread will provide a positive long term return.

How To Use the Future Value Calendar Spread Tables

Your greatest challenge is to quickly and effectively learn what the figures in the Future Value Calendar Spread Tables signify. Remember, in designing these tables, we make the following assumptions:

- The underlying common stock price moves randomly based on its volatility from the point where you entered the spread strategy.

- The calendar spread would be held until the expiration of the shorter term option, which you normally would write (sell).

- The values presented in the tables are the spread differential when the shorter term option expires based on thousands of simulated years. These are not the normal values or the market values of the spread.

- Commissions are not included in the tables.

At this point, we will demonstrate the use of the tables by going back to the original time spread example at the beginning of this chapter.

Example I

Suppose again the following prices exist as of the middle of May.

Xerox (XRX) is 45	**Aug 45 call**	**Nov 45 call**
	2	3

Projected volatility = 30%

Here we have a calendar spread with a difference of one point ($100). How do we know if this is a profitable calendar spread that in the long run will pay off with a good return? Let's check our Future Value Calendar Spread Tables and look into the crystal ball of the future. Let's look at the Calendar Spread Table on Page T80. As in the Future Value Pricing Tables, there are three volatility levels, and as in Chapter 7, the same volatility categories apply:

$$
\left.
\begin{array}{l}
\text{High Volatility} = 40\% - 60\% \\
\text{Average Volatility} = 23\% - 39\% \\
\text{Low Volatility} = 5\% - 22\%
\end{array}
\right\} \quad \text{annually}
$$

Looking at the Average Volatility portion of the tables, we see that when the stock price is at 45 with 3 months left in the shorter term option and six months left in the longer term option, the *future value* of the time spread is 1.9 ($190). This is the *future value* in that after thousands of trials, the average spread when the Xerox Aug 45 call expired would be 1.9.

Therefore, this spread is a good ploy. The expected profit would be .9 (1.9 − 1 = .9) or $90, for on average the spread would widen from 1 to 1.9 in the long run.

To elaborate further, we will walk through some more examples. Remember, you want the *actual* spread to be smaller than the spread differential in the Future Value Tables. You want the spread to widen before the shorter term option expires.

Example II

Suppose the following theoretical prices exist as of the middle of April:

Disney at 45	**Oct 50 call**	**Jan 50 call**
	2½	4

The spread in this strategy is 1½ points. To measure the future spread, let's look at the following theoretical data and look up the *future value* of the spread in the tables.

Option Exercise Price. 50
Projected Volatility of Underlying Stock Price. 45%
Price of Disney Common Stock. 45
Current Month. . . . . .April
Shorter Term Option — Expiration Month. . . . . .October
Time Remaining in Shorter Term Option. . . . . .6 months
Time Remaining in Longer Term Option. . . . . .9 months
Volatility Level in Tables. . . . . .High

By referring to Page T81, we find that the *future value* of this calendar spread between the Disney Oct 50 call and the Disney Jan 50 call should be 1.4. In other words, over thousands of trial simulations, the *average* spread when this calendar spread is held until the expiration of the shorter term option is 1.4 ($140). The *future value* of the Disney spread is close to the actual value. Therefore, this time spread is *not* a worthwhile venture; nothing will be gained in the long run except a lot of commission costs.

```
      CALENDAR SPREAD TABLE
             Call Options
         Exercise Price is 50
           High Volatility

         Number of Months Before the Longer Term
Stock              Options Expire
Price
         3      4      5      6      7      8      9
    Number of Months Before the Shorter Term Options Expire
         ·0     1      2      3      4      5      6
45      [2.0]  1.8    1.7    1.6    1.5    1.5   [1.4]
```

Example III

In this example, we will use a *put* calendar spread. Suppose the following prices exist as of late February:

ABC at 35	**May 30 Put**	**Aug 30 Put**
	1	1¼

The spread in this case is ¼ of a point ($25). To measure the *future value* of the spread, review the following facts and look up the value in the Calendar Spread Tables.

```
Option Exercise Price.................................30
Projected Volatility of Underlying Stock Price..........28%
Price of ABC Common Stock.........................35
Time Remaining in Shorter Term Option...........3 months
Time Remaining in Longer Term Option............6 months
Volatility Level in Tables........................Average
```

By referring to Page T92, we find the *future value* of the calendar spread between the ABC May 30 put and the Aug 30 put is .4, almost 7/16 of a point, ($40).

CALENDAR SPREAD TABLE
Put Options
Exercise Price is 30
Average Volatility

Stock Price	Number of Months Before the Longer Term Options Expire						
	3	4	5	6	7	8	9
	Number of Months Before the Shorter Term Options Expire						
	0	1	2	3	4	5	6
35	0.2	0.3	0.4	0.4	0.4	0.4	0.4

Here the spread will probably widen before the strategy ends. If you can minimize the commission costs, this could be a strategy to consider. The long term gross profit per position is $15.

Targeting Spread Strategies

The Future Value Calendar Spread Tables have another special feature. In the first column, time remaining in the shorter term option is zero, and three months remain in the longer term option. The longer term option is the option you would be holding in a spread strategy. The value of that option is the fair market value based on past empirical evidence (past prices in the options markets). For those who feel they can target at what price level the underlying common stock will be when the option expires, this column will provide some guidance as it indicates the final spread at each stock price level. For example, you enter a call calendar spread with an exercise price of 50 with a stock price possessing high volatility, and you target the stock price to be at 45 when the shorter term expires. A quick glance at Page T81, column 1 will show you that the spread will be worth 2.0.

Maximize Your Profits Through Active Surveillance

Calendar spreads, like any other strategy, can move into profit zones at any time during the life of the strategy. On many occasions the best time to take profits is during the life of the strategy. Remember, the spread will widen to its maximum width per the time left in each option when the underlying stock price reaches the *exercise price* for the spread. If there is enough profit when that price is reached during the life of the strategy, you should take the money and run.

One other important point — if during the life of the strategy, the time value of the shorter term option disappears because the stock price is in-the-money or way out-of-the-money, the calendar spread should be closed out for the following reasons:

1. to avoid exercise
2. to avoid further damage to the longer term option

So, active and close surveillance of your calendar spreads is a prerequisite to success. When the spread widens and target profits develop, they should be taken immediately.

Beware Of Paper Tigers

Calendar spreads can look beautiful mapped out on paper, but a calendar spread on paper may be impossible to implement for the following reasons:

• Calendar spreads that you map out from the newspaper may not exist in the market. Option prices in the newspaper may be prices that occurred several hours before the market closed. This event occurs in options that have little liquidity and, therefore trade infrequently.

• Option prices listed in the newspaper are the last price before the close of the market. They may not depict the real spread which is the *bid* of the shorter term option and *asked* of the longer term option. These figures are not available in any publication, but are needed to determine what the real spread is at any point in time. Your broker can provide you with that up-to-date information.

- *Trading* calendar spreads can give an option player nightmares. Moving into and out of most spreads is quite difficult, and while doing so, an option player is prone to trading errors that will destroy the spread strategy. Trading skills and discipline are an absolute necessity when working with calendar spreads. If you don't have the trading skills, get an options broker who does. (Review Chapter 21 of THE COMPLEAT OPTION PLAYER.)

- Calendar spreads on paper never display the high commission costs that are incurred with these types of strategies due to the fact that each calendar spread will normally incur three to four commissions during its life. Such high commissions make many spreads impractical. All-out attempts must be made to reduce commission costs by working with larger sized orders and getting maximum discounts on commission charges.

Calendar spreading can be a great strategy on paper, but because of the above factors, any spreads you attempt to enter must have plenty of room for error.

Your Guide To Creative Strategies

The Future Value Calendar Spread Tables that are demonstrated in this chapter will provide guidance not only in the area of laying out a one-on-one calendar spread, but will also provide guidance to far more creative strategies. These strategies might include a ratio calendar spread where you write more options than you buy, or a *reverse* calendar spread where you write a longer term option and buy a shorter term option. These more exotic strategies can pay off with big rewards, and the Future Value Calendar Spread Tables in this book will provide a basis for telling you right off the bat whether to design a ratio or a reverse spread.

The reverse spread has some interesting features in that when an actual spread is far too wide, there is a pretty good potential

74

for it to narrow, and then the reverse spread becomes quite attractive. However, the problem with the reverse spread is that when you write the longer term option and you buy the shorter term option, you have to put up the sizeable naked writing margin requirement for the option you have written. This is a heavy bill of fare, and unless you have extra Treasury Bills lying around, the strategy really has limited applicability.

We discussed ratio spreads in THE COMPLEAT OPTION PLAYER, and they do have a lot of good features. Again, the Future Value Calendar Spread Tables in this book will provide a basis for the design of these types of strategies. Use them.

Chapter 12

Straddle and Win

The options game allows the creative player to go wild with new, different ane unique strategies. Spreading opens up unlimited possibilities for the game player. One of the less publicized strategies that has a lot of potential is the *straddle*. As in other complicated strategies, it has some of the same drawbacks, including commissions and trading difficulties.

A Straddle Defined

The straddle is a strategy where a put and a call have the same underlying common stock and the same exercise price.

- The straddle *buyer* is hoping for violent action in the common stock price, both up and down, so that he can take profits on both the call and the put side of the strategy.

- The straddle *writer* is hoping that the stock price stays within a narrow range and both the put and the call lose much of their value and expire worthless.

Flexibility For The Option Buyer

Straddles are excellent vehicles for option buyers, especially if the buyer is able to key in on highly volatile common stocks — stock prices that move in an erratic and violent manner. Straddles provide additional flexibility to the option buyer in that he does not have to call the direction of the stock price move; all he has to predict is that in the short term the stock price will move and move big.

Why Write Naked Straddles?

The writing of a naked straddle is similar to the writing of a naked option, except that there are three advantages for the naked straddle writer:

1. The writer of the naked straddle receives almost twice as much time value; he receives:

   • the premium from the call
   • and the premium from the put.

   Of course, his risk on the upside and the downside are the same as that of the standard naked writer of either a put or a call.

2. The naked straddle writer is required to put up approximately half as much margin as compared to standard naked writing. Therefore, he is getting double the return on his dollar of investment.

3. Treasury Bills can be used as margin.

The dark side of naked straddle writing is that if the stock price moves violently, the writer still retains that unlimited risk on the upside and extensive risk on the downside.

How To Use The Future Value Straddle Tables

The Future Value Straddle Tables are developed along the same lines as the other tables in this text. We again assume random stock price action, a hold until expiration strategy, and the same three volatility categories for the underlying common stock price:

High = 40% – 60%
Average = 23% – 39%   } annually
Low = 5% – 22%

The Straddle prices as indicated in the tables are the prices of the put and the call added together. For example, if the put is priced at 2 and the call is priced at 3, then the straddle price is 5 (3 + 2 = 5). Comparing that price to the *future value* in the tables will indicate whether the price of 5 is a good buy or a good sell.

Let's look at a few theoretical examples to determine how to measure the *future value* of a straddle.

Example I:

Suppose we have the following theoretical data regarding the CBS February 40 put and call:

Option Exercise Price..................................40
Projected Volatility of Underlying Stock Price...........30%
Price of CBS Common Stock...........................40
Current Month...................................October
Time Remaining in the Put and Call Life............4 months
Volatility Level in Tables.........................Average

What would be the *future value* of the CBS 40 straddle? By referring to Page T109, you will be able to look into the future and determine that value, which is 3.6.

```
                    STRADDLE TABLE
                   Exercise Price is 40
                   Average Volatility
   Stock
   Price      Number of Months Before the Options Expire
          1    2    3    4    5    6    7    8    9
   40    1.6  2.5  3.0  3.6  3.9  4.1  4.4  4.7  5.1
```

If the actual straddle price is above 3.6, straddle writing in the long run will provide a positive return on investment. The reverse would be true of the straddle buyer.

Example II:

Suppose we have the following theoretical data in late November regarding the Monsanto Jan 60 put and call:

```
Option Exercise Price..................................60
Projected Volatility of Underlying Stock Price...........20%
Current Month..............................November
Price of Monsanto Common Stock......................58
Time Remaining in the Put and Call Life...........2 months
Volatility Level......................................Low
```

Again, let's turn the tables on the options market and look into the future. By referring to Page T112, you will discover that the *future value* of the Monsanto Jan 60 straddle is 3.1 ($310).

Comparing the actual straddle price to the *future value* will indicate whether the straddle is a good buy or a good candidate for writing. Beginning with the *future value* of the straddle, remember to add in the cost of commissions and trading difficulties in determining your return on investment.

One final comment before we move on. Remember that the *future value* of the straddle is the long term intrinsic value of the straddle when it expires. When buying or writing, you must get a price that provides a comfortable profit above or below the *future value* price.

The Secrets of Straddling

For Options Buyers Only

There are two secrets to success in straddle buying:

1. Volatility is all important. The more time you spend on projecting volatility, the more successful you will be. When you buy straddles, the stock price must perform like a wild horse moving erratically and dramatically all the time.

2. Once you have identified the real swingers in the market, you have to make sure that you purchase straddles that are underpriced according to their *future value.* Using the Future Value Tables in this text, only enter straddle positions where the option price is at least 25% *below* the *future value.*

For Straddle Writers Only

There are three important requirements for successful straddle writing:

1. Write only highly overpriced straddles, using our Future Value Straddle Tables. Only write straddles that are priced at least 25% *over* the *future value* of the straddle.

2. Make sure that you have keyed in on the future volatility of the common stock price and that there are no developing factors that will cause increased volatility in the underlying stock price. Surveillance of volatility is critical to your success when writing straddles. Any change in the volatility pattern of the underlying common stock requires swift and drastic action on your part. Volatility is your greatest *danger.*

3. Establish a solid game plan. Writing straddles is like writing any other type of naked option configuration; you

are faced with unlimited risk. Bail-out points must be set to limit losses, and you must have the discipline of an Olympic athlete.

One final word of caution to straddle writers. Unlike other types of naked writing or options writing, the straddle writer is exposed to a thinner range of profitability. Both options that he writes are probably close-to-the-money. Any significant percentage move of the stock price over the short term could cause extensive damage.

Chapter 13

The Winning Combination

The straddle is a highly versatile investment vehicle, but now we come upon the strategy that the author feels is the most dynamic and powerful of all the option strategies; this strategy is called the *combination*. Another term used to designate the combination is the naked spread as described in Chapter 17 of THE COMPLEAT OPTION PLAYER.

The Combination Defined

The combination has many characteristics that are similar to the straddle. The buyer of the combination would buy a put and a call but not at the same exercise price. The *put* would be at an exercise price that is *lower* than the call price; the *call* would have an exercise price that is *higher* than the put. An example of a combination would be a 45 put and a 50 call. Normally the combination would have the same expiration date for both the put and the call as in the case of a straddle with the same underlying stock.

Buying Versus Writing

The naked spread or combination is probably one of the most powerful and unique option strategies available for the writer, but not for the buyer. The *buyer* is fighting one big disadvantage; to profit from the purchase of a combination, he normally needs a pretty good move from the underlying stock price, far more than with a straddle. Again, this move would be contingent upon the price he pays for the combination. The *writer* of the combination is in the reverse position. Only a big move by the underlying common stock price will cause him any problems, because, unlike straddles, the naked writer has between five and ten points of stock price to work with.

Writing Combinations — The Advantages

There are some big advantages to writing combinations:

1. You are not as vulnerable to a large move in the common stock price with a combination. There is a high probability you will never have to bail-out of the strategy.

2. There is again, as in the writing of straddles, a double dose of time value, in that you receive the premium for both the put and the call.

3. There is a margin advantage. The margin requirement for writing a combination is one half of the margin requirement for writing an individual put or call. In other words, by writing a put and a call at the same time for the same underlying common stock, the margin requirement is close to what it would be if you were to write just one put or one call.

4. There is the Treasury Bill advantage. Treasury Bills can again be used as margin for the writing of naked combinations. When Treasury Bill rates are high, writing combinations receives an additional bonus in the form of the interest return from Treasury Bills that are put up for margin.

5. The combination can be designed to lock in a wide profit zone where the chances of profiting are excellent and the risks of a loss are quite small. (See Table 3.)

Designing a Combination

We have taken an example of a combination from THE COMPLEAT OPTION PLAYER and placed it in Table 3, Page 86 so that you can see how a combination (naked spread) looks when it is mapped out. There are many excellent features to this strategy, but like any other naked writing strategy, it still maintains that heavy risk on both the upside and the downside at the end of the profit zones. Therefore, in designing a combination, bail-out points must be set and strictly adhered to.

The Future Value Combination Tables

We have computer simulated the combination, as we have with all the other unique strategies in this text, so that you can target in on a good combination quickly without spending time mapping it out. (Table 3.) These simulation tables have been designed so that you can easily pinpoint when a combination is out-of-line and when a combination is an excellent candidate for buying or for writing.

How To Use The Future Value Combination Tables

The Future Value Combination Tables are developed in the same manner as the Future Value Straddle Tables. We again assume random stock price action and a hold until expiration strategy with the same three volatility categories for the underlying common stock price:

$$
\left. \begin{array}{rcl}
\text{High} & = & 40\% - 60\% \\
\text{Average} & = & 23\% - 39\% \\
\text{Low} & = & 5\% - 22\%
\end{array} \right\} \quad \text{Annually}
$$

85

Table 3

```
┌─────────────────────────────────────────────────────────────────────────┐
│                                                                           │
│                         THE NAKED SPREAD                                  │
│                                                                           │
│         Sell    1     Xerox    Jul    70    Call    at 4                  │
│         Sell    1     Xerox    Jul    60    Put     at 3                  │
│                                                                           │
│      The Xerox common stock price is 65 at the time of entry on May 1 for │
│   this theoretical strategy.                                              │
│      The Initial Margin Requirement would be $750.                        │
│      The Profit-Loss Table is presented below.                            │
│                                                                           │
│   XEROX Price at the                        Gross                   Loss  │
│   End of July                               Profit                        │
│                                                                           │
│      80                                                            ($300)  │
│      79                                                             (200)  │
│      78                                                             (100)  │
│      77  Bail-out Point . . . . . . . . . . . . . . . .0                   │
│      76                            ▲              100                      │
│      75                            ┊              200                      │
│      74                            ┊              300                      │
│      73                            ┊              400                      │
│      72                            ┊              500                      │
│      71                            ┊              600                      │
│      70                            ┊              700                      │
│      69                            ┊              700                      │
│      68                            ┊              700                      │
│      67                            ┊              700                      │
│      66                     Profit               700                      │
│      65  Present Price      Zone                 700                      │
│      64                                          700                      │
│      63                            ┊              700                      │
│      62                            ┊              700                      │
│      61                            ┊              700                      │
│      60                            ┊              700                      │
│      59                            ┊              600                      │
│      58                            ┊              500                      │
│      57                            ┊              400                      │
│      56                            ┊              300                      │
│      55                            ┊              200                      │
│      54                            ▼              100                      │
│      53  Bail-out Point. . . . . . . . . . . . . . . .0                    │
│      52                                                            (100)   │
│      51                                                            (200)   │
│      50                                                            (300)   │
│                                                                           │
│      With this strategy, if the Xerox price is between 53 and 77 at the    │
│   end of July when the options expire, a gross profit will be realized. If │
│   the Xerox stock price moves to 77 or 53 before, we should bail out of    │
│   both naked options to minimize potential losses. Commission costs are    │
│   not included in this profit-loss scenario.                              │
│                                                                           │
└─────────────────────────────────────────────────────────────────────────┘
```

86

The combination price as indicated in the tables is the price of the put and the call *added together,* both with different exercise prices. For example, if the 50 put is priced at 3 and the 60 call is priced at 4, then the combination price is 7, (3 + 4 = 7), or $700. Comparing the price of 7 to the *future value* of the combination in the tables will indicate whether the combination is a good purchase or writing candidate.

The tables have been set up with five point combinations up to a price of 50 and ten point combinations for prices of 50 and above. Now let's evaluate a few theoretical examples to determine how to measure the *future value* of a combination (naked spread).

Example I:

Suppose we have the following data for the Eastman Kodak July 50 put and the Eastman Kodak July 60 call in late January:

```
Option Exercise Price for the Put.......................50
Option Exercise Price for the Call......................60
Projected Volatility of Underlying Stock Price..........30%
Price of Eastman Kodak Common Stock.................55
Current Month....................................January
Time Remaining in the Put and Call Options.........6 months
Volatility Level..................................Average
```

What would be the *future value* of the Eastman Kodak 50-60 combination? By referring to Page T126, you will find that the *future value* of this combination in the long term should be 2.8 ($280), or about 2¾.

COMBINATION TABLE
Exercise Price of the Call is 60
Exercise Price of the Put is 50
Average Volatility

Stock	Number of Months Before the Options Expire								
Price	1	2	3	4	5	6	7	8	9
55	0.2	0.9	1.4	2.1	2.4	2.8	3.1	3.5	3.9

If the actual price was above 2¾, writing the combination would provide a positive return in the long run.

Example II:

Suppose we have the following theoretical figures in late September regarding the Boise Cascade November 35 put and the November 40 call:

Option Exercise Price of the Put........................35
Option Exercise Price of the Call.......................40
Projected Volatility of Underlying Stock Price..........45%
Price of Boise Cascade Common Stock...................37
Current Month.............................September
Time Remaining in the Put and Call Options.........2 months
Volatility Level.................................High

By referring to Page T123 of the tables, we find the *future value* of this combination to be 2.5 ($250), about 2½.

NOTE: Volatility is still an important factor and should be carefully targeted to insure the *future value* of the strategy.

Guidelines For Success With Combinations

For Option Buyers

Option buyers should be wary when they use the combination. The keys to success in buying combinations are twofold:

1. You must purchase combinations for common stocks that will have violent future price volatility.

2. You must buy combinations that are underpriced according to the Future Value Combination Tables in this book.

Finding the perfect combination for your strategy with these two prerequisites is a difficult task, and rarely do you find a stock price with great volatility and low priced combinations. If you can find a combination at an extremely low price on a stock that will move violently, you could have a big winner.

A Writer's Paradise

To the writer, the combination is like going to heaven. When you write combinations, all the ideal features of option writing are present. You will have many winners; rarely will you get bounced out of your strategy, and you only have to put up half the margin that would normally be required for a standard put or call writing strategy.

The key steps to success in writing combinations include the following:

1. Write only combinations that are priced at least 25% over their *future value* as indicated in the Future Value Combination Tables.

2. Carefully measure the volatility of the underlying common stock price.

3. Carefully map out your strategy to identify the bail-out points as featured in Table 3.

4. Follow your game plan to the letter.

If you follow these four key steps, in the long run you will prosper by writing naked combinations. The time and effort that are required for developing a game plan and mapping out the combination are critical to the success of the strategy. Any type of naked writing strategy *must* be mapped out in advance. The only way you can protect yourself against the risks of naked writing is to set points where you will bail out of your strategies when the stock price leaves the profit zone. With the naked combination these points are ideally determined by taking the total premium that you receive from writing both options, and subtracting it from your downside exercise price and adding it to your upside exercise price. By doing this, you will come up with your downside bail-out point and your upside bail-out point. In Table 3 these two bail-out points are 53 and 77. The process is quite easy, although it may look complex at first. Practice and make sure that you lay out the strategy before you ever consider entering it.

In Conclusion

Writing combinations can be the best that the options market can offer the investor. However, if you do not have a viable game plan, do not watch for overpriced options to write, and do not carefully measure the volatility of the underlying common stock price, it could be the worst investment you ever made.

Chapter 14

The Professional's Guide to Covered Writing

Where the Institutions Play!

The most popular and publicized options strategy today is covered option writing. Most conservative investors who have entered the options game have done so through the covered writing channel. The institutions are also using covered writing as their gateway to the options markets. The unique features of options are ideal for hedging portfolios and providing better returns for the institutional coffers. Banks, insurance companies, mutual funds, and pension funds are all entering the options markets, hoping that here lies their Shangri La, a way to out-perform their competitors and to appease the appetites of their constituency.

However, the process has been slow. Although there are now fifty or more pension funds involved in option writing, they have not really aggressively entered the options markets.

Covered option writing, a strategy whereby you hold the common stock and write one call option against each 100 shares, has moved through a short and turbulent history. Initially several barriers prevented the easy entry of institutions into this arena, but in recent times, most of these barriers have been removed.

Is Covered Writing Worthwhile?

There has been a lot of financial rhetoric about covered writing, both from those who are for it and from those who are against it. Brokers continue to tout covered writing as a perfect strategy where you can never lose. With all these opinions floating around, it is difficult to get a clear picture of the full capabilities of the strategy, the true return, and finally to determine if the strategy suits your needs, whether you are an institutional investor or an individual.

There are many misgivings about using options in institutional and individual portfolios. These include:

- Does covered option writing meet the "prudent man" rule?
- Is writing against common stock only good in down markets?
- Are there too many institutions entering the game, and will they burn out the opportunities?
- Are the long term results from covered writing worth all the time and effort?
- Will covered writing really replace the loss of potential profits that are capped when you write options against common stock?
- Are there enough skilled professionals around to handle the job?
- Have the options markets become so efficient that there are rarely good covered option writing positions available?

These and many other questions are being asked about covered option writing.

What do the Studies Say?

To answer these doubts, scientists and consulting firms have delved into the market and have carried out some extensive and well documented studies to identify whether or not institutions should consider entering the options game. The results of these works are mixed and conflicting.

We discussed in Chapter 9 the Scholes, Merton, Gladstein study which calculated the effectiveness of buying options during the period from 1963 to 1975. In their examination of this period, they also discovered that the writing of covered options against the stocks in the Dow Jones Industrial Average showed 2.9% return for each six month period, as compared to a 4.1% return for each six month period for the same common stocks without options written against them. The study indicated that covered option writing did *not* provide a better return than merely holding the common stocks. It did pinpoint the fact that in a covered option writing portfolio the volatility and risk are greatly reduced from that of a portfolio comprised wholly of common stocks. This reduction in risk can range anywhere from five to ten times less than the usual amount of risk found in a common stock portfolio.*

Another study put out by one of the more prestigious accounting firms indicates that there are good values in the options markets and that covered option strategies that are skillfully implemented will provide good return to a common stock portfolio. Possibly you should underline the words *skillfully implemented*. This subject will be covered in the following chapters. This study goes on to show that you can increase your overall return by writing options on the underlying common stock by as much as 2% a year over a common stock portfolio.

*Ibid., p119-120.

Why Covered Writing?

From these studies we find two major advantages to covered option writing:

1. With proper selection and implementation of covered writing strategies, increased returns can be generated over traditional common stock portfolios.
2. Covered writing strategies most definitely reduce the risk and volatility of a common stock portfolio in the short term.

These two advantages are especially important to the institutional manager who is always concerned with the risk to his portfolio and the betterment of the total return. In order to receive the benefits of these advantages, the institutional manager, and, indeed, the average investor must develop the proper skills. They must dismiss much of the financial rhetoric regarding covered writing that is floating around.

Skilled Money Managers Needed

As mentioned, up to this point in time, institutions have been dabbling in the options markets. In many cases, their money managers lack the experience that is necessary to utilize options properly and as a result, their performances are disappointing. There have been several mutual funds that have entered the covered option writing game, and some of their returns have not been up to par. Many have underperformed the stock market indices, and overall they have shown stodgy results. As in any other investment activity, the skill of the investment manager is a critical determinant of the success of the investment strategy. In dealing with options, which are complicated, intricate investment vehicles, a competent investment manager is even more important.

Most managers who enter covered writing are taking the wrong approach. They do not understand the game, they do not understand how to evaluate covered writing strategies, and they do not understand how to tactically move in and out of option writing strategies.

Investment Skill is All Important

Again, the difference between success or failure in this conservative investment activity is the proper skill of the investment manager, whether it is the individual himself, the money manager, or the stock broker. *You* can learn the correct approach! In the following chapters you will be enlightened by some unheard of considerations in writing covered options. Among other points we will describe an important hidden cost of option writing that must be considered in any covered option writing decisions. A set of *tables* has been developed to carefully guide you through the covered option writing process to make sure that when you enter a strategy, you will be entering one that will provide a healthy positive return and reduce risk in the long run.

Chapter 15

The Hidden Costs of Covered Option Writing

There are no free lunches in the options game, especially in covered option writing. Many brokers have touted covered option writing as a way to increase the returns on your portfolio with a significant decrease in risk. They have indicated that covered option writing is a conservative, safe method of holding a common stock portfolio and increasing the return on the portfolio. Beyond this rhetoric, longitudinal studies have indicated conflicting performance reports regarding covered option writing. Little has been done to evaluate the true risk-reward considerations when you are writing covered options.

The Computer Does the Job

In an effort to improve your performance in writing covered options, we carried out extensive computer simulations to:

- Identify the best way to measure and evaluate a covered option writing strategy.

96

- Find the best tactics to be used in implementing and maintaining a covered option writing portfolio.

Our studies disclosed some very shocking and revealing information.

A Major Finding

> *The major finding of our simulations is that there is a hidden cost* in covered option writing, one that is much higher than you would anticipate. That cost is created by the loss of opportunity on the upside, combined with extensive *downside risk* which is only reduced by the premium received from writing an option against the common stock.

This major finding will be quite important to you as you evaluate whether or not to enter covered option writing strategies. This cost factor indicates that in many cases covered option writing would provide a negative return in the long run. In fact, one of the most revealing pieces of information uncovered by the simulations was that *high* price volatility stocks have a much higher hidden cost in covered option writing than do the *low* volatility stocks. This is because far more potential profit on the upside is capped and shut off to the covered option writer. Yet the same downside risk is reduced only by the amount of the premium of the options that are written against the common stock. All the rhetoric that we hear about covered option writing *totally ignores the hidden costs,* cost factors that are far more significant than formerly recognized and that in the long run can result in a negative or sub-par performance.

Assumptions

In the process of developing our computer simulations, we again made the following assumptions:

1. Random movement of the underlying stock price
2. A *write* and *hold* covered writing strategy

The second assumption may not hold true for *all* professional covered option writers or individuals who do covered option writing. The write and hold strategy involves buying the

98

underlying common stock, writing one option against each 100 shares, and holding the option *until expiration,* regardless of the price action of the underlying common stock. The good portfolio manager who is utilizing covered option writing will not always hold options until expiration. If the stock price is moving down rapidly, he will roll over and write additional options to try to reduce some of the downside risk.

Normally the effectiveness of this rolling over activity is highly dependent upon the skill and experience of the investment manager or covered writer who is handling the enterprise. For many, and especially for the individual investor who does not have a large position, buying the underlying common stock, writing options against those postitions and holding the options until expiration may be the wiser strategy. This is true especially when we consider the commission costs and the trading difficulties that the individual investor may encounter in trying any complicated tactics in managing his portfolio.

The Results

Therefore, using the two assumptions, random market and a write and hold until expiration scenario, we simulated thousands of years of covered writing activities with different volatility levels of the underlying common stock. The True Cost Covered Option Writing Tables beginning on Page T132 show you the results of our simulations. They disclose what the price of the option that you are writing must be, at each price level of the underlying common stock in order to *break even* in the long run. It must be emphasized that the price disclosed is one that is necessary, not to make any profit or return, but just to *break even.* NOTE: These simulations did not include dividend yield; therefore, this would be an added return to the proposed strategy.

The Wrong Approach

Up to this point in time, covered option writing has been evaluated on the return that an option will provide. This has been done without considering the *downside risk* and only assuming that the option will expire and that the stock price will not move downward. For example, if you were to purchase one hundred shares of stock at 50 and write a six month call option with an exercise price of 50 that is selling at 5 against that stock, assuming no yield, your return on that investment would be 10% for that six month period of time. The covered writer would look at that as a 10% return for six months or a 20% return for a year and use that as his basis of comparison. This approach for evaluating covered writing strategies is *incorrect* based on our new findings.

The Correct Approach

The *hidden cost* we have been discussing must be considered in the decision making process. To help you view the hidden costs for covered writing in developing strategies, we again have laid out a beautiful set of tables, which should guide you through the evaluation process. Using these tables, you should be able to take an objective look at the potential of each covered writing strategy and from there select those strategies that will provide you with the return that you have been seeking.

The following chapter will demonstrate how to use the True Cost Covered Option Writing Tables. These tables will help you to design and measure the *true* return of a covered option writing strategy. You will learn to design and measure the *true* return of a strategy, taking into consideration the *hidden costs* of covered option writing. So, if you are an institutional money manager or an individual who does extensive amounts of covered writing, the next chapter is probably the most important one.

Chapter 16

Uncovering Covered Writing

The True Cost Covered Option Writing Tables should become the most important tool of the covered option writer. The figures in these tables should be the pivotal point in determining whether you will enter a covered writing strategy and what the *true* return will be from that position. Without the tables the covered writer is not considering the most important factor — the HIDDEN COST — in the investment activity; and consequently, long term results will suffer.

How to Use the True Cost Covered Option Writing Tables

As with all the tables in this book, the underlying common stock price must be classified according to one of three projected volatility levels for the year:

$$
\left. \begin{array}{l}
\text{High Volatility} = 40\% - 60\% \\
\text{Average Volatility} = 23\% - 39\% \\
\text{Low Volatility} = 5\% - 22\%
\end{array} \right\} \quad \text{Annually}
$$

Now let's review a theoretical example to demonstrate how to use the True Cost Covered Option Writing Tables.

Example I:

Suppose the following facts exist as of the middle of May for the Ford Motor October 40 call:

Option Exercise Price................................40
Projected Volatility of Underlying Stock Price...........18%
Price of Ford Common Stock.........................38
Current Month......................................May
Time Remaining in Option Life..................4 months
Volatility Level in Tables.............................Low

By referring to Page T139, you will find that the cost of writing a Ford Oct 40 call against 100 shares of Ford Common stock when its price is 38 is 0.6 (5/8).

COVERED OPTION
WRITING TABLE
Exercise Price is 40
Low Volatility

Stock
Price   Number of Months Before the Options Expire

	1	2	3	4	5	6	7	8	9
38	0.1	0.3	0.4	0.6	0.7	0.8	0.8	0.9	1.0

If you write an option at 5/8 and hold until expiration, your long term result will be to break even. (Again, by long term we mean the identical strategy run over and over thousands of times would result in no gain or loss if all profits and losses were added together.) A price above the price of 5/8 would provide the corresponding return less the true cost. A price below 5/8 would have a correspondingly negative return excluding dividends or commissions.

102

How to Measure the True Return from Covered Writing

Now let's take another example, (using the tables) and demonstrate how to measure the true return from covered writing.

Example II:

Suppose the following facts exist regarding the Westinghouse July 25 call in late February:

Option Exercise Price.................................25
Projected Volatility of Underlying Stock Price...........29%
Price of Westinghouse Common Stock....................24
Current Month................................February
Time Remaining in Option's Life.................5 months
Volatility Level in Tables.........................Average
Market Price of Westinghouse July 25 Call...........2 ($200)

By referring to the Average Volatility Table on Page T136, we find that the true cost of covered writing the Westinghouse July 25 call is .9 ($90) or close to 7/8.

Knowing the cost of the covered option, we are able to compare that to the market price of the option which is 2 ($200). Thus we can determine the true return.

Market price of Westinghouse Jul 25 Call..................2
True cost of Westinghouse Jul 25 Call (Subtract)........ −7/8
Profit or Loss from Writing the Option........profit ..1⅛

By subtacting the true cost of covered writing the Westinghouse July 25 call at ⅞ from the market price of the option, we can determine the true long term profit or loss from writing the option. In this case the true long term profit is close to 1⅛ ($110). One hundred ten dollars ($110) plus the dividend yield will give us our total return on our investment in the covered option writing strategy.

```
100shares of Westinghouse at $24...........$2400
Less Westinghouse July call price...........− 200
   Total Investment.......................$2200
True return after subtracting true cost
of covered writing the Westinghouse July call = $110
True % return on investment for 5 months
                     $110/$2200    =    5 %
Annualized return...........12% before dividends
```

Using the analysis presented above, you can now determine the *true* long term return on a covered writing strategy, rather than a false return which deceives the public and ignores the hidden cost of covered writing (the downside risk). The procedure to determine the true cost looks a little complex at first, but it is quite easy after a little practice. Just remember to subtract the true cost of the option from the market price. The difference, if it is positive, is your long term return from the covered option writing investment (for each 100 shares). If the result of the subtraction is negative, the covered writing strategy is a loser in the long run unless dividends can reverse that negative return. In any case, always add dividends after you have determined the return on investment.

Another example may make this picture a little clearer.

Example III:

Suppose the following facts exist regarding the Honeywell May 80 call in late September:

```
Option Exercise Price................................80
Price of Honeywell Common Stock.....................75
Current Month...............................September
Time Remaining in Option Life....................8 months
Projected Volatility of Underlying Stock Price...........45%
Volatility Level in Tables...........................High
Market Price of the Honeywell May 80 Call..........6 ($600)
```

By referring to Page T144 in the High Volatility category, you will find the true cost of the Honeywell May 80 call when you write it against 100 shares and hold it to expiration. The *true* cost is 7.3 ($730), or 7¼.

```
                    COVERED OPTION
                    WRITING TABLE
                   Exercise Price is 80
                     High Volatility
Stock
Price       Number of Months Before the Options Expire
         1     2     3     4     5     6     7     8      9
75      1.6   3.0   4.0   5.0   5.6   6.1   6.6  |7.3|   8.0
```

Such a cost figure would indicate a negative return over the long term of 1.3 ($130) per 100 shares (6 − 7.3 = −1.3). The Honeywell May 80 call is not an acceptable call for covered writing when it is at a market price of 6.

Improving Your Covered Writing Returns

The following tactics will help you improve your returns from covered option writing:

• DO NOT get locked into a covered writing portfolio where you must write all the time. When you are forced to write options against common stock, you are forced to select options that may be priced under their *true cost*. Therefore, in the long run these positions will end up with a negative return. (Mutual funds that are using covered option writing are facing this dilemma.) As with any other option strategy, you must be patient and wait for the right time. In this case, the time is right when option prices are above their *true cost* as shown in the True Cost Covered Option Writing Tables.

105

- DO NOT enter covered option writing strategies in the early stages of bear markets. Covered writers must realize that downside risk is more dangerous to them than common stock buyers because the potential profits that would offset the downside risk are capped off.

- DO use the True Cost Covered Option Writing Tables. Only write options that provide a comfortable return above the *true cost* of writing the option.

- DO provide more active surveillance of your option writing portfolio. Roll into new positions as the time values of covered options diminish. DO NOT wait until expiration to write new options.

- DO select underlying common stocks with minimal downside risk. Downside risk is the *hidden cost* of covered option writing.

- DO consider the *put alternative.* Writing naked puts may be a better alternative than covered writing, and with no additional risk. Check the pros and cons of this strategy in the next chapter.

Using the True Cost Covered Option Writing Tables you can eliminate poor covered option writing strategies. At first glance strategies may look attractive, but as in Example III, they *may not be profitable.* After you have studied the True Cost Covered Option Writing Tables for a while, you will discover that you must be very selective in entering covered writing strategies. When you look closely at the tables, you will find that many such strategies will not provide an acceptable return.

Consider the put alternative

Chapter 17

The Put Alternative

The previous chapter probably has deflated some of the glamour that is normally attached to covered option writing strategies. This chapter will provide you with an alternative which is as conservative as covered option writing, but may provide you with a far better return. That alternative, believe it or not, is *to write naked put options.*

Writing Puts Simulates Covered Writing

Now wait before you close the book. Writing naked puts, when the put is written at-the-money, almost perfectly simulates a covered option writing strategy. (When writing naked puts that are out-of-the-money, the results are the same with one exception. You lose the capital gains potential from owning the underlying common stock but have reduced the risk of the position by the amount the stock price is out-of-the-money.)

Just sit back for a moment and think about the similarities. Remember, with covered option writing your risk is the downside exposure of the hundred shares of stock that you own.

The same exposure exists in naked put writing, and in each case the option premiums offset some of the risk and provide income. Now, looking at these similarities, maybe the risk of naked writing has been over-emphasized and the risk of covered writing has been under-emphasized. As it turns out, when it comes to writing naked puts, the risks are almost identical to covered writing.

Advantages of Writing Naked Puts Over Covered Writing

- You receive almost three times the return on investment (based on option premiums).
- Writing naked puts involves less commissions. (You do not have to purchase the common stock.)
- There is less trading difficulty when you write naked puts (there is only one transaction rather than two.)
- You are able to use Treasury Bills as collateral.

Disadvantages of Writing Naked Puts over Covered Writing

- You do not receive the dividends from the common stock.
- You lose some capital gain potential in the common stock at certain times. (When the stock price is out-of-the-money, the difference between the stock price and the exercise price is lost if the stock price moves to the exercise price.)
- Puts are usually lower priced than calls.
- Your risk per dollar of investment increases, but the risk per position does not.

Comparing the Pros to the Cons

The major advantage of writing naked puts is that you do not have to purchase the common stock. You only have to follow the naked writing margin rules that require putting up approximately 30% of the underlying stock value in the form of cash, Treasury Bills, or securities. Without the common stock you eliminate a lot of commissions and trading difficulties. In addition, you are now able to provide a lot more income per dollar of investment.

The disadvantages are quite minor in comparison. The loss of dividends can be offset by income from Treasury Bills. The increased risk is only the result of greater leverage from writing naked puts. Puts are usually lower priced than calls. so the writer must be more selective when targeting in on put writing candidates. The loss of capital gains potential with an out-of-the-money covered option writing strategy is offset by the reduction in risk with an out-of-the-money naked put writing strategy.

So when you compare the pros to the cons, put writing becomes highly attractive. One word of caution, however, when you are writing naked puts, just as when you are carrying out a covered writing strategy, you must write puts that have *inherent profitability.* As with writing calls, you must write puts that are higher priced than their *future intrinsic value* as indicated in our Future Value Put Pricing Tables. To write puts that are under their *future value* will result in long term losses.

The Art of Writing Naked Puts

If you decide to include naked put writing in your portfolio to improve income returns, your next step is to identify what strategy and tactics should be used in developing a naked put writing portfolio. Follow the same steps and procedures that are indicated in Chapters 7, 8 and 10. The Future Value Put Pricing Tables starting on Page T22 and the High Price Option Tables starting on Page T57 will provide invaluable tools that must be used in order to insure a portfolio that will produce long term profitability.

111

Measuring Return on Investment

In measuring your return on investment, you should closely monitor the Future Value Put Pricing Tables. They tell you what price the option should be in order to *break even*. The amount of premium beyond the *breakeven value* in the tables is the figure you should use to measure your long term return on investment.

Beware Of The Risks

The writing of naked puts can be easier to implement than a covered option writing strategy, but only if you use the tables in this book and only if you realize — because of the greater leverage possible — that there will be increased downside risks. As in any other naked writing strategy, naked puts have the potential for significant risk and, therefore, should be handled with kid gloves. Nevertheless, from our analysis, the risks of put writing are not greater than the risks of covered writing.

In conclusion, *naked put writing* with proper selectivity can be a better alternative than covered writing. The novelty and innovative nature of put writing should not scare the investor or money manager away from this powerful, but prudent strategy.

Chapter 18

Advanced Trading Tactics

Our concern so far has been with the selection of option strategies that have long term profit potential. However, the experienced option player knows that the selection of strategies is only half the game. The implementation, maintenance, and surveillance of these strategies is as important as the selection process, if not more so. In THE COMPLEAT OPTION PLAYER we spent a considerable amount of time discussing trading tactics, strategies, and other aspects of the trading arena that we cannot overlook.

Referring back to that book is an important part of your learning process. We are not going to cover the same tactics in this book, but we will discuss some important advanced aspects of trading that are being overlooked in the options market and will provide even more firing power to your options toolkit.

The Individual Player's Big Advantage

Unlike the stock market or most other investment markets that we encounter, the options markets offer the investor and the option player a unique advantage, which few know about. This advantage is only available on specific exchanges, which include The Chicago Board Options Exchange and the Pacific Options Exchange; they do not have a specialist system as do the stock exchange and some of the other options exchanges.

The advantage we are referring to is the ability of the option player to put a *limit order* into the Board broker's book (reference THE COMPLEAT OPTION PLAYER, Chapter 21). When the order is entered in that book, it receives *top priority* consideration over all other orders. What does that mean? It means that the market makers on the floor of these Exchanges do not have priority over your order, nor do they see your order in the book. Therefore, the patient option player even if he is not on the floor of the exchange, can wait for opportunities, and the probability of a specialist stealing these opportunities from him is eliminated.

You will better understand this concept if you comprehend the setup for options trading on the above mentioned exchange floors where there is a market maker system. It differs dramatically from what happens on the floors of the stock exchange and on the floor of the American Options Exchange where specialists rule the roost. The specialist can see your order in the book and, therefore, knows exactly when to steal the good opportunities away from you. In the case of the Chicago Board Options Exchange and the Pacific Options Exchange, the Board broker is not a specialist. He is an employee of the Exchange whose only purpose is to run the individual auctions and to make sure everybody gets a fair shake.

There are many market makers who trade for their own accounts and are continually looking for bargains and taking advantage of market orders and poorly placed limit orders that are

114

filtered onto the floor from individual investors. The priority consideration allows and enables individual investors to have an even better opportunity than the market makers to take advantage of out-of-line options or out-of-line strategies. In other words, trading from your home with well placed orders, you can have a better advantage than the market makers have on the floors of the options exchanges.

With this priority advantage you can now begin to fish for outstanding opportunities. Place orders below or above the market price, at a price you believe may be reached on short term fluctuations. Patience and the ability to fish carefully for these opportunities are two keys to success in options trading. Remember the *priority advantage.* If you don't understand it, ask your broker about it.

The Golden Rule Of Options Trading

With the priority advantage, which is available on the above mentioned options exchanges, and with the nature of option strategies, you need one specific quality to be a successful option trader. If you have looked at all the many tables in this book and if you are planning on using these tables to guide you to victory in the options game, the obvious characteristic that you will need is **patience.**

The only way to prosper in the options markets, the only way to *turn the tables on the options markets,* is to take advantage of options and option strategies that are out-of-line, that are counter to the crowd and to the masses and that will provide a good margin of long term profitability.

To do this requires tremendous patience on your part. If you are involved in covered option writing strategies, there will be times when you should *not* be writing options. You may have to wait weeks, months, and, in some cases, years before you resume that behavior. If you are an option buyer, there are times when option buying is out of the question. There are other times when option prices will be highly depressed, and then you

Use the priority advantage

should definitely go out and get a lot of fishing poles in the water. But, again, patience. Do you have the ability to wait a week, a month, a year?

Although normally difficult to evaluate, calendar spreads can be easily appraised and closely watched with the tables in this text. Here again, opportunities fade and blossom and them fade once more.

Calendar spreads need a good margin of profit because of the trading difficulties of moving in and out of these strategies. To repeat, *patience* is needed to find those spreads that give you the biggest payoff and provide a good margin of error.

To summarize, as in the stock market, the successful options investor is one who identifies opportunities before anybody else does. Rarely do you win if you follow the crowd. The beauty of the options market, as opposed to other markets, is that it is far easier to identify when options or option strategies are out-of-line. With this book that task will be made far easier. But to be successful, you must have the patience to wait for the right price, to wait for the right spread, and to wait for the right opportunity. That is the golden rule of options trading — **patience.**

There are many other trading tactics that we discussed more extensively in THE COMPLEAT OPTION PLAYER, and they would be worthwhile reviewing as you try to improve and hone your trading skills.

Chapter 19

Enter The Home Computer

The power of the computer is one that cannot be ignored during this age of advanced technology. A computing capability, which was once priced at over a million dollars, can now be purchased in the form of a home computer or "personal" computer for as little as $1,000.

What can a home computer do? Many wondrous things for the option player, including:

1. Option strategy surveillance
2. Commission analysis
3. Bookkeeping functions
4. A price quote system
5. Strategy designs
6. Strategy simulations
7. A technical prediction of market activity
8. Computer selection of options and option strategies,

and countless other analytical activities that will aid the option player in winning this game. The home computer will become part of all of our lives in the next ten years. Those who use the computer as an aid in dealing with options will succeed; those who do not will be unable to compete.

This book has taken some of the wondrous findings and features of the computer and placed them in an easy-to-read table form, a reference form that is a better information system than the computer itself. However, if you want to go beyond this book, the home computer is your next step. A computer, such as the Apple computer, can be hooked up to the stock market and Dow Jones news wire to receive — on a real time basis — almost immediate quotes (15 minute delay) and news items.

With a home computer the only problem you will face is to get the proper software (programs that perform the above mentioned tasks). There are many new programs being developed today to analyze and manage stock portfolios. Similar programs should also soon be available for stock options. For those who know how to program, the applications of the home computer to the options game are limited only by his imagination.

So the next step for the option player with THE OPTION PLAYER'S ADVANCED GUIDEBOOK in hand is to consider investing in a home computer. As computer technology advances, the home computer will become the most important tool of the option player.

Appendix

The Player's Guide to Applied Probabilities

Throughout this book we have emphasized the major keys to success in the option markets:

— The ability to evaluate the inherent profitability of an option strategy before you enter that strategy

— The flexibility to move from one option investment mode to another as option strategies become out-of-line with their *future value.*

To capitalize on these premises, you have discovered several sets of Future Value Tables in the text. However, some players will wish to go beyond the tools thus far presented. Many option players feel they can accurately predict stock price action in the near future. Consequently, this section is designed for these players.

When you have a good feel for the future price action of the underlying stock, you must convert that "feeling" into some concrete figures that will tell you which option strategy to select in order to be profitable in the options game. To do this, a short course on *probabilities* and *probability* theory is necessary.

Now, wait before you leave! The author plans to present this scary subject in an easy-to digest manner. Knowledge of probabilities may sound more like a scientific endeavor to be performed by engineers, scientists and mathematicians. Yet it can be useful and effective for the layman and for the option player. So what we need is a little patience and a few minutes of your time to take this short course in probability theory, a short, *easy* course.

An Easy Course in Applied Probabilities

In order to evaluate the profitability of a specific option or option strategy in advance, the usual procedure is to identify what the future price action of a common stock will be. Although that sounds quite simple, it is difficult to precisely and consistently predict stock price action. Many of you will say that you can, but if you really look at your record, you would probably find that it is not as consistent nor as accurate as you thought.

Hence, enter the use of probability techniques. Probability theory will enable you to provide a better black and white analysis of what will happen to the stock prices in your strategies. Therefore, you will be able to predict much more accurately the profitability of your option positions in these strategies.

The Procedure

In order to complete this task, we are going to look at the area called *subjective probabilities.* Normally when we talk about probabilities we think of the flipping of a coin or the probability of throwing a seven on the roll of the dice. Yet we hear of other probabilities constantly in our daily lives, such as in the weather forecast when the forecaster predicts the percentage probability for rain, or in sports, the probability that the Green Bay Packers will beat the New Orleans Saints.

These same types of probabilities may be applied in analyzing your option strategies. Add to this your intuitive ability to predict stock prices, and in many cases you can clearly predict the profitability of an option strategy.

As an example, let's say that we are looking at Xerox common stock priced at 60, and let's also assume that our option strategy is to purchase a Xerox July 60 call option for 3 ($300) with three months left in its life. Now, how do we evaluate whether that purchase of an option for 3 is a profitable purchase? We can say, well, we believe the stock price is going to go up. But what does that mean? It does not mean any more than an intuitive feeling that the Xerox stock price will move upward in the next three months. It does not provide any kind of a clearcut game plan on our part; it doesn't even indicate what our profit objective will be.

On Your Way to A Pen and Paper Analysis

Now let us apply probability theory to this simple strategy. First let us establish a game plan where we will hold the Xerox July 60 call option until expiration. Using technical analysis, combined with an ongoing continual analysis of the Xerox fundamentals and plenty of homework on the other aspects of the market, we decide there is a 10% chance that Xerox will be at 70 at the end of July, a 20% chance it will be at 65, a 40% chance it will be at 63, and a 30% chance that Xerox will not be above 60 when the call option expires.

Xerox Stock Price	Probability of Xerox Being at the Stock Price in 3 Months
70	10%
65	20%
63	40%
Below 60	30%
	100%

How did we come up with these probabilities? In a sense they were taken out of the air. Hopefully good homework on your part will make these probabilities more than just guesswork. The

123

whole theory is based on taking your intuituve feeling, homework, and analysis and putting them down on paper.

How do we use these subjective probabilities to identify the profitability of our strategy? Let's add one more feature in mapping out this strategy. The profit or loss at each price level of the stock is as follows:

Xerox Stock Price When Option Expires	Probability	Profit or Loss
70	10%	+ $700
65	20%	+ $200
63	40%	0
Below 60	30%	(− $300)

Note: Commissions not included

The Magic Decision Rule

Now we are ready to gaze into the crystal ball and find what the future holds. To do this, we will open the statistics book a little wider and pull out a special rule called THE BAYSIAN DECISION RULE. This rule will provide our answer to the future. Rather than scare you with the formula, let's walk through this procedure in a nice and easy fashion.

First, let's take the 30% probability of losing all of our investment and multiply it times the $300 loss:

($300) Loss
× 30% Probability Xerox is at or below 60 when option expires
_____
($90) Loss

Now let's do the same with all the other probabilities and profits or losses at each stock price level:

124

When Xerox Stock Price is at 63

$$\begin{array}{r} 0 \quad \text{Profit or Loss} \\ \times\ 40\% \\ \hline 0 \end{array}$$

When Xerox Stock Price is at 65

$$\begin{array}{r} \$200 \quad \text{Profit} \\ \times\quad 20\% \\ \hline \$40 \end{array}$$

When Xerox Stock Price is at 70

$$\begin{array}{r} \$700 \quad \text{Profit} \\ \times\quad 10\% \\ \hline \$70 \end{array}$$

Now let's add up all the results of these multiplications:

```
- $90..............................Xerox at 60 or lower
    0.. ..............................Xerox at 63
+  40.......................................Xerox at 65
+  70.......................................Xerox at 70
+ $20    Profit or Loss (Expected Value)
```

The result of this multiplication and addition process is called our *expected value* — in layman's terms, our potential profit or loss. The profit or loss is the average profit or loss if we were to enter the same *exact* strategy thousands of times and determine the average return. In our example, the return on average would be $20 in the long run for a $300 investment, and let's emphasize THE LONG RUN.

125

The Advantage Of Probability Theory

Now you have a clear picture of the profitability of the strategy that initially looked pretty lucrative. Once you laid it out on paper and applied the Magic Decision Rule, however, the long run profitability looks very thin. This procedure, (which takes only a few minutes to complete) can give you an invaluable glance at the future. Again, remember the subjective probability must be developed through your own analysis of potential stock price action.

Seeing The Price Action As It Is

Taking a realistic look at the stock price action of your playable stock is critical. Don't let your enthusiasm for a stock cloud your future projection of its price action. No stock price has a 100% chance of going up. As in horse racing, there are no "sure things" in the stock market. You must take a sobering look at the action of a stock price before coming up with your subjective probabilities. Using probability theory, we are able to come much closer to estimating the profitability of an option strategy. At least we can get a much clearer picture of our potential profits or losses. The only problem with subjective probabilities is that they are highly dependent upon our own estimate of stock price action in the future. If more emotion than homework is involved in the process, all of our work will lead us astray. Making rational, well researched decisions is critical in developing subjective probabilities. Many do not have this capacity or are just unable to translate their intuitive feel and homework into hard figures.

Developing More Concrete Probabilities

So where do we go from here? For those who are in touch with the market and know the common stocks they follow quite well, subjective probabilities will pay off with big rewards and will pinpoint the best option strategy available at any one time. But probably a more important advantage is that they will get you off of losing strategies, especially those that lure you in with high profit potential, but require unrealistic performance from the underlying stock price.

For those who are unable to convert their intuitive feelings for a stock price into subjective probabilities, we have provided some *real probabilities* based on our simulations. The High Price Tables and the Future Value Tables provide *concrete* probabilities and data for the Magic Decision Rule.

To demonstrate: Mr. Jones purchases a Honeywell Aug 70 call option at 3 ($300). The *future value* based on our Future Values Tables is $250 (2.5) when it expires; however, the *average high price* according to our High Price Tables is $700, and according to the same tables, there is a 40% chance of reaching that price. Mr. Jones decides to put in a limit order to sell his option at $700 or else to hold until expiration if the price is not reached. With these facts, *has* Mr. Jones entered a profitable strategy?

Let's use the Magic Decision Rule to find out. First let's map out the strategy. There are two possible outcomes:

(1) A $400 profit if the high price is reached
(2) A $50 loss if the high price is never reached (in the long run based on the *future value*)

Probability		Profit or Loss
40%	×	$400 Profit ($700 − $300 = $400)
60%	×	($50) Loss ($250 − $300 = −$50)

There is a 40% probability that the high price will be attained and therefore a 60% chance that the option will not reach the high price before its expiration date.

127

To determine the true return, we multiply the probability times the profit or loss from each outcome.

Outcome #1

$400 Profit
× 40%
$160 Profit

$160 Profit
Less ($30) Loss
$130 Profit

Outcome #2

$50 Loss
× 60%
($30) Loss

The *expected return* after applying the magic rule is $130. This strategy then in the long run would show a profitable return.

We have provided several ways to use the probability theory to more accurately measure the *true* return from an option strategy. The more time and effort that you expend in measuring the *true* return of a potential option strategy, the more successful you will be in the options markets.

THE FUTURE
VALUE TABLES

THE FUTURE VALUE
CALL PRICING TABLES

Decimal to Fraction Conversion Chart		
Table Shows		Market Fraction
.1	=	1/16
.1	=	1/8
.2	=	3/16
.2	=	1/4
.3	=	5/16
.4	=	3/8
.4	=	7/16
.5	=	1/2
.6	=	9/16
.6	=	5/8
.7	=	11/16
.8	=	3/4
.8	=	13/16
.9	=	7/8
.9	=	15/16

*The Future Value Tables are generated by computer simulation. Due to the nature of the computer simulation techniques that we used there may be slight aberrations in the option prices presented. Therefore you should allow a variance of plus or minus 10% of these option prices. In a few cases, some of the less important, peripheral option prices may vary more than 10%.

CALL PRICING TABLE

Exercise Price is (10)

Low Volatility

STOCK PRICE — NUMBER OF MONTHS BEFORE THE OPTIONS EXPIRE

STOCK PRICE	1	2	3	4	5	6	7	8	9
0	0.0	0.0	0.0	0.0	0.0	0.0	0.0	0.0	0.0
1	0.0	0.0	0.0	0.0	0.0	0.0	0.0	0.0	0.0
2	0.0	0.0	0.0	0.0	0.0	0.0	0.0	0.0	0.0
3	0.0	0.0	0.0	0.0	0.0	0.0	0.0	0.0	0.0
4	0.0	0.0	0.0	0.0	0.0	0.0	0.0	0.0	0.0
5	0.0	0.0	0.0	0.0	0.0	0.0	0.0	0.0	0.0
6	0.0	0.0	0.0	0.0	0.0	0.0	0.0	0.0	0.0
7	0.0	0.0	0.0	0.0	0.0	0.0	0.0	0.0	0.0
8	0.0	0.0	0.0	0.0	0.0	0.0	0.0	0.0	0.0
9	0.0	0.0	0.0	0.0	0.0	0.0	0.0	0.0	0.0
10	0.1	0.1	0.1	0.2	0.2	0.2	0.2	0.2	0.3
11	0.9	0.9	0.9	1.0	1.0	1.0	1.0	1.0	1.0
12	1.9	1.9	1.9	1.9	1.9	1.9	1.9	1.9	2.0
13	2.9	2.9	2.9	2.9	2.9	2.9	2.9	2.9	3.0
14	3.9	3.9	3.9	3.9	3.9	3.9	3.9	3.9	4.0
15	4.9	4.9	4.9	4.9	4.9	4.9	4.9	4.9	5.0

Average Volatility

STOCK PRICE — NUMBER OF MONTHS BEFORE THE OPTIONS EXPIRE

STOCK PRICE	1	2	3	4	5	6	7	8	9
0	0.0	0.0	0.0	0.0	0.0	0.0	0.0	0.0	0.0
1	0.0	0.0	0.0	0.0	0.0	0.0	0.0	0.0	0.0
2	0.0	0.0	0.0	0.0	0.0	0.0	0.0	0.0	0.0
3	0.0	0.0	0.0	0.0	0.0	0.0	0.0	0.0	0.0
4	0.0	0.0	0.0	0.0	0.0	0.0	0.0	0.0	0.0
5	0.0	0.0	0.0	0.0	0.0	0.0	0.0	0.0	0.0
6	0.0	0.0	0.0	0.0	0.0	0.0	0.0	0.0	0.0
7	0.0	0.0	0.0	0.0	0.0	0.0	0.0	0.0	0.0
8	0.0	0.0	0.0	0.0	0.0	0.0	0.0	0.0	0.0
9	0.0	0.0	0.0	0.0	0.0	0.0	0.1	0.1	0.1
10	0.1	0.2	0.2	0.3	0.3	0.3	0.3	0.4	0.4
11	0.9	0.9	1.0	1.0	1.0	1.0	1.0	1.1	1.1
12	1.9	1.9	1.9	1.9	1.9	1.9	1.9	1.9	2.0
13	2.9	2.9	2.9	2.9	2.9	2.9	2.9	2.9	3.0
14	3.9	3.9	3.9	3.9	3.9	3.9	3.9	3.9	4.0
15	4.9	4.9	4.9	4.9	4.9	4.9	4.9	4.9	5.0

High Volatility

STOCK PRICE — NUMBER OF MONTHS BEFORE THE OPTIONS EXPIRE

STOCK PRICE	1	2	3	4	5	6	7	8	9
0	0.0	0.0	0.0	0.0	0.0	0.0	0.0	0.0	0.0
1	0.0	0.0	0.0	0.0	0.0	0.0	0.0	0.0	0.0
2	0.0	0.0	0.0	0.0	0.0	0.0	0.0	0.0	0.0
3	0.0	0.0	0.0	0.0	0.0	0.0	0.0	0.0	0.0
4	0.0	0.0	0.0	0.0	0.0	0.0	0.0	0.0	0.0
5	0.0	0.0	0.0	0.0	0.0	0.0	0.0	0.0	0.0
6	0.0	0.0	0.0	0.0	0.0	0.0	0.0	0.0	0.0
7	0.0	0.0	0.0	0.0	0.0	0.0	0.0	0.1	0.1
8	0.0	0.0	0.0	0.1	0.1	0.1	0.1	0.2	0.2
9	0.0	0.1	0.1	0.2	0.3	0.3	0.3	0.4	0.4
10	0.2	0.4	0.5	0.5	0.6	0.6	0.7	0.7	0.8
11	1.0	1.1	1.1	1.2	1.3	1.3	1.3	1.4	1.4
12	1.9	1.9	2.0	2.0	2.1	2.1	2.1	2.1	2.2
13	2.9	2.9	2.9	2.9	3.0	3.0	3.0	3.0	3.0
14	3.9	3.9	3.9	3.9	3.9	3.9	3.9	3.9	3.9
15	4.9	4.9	4.9	4.9	4.9	4.9	4.9	4.9	4.9

T3

CALL PRICING TABLE

Exercise Price is (15)

Low Volatility

STOCK PRICE — NUMBER OF MONTHS BEFORE THE OPTIONS EXPIRE

STOCK PRICE	1	2	3	4	5	6	7	8	9
5	0.0	0.0	0.0	0.0	0.0	0.0	0.0	0.0	0.0
6	0.0	0.0	0.0	0.0	0.0	0.0	0.0	0.0	0.0
7	0.0	0.0	0.0	0.0	0.0	0.0	0.0	0.0	0.0
8	0.0	0.0	0.0	0.0	0.0	0.0	0.0	0.0	0.0
9	0.0	0.0	0.0	0.0	0.0	0.0	0.0	0.0	0.0
10	0.0	0.0	0.0	0.0	0.0	0.0	0.0	0.0	0.0
11	0.0	0.0	0.0	0.0	0.0	0.0	0.0	0.0	0.0
12	0.0	0.0	0.0	0.0	0.0	0.0	0.0	0.0	0.0
13	0.0	0.0	0.0	0.0	0.0	0.0	0.0	0.0	0.0
14	0.0	0.0	0.0	0.0	0.1	0.1	0.1	0.1	0.1
15	0.1	0.2	0.2	0.3	0.3	0.4	0.4	0.4	0.5
16	0.9	1.0	1.0	1.0	1.0	1.1	1.1	1.1	1.1
17	1.9	1.9	1.9	1.9	1.9	1.9	1.9	2.0	2.0
18	2.9	2.9	2.9	2.9	2.9	2.9	2.9	2.9	2.9
19	3.9	3.9	3.9	3.9	3.9	3.9	3.9	3.9	3.9
20	4.9	4.9	4.9	4.9	4.9	4.9	4.9	4.9	4.9

Average Volatility

STOCK PRICE — NUMBER OF MONTHS BEFORE THE OPTIONS EXPIRE

STOCK PRICE	1	2	3	4	5	6	7	8	9
5	0.0	0.0	0.0	0.0	0.0	0.0	0.0	0.0	0.0
6	0.0	0.0	0.0	0.0	0.0	0.0	0.0	0.0	0.0
7	0.0	0.0	0.0	0.0	0.0	0.0	0.0	0.0	0.0
8	0.0	0.0	0.0	0.0	0.0	0.0	0.0	0.0	0.0
9	0.0	0.0	0.0	0.0	0.0	0.0	0.0	0.0	0.0
10	0.0	0.0	0.0	0.0	0.0	0.0	0.0	0.0	0.0
11	0.0	0.0	0.0	0.0	0.0	0.0	0.0	0.0	0.0
12	0.0	0.0	0.0	0.0	0.0	0.0	0.0	0.0	0.0
13	0.0	0.0	0.0	0.0	0.1	0.1	0.1	0.1	0.2
14	0.0	0.0	0.1	0.2	0.2	0.2	0.3	0.3	0.3
15	0.2	0.3	0.4	0.5	0.5	0.6	0.6	0.7	0.7
16	1.0	1.0	1.1	1.1	1.2	1.2	1.2	1.3	1.3
17	1.9	1.9	1.9	2.0	2.0	2.0	2.1	2.1	2.1
18	2.9	2.9	2.9	2.9	2.9	2.9	2.9	3.0	3.0
19	3.9	3.9	3.9	3.9	3.9	3.9	3.9	3.9	3.9
20	4.9	4.9	4.9	4.9	4.9	4.9	4.9	4.9	4.9

High Volatility

STOCK PRICE — NUMBER OF MONTHS BEFORE THE OPTIONS EXPIRE

STOCK PRICE	1	2	3	4	5	6	7	8	9
5	0.0	0.0	0.0	0.0	0.0	0.0	0.0	0.0	0.0
6	0.0	0.0	0.0	0.0	0.0	0.0	0.0	0.0	0.0
7	0.0	0.0	0.0	0.0	0.0	0.0	0.0	0.0	0.0
8	0.0	0.0	0.0	0.0	0.0	0.0	0.0	0.0	0.0
9	0.0	0.0	0.0	0.0	0.0	0.0	0.0	0.1	0.1
10	0.0	0.0	0.0	0.0	0.0	0.1	0.1	0.1	0.2
11	0.0	0.0	0.0	0.1	0.1	0.1	0.2	0.2	0.3
12	0.0	0.0	0.1	0.2	0.2	0.3	0.3	0.4	0.4
13	0.0	0.1	0.2	0.3	0.4	0.4	0.5	0.6	0.7
14	0.1	0.3	0.4	0.6	0.6	0.7	0.8	0.9	1.0
15	0.4	0.6	0.8	0.9	1.0	1.1	1.2	1.3	1.4
16	1.1	1.3	1.4	1.6	1.6	1.7	1.8	1.9	2.0
17	2.0	2.1	2.2	2.3	2.4	2.4	2.5	2.5	2.6
18	2.9	3.0	3.0	3.1	3.2	3.2	3.3	3.3	3.4
19	3.9	3.9	3.9	4.0	4.0	4.1	4.1	4.2	4.2
20	4.9	4.9	4.9	4.9	4.9	5.0	5.0	5.0	5.1

CALL PRICING TABLE

Exercise Price is (20)

Low Volatility

STOCK PRICE

NUMBER OF MONTHS BEFORE THE OPTIONS EXPIRE

STOCK PRICE	1	2	3	4	5	6	7	8	9
10	0.0	0.0	0.0	0.0	0.0	0.0	0.0	0.0	0.0
11	0.0	0.0	0.0	0.0	0.0	0.0	0.0	0.0	0.0
12	0.0	0.0	0.0	0.0	0.0	0.0	0.0	0.0	0.0
13	0.0	0.0	0.0	0.0	0.0	0.0	0.0	0.0	0.0
14	0.0	0.0	0.0	0.0	0.0	0.0	0.0	0.0	0.0
15	0.0	0.0	0.0	0.0	0.0	0.0	0.0	0.0	0.0
16	0.0	0.0	0.0	0.0	0.0	0.0	0.0	0.0	0.0
17	0.0	0.0	0.0	0.0	0.0	0.0	0.0	0.0	0.0
18	0.0	0.0	0.0	0.0	0.0	0.0	0.1	0.1	0.1
19	0.0	0.0	0.1	0.1	0.2	0.2	0.2	0.3	0.3
20	0.2	0.3	0.4	0.5	0.5	0.5	0.6	0.6	0.7
21	0.9	1.0	1.1	1.1	1.2	1.2	1.2	1.3	1.3
22	1.9	1.9	1.9	2.0	2.0	2.0	2.0	2.1	2.1
23	2.9	2.9	2.9	2.9	2.9	2.9	2.9	2.9	3.0
24	3.9	3.9	3.9	3.9	3.9	3.9	3.9	3.9	3.9
25	4.9	4.9	4.9	4.9	4.9	4.9	4.9	4.9	4.9

Average Volatility

STOCK PRICE

NUMBER OF MONTHS BEFORE THE OPTIONS EXPIRE

STOCK PRICE	1	2	3	4	5	6	7	8	9
10	0.0	0.0	0.0	0.0	0.0	0.0	0.0	0.0	0.0
11	0.0	0.0	0.0	0.0	0.0	0.0	0.0	0.0	0.0
12	0.0	0.0	0.0	0.0	0.0	0.0	0.0	0.0	0.0
13	0.0	0.0	0.0	0.0	0.0	0.0	0.0	0.0	0.0
14	0.0	0.0	0.0	0.0	0.0	0.0	0.0	0.0	0.0
15	0.0	0.0	0.0	0.0	0.0	0.0	0.0	0.0	0.0
16	0.0	0.0	0.0	0.0	0.0	0.0	0.0	0.1	0.1
17	0.0	0.0	0.0	0.0	0.1	0.1	0.1	0.2	0.2
18	0.0	0.0	0.1	0.1	0.2	0.2	0.3	0.3	0.4
19	0.0	0.1	0.2	0.3	0.4	0.4	0.5	0.5	0.6
20	0.3	0.5	0.6	0.7	0.8	0.8	0.9	0.9	1.0
21	1.0	1.1	1.2	1.3	1.4	1.4	1.5	1.5	1.6
22	1.9	2.0	2.0	2.1	2.2	2.2	2.2	2.3	2.3
23	2.9	2.9	2.9	3.0	3.0	3.0	3.1	3.1	3.2
24	3.9	3.9	3.9	3.9	3.9	3.9	4.0	4.0	4.0
25	4.9	4.9	4.9	4.9	4.9	4.9	4.9	4.9	4.9

High Volatility

STOCK PRICE

NUMBER OF MONTHS BEFORE THE OPTIONS EXPIRE

STOCK PRICE	1	2	3	4	5	6	7	8	9
10	0.0	0.0	0.0	0.0	0.0	0.0	0.0	0.0	0.1
11	0.0	0.0	0.0	0.0	0.0	0.0	0.0	0.1	0.1
12	0.0	0.0	0.0	0.0	0.0	0.0	0.1	0.1	0.2
13	0.0	0.0	0.0	0.0	0.1	0.1	0.1	0.2	0.3
14	0.0	0.0	0.0	0.1	0.1	0.2	0.2	0.3	0.4
15	0.0	0.0	0.1	0.2	0.2	0.3	0.3	0.4	0.5
16	0.0	0.1	0.2	0.3	0.4	0.4	0.5	0.6	0.7
17	0.0	0.2	0.3	0.4	0.5	0.6	0.7	0.8	0.9
18	0.1	0.3	0.4	0.6	0.7	0.7	0.8	1.0	1.1
19	0.2	0.5	0.7	0.9	1.0	1.1	1.2	1.4	1.5
20	0.6	0.9	1.1	1.4	1.5	1.6	1.7	1.8	1.9
21	1.2	1.5	1.7	1.9	2.0	2.2	2.2	2.4	2.5
22	2.1	2.3	2.4	2.6	2.7	2.7	2.9	3.0	3.1
23	2.9	3.1	3.2	3.4	3.5	3.6	3.6	3.7	3.8
24	3.9	4.0	4.1	4.2	4.3	4.4	4.4	4.5	4.6
25	4.9	4.9	5.0	5.1	5.1	5.2	5.2	5.3	5.4

CALL PRICING TABLE

Exercise Price is ⓔ25

Low Volatility

STOCK PRICE — NUMBER OF MONTHS BEFORE THE OPTIONS EXPIRE

Stock Price	1	2	3	4	5	6	7	8	9
15	0.0	0.0	0.0	0.0	0.0	0.0	0.0	0.0	0.0
16	0.0	0.0	0.0	0.0	0.0	0.0	0.0	0.0	0.0
17	0.0	0.0	0.0	0.0	0.0	0.0	0.0	0.0	0.0
18	0.0	0.0	0.0	0.0	0.0	0.0	0.0	0.0	0.0
19	0.0	0.0	0.0	0.0	0.0	0.0	0.0	0.0	0.0
20	0.0	0.0	0.0	0.0	0.0	0.0	0.0	0.0	0.0
21	0.0	0.0	0.0	0.0	0.0	0.0	0.0	0.0	0.0
22	0.0	0.0	0.0	0.0	0.0	0.0	0.1	0.1	0.1
23	0.0	0.0	0.0	0.1	0.1	0.1	0.2	0.2	0.3
24	0.0	0.1	0.2	0.2	0.3	0.3	0.4	0.4	0.5
25	0.2	0.4	0.5	0.6	0.7	0.7	0.7	0.8	0.9
26	1.0	1.1	1.2	1.2	1.3	1.3	1.4	1.4	1.5
27	1.9	2.0	2.0	2.0	2.1	2.1	2.1	2.2	2.2
28	2.9	2.9	2.9	2.9	3.0	3.0	3.0	3.0	3.1
29	3.9	3.9	3.9	3.9	3.9	3.9	3.9	3.9	3.9
30	4.9	4.9	4.9	4.9	4.9	4.9	4.9	4.9	4.9

Average Volatility

STOCK PRICE — NUMBER OF MONTHS BEFORE THE OPTIONS EXPIRE

Stock Price	1	2	3	4	5	6	7	8	9
15	0.0	0.0	0.0	0.0	0.0	0.0	0.0	0.0	0.0
16	0.0	0.0	0.0	0.0	0.0	0.0	0.0	0.0	0.0
17	0.0	0.0	0.0	0.0	0.0	0.0	0.0	0.0	0.0
18	0.0	0.0	0.0	0.0	0.0	0.0	0.0	0.0	0.1
19	0.0	0.0	0.0	0.0	0.0	0.0	0.1	0.1	0.2
20	0.0	0.0	0.0	0.0	0.0	0.0	0.1	0.1	0.2
21	0.0	0.0	0.0	0.0	0.0	0.1	0.1	0.2	0.3
22	0.0	0.0	0.0	0.1	0.1	0.2	0.2	0.3	0.4
23	0.0	0.1	0.2	0.3	0.3	0.4	0.4	0.5	0.6
24	0.1	0.3	0.4	0.5	0.6	0.7	0.7	0.8	0.9
25	0.4	0.6	0.8	0.9	1.0	1.1	1.1	1.2	1.3
26	1.1	1.3	1.4	1.5	1.6	1.7	1.7	1.8	1.9
27	2.0	2.1	2.2	2.3	2.3	2.4	2.4	2.5	2.6
28	2.9	3.0	3.0	3.1	3.1	3.2	3.2	3.3	3.4
29	3.9	3.9	3.9	4.0	4.0	4.0	4.1	4.1	4.2
30	4.9	4.9	4.9	4.9	4.9	4.9	5.0	5.0	5.0

High Volatility

STOCK PRICE — NUMBER OF MONTHS BEFORE THE OPTIONS EXPIRE

Stock Price	1	2	3	4	5	6	7	8	9
15	0.0	0.0	0.0	0.0	0.0	0.1	0.1	0.2	0.3
16	0.0	0.0	0.0	0.0	0.1	0.1	0.2	0.3	0.4
17	0.0	0.0	0.0	0.1	0.2	0.2	0.3	0.4	0.5
18	0.0	0.0	0.1	0.2	0.3	0.3	0.4	0.5	0.6
19	0.0	0.0	0.1	0.3	0.4	0.4	0.5	0.6	0.7
20	0.0	0.1	0.2	0.4	0.5	0.6	0.7	0.8	0.9
21	0.0	0.2	0.3	0.5	0.6	0.7	0.8	1.0	1.1
22	0.1	0.3	0.5	0.7	0.8	1.0	1.1	1.2	1.4
23	0.2	0.5	0.7	1.0	1.1	1.2	1.4	1.5	1.7
24	0.4	0.8	1.0	1.3	1.5	1.6	1.7	1.9	2.1
25	0.8	1.2	1.5	1.7	1.9	2.0	2.2	2.3	2.5
26	1.4	1.8	2.0	2.3	2.5	2.6	2.7	2.9	3.1
27	2.2	2.5	2.7	3.0	3.1	3.2	3.3	3.5	3.7
28	3.0	3.3	3.5	3.7	3.8	4.0	4.0	4.2	4.4
29	3.9	4.1	4.3	4.5	4.6	4.7	4.8	4.9	5.1
30	4.9	5.0	5.1	5.3	5.4	5.5	5.6	5.7	5.9

CALL PRICING TABLE

Exercise Price is (30)

Low Volatility

STOCK PRICE — NUMBER OF MONTHS BEFORE THE OPTIONS EXPIRE

STOCK PRICE	1	2	3	4	5	6	7	8	9
20	0.0	0.0	0.0	0.0	0.0	0.0	0.0	0.0	0.0
21	0.0	0.0	0.0	0.0	0.0	0.0	0.0	0.0	0.0
22	0.0	0.0	0.0	0.0	0.0	0.0	0.0	0.0	0.0
23	0.0	0.0	0.0	0.0	0.0	0.0	0.0	0.0	0.0
24	0.0	0.0	0.0	0.0	0.0	0.0	0.0	0.0	0.0
25	0.0	0.0	0.0	0.0	0.0	0.0	0.0	0.0	0.1
26	0.0	0.0	0.0	0.0	0.0	0.0	0.1	0.1	0.1
27	0.0	0.0	0.0	0.1	0.1	0.1	0.2	0.2	0.2
28	0.0	0.0	0.1	0.2	0.2	0.2	0.3	0.3	0.4
29	0.0	0.2	0.3	0.4	0.4	0.5	0.5	0.6	0.7
30	0.3	0.5	0.6	0.7	0.8	0.8	0.9	1.0	1.1
31	1.0	1.2	1.3	1.4	1.4	1.5	1.5	1.6	1.7
32	1.9	2.0	2.1	2.1	2.2	2.2	2.3	2.3	2.4
33	2.9	2.9	3.0	3.0	3.0	3.0	3.1	3.1	3.2
34	3.9	3.9	3.9	3.9	3.9	3.9	4.0	4.0	4.1
35	4.9	4.9	4.9	4.9	4.9	4.9	4.9	4.9	5.0

Average Volatility

STOCK PRICE — NUMBER OF MONTHS BEFORE THE OPTIONS EXPIRE

STOCK PRICE	1	2	3	4	5	6	7	8	9
20	0.0	0.0	0.0	0.0	0.0	0.0	0.0	0.0	0.0
21	0.0	0.0	0.0	0.0	0.0	0.0	0.0	0.0	0.0
22	0.0	0.0	0.0	0.0	0.0	0.0	0.0	0.0	0.1
23	0.0	0.0	0.0	0.0	0.0	0.0	0.1	0.1	0.1
24	0.0	0.0	0.0	0.0	0.1	0.1	0.2	0.2	0.3
25	0.0	0.0	0.0	0.1	0.1	0.2	0.2	0.2	0.3
26	0.0	0.0	0.1	0.1	0.2	0.3	0.3	0.4	0.4
27	0.0	0.1	0.2	0.3	0.3	0.4	0.4	0.5	0.6
28	0.0	0.2	0.3	0.4	0.5	0.6	0.7	0.8	0.8
29	0.2	0.4	0.5	0.7	0.8	0.9	1.1	1.1	1.2
30	0.5	0.8	0.9	1.1	1.2	1.3	1.4	1.5	1.6
31	1.2	1.4	1.5	1.7	1.8	1.9	2.0	2.1	2.2
32	2.0	2.2	2.3	2.4	2.5	2.6	2.7	2.7	2.8
33	2.9	3.0	3.1	3.2	3.3	3.4	3.4	3.5	3.6
34	3.9	3.9	4.0	4.1	4.1	4.2	4.2	4.3	4.4
35	4.9	4.9	4.9	5.0	5.0	5.1	5.1	5.2	5.2

High Volatility

STOCK PRICE — NUMBER OF MONTHS BEFORE THE OPTIONS EXPIRE

STOCK PRICE	1	2	3	4	5	6	7	8	9
20	0.0	0.0	0.0	0.1	0.2	0.3	0.3	0.4	0.6
21	0.0	0.0	0.1	0.2	0.3	0.4	0.4	0.6	0.7
22	0.0	0.0	0.1	0.3	0.4	0.5	0.5	0.7	0.8
23	0.0	0.1	0.2	0.4	0.5	0.6	0.7	0.8	1.0
24	0.0	0.1	0.3	0.5	0.6	0.7	0.8	1.0	1.2
25	0.0	0.2	0.4	0.6	0.8	0.9	1.0	1.2	1.4
26	0.1	0.4	0.6	0.8	1.0	1.1	1.2	1.4	1.6
27	0.2	0.5	0.8	1.1	1.2	1.3	1.5	1.7	1.9
28	0.3	0.7	1.0	1.3	1.5	1.7	1.8	2.0	2.3
29	0.6	1.0	1.3	1.7	1.9	2.0	2.2	2.4	2.6
30	0.9	1.5	1.8	2.1	2.3	2.5	2.6	2.9	3.1
31	1.6	2.1	2.4	2.7	2.9	3.0	3.2	3.4	3.7
32	2.3	2.7	3.0	3.2	3.3	3.7	3.8	4.0	4.3
33	3.1	3.5	3.7	4.0	4.2	4.3	4.5	4.7	4.9
34	4.0	4.3	4.5	4.8	4.9	5.1	5.2	5.4	5.6
35	4.9	5.2	5.3	5.6	5.7	5.8	6.0	6.2	6.3

CALL PRICING TABLE

Low Volatility

STOCK PRICE — NUMBER OF MONTHS BEFORE THE OPTIONS EXPIRE

STOCK PRICE	1	2	3	4	5	6	7	8	9
25	0.0	0.0	0.0	0.0	0.0	0.0	0.0	0.0	0.0
26	0.0	0.0	0.0	0.0	0.0	0.0	0.0	0.0	0.0
27	0.0	0.0	0.0	0.0	0.0	0.0	0.0	0.0	0.0
28	0.0	0.0	0.0	0.0	0.0	0.0	0.0	0.0	0.0
29	0.0	0.0	0.0	0.0	0.0	0.0	0.0	0.0	0.1
30	0.0	0.0	0.0	0.0	0.0	0.0	0.0	0.0	0.1
31	0.0	0.0	0.0	0.0	0.0	0.1	0.1	0.1	0.2
32	0.0	0.0	0.1	0.1	0.2	0.2	0.3	0.3	0.4
33	0.0	0.1	0.2	0.3	0.3	0.4	0.4	0.5	0.6
34	0.1	0.2	0.4	0.5	0.6	0.6	0.7	0.8	0.9
35	0.4	0.6	0.7	0.9	1.0	1.0	1.1	1.2	1.3
36	1.1	1.2	1.4	1.6	1.6	1.6	1.7	1.8	1.9
37	1.9	2.0	2.1	2.2	2.3	2.4	2.4	2.5	2.6
38	2.9	2.9	3.0	3.1	3.1	3.2	3.2	3.3	3.3
39	3.9	3.9	3.9	4.0	4.0	4.0	4.1	4.1	4.2
40	4.9	4.9	4.9	4.9	4.9	4.9	5.0	5.0	5.0

Average Volatility

STOCK PRICE — NUMBER OF MONTHS BEFORE THE OPTIONS EXPIRE

STOCK PRICE	1	2	3	4	5	6	7	8	9
25	0.0	0.0	0.0	0.0	0.0	0.0	0.0	0.0	0.0
26	0.0	0.0	0.0	0.0	0.0	0.0	0.0	0.1	0.1
27	0.0	0.0	0.0	0.0	0.0	0.0	0.0	0.1	0.2
28	0.0	0.0	0.0	0.0	0.1	0.1	0.1	0.2	0.3
29	0.0	0.0	0.0	0.1	0.1	0.2	0.2	0.3	0.4
30	0.0	0.0	0.1	0.2	0.2	0.3	0.3	0.4	0.5
31	0.0	0.1	0.2	0.3	0.3	0.4	0.5	0.6	0.7
32	0.0	0.1	0.3	0.4	0.5	0.6	0.6	0.7	0.9
33	0.1	0.3	0.4	0.6	0.7	0.8	0.9	1.0	1.1
34	0.2	0.5	0.7	0.9	1.0	1.1	1.2	1.3	1.5
35	0.6	0.9	1.1	1.3	1.4	1.6	1.6	1.8	1.9
36	1.2	1.5	1.7	1.9	2.0	2.1	2.2	2.3	2.5
37	2.1	2.3	2.4	2.6	2.7	2.8	2.9	3.0	3.1
38	3.0	3.1	3.2	3.4	3.5	3.6	3.6	3.7	3.9
39	3.9	4.0	4.1	4.2	4.3	4.4	4.4	4.5	4.6
40	4.9	4.9	5.0	5.1	5.1	5.2	5.2	5.3	5.4

High Volatility

STOCK PRICE — NUMBER OF MONTHS BEFORE THE OPTIONS EXPIRE

STOCK PRICE	1	2	3	4	5	6	7	8	9
25	0.0	0.0	0.1	0.3	0.4	0.5	0.6	0.7	0.9
26	0.0	0.0	0.2	0.4	0.5	0.6	0.7	0.9	1.0
27	0.0	0.1	0.3	0.5	0.6	0.7	0.8	1.0	1.2
28	0.0	0.2	0.4	0.6	0.8	0.9	1.0	1.2	1.4
29	0.0	0.3	0.5	0.8	0.9	1.0	1.2	1.4	1.6
30	0.1	0.4	0.6	0.9	1.1	1.2	1.4	1.6	1.8
31	0.2	0.5	0.8	1.1	1.3	1.5	1.6	1.9	2.1
32	0.3	0.7	1.0	1.4	1.6	1.8	1.9	2.2	2.4
33	0.4	1.0	1.3	1.7	1.9	2.1	2.3	2.5	2.8
34	0.7	1.3	1.7	2.1	2.3	2.5	2.7	2.9	3.2
35	1.1	1.7	2.1	2.5	2.8	3.0	3.1	3.4	3.7
36	1.7	2.3	2.7	3.1	3.3	3.5	3.7	3.9	4.2
37	2.4	3.0	3.3	3.7	4.0	4.1	4.3	4.5	4.8
38	3.2	3.7	4.0	4.4	4.6	4.8	5.0	5.2	5.4
39	4.1	4.5	4.8	5.1	5.3	5.5	5.6	5.9	6.1
40	5.0	5.3	5.6	5.9	6.1	6.2	6.4	6.6	6.8

CALL PRICING TABLE

Exercise Price is (40)

STOCK PRICE

Low Volatility
NUMBER OF MONTHS BEFORE THE OPTIONS EXPIRE

	1	2	3	4	5	6	7	8	9
30	0.0	0.0	0.0	0.0	0.0	0.0	0.0	0.0	0.0
31	0.0	0.0	0.0	0.0	0.0	0.0	0.0	0.0	0.0
32	0.0	0.0	0.0	0.0	0.0	0.0	0.0	0.0	0.0
33	0.0	0.0	0.0	0.0	0.0	0.0	0.0	0.0	0.1
34	0.0	0.0	0.0	0.0	0.0	0.0	0.0	0.1	0.1
35	0.0	0.0	0.0	0.0	0.0	0.1	0.1	0.1	0.2
36	0.0	0.0	0.0	0.1	0.1	0.1	0.2	0.2	0.3
37	0.0	0.0	0.1	0.2	0.2	0.3	0.3	0.4	0.4
38	0.0	0.1	0.2	0.3	0.4	0.4	0.5	0.6	0.7
39	0.1	0.3	0.4	0.6	0.6	0.7	0.8	0.8	1.0
40	0.4	0.6	0.8	1.0	1.0	1.1	1.2	1.3	1.4
41	1.1	1.3	1.4	1.6	1.6	1.7	1.8	1.8	2.0
42	2.0	2.1	2.2	2.3	2.4	2.4	2.5	2.5	2.7
43	2.9	3.0	3.0	3.1	3.2	3.2	3.3	3.3	3.4
44	3.9	3.9	3.9	4.0	4.0	4.1	4.1	4.2	4.2
45	4.9	4.9	4.8	4.9	4.9	5.0	5.0	5.0	5.1

STOCK PRICE

Average Volatility
NUMBER OF MONTHS BEFORE THE OPTIONS EXPIRE

	1	2	3	4	5	6	7	8	9
30	0.0	0.0	0.0	0.0	0.0	0.0	0.0	0.1	0.2
31	0.0	0.0	0.0	0.0	0.0	0.1	0.1	0.2	0.2
32	0.0	0.0	0.0	0.0	0.1	0.1	0.2	0.2	0.3
33	0.0	0.0	0.0	0.1	0.1	0.2	0.3	0.3	0.4
34	0.0	0.0	0.1	0.2	0.2	0.3	0.4	0.5	0.6
35	0.0	0.0	0.1	0.3	0.4	0.4	0.5	0.6	0.7
36	0.0	0.1	0.3	0.4	0.5	0.6	0.6	0.8	0.9
37	0.0	0.2	0.4	0.6	0.7	0.8	0.8	1.0	1.1
38	0.1	0.4	0.6	0.8	0.9	1.0	1.1	1.3	1.4
39	0.3	0.7	0.9	1.1	1.2	1.4	1.5	1.6	1.8
40	0.7	1.1	1.3	1.5	1.7	1.8	1.9	2.1	2.2
41	1.3	1.7	1.9	2.1	2.2	2.4	2.5	2.6	2.8
42	2.1	2.4	2.6	2.8	2.9	3.0	3.1	3.3	3.4
43	3.0	3.2	3.4	3.5	3.6	3.8	3.8	4.0	4.1
44	3.9	4.1	4.2	4.3	4.4	4.5	4.6	4.7	4.9
45	4.9	5.0	5.0	5.2	5.3	5.4	5.4	5.5	5.7

STOCK PRICE

High Volatility
NUMBER OF MONTHS BEFORE THE OPTIONS EXPIRE

	1	2	3	4	5	6	7	8	9
30	0.0	0.1	0.3	0.5	0.7	0.8	0.9	1.1	1.3
31	0.0	0.1	0.3	0.6	0.8	0.9	1.0	1.2	1.4
32	0.0	0.2	0.4	0.7	0.9	1.0	1.2	1.4	1.6
33	0.0	0.3	0.6	0.9	1.1	1.2	1.3	1.6	1.8
34	0.1	0.4	0.7	1.0	1.3	1.4	1.6	1.8	2.1
35	0.1	0.6	0.9	1.2	1.5	1.6	1.8	2.0	2.3
36	0.3	0.7	1.1	1.5	1.7	1.9	2.1	2.3	2.6
37	0.4	0.9	1.3	1.8	2.0	2.2	2.4	2.7	3.0
38	0.6	1.2	1.6	2.1	2.4	2.5	2.7	3.0	3.3
39	0.9	1.6	2.0	2.5	2.8	2.9	3.1	3.4	3.8
40	1.3	2.0	2.5	2.9	3.2	3.4	3.6	3.9	4.2
41	1.9	2.6	3.0	3.5	3.8	4.0	4.2	4.4	4.8
42	2.6	3.2	3.6	4.1	4.4	4.5	4.8	5.0	5.3
43	3.4	3.9	4.3	4.8	5.0	5.2	5.7	5.7	6.0
44	4.2	4.7	5.1	5.5	5.7	5.9	6.1	6.3	6.6
45	5.0	5.5	5.8	6.2	6.4	6.6	6.8	7.0	7.3

CALL PRICING TABLE

Exercise Price is (45)

Low Volatility

STOCK PRICE — NUMBER OF MONTHS BEFORE THE OPTIONS EXPIRE

	1	2	3	4	5	6	7	8	9
35	0.0	0.0	0.0	0.0	0.0	0.0	0.0	0.0	0.0
36	0.0	0.0	0.0	0.0	0.0	0.0	0.0	0.0	0.0
37	0.0	0.0	0.0	0.0	0.0	0.0	0.0	0.0	0.1
38	0.0	0.0	0.0	0.0	0.0	0.0	0.0	0.0	0.1
39	0.0	0.0	0.0	0.0	0.0	0.0	0.0	0.1	0.1
40	0.0	0.0	0.0	0.1	0.1	0.1	0.1	0.1	0.2
41	0.0	0.0	0.0	0.1	0.2	0.2	0.2	0.2	0.3
42	0.0	0.1	0.1	0.3	0.3	0.4	0.4	0.5	0.6
43	0.0	0.2	0.3	0.4	0.5	0.6	0.6	0.7	0.8
44	0.2	0.4	0.5	0.7	0.8	0.9	0.9	1.0	1.2
45	0.5	0.7	0.9	1.1	1.2	1.3	1.4	1.5	1.6
46	1.1	1.4	1.5	1.7	1.8	1.9	1.9	2.0	2.2
47	2.0	2.1	2.3	2.4	2.5	2.6	2.6	2.7	2.8
48	2.9	3.0	3.1	3.2	3.3	3.3	3.4	3.5	3.6
49	3.9	3.9	4.0	4.1	4.1	4.1	4.2	4.3	4.4
50	4.9	4.9	4.9	5.0	5.0	5.0	5.1	5.1	5.2

Average Volatility

STOCK PRICE — NUMBER OF MONTHS BEFORE THE OPTIONS EXPIRE

	1	2	3	4	5	6	7	8	9
35	0.0	0.0	0.0	0.0	0.0	0.1	0.1	0.2	0.3
36	0.0	0.0	0.0	0.0	0.1	0.2	0.2	0.3	0.4
37	0.0	0.0	0.0	0.1	0.2	0.2	0.3	0.4	0.5
38	0.0	0.0	0.1	0.2	0.3	0.3	0.4	0.5	0.6
39	0.0	0.0	0.1	0.3	0.4	0.5	0.5	0.6	0.8
40	0.0	0.1	0.2	0.4	0.5	0.6	0.7	0.8	0.9
41	0.0	0.2	0.4	0.5	0.7	0.8	0.8	1.0	1.1
42	0.1	0.3	0.5	0.7	0.9	1.0	1.1	1.2	1.4
43	0.2	0.5	0.7	1.0	1.1	1.3	1.4	1.5	1.7
44	0.4	0.8	1.0	1.3	1.5	1.6	1.7	1.9	2.1
45	0.8	1.2	1.5	1.7	1.9	2.1	2.2	2.3	2.6
46	1.4	1.8	2.0	2.3	2.5	2.6	2.7	2.9	3.1
47	2.2	2.5	2.7	3.0	3.1	3.3	3.4	3.5	3.7
48	3.0	3.3	3.5	3.7	3.9	4.0	4.1	4.2	4.4
49	3.9	4.1	4.3	4.5	4.6	4.7	4.8	5.0	5.1
50	4.9	5.0	5.1	5.3	5.4	5.6	5.6	5.7	5.9

High Volatility

STOCK PRICE — NUMBER OF MONTHS BEFORE THE OPTIONS EXPIRE

	1	2	3	4	5	6	7	8	9
35	0.0	0.2	0.4	0.7	0.9	1.0	1.2	1.4	1.7
36	0.0	0.3	0.5	0.8	1.1	1.2	1.3	1.6	1.9
37	0.0	0.4	0.6	1.0	1.2	1.3	1.5	1.8	2.1
38	0.1	0.5	0.8	1.1	1.4	1.5	1.7	2.0	2.3
39	0.1	0.6	0.9	1.3	1.6	1.7	2.0	2.2	2.6
40	0.2	0.8	1.1	1.6	1.9	2.0	2.2	2.5	2.9
41	0.4	0.9	1.3	1.8	2.1	2.3	2.5	2.8	3.2
42	0.5	1.2	1.6	2.1	2.5	2.6	2.9	3.2	3.5
43	0.7	1.5	2.0	2.5	2.8	3.0	3.2	3.5	3.9
44	1.1	1.9	2.3	2.9	3.2	3.4	3.6	4.0	4.3
45	1.5	2.3	2.8	3.3	3.7	3.8	4.1	4.4	4.8
46	2.1	2.9	3.3	3.9	4.2	4.4	4.7	5.0	5.3
47	2.7	3.5	4.0	4.5	4.8	5.0	5.2	5.5	5.9
48	3.5	4.2	4.6	5.1	5.5	5.6	5.9	6.2	6.5
49	4.3	4.9	5.3	5.8	6.1	6.3	6.5	6.8	7.2
50	5.2	5.7	6.1	6.5	6.8	7.0	7.2	7.5	7.8

CALL PRICING TABLE

Exercise Price is (50)

Low Volatility

STOCK PRICE — NUMBER OF MONTHS BEFORE THE OPTIONS EXPIRE

STOCK PRICE	1	2	3	4	5	6	7	8	9
35	0.0	0.0	0.0	0.0	0.0	0.0	0.0	0.0	0.0
36	0.0	0.0	0.0	0.0	0.0	0.0	0.0	0.0	0.0
37	0.0	0.0	0.0	0.0	0.0	0.0	0.0	0.0	0.0
38	0.0	0.0	0.0	0.0	0.0	0.0	0.0	0.0	0.0
39	0.0	0.0	0.0	0.0	0.0	0.0	0.0	0.0	0.0
40	0.0	0.0	0.0	0.0	0.0	0.0	0.0	0.0	0.0
41	0.0	0.0	0.0	0.0	0.0	0.0	0.0	0.0	0.1
42	0.0	0.0	0.0	0.0	0.0	0.0	0.0	0.1	0.1
43	0.0	0.0	0.0	0.0	0.0	0.0	0.1	0.1	0.2
44	0.0	0.0	0.0	0.0	0.1	0.1	0.2	0.2	0.3
45	0.0	0.0	0.0	0.1	0.2	0.2	0.3	0.3	0.4
46	0.0	0.0	0.1	0.2	0.3	0.3	0.4	0.5	0.6
47	0.0	0.1	0.2	0.3	0.4	0.5	0.6	0.6	0.8
48	0.1	0.2	0.4	0.5	0.6	0.7	0.8	0.9	1.0
49	0.2	0.5	0.6	0.8	0.9	1.0	1.1	1.2	1.4
50	0.5	0.8	1.0	1.2	1.4	1.4	1.5	1.6	1.8
51	1.2	1.5	1.6	1.8	1.9	2.0	2.1	2.2	2.4
52	2.0	2.2	2.4	2.5	2.6	2.7	2.8	2.9	3.0
53	2.9	3.1	3.2	3.3	3.4	3.5	3.5	3.6	3.8
54	3.9	4.0	4.0	4.1	4.2	4.3	4.3	4.4	4.5
55	4.9	4.9	4.9	5.0	5.1	5.1	5.2	5.2	5.4

Average Volatility

STOCK PRICE — NUMBER OF MONTHS BEFORE THE OPTIONS EXPIRE

STOCK PRICE	1	2	3	4	5	6	7	8	9
35	0.0	0.0	0.0	0.0	0.0	0.0	0.0	0.0	0.1
36	0.0	0.0	0.0	0.0	0.0	0.0	0.0	0.0	0.1
37	0.0	0.0	0.0	0.0	0.0	0.0	0.0	0.1	0.1
38	0.0	0.0	0.0	0.0	0.0	0.0	0.1	0.1	0.2
39	0.0	0.0	0.0	0.0	0.0	0.1	0.1	0.2	0.3
40	0.0	0.0	0.0	0.0	0.1	0.2	0.2	0.3	0.4
41	0.0	0.0	0.0	0.1	0.2	0.2	0.3	0.4	0.5
42	0.0	0.0	0.0	0.1	0.2	0.3	0.4	0.5	0.6
43	0.0	0.0	0.1	0.2	0.3	0.4	0.5	0.6	0.7
44	0.0	0.1	0.2	0.3	0.4	0.5	0.6	0.7	0.8
45	0.0	0.1	0.3	0.5	0.6	0.7	0.7	0.9	1.0
46	0.0	0.2	0.4	0.6	0.7	0.8	0.9	1.1	1.2
47	0.1	0.4	0.6	0.8	1.0	1.1	1.2	1.3	1.5
48	0.2	0.6	0.8	1.1	1.3	1.4	1.5	1.7	1.8
49	0.4	0.9	1.1	1.4	1.6	1.7	1.9	2.0	2.2
50	0.8	1.3	1.6	1.8	2.0	2.2	2.3	2.5	2.7
51	1.4	1.9	2.1	2.4	2.6	2.7	2.9	3.0	3.2
52	2.2	2.6	2.8	3.1	3.2	3.4	3.5	3.7	3.8
53	3.0	3.4	3.6	3.8	4.0	4.1	4.2	4.3	4.5
54	3.9	4.2	4.4	4.6	4.7	4.8	4.9	5.1	5.2
55	4.9	5.1	5.2	5.4	5.5	5.6	5.7	5.8	6.0

High Volatility

STOCK PRICE — NUMBER OF MONTHS BEFORE THE OPTIONS EXPIRE

STOCK PRICE	1	2	3	4	5	6	7	8	9
35	0.0	0.0	0.1	0.3	0.5	0.6	0.7	0.9	1.1
36	0.0	0.0	0.2	0.4	0.6	0.7	0.8	1.0	1.3
37	0.0	0.1	0.2	0.5	0.7	0.8	0.9	1.2	1.4
38	0.0	0.1	0.3	0.6	0.8	0.9	1.1	1.3	1.6
39	0.0	0.2	0.4	0.7	0.9	1.0	1.2	1.4	1.7
40	0.0	0.2	0.5	0.8	1.0	1.2	1.3	1.6	1.9
41	0.0	0.3	0.6	1.0	1.2	1.3	1.5	1.8	2.1
42	0.0	0.4	0.7	1.1	1.3	1.5	1.7	2.0	2.3
43	0.1	0.5	0.9	1.3	1.5	1.7	1.9	2.2	2.6
44	0.2	0.7	1.0	1.5	1.8	2.0	2.2	2.5	2.8
45	0.3	0.8	1.3	1.7	2.0	2.2	2.4	2.8	3.1
46	0.4	1.0	1.5	2.0	2.3	2.5	2.7	3.1	3.5
47	0.6	1.3	1.8	2.3	2.6	2.9	3.1	3.4	3.8
48	0.8	1.6	2.1	2.7	3.0	3.2	3.4	3.8	4.2
49	1.2	2.0	2.5	3.1	3.4	3.6	3.9	4.2	4.6
50	1.6	2.4	3.0	3.5	3.9	4.1	4.3	4.7	5.1
51	2.2	3.0	3.5	4.1	4.4	4.6	4.9	5.2	5.6
52	2.8	3.6	4.1	4.7	5.0	5.2	5.5	5.8	6.2
53	3.6	4.3	4.8	5.3	5.6	5.9	6.1	6.4	6.8
54	4.4	5.0	5.5	6.0	6.3	6.5	6.8	7.1	7.4
55	5.2	5.8	6.2	6.7	7.0	7.2	7.4	7.8	8.1

CALL PRICING TABLE

Exercise Price is (55)

Low Volatility

STOCK PRICE — NUMBER OF MONTHS BEFORE THE OPTIONS EXPIRE

Stock Price	1	2	3	4	5	6	7	8	9
40	0.0	0.0	0.0	0.0	0.0	0.0	0.0	0.0	0.0
41	0.0	0.0	0.0	0.0	0.0	0.0	0.0	0.0	0.0
42	0.0	0.0	0.0	0.0	0.0	0.0	0.0	0.0	0.0
43	0.0	0.0	0.0	0.0	0.0	0.0	0.0	0.0	0.0
44	0.0	0.0	0.0	0.0	0.0	0.0	0.0	0.0	0.0
45	0.0	0.0	0.0	0.0	0.0	0.0	0.0	0.0	0.1
46	0.0	0.0	0.0	0.0	0.0	0.0	0.0	0.1	0.1
47	0.0	0.0	0.0	0.0	0.0	0.1	0.1	0.1	0.2
48	0.0	0.0	0.0	0.0	0.1	0.1	0.2	0.2	0.3
49	0.0	0.0	0.0	0.1	0.2	0.2	0.3	0.3	0.4
50	0.0	0.0	0.1	0.2	0.3	0.3	0.4	0.4	0.5
51	0.0	0.1	0.2	0.3	0.4	0.4	0.5	0.6	0.7
52	0.0	0.2	0.3	0.4	0.5	0.6	0.7	0.8	0.9
53	0.1	0.3	0.5	0.7	0.8	0.9	0.9	1.1	1.2
54	0.3	0.5	0.7	1.0	1.1	1.2	1.3	1.4	1.5
55	0.6	0.9	1.1	1.4	1.5	1.6	1.7	1.8	2.0
56	1.3	1.5	1.7	2.0	2.1	2.2	2.3	2.4	2.6
57	2.1	2.3	2.4	2.6	2.8	2.9	2.9	3.1	3.2
58	2.9	3.1	3.2	3.4	3.5	3.6	3.7	3.8	3.9
59	3.9	4.0	4.1	4.2	4.3	4.4	4.4	4.6	4.7
60	4.9	4.9	5.0	5.1	5.2	5.2	5.3	5.4	5.5

Average Volatility

STOCK PRICE — NUMBER OF MONTHS BEFORE THE OPTIONS EXPIRE

Stock Price	1	2	3	4	5	6	7	8	9
40	0.0	0.0	0.0	0.0	0.0	0.0	0.0	0.1	0.1
41	0.0	0.0	0.0	0.0	0.0	0.0	0.1	0.1	0.2
42	0.0	0.0	0.0	0.0	0.0	0.0	0.1	0.2	0.3
43	0.0	0.0	0.0	0.0	0.1	0.1	0.1	0.2	0.3
44	0.0	0.0	0.0	0.0	0.1	0.2	0.2	0.3	0.4
45	0.0	0.0	0.0	0.1	0.2	0.2	0.3	0.4	0.5
46	0.0	0.0	0.0	0.2	0.3	0.3	0.4	0.5	0.6
47	0.0	0.0	0.1	0.2	0.4	0.4	0.5	0.6	0.8
48	0.0	0.1	0.2	0.3	0.5	0.5	0.6	0.8	0.9
49	0.0	0.1	0.3	0.5	0.6	0.7	0.8	0.9	1.1
50	0.0	0.2	0.4	0.6	0.7	0.8	0.9	1.1	1.3
51	0.1	0.3	0.5	0.8	0.9	1.0	1.2	1.3	1.5
52	0.2	0.5	0.7	1.0	1.2	1.3	1.4	1.6	1.8
53	0.3	0.7	1.0	1.3	1.5	1.6	1.7	1.9	2.1
54	0.5	1.0	1.3	1.6	1.8	1.9	2.1	2.3	2.5
55	0.9	1.4	1.7	2.1	2.3	2.4	2.6	2.8	3.0
56	1.5	2.0	2.3	2.6	2.8	2.9	3.1	3.3	3.5
57	2.3	2.7	3.0	3.3	3.5	3.6	3.7	3.9	4.1
58	3.1	3.5	3.7	4.0	4.2	4.3	4.4	4.6	4.8
59	4.0	4.3	4.5	4.7	4.9	5.0	5.1	5.3	5.5
60	4.9	5.1	5.3	5.5	5.7	5.8	5.9	6.1	6.2

High Volatility

STOCK PRICE — NUMBER OF MONTHS BEFORE THE OPTIONS EXPIRE

Stock Price	1	2	3	4	5	6	7	8	9
40	0.0	0.1	0.2	0.5	0.7	0.8	1.0	1.2	1.5
41	0.0	0.1	0.3	0.6	0.8	0.9	1.1	1.3	1.6
42	0.0	0.1	0.4	0.7	0.9	1.0	1.2	1.5	1.8
43	0.0	0.2	0.5	0.8	1.1	1.1	1.4	1.6	1.9
44	0.0	0.3	0.6	0.9	1.2	1.3	1.5	1.8	2.1
45	0.0	0.4	0.7	1.1	1.3	1.4	1.7	2.0	2.3
46	0.1	0.5	0.8	1.2	1.5	1.6	1.9	2.2	2.5
47	0.1	0.6	1.0	1.4	1.7	1.8	2.1	2.4	2.8
48	0.2	0.7	1.1	1.6	1.9	2.0	2.3	2.7	3.1
49	0.3	0.9	1.3	1.8	2.2	2.3	2.6	2.9	3.4
50	0.4	1.0	1.5	2.1	2.4	2.6	2.9	3.2	3.7
51	0.6	1.3	1.8	2.4	2.7	2.9	3.2	3.6	4.0
52	0.7	1.5	2.1	2.7	3.1	3.2	3.5	3.9	4.4
53	1.0	1.8	2.4	3.0	3.4	3.6	3.9	4.3	4.8
54	1.3	2.2	2.8	3.5	3.9	4.0	4.4	4.7	5.2
55	1.8	2.7	3.3	3.9	4.3	4.5	4.8	5.2	5.7
56	2.3	3.2	3.8	4.5	4.9	5.0	5.4	5.8	6.2
57	3.0	3.8	4.4	5.1	5.4	5.6	5.9	6.3	6.8
58	3.7	4.5	5.1	5.7	6.1	6.2	6.6	6.9	7.4
59	4.5	5.2	5.8	6.4	6.7	6.9	7.2	7.6	8.0
60	5.3	6.0	6.5	7.1	7.4	7.5	7.9	8.2	8.7

CALL PRICING TABLE

Exercise Price is 60

Low Volatility

STOCK PRICE — NUMBER OF MONTHS BEFORE THE OPTIONS EXPIRE

STOCK PRICE	1	2	3	4	5	6	7	8	9
45	0.0	0.0	0.0	0.0	0.0	0.0	0.0	0.0	0.0
46	0.0	0.0	0.0	0.0	0.0	0.0	0.0	0.0	0.0
47	0.0	0.0	0.0	0.0	0.0	0.0	0.0	0.0	0.0
48	0.0	0.0	0.0	0.0	0.0	0.0	0.0	0.0	0.0
49	0.0	0.0	0.0	0.0	0.0	0.0	0.0	0.0	0.1
50	0.0	0.0	0.0	0.0	0.0	0.0	0.0	0.1	0.1
51	0.0	0.0	0.0	0.0	0.0	0.1	0.1	0.1	0.2
52	0.0	0.0	0.0	0.0	0.1	0.1	0.2	0.2	0.3
53	0.0	0.0	0.0	0.1	0.1	0.2	0.2	0.3	0.4
54	0.0	0.0	0.1	0.2	0.2	0.3	0.4	0.4	0.5
55	0.0	0.0	0.1	0.3	0.3	0.4	0.5	0.6	0.7
56	0.0	0.1	0.2	0.4	0.5	0.6	0.6	0.7	0.9
57	0.0	0.2	0.4	0.5	0.7	0.7	0.8	1.0	1.1
58	0.1	0.4	0.6	0.8	0.9	1.0	1.1	1.2	1.4
59	0.3	0.6	0.8	1.1	1.2	1.3	1.4	1.6	1.7
60	0.7	1.0	1.3	1.5	1.8	1.8	1.9	2.0	2.2
61	1.3	1.6	1.8	2.1	2.2	2.3	2.5	2.6	2.8
62	2.1	2.4	2.5	2.7	2.9	3.0	3.1	3.2	3.4
63	3.0	3.2	3.3	3.5	3.7	3.7	3.8	4.0	4.1
64	3.9	4.0	4.2	4.3	4.4	4.5	4.6	4.7	4.8
65	4.9	4.9	5.0	5.1	5.3	5.3	5.4	5.5	5.6

Average Volatility

STOCK PRICE — NUMBER OF MONTHS BEFORE THE OPTIONS EXPIRE

STOCK PRICE	1	2	3	4	5	6	7	8	9
45	0.0	0.0	0.0	0.0	0.0	0.0	0.1	0.1	0.2
46	0.0	0.0	0.0	0.0	0.0	0.1	0.1	0.2	0.3
47	0.0	0.0	0.0	0.0	0.1	0.1	0.2	0.3	0.4
48	0.0	0.0	0.0	0.1	0.1	0.2	0.3	0.4	0.5
49	0.0	0.0	0.0	0.1	0.2	0.3	0.3	0.4	0.6
50	0.0	0.0	0.1	0.2	0.3	0.3	0.4	0.6	0.7
51	0.0	0.0	0.1	0.3	0.4	0.4	0.5	0.7	0.8
52	0.0	0.0	0.2	0.3	0.5	0.6	0.7	0.8	1.0
53	0.0	0.1	0.3	0.5	0.6	0.7	0.8	0.9	1.1
54	0.0	0.2	0.4	0.6	0.7	0.8	0.9	1.1	1.3
55	0.0	0.3	0.5	0.7	0.9	1.0	1.1	1.3	1.5
56	0.1	0.4	0.7	0.9	1.1	1.2	1.4	1.6	1.8
57	0.2	0.6	0.9	1.2	1.4	1.5	1.6	1.9	2.1
58	0.4	0.8	1.1	1.5	1.7	1.8	2.0	2.2	2.4
59	0.6	1.1	1.5	1.8	2.0	2.2	2.4	2.6	2.8
60	1.0	1.6	1.9	2.3	2.5	2.7	2.8	3.0	3.3
61	1.6	2.1	2.5	2.8	3.0	3.2	3.4	3.6	3.8
62	2.4	2.8	3.1	3.5	3.7	3.8	4.0	4.2	4.4
63	3.2	3.6	3.9	4.2	4.4	4.5	4.7	4.9	5.1
64	4.0	4.4	4.6	4.9	5.1	5.2	5.4	5.6	5.8
65	4.9	5.2	5.4	5.7	5.8	6.0	6.1	6.3	6.5

High Volatility

STOCK PRICE — NUMBER OF MONTHS BEFORE THE OPTIONS EXPIRE

STOCK PRICE	1	2	3	4	5	6	7	8	9
45	0.0	0.1	0.4	0.7	0.9	1.1	1.2	1.5	1.8
46	0.0	0.2	0.4	0.8	1.1	1.2	1.4	1.7	2.0
47	0.0	0.2	0.5	0.9	1.2	1.4	1.5	1.8	2.2
48	0.0	0.3	0.6	1.1	1.3	1.5	1.7	2.0	2.3
49	0.0	0.4	0.8	1.2	1.5	1.7	1.8	2.2	2.5
50	0.1	0.5	0.9	1.3	1.6	1.8	2.0	2.4	2.8
51	0.1	0.6	1.0	1.5	1.8	2.0	2.2	2.6	3.0
52	0.2	0.7	1.2	1.7	2.0	2.3	2.5	2.8	3.3
53	0.3	0.9	1.3	1.9	2.3	2.5	2.7	3.1	3.5
54	0.4	1.1	1.6	2.2	2.5	2.8	3.0	3.4	3.8
55	0.5	1.3	1.8	2.4	2.8	3.1	3.3	3.7	4.2
56	0.7	1.5	2.1	2.7	3.1	3.4	3.6	4.1	4.5
57	0.9	1.8	2.4	3.1	3.5	3.7	4.0	4.4	4.9
58	1.2	2.1	2.7	3.4	3.8	4.1	4.4	4.8	5.3
59	1.5	2.5	3.2	3.9	4.3	4.6	4.8	5.3	5.7
60	1.9	3.0	3.6	4.3	4.7	5.0	5.3	5.7	6.2
61	2.5	3.5	4.2	4.9	5.3	5.6	5.8	6.3	6.8
62	3.2	4.1	4.8	5.4	5.8	6.1	6.4	6.9	7.3
63	3.9	4.8	5.4	6.1	6.5	6.7	7.0	7.4	7.9
64	4.6	5.5	6.1	6.7	7.1	7.4	7.7	8.1	8.5
65	5.4	6.2	6.8	7.4	7.8	8.1	8.3	8.7	9.2

CALL PRICING TABLE

Exercise Price is (65)

Low Volatility

NUMBER OF MONTHS BEFORE THE OPTIONS EXPIRE

Stock Price	1	2	3	4	5	6	7	8	9
50	0.0	0.0	0.0	0.0	0.0	0.0	0.0	0.0	0.0
51	0.0	0.0	0.0	0.0	0.0	0.0	0.0	0.0	0.0
52	0.0	0.0	0.0	0.0	0.0	0.0	0.0	0.0	0.1
53	0.0	0.0	0.0	0.0	0.0	0.0	0.0	0.0	0.1
54	0.0	0.0	0.0	0.0	0.0	0.0	0.0	0.1	0.2
55	0.0	0.0	0.0	0.0	0.0	0.1	0.1	0.2	0.2
56	0.0	0.0	0.0	0.0	0.1	0.1	0.2	0.2	0.3
57	0.0	0.0	0.0	0.1	0.1	0.2	0.2	0.3	0.4
58	0.0	0.0	0.0	0.1	0.2	0.3	0.3	0.4	0.5
59	0.0	0.0	0.1	0.2	0.3	0.4	0.4	0.6	0.7
60	0.0	0.1	0.2	0.3	0.4	0.5	0.6	0.7	0.8
61	0.0	0.2	0.3	0.5	0.6	0.7	0.7	0.9	1.0
62	0.1	0.3	0.4	0.7	0.8	0.9	1.0	1.1	1.3
63	0.2	0.4	0.7	0.9	1.0	1.2	1.2	1.4	1.6
64	0.4	0.7	1.0	1.2	1.4	1.5	1.6	1.8	2.0
65	0.7	1.1	1.4	1.7	1.8	1.9	2.0	2.2	2.4
66	1.4	1.7	2.0	2.2	2.4	2.5	2.6	2.8	3.0
67	2.1	2.4	2.7	2.9	3.1	3.2	3.2	3.4	3.6
68	3.0	3.2	3.4	3.7	3.8	3.9	3.9	4.1	4.3
69	3.9	4.1	4.3	4.4	4.5	4.6	4.7	4.9	5.0
70	4.9	5.0	5.1	5.3	5.4	5.4	5.5	5.7	5.8

Average Volatility

STOCK PRICE — NUMBER OF MONTHS BEFORE THE OPTIONS EXPIRE

Stock Price	1	2	3	4	5	6	7	8	9
50	0.0	0.0	0.0	0.0	0.1	0.1	0.2	0.2	0.4
51	0.0	0.0	0.0	0.0	0.1	0.1	0.2	0.3	0.4
52	0.0	0.0	0.0	0.1	0.2	0.2	0.3	0.4	0.5
53	0.0	0.0	0.0	0.1	0.2	0.3	0.4	0.5	0.6
54	0.0	0.0	0.1	0.2	0.3	0.4	0.5	0.6	0.8
55	0.0	0.0	0.1	0.3	0.4	0.4	0.6	0.7	0.9
56	0.0	0.0	0.2	0.4	0.5	0.6	0.7	0.8	1.0
57	0.0	0.1	0.3	0.5	0.6	0.7	0.8	1.0	1.2
58	0.0	0.2	0.4	0.6	0.7	0.8	1.0	1.1	1.3
59	0.0	0.3	0.5	0.7	0.9	1.0	1.1	1.3	1.6
60	0.1	0.4	0.6	0.7	0.9	1.0	1.1	1.3	1.6
61	0.2	0.5	0.8	1.1	1.3	1.4	1.6	1.8	2.1
62	0.3	0.7	1.0	1.3	1.6	1.7	1.9	2.1	2.4
63	0.5	0.9	1.3	1.7	1.9	2.0	2.2	2.5	2.7
64	0.7	1.3	1.7	2.0	2.3	2.4	2.6	2.9	3.2
65	1.1	1.7	2.1	2.5	2.7	2.8	3.1	3.3	3.6
66	1.7	2.3	2.7	3.0	3.3	3.4	3.6	3.9	4.2
67	2.5	2.9	3.3	3.6	3.9	4.0	4.2	4.5	4.8
68	3.3	3.7	4.0	4.3	4.6	4.7	4.9	5.1	5.4
69	4.1	4.5	4.8	5.1	5.3	5.4	5.6	5.8	6.1
70	5.0	5.3	5.6	5.8	6.0	6.1	6.3	6.5	6.8

High Volatility

STOCK PRICE — NUMBER OF MONTHS BEFORE THE OPTIONS EXPIRE

Stock Price	1	2	3	4	5	6	7	8	9
50	0.0	0.2	0.5	0.9	1.2	1.4	1.5	1.9	2.2
51	0.0	0.3	0.6	1.0	1.3	1.5	1.7	2.0	2.4
52	0.0	0.4	0.7	1.2	1.5	1.7	1.8	2.2	2.6
53	0.0	0.4	0.8	1.3	1.6	1.8	2.0	2.4	2.8
54	0.1	0.5	1.0	1.4	1.8	2.0	2.2	2.6	3.0
55	0.1	0.6	1.1	1.6	2.0	2.2	2.4	2.8	3.2
56	0.2	0.8	1.2	1.8	2.2	2.4	2.6	3.1	3.5
57	0.3	0.9	1.4	2.0	2.4	2.7	2.9	3.3	3.8
58	0.4	1.1	1.6	2.2	2.6	2.9	3.1	3.6	4.1
59	0.5	1.2	1.8	2.5	2.9	3.2	3.4	3.9	4.4
60	0.6	1.5	2.1	2.8	3.2	3.5	3.8	4.2	4.7
61	0.8	1.7	2.4	3.1	3.6	3.9	4.1	4.6	5.1
62	1.0	2.0	2.7	3.5	3.9	4.2	4.5	5.0	5.4
63	1.3	2.4	3.1	3.8	4.3	4.6	4.9	5.4	5.9
64	1.7	2.7	3.5	4.3	4.7	5.1	5.3	5.8	6.3
65	2.1	3.2	4.0	4.7	5.2	5.5	5.8	6.3	6.8
66	2.7	3.8	4.5	5.3	5.7	6.1	6.3	6.8	7.3
67	3.3	4.3	5.1	5.9	6.3	6.6	6.9	7.4	7.9
68	4.0	5.0	5.7	6.5	6.9	7.2	7.5	8.0	8.5
69	4.8	5.7	6.4	7.1	7.6	7.9	8.1	8.6	9.1
70	5.6	6.4	7.1	7.8	8.2	8.5	8.7	9.3	9.7

CALL PRICING TABLE

Exercise Price is 70

Low Volatility

STOCK PRICE	NUMBER OF MONTHS BEFORE THE OPTIONS EXPIRE								
	1	2	3	4	5	6	7	8	9
55	0.0	0.0	0.0	0.0	0.0	0.0	0.0	0.0	0.0
56	0.0	0.0	0.0	0.0	0.0	0.0	0.0	0.0	0.1
57	0.0	0.0	0.0	0.0	0.0	0.0	0.0	0.1	0.1
58	0.0	0.0	0.0	0.0	0.0	0.0	0.0	0.1	0.2
59	0.0	0.0	0.0	0.0	0.0	0.0	0.1	0.2	0.2
60	0.0	0.0	0.0	0.0	0.1	0.1	0.1	0.2	0.3
61	0.0	0.0	0.0	0.1	0.1	0.2	0.2	0.3	0.4
62	0.0	0.0	0.0	0.1	0.2	0.3	0.3	0.4	0.5
63	0.0	0.0	0.1	0.2	0.3	0.4	0.4	0.5	0.7
64	0.0	0.0	0.1	0.3	0.4	0.5	0.5	0.7	0.8
65	0.0	0.1	0.2	0.4	0.5	0.6	0.7	0.8	1.0
66	0.0	0.2	0.4	0.6	0.7	0.8	0.9	1.0	1.2
67	0.1	0.3	0.5	0.8	0.9	1.0	1.1	1.3	1.5
68	0.2	0.5	0.7	1.0	1.2	1.3	1.4	1.6	1.8
69	0.4	0.8	1.1	1.4	1.5	1.7	1.8	2.0	2.2
70	0.8	1.2	1.5	1.8	2.0	2.1	2.2	2.4	2.6
71	1.4	1.8	2.1	2.4	2.6	2.7	2.8	3.0	3.2
72	2.2	2.5	2.7	3.0	3.2	3.3	3.4	3.6	3.8
73	3.0	3.3	3.5	3.8	3.9	4.0	4.1	4.3	4.5
74	3.9	4.1	4.3	4.5	4.7	4.8	4.8	5.0	5.2
75	4.9	5.0	5.1	5.4	5.5	5.6	5.6	5.8	5.9

Average Volatility

STOCK PRICE	NUMBER OF MONTHS BEFORE THE OPTIONS EXPIRE								
	1	2	3	4	5	6	7	8	9
55	0.0	0.0	0.0	0.1	0.1	0.2	0.2	0.4	0.5
56	0.0	0.0	0.0	0.1	0.2	0.2	0.3	0.4	0.6
57	0.0	0.0	0.0	0.1	0.2	0.3	0.4	0.5	0.7
58	0.0	0.0	0.1	0.2	0.3	0.4	0.5	0.6	0.8
59	0.0	0.0	0.1	0.3	0.4	0.5	0.7	0.7	0.9
60	0.0	0.0	0.2	0.4	0.5	0.6	0.7	0.9	1.1
61	0.0	0.1	0.2	0.5	0.6	0.7	0.8	1.0	1.2
62	0.0	0.2	0.3	0.6	0.7	0.9	1.0	1.2	1.4
63	0.0	0.2	0.5	0.7	0.9	1.0	1.1	1.3	1.6
64	0.0	0.3	0.6	0.9	1.1	1.2	1.3	1.5	1.8
65	0.1	0.5	0.7	1.0	1.3	1.4	1.5	1.8	2.0
66	0.2	0.6	0.9	1.3	1.5	1.7	1.8	2.1	2.3
67	0.4	0.8	1.2	1.5	1.8	2.0	2.1	2.4	2.7
68	0.5	1.1	1.4	1.9	2.2	2.3	2.4	2.7	3.0
69	0.8	1.4	1.8	2.2	2.5	2.7	2.8	3.1	3.4
70	1.2	1.9	2.3	2.7	3.0	3.2	3.3	3.6	3.9
71	1.8	2.4	2.8	3.2	3.5	3.7	3.8	4.2	4.5
72	2.5	3.1	3.4	3.9	4.1	4.3	4.4	4.7	5.0
73	3.3	3.8	4.1	4.5	4.8	5.0	5.1	5.4	5.7
74	4.2	4.6	4.9	5.3	5.5	5.7	5.8	6.1	6.3
75	5.0	5.4	5.7	6.0	6.2	6.4	6.5	6.8	7.0

High Volatility

STOCK PRICE	NUMBER OF MONTHS BEFORE THE OPTIONS EXPIRE								
	1	2	3	4	5	6	7	8	9
55	0.0	0.3	0.7	1.1	1.5	1.7	1.9	2.2	2.6
56	0.0	0.4	0.8	1.3	1.6	1.8	2.0	2.3	2.8
57	0.0	0.5	0.9	1.4	1.7	2.0	2.2	2.5	3.0
58	0.1	0.6	1.0	1.5	1.9	2.1	2.4	2.7	3.3
59	0.1	0.7	1.1	1.7	2.1	2.3	2.6	2.9	3.5
60	0.2	0.8	1.3	1.9	2.3	2.5	2.8	3.2	3.7
61	0.3	1.0	1.5	2.1	2.5	2.8	3.0	3.4	4.0
62	0.4	1.1	1.6	2.3	2.7	3.0	3.3	3.7	4.3
63	0.5	1.3	1.9	2.5	3.0	3.3	3.6	4.0	4.6
64	0.6	1.5	2.1	2.8	3.3	3.6	3.9	4.3	4.9
65	0.8	1.7	2.4	3.1	3.6	3.9	4.2	4.6	5.3
66	1.0	2.0	2.7	3.5	4.0	4.3	4.6	5.0	5.6
67	1.2	2.3	3.0	3.8	4.3	4.6	4.9	5.4	6.0
68	1.5	2.7	3.4	4.2	4.7	5.0	5.4	5.8	6.5
69	1.9	3.1	3.8	4.6	5.2	5.5	5.8	6.2	6.9
70	2.3	3.5	4.3	5.1	5.6	6.0	6.3	6.7	7.4
71	2.9	4.1	4.8	5.6	6.2	6.5	6.8	7.2	7.9
72	3.5	4.7	5.4	6.2	6.7	7.1	7.4	7.8	8.5
73	4.2	5.3	6.0	6.8	7.3	7.7	8.0	8.4	9.1
74	4.9	6.0	6.7	7.5	8.0	8.3	8.6	9.0	9.7
75	5.7	6.7	7.4	8.1	8.6	8.9	9.2	9.6	10.

CALL PRICING TABLE

Exercise Price is (75)

Low Volatility

STOCK PRICE — NUMBER OF MONTHS BEFORE THE OPTIONS EXPIRE

STOCK PRICE	1	2	3	4	5	6	7	8	9
60	0.0	0.0	0.0	0.0	0.0	0.0	0.0	0.0	0.1
61	0.0	0.0	0.0	0.0	0.0	0.0	0.0	0.1	0.1
62	0.0	0.0	0.0	0.0	0.0	0.0	0.1	0.1	0.2
63	0.0	0.0	0.0	0.0	0.0	0.1	0.1	0.2	0.3
64	0.0	0.0	0.0	0.0	0.1	0.1	0.2	0.2	0.3
65	0.0	0.0	0.0	0.1	0.1	0.2	0.2	0.3	0.4
66	0.0	0.0	0.0	0.1	0.2	0.3	0.3	0.4	0.5
67	0.0	0.0	0.1	0.2	0.3	0.3	0.4	0.5	0.7
68	0.0	0.0	0.1	0.3	0.4	0.5	0.5	0.7	0.8
69	0.0	0.1	0.2	0.4	0.5	0.6	0.7	0.8	1.0
70	0.0	0.2	0.3	0.5	0.6	0.7	0.8	1.0	1.1
71	0.0	0.3	0.4	0.7	0.8	0.9	1.0	1.2	1.4
72	0.1	0.4	0.6	0.9	1.0	1.2	1.3	1.5	1.7
73	0.3	0.6	0.8	1.2	1.3	1.5	1.6	1.8	2.0
74	0.5	0.9	1.2	1.5	1.7	1.8	1.9	2.2	2.4
75	0.9	1.3	1.6	2.0	2.1	2.3	2.4	2.6	2.8
76	1.5	1.9	2.2	2.5	2.7	2.8	3.0	3.2	3.4
77	2.2	2.6	2.8	3.2	3.3	3.5	3.6	3.8	4.0
78	3.1	3.4	3.6	3.9	4.0	4.1	4.3	4.5	4.7
79	4.0	4.2	4.4	4.7	4.8	4.9	5.0	5.2	5.4
80	4.9	5.1	5.2	5.5	5.6	5.7	5.8	6.0	6.1

Average Volatility

STOCK PRICE — NUMBER OF MONTHS BEFORE THE OPTIONS EXPIRE

STOCK PRICE	1	2	3	4	5	6	7	8	9
60	0.0	0.0	0.0	0.1	0.2	0.3	0.4	0.5	0.6
61	0.0	0.0	0.0	0.2	0.3	0.4	0.4	0.6	0.8
62	0.0	0.0	0.1	0.2	0.3	0.4	0.5	0.7	0.9
63	0.0	0.0	0.1	0.3	0.4	0.5	0.6	0.8	1.0
64	0.0	0.0	0.2	0.4	0.5	0.6	0.8	0.9	1.1
65	0.0	0.1	0.2	0.5	0.6	0.8	0.9	1.0	1.3
66	0.0	0.1	0.3	0.6	0.8	0.9	1.0	1.2	1.4
67	0.0	0.2	0.4	0.7	0.9	1.0	1.2	1.3	1.6
68	0.0	0.3	0.6	0.8	1.1	1.2	1.3	1.5	1.8
69	0.1	0.4	0.7	1.0	1.2	1.4	1.5	1.8	2.0
70	0.2	0.6	0.9	1.2	1.5	1.6	1.8	2.0	2.3
71	0.3	0.7	1.1	1.4	1.7	1.9	2.1	2.3	2.6
72	0.4	0.9	1.3	1.7	2.0	2.2	2.4	2.6	3.0
73	0.6	1.2	1.6	2.1	2.4	2.5	2.7	3.0	3.3
74	0.9	1.6	2.0	2.4	2.8	2.9	3.1	3.4	3.7
75	1.3	2.0	2.5	2.9	3.2	3.4	3.6	3.9	4.2
76	1.9	2.6	3.0	3.5	3.8	3.9	4.1	4.4	4.8
77	2.6	3.2	3.6	4.1	4.4	4.5	4.7	5.0	5.3
78	3.4	3.9	4.3	4.7	5.0	5.2	5.4	5.6	6.0
79	4.2	4.7	5.0	5.4	5.7	5.9	6.1	6.3	6.6
80	5.1	5.5	5.8	6.2	6.4	6.6	6.8	7.0	7.3

High Volatility

STOCK PRICE — NUMBER OF MONTHS BEFORE THE OPTIONS EXPIRE

STOCK PRICE	1	2	3	4	5	6	7	8	9
60	0.0	0.5	0.9	1.4	1.7	2.0	2.2	2.5	3.0
61	0.0	0.5	1.0	1.5	1.9	2.1	2.4	2.7	3.2
62	0.1	0.6	1.1	1.7	2.0	2.3	2.6	2.9	3.4
63	0.1	0.8	1.2	1.8	2.2	2.5	2.8	3.1	3.7
64	0.2	0.9	1.4	2.0	2.4	2.7	3.0	3.3	3.9
65	0.3	1.0	1.5	2.2	2.6	2.9	3.2	3.6	4.2
66	0.4	1.2	1.7	2.4	2.9	3.2	3.5	3.8	4.5
67	0.5	1.3	1.9	2.6	3.1	3.4	3.8	4.1	4.8
68	0.6	1.5	2.2	2.9	3.4	3.7	4.1	4.4	5.1
69	0.7	1.7	2.4	3.2	3.7	4.0	4.4	4.8	5.4
70	0.9	2.0	2.7	3.5	4.0	4.4	4.7	5.1	5.8
71	1.1	2.3	3.0	3.8	4.4	4.7	5.1	5.5	6.1
72	1.4	2.6	3.4	4.2	4.7	5.1	5.4	5.9	6.5
73	1.7	2.9	3.7	4.6	5.2	5.5	5.9	6.3	7.0
74	2.0	3.4	4.2	5.0	5.6	5.9	6.3	6.7	7.4
75	2.5	3.8	4.6	5.5	6.1	6.4	6.8	7.2	7.9
76	3.1	4.4	5.2	6.0	6.6	7.0	7.3	7.7	8.4
77	3.7	5.0	5.8	6.6	7.2	7.5	7.9	8.3	9.0
78	4.4	5.6	6.4	7.2	7.8	8.1	8.5	8.9	9.6
79	5.1	6.3	7.0	7.8	8.4	8.7	9.1	9.5	10.
80	5.9	7.0	7.7	8.5	9.0	9.4	9.7	10.	10.

CALL PRICING TABLE

Exercise Price is (80)

Low Volatility

STOCK PRICE — NUMBER OF MONTHS BEFORE THE OPTIONS EXPIRE

	1	2	3	4	5	6	7	8	9
65	0.0	0.0	0.0	0.0	0.0	0.0	0.0	0.1	0.1
66	0.0	0.0	0.0	0.0	0.0	0.0	0.1	0.1	0.2
67	0.0	0.0	0.0	0.0	0.0	0.1	0.1	0.2	0.3
68	0.0	0.0	0.0	0.0	0.1	0.1	0.2	0.2	0.3
69	0.0	0.0	0.0	0.1	0.1	0.2	0.2	0.3	0.4
70	0.0	0.0	0.0	0.1	0.2	0.2	0.3	0.4	0.5
71	0.0	0.0	0.0	0.2	0.3	0.3	0.4	0.5	0.7
72	0.0	0.0	0.1	0.3	0.4	0.4	0.5	0.6	0.8
73	0.0	0.1	0.2	0.4	0.5	0.6	0.6	0.8	0.9
74	0.0	0.1	0.3	0.5	0.6	0.7	0.8	0.9	1.1
75	0.0	0.2	0.4	0.6	0.8	0.9	1.0	1.1	1.3
76	0.1	0.3	0.5	0.8	0.9	1.1	1.2	1.3	1.6
77	0.2	0.5	0.7	1.0	1.2	1.3	1.4	1.6	1.8
78	0.3	0.7	0.9	1.3	1.5	1.6	1.8	1.9	2.2
79	0.5	1.0	1.3	1.7	1.9	2.0	2.1	2.3	2.6
80	0.9	1.4	1.7	2.1	2.3	2.4	2.6	2.8	3.0
81	1.5	2.0	2.3	2.7	2.9	3.0	3.1	3.3	3.6
82	2.3	2.7	2.9	3.3	3.5	3.6	3.8	3.9	4.2
83	3.1	3.4	3.7	4.0	4.2	4.3	4.4	4.6	4.8
84	4.0	4.3	4.5	4.8	4.9	5.0	5.2	5.3	5.5
85	4.9	5.1	5.3	5.6	5.7	5.8	5.9	6.1	6.3

Average Volatility

STOCK PRICE — NUMBER OF MONTHS BEFORE THE OPTIONS EXPIRE

	1	2	3	4	5	6	7	8	9
65	0.0	0.0	0.0	0.2	0.3	0.4	0.5	0.6	0.8
66	0.0	0.0	0.1	0.2	0.4	0.5	0.6	0.7	0.9
67	0.0	0.0	0.1	0.3	0.5	0.6	0.7	0.8	1.0
68	0.0	0.0	0.2	0.4	0.5	0.7	0.8	0.9	1.2
69	0.0	0.1	0.2	0.5	0.7	0.8	0.9	1.1	1.3
70	0.0	0.1	0.3	0.6	0.8	0.9	1.0	1.2	1.5
71	0.0	0.2	0.4	0.7	0.9	1.1	1.2	1.4	1.6
72	0.0	0.3	0.5	0.8	1.0	1.2	1.3	1.5	1.8
73	0.1	0.4	0.6	1.0	1.2	1.4	1.5	1.7	2.1
74	0.1	0.5	0.8	1.2	1.4	1.6	1.8	2.0	2.3
75	0.2	0.7	1.0	1.4	1.6	1.8	2.0	2.2	2.6
76	0.3	0.8	1.2	1.6	1.9	2.1	2.3	2.5	2.9
77	0.5	1.1	1.4	1.9	2.2	2.4	2.6	2.9	3.3
78	0.7	1.4	1.8	2.3	2.6	2.8	3.0	3.2	3.6
79	1.0	1.7	2.1	2.6	3.0	3.2	3.4	3.7	4.1
80	1.4	2.2	2.6	3.1	3.4	3.7	3.9	4.1	4.5
81	2.0	2.7	3.1	3.7	4.0	4.2	4.4	4.7	5.1
82	2.7	3.4	3.7	4.3	4.6	4.8	5.0	5.2	5.7
83	3.5	4.1	4.4	4.9	5.2	5.5	5.6	5.9	6.3
84	4.3	4.8	5.1	5.6	5.9	6.1	6.3	6.5	6.9
85	5.1	5.6	5.9	6.4	6.6	6.9	7.0	7.2	7.6

High Volatility

STOCK PRICE — NUMBER OF MONTHS BEFORE THE OPTIONS EXPIRE

	1	2	3	4	5	6	7	8	9
65	0.0	0.6	1.1	1.6	2.0	2.3	2.6	3.0	3.5
66	0.1	0.7	1.2	1.7	2.2	2.5	2.7	3.2	3.7
67	0.1	0.8	1.3	1.9	2.4	2.6	2.9	3.4	3.9
68	0.2	0.9	1.4	2.1	2.6	2.8	3.2	3.6	4.2
69	0.3	1.0	1.6	2.2	2.8	3.1	3.4	3.9	4.5
70	0.4	1.2	1.8	2.5	3.0	3.3	3.6	4.1	4.7
71	0.5	1.3	2.0	2.7	3.2	3.6	3.9	4.4	5.0
72	0.6	1.5	2.2	2.9	3.5	3.8	4.2	4.7	5.3
73	0.7	1.7	2.4	3.2	3.8	4.1	4.5	5.0	5.7
74	0.8	1.9	2.7	3.5	4.1	4.5	4.8	5.4	6.0
75	1.0	2.2	3.0	3.8	4.5	4.8	5.2	5.7	6.4
76	1.3	2.5	3.3	4.2	4.8	5.2	5.5	6.1	6.8
77	1.5	2.8	3.7	4.5	5.2	5.5	5.9	6.5	7.2
78	1.8	3.2	4.1	4.9	5.6	6.0	6.3	6.9	7.6
79	2.2	3.6	4.5	5.4	6.0	6.4	6.8	7.4	8.1
80	2.7	4.1	5.0	5.8	6.5	6.9	7.2	7.8	8.5
81	3.2	4.6	5.5	6.4	7.0	7.4	7.8	8.4	9.1
82	3.9	5.2	6.1	6.9	7.6	8.0	8.3	8.9	9.6
83	4.5	5.8	6.7	7.5	8.2	8.6	8.9	9.5	10.
84	5.2	6.5	7.3	8.2	8.8	9.2	9.5	10.	10.
85	6.0	7.2	8.0	8.8	9.5	9.8	10.	10.	11.

CALL PRICING TABLE

Exercise Price is (85)

Low Volatility

STOCK PRICE — NUMBER OF MONTHS BEFORE THE OPTIONS EXPIRE

	1	2	3	4	5	6	7	8	9
70	0.0	0.0	0.0	0.0	0.0	0.0	0.1	0.1	0.2
71	0.0	0.0	0.0	0.0	0.0	0.1	0.1	0.2	0.3
72	0.0	0.0	0.0	0.0	0.1	0.1	0.2	0.2	0.4
73	0.0	0.0	0.0	0.0	0.1	0.1	0.2	0.3	0.4
74	0.0	0.0	0.0	0.1	0.2	0.2	0.2	0.3	0.5
75	0.0	0.0	0.0	0.2	0.3	0.3	0.4	0.5	0.7
76	0.0	0.0	0.1	0.2	0.3	0.4	0.5	0.6	0.8
77	0.0	0.0	0.1	0.3	0.4	0.5	0.6	0.7	0.9
78	0.0	0.1	0.2	0.4	0.6	0.7	0.8	0.9	1.1
79	0.0	0.2	0.3	0.6	0.7	0.8	0.9	1.0	1.3
80	0.0	0.3	0.4	0.7	0.9	1.0	1.1	1.2	1.5
81	0.1	0.4	0.6	0.9	1.1	1.2	1.3	1.5	1.7
82	0.2	0.5	0.8	1.1	1.3	1.5	1.6	1.8	2.0
83	0.3	0.8	1.1	1.4	1.6	1.8	1.9	2.1	2.4
84	0.6	1.1	1.4	1.8	2.0	2.2	2.3	2.5	2.8
85	1.0	1.5	1.8	2.2	2.5	2.6	2.8	2.9	3.2
86	1.6	2.1	2.4	2.8	3.0	3.2	3.3	3.5	3.8
87	2.3	2.8	3.1	3.4	3.6	3.8	3.9	4.1	4.4
88	3.1	3.5	3.8	4.1	4.3	4.5	4.6	4.8	5.0
89	4.0	4.3	4.5	4.9	5.1	5.2	5.3	5.5	5.7
90	4.9	5.2	5.4	5.7	5.8	5.9	6.1	6.2	6.5

Average Volatility

STOCK PRICE — NUMBER OF MONTHS BEFORE THE OPTIONS EXPIRE

	1	2	3	4	5	6	7	8	9
70	0.0	0.0	0.1	0.2	0.4	0.5	0.6	0.8	1.0
71	0.0	0.0	0.1	0.3	0.5	0.6	0.7	0.9	1.1
72	0.0	0.0	0.2	0.4	0.6	0.7	0.8	1.0	1.2
73	0.0	0.1	0.3	0.5	0.7	0.8	0.9	1.1	1.4
74	0.0	0.1	0.3	0.6	0.8	0.9	1.1	1.2	1.5
75	0.0	0.2	0.4	0.7	0.9	1.1	1.2	1.4	1.7
76	0.0	0.3	0.5	0.8	1.1	1.2	1.3	1.6	1.9
77	0.0	0.4	0.7	1.0	1.2	1.4	1.5	1.8	2.1
78	0.1	0.5	0.8	1.1	1.4	1.6	1.7	2.0	2.3
79	0.2	0.6	1.0	1.3	1.6	1.8	2.0	2.2	2.6
80	0.3	0.8	1.1	1.5	1.8	2.0	2.2	2.5	2.9
81	0.4	1.0	1.4	1.8	2.1	2.3	2.5	2.8	3.2
82	0.6	1.2	1.7	2.1	2.4	2.7	2.9	3.2	3.5
83	0.8	1.5	2.0	2.4	2.8	3.0	3.2	3.5	3.9
84	1.1	1.9	2.4	2.8	3.2	3.4	3.6	4.0	4.3
85	1.5	2.3	2.8	3.3	3.7	3.9	4.1	4.4	4.8
86	2.1	2.9	3.4	3.9	4.2	4.4	4.7	5.0	5.3
87	2.8	3.5	4.0	4.5	4.8	5.0	5.2	5.5	5.9
88	3.5	4.2	4.7	5.1	5.5	5.7	5.9	6.2	6.5
89	4.3	4.9	5.4	5.8	6.1	6.3	6.5	6.8	7.2
90	5.2	5.7	6.1	6.5	6.8	7.0	7.2	7.5	7.9

High Volatility

STOCK PRICE — NUMBER OF MONTHS BEFORE THE OPTIONS EXPIRE

	1	2	3	4	5	6	7	8	9
70	0.1	0.7	1.3	1.9	2.3	2.6	2.9	3.4	3.9
71	0.1	0.8	1.4	2.0	2.5	2.8	3.1	3.6	4.1
72	0.2	1.0	1.5	2.2	2.7	3.0	3.3	3.8	4.4
73	0.3	1.1	1.7	2.4	2.9	3.2	3.6	4.1	4.6
74	0.4	1.2	1.8	2.6	3.1	3.5	3.8	4.3	4.9
75	0.5	1.4	2.0	2.8	3.3	3.7	4.1	4.6	5.2
76	0.6	1.5	2.2	3.0	3.6	4.0	4.4	4.9	5.5
77	0.7	1.7	2.5	3.3	3.9	4.3	4.7	5.2	5.8
78	0.8	1.9	2.7	3.6	4.2	4.6	5.0	5.5	6.2
79	1.0	2.2	3.0	3.9	4.5	4.9	5.3	5.9	6.5
80	1.2	2.5	3.3	4.2	4.8	5.3	5.7	6.2	6.9
81	1.4	2.8	3.6	4.6	5.2	5.6	6.0	6.6	7.3
82	1.7	3.1	4.0	4.9	5.6	6.0	6.4	7.0	7.7
83	2.0	3.5	4.4	5.3	6.0	6.4	6.8	7.4	8.1
84	2.4	3.9	4.8	5.8	6.4	6.9	7.3	7.9	8.6
85	2.9	4.4	5.3	6.3	6.9	7.4	7.8	8.4	9.1
86	3.4	4.9	5.8	6.8	7.5	7.9	8.3	8.9	9.1
87	4.0	5.5	6.4	7.4	8.0	8.5	8.9	9.4	10.
88	4.7	6.1	7.0	7.9	8.6	9.0	9.4	10.	10.
89	5.4	6.8	7.6	8.6	9.2	9.6	10.	10.	11.
90	6.2	7.5	8.3	9.2	9.9	10.	10.	11.	11.

CALL PRICING TABLE

Exercise Price is (90)

Low Volatility

STOCK PRICE	NUMBER OF MONTHS BEFORE THE OPTIONS EXPIRE								
	1	2	3	4	5	6	7	8	9
75	0.0	0.0	0.0	0.0	0.0	0.1	0.1	0.2	0.3
76	0.0	0.0	0.0	0.0	0.1	0.1	0.2	0.2	0.4
77	0.0	0.0	0.0	0.0	0.1	0.2	0.2	0.3	0.4
78	0.0	0.0	0.0	0.0	0.1	0.2	0.3	0.4	0.5
79	0.0	0.0	0.0	0.0	0.1	0.2	0.4	0.5	0.7
80	0.0	0.0	0.1	0.2	0.3	0.4	0.5	0.6	0.8
81	0.0	0.0	0.1	0.3	0.4	0.5	0.6	0.7	0.9
82	0.0	0.1	0.2	0.4	0.5	0.6	0.7	0.9	1.0
83	0.0	0.1	0.3	0.5	0.7	0.8	0.9	1.0	1.2
84	0.0	0.2	0.4	0.6	0.8	0.9	1.0	1.2	1.4
85	0.0	0.3	0.5	0.8	1.0	1.1	1.2	1.4	1.6
86	0.1	0.5	0.7	1.0	1.2	1.3	1.5	1.7	1.9
87	0.2	0.6	0.9	1.2	1.5	1.6	1.7	2.0	2.2
88	0.4	0.9	1.2	1.6	1.8	1.9	2.1	2.3	2.6
89	0.7	1.2	1.5	1.9	2.2	2.3	2.5	2.7	3.0
90	1.1	1.6	2.0	2.4	2.6	2.8	2.9	3.2	3.4
91	1.7	2.2	2.5	2.9	3.2	3.3	3.5	3.7	4.0
92	2.4	2.9	3.2	3.6	3.8	3.9	4.1	4.3	4.6
93	3.2	3.6	3.9	4.2	4.5	4.6	4.7	5.0	5.2
94	4.0	4.4	4.7	5.0	5.2	5.3	5.4	5.6	5.9
95	4.9	5.2	5.5	5.8	5.9	6.1	6.2	6.4	6.6

Average Volatility

STOCK PRICE	NUMBER OF MONTHS BEFORE THE OPTIONS EXPIRE								
	1	2	3	4	5	6	7	8	9
75	0.0	0.0	0.1	0.3	0.5	0.6	0.7	0.9	1.1
76	0.0	0.0	0.2	0.4	0.6	0.7	0.8	1.0	1.3
77	0.0	0.1	0.3	0.5	0.7	0.8	1.0	1.1	1.4
78	0.0	0.1	0.3	0.6	0.8	0.9	1.1	1.3	1.6
79	0.0	0.2	0.4	0.7	0.9	1.1	1.2	1.4	1.7
80	0.0	0.3	0.5	0.8	1.1	1.2	1.4	1.6	1.9
81	0.0	0.3	0.6	1.0	1.2	1.4	1.5	1.7	2.1
82	0.1	0.5	0.8	1.1	1.4	1.6	1.7	1.9	2.3
83	0.1	0.6	0.9	1.3	1.6	1.8	1.9	2.2	2.6
84	0.2	0.7	1.1	1.5	1.8	2.0	2.2	2.4	2.8
85	0.3	0.9	1.3	1.7	2.1	2.3	2.5	2.7	3.1
86	0.5	1.1	1.5	2.0	2.3	2.6	2.8	3.0	3.5
87	0.6	1.3	1.8	2.3	2.7	2.9	3.1	3.4	3.8
88	0.9	1.6	2.2	2.7	3.0	3.2	3.5	3.8	4.2
89	1.2	2.0	2.6	3.1	3.5	3.7	3.9	4.2	4.6
90	1.6	2.5	3.0	3.5	3.9	4.1	4.4	4.6	5.1
91	2.2	3.0	3.6	4.1	4.5	4.7	4.9	5.2	5.7
92	2.9	3.7	4.2	4.7	5.0	5.3	5.5	5.8	6.2
93	3.6	4.3	4.8	5.3	5.7	5.9	6.1	6.4	6.8
94	4.4	5.1	5.5	6.0	6.4	6.6	6.8	7.0	7.5
95	5.3	5.8	6.3	6.7	7.1	7.2	7.5	7.7	8.2

High Volatility

STOCK PRICE	NUMBER OF MONTHS BEFORE THE OPTIONS EXPIRE								
	1	2	3	4	5	6	7	8	9
75	0.1	0.9	1.5	2.1	2.6	2.9	3.3	3.8	4.3
76	0.2	1.0	1.6	2.3	2.8	3.1	3.5	4.0	4.6
77	0.3	1.1	1.7	2.5	3.0	3.4	3.7	4.3	4.8
78	0.4	1.2	1.9	2.7	3.2	3.6	4.0	4.6	5.1
79	0.6	1.4	2.1	2.9	3.5	3.7	4.1	5.1	5.7
80	0.6	1.5	2.3	3.1	3.7	4.1	4.5	5.4	6.0
81	0.7	1.7	2.5	3.4	4.0	4.4	4.8	5.7	6.3
82	0.8	1.9	2.7	3.6	4.3	4.7	5.1	5.7	6.6
83	0.9	2.2	3.0	3.9	4.6	5.0	5.4	6.1	6.6
84	1.1	2.4	3.3	4.3	4.9	5.3	5.8	6.4	7.0
85	1.3	2.7	3.6	4.6	5.3	5.7	6.1	6.8	7.4
86	1.6	3.0	3.9	4.9	5.6	6.0	6.4	7.2	7.7
87	1.9	3.4	4.3	5.3	6.0	6.4	6.9	7.6	8.2
88	2.2	3.7	4.7	5.7	6.5	6.9	7.3	8.0	8.6
89	2.6	4.2	5.1	6.2	6.9	7.3	7.8	8.5	9.1
90	3.1	4.6	5.6	6.7	7.4	7.8	8.3	9.0	9.5
91	3.6	5.2	6.1	7.2	7.9	8.3	8.8	9.5	10.
92	4.2	5.7	6.7	7.8	8.5	8.9	9.4	10.	10.
93	4.9	6.4	7.3	8.4	9.1	9.5	9.9	10.	11.
94	5.6	7.0	7.9	9.0	9.7	10.	10.	11.	11.
95	6.3	7.7	8.6	9.6	10.	10.	11.	11.	12.

CALL PRICING TABLE

Exercise Price is (95)

Low Volatility

STOCK PRICE	1	2	3	4	5	6	7	8	9
80	0.0	0.0	0.0	0.0	0.1	0.1	0.2	0.2	0.4
81	0.0	0.0	0.0	0.0	0.1	0.2	0.2	0.3	0.5
82	0.0	0.0	0.0	0.1	0.2	0.2	0.3	0.4	0.5
83	0.0	0.0	0.0	0.1	0.2	0.3	0.4	0.5	0.7
84	0.0	0.0	0.1	0.2	0.3	0.4	0.5	0.6	0.8
85	0.0	0.0	0.1	0.3	0.4	0.5	0.6	0.7	0.9
86	0.0	0.0	0.2	0.4	0.5	0.6	0.7	0.8	1.0
87	0.0	0.1	0.3	0.5	0.6	0.7	0.8	0.9	1.2
88	0.0	0.2	0.4	0.6	0.8	0.9	1.0	1.1	1.4
89	0.0	0.3	0.5	0.7	0.9	1.0	1.2	1.3	1.6
90	0.1	0.4	0.6	0.9	1.1	1.2	1.4	1.5	1.8
91	0.2	0.5	0.8	1.1	1.3	1.5	1.6	1.8	2.1
92	0.3	0.7	1.0	1.4	1.6	1.8	1.9	2.1	2.4
93	0.4	1.0	1.3	1.7	1.9	2.1	2.3	2.4	2.8
94	0.7	1.3	1.7	2.0	2.3	2.5	2.7	2.8	3.2
95	1.1	1.7	2.1	2.5	2.8	2.9	3.1	3.3	3.6
96	1.7	2.3	2.7	3.0	3.3	3.5	3.7	3.8	4.2
97	2.4	3.0	3.3	3.7	3.9	4.1	4.3	4.4	4.8
98	3.2	3.7	4.0	4.3	4.6	4.8	4.9	5.1	5.4
99	4.1	4.5	4.8	5.1	5.3	5.5	5.6	5.7	6.1

NUMBER OF MONTHS BEFORE THE OPTIONS EXPIRE

Average Volatility

STOCK PRICE	1	2	3	4	5	6	7	8	9
80	0.0	0.0	0.2	0.4	0.6	0.7	0.9	1.1	1.3
81	0.0	0.1	0.3	0.5	0.7	0.9	1.0	1.2	1.5
82	0.0	0.1	0.3	0.6	0.8	1.0	1.1	1.3	1.6
83	0.0	0.2	0.4	0.7	0.9	1.1	1.2	1.5	1.8
84	0.0	0.2	0.5	0.8	1.1	1.2	1.4	1.6	1.9
85	0.0	0.3	0.6	0.9	1.2	1.4	1.5	1.8	2.1
86	0.0	0.4	0.7	1.1	1.4	1.6	1.7	2.0	2.3
87	0.1	0.5	0.9	1.2	1.6	1.8	1.9	2.2	2.6
88	0.2	0.7	1.0	1.4	1.8	2.0	2.2	2.5	2.8
89	0.3	0.8	1.2	1.6	2.0	2.2	2.4	2.7	3.1
90	0.4	1.0	1.4	1.9	2.3	2.5	2.7	3.0	3.4
91	0.5	1.2	1.7	2.1	2.6	2.8	3.0	3.3	3.8
92	0.7	1.5	2.0	2.5	2.9	3.2	3.4	3.7	4.1
93	1.0	1.8	2.3	2.8	3.3	3.5	3.7	4.1	4.5
94	1.3	2.2	2.6	3.2	3.7	3.9	4.2	4.5	5.0
95	1.7	2.6	3.2	3.7	4.1	4.4	4.6	5.0	5.4
96	2.3	3.2	3.7	4.2	4.7	5.0	5.2	5.5	6.0
97	3.0	3.8	4.3	4.8	5.3	5.5	5.7	6.1	6.6
98	3.7	4.5	5.0	5.5	5.9	6.1	6.4	6.7	7.2
99	4.5	5.2	5.7	6.1	6.6	6.8	7.0	7.4	7.8

NUMBER OF MONTHS BEFORE THE OPTIONS EXPIRE

High Volatility

STOCK PRICE	1	2	3	4	5	6	7	8	9
80	0.2	1.0	1.7	2.4	2.9	3.3	3.6	4.2	4.9
81	0.3	1.2	1.8	2.6	3.1	3.5	3.9	4.4	5.1
82	0.3	1.3	2.0	2.8	3.3	3.7	4.1	4.7	5.4
83	0.4	1.4	2.2	3.0	3.6	4.0	4.4	4.9	5.7
84	0.5	1.6	2.4	3.3	3.8	4.2	4.6	5.2	6.0
85	0.6	1.8	2.6	3.5	4.1	4.5	4.9	5.5	6.3
86	0.8	2.0	2.8	3.8	4.3	4.8	5.1	5.8	6.6
87	0.9	2.2	3.0	4.1	4.6	5.1	5.5	6.1	6.9
88	1.1	2.4	3.3	4.4	5.0	5.4	5.8	6.5	7.3
89	1.2	2.7	3.6	4.7	5.3	5.8	6.2	6.8	7.6
90	1.5	3.0	3.9	5.0	5.6	6.1	6.5	7.2	8.0
91	1.7	3.3	4.3	5.4	6.0	6.5	6.9	7.6	8.4
92	2.0	3.6	4.6	5.8	6.4	6.9	7.3	8.0	8.8
93	2.4	4.0	5.1	6.2	6.8	7.4	7.8	8.2	9.3
94	2.8	4.5	5.5	6.6	7.3	7.8	8.2	8.7	9.7
95	3.2	4.9	6.0	7.1	7.8	8.3	8.7	8.9	9.7
96	3.8	5.5	6.5	7.6	8.3	8.8	9.2	9.4	10.
97	4.4	6.0	7.1	8.2	8.9	9.4	9.8	9.9	10.
98	5.0	6.7	7.7	8.8	9.4	10.	10.	11.	11.
99	5.7	7.3	8.3	9.4	10.	10.	11.	11.	12.

NUMBER OF MONTHS BEFORE THE OPTIONS EXPIRE

CALL PRICING TABLE

Exercise Price is ⑩⑩

Low Volatility

STOCK PRICE — NUMBER OF MONTHS BEFORE THE OPTIONS EXPIRE

	1	2	3	4	5	6	7	8	9
85	0.0	0.0	0.0	0.0	0.1	0.2	0.2	0.3	0.5
86	0.0	0.0	0.0	0.1	0.2	0.2	0.3	0.4	0.5
87	0.0	0.0	0.0	0.1	0.2	0.3	0.4	0.5	0.6
88	0.0	0.0	0.0	0.2	0.3	0.4	0.5	0.6	0.8
89	0.0	0.0	0.1	0.3	0.4	0.5	0.6	0.7	0.9
90	0.0	0.0	0.1	0.3	0.5	0.6	0.7	0.8	1.0
91	0.0	0.1	0.2	0.4	0.6	0.7	0.8	1.0	1.1
92	0.0	0.1	0.3	0.6	0.7	0.8	1.0	1.1	1.3
93	0.0	0.2	0.4	0.7	0.9	1.0	1.1	1.3	1.5
94	0.0	0.3	0.5	0.8	1.0	1.2	1.3	1.5	1.7
95	0.1	0.4	0.7	1.0	1.2	1.4	1.5	1.7	2.0
96	0.2	0.6	0.9	1.2	1.5	1.6	1.8	2.0	2.3
97	0.3	0.8	1.1	1.5	1.7	1.9	2.1	2.3	2.6
98	0.5	1.0	1.4	1.8	2.1	2.3	2.4	2.7	2.9
99	0.8	1.4	1.8	2.2	2.5	2.6	2.8	3.1	3.4
100	1.2	1.8	2.2	2.7	2.9	3.1	3.3	3.5	3.8
101	1.8	2.4	2.8	3.2	3.5	3.7	3.8	4.1	4.4
102	2.5	3.0	3.4	3.8	4.1	4.3	4.4	4.7	5.0
103	3.3	3.8	4.1	4.5	4.7	4.9	5.1	5.3	5.6
104	4.1	4.5	4.8	5.2	5.4	5.6	5.8	6.0	6.3
105	5.0	5.4	5.6	6.0	6.2	6.3	6.5	6.7	7.0

Average Volatility

STOCK PRICE — NUMBER OF MONTHS BEFORE THE OPTIONS EXPIRE

	1	2	3	4	5	6	7	8	9
85	0.0	0.1	0.3	0.5	0.7	0.9	1.0	1.2	1.5
86	0.0	0.1	0.3	0.6	0.8	1.0	1.2	1.4	1.6
87	0.0	0.2	0.4	0.7	0.9	1.1	1.3	1.5	1.8
88	0.0	0.2	0.5	0.8	1.1	1.2	1.4	1.7	1.9
89	0.0	0.3	0.6	0.9	1.2	1.4	1.6	1.8	2.1
90	0.0	0.4	0.7	1.1	1.3	1.5	1.7	2.0	2.3
91	0.1	0.5	0.9	1.2	1.5	1.7	1.9	2.2	2.5
92	0.1	0.6	1.0	1.4	1.7	1.9	2.2	2.5	2.8
93	0.2	0.8	1.2	1.6	1.9	2.2	2.4	2.7	3.0
94	0.3	0.9	1.3	1.8	2.2	2.4	2.7	3.0	3.3
95	0.5	1.1	1.6	2.0	2.4	2.7	3.0	3.3	3.7
96	0.6	1.3	1.8	2.3	2.8	3.0	3.3	3.6	4.0
97	0.8	1.6	2.2	2.7	3.1	3.4	3.6	4.0	4.4
98	1.1	1.9	2.5	3.0	3.5	3.7	4.0	4.4	4.8
99	1.4	2.3	2.9	3.4	3.9	4.2	4.4	4.8	5.2
100	1.8	2.8	3.4	3.9	4.4	4.6	4.9	5.3	5.7
101	2.4	3.3	3.9	4.4	4.9	5.2	5.4	5.8	6.2
102	3.1	3.9	4.5	5.0	5.5	5.8	6.0	6.4	6.8
103	3.8	4.6	5.2	5.7	6.1	6.4	6.6	7.0	7.4
104	4.6	5.3	5.8	6.3	6.8	7.0	7.3	7.6	8.0
105	5.4	6.1	6.6	7.0	7.5	7.7	8.0	8.3	8.7

High Volatility

STOCK PRICE — NUMBER OF MONTHS BEFORE THE OPTIONS EXPIRE

	1	2	3	4	5	6	7	8	9
85	0.3	1.2	1.9	2.7	3.2	3.7	4.1	4.7	5.2
86	0.3	1.3	2.0	2.9	3.4	3.9	4.3	4.9	5.4
87	0.4	1.5	2.2	3.1	3.6	4.1	4.5	5.2	5.7
88	0.5	1.6	2.4	3.4	3.9	4.4	4.8	5.5	6.0
89	0.6	1.8	2.6	3.6	4.1	4.7	5.1	5.7	6.3
90	0.8	2.0	2.8	3.9	4.4	4.9	5.4	6.1	6.6
91	0.9	2.2	3.1	4.1	4.7	5.2	5.7	6.4	6.9
92	1.0	2.4	3.3	4.4	5.0	5.6	6.0	6.7	7.3
93	1.2	2.6	3.6	4.8	5.3	5.9	6.3	7.0	7.6
94	1.4	2.9	3.9	5.1	5.7	6.2	6.7	7.4	8.0
95	1.6	3.2	4.3	5.4	6.0	6.6	7.0	7.8	8.3
96	1.9	3.6	4.6	5.8	6.4	7.0	7.4	8.2	8.8
97	2.2	3.9	5.0	6.2	6.8	7.4	7.8	8.6	9.2
98	2.5	4.3	5.4	6.6	7.2	7.8	8.3	9.0	9.6
99	2.9	4.7	5.9	7.1	7.7	8.3	8.7	9.5	10.
100	3.4	5.2	6.3	7.6	8.1	8.8	9.2	10.	10.
101	4.0	5.7	6.9	8.1	8.7	9.3	9.7	10.	11.
102	4.6	6.3	7.4	8.6	9.2	9.8	10.	11.	11.
103	5.2	6.9	8.0	9.2	9.8	10.	10.	11.	12.
104	5.9	7.6	8.6	9.8	10.	11.	11.	12.	12.
105	6.6	8.2	9.3	10.	11.	11.	12.	12.	13.

THE FUTURE VALUE
PUT PRICING TABLES

Decimal to Fraction Conversion Chart		
Table Shows		Market Fraction
.1	=	1/16
.1	=	1/8
.2	=	3/16
.2	=	1/4
.3	=	5/16
.4	=	3/8
.4	=	7/16
.5	=	1/2
.6	=	9/16
.6	=	5/8
.7	=	11/16
.8	=	3/4
.8	=	13/16
.9	=	7/8
.9	=	15/16

*The Future Value Tables are generated by computer simulation. Due to the nature of the computer simulation techniques that we used there may be slight aberrations in the option prices presented. Therefore you should allow a variance of plus or minus 10% of these option prices. In a few cases, some of the less important, peripheral option prices may vary more than 10%.

PUT PRICING TABLE

Exercise Price is ⑩

Low Volatility

STOCK PRICE — NUMBER OF MONTHS BEFORE THE OPTIONS EXPIRE

STOCK PRICE	1	2	3	4	5	6	7	8	9
20	0.0	0.0	0.0	0.0	0.0	0.0	0.0	0.0	0.0
19	0.0	0.0	0.0	0.0	0.0	0.0	0.0	0.0	0.0
18	0.0	0.0	0.0	0.0	0.0	0.0	0.0	0.0	0.0
17	0.0	0.0	0.0	0.0	0.0	0.0	0.0	0.0	0.0
16	0.0	0.0	0.0	0.0	0.0	0.0	0.0	0.0	0.0
15	0.0	0.0	0.0	0.0	0.0	0.0	0.0	0.0	0.0
14	0.0	0.0	0.0	0.0	0.0	0.0	0.0	0.0	0.0
13	0.0	0.0	0.0	0.0	0.0	0.0	0.0	0.0	0.0
12	0.0	0.0	0.0	0.0	0.0	0.0	0.0	0.0	0.0
11	0.0	0.0	0.0	0.0	0.0	0.0	0.0	0.0	0.0
10	0.1	0.1	0.1	0.2	0.2	0.2	0.2	0.2	0.3
9	1.0	1.0	1.0	1.0	1.0	1.0	1.0	1.0	1.0
8	2.0	2.0	2.0	2.0	2.0	2.0	2.0	2.0	2.0
7	3.0	3.0	3.0	3.0	3.0	3.0	3.0	3.0	3.0
6	4.0	4.0	4.0	4.0	4.0	4.0	4.0	4.0	4.0
5	5.0	5.0	5.0	5.0	5.0	5.0	5.0	5.0	5.0

Average Volatility

STOCK PRICE — NUMBER OF MONTHS BEFORE THE OPTIONS EXPIRE

STOCK PRICE	1	2	3	4	5	6	7	8	9
20	0.0	0.0	0.0	0.0	0.0	0.0	0.0	0.0	0.0
19	0.0	0.0	0.0	0.0	0.0	0.0	0.0	0.0	0.0
18	0.0	0.0	0.0	0.0	0.0	0.0	0.0	0.0	0.0
17	0.0	0.0	0.0	0.0	0.0	0.0	0.0	0.0	0.0
16	0.0	0.0	0.0	0.0	0.0	0.0	0.0	0.0	0.0
15	0.0	0.0	0.0	0.0	0.0	0.0	0.0	0.0	0.0
14	0.0	0.0	0.0	0.0	0.0	0.0	0.0	0.0	0.0
13	0.0	0.0	0.0	0.0	0.0	0.0	0.0	0.0	0.0
12	0.0	0.0	0.0	0.0	0.0	0.0	0.0	0.0	0.0
11	0.0	0.0	0.0	0.0	0.0	0.0	0.1	0.1	0.1
10	0.1	0.2	0.2	0.3	0.3	0.3	0.3	0.4	0.4
9	1.0	1.0	1.0	1.0	1.0	1.0	1.0	1.0	1.0
8	2.0	2.0	2.0	2.0	2.0	2.0	2.0	2.0	2.0
7	3.0	3.0	3.0	3.0	3.0	3.0	3.0	3.0	3.0
6	4.0	4.0	4.0	4.0	4.0	4.0	4.0	4.0	4.0
5	5.0	5.0	5.0	5.0	5.0	5.0	5.0	5.0	5.0

High Volatility

STOCK PRICE — NUMBER OF MONTHS BEFORE THE OPTIONS EXPIRE

STOCK PRICE	1	2	3	4	5	6	7	8	9
20	0.0	0.0	0.0	0.0	0.0	0.0	0.0	0.0	0.0
19	0.0	0.0	0.0	0.0	0.0	0.0	0.0	0.0	0.0
18	0.0	0.0	0.0	0.0	0.0	0.0	0.0	0.0	0.0
17	0.0	0.0	0.0	0.0	0.0	0.0	0.0	0.0	0.0
16	0.0	0.0	0.0	0.0	0.0	0.0	0.0	0.0	0.0
15	0.0	0.0	0.0	0.0	0.0	0.0	0.0	0.0	0.0
14	0.0	0.0	0.0	0.0	0.0	0.0	0.0	0.0	0.0
13	0.0	0.0	0.0	0.0	0.0	0.0	0.0	0.1	0.1
12	0.0	0.0	0.0	0.1	0.1	0.1	0.1	0.2	0.2
11	0.0	0.1	0.1	0.2	0.3	0.3	0.3	0.4	0.4
10	0.2	0.4	0.5	0.5	0.6	0.6	0.7	0.7	0.8
9	1.0	1.0	1.0	1.1	1.2	1.2	1.2	1.3	1.3
8	2.0	2.0	2.0	2.0	2.0	2.0	2.0	2.0	2.1
7	3.0	3.0	3.0	3.0	3.0	3.0	3.0	3.0	3.0
6	4.0	4.0	4.0	4.0	4.0	4.0	4.0	4.0	4.0
5	5.0	5.0	5.0	5.0	5.0	5.0	5.0	5.0	5.0

PUT PRICING TABLE

Exercise Price is ⑮

Low Volatility

STOCK PRICE	NUMBER OF MONTHS BEFORE THE OPTIONS EXPIRE								
	1	2	3	4	5	6	7	8	9
25	0.0	0.0	0.0	0.0	0.0	0.0	0.0	0.0	0.0
24	0.0	0.0	0.0	0.0	0.0	0.0	0.0	0.0	0.0
23	0.0	0.0	0.0	0.0	0.0	0.0	0.0	0.0	0.0
22	0.0	0.0	0.0	0.0	0.0	0.0	0.0	0.0	0.0
21	0.0	0.0	0.0	0.0	0.0	0.0	0.0	0.0	0.0
20	0.0	0.0	0.0	0.0	0.0	0.0	0.0	0.0	0.0
19	0.0	0.0	0.0	0.0	0.0	0.0	0.0	0.0	0.0
18	0.0	0.0	0.0	0.0	0.0	0.0	0.0	0.0	0.0
17	0.0	0.0	0.0	0.0	0.0	0.0	0.0	0.0	0.0
16	0.0	0.0	0.0	0.0	0.1	0.1	0.1	0.1	0.1
15	0.1	0.2	0.2	0.3	0.3	0.4	0.4	0.4	0.5
14	1.0	1.0	1.0	1.0	1.0	1.0	1.0	1.0	1.0
13	2.0	2.0	2.0	2.0	2.0	2.0	2.0	2.0	2.0
12	3.0	3.0	3.0	3.0	3.0	3.0	3.0	3.0	3.0
11	4.0	4.0	4.0	4.0	4.0	4.0	4.0	4.0	4.0
10	5.0	5.0	5.0	5.0	5.0	5.0	5.0	5.0	5.0

Average Volatility

STOCK PRICE	NUMBER OF MONTHS BEFORE THE OPTIONS EXPIRE								
	1	2	3	4	5	6	7	8	9
25	0.0	0.0	0.0	0.0	0.0	0.0	0.0	0.0	0.0
24	0.0	0.0	0.0	0.0	0.0	0.0	0.0	0.0	0.0
23	0.0	0.0	0.0	0.0	0.0	0.0	0.0	0.0	0.0
22	0.0	0.0	0.0	0.0	0.0	0.0	0.0	0.0	0.0
21	0.0	0.0	0.0	0.0	0.0	0.0	0.0	0.0	0.0
20	0.0	0.0	0.0	0.0	0.0	0.0	0.0	0.0	0.0
19	0.0	0.0	0.0	0.0	0.0	0.0	0.0	0.0	0.0
18	0.0	0.0	0.0	0.0	0.0	0.0	0.0	0.0	0.0
17	0.0	0.0	0.0	0.0	0.1	0.1	0.1	0.1	0.2
16	0.0	0.0	0.1	0.2	0.2	0.2	0.3	0.3	0.3
15	0.2	0.3	0.4	0.5	0.5	0.6	0.6	0.7	0.7
14	1.0	1.0	1.0	1.0	1.1	1.1	1.1	1.2	1.2
13	2.0	2.0	2.0	2.0	2.0	2.0	2.0	2.0	2.0
12	3.0	3.0	3.0	3.0	3.0	3.0	3.0	3.0	3.0
11	4.0	4.0	4.0	4.0	4.0	4.0	4.0	4.0	4.0
10	5.0	5.0	5.0	5.0	5.0	5.0	5.0	5.0	5.0

High Volatility

STOCK PRICE	NUMBER OF MONTHS BEFORE THE OPTIONS EXPIRE								
	1	2	3	4	5	6	7	8	9
25	0.0	0.0	0.0	0.0	0.0	0.0	0.0	0.0	0.0
24	0.0	0.0	0.0	0.0	0.0	0.0.	0.0	0.0	0.0
23	0.0	0.0	0.0	0.0	0.0	0.0	0.0	0.0	0.0
22	0.0	0.0	0.0	0.0	0.0	0.0	0.0	0.0	0.0
21	0.0	0.0	0.0	0.0	0.0	0.0	0.0	0.0	0.0
20	0.0	0.0	0.0	0.0	0.0	0.1	0.1	0.1	0.1
19	0.0	0.0	0.0	0.1	0.1	0.1	0.2	0.2	0.3
18	0.0	0.0	0.1	0.2	0.2	0.3	0.3	0.4	0.4
17	0.0	0.1	0.2	0.3	0.4	0.4	0.5	0.6	0.7
16	0.1	0.3	0.4	0.6	0.6	0.7	0.8	0.9	1.0
15	0.4	0.6	0.8	0.9	1.0	1.1	1.2	1.3	1.4
14	1.0	1.2	1.3	1.5	1.5	1.6	1.7	1.8	1.9
13	2.0	2.0	2.1	2.2	2.3	2.3	2.4	2.4	2.5
12	3.0	3.0	3.0	3.0	3.1	3.1	3.2	3.2	3.3
11	4.0	4.0	4.0	4.0	4.0	4.0	4.0	4.1	4.1
10	5.0	5.0	5.0	5.0	5.0	5.0	5.0	5.0	5.0

T24

PUT PRICING TABLE

Exercise Price is (20)

Low Volatility

STOCK PRICE — NUMBER OF MONTHS BEFORE THE OPTIONS EXPIRE

STOCK PRICE	1	2	3	4	5	6	7	8	9
30	0.0	0.0	0.0	0.0	0.0	0.0	0.0	0.0	0.0
29	0.0	0.0	0.0	0.0	0.0	0.0	0.0	0.0	0.0
28	0.0	0.0	0.0	0.0	0.0	0.0	0.0	0.0	0.0
27	0.0	0.0	0.0	0.0	0.0	0.0	0.0	0.0	0.0
26	0.0	0.0	0.0	0.0	0.0	0.0	0.0	0.0	0.0
25	0.0	0.0	0.0	0.0	0.0	0.0	0.0	0.0	0.0
24	0.0	0.0	0.0	0.0	0.0	0.0	0.0	0.0	0.0
23	0.0	0.0	0.0	0.0	0.0	0.0	0.0	0.0	0.0
22	0.0	0.0	0.0	0.0	0.0	0.0	0.1	0.1	0.1
21	0.0	0.0	0.1	0.1	0.2	0.2	0.2	0.3	0.3
20	0.2	0.3	0.4	0.5	0.5	0.5	0.6	0.6	0.7
19	1.0	1.0	1.0	1.0	1.1	1.1	1.1	1.2	1.2
18	2.0	2.0	2.0	2.0	2.0	2.0	2.0	2.0	2.0
17	3.0	3.0	3.0	3.0	3.0	3.0	3.0	3.0	3.0
16	4.0	4.0	4.0	4.0	4.0	4.0	4.0	4.0	4.0
15	5.0	5.0	5.0	5.0	5.0	5.0	5.0	5.0	5.0

Average Volatility

STOCK PRICE — NUMBER OF MONTHS BEFORE THE OPTIONS EXPIRE

STOCK PRICE	1	2	3	4	5	6	7	8	9
30	0.0	0.0	0.0	0.0	0.0	0.0	0.0	0.0	0.0
29	0.0	0.0	0.0	0.0	0.0	0.0	0.0	0.0	0.0
28	0.0	0.0	0.0	0.0	0.0	0.0	0.0	0.0	0.0
27	0.0	0.0	0.0	0.0	0.0	0.0	0.0	0.0	0.0
26	0.0	0.0	0.0	0.0	0.0	0.0	0.0	0.0	0.0
25	0.0	0.0	0.0	0.0	0.0	0.0	0.0	0.0	0.0
24	0.0	0.0	0.0	0.0	0.0	0.0	0.0	0.1	0.1
23	0.0	0.0	0.0	0.0	0.1	0.1	0.1	0.2	0.2
22	0.0	0.0	0.1	0.1	0.2	0.2	0.3	0.3	0.4
21	0.0	0.1	0.2	0.3	0.4	0.4	0.5	0.5	0.6
20	0.3	0.5	0.6	0.7	0.8	0.8	0.9	0.9	1.0
19	1.0	1.0	1.1	1.2	1.3	1.3	1.4	1.4	1.5
18	2.0	2.0	2.0	2.0	2.1	2.1	2.1	2.2	2.2
17	3.0	3.0	3.0	3.0	3.0	3.0	3.0	3.0	3.1
16	4.0	4.0	4.0	4.0	4.0	4.0	4.0	4.0	4.0
15	5.0	5.0	5.0	5.0	5.0	5.0	5.0	5.0	5.0

High Volatility

STOCK PRICE — NUMBER OF MONTHS BEFORE THE OPTIONS EXPIRE

STOCK PRICE	1	2	3	4	5	6	7	8	9
30	0.0	0.0	0.0	0.0	0.0	0.0	0.0	0.0	0.1
29	0.0	0.0	0.0	0.0	0.0	0.0	0.0	0.0	0.1
28	0.0	0.0	0.0	0.0	0.0	0.0	0.1	0.1	0.2
27	0.0	0.0	0.0	0.0	0.1	0.1	0.1	0.2	0.4
26	0.0	0.0	0.0	0.1	0.1	0.2	0.2	0.3	0.5
25	0.0	0.0	0.1	0.2	0.2	0.3	0.3	0.5	0.6
24	0.0	0.1	0.2	0.3	0.4	0.4	0.6	0.7	0.8
23	0.0	0.2	0.3	0.4	0.5	0.6	0.8	0.9	1.0
22	0.1	0.3	0.4	0.6	0.7	0.8	0.9	1.1	1.2
21	0.2	0.5	0.7	0.9	1.0	1.1	1.2	1.4	1.5
20	0.6	0.9	1.1	1.3	1.5	1.6	1.7	1.8	1.9
19	1.1	1.4	1.6	1.8	1.9	2.1	2.1	2.3	2.4
18	2.0	2.2	2.3	2.5	2.6	2.7	2.8	2.9	2.9
17	3.0	3.0	3.1	3.3	3.4	3.5	3.5	3.5	3.6
16	4.0	4.0	4.0	4.1	4.2	4.3	4.3	4.4	4.4
15	5.0	5.0	5.0	5.0	5.0	5.1	5.1	5.2	5.3

PUT PRICING TABLE

Exercise Price is (25)

Low Volatility

STOCK PRICE — NUMBER OF MONTHS BEFORE THE OPTIONS EXPIRE

STOCK PRICE	1	2	3	4	5	6	7	8	9
35	0.0	0.0	0.0	0.0	0.0	0.0	0.0	0.0	0.0
34	0.0	0.0	0.0	0.0	0.0	0.0	0.0	0.0	0.0
33	0.0	0.0	0.0	0.0	0.0	0.0	0.0	0.0	0.0
32	0.0	0.0	0.0	0.0	0.0	0.0	0.0	0.0	0.0
31	0.0	0.0	0.0	0.0	0.0	0.0	0.0	0.0	0.0
30	0.0	0.0	0.0	0.0	0.0	0.0	0.0	0.0	0.0
29	0.0	0.0	0.0	0.0	0.0	0.0	0.0	0.0	0.0
28	0.0	0.0	0.0	0.0	0.0	0.0	0.1	0.1	0.1
27	0.0	0.0	0.0	0.1	0.1	0.1	0.2	0.2	0.3
26	0.0	0.1	0.2	0.2	0.3	0.3	0.4	0.4	0.5
25	0.2	0.4	0.5	0.6	0.7	0.7	0.7	0.8	0.9
24	1.0	1.0	1.1	1.1	1.2	1.2	1.3	1.3	1.4
23	2.0	2.0	2.0	2.0	2.0	2.0	2.0	2.1	2.1
22	3.0	3.0	3.0	3.0	3.0	3.0	3.0	3.0	3.0
21	4.0	4.0	4.0	4.0	4.0	4.0	4.0	4.0	4.0
20	5.0	5.0	5.0	5.0	5.0	5.0	5.0	5.0	5.0

Average Volatility

STOCK PRICE — NUMBER OF MONTHS BEFORE THE OPTIONS EXPIRE

STOCK PRICE	1	2	3	4	5	6	7	8	9
35	0.0	0.0	0.0	0.0	0.0	0.0	0.0	0.0	0.0
34	0.0	0.0	0.0	0.0	0.0	0.0	0.0	0.0	0.0
33	0.0	0.0	0.0	0.0	0.0	0.0	0.0	0.0	0.0
32	0.0	0.0	0.0	0.0	0.0	0.0	0.0	0.0	0.0
31	0.0	0.0	0.0	0.0	0.0	0.0	0.0	0.0	0.1
30	0.0	0.0	0.0	0.0	0.0	0.0	0.1	0.1	0.2
29	0.0	0.0	0.0	0.0	0.1	0.1	0.2	0.2	0.3
28	0.0	0.0	0.1	0.1	0.2	0.2	0.3	0.3	0.4
27	0.0	0.1	0.2	0.3	0.3	0.4	0.4	0.5	0.6
26	0.1	0.3	0.4	0.5	0.6	0.7	0.7	0.8	0.9
25	0.4	0.6	0.8	0.9	1.0	1.1	1.1	1.2	1.3
24	1.0	1.2	1.3	1.4	1.5	1.6	1.6	1.7	1.8
23	2.0	2.0	2.1	2.2	2.2	2.3	2.3	2.4	2.5
22	3.0	3.0	3.0	3.0	3.0	3.1	3.1	3.2	3.3
21	4.0	4.0	4.0	4.0	4.0	4.0	4.0	4.0	4.1
20	5.0	5.0	5.0	5.0	5.0	5.0	5.0	5.0	5.0

High Volatility

STOCK PRICE — NUMBER OF MONTHS BEFORE THE OPTIONS EXPIRE

STOCK PRICE	1	2	3	4	5	6	7	8	9
35	0.0	0.0	0.0	0.0	0.0	0.1	0.1	0.2	0.4
34	0.0	0.0	0.0	0.0	0.1	0.1	0.2	0.4	0.5
33	0.0	0.0	0.0	0.1	0.2	0.2	0.3	0.5	0.6
32	0.0	0.0	0.1	0.2	0.3	0.3	0.5	0.6	0.7
31	0.0	0.0	0.1	0.3	0.4	0.4	0.6	0.7	0.8
30	0.0	0.1	0.2	0.4	0.6	0.7	0.8	0.9	1.0
29	0.0	0.2	0.3	0.5	0.6	0.8	0.9	1.1	1.2
28	0.1	0.3	0.5	0.7	0.8	1.1	1.2	1.3	1.5
27	0.2	0.5	0.7	1.0	1.1	1.2	1.5	1.6	1.8
26	0.4	0.8	1.0	1.3	1.5	1.6	1.7	1.9	2.1
25	0.8	1.2	1.5	1.7	1.9	2.0	2.2	2.3	2.5
24	1.3	1.7	1.9	2.2	2.4	2.5	2.6	2.8	3.0
23	2.1	2.4	2.6	2.9	3.0	3.1	3.1	3.3	3.5
22	3.0	3.2	3.4	3.6	3.7	3.8	3.8	4.0	4.2
21	4.0	4.0	4.2	4.4	4.5	4.5	4.6	4.7	4.9
20	5.0	5.0	5.0	5.2	5.3	5.4	5.4	5.5	5.7

T26

PUT PRICING TABLE

Exercise Price is ㉚

Low Volatility

STOCK PRICE — NUMBER OF MONTHS BEFORE THE OPTIONS EXPIRE

Stock Price	1	2	3	4	5	6	7	8	9
40	0.0	0.0	0.0	0.0	0.0	0.0	0.0	0.0	0.0
39	0.0	0.0	0.0	0.0	0.0	0.0	0.0	0.0	0.0
38	0.0	0.0	0.0	0.0	0.0	0.0	0.0	0.0	0.0
37	0.0	0.0	0.0	0.0	0.0	0.0	0.0	0.0	0.0
36	0.0	0.0	0.0	0.0	0.0	0.0	0.0	0.0	0.0
35	0.0	0.0	0.0	0.0	0.0	0.0	0.0	0.0	0.0
34	0.0	0.0	0.0	0.0	0.0	0.0	0.1	0.1	0.1
33	0.0	0.0	0.0	0.1	0.1	0.1	0.2	0.2	0.2
32	0.0	0.0	0.1	0.2	0.2	0.2	0.3	0.3	0.4
31	0.0	0.2	0.3	0.4	0.4	0.5	0.5	0.6	0.7
30	0.3	0.5	0.6	0.7	0.8	0.8	0.9	1.0	1.1
29	1.0	1.1	1.2	1.3	1.3	1.4	1.4	1.5	1.6
28	2.0	2.0	2.0	2.0	2.1	2.1	2.2	2.2	2.3
27	3.0	3.0	3.0	3.0	3.0	3.0	3.0	3.0	3.1
26	4.0	4.0	4.0	4.0	4.0	4.0	4.0	4.0	4.0
25	5.0	5.0	5.0	5.0	5.0	5.0	5.0	5.0	5.0

Average Volatility

STOCK PRICE — NUMBER OF MONTHS BEFORE THE OPTIONS EXPIRE

Stock Price	1	2	3	4	5	6	7	8	9
40	0.0	0.0	0.0	0.0	0.0	0.0	0.0	0.0	0.0
39	0.0	0.0	0.0	0.0	0.0	0.0	0.0	0.0	0.0
38	0.0	0.0	0.0	0.0	0.0	0.0	0.0	0.0	0.1
37	0.0	0.0	0.0	0.0	0.0	0.0	0.0	0.1	0.1
36	0.0	0.0	0.0	0.0	0.0	0.0	0.1	0.2	0.2
35	0.0	0.0	0.0	0.1	0.1	0.2	0.2	0.2	0.3
34	0.0	0.0	0.1	0.1	0.2	0.3	0.3	0.4	0.4
33	0.0	0.1	0.2	0.3	0.3	0.4	0.4	0.5	0.6
32	0.0	0.2	0.3	0.4	0.5	0.6	0.7	0.8	0.8
31	0.2	0.4	0.5	0.7	0.8	0.9	1.0	1.1	1.2
30	0.5	0.8	0.9	1.1	1.2	1.3	1.4	1.5	1.6
29	1.1	1.3	1.4	1.6	1.7	1.8	1.9	2.0	2.1
28	2.0	2.1	2.2	2.3	2.4	2.5	2.6	2.6	2.7
27	3.0	3.0	3.0	3.1	3.2	3.3	3.3	3.4	3.5
26	4.0	4.0	4.0	4.0	4.0	4.1	4.1	4.2	4.3
25	5.0	5.0	5.0	5.0	5.0	5.0	5.0	5.1	5.1

High Volatility

STOCK PRICE — NUMBER OF MONTHS BEFORE THE OPTIONS EXPIRE

Stock Price	1	2	3	4	5	6	7	8	9
40	0.0	0.0	0.0	0.1	0.2	0.4	0.4	0.5	0.8
39	0.0	0.0	0.1	0.2	0.3	0.5	0.5	0.7	0.9
38	0.0	0.0	0.1	0.3	0.5	0.6	0.6	0.8	1.0
37	0.0	0.1	0.2	0.4	0.6	0.7	0.8	0.9	1.2
36	0.0	0.1	0.3	0.6	0.7	0.8	0.9	1.2	1.4
35	0.0	0.2	0.4	0.7	0.9	1.0	1.1	1.4	1.6
34	0.1	0.4	0.6	0.9	1.1	1.2	1.3	1.5	1.8
33	0.2	0.5	0.8	1.2	1.3	1.4	1.6	1.8	2.0
32	0.3	0.7	1.0	1.3	1.6	1.8	1.9	2.1	2.4
31	0.6	1.0	1.3	1.7	1.9	2.0	2.2	2.4	2.6
30	0.9	1.5	1.8	2.1	2.3	2.5	2.6	2.9	3.1
29	1.5	2.0	2.3	2.6	2.8	2.9	3.1	3.3	3.6
28	2.2	2.6	2.9	3.2	3.4	3.5	3.6	3.8	4.1
27	3.0	3.4	3.6	3.9	4.0	4.1	4.3	4.5	4.7
26	4.0	4.2	4.4	4.6	4.7	4.9	5.0	5.2	5.3
25	5.0	5.1	5.2	5.5	5.5	5.6	5.8	6.0	6.0

PUT PRICING TABLE

Exercise Price is (35)

Low Volatility

STOCK PRICE	NUMBER OF MONTHS BEFORE THE OPTIONS EXPIRE								
	1	2	3	4	5	6	7	8	9
45	0.0	0.0	0.0	0.0	0.0	0.0	0.0	0.0	0.0
44	0.0	0.0	0.0	0.0	0.0	0.0	0.0	0.0	0.0
43	0.0	0.0	0.0	0.0	0.0	0.0	0.0	0.0	0.0
42	0.0	0.0	0.0	0.0	0.0	0.0	0.0	0.0	0.1
41	0.0	0.0	0.0	0.0	0.0	0.0	0.0	0.1	0.1
40	0.0	0.0	0.0	0.0	0.0	0.0	0.1	0.1	0.1
39	0.0	0.0	0.0	0.0	0.1	0.1	0.1	0.2	0.2
38	0.0	0.0	0.1	0.1	0.2	0.2	0.3	0.3	0.4
37	0.0	0.1	0.2	0.3	0.3	0.4	0.4	0.5	0.6
36	0.1	0.2	0.4	0.5	0.6	0.6	0.7	0.8	0.9
35	0.4	0.6	0.7	0.9	1.0	1.0	1.1	1.2	1.3
34	1.0	1.1	1.3	1.4	1.5	1.5	1.6	1.7	1.8
33	2.0	2.0	2.0	2.1	2.2	2.3	2.3	2.4	2.5
32	3.0	3.0	3.0	3.0	3.0	3.1	3.1	3.2	3.2
31	4.0	4.0	4.0	4.0	4.0	4.0	4.0	4.0	4.1
30	5.0	5.0	5.0	5.0	5.0	5.0	5.0	5.0	5.0

Average Volatility

STOCK PRICE	NUMBER OF MONTHS BEFORE THE OPTIONS EXPIRE								
	1	2	3	4	5	6	7	8	9
45	0.0	0.0	0.0	0.0	0.0	0.0	0.0	0.0	0.0
44	0.0	0.0	0.0	0.0	0.0	0.0	0.0	0.1	0.1
43	0.0	0.0	0.0	0.0	0.0	0.0	0.1	0.1	0.2
42	0.0	0.0	0.0	0.0	0.1	0.1	0.1	0.2	0.3
41	0.0	0.0	0.0	0.1	0.1	0.2	0.2	0.3	0.4
40	0.0	0.0	0.0	0.1	0.2	0.3	0.3	0.4	0.5
39	0.0	0.1	0.2	0.3	0.3	0.4	0.5	0.6	0.7
38	0.0	0.1	0.3	0.4	0.5	0.6	0.6	0.7	0.9
37	0.1	0.3	0.4	0.6	0.7	0.8	0.9	1.0	1.1
36	0.2	0.5	0.7	0.9	1.0	1.1	1.2	1.3	1.5
35	0.6	0.9	1.1	1.3	1.4	1.6	1.6	1.8	1.9
34	1.1	1.4	1.6	1.8	1.9	2.0	2.1	2.2	2.4
33	2.0	2.2	2.3	2.5	2.6	2.7	2.8	2.9	3.0
32	3.0	3.0	3.1	3.3	3.4	3.5	3.5	3.6	3.8
31	4.0	4.0	4.0	4.1	4.2	4.3	4.3	4.4	4.5
30	5.0	5.0	5.0	5.0	5.0	5.1	5.1	5.2	5.3

High Volatility

STOCK PRICE	NUMBER OF MONTHS BEFORE THE OPTIONS EXPIRE								
	1	2	3	4	5	6	7	8	9
45	0.0	0.0	0.1	0.3	0.5	0.6	0.7	0.9	1.1
44	0.0	0.0	0.2	0.5	0.6	0.7	0.8	1.1	1.2
43	0.0	0.1	0.3	0.6	0.7	0.8	0.9	1.2	1.4
42	0.0	0.2	0.4	0.7	0.9	1.0	1.2	1.4	1.6
41	0.0	0.3	0.5	0.9	1.0	1.1	1.4	1.6	1.8
40	0.1	0.4	0.6	1.0	1.2	1.3	1.6	1.8	2.0
39	0.2	0.5	0.8	1.2	1.4	1.6	1.7	2.1	2.3
38	0.3	0.7	1.0	1.5	1.7	1.9	2.0	2.3	2.6
37	0.4	1.0	1.3	1.7	2.0	2.2	2.4	2.6	2.9
36	0.7	1.3	1.7	2.1	2.3	2.5	2.7	2.9	3.2
35	1.1	1.7	2.1	2.5	2.8	3.0	3.1	3.4	3.7
34	1.6	2.2	2.6	3.0	3.2	3.4	3.6	3.8	4.1
33	2.3	2.9	3.2	3.6	3.8	3.9	4.1	4.3	4.6
32	3.1	3.6	3.9	4.2	4.4	4.6	4.8	5.0	5.1
31	4.0	4.4	4.7	4.9	5.1	5.3	5.4	5.6	5.8
30	5.0	5.2	5.5	5.7	5.9	6.0	6.2	6.3	6.5

PUT PRICING TABLE

Exercise Price is (40)

Low Volatility

STOCK PRICE

NUMBER OF MONTHS BEFORE THE OPTIONS EXPIRE

	1	2	3	4	5	6	7	8	9
50	0.0	0.0	0.0	0.0	0.0	0.0	0.0	0.0	0.0
49	0.0	0.0	0.0	0.0	0.0	0.0	0.0	0.0	0.0
48	0.0	0.0	0.0	0.0	0.0	0.0	0.0	0.0	0.0
47	0.0	0.0	0.0	0.0	0.0	0.0	0.0	0.0	0.0
46	0.0	0.0	0.0	0.0	0.0	0.0	0.0	0.1	0.1
45	0.0	0.0	0.0	0.0	0.0	0.1	0.1	0.1	0.2
44	0.0	0.0	0.0	0.1	0.1	0.1	0.2	0.2	0.3
43	0.0	0.0	0.1	0.2	0.2	0.3	0.3	0.4	0.4
42	0.0	0.1	0.2	0.3	0.4	0.4	0.5	0.6	0.7
41	0.1	0.3	0.4	0.6	0.6	0.7	0.8	0.8	1.0
40	0.4	0.6	0.8	1.0	1.0	1.1	1.2	1.3	1.4
39	1.0	1.2	1.3	1.5	1.5	1.6	1.7	1.7	1.9
38	2.0	2.0	2.1	2.2	2.3	2.3	2.4	2.4	2.6
37	3.0	3.0	3.0	3.0	3.1	3.1	3.2	3.2	3.3
36	4.0	4.0	4.0	4.0	4.0	4.0	4.0	4.1	4.1
35	5.0	5.0	5.0	5.0	5.0	5.0	5.0	5.0	5.0

Average Volatility

STOCK PRICE

NUMBER OF MONTHS BEFORE THE OPTIONS EXPIRE

	1	2	3	4	5	6	7	8	9
50	0.0	0.0	0.0	0.0	0.0	0.0	0.0	0.1	0.2
49	0.0	0.0	0.0	0.0	0.0	0.1	0.1	0.2	0.2
48	0.0	0.0	0.0	0.0	0.1	0.1	0.2	0.2	0.3
47	0.0	0.0	0.0	0.1	0.1	0.2	0.3	0.3	0.4
46	0.0	0.0	0.1	0.2	0.2	0.3	0.4	0.5	0.6
45	0.0	0.0	0.1	0.3	0.4	0.4	0.5	0.6	0.7
44	0.0	0.1	0.3	0.4	0.5	0.6	0.6	0.8	0.9
43	0.0	0.2	0.4	0.6	0.7	0.8	0.8	1.0	1.1
42	0.1	0.4	0.6	0.8	0.9	1.0	1.1	1.3	1.4
41	0.3	0.7	0.9	1.1	1.2	1.4	1.5	1.6	1.8
40	0.7	1.1	1.3	1.5	1.7	1.8	1.9	2.1	2.2
39	1.2	1.6	1.8	2.0	2.1	2.3	2.4	2.5	2.7
38	2.0	2.3	2.5	2.7	2.8	2.9	3.0	3.2	3.3
37	3.0	3.1	3.3	3.4	3.5	3.7	3.7	3.9	4.0
36	4.0	4.0	4.1	4.2	4.3	4.4	4.5	4.6	4.8
35	5.0	5.0	5.0	5.1	5.2	5.3	5.3	5.4	5.6

High Volatility

STOCK PRICE

NUMBER OF MONTHS BEFORE THE OPTIONS EXPIRE

	1	2	3	4	5	6	7	8	9
50	0.0	0.1	0.3	0.6	0.8	1.0	1.1	1.3	1.6
49	0.0	0.1	0.3	0.7	0.9	1.1	1.2	1.4	1.7
48	0.0	0.2	0.4	0.8	1.0	1.2	1.4	1.6	1.9
47	0.0	0.3	0.7	1.0	1.2	1.4	1.5	1.8	2.1
46	0.1	0.4	0.8	1.1	1.4	1.6	1.8	2.0	2.4
45	0.1	0.6	1.0	1.3	1.6	1.8	2.0	2.2	2.5
44	0.3	0.7	1.2	1.6	1.8	2.0	2.3	2.4	2.8
43	0.4	0.9	1.3	1.9	2.1	2.3	2.5	2.9	3.2
42	0.6	1.2	1.6	2.2	2.5	2.6	2.8	3.1	3.4
41	0.9	1.6	2.0	2.5	2.8	2.9	3.1	3.4	3.8
40	1.3	2.0	2.5	2.9	3.2	3.4	3.6	3.9	4.2
39	1.8	2.5	2.9	3.4	3.7	3.9	4.1	4.3	4.7
38	2.5	3.1	3.5	3.9	4.2	4.3	4.6	4.8	5.1
37	3.3	3.8	4.2	4.6	4.8	5.0	5.2	5.4	5.7
36	4.1	4.6	4.9	5.3	5.5	5.7	5.8	6.0	6.3
35	5.0	5.4	5.7	6.0	6.2	6.4	6.5	6.7	7.0

PUT PRICING TABLE

Exercise Price is ⑤ 45

Low Volatility

STOCK PRICE — NUMBER OF MONTHS BEFORE THE OPTIONS EXPIRE

	1	2	3	4	5	6	7	8	9
55	0.0	0.0	0.0	0.0	0.0	0.0	0.0	0.0	0.0
54	0.0	0.0	0.0	0.0	0.0	0.0	0.0	0.0	0.0
53	0.0	0.0	0.0	0.0	0.0	0.0	0.0	0.0	0.1
52	0.0	0.0	0.0	0.0	0.0	0.0	0.0	0.1	0.1
51	0.0	0.0	0.0	0.0	0.0	0.0	0.1	0.1	0.2
50	0.0	0.0	0.0	0.1	0.1	0.1	0.2	0.2	0.3
49	0.0	0.0	0.0	0.1	0.2	0.2	0.3	0.3	0.4
48	0.0	0.1	0.1	0.3	0.3	0.4	0.4	0.5	0.6
47	0.0	0.2	0.3	0.4	0.5	0.6	0.6	0.7	0.8
46	0.2	0.4	0.5	0.7	0.8	0.9	0.9	1.0	1.2
45	0.5	0.7	0.9	1.1	1.2	1.3	1.4	1.5	1.6
44	1.0	1.3	1.4	1.6	1.7	1.8	1.8	1.9	2.1
43	2.0	2.0	2.2	2.3	2.4	2.5	2.5	2.6	2.7
42	3.0	3.0	3.1	3.1	3.2	3.2	3.3	3.4	3.5
41	4.0	4.0	4.0	4.0	4.0	4.1	4.1	4.2	4.3
40	5.0	5.0	5.0	5.0	5.0	5.0	5.0	5.0	5.1

Average Volatility

STOCK PRICE — NUMBER OF MONTHS BEFORE THE OPTIONS EXPIRE

	1	2	3	4	5	6	7	8	9
55	0.0	0.0	0.0	0.0	0.0	0.1	0.1	0.2	0.3
54	0.0	0.0	0.0	0.0	0.1	0.2	0.2	0.3	0.4
53	0.0	0.0	0.0	0.1	0.2	0.2	0.3	0.4	0.5
52	0.0	0.0	0.1	0.2	0.3	0.3	0.4	0.5	0.6
51	0.0	0.0	0.1	0.3	0.4	0.5	0.5	0.6	0.9
50	0.0	0.1	0.2	0.4	0.5	0.6	0.7	0.8	1.0
49	0.0	0.2	0.4	0.5	0.7	0.8	0.8	1.0	1.1
48	0.1	0.3	0.5	0.7	0.9	1.0	1.1	1.2	1.4
47	0.2	0.5	0.7	1.0	1.1	1.3	1.4	1.5	1.7
46	0.4	0.8	1.0	1.3	1.5	1.6	1.7	1.9	2.1
45	0.8	1.2	1.5	1.7	1.9	2.1	2.2	2.3	2.6
44	1.3	1.7	1.9	2.2	2.4	2.5	2.6	2.8	3.0
43	2.1	2.4	2.6	2.9	3.0	3.2	3.3	3.4	3.6
42	3.0	3.2	3.4	3.6	3.8	3.9	4.0	4.1	4.3
41	4.0	4.0	4.2	4.4	4.5	4.6	4.7	4.9	5.0
40	5.0	5.0	5.0	5.2	5.3	5.5	5.5	5.6	5.8

High Volatility

STOCK PRICE — NUMBER OF MONTHS BEFORE THE OPTIONS EXPIRE

	1	2	3	4	5	6	7	8	9
55	0.0	0.2	0.4	0.8	1.1	1.2	1.4	1.7	2.0
54	0.0	0.3	0.6	0.9	1.3	1.4	1.5	1.9	2.2
53	0.0	0.4	0.7	1.1	1.4	1.5	1.7	2.1	2.4
52	0.1	0.5	0.9	1.2	1.6	1.7	1.9	2.3	2.6
51	0.1	0.6	1.0	1.4	1.8	1.9	2.2	2.4	2.9
50	0.2	0.8	1.2	1.7	2.1	2.2	2.4	2.7	3.2
49	0.4	0.9	1.4	1.9	2.2	2.5	2.7	3.0	3.4
48	0.5	1.2	1.7	2.2	2.6	2.7	3.0	3.4	3.7
47	0.7	1.5	2.0	2.6	2.9	3.1	3.3	3.6	4.0
46	1.1	1.9	2.3	2.9	3.2	3.4	3.6	4.0	4.3
45	1.5	2.3	2.8	3.3	3.7	3.8	4.1	4.4	4.8
44	2.0	2.8	3.2	3.8	4.1	4.3	4.6	4.9	5.2
43	2.6	3.4	3.9	4.3	4.6	4.8	5.0	5.3	5.7
42	3.4	4.1	4.4	4.9	5.3	5.4	5.7	5.9	6.2
41	4.2	4.8	5.1	5.6	5.9	6.0	6.2	6.5	6.9
40	5.1	5.6	5.9	6.3	6.6	6.7	6.9	7.2	7.4

PUT PRICING TABLE

Exercise Price is 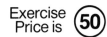 **50**

Low Volatility

| STOCK PRICE | \
NUMBER OF MONTHS BEFORE THE OPTIONS EXPIRE | | | | | | | |
| --- | --- | --- | --- | --- | --- | --- | --- | --- |
| | **1** | **2** | **3** | **4** | **5** | **6** | **7** | **8** | **9** |
| 65 | 0.0 | 0.0 | 0.0 | 0.0 | 0.0 | 0.0 | 0.0 | 0.0 | 0.0 |
| 64 | 0.0 | 0.0 | 0.0 | 0.0 | 0.0 | 0.0 | 0.0 | 0.0 | 0.0 |
| 63 | 0.0 | 0.0 | 0.0 | 0.0 | 0.0 | 0.0 | 0.0 | 0.0 | 0.0 |
| 62 | 0.0 | 0.0 | 0.0 | 0.0 | 0.0 | 0.0 | 0.0 | 0.0 | 0.0 |
| 61 | 0.0 | 0.0 | 0.0 | 0.0 | 0.0 | 0.0 | 0.0 | 0.0 | 0.0 |
| 60 | 0.0 | 0.0 | 0.0 | 0.0 | 0.0 | 0.0 | 0.0 | 0.0 | 0.0 |
| 59 | 0.0 | 0.0 | 0.0 | 0.0 | 0.0 | 0.0 | 0.0 | 0.0 | 0.1 |
| 58 | 0.0 | 0.0 | 0.0 | 0.0 | 0.0 | 0.0 | 0.0 | 0.1 | 0.1 |
| 57 | 0.0 | 0.0 | 0.0 | 0.0 | 0.0 | 0.1 | 0.1 | 0.1 | 0.2 |
| 56 | 0.0 | 0.0 | 0.0 | 0.0 | 0.1 | 0.1 | 0.2 | 0.2 | 0.3 |
| 55 | 0.0 | 0.0 | 0.0 | 0.1 | 0.2 | 0.2 | 0.3 | 0.3 | 0.4 |
| 54 | 0.0 | 0.0 | 0.1 | 0.2 | 0.3 | 0.3 | 0.4 | 0.5 | 0.6 |
| 53 | 0.0 | 0.1 | 0.2 | 0.3 | 0.4 | 0.5 | 0.6 | 0.6 | 0.8 |
| 52 | 0.1 | 0.2 | 0.4 | 0.5 | 0.6 | 0.7 | 0.8 | 0.9 | 1.0 |
| 51 | 0.2 | 0.5 | 0.6 | 0.8 | 0.9 | 1.0 | 1.1 | 1.2 | 1.4 |
| 50 | 0.5 | 0.8 | 1.0 | 1.2 | 1.4 | 1.4 | 1.5 | 1.6 | 1.8 |
| 49 | 1.1 | 1.4 | 1.5 | 1.7 | 1.8 | 1.9 | 2.0 | 2.1 | 2.3 |
| 48 | 2.0 | 2.1 | 2.3 | 2.4 | 2.5 | 2.6 | 2.7 | 2.8 | 2.9 |
| 47 | 3.0 | 3.0 | 3.1 | 3.2 | 3.3 | 3.4 | 3.4 | 3.5 | 3.7 |
| 46 | 4.0 | 4.0 | 4.0 | 4.0 | 4.1 | 4.2 | 4.2 | 4.3 | 4.4 |
| 45 | 5.0 | 5.0 | 5.0 | 5.0 | 5.0 | 5.0 | 5.1 | 5.1 | 5.3 |

Average Volatility

| STOCK PRICE | \
NUMBER OF MONTHS BEFORE THE OPTIONS EXPIRE | | | | | | | |
| --- | --- | --- | --- | --- | --- | --- | --- | --- |
| | **1** | **2** | **3** | **4** | **5** | **6** | **7** | **8** | **9** |
| 65 | 0.0 | 0.0 | 0.0 | 0.0 | 0.0 | 0.0 | 0.0 | 0.0 | 0.1 |
| 64 | 0.0 | 0.0 | 0.0 | 0.0 | 0.0 | 0.0 | 0.0 | 0.0 | 0.1 |
| 63 | 0.0 | 0.0 | 0.0 | 0.0 | 0.0 | 0.0 | 0.0 | 0.1 | 0.1 |
| 62 | 0.0 | 0.0 | 0.0 | 0.0 | 0.0 | 0.0 | 0.1 | 0.1 | 0.2 |
| 61 | 0.0 | 0.0 | 0.0 | 0.0 | 0.0 | 0.1 | 0.1 | 0.2 | 0.3 |
| 60 | 0.0 | 0.0 | 0.0 | 0.0 | 0.1 | 0.1 | 0.2 | 0.2 | 0.4 |
| 59 | 0.0 | 0.0 | 0.0 | 0.1 | 0.2 | 0.2 | 0.3 | 0.4 | 0.5 |
| 58 | 0.0 | 0.0 | 0.0 | 0.2 | 0.2 | 0.3 | 0.4 | 0.5 | 0.6 |
| 57 | 0.0 | 0.0 | 0.1 | 0.2 | 0.3 | 0.4 | 0.5 | 0.6 | 0.7 |
| 56 | 0.0 | 0.1 | 0.2 | 0.3 | 0.4 | 0.5 | 0.6 | 0.7 | 0.8 |
| 55 | 0.0 | 0.1 | 0.3 | 0.5 | 0.6 | 0.7 | 0.7 | 0.9 | 1.1 |
| 54 | 0.0 | 0.2 | 0.4 | 0.6 | 0.7 | 0.8 | 0.9 | 1.1 | 1.2 |
| 53 | 0.1 | 0.4 | 0.6 | 0.8 | 1.0 | 1.1 | 1.2 | 1.3 | 1.5 |
| 52 | 0.2 | 0.6 | 0.8 | 1.1 | 1.3 | 1.4 | 1.5 | 1.7 | 1.8 |
| 51 | 0.4 | 0.9 | 1.1 | 1.4 | 1.6 | 1.7 | 1.9 | 2.0 | 2.2 |
| 50 | 0.8 | 1.3 | 1.6 | 1.8 | 2.0 | 2.2 | 2.3 | 2.5 | 2.7 |
| 49 | 1.3 | 1.8 | 2.0 | 2.3 | 2.5 | 2.6 | 2.8 | 2.9 | 3.1 |
| 48 | 2.1 | 2.5 | 2.7 | 3.0 | 3.1 | 3.3 | 3.4 | 3.7 | 3.7 |
| 47 | 3.0 | 3.3 | 3.5 | 3.7 | 3.9 | 4.0 | 4.1 | 4.2 | 4.4 |
| 46 | 4.0 | 4.1 | 4.3 | 4.5 | 4.6 | 4.7 | 4.8 | 5.0 | 5.1 |
| 45 | 5.0 | 5.0 | 5.1 | 5.3 | 5.4 | 5.5 | 5.6 | 5.7 | 5.9 |

High Volatility

| STOCK PRICE | \
NUMBER OF MONTHS BEFORE THE OPTIONS EXPIRE | | | | | | | |
| --- | --- | --- | --- | --- | --- | --- | --- | --- |
| | **1** | **2** | **3** | **4** | **5** | **6** | **7** | **8** | **9** |
| 65 | 0.0 | 0.0 | 0.1 | 0.3 | 0.6 | 0.7 | 0.9 | 1.1 | 1.4 |
| 64 | 0.0 | 0.0 | 0.2 | 0.5 | 0.7 | 0.8 | 1.0 | 1.2 | 1.6 |
| 63 | 0.0 | 0.1 | 0.2 | 0.6 | 0.8 | 1.0 | 1.1 | 1.5 | 1.7 |
| 62 | 0.0 | 0.1 | 0.3 | 0.7 | 0.9 | 1.1 | 1.3 | 1.6 | 1.9 |
| 61 | 0.0 | 0.2 | 0.4 | 0.8 | 1.0 | 1.2 | 1.4 | 1.7 | 2.0 |
| 60 | 0.0 | 0.2 | 0.6 | 0.9 | 1.2 | 1.4 | 1.5 | 1.9 | 2.2 |
| 59 | 0.0 | 0.3 | 0.7 | 1.1 | 1.4 | 1.5 | 1.7 | 2.1 | 2.4 |
| 58 | 0.0 | 0.4 | 0.8 | 1.2 | 1.5 | 1.7 | 1.9 | 2.3 | 2.6 |
| 57 | 0.1 | 0.5 | 1.0 | 1.4 | 1.7 | 1.9 | 2.1 | 2.5 | 2.9 |
| 56 | 0.2 | 0.7 | 1.1 | 1.6 | 2.0 | 2.2 | 2.4 | 2.8 | 3.1 |
| 55 | 0.3 | 0.8 | 1.4 | 1.8 | 2.2 | 2.4 | 2.6 | 3.0 | 3.4 |
| 54 | 0.4 | 1.0 | 1.6 | 2.1 | 2.4 | 2.7 | 2.9 | 3.3 | 3.7 |
| 53 | 0.6 | 1.3 | 1.9 | 2.4 | 2.7 | 3.0 | 3.2 | 3.6 | 4.0 |
| 52 | 0.8 | 1.6 | 2.1 | 2.8 | 3.1 | 3.3 | 3.5 | 3.9 | 4.3 |
| 51 | 1.2 | 2.0 | 2.5 | 3.1 | 3.4 | 3.6 | 3.9 | 4.2 | 4.6 |
| 50 | 1.6 | 2.4 | 3.0 | 3.5 | 3.9 | 4.1 | 4.3 | 4.7 | 5.1 |
| 49 | 2.1 | 2.9 | 3.4 | 4.0 | 4.3 | 4.5 | 4.8 | 5.1 | 5.5 |
| 48 | 2.7 | 3.5 | 4.0 | 4.5 | 4.8 | 5.0 | 5.3 | 5.6 | 6.0 |
| 47 | 3.5 | 4.2 | 4.6 | 5.1 | 5.4 | 5.7 | 5.9 | 6.1 | 6.5 |
| 46 | 4.3 | 4.9 | 5.3 | 5.8 | 6.1 | 6.3 | 6.5 | 6.8 | 7.1 |
| 45 | 5.1 | 5.7 | 6.0 | 6.5 | 6.8 | 6.9 | 7.1 | 7.5 | 7.7 |

PUT PRICING TABLE

Exercise Price is (55)

Low Volatility

STOCK PRICE — NUMBER OF MONTHS BEFORE THE OPTIONS EXPIRE

	1	2	3	4	5	6	7	8	9
70	0.0	0.0	0.0	0.0	0.0	0.0	0.0	0.0	0.0
69	0.0	0.0	0.0	0.0	0.0	0.0	0.0	0.0	0.0
68	0.0	0.0	0.0	0.0	0.0	0.0	0.0	0.0	0.0
67	0.0	0.0	0.0	0.0	0.0	0.0	0.0	0.0	0.0
66	0.0	0.0	0.0	0.0	0.0	0.0	0.0	0.0	0.0
65	0.0	0.0	0.0	0.0	0.0	0.0	0.0	0.0	0.1
64	0.0	0.0	0.0	0.0	0.0	0.0	0.0	0.1	0.1
63	0.0	0.0	0.0	0.0	0.0	0.0	0.1	0.1	0.2
62	0.0	0.0	0.0	0.0	0.1	0.1	0.2	0.2	0.3
61	0.0	0.0	0.0	0.1	0.2	0.2	0.3	0.3	0.4
60	0.0	0.0	0.1	0.2	0.3	0.3	0.4	0.4	0.5
59	0.0	0.1	0.2	0.3	0.4	0.4	0.5	0.6	0.7
58	0.0	0.2	0.3	0.4	0.5	0.6	0.7	0.8	0.9
57	0.1	0.3	0.5	0.7	0.8	0.9	0.9	1.1	1.2
56	0.3	0.5	0.7	1.0	1.1	1.2	1.3	1.4	1.5
55	0.6	0.9	1.1	1.4	1.5	1.6	1.7	1.8	2.0
54	1.2	1.4	1.6	1.9	2.0	2.1	2.2	2.3	2.5
53	2.0	2.2	2.3	2.5	2.7	2.8	2.8	3.0	3.1
52	3.0	3.0	3.1	3.1	3.3	3.4	3.5	3.6	3.8
51	4.0	4.0	4.0	4.1	4.2	4.3	4.3	4.5	4.6
50	5.0	5.0	5.0	5.0	5.1	5.1	5.2	5.3	5.4

Average Volatility

STOCK PRICE — NUMBER OF MONTHS BEFORE THE OPTIONS EXPIRE

	1	2	3	4	5	6	7	8	9
70	0.0	0.0	0.0	0.0	0.0	0.0	0.0	0.1	0.1
69	0.0	0.0	0.0	0.0	0.0	0.0	0.1	0.1	0.2
68	0.0	0.0	0.0	0.0	0.0	0.1	0.1	0.2	0.3
67	0.0	0.0	0.0	0.0	0.1	0.1	0.1	0.2	0.3
66	0.0	0.0	0.0	0.0	0.1	0.2	0.2	0.3	0.4
65	0.0	0.0	0.0	0.1	0.2	0.2	0.3	0.4	0.5
64	0.0	0.0	0.0	0.2	0.3	0.3	0.4	0.5	0.6
63	0.0	0.0	0.1	0.2	0.4	0.4	0.5	0.6	0.9
62	0.0	0.1	0.2	0.3	0.5	0.5	0.6	0.9	1.0
61	0.0	0.1	0.3	0.5	0.6	0.7	0.8	0.9	1.2
60	0.0	0.2	0.4	0.6	0.7	0.8	0.9	1.2	1.4
59	0.1	0.3	0.5	0.8	0.9	1.0	1.2	1.3	1.6
58	0.2	0.5	0.7	1.0	1.2	1.3	1.4	1.6	1.8
57	0.3	0.7	1.0	1.3	1.5	1.6	1.7	1.9	2.1
56	0.5	1.0	1.3	1.6	1.8	1.9	2.1	2.3	2.5
55	0.9	1.4	1.7	2.1	2.3	2.4	2.6	2.8	3.0
54	1.4	1.9	2.2	2.5	2.7	2.8	3.0	3.2	3.4
53	2.2	2.6	2.9	3.2	3.4	3.5	3.6	3.8	4.0
52	3.0	3.4	3.6	3.9	4.1	4.2	4.3	4.5	4.7
51	4.0	4.2	4.4	4.6	4.8	4.9	5.0	5.2	5.3
50	5.0	5.0	5.2	5.4	5.6	5.7	5.8	6.0	6.0

High Volatility

STOCK PRICE — NUMBER OF MONTHS BEFORE THE OPTIONS EXPIRE

	1	2	3	4	5	6	7	8	9
70	0.0	0.1	0.2	0.6	0.8	1.0	1.2	1.5	1.9
69	0.0	0.1	0.3	0.7	1.0	1.1	1.3	1.6	2.0
68	0.0	0.1	0.4	0.8	1.1	1.2	1.4	1.8	2.2
67	0.0	0.2	0.6	0.9	1.3	1.3	1.7	1.9	2.3
66	0.0	0.3	0.7	1.0	1.4	1.5	1.8	2.1	2.5
65	0.0	0.4	0.8	1.3	1.5	1.6	2.0	2.3	2.7
64	0.1	0.5	0.9	1.3	1.7	1.8	2.2	2.5	2.9
63	0.1	0.6	1.1	1.6	1.9	2.0	2.4	2.7	3.2
62	0.2	0.7	1.2	1.8	2.1	2.2	2.5	3.0	3.4
61	0.3	0.9	1.4	1.9	2.4	2.5	2.8	3.2	3.7
60	0.4	1.0	1.6	2.2	2.6	2.8	3.1	3.4	4.0
59	0.6	1.3	1.9	2.5	2.8	3.1	3.4	3.8	4.2
58	0.7	1.5	2.2	2.8	3.2	3.3	3.6	4.1	4.6
57	1.0	1.8	2.4	3.1	3.5	3.7	4.0	4.4	4.9
56	1.3	2.2	2.8	3.5	3.9	4.0	4.4	4.7	5.2
55	1.8	2.7	3.3	3.9	4.3	4.5	4.8	5.2	5.7
54	2.2	3.1	3.7	4.4	4.8	4.9	5.3	5.7	6.1
53	2.9	3.7	4.3	4.9	5.2	5.4	5.7	6.1	6.6
52	3.6	4.4	4.9	5.5	5.9	6.0	6.4	6.6	7.1
51	4.4	5.1	5.6	6.2	6.5	6.6	6.9	7.3	7.7
50	5.2	5.9	6.3	6.9	7.1	7.2	7.6	7.9	8.3

T32

PUT PRICING TABLE

Exercise Price is (60)

Low Volatility

NUMBER OF MONTHS BEFORE THE OPTIONS EXPIRE

STOCK PRICE	1	2	3	4	5	6	7	8	9
75	0.0	0.0	0.0	0.0	0.0	0.0	0.0	0.0	0.0
74	0.0	0.0	0.0	0.0	0.0	0.0	0.0	0.0	0.0
73	0.0	0.0	0.0	0.0	0.0	0.0	0.0	0.0	0.0
72	0.0	0.0	0.0	0.0	0.0	0.0	0.0	0.0	0.0
71	0.0	0.0	0.0	0.0	0.0	0.0	0.0	0.0	0.1
70	0.0	0.0	0.0	0.0	0.0	0.0	0.0	0.1	0.1
69	0.0	0.0	0.0	0.0	0.0	0.1	0.1	0.1	0.2
68	0.0	0.0	0.0	0.0	0.1	0.1	0.2	0.2	0.3
67	0.0	0.0	0.0	0.1	0.1	0.2	0.2	0.3	0.4
66	0.0	0.0	0.1	0.2	0.2	0.3	0.4	0.4	0.5
65	0.0	0.0	0.1	0.3	0.3	0.4	0.5	0.6	0.7
64	0.0	0.1	0.2	0.4	0.5	0.6	0.6	0.7	0.9
63	0.0	0.2	0.4	0.5	0.7	0.7	0.8	1.0	1.1
62	0.1	0.4	0.6	0.8	0.9	1.0	1.1	1.2	1.4
61	0.3	0.6	0.8	1.1	1.2	1.3	1.4	1.6	1.7
60	0.7	1.0	1.3	1.5	1.7	1.8	1.9	2.0	2.2
59	1.2	1.5	1.7	2.0	2.1	2.2	2.4	2.5	2.7
58	2.0	2.3	2.4	2.6	2.8	2.9	3.0	3.1	3.3
57	3.0	3.1	3.2	3.4	3.6	3.6	3.7	3.9	4.0
56	4.0	4.0	4.1	4.2	4.3	4.4	4.5	4.6	4.7
55	5.0	5.0	5.0	5.0	5.2	5.2	5.3	5.4	5.5

Average Volatility

STOCK PRICE
NUMBER OF MONTHS BEFORE THE OPTIONS EXPIRE

STOCK PRICE	1	2	3	4	5	6	7	8	9
75	0.0	0.0	0.0	0.0	0.0	0.0	0.1	0.1	0.2
74	0.0	0.0	0.0	0.0	0.0	0.1	0.1	0.2	0.3
73	0.0	0.0	0.0	0.0	0.1	0.1	0.2	0.3	0.4
72	0.0	0.0	0.0	0.1	0.1	0.2	0.3	0.4	0.6
71	0.0	0.0	0.0	0.1	0.2	0.3	0.3	0.4	0.7
70	0.0	0.0	0.1	0.2	0.3	0.3	0.4	0.7	0.8
69	0.0	0.0	0.1	0.3	0.4	0.4	0.5	0.8	0.9
68	0.0	0.0	0.2	0.3	0.5	0.6	0.7	0.9	1.1
67	0.0	0.1	0.3	0.5	0.6	0.7	0.8	1.0	1.2
66	0.0	0.2	0.4	0.6	0.7	0.8	0.9	1.2	1.4
65	0.0	0.3	0.5	0.7	0.9	1.0	1.1	1.4	1.6
64	0.1	0.4	0.7	0.9	1.1	1.2	1.4	1.7	1.9
63	0.2	0.6	0.9	1.2	1.4	1.5	1.6	1.9	2.2
62	0.4	0.8	1.1	1.5	1.7	1.8	2.0	2.2	2.4
61	0.6	1.1	1.5	1.8	2.0	2.2	2.4	2.6	2.8
60	1.0	1.6	1.9	2.3	2.5	2.7	2.8	3.0	3.3
59	1.5	2.0	2.4	2.7	2.9	3.1	3.3	3.5	3.7
58	2.3	2.7	3.0	3.4	3.6	3.7	3.9	4.1	4.3
57	3.1	3.5	3.8	4.1	4.4	4.4	4.6	4.8	4.9
56	4.0	4.3	4.5	4.8	5.0	5.1	5.3	5.4	5.6
55	5.0	5.1	5.3	5.6	5.7	5.9	6.0	6.1	6.3

High Volatility

STOCK PRICE
NUMBER OF MONTHS BEFORE THE OPTIONS EXPIRE

STOCK PRICE	1	2	3	4	5	6	7	8	9
75	0.0	0.1	0.5	0.8	1.1	1.3	1.5	1.8	2.2
74	0.0	0.2	0.4	0.9	1.3	1.4	1.7	2.0	2.4
73	0.0	0.2	0.6	1.0	1.4	1.7	1.8	2.1	2.6
72	0.0	0.3	0.7	1.3	1.5	1.8	2.0	2.4	2.7
71	0.0	0.4	0.9	1.4	1.7	2.0	2.1	2.6	2.9
70	0.1	0.5	1.0	1.5	1.8	2.1	2.3	2.8	3.2
69	0.1	0.6	1.1	1.7	2.0	2.3	2.5	2.9	3.4
68	0.2	0.7	1.3	1.9	2.2	2.6	2.8	3.1	3.7
67	0.3	1.0	1.4	2.1	2.5	2.7	3.0	3.4	3.9
66	0.4	1.2	1.7	2.4	2.7	3.0	3.3	3.7	4.1
65	0.5	1.4	1.9	2.6	3.0	3.3	3.5	4.0	4.5
64	0.7	1.6	2.2	2.8	3.3	3.6	3.8	4.3	4.8
63	0.9	1.8	2.5	3.2	3.6	3.8	4.2	4.6	5.1
62	1.2	2.1	2.7	3.5	3.9	4.2	4.5	4.9	5.4
61	1.5	2.5	3.2	3.9	4.3	4.6	4.8	5.3	5.7
60	1.9	3.0	3.6	4.3	4.7	5.0	5.3	5.8	6.2
59	2.4	3.4	4.1	4.8	5.2	5.5	5.7	6.2	6.7
58	3.1	4.0	4.7	5.2	5.9	5.9	6.2	6.7	7.1
57	3.8	4.7	5.2	5.9	6.3	6.5	6.8	7.1	7.6
56	4.5	5.4	5.9	6.5	6.8	7.1	7.4	7.8	8.2
55	5.3	6.1	6.6	7.2	7.5	7.8	8.0	8.3	8.8

PUT PRICING TABLE

Exercise Price is **65**

Low Volatility

STOCK PRICE — NUMBER OF MONTHS BEFORE THE OPTIONS EXPIRE

STOCK PRICE	1	2	3	4	5	6	7	8	9
80	0.0	0.0	0.0	0.0	0.0	0.0	0.0	0.0	0.0
79	0.0	0.0	0.0	0.0	0.0	0.0	0.0	0.0	0.0
78	0.0	0.0	0.0	0.0	0.0	0.0	0.0	0.0	0.1
77	0.0	0.0	0.0	0.0	0.0	0.0	0.0	0.0	0.1
76	0.0	0.0	0.0	0.0	0.0	0.0	0.0	0.1	0.2
75	0.0	0.0	0.0	0.0	0.0	0.1	0.1	0.2	0.2
74	0.0	0.0	0.0	0.0	0.1	0.1	0.2	0.2	0.3
73	0.0	0.0	0.0	0.1	0.1	0.2	0.2	0.3	0.4
72	0.0	0.0	0.0	0.1	0.2	0.3	0.3	0.4	0.5
71	0.0	0.0	0.1	0.2	0.3	0.4	0.4	0.6	0.7
70	0.0	0.1	0.2	0.3	0.4	0.5	0.6	0.7	0.8
69	0.0	0.2	0.3	0.5	0.6	0.7	0.7	0.9	1.0
68	0.1	0.3	0.4	0.7	0.8	0.9	1.0	1.1	1.3
67	0.2	0.4	0.7	0.9	1.0	1.2	1.2	1.4	1.6
66	0.4	0.7	1.0	1.2	1.4	1.5	1.6	1.8	2.0
65	0.7	1.1	1.4	1.7	1.8	1.9	2.0	2.2	2.4
64	1.3	1.6	1.9	2.1	2.3	2.4	2.5	2.7	2.9
63	2.0	2.3	2.6	2.8	3.0	3.1	3.1	3.3	3.5
62	3.0	3.1	3.3	3.6	3.7	3.8	3.8	4.0	4.2
61	4.0	4.0	4.2	4.3	4.4	4.5	4.6	4.8	4.9
60	5.0	5.0	5.0	5.2	5.3	5.3	5.4	5.6	5.7

Average Volatility

STOCK PRICE — NUMBER OF MONTHS BEFORE THE OPTIONS EXPIRE

STOCK PRICE	1	2	3	4	5	6	7	8	9
80	0.0	0.0	0.0	0.0	0.1	0.1	0.2	0.2	0.4
79	0.0	0.0	0.0	0.0	0.1	0.1	0.2	0.3	0.4
78	0.0	0.0	0.0	0.1	0.1	0.2	0.3	0.4	0.6
77	0.0	0.0	0.0	0.1	0.2	0.2	0.3	0.4	0.7
76	0.0	0.0	0.1	0.2	0.3	0.4	0.5	0.7	0.9
75	0.0	0.0	0.1	0.3	0.4	0.4	0.6	0.8	1.0
74	0.0	0.0	0.2	0.4	0.5	0.6	0.7	0.9	1.1
73	0.0	0.1	0.3	0.5	0.6	0.7	0.8	1.1	1.3
72	0.0	0.2	0.4	0.6	0.7	0.8	1.1	1.2	1.4
71	0.0	0.3	0.5	0.7	0.9	1.0	1.2	1.4	1.7
70	0.1	0.4	0.6	0.9	1.1	1.2	1.4	1.7	1.9
69	0.2	0.5	0.8	1.1	1.3	1.4	1.6	1.9	2.2
68	0.3	0.7	1.0	1.3	1.6	1.7	1.9	2.1	2.5
67	0.5	0.9	1.3	1.7	1.9	2.0	2.2	2.5	2.7
66	0.7	1.3	1.7	2.0	2.3	2.4	2.6	2.9	3.2
65	1.1	1.7	2.1	2.5	2.7	2.8	3.1	3.3	3.6
64	1.6	2.2	2.6	2.9	3.2	3.3	3.5	3.8	4.1
63	2.4	2.8	3.2	3.5	3.8	3.9	4.1	4.4	4.7
62	3.2	3.6	3.9	4.2	4.5	4.6	4.8	5.0	5.2
61	4.0	4.4	4.7	5.0	5.2	5.3	5.5	5.6	5.9
60	5.0	5.2	5.5	5.7	5.9	6.0	6.2	6.3	6.6

High Volatility

STOCK PRICE — NUMBER OF MONTHS BEFORE THE OPTIONS EXPIRE

STOCK PRICE	1	2	3	4	5	6	7	8	9
80	0.0	0.2	0.6	1.1	1.4	1.7	1.8	2.3	2.7
79	0.0	0.3	0.7	1.2	1.5	1.8	2.0	2.4	2.9
78	0.0	0.4	0.8	1.4	1.8	2.0	2.1	2.6	3.1
77	0.0	0.4	0.9	1.5	1.8	2.1	2.3	2.8	3.3
76	0.1	0.5	1.1	1.6	2.1	2.3	2.5	3.0	3.5
75	0.1	0.6	1.2	1.8	2.3	2.5	2.7	3.2	3.6
74	0.2	0.9	1.3	2.0	2.5	2.7	2.9	3.5	3.9
73	0.3	1.0	1.5	2.2	2.6	3.0	3.2	3.7	4.2
72	0.4	1.2	1.7	2.4	2.8	3.2	3.4	3.9	4.5
71	0.5	1.3	1.9	2.7	3.1	3.4	3.7	4.2	4.8
70	0.6	1.6	2.2	3.0	3.4	3.7	4.0	4.5	5.0
69	0.8	1.8	2.5	3.2	3.8	4.1	4.3	4.8	5.4
68	1.0	2.0	2.8	3.6	4.0	4.3	4.7	5.2	5.6
67	1.3	2.4	3.1	3.9	4.4	4.7	5.0	5.5	6.0
66	1.7	2.7	3.5	4.3	4.7	5.1	5.3	5.8	6.3
65	2.1	3.2	4.0	4.7	5.2	5.5	5.8	6.3	6.8
64	2.6	3.7	4.4	5.2	5.6	6.0	6.2	6.7	7.2
63	3.2	4.2	5.0	5.7	6.1	6.4	6.7	7.2	7.7
62	3.9	4.9	5.5	6.3	6.7	7.0	7.2	7.7	8.2
61	4.7	5.5	6.2	6.9	7.3	7.6	7.8	8.3	8.7
60	5.5	6.2	6.9	7.5	7.9	8.2	8.4	8.9	9.3

PUT PRICING TABLE

Exercise Price is 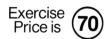 70

Low Volatility

STOCK PRICE — NUMBER OF MONTHS BEFORE THE OPTIONS EXPIRE

STOCK PRICE	1	2	3	4	5	6	7	8	9
85	0.0	0.0	0.0	0.0	0.0	0.0	0.0	0.0	0.0
84	0.0	0.0	0.0	0.0	0.0	0.0	0.0	0.0	0.1
83	0.0	0.0	0.0	0.0	0.0	0.0	0.0	0.1	0.1
82	0.0	0.0	0.0	0.0	0.0	0.0	0.0	0.1	0.2
81	0.0	0.0	0.0	0.0	0.0	0.1	0.1	0.2	0.2
80	0.0	0.0	0.0	0.0	0.1	0.1	0.1	0.2	0.3
79	0.0	0.0	0.0	0.0	0.1	0.2	0.2	0.3	0.4
78	0.0	0.0	0.0	0.1	0.1	0.2	0.3	0.4	0.5
77	0.0	0.0	0.1	0.2	0.3	0.3	0.4	0.5	0.7
76	0.0	0.0	0.1	0.3	0.4	0.5	0.5	0.7	0.8
75	0.0	0.1	0.2	0.4	0.5	0.6	0.7	0.8	1.0
74	0.0	0.2	0.4	0.6	0.7	0.8	0.9	1.0	1.2
73	0.1	0.3	0.5	0.8	0.9	1.0	1.1	1.3	1.5
72	0.2	0.5	0.7	1.0	1.2	1.3	1.4	1.6	1.8
71	0.4	0.8	1.1	1.4	1.5	1.7	1.8	2.0	2.2
70	0.8	1.2	1.5	1.8	2.0	2.1	2.2	2.4	2.6
69	1.3	1.7	2.0	2.3	2.5	2.6	2.7	2.9	3.1
68	2.1	2.4	2.6	2.9	3.1	3.2	3.3	3.5	3.7
67	3.0	3.2	3.4	3.7	3.8	3.9	4.0	4.2	4.4
66	4.0	4.0	4.2	4.4	4.6	4.7	4.7	4.9	5.1
65	5.0	5.0	5.0	5.3	5.4	5.5	5.5	5.7	5.8

Average Volatility

STOCK PRICE — NUMBER OF MONTHS BEFORE THE OPTIONS EXPIRE

STOCK PRICE	1	2	3	4	5	6	7	8	9
85	0.0	0.0	0.0	0.1	0.1	0.2	0.2	0.4	0.6
84	0.0	0.0	0.0	0.1	0.2	0.2	0.3	0.4	0.7
83	0.0	0.0	0.0	0.1	0.2	0.3	0.4	0.5	0.8
82	0.0	0.0	0.1	0.2	0.3	0.4	0.5	0.7	0.9
81	0.0	0.0	0.1	0.3	0.4	0.5	0.6	0.8	1.0
80	0.0	0.0	0.2	0.4	0.5	0.6	0.8	1.0	1.2
79	0.0	0.1	0.2	0.5	0.6	0.7	0.9	1.1	1.3
78	0.0	0.2	0.3	0.6	0.7	1.0	1.1	1.3	1.5
77	0.0	0.2	0.5	0.7	0.9	1.1	1.2	1.4	1.7
76	0.0	0.3	0.6	0.9	1.1	1.3	1.4	1.6	1.9
75	0.1	0.5	0.7	1.0	1.3	1.5	1.6	1.9	2.1
74	0.2	0.6	0.9	1.3	1.5	1.7	1.9	2.2	2.4
73	0.4	0.8	1.2	1.5	1.8	2.0	2.1	2.5	2.8
72	0.5	1.1	1.4	1.9	2.1	2.3	2.4	2.7	3.0
71	0.8	1.4	1.8	2.2	2.5	2.7	2.8	3.1	3.4
70	1.2	1.9	2.3	2.7	3.0	3.2	3.3	3.6	3.9
69	1.7	2.3	2.7	3.1	3.4	3.6	3.7	4.1	4.4
68	2.4	3.0	3.3	3.8	4.0	4.2	4.3	4.6	4.9
67	3.2	3.7	4.0	4.4	4.7	4.9	5.0	5.2	5.5
66	4.1	4.5	4.8	5.2	5.4	5.6	5.6	5.9	6.1
65	5.0	5.3	5.6	5.9	6.1	6.3	6.3	6.6	6.8

High Volatility

STOCK PRICE — NUMBER OF MONTHS BEFORE THE OPTIONS EXPIRE

STOCK PRICE	1	2	3	4	5	6	7	8	9
85	0.0	0.3	0.8	1.3	1.8	2.0	2.3	2.6	3.1
84	0.0	0.4	0.9	1.5	1.9	2.1	2.4	2.7	3.3
83	0.0	0.5	1.0	1.6	2.0	2.3	2.6	2.9	3.5
82	0.1	0.7	1.1	1.7	2.2	2.6	2.8	3.1	3.8
81	0.1	0.8	1.2	1.9	2.4	2.6	3.0	3.3	4.0
80	0.2	0.9	1.4	2.1	2.6	2.8	3.2	3.6	4.2
79	0.3	1.1	1.6	2.3	2.8	3.1	3.3	3.8	4.5
78	0.4	1.2	1.7	2.5	3.0	3.3	3.6	4.1	4.7
77	0.5	1.4	2.0	2.7	3.3	3.6	3.9	4.4	5.0
76	0.6	1.6	2.2	3.0	3.5	3.9	4.2	4.6	5.3
75	0.8	1.8	2.5	3.3	3.8	4.1	4.5	4.9	5.6
74	1.0	2.1	2.8	3.7	4.2	4.5	4.8	5.2	5.9
73	1.2	2.3	3.1	3.9	4.4	4.7	5.1	5.6	6.2
72	1.5	2.7	3.4	4.3	4.8	5.1	5.5	5.9	6.6
71	1.9	3.1	3.8	4.6	5.2	5.5	5.8	6.2	6.9
70	2.3	3.5	4.3	5.1	5.6	6.0	6.3	6.7	7.4
69	2.8	4.0	4.7	5.5	6.1	6.4	6.7	7.1	7.8
68	3.4	4.6	5.3	6.0	6.5	6.9	7.2	7.6	8.3
67	4.1	5.2	5.8	6.6	7.1	7.4	7.7	8.1	8.8
66	4.8	5.8	6.5	7.3	7.7	8.0	8.3	8.7	9.3
65	5.6	6.5	7.2	7.8	8.3	8.6	8.9	9.2	9.6

PUT PRICING TABLE

Exercise Price is (75)

Low Volatility

STOCK PRICE — NUMBER OF MONTHS BEFORE THE OPTIONS EXPIRE

STOCK PRICE	1	2	3	4	5	6	7	8	9
90	0.0	0.0	0.0	0.0	0.0	0.0	0.0	0.0	0.1
89	0.0	0.0	0.0	0.0	0.0	0.0	0.0	0.1	0.1
88	0.0	0.0	0.0	0.0	0.0	0.0	0.1	0.1	0.2
87	0.0	0.0	0.0	0.0	0.0	0.1	0.1	0.2	0.3
86	0.0	0.0	0.0	0.0	0.1	0.1	0.2	0.2	0.3
85	0.0	0.0	0.0	0.1	0.1	0.2	0.2	0.3	0.4
84	0.0	0.0	0.0	0.1	0.2	0.3	0.3	0.4	0.5
83	0.0	0.0	0.1	0.2	0.3	0.3	0.4	0.5	0.7
82	0.0	0.0	0.1	0.3	0.4	0.5	0.5	0.7	0.8
81	0.0	0.1	0.2	0.4	0.5	0.6	0.7	0.8	1.0
80	0.0	0.2	0.3	0.5	0.6	0.7	0.8	1.0	1.1
79	0.0	0.3	0.4	0.7	0.8	0.9	1.0	1.2	1.4
78	0.1	0.4	0.6	0.9	1.0	1.2	1.3	1.5	1.7
77	0.3	0.6	0.8	1.2	1.3	1.5	1.6	1.8	2.0
76	0.5	0.9	1.2	1.5	1.7	1.8	1.9	2.2	2.4
75	0.9	1.3	1.6	2.0	2.1	2.3	2.4	2.6	2.8
74	1.4	1.8	2.1	2.4	2.6	2.7	2.9	3.1	3.3
73	2.1	2.5	2.7	3.1	3.2	3.4	3.5	3.7	3.9
72	3.0	3.3	3.5	3.8	3.9	4.0	4.2	4.4	4.6
71	4.0	4.1	4.3	4.6	4.7	4.8	4.9	5.1	5.3
70	5.0	5.0	5.1	5.4	5.5	5.6	5.7	5.9	6.0

Average Volatility

STOCK PRICE — NUMBER OF MONTHS BEFORE THE OPTIONS EXPIRE

STOCK PRICE	1	2	3	4	5	6	7	8	9
90	0.0	0.0	0.0	0.1	0.2	0.3	0.4	0.6	0.7
89	0.0	0.0	0.0	0.2	0.3	0.4	0.4	0.7	0.9
88	0.0	0.0	0.1	0.2	0.3	0.4	0.5	0.8	1.0
87	0.0	0.0	0.1	0.3	0.4	0.5	0.6	0.9	1.1
86	0.0	0.0	0.2	0.4	0.5	0.6	0.9	1.0	1.2
85	0.0	0.1	0.2	0.5	0.6	0.9	1.0	1.1	1.4
84	0.0	0.1	0.3	0.6	0.8	1.0	1.1	1.3	1.5
83	0.0	0.2	0.4	0.7	0.9	1.1	1.3	1.4	1.7
82	0.0	0.3	0.6	0.8	1.2	1.3	1.4	1.6	1.9
81	0.1	0.4	0.7	1.0	1.2	1.5	1.6	1.9	2.1
80	0.2	0.6	0.9	1.2	1.6	1.7	1.9	2.1	2.4
79	0.3	0.7	1.1	1.4	1.7	2.0	2.2	2.4	2.7
78	0.4	0.9	1.3	1.7	2.0	2.2	2.4	2.7	3.1
77	0.6	1.2	1.6	2.1	2.4	2.5	2.7	3.0	3.3
76	0.9	1.6	2.0	2.4	2.8	2.9	3.1	3.4	3.7
75	1.3	2.0	2.5	2.9	3.2	3.4	3.6	3.9	4.2
74	1.8	2.5	2.9	3.4	3.7	3.8	4.0	4.3	4.7
73	2.5	3.1	3.5	4.0	4.3	4.4	4.6	4.9	5.2
72	3.3	3.8	4.2	4.6	4.9	5.1	5.3	5.4	5.8
71	4.1	4.6	4.9	5.3	5.6	5.7	5.9	6.1	6.4
70	5.0	5.4	5.7	6.1	6.3	6.4	6.6	6.8	7.1

High Volatility

STOCK PRICE — NUMBER OF MONTHS BEFORE THE OPTIONS EXPIRE

STOCK PRICE	1	2	3	4	5	6	7	8	9
90	0.0	0.6	1.0	1.6	2.0	2.4	2.6	3.0	3.6
89	0.0	0.5	1.1	1.7	2.2	2.4	2.8	3.2	3.7
88	0.1	0.7	1.2	1.9	2.3	2.6	3.0	3.4	3.9
87	0.1	0.9	1.3	2.0	2.5	2.9	3.2	3.5	4.2
86	0.2	1.0	1.6	2.2	2.7	3.0	3.4	3.7	4.4
85	0.3	1.1	1.7	2.4	2.9	3.2	3.6	4.0	4.7
84	0.4	1.3	1.9	2.6	3.2	3.5	3.9	4.2	5.0
83	0.5	1.4	2.1	2.8	3.4	3.7	4.2	4.5	5.3
82	0.6	1.6	2.4	3.1	3.7	4.0	4.4	4.8	5.5
81	0.7	1.8	2.5	3.4	3.9	4.3	4.7	5.1	5.8
80	0.9	2.1	2.8	3.7	4.2	4.6	5.0	5.4	6.1
79	1.1	2.4	3.1	4.0	4.6	4.9	5.3	5.7	6.4
78	1.4	2.7	3.5	4.3	4.8	5.3	5.6	6.1	6.7
77	1.7	2.9	3.7	4.7	5.3	5.6	6.0	6.4	7.1
76	2.0	3.4	4.2	5.0	5.6	5.9	6.3	6.7	7.4
75	2.5	3.8	4.6	5.5	6.1	6.4	6.8	7.2	7.9
74	3.0	4.3	5.1	5.9	6.5	6.9	7.2	7.6	8.3
73	3.6	4.9	5.6	6.4	7.0	7.3	7.7	8.1	8.8
72	4.3	5.4	6.2	7.0	7.6	7.8	8.2	8.6	9.3
71	5.0	6.1	6.8	7.5	8.1	8.4	8.8	9.2	9.6
70	5.8	6.8	7.5	8.2	8.7	9.1	9.3	9.6	9.6

PUT PRICING TABLE

Exercise Price is 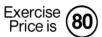 80

Low Volatility

STOCK PRICE — NUMBER OF MONTHS BEFORE THE OPTIONS EXPIRE

STOCK PRICE	1	2	3	4	5	6	7	8	9
95	0.0	0.0	0.0	0.0	0.0	0.0	0.0	0.1	0.1
94	0.0	0.0	0.0	0.0	0.0	0.0	0.1	0.1	0.2
93	0.0	0.0	0.0	0.0	0.0	0.1	0.1	0.2	0.3
92	0.0	0.0	0.0	0.0	0.1	0.1	0.2	0.2	0.3
91	0.0	0.0	0.0	0.1	0.1	0.2	0.2	0.3	0.4
90	0.0	0.0	0.0	0.1	0.2	0.2	0.3	0.4	0.5
89	0.0	0.0	0.0	0.2	0.3	0.3	0.4	0.5	0.7
88	0.0	0.0	0.1	0.3	0.4	0.4	0.5	0.6	0.8
87	0.0	0.1	0.2	0.4	0.5	0.6	0.6	0.8	0.9
86	0.0	0.1	0.3	0.5	0.6	0.7	0.8	0.8	1.1
85	0.0	0.2	0.4	0.6	0.8	0.9	1.0	1.1	1.3
84	0.1	0.3	0.5	0.8	0.9	1.1	1.2	1.3	1.6
83	0.2	0.5	0.7	1.0	1.2	1.3	1.4	1.6	1.8
82	0.3	0.7	0.9	1.3	1.5	1.6	1.8	1.9	2.2
81	0.5	1.0	1.3	1.7	1.9	2.0	2.1	2.3	2.6
80	0.9	1.4	1.7	2.1	2.3	2.4	2.6	2.8	3.0
79	1.4	1.9	2.2	2.6	2.8	2.9	3.0	3.2	3.5
78	2.2	2.6	2.8	3.2	3.4	3.5	3.7	3.8	4.1
77	3.0	3.3	3.6	3.9	4.1	4.2	4.3	4.5	4.7
76	4.0	4.2	4.4	4.7	4.8	4.9	5.1	5.2	5.4
75	5.0	5.0	5.2	5.5	5.6	5.7	5.8	6.0	6.2

Average Volatility

STOCK PRICE — NUMBER OF MONTHS BEFORE THE OPTIONS EXPIRE

STOCK PRICE	1	2	3	4	5	6	7	8	9
95	0.0	0.0	0.0	0.2	0.3	0.4	0.5	0.7	0.9
94	0.0	0.0	0.1	0.2	0.4	0.5	0.7	0.8	1.0
93	0.0	0.0	0.1	0.3	0.5	0.6	0.8	0.9	1.1
92	0.0	0.0	0.2	0.4	0.5	0.8	0.9	1.0	1.3
91	0.0	0.1	0.2	0.5	0.7	0.9	1.0	1.2	1.4
90	0.0	0.1	0.3	0.6	0.9	1.0	1.1	1.3	1.6
89	0.0	0.2	0.4	0.7	1.0	1.2	1.3	1.5	1.7
88	0.0	0.3	0.5	0.8	1.1	1.3	1.4	1.6	1.9
87	0.1	0.4	0.6	1.0	1.3	1.5	1.6	1.8	2.2
86	0.1	0.5	0.8	1.2	1.5	1.7	1.9	2.1	2.4
85	0.2	0.7	1.0	1.4	1.7	1.9	2.1	2.3	2.7
84	0.3	0.8	1.2	1.6	1.9	2.2	2.4	2.6	3.0
83	0.5	1.1	1.4	1.9	2.2	2.4	2.6	3.0	3.4
82	0.7	1.4	1.8	2.3	2.6	2.8	3.0	3.2	3.6
81	1.0	1.7	2.1	2.6	2.8	3.2	3.4	3.7	4.1
80	1.4	2.2	2.6	3.1	3.4	3.7	3.9	4.1	4.5
79	1.9	2.6	3.0	3.6	3.9	4.1	4.3	4.6	5.0
78	2.6	3.3	3.6	4.2	4.5	4.7	4.9	5.1	5.6
77	3.4	4.0	4.3	4.8	5.1	5.4	5.5	5.7	6.1
76	4.2	4.7	5.0	5.5	5.8	5.9	6.1	6.3	6.7
75	5.0	5.5	5.8	6.3	6.5	6.7	6.8	7.0	7.4

High Volatility

STOCK PRICE — NUMBER OF MONTHS BEFORE THE OPTIONS EXPIRE

STOCK PRICE	1	2	3	4	5	6	7	8	9
95	0.0	0.7	1.3	1.9	2.3	2.7	3.0	3.5	4.1
94	0.1	0.8	1.4	1.9	2.5	2.9	3.1	3.7	4.3
93	0.1	0.9	1.5	2.2	2.7	3.0	3.3	3.9	4.5
92	0.2	1.0	1.6	2.4	2.9	3.2	3.6	4.1	4.8
91	0.3	1.1	1.8	2.5	3.1	3.5	3.8	4.4	5.1
90	0.4	1.3	2.0	2.8	3.3	3.7	4.0	4.6	5.2
89	0.5	1.4	2.2	3.0	3.5	4.0	4.3	4.8	5.5
88	0.6	1.6	2.4	3.1	3.8	4.1	4.6	5.1	6.1
87	0.7	1.8	2.6	3.4	4.1	4.4	4.8	5.4	6.1
86	0.8	2.0	2.9	3.7	4.4	4.8	5.1	5.8	6.8
85	1.0	2.3	3.1	4.0	4.7	5.1	5.5	6.0	6.8
84	1.3	2.6	3.4	4.4	5.0	5.4	5.7	6.4	7.1
83	1.5	2.9	3.8	4.6	5.3	5.7	6.1	6.7	7.4
82	1.8	3.2	4.2	5.0	5.7	6.1	6.4	7.0	7.7
81	2.2	3.6	4.5	5.4	6.0	6.4	6.8	7.4	8.2
80	2.7	4.1	5.0	5.8	6.5	6.9	7.2	7.8	8.5
79	3.1	4.5	5.4	6.3	6.9	7.3	7.7	8.3	8.9
78	3.8	5.1	5.9	6.7	7.4	7.8	8.1	8.7	9.4
77	4.4	5.6	6.5	7.3	8.0	8.3	8.6	9.2	9.7
76	5.1	6.3	7.1	7.9	8.5	8.9	9.2	9.7	9.7
75	5.9	7.0	7.8	8.5	9.2	9.5	9.6	9.6	10.

PUT PRICING TABLE

Exercise Price is (85)

Low Volatility

STOCK PRICE — NUMBER OF MONTHS BEFORE THE OPTIONS EXPIRE

STOCK PRICE	1	2	3	4	5	6	7	8	9
99	0.0	0.0	0.0	0.0	0.0	0.1	0.1	0.2	0.3
98	0.0	0.0	0.0	0.0	0.1	0.1	0.2	0.2	0.4
97	0.0	0.0	0.0	0.1	0.1	0.2	0.2	0.3	0.4
96	0.0	0.0	0.0	0.1	0.2	0.2	0.3	0.4	0.5
95	0.0	0.0	0.0	0.2	0.3	0.3	0.4	0.5	0.7
94	0.0	0.0	0.1	0.2	0.3	0.4	0.5	0.6	0.8
93	0.0	0.0	0.1	0.3	0.4	0.5	0.6	0.7	0.9
92	0.0	0.1	0.2	0.4	0.6	0.7	0.8	0.9	1.1
91	0.0	0.2	0.3	0.6	0.7	0.8	0.9	1.0	1.3
90	0.0	0.3	0.4	0.7	0.9	1.0	1.1	1.2	1.5
89	0.1	0.4	0.6	0.9	1.1	1.2	1.3	1.5	1.7
88	0.2	0.5	0.8	1.1	1.3	1.5	1.6	1.8	2.0
87	0.3	0.8	1.1	1.4	1.6	1.8	1.9	2.1	2.4
86	0.6	1.1	1.4	1.8	2.0	2.2	2.3	2.5	2.8
85	1.0	1.5	1.8	2.2	2.5	2.6	2.8	2.9	3.2
84	1.5	2.0	2.3	2.7	2.9	3.1	3.2	3.4	3.7
83	2.2	2.7	3.0	3.3	3.5	3.7	3.8	4.0	4.3
82	3.0	3.4	3.7	4.0	4.2	4.4	4.5	4.7	4.9
81	4.0	4.2	4.4	4.8	5.0	5.1	5.2	5.4	5.6
80	5.0	5.1	5.3	5.6	5.7	5.8	6.0	6.1	6.4

Average Volatility

STOCK PRICE — NUMBER OF MONTHS BEFORE THE OPTIONS EXPIRE

STOCK PRICE	1	2	3	4	5	6	7	8	9
99	0.0	0.0	0.1	0.3	0.5	0.6	0.8	1.0	1.2
98	0.0	0.0	0.2	0.4	0.6	0.8	0.9	1.1	1.3
97	0.0	0.1	0.3	0.5	0.7	0.9	1.0	1.2	1.5
96	0.0	0.1	0.3	0.6	0.9	1.0	1.2	1.3	1.6
95	0.0	0.2	0.4	0.7	1.0	1.2	1.3	1.5	1.9
94	0.0	0.3	0.5	0.8	1.2	1.3	1.4	1.7	2.1
93	0.0	0.4	0.7	1.0	1.3	1.5	1.6	1.9	2.2
92	0.1	0.5	0.8	1.1	1.5	1.7	1.8	2.1	2.4
91	0.2	0.6	1.0	1.3	1.7	1.9	2.1	2.3	2.7
90	0.3	0.8	1.1	1.5	1.9	2.1	2.3	2.6	3.0
89	0.4	1.0	1.4	1.8	2.1	2.4	2.6	2.9	3.3
88	0.6	1.2	1.7	2.1	2.4	2.7	3.0	3.3	3.6
87	0.8	1.5	2.0	2.4	2.8	3.0	3.2	3.5	3.9
86	1.1	1.9	2.4	2.8	3.2	3.4	3.6	4.0	4.3
85	1.5	2.3	2.8	3.3	3.7	3.9	4.1	4.4	4.8
84	2.0	2.8	3.3	3.8	4.1	4.3	4.6	4.9	5.2
83	2.7	3.4	3.9	4.4	4.7	4.9	5.1	5.4	5.8
82	3.4	4.1	4.6	5.0	5.4	5.6	5.7	6.0	6.3
81	4.2	4.8	5.3	5.7	6.0	6.1	6.3	6.6	7.0
80	5.1	5.6	6.0	6.4	6.6	6.8	7.0	7.3	7.7

High Volatility

STOCK PRICE — NUMBER OF MONTHS BEFORE THE OPTIONS EXPIRE

STOCK PRICE	1	2	3	4	5	6	7	8	9
99	0.1	0.9	1.6	2.3	2.9	3.2	3.6	4.1	4.7
98	0.2	1.1	1.7	2.5	3.1	3.4	3.8	4.3	5.0
97	0.3	1.2	1.9	2.7	3.3	3.6	4.1	4.6	5.2
96	0.4	1.3	2.0	2.9	3.5	3.9	4.2	4.8	5.5
95	0.5	1.5	2.2	3.1	3.6	4.1	4.5	5.1	5.8
94	0.6	1.6	2.4	3.3	3.9	4.4	4.8	5.4	6.0
93	0.7	1.8	2.7	3.6	4.2	4.7	5.1	5.6	6.3
92	0.8	2.0	2.9	3.8	4.5	4.9	5.4	5.9	6.7
91	1.0	2.3	3.2	4.1	4.8	5.2	5.6	6.3	6.9
90	1.2	2.6	3.4	4.4	5.0	5.6	6.0	6.5	7.3
89	1.4	2.9	3.7	4.8	5.4	5.8	6.2	6.9	7.6
88	1.7	3.2	4.1	5.0	5.7	6.2	6.6	7.2	7.9
87	2.0	3.5	4.5	5.4	6.1	6.5	6.9	7.5	8.2
86	2.4	3.9	4.8	5.8	6.4	6.9	7.3	7.9	8.7
85	2.9	4.4	5.3	6.3	6.9	7.4	7.8	8.4	9.1
84	3.3	4.8	5.7	6.7	7.4	7.8	8.2	8.8	9.4
83	3.9	5.4	6.2	7.2	7.8	8.3	8.7	9.2	9.8
82	4.6	5.9	6.8	7.7	8.4	8.7	9.1	9.7	9.7
81	5.3	6.6	7.4	8.3	8.9	9.3	9.7	9.7	10.
80	6.1	7.3	8.1	8.9	9.6	9.7	9.7	10.	10.

PUT PRICING TABLE

Exercise Price is 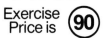 90

Low Volatility

STOCK PRICE — NUMBER OF MONTHS BEFORE THE OPTIONS EXPIRE

STOCK PRICE	1	2	3	4	5	6	7	8	9
105	0.0	0.0	0.0	0.0	0.0	0.1	0.1	0.2	0.3
104	0.0	0.0	0.0	0.0	0.1	0.1	0.2	0.2	0.4
103	0.0	0.0	0.0	0.0	0.1	0.2	0.2	0.3	0.4
102	0.0	0.0	0.0	0.1	0.2	0.2	0.3	0.4	0.5
101	0.0	0.0	0.0	0.1	0.2	0.3	0.4	0.5	0.7
100	0.0	0.0	0.1	0.2	0.3	0.4	0.5	0.6	0.8
99	0.0	0.0	0.1	0.3	0.4	0.5	0.6	0.7	0.9
98	0.0	0.1	0.2	0.4	0.5	0.6	0.7	0.9	1.0
97	0.0	0.1	0.3	0.5	0.7	0.8	0.9	1.0	1.2
96	0.0	0.2	0.4	0.6	0.8	0.9	1.0	1.2	1.4
95	0.0	0.3	0.5	0.8	1.0	1.1	1.2	1.4	1.6
94	0.1	0.5	0.7	1.0	1.2	1.3	1.5	1.7	1.9
93	0.2	0.6	0.9	1.2	1.5	1.6	1.7	2.0	2.2
92	0.4	0.9	1.2	1.6	1.8	1.9	2.1	2.3	2.6
91	0.7	1.2	1.5	1.9	2.2	2.3	2.5	2.7	3.0
90	1.1	1.6	2.0	2.4	2.6	2.8	2.9	3.2	3.4
89	1.6	2.1	2.4	2.8	3.1	3.2	3.4	3.6	3.9
88	2.3	2.8	3.1	3.5	3.7	3.8	4.0	4.2	4.5
87	3.1	3.5	3.8	4.1	4.4	4.5	4.6	4.9	5.1
86	4.0	4.3	4.6	4.9	5.1	5.2	5.3	5.5	5.8
85	5.0	5.1	5.4	5.7	5.8	6.0	6.1	6.3	6.5

Average Volatility

STOCK PRICE — NUMBER OF MONTHS BEFORE THE OPTIONS EXPIRE

STOCK PRICE	1	2	3	4	5	6	7	8	9
105	0.0	0.0	0.1	0.3	0.5	0.7	0.8	1.0	1.2
104	0.0	0.0	0.2	0.4	0.6	0.8	0.9	1.1	1.5
103	0.0	0.1	0.3	0.5	0.8	0.9	1.1	1.2	1.6
102	0.0	0.1	0.3	0.6	0.9	1.0	1.2	1.4	1.8
101	0.0	0.2	0.4	0.7	1.0	1.2	1.3	1.5	1.9
100	0.0	0.3	0.5	0.8	1.2	1.3	1.5	1.7	2.1
99	0.0	0.3	0.6	1.1	1.3	1.5	1.5	1.8	2.3
98	0.1	0.5	0.8	1.1	1.5	1.7	1.8	2.0	2.5
97	0.1	0.6	0.9	1.4	1.7	1.9	2.0	2.3	2.8
96	0.2	0.7	1.1	1.6	1.9	2.1	2.3	2.5	2.9
95	0.3	0.9	1.3	1.7	2.2	2.4	2.6	2.8	3.2
94	0.5	1.1	1.5	2.0	2.4	2.7	2.9	3.1	3.6
93	0.6	1.3	1.8	2.3	2.7	2.9	3.2	3.5	3.9
92	0.9	1.6	2.2	2.7	3.0	3.2	3.5	3.8	4.2
91	1.2	2.0	2.6	3.1	3.5	3.7	3.9	4.2	4.6
90	1.6	2.5	3.0	3.5	3.9	4.1	4.4	4.6	5.1
89	2.1	2.9	3.5	4.0	4.4	4.6	4.8	5.1	5.6
88	2.8	3.6	4.1	4.6	4.9	5.2	5.4	5.7	6.1
87	3.5	4.2	4.7	5.2	5.6	5.8	5.9	6.2	6.6
86	4.3	5.0	5.4	5.9	6.2	6.4	6.6	6.8	7.3
85	5.2	5.7	6.2	6.6	6.9	7.0	7.3	7.5	8.0

High Volatility

STOCK PRICE — NUMBER OF MONTHS BEFORE THE OPTIONS EXPIRE

STOCK PRICE	1	2	3	4	5	6	7	8	9
105	0.1	1.0	1.7	2.4	3.0	3.3	3.8	4.4	5.0
104	0.2	1.1	1.8	2.6	3.2	3.5	4.0	4.6	5.3
103	0.3	1.2	1.9	2.8	3.4	3.8	4.2	4.9	5.4
102	0.4	1.3	2.1	3.0	3.6	4.0	4.5	5.2	5.7
101	0.4	1.5	2.3	3.2	3.9	4.2	4.7	5.3	6.0
100	0.6	1.6	2.5	3.4	4.1	4.5	5.0	5.6	6.3
99	0.7	1.8	2.7	3.7	4.4	4.8	5.2	5.9	6.6
98	0.8	2.0	2.9	3.9	4.6	5.0	5.4	6.1	6.8
97	0.9	2.3	3.2	4.2	4.9	5.3	5.8	6.5	7.1
96	1.1	2.5	3.5	4.5	5.2	5.6	6.1	6.8	7.4
95	1.3	2.8	3.8	4.8	5.5	6.0	6.7	7.1	7.8
94	1.6	3.1	4.0	5.1	5.8	6.2	6.7	7.5	8.0
93	1.9	3.5	4.4	5.4	6.2	6.6	7.1	7.8	8.4
92	2.2	3.7	4.8	5.8	6.6	7.0	7.4	8.1	8.7
91	2.6	4.2	5.1	6.2	6.9	7.3	7.8	8.5	9.2
90	3.1	4.6	5.6	6.7	7.4	7.8	8.3	9.0	9.5
89	3.5	5.1	6.0	7.1	7.8	8.2	8.7	9.4	9.9
88	4.1	5.6	6.5	7.6	8.3	8.7	9.2	9.8	9.8
87	4.8	6.2	7.1	8.2	8.8	9.2	9.6	9.7	10.
86	5.5	6.8	7.7	8.7	9.4	9.7	9.7	10.	10.
85	6.2	7.5	8.4	9.3	9.7	9.7	10.	10.	11.

PUT PRICING TABLE

Exercise Price is (95)

Low Volatility

STOCK PRICE — NUMBER OF MONTHS BEFORE THE OPTIONS EXPIRE

	1	2	3	4	5	6	7	8	9
110	0.0	0.0	0.0	0.0	0.1	0.1	0.2	0.2	0.4
109	0.0	0.0	0.0	0.0	0.1	0.2	0.2	0.3	0.5
108	0.0	0.0	0.0	0.1	0.2	0.2	0.3	0.4	0.5
107	0.0	0.0	0.0	0.1	0.2	0.3	0.4	0.5	0.7
106	0.0	0.0	0.1	0.2	0.3	0.4	0.5	0.6	0.8
105	0.0	0.0	0.1	0.3	0.4	0.5	0.6	0.7	0.9
104	0.0	0.0	0.2	0.4	0.5	0.6	0.7	0.8	1.0
103	0.0	0.1	0.3	0.5	0.6	0.7	0.8	0.9	1.3
102	0.0	0.2	0.4	0.6	0.8	0.9	1.0	1.1	1.5
101	0.0	0.3	0.5	0.7	0.9	1.0	1.2	1.3	1.7
100	0.1	0.4	0.6	0.9	1.1	1.2	1.4	1.5	1.8
99	0.2	0.5	0.8	1.1	1.3	1.5	1.6	1.8	2.1
98	0.3	0.7	1.0	1.4	1.6	1.8	1.9	2.1	2.4
97	0.4	1.0	1.3	1.7	1.9	2.1	2.3	2.4	2.8
96	0.7	1.3	1.7	2.0	2.3	2.5	2.7	2.8	3.2
95	1.1	1.7	2.1	2.5	2.8	2.9	3.1	3.3	3.6
94	1.6	2.2	2.6	2.9	3.2	3.4	3.6	3.7	4.1
93	2.3	2.9	3.2	3.6	3.8	4.0	4.2	4.3	4.7
92	3.1	3.6	3.9	4.2	4.5	4.7	4.8	5.0	5.3
91	4.0	4.4	4.7	5.0	5.2	5.4	5.5	5.6	6.0
90	5.0	5.2	5.5	5.7	6.0	6.1	6.2	6.4	6.7

Average Volatility

STOCK PRICE — NUMBER OF MONTHS BEFORE THE OPTIONS EXPIRE

	1	2	3	4	5	6	7	8	9
110	0.0	0.0	0.2	0.4	0.6	0.8	1.0	1.2	1.5
109	0.0	0.1	0.3	0.5	0.8	1.0	1.1	1.3	1.7
108	0.0	0.1	0.3	0.6	0.9	1.1	1.2	1.4	1.8
107	0.0	0.2	0.4	0.7	1.0	1.2	1.3	1.6	2.0
106	0.0	0.2	0.5	0.8	1.2	1.3	1.5	1.7	2.1
105	0.0	0.3	0.6	0.9	1.3	1.5	1.6	1.9	2.3
104	0.0	0.4	0.7	1.2	1.5	1.7	1.8	2.1	2.5
103	0.1	0.5	0.9	1.3	1.7	1.9	2.0	2.3	2.8
102	0.2	0.7	1.0	1.5	1.9	2.1	2.3	2.6	3.0
101	0.3	0.8	1.2	1.7	2.1	2.3	2.5	2.8	3.2
100	0.4	1.0	1.4	2.0	2.4	2.6	2.8	3.1	3.5
99	0.5	1.2	1.7	2.1	2.7	2.9	3.1	3.4	3.9
98	0.7	1.5	2.0	2.5	2.9	3.3	3.5	3.8	4.2
97	1.0	1.8	2.3	2.8	3.3	3.5	3.7	4.1	4.5
96	1.3	2.2	2.7	3.2	3.7	3.9	4.2	4.5	5.0
95	1.7	2.6	3.2	3.7	4.1	4.4	4.6	5.0	5.4
94	2.2	3.1	3.6	4.1	4.6	4.9	5.1	5.4	5.9
93	2.9	3.7	4.2	4.7	5.2	5.4	5.6	6.0	6.5
92	3.6	4.4	4.9	5.4	5.8	6.0	6.2	6.5	7.0
91	4.4	5.1	5.6	6.0	6.4	6.6	6.8	7.2	7.6
90	5.2	5.8	6.3	6.7	7.1	7.3	7.5	7.8	8.3

High Volatility

STOCK PRICE — NUMBER OF MONTHS BEFORE THE OPTIONS EXPIRE

	1	2	3	4	5	6	7	8	9
110	0.2	1.1	1.9	2.7	3.3	3.8	4.1	4.8	5.6
109	0.3	1.3	2.0	2.9	3.5	4.0	4.4	5.0	5.8
108	0.3	1.4	2.2	3.1	3.7	4.2	4.6	5.3	6.1
107	0.4	1.5	2.4	3.3	4.0	4.5	4.9	5.5	6.4
106	0.5	1.7	2.6	3.6	4.2	4.6	5.1	5.8	6.6
105	0.6	1.9	2.8	3.8	4.5	4.9	5.4	6.0	6.9
104	0.8	2.1	3.0	4.1	4.7	5.2	5.6	6.3	7.2
103	0.9	2.3	3.2	4.4	4.9	5.5	5.9	6.6	7.4
102	1.1	2.5	3.5	4.7	5.3	5.7	6.2	6.9	7.8
101	1.2	2.8	3.8	4.9	5.6	6.1	6.5	7.2	8.0
100	1.5	3.1	4.1	5.2	5.8	6.4	6.8	7.5	8.4
99	1.7	3.4	4.4	5.6	6.2	6.7	7.1	7.9	8.7
98	2.0	3.7	4.7	5.9	6.6	7.1	7.5	8.2	9.0
97	2.4	4.0	5.2	6.3	6.9	7.5	7.9	8.5	9.4
96	2.8	4.5	5.5	6.6	7.3	7.8	8.2	8.9	9.8
95	3.2	4.9	6.0	7.1	7.8	8.3	8.7	9.4	10.
94	3.7	5.4	6.4	7.5	8.2	8.7	9.1	9.8	9.9
93	4.3	5.9	6.9	8.0	8.7	9.2	9.6	9.8	10.
92	4.9	6.5	7.5	8.6	9.1	9.7	9.7	10.	10.
91	5.6	7.1	8.1	9.1	9.7	9.7	10.	10.	11.
90	6.4	7.8	8.6	9.7	9.7	10.	10.	11.	12.

PUT PRICING TABLE

Exercise Price is (100)

Low Volatility

STOCK PRICE — NUMBER OF MONTHS BEFORE THE OPTIONS EXPIRE

	1	2	3	4	5	6	7	8	9
115	0.0	0.0	0.0	0.0	0.1	0.2	0.2	0.3	0.5
114	0.0	0.0	0.0	0.1	0.2	0.2	0.3	0.4	0.5
113	0.0	0.0	0.0	0.1	0.2	0.3	0.4	0.5	0.6
112	0.0	0.0	0.0	0.2	0.3	0.4	0.5	0.6	0.8
111	0.0	0.0	0.1	0.3	0.4	0.5	0.6	0.7	0.9
110	0.0	0.0	0.1	0.3	0.5	0.6	0.7	0.8	1.1
109	0.0	0.1	0.2	0.4	0.6	0.7	0.8	1.0	1.1
108	0.0	0.1	0.3	0.6	0.7	0.8	1.0	1.1	1.4
107	0.0	0.2	0.4	0.7	0.9	1.0	1.1	1.3	1.6
106	0.0	0.3	0.5	0.8	1.0	1.2	1.3	1.5	1.8
105	0.1	0.4	0.7	1.0	1.2	1.4	1.5	1.7	2.1
104	0.2	0.6	0.9	1.2	1.5	1.6	1.8	2.0	2.3
103	0.3	0.8	1.1	1.5	1.7	1.9	2.1	2.3	2.6
102	0.5	1.0	1.4	1.8	2.1	2.3	2.4	2.7	2.9
101	0.8	1.4	1.8	2.2	2.5	2.6	2.8	3.1	3.4
100	1.2	1.8	2.2	2.7	2.9	3.1	3.3	3.5	3.8
99	1.7	2.3	2.7	3.1	3.4	3.6	3.7	4.0	4.3
98	2.4	2.9	3.3	3.7	4.0	4.2	4.3	4.6	4.9
97	3.2	3.7	4.0	4.4	4.6	4.8	5.0	5.2	5.5
96	4.0	4.4	4.7	5.1	5.3	5.5	5.7	5.9	6.2
95	5.0	5.3	5.5	5.9	6.1	6.2	6.4	6.6	6.9

Average Volatility

STOCK PRICE — NUMBER OF MONTHS BEFORE THE OPTIONS EXPIRE

	1	2	3	4	5	6	7	8	9
115	0.0	0.1	0.3	0.5	0.8	1.0	1.1	1.4	1.7
114	0.0	0.1	0.3	0.6	0.9	1.1	1.3	1.5	1.8
113	0.0	0.2	0.4	0.7	1.0	1.2	1.4	1.6	2.0
112	0.0	0.2	0.5	0.8	1.2	1.3	1.5	1.9	2.1
111	0.0	0.3	0.6	0.9	1.3	1.5	1.7	1.9	2.3
110	0.0	0.4	0.7	1.2	1.4	1.6	1.8	2.2	2.5
109	0.1	0.5	0.9	1.3	1.6	1.8	2.0	2.3	2.7
108	0.1	0.6	1.0	1.5	1.8	2.0	2.3	2.7	3.0
107	0.2	0.8	1.2	1.7	2.0	2.3	2.5	2.8	3.2
106	0.3	0.9	1.3	1.9	2.3	2.5	2.8	3.1	3.4
105	0.5	1.1	1.6	2.1	2.5	2.8	3.1	3.4	3.8
104	0.6	1.3	1.8	2.3	2.9	3.1	3.4	3.7	4.1
103	0.8	1.6	2.2	2.7	3.1	3.5	3.7	4.1	4.5
102	1.1	1.9	2.5	3.0	3.5	3.7	4.0	4.4	4.8
101	1.4	2.3	2.9	3.4	3.9	4.2	4.4	4.8	5.2
100	1.8	2.8	3.4	3.9	4.4	4.6	4.9	5.3	5.7
99	2.3	3.2	3.8	4.3	4.8	5.1	5.3	5.7	6.1
98	3.0	3.8	4.4	4.9	5.4	5.7	5.9	6.3	6.7
97	3.7	4.5	5.1	5.6	6.0	6.2	6.4	6.8	7.2
96	4.5	5.2	5.7	6.2	6.6	6.8	7.1	7.4	7.8
95	5.3	6.0	6.5	6.9	7.3	7.5	7.8	8.1	8.5

High Volatility

STOCK PRICE — NUMBER OF MONTHS BEFORE THE OPTIONS EXPIRE

	1	2	3	4	5	6	7	8	9
115	0.3	1.3	2.1	3.1	3.6	4.2	4.7	5.4	5.9
114	0.3	1.4	2.2	3.3	3.8	4.4	4.9	5.5	6.1
113	0.4	1.6	2.4	3.5	4.0	4.6	5.0	5.8	6.4
112	0.5	1.7	2.6	3.8	4.3	4.9	5.3	6.1	6.7
111	0.6	1.9	2.8	3.9	4.5	5.2	5.6	6.3	6.9
110	0.8	2.2	3.0	4.2	4.8	5.3	5.9	6.7	7.2
109	0.9	2.3	3.3	4.4	5.1	5.6	6.2	6.9	7.5
108	1.0	2.5	3.5	4.7	5.4	6.0	6.4	7.2	7.8
107	1.2	2.7	3.8	5.1	5.6	6.3	6.7	7.4	8.1
106	1.4	3.0	4.1	5.4	6.0	6.5	7.1	7.8	8.4
105	1.6	3.3	4.5	5.6	6.3	6.9	7.3	8.1	8.7
104	1.9	3.7	4.7	6.0	6.6	7.2	7.6	8.5	9.1
103	2.2	4.0	5.1	6.3	7.0	7.6	8.0	8.8	9.4
102	2.5	4.3	5.5	6.7	7.3	7.9	8.4	9.1	9.7
101	2.9	4.7	5.9	7.1	7.7	8.3	8.7	9.5	10.
100	3.4	5.2	6.3	7.6	8.1	8.8	9.2	10.	10.
99	3.9	5.6	6.8	8.0	8.6	9.2	9.6	9.9	10.
98	4.5	6.2	7.2	8.4	9.0	9.6	9.8	10.	10.
97	5.1	6.7	7.8	9.0	9.5	9.7	9.7	10.	11.
96	5.8	7.4	8.4	9.5	9.7	10.	10.	11.	11.
95	6.5	8.0	9.0	9.7	10.	10.	11.	11.	12.

THE HIGH PRICE
CALL TABLES

	Decimal to Fraction	
	Conversion Chart	
Table		Market
Shows		Fraction
.1	=	1/16
.1	=	1/8
.2	=	3/16
.2	=	1/4
.3	=	5/16
.4	=	3/8
.4	=	7/16
.5	=	1/2
.6	=	9/16
.6	=	5/8
.7	=	11/16
.8	=	3/4
.8	=	13/16
.9	=	7/8
.9	=	15/16

*The Future Value Tables are generated by computer simulation. Due to the nature of the computer simulation techniques that we used there may be slight aberrations in the option prices presented. Therefore you should allow yourself a variance of plus or minus 10% of these option prices. In a few cases, some of the less important, peripheral option prices may vary more than 10%.

HIGH PRICE CALL TABLE

Exercise Price is ⑩

Average Volatility

STOCK PRICE — NUMBER OF MONTHS BEFORE THE OPTIONS EXPIRE

STOCK PRICE	1	2	3	4	5	6	7	8	9
0	0.0	0.0	0.0	0.0	0.0	0.0	0.0	0.0	0.0
0	1 %	1 %	1 %	1 %	1 %	1 %	1 %	1 %	1 %
1	0.0	0.0	0.0	0.0	0.0	0.0	0.0	0.0	0.0
1	1 %	1 %	1 %	1 %	1 %	1 %	1 %	1 %	1 %
2	0.0	0.0	0.0	0.0	0.0	0.0	0.0	0.0	0.0
2	1 %	1 %	1 %	1 %	1 %	1 %	1 %	1 %	1 %
3	0.0	0.0	0.0	0.0	0.0	0.0	0.0	0.0	0.0
3	1 %	1 %	1 %	1 %	1 %	1 %	1 %	1 %	1 %
4	0.0	0.0	0.0	0.0	0.0	0.0	0.0	0.0	0.0
4	1 %	1 %	1 %	1 %	1 %	1 %	1 %	1 %	1 %
5	0.0	0.0	0.0	0.0	0.0	0.0	0.0	0.0	0.0
5	1 %	1 %	1 %	1 %	1 %	1 %	0 %	2 %	3 %
6	0.0	0.0	0.0	0.0	0.0	0.0	0.0	0.0	0.0
6	1 %	1 %	1 %	0 %	4 %	4 %	6 %	7 %	13%
7	0.0	0.0	0.0	0.0	0.0	0.0	0.0	0.0	0.1
7	1 %	1 %	4 %	8 %	12%	18%	21%	25%	27%
8	0.0	0.0	0.0	0.0	0.1	0.2	0.2	0.3	
8	1 %	8 %	21%	27%	34%	39%	38%	39%	39%
9	0.0	0.1	0.2	0.3	0.4	0.5	0.6	0.6	0.7
9	26%	39%	41%	41%	39%	41%	39%	40%	40%
10	0.4	0.6	0.7	0.9	1.0	1.1	1.1	1.2	1.3
10	35%	36%	38%	38%	41%	41%	41%	40%	39%
11	1.3	1.5	1.6	1.7	1.8	1.9	2.0	2.0	2.2
11	40%	40%	41%	41%	41%	42%	42%	43%	40%
12	2.3	2.4	2.5	2.7	2.8	2.9	2.9	3.0	3.1
12	40%	40%	40%	40%	40%	40%	40%	41%	41%
13	3.3	3.5	3.6	3.7	3.9	3.9	4.0	4.1	4.2
13	40%	41%	41%	40%	38%	40%	39%	43%	40%
14	4.3	4.5	4.6	4.8	4.9	5.0	5.1	5.2	5.3
14	40%	40%	41%	41%	39%	41%	41%	42%	41%
15	5.3	5.5	5.6	5.8	6.0	6.1	6.2	6.3	6.4
15	40%	42%	41%	42%	39%	41%	41%	41%	39%

High Volatility

STOCK PRICE — NUMBER OF MONTHS BEFORE THE OPTIONS EXPIRE

STOCK PRICE	1	2	3	4	5	6	7	8	9
0	0.0	0.0	0.0	0.0	0.0	0.0	0.0	0.0	0.0
0	1 %	1 %	1 %	1 %	1 %	1 %	1 %	1 %	1 %
1	0.0	0.0	0.0	0.0	0.0	0.0	0.0	0.0	0.0
1	1 %	1 %	1 %	1 %	1 %	1 %	1 %	1 %	0 %
2	0.0	0.0	0.0	0.0	0.0	0.0	0.0	0.0	0.0
2	1 %	1 %	1 %	1 %	1 %	1 %	1 %	1 %	1 %
3	0.0	0.0	0.0	0.0	0.0	0.0	0.0	0.0	0.0
3	1 %	1 %	1 %	1 %	0 %	1 %	1 %	2 %	2 %
4	0.0	0.0	0.0	0.0	0.0	0.0	0.0	0.0	0.0
4	1 %	1 %	1 %	1 %	1 %	2 %	3 %	7 %	9 %
5	0.0	0.0	0.0	0.0	0.0	0.0	0.0	0.0	0.1
5	1 %	1 %	1 %	2 %	5 %	9 %	9 %	13%	16%
6	0.0	0.0	0.0	0.0	0.0	0.0	0.0	0.1	0.2
6	1 %	1 %	4 %	9 %	13%	17%	19%	24%	25%
7	0.0	0.0	0.0	0.1	0.2	0.2	0.3	0.3	0.5
7	1 %	8 %	14%	23%	25%	28%	32%	37%	34%
8	0.0	0.1	0.2	0.3	0.4	0.5	0.6	0.7	0.9
8	9 %	24%	33%	36%	35%	35%	38%	38%	35%
9	0.1	0.4	0.5	0.7	0.9	1.0	1.1	1.2	1.4
9	38%	38%	38%	36%	33%	36%	35%	40%	36%
10	0.6	1.0	1.1	1.4	1.6	1.7	1.8	1.9	2.1
10	39%	41%	39%	41%	40%	40%	40%	42%	41%
11	1.5	1.8	2.0	2.2	2.4	2.6	2.7	2.8	3.0
11	43%	43%	43%	43%	42%	42%	42%	43%	42%
12	2.5	2.8	3.0	3.2	3.4	3.6	3.6	3.8	4.0
12	43%	44%	43%	43%	43%	43%	43%	43%	43%
13	3.5	3.9	4.0	4.3	4.5	4.6	4.7	4.8	5.1
13	43%	44%	43%	43%	43%	43%	43%	44%	43%
14	4.5	4.9	5.1	5.3	5.5	5.7	5.8	5.9	6.2
14	43%	43%	43%	43%	43%	43%	44%	44%	43%
15	5.5	5.9	6.1	6.4	6.6	6.8	6.9	7.0	7.3
15	43%	43%	43%	43%	43%	41%	43%	44%	42%

HIGH PRICE CALL TABLE

Exercise Price is (15)

Average Volatility

STOCK PRICE — NUMBER OF MONTHS BEFORE THE OPTIONS EXPIRE

STOCK PRICE	1	2	3	4	5	6	7	8	9
5	0.0	0.0	0.0	0.0	0.0	0.0	0.0	0.0	0.0
5	1 %	1 %	1 %	1 %	1 %	1 %	1 %	1 %	1 %
6	0.0	0.0	0.0	0.0	0.0	0.0	0.0	0.0	0.0
6	1 %	1 %	1 %	1 %	1 %	1 %	1 %	1 %	1 %
7	0.0	0.0	0.0	0.0	0.0	0.0	0.0	0.0	0.0
7	1 %	1 %	1 %	1 %	1 %	1 %	0 %	1 %	4 %
8	0.0	0.0	0.0	0.0	0.0	0.0	0.0	0.0	0.0
8	1 %	1 %	1 %	1 %	1 %	1 %	4 %	4 %	7 %
9	0.0	0.0	0.0	0.0	0.0	0.0	0.0	0.0	0.0
9	1 %	1 %	1 %	1 %	4 %	4 %	8 %	10%	17%
10	0.0	0.0	0.0	0.0	0.0	0.0	0.0	0.0	0.1
10	1 %	1 %	1 %	4 %	9 %	14%	20%	21%	24%
11	0.0	0.0	0.0	0.0	0.0	0.1	0.1	0.2	0.2
11	1 %	4 %	8 %	17%	22%	26%	28%	34%	37%
12	0.0	0.0	0.0	0.1	0.2	0.3	0.3	0.4	0.5
12	1 %	12%	23%	30%	37%	38%	38%	39%	39%
13	0.0	0.1	0.2	0.4	0.5	0.6	0.7	0.8	1.0
13	15%	35%	39%	39%	39%	40%	40%	39%	39%
14	0.1	0.4	0.6	0.8	1.0	1.1	1.2	1.3	1.5
14	40%	40%	39%	39%	39%	40%	38%	37%	36%
15	0.6	0.9	1.2	1.4	1.6	1.7	1.8	2.0	2.1
15	36%	38%	38%	39%	41%	40%	41%	39%	40%
16	1.5	1.8	2.0	2.3	2.4	2.6	2.7	2.8	3.0
16	41%	40%	41%	40%	39%	39%	38%	39%	41%
17	2.5	2.8	3.0	3.2	3.3	3.5	3.6	3.7	3.9
17	41%	40%	40%	41%	41%	42%	39%	38%	38%
18	3.5	3.7	3.9	4.1	4.3	4.4	4.5	4.7	4.9
18	41%	41%	40%	40%	40%	40%	40%	41%	42%
19	4.5	4.8	5.0	5.2	5.4	5.5	5.6	5.8	6.0
19	41%	40%	41%	40%	40%	41%	41%	41%	41%
20	5.5	5.8	6.0	6.2	6.4	6.5	6.7	6.9	7.0
20	40%	40%	40%	40%	41%	41%	40%	40%	41%

High Volatility

STOCK PRICE — NUMBER OF MONTHS BEFORE THE OPTIONS EXPIRE

STOCK PRICE	1	2	3	4	5	6	7	8	9
5	0.0	0.0	0.0	0.0	0.0	0.0	0.0	0.0	0.0
5	1 %	1 %	1 %	1 %	1 %	2 %	2 %	5 %	8 %
6	0.0	0.0	0.0	0.0	0.0	0.0	0.0	0.0	0.1
6	1 %	1 %	1 %	1 %	2 %	3 %	7 %	8 %	11%
7	0.0	0.0	0.0	0.0	0.0	0.0	0.0	0.1	0.1
7	1 %	1 %	1 %	2 %	6 %	9 %	9 %	12%	14%
8	0.0	0.0	0.0	0.0	0.0	0.0	0.1	0.2	0.3
8	1 %	1 %	2 %	7 %	10%	12%	14%	19%	21%
9	0.0	0.0	0.0	0.0	0.1	0.1	0.2	0.3	0.4
9	1 %	2 %	7 %	12%	17%	19%	24%	26%	29%
10	0.0	0.0	0.0	0.1	0.2	0.3	0.4	0.5	0.7
10	1 %	7 %	12%	19%	24%	27%	29%	30%	34%
11	0.0	0.0	0.1	0.3	0.4	0.5	0.7	0.8	1.0
11	2 %	13%	23%	29%	35%	36%	37%	38%	36%
12	0.0	0.1	0.3	0.6	0.8	0.9	1.1	1.3	1.5
12	10%	26%	35%	35%	36%	36%	36%	36%	36%
13	0.1	0.4	0.7	1.0	1.3	1.4	1.6	1.8	2.1
13	26%	36%	35%	35%	33%	33%	35%	36%	37%
14	0.4	0.9	1.2	1.6	1.8	2.0	2.2	2.4	2.7
14	38%	34%	37%	39%	40%	40%	38%	37%	38%
15	1.0	1.6	1.9	2.3	2.5	2.7	2.9	3.2	3.5
15	42%	42%	39%	43%	42%	41%	41%	41%	40%
16	1.9	2.4	2.8	3.2	3.4	3.6	3.8	4.1	4.4
16	43%	43%	43%	43%	42%	41%	42%	42%	42%
17	2.9	3.4	3.7	4.1	4.4	4.5	4.7	5.0	5.3
17	43%	43%	43%	43%	43%	43%	43%	44%	43%
18	3.9	4.4	4.7	5.1	5.4	5.5	5.7	6.0	6.3
18	43%	43%	43%	44%	43%	43%	43%	44%	43%
19	4.9	5.4	5.8	6.1	6.4	6.6	6.8	7.1	7.4
19	43%	43%	43%	43%	43%	43%	43%	43%	43%
20	5.9	6.4	6.8	7.2	7.5	7.7	7.9	8.2	8.5
20	43%	43%	43%	43%	43%	43%	43%	43%	43%

HIGH PRICE CALL TABLE

Exercise Price is 20

Average Volatility

STOCK PRICE — NUMBER OF MONTHS BEFORE THE OPTIONS EXPIRE

STOCK PRICE	1	2	3	4	5	6	7	8	9
10	0.0	0.0	0.0	0.0	0.0	0.0	0.0	0.0	0.0
10	1 %	1 %	1 %	1 %	1 %	1 %	4 %	4 %	5 %
11	0.0	0.0	0.0	0.0	0.0	0.0	0.0	0.0	0.0
11	1 %	1 %	1 %	1 %	1 %	4 %	4 %	6 %	9 %
12	0.0	0.0	0.0	0.0	0.0	0.0	0.0	0.0	0.0
12	1 %	1 %	1 %	1 %	4 %	7 %	8 %	11%	17%
13	0.0	0.0	0.0	0.0	0.0	0.0	0.0	0.1	0.1
13	1 %	1 %	1 %	4 %	8 %	12%	17%	20%	24%
14	0.0	0.0	0.0	0.0	0.0	0.0	0.1	0.1	0.2
14	1 %	1 %	4 %	8 %	18%	22%	24%	27%	32%
15	0.0	0.0	0.0	0.0	0.1	0.2	0.3	0.4	0.5
15	1 %	4 %	12%	21%	25%	28%	34%	35%	37%
16	0.0	0.0	0.0	0.2	0.3	0.4	0.5	0.6	0.8
16	1 %	13%	25%	32%	37%	39%	39%	40%	40%
17	0.0	0.1	0.2	0.4	0.6	0.7	0.9	1.0	1.2
17	8 %	26%	37%	39%	39%	39%	41%	39%	39%
18	0.1	0.3	0.5	0.8	1.0	1.2	1.3	1.5	1.7
18	30%	39%	39%	39%	39%	39%	39%	40%	39%
19	0.3	0.7	1.0	1.3	1.5	1.7	1.9	2.1	2.3
19	40%	39%	40%	37%	36%	37%	35%	35%	36%
20	0.9	1.3	1.6	1.9	2.2	2.4	2.5	2.7	3.0
20	36%	37%	38%	40%	41%	41%	39%	40%	41%
21	1.7	2.2	2.5	2.8	3.0	3.2	3.4	3.6	3.8
21	40%	42%	42%	41%	41%	40%	41%	40%	40%
22	2.7	3.1	3.4	3.6	3.9	4.0	4.2	4.4	4.6
22	40%	40%	41%	40%	42%	41%	41%	41%	41%
23	3.7	4.1	4.3	4.6	4.9	5.0	5.2	5.4	5.6
23	41%	40%	40%	40%	40%	41%	40%	40%	40%
24	4.7	5.1	5.3	5.6	5.8	6.0	6.1	6.4	6.6
24	41%	41%	40%	41%	41%	40%	40%	40%	42%
25	5.7	6.1	6.3	6.7	6.9	7.1	7.2	7.5	7.7
25	41%	40%	40%	40%	41%	40%	41%	41%	41%

High Volatility

STOCK PRICE — NUMBER OF MONTHS BEFORE THE OPTIONS EXPIRE

STOCK PRICE	1	2	3	4	5	6	7	8	9
10	0.0	0.0	0.0	0.0	0.0	0.1	0.1	0.2	0.3
10	1 %	1 %	2 %	6 %	9 %	12%	13%	17%	19%
11	0.0	0.0	0.0	0.0	0.1	0.2	0.2	0.3	0.5
11	1 %	1 %	3 %	10%	11%	14%	18%	20%	23%
12	0.0	0.0	0.0	0.1	0.2	0.3	0.4	0.5	0.7
12	1 %	2 %	8 %	12%	17%	19%	23%	25%	30%
13	0.0	0.0	0.0	0.2	0.3	0.4	0.6	0.7	1.0
13	1 %	6 %	11%	19%	22%	25%	28%	29%	31%
14	0.0	0.0	0.1	0.3	0.5	0.6	0.8	1.0	1.2
14	1 %	11%	19%	26%	29%	34%	35%	36%	35%
15	0.0	0.1	0.3	0.6	0.8	1.0	1.1	1.4	1.7
15	3 %	19%	25%	31%	35%	35%	37%	37%	35%
16	0.0	0.2	0.5	0.8	1.1	1.3	1.5	1.8	2.1
16	12%	28%	35%	36%	37%	36%	38%	36%	33%
17	0.1	0.5	0.9	1.3	1.6	1.9	2.1	2.4	2.7
17	23%	35%	35%	36%	32%	34%	33%	37%	35%
18	0.3	0.9	1.4	1.8	2.1	2.4	2.6	2.9	3.3
18	36%	36%	34%	37%	35%	37%	37%	40%	37%
19	0.8	1.5	2.0	2.5	2.8	3.1	3.3	3.6	4.0
19	37%	37%	39%	40%	35%	35%	38%	40%	41%
20	1.4	2.2	2.7	3.2	3.5	3.8	4.1	4.4	4.8
20	42%	40%	40%	42%	42%	42%	42%	40%	37%
21	2.3	3.0	3.5	4.0	4.4	4.7	4.9	5.2	5.7
21	43%	43%	44%	43%	41%	40%	41%	42%	40%
22	3.3	4.0	4.4	5.0	5.3	5.6	5.8	6.1	6.6
22	43%	43%	43%	43%	44%	43%	43%	43%	43%
23	4.3	5.0	5.4	6.0	6.3	6.6	6.8	7.1	7.6
23	43%	43%	43%	43%	43%	43%	43%	43%	43%
24	5.2	6.0	6.4	6.9	7.3	7.6	7.8	8.1	8.6
24	43%	43%	43%	44%	43%	43%	43%	43%	43%
25	6.3	7.0	7.5	8.0	8.3	8.6	8.9	9.2	9.7
25	43%	43%	43%	43%	43%	43%	43%	43%	43%

HIGH PRICE CALL TABLE

Exercise Price is 25

Average Volatility

STOCK PRICE — NUMBER OF MONTHS BEFORE THE OPTIONS EXPIRE

STOCK PRICE	1	2	3	4	5	6	7	8	9
15	0.0	0.0	0.0	0.0	0.0	0.0	0.0	0.0	0.1
15	1%	1%	1%	3%	4%	7%	9%	12%	19%
16	0.0	0.0	0.0	0.0	0.0	0.0	0.0	0.1	0.2
16	1%	1%	1%	4%	8%	10%	16%	20%	23%
17	0.0	0.0	0.0	0.0	0.0	0.1	0.1	0.2	0.3
17	1%	1%	4%	8%	14%	20%	22%	24%	26%
18	0.0	0.0	0.0	0.0	0.1	0.1	0.2	0.3	0.5
18	1%	4%	6%	17%	21%	24%	26%	31%	35%
19	0.0	0.0	0.0	0.1	0.2	0.3	0.4	0.5	0.7
19	1%	5%	18%	24%	29%	33%	37%	38%	39%
20	0.0	0.0	0.1	0.3	0.4	0.5	0.7	0.9	1.1
20	1%	16%	24%	32%	35%	37%	39%	39%	39%
21	0.0	0.1	0.2	0.5	0.7	0.9	1.0	1.2	1.5
21	7%	24%	35%	39%	39%	39%	39%	39%	40%
22	0.0	0.3	0.5	0.8	1.1	1.3	1.5	1.7	1.9
22	22%	38%	40%	40%	40%	39%	39%	39%	39%
23	0.2	0.6	0.9	1.3	1.6	1.8	2.0	2.2	2.5
23	39%	39%	39%	38%	38%	39%	38%	37%	35%
24	0.6	1.1	1.5	1.8	2.1	2.4	2.6	2.8	3.1
24	39%	38%	36%	35%	37%	35%	35%	37%	38%
25	1.1	1.7	2.1	2.5	2.8	3.0	3.2	3.5	3.8
25	36%	38%	38%	40%	43%	40%	39%	40%	41%
26	2.0	2.5	2.9	3.3	3.6	3.8	4.1	4.4	4.7
26	40%	42%	43%	41%	39%	42%	42%	42%	41%
27	2.9	3.5	3.8	4.2	4.5	4.7	5.0	5.2	5.5
27	40%	41%	40%	40%	41%	40%	41%	41%	39%
28	3.9	4.4	4.8	5.1	5.4	5.6	5.8	6.1	6.4
28	41%	40%	40%	40%	41%	42%	41%	40%	38%
29	4.9	5.4	5.8	6.1	6.4	6.6	6.8	7.1	7.4
29	42%	41%	40%	40%	40%	40%	40%	40%	40%
30	5.9	6.4	6.7	7.1	7.4	7.6	7.8	8.0	8.4
30	41%	41%	40%	40%	40%	40%	40%	40%	40%

High Volatility

STOCK PRICE — NUMBER OF MONTHS BEFORE THE OPTIONS EXPIRE

STOCK PRICE	1	2	3	4	5	6	7	8	9
15	0.0	0.0	0.0	0.1	0.3	0.4	0.5	0.7	0.9
15	1%	2%	9%	13%	17%	19%	24%	26%	29%
16	0.0	0.0	0.1	0.3	0.4	0.6	0.7	0.9	1.2
16	1%	6%	12%	17%	20%	24%	28%	29%	32%
17	0.0	0.0	0.1	0.4	0.6	0.7	0.9	1.2	1.5
17	0%	9%	16%	20%	26%	30%	32%	36%	35%
18	0.0	0.1	0.3	0.6	0.8	1.0	1.3	1.6	1.9
18	2%	13%	19%	27%	31%	32%	35%	36%	34%
19	0.0	0.2	0.4	0.8	1.1	1.3	1.6	2.0	2.3
19	6%	20%	29%	33%	35%	35%	35%	35%	32%
20	0.0	0.4	0.7	1.2	1.5	1.8	2.1	2.4	2.8
20	12%	26%	34%	36%	36%	36%	35%	35%	33%
21	0.1	0.6	1.0	1.6	2.0	2.3	2.6	2.9	3.4
21	19%	35%	37%	37%	34%	33%	33%	35%	35%
22	0.3	1.0	1.5	2.1	2.5	2.8	3.2	3.6	4.0
22	36%	35%	36%	34%	37%	36%	36%	36%	36%
23	0.7	1.5	2.1	2.7	3.1	3.4	3.8	4.2	4.6
23	36%	35%	37%	37%	38%	40%	37%	36%	38%
24	1.2	2.1	2.7	3.3	3.8	4.1	4.4	4.9	5.4
24	35%	37%	41%	36%	36%	39%	39%	40%	40%
25	1.8	2.8	3.4	4.1	4.6	4.9	5.2	5.7	6.2
25	42%	41%	42%	42%	42%	42%	42%	40%	36%
26	2.7	3.6	4.2	4.9	5.4	5.7	6.1	6.5	7.0
26	43%	43%	43%	43%	41%	40%	39%	39%	40%
27	3.6	4.6	5.2	5.9	6.3	6.6	7.0	7.4	8.0
27	43%	43%	43%	43%	42%	43%	43%	42%	42%
28	4.6	5.5	6.1	6.8	7.3	7.6	7.9	8.4	8.9
28	44%	43%	43%	43%	43%	43%	43%	43%	43%
29	5.6	6.5	7.1	7.8	8.3	8.6	8.9	9.4	9.9
29	44%	43%	43%	43%	43%	43%	43%	43%	43%
30	6.6	7.5	8.1	8.8	9.3	9.6	9.9	10.	10.
30	43%	43%	43%	43%	43%	43%	43%	43%	43%

HIGH PRICE CALL TABLE

Exercise Price is ⓵⓪ (30)

Average Volatility

STOCK PRICE — NUMBER OF MONTHS BEFORE THE OPTIONS EXPIRE

STOCK PRICE	1	2	3	4	5	6	7	8	9
20	0.0	0.0	0.0	0.0	0.0	0.1	0.1	0.2	0.3
20	1%	1%	4%	7%	10%	18%	19%	25%	25%
21	0.0	0.0	0.0	0.0	0.1	0.2	0.2	0.4	0.5
21	1%	1%	4%	10%	20%	23%	25%	26%	31%
22	0.0	0.0	0.0	0.1	0.2	0.3	0.4	0.5	0.7
22	1%	4%	9%	20%	25%	26%	30%	34%	35%
23	0.0	0.0	0.0	0.2	0.3	0.4	0.6	0.8	1.0
23	1%	7%	19%	24%	30%	34%	35%	37%	38%
24	0.0	0.0	0.1	0.3	0.5	0.6	0.8	1.0	1.3
24	1%	17%	24%	32%	37%	39%	39%	39%	40%
25	0.0	0.1	0.3	0.6	0.8	1.0	1.2	1.5	1.7
25	5%	24%	33%	36%	40%	39%	39%	40%	39%
26	0.0	0.2	0.5	0.9	1.1	1.4	1.6	1.9	2.1
26	18%	34%	39%	39%	39%	40%	39%	39%	39%
27	0.1	0.5	0.9	1.3	1.6	1.9	2.1	2.4	2.7
27	33%	40%	39%	39%	38%	38%	39%	38%	38%
28	0.4	0.9	1.3	1.8	2.1	2.4	2.6	3.0	3.3
28	39%	39%	39%	36%	37%	36%	36%	34%	35%
29	0.8	1.4	1.9	2.4	2.7	3.0	3.2	3.5	3.9
29	40%	40%	37%	36%	36%	35%	39%	39%	38%
30	1.4	2.1	2.5	3.0	3.4	3.7	3.9	4.2	4.6
30	37%	38%	38%	40%	43%	41%	40%	42%	41%
31	2.2	2.9	3.3	3.8	4.2	4.5	4.7	5.1	5.5
31	41%	42%	43%	41%	41%	42%	41%	42%	42%
32	3.2	3.8	4.2	4.8	5.1	5.4	5.6	6.0	6.4
32	40%	41%	40%	40%	40%	40%	39%	39%	39%
33	4.1	4.7	5.1	5.6	5.9	6.2	6.4	6.8	7.2
33	41%	40%	40%	40%	41%	41%	42%	42%	41%
34	5.1	5.7	6.1	6.6	6.9	7.2	7.4	7.8	8.2
34	41%	40%	40%	40%	41%	40%	41%	41%	38%
35	6.1	6.7	7.1	7.6	7.9	8.2	8.4	8.8	9.1
35	41%	41%	40%	40%	40%	40%	40%	40%	40%

High Volatility

STOCK PRICE — NUMBER OF MONTHS BEFORE THE OPTIONS EXPIRE

STOCK PRICE	1	2	3	4	5	6	7	8	9
20	0.0	0.0	0.2	0.4	0.7	0.9	1.1	1.4	1.7
20	1%	8%	14%	20%	26%	29%	30%	32%	33%
21	0.0	0.1	0.3	0.6	0.9	1.1	1.4	1.7	2.1
21	1%	12%	20%	26%	30%	31%	34%	35%	35%
22	0.0	0.1	0.4	0.8	1.1	1.4	1.7	2.1	2.5
22	2%	16%	25%	31%	33%	35%	35%	35%	34%
23	0.0	0.3	0.6	1.1	1.5	1.8	2.1	2.5	3.0
23	7%	20%	30%	31%	33%	35%	35%	36%	32%
24	0.0	0.4	0.9	1.4	1.9	2.2	2.6	3.0	3.5
24	12%	29%	34%	36%	34%	36%	35%	32%	32%
25	0.1	0.7	1.2	1.9	2.3	2.7	3.0	3.5	4.0
25	20%	33%	35%	34%	32%	32%	33%	35%	36%
26	0.3	1.0	1.7	2.4	2.9	3.2	3.6	4.1	4.6
26	30%	36%	36%	34%	35%	36%	36%	37%	38%
27	0.6	1.5	2.2	2.9	3.5	3.8	4.2	4.7	5.3
27	36%	36%	33%	36%	35%	37%	39%	36%	37%
28	1.0	2.0	2.8	3.5	4.1	4.5	4.8	5.4	5.9
28	37%	34%	37%	40%	37%	35%	38%	39%	40%
29	1.6	2.7	3.4	4.2	4.8	5.2	5.6	6.1	6.7
29	34%	38%	40%	37%	38%	41%	40%	40%	41%
30	2.2	3.4	4.2	5.0	5.5	5.9	6.3	6.9	7.5
30	42%	40%	41%	42%	42%	42%	42%	38%	37%
31	3.1	4.2	5.0	5.8	6.4	6.8	7.2	7.8	8.4
31	43%	43%	43%	43%	41%	39%	41%	39%	39%
32	4.1	5.2	5.9	6.7	7.3	7.7	8.1	8.7	9.3
32	43%	43%	43%	43%	42%	42%	42%	42%	42%
33	5.0	6.1	6.9	7.6	8.2	8.6	9.0	9.6	10.
33	43%	43%	43%	43%	43%	43%	44%	43%	43%
34	6.0	7.1	7.8	8.6	9.2	9.6	10.	10.	11.
34	43%	43%	44%	43%	43%	43%	43%	43%	43%
35	7.0	8.1	8.8	9.6	10.	10.	11.	11.	12.
35	43%	43%	43%	43%	43%	43%	43%	43%	43%

HIGH PRICE CALL TABLE

Exercise Price is (35)

Average Volatility

NUMBER OF MONTHS BEFORE THE OPTIONS EXPIRE

STOCK PRICE	1	2	3	4	5	6	7	8	9
25	0.0	0.0	0.0	0.1	0.1	0.2	0.4	0.5	0.7
25	1%	4%	7%	16%	21%	25%	26%	31%	32%
26	0.0	0.0	0.0	0.1	0.3	0.4	0.5	0.7	0.9
26	1%	4%	11%	21%	25%	27%	32%	34%	35%
27	0.0	0.0	0.1	0.2	0.4	0.6	0.7	1.0	1.2
27	1%	9%	19%	24%	32%	34%	36%	38%	39%
28	0.0	0.0	0.2	0.4	0.6	0.8	1.0	1.3	1.6
28	2%	17%	24%	32%	35%	38%	39%	39%	39%
29	0.0	0.1	0.3	0.6	0.9	1.1	1.3	1.6	2.0
29	4%	25%	33%	38%	39%	39%	39%	39%	39%
30	0.0	0.2	0.6	0.9	1.2	1.5	1.8	2.1	2.4
30	12%	32%	38%	39%	40%	39%	39%	39%	38%
31	0.1	0.5	0.9	1.3	1.6	2.0	2.2	2.5	2.9
31	25%	38%	39%	40%	39%	39%	39%	39%	38%
32	0.2	0.8	1.3	1.8	2.2	2.4	2.7	3.1	3.5
32	38%	40%	39%	38%	37%	38%	39%	37%	35%
33	0.6	1.3	1.8	2.3	2.7	3.0	3.3	3.7	4.1
33	39%	38%	38%	36%	36%	35%	35%	35%	35%
34	1.0	1.8	2.3	2.9	3.3	3.6	3.9	4.3	4.7
34	39%	36%	36%	35%	37%	38%	40%	40%	39%
35	1.6	2.4	3.0	3.6	4.0	4.3	4.6	5.0	5.5
35	37%	39%	38%	40%	43%	41%	40%	43%	43%
36	2.4	3.2	3.8	4.4	4.8	5.1	5.4	5.9	6.3
36	40%	41%	41%	41%	42%	42%	43%	42%	42%
37	3.4	4.2	4.7	5.3	5.7	6.0	6.4	6.8	7.2
37	40%	41%	40%	41%	40%	38%	39%	40%	38%
38	4.4	5.1	5.6	6.2	6.6	6.9	7.2	7.6	8.0
38	40%	41%	40%	41%	40%	40%	41%	38%	38%
39	5.3	6.1	6.6	7.1	7.5	7.8	8.1	8.5	8.9
39	41%	40%	40%	40%	42%	41%	42%	43%	39%
40	6.3	7.1	7.5	8.1	8.5	8.8	9.1	9.5	9.9
40	41%	40%	41%	41%	40%	40%	40%	41%	40%

High Volatility

STOCK PRICE — NUMBER OF MONTHS BEFORE THE OPTIONS EXPIRE

STOCK PRICE	1	2	3	4	5	6	7	8	9
25	0.0	0.1	0.4	0.9	1.2	1.5	1.8	2.2	2.7
25	4%	20%	24%	31%	32%	32%	32%	32%	32%
26	0.0	0.2	0.6	1.1	1.5	1.8	2.1	2.6	3.1
26	3%	23%	26%	32%	32%	33%	34%	33%	32%
27	0.0	0.4	0.8	1.4	1.8	2.2	2.6	3.1	3.6
27	9%	25%	32%	32%	32%	34%	33%	32%	33%
28	0.0	0.6	1.1	1.8	2.3	2.6	3.0	3.6	4.1
28	15%	31%	32%	32%	32%	32%	34%	35%	34%
29	0.1	0.8	1.4	2.2	2.7	3.1	3.6	4.1	4.7
29	23%	33%	32%	32%	33%	34%	34%	35%	35%
30	0.3	1.1	1.8	2.7	3.2	3.6	4.1	4.6	5.3
30	30%	32%	32%	34%	35%	36%	36%	35%	35%
31	0.5	1.5	2.3	3.2	3.8	4.2	4.7	5.3	5.9
31	33%	32%	35%	36%	35%	37%	35%	35%	36%
32	0.9	2.1	2.9	3.8	4.4	4.8	5.3	5.9	6.6
32	33%	36%	34%	37%	35%	36%	36%	37%	38%
33	1.4	2.6	3.5	4.4	5.1	5.5	6.0	6.6	7.2
33	35%	37%	37%	37%	38%	37%	38%	38%	39%
34	2.0	3.3	4.2	5.1	5.8	6.2	6.7	7.4	8.0
34	36%	39%	40%	40%	39%	40%	39%	40%	37%
35	2.6	4.0	4.9	5.9	6.5	7.0	7.5	8.1	8.8
35	40%	40%	40%	41%	40%	40%	39%	39%	39%
36	3.5	4.8	5.7	6.7	7.4	7.8	8.3	9.0	9.7
36	41%	40%	40%	40%	41%	40%	40%	40%	40%
37	4.4	5.8	6.6	7.7	8.3	8.7	9.2	9.9	10.
37	42%	41%	40%	41%	40%	40%	40%	41%	40%
38	5.4	6.7	7.6	8.6	9.2	9.7	10.	10.	11.
38	41%	41%	40%	40%	40%	40%	40%	40%	40%
39	6.4	7.7	8.5	9.5	10.	10.	11.	11.	12.
39	42%	41%	41%	41%	40%	40%	40%	41%	41%
40	7.4	8.7	9.5	10.	11.	11.	12.	12.	13.
40	41%	41%	41%	40%	40%	40%	40%	40%	40%

HIGH PRICE CALL TABLE

Exercise Price is (40)

Average Volatility

STOCK PRICE — NUMBER OF MONTHS BEFORE THE OPTIONS EXPIRE

STOCK PRICE	1	2	3	4	5	6	7	8	9
30	0.0	0.0	0.0	0.2	0.3	0.5	0.7	0.9	1.2
30	1 %	4 %	13%	22%	26%	30%	33%	35%	36%
31	0.0	0.0	0.1	0.3	0.5	0.7	0.9	1.2	1.5
31	1 %	9 %	19%	25%	31%	34%	35%	38%	38%
32	0.0	0.0	0.2	0.4	0.7	0.9	1.2	1.5	1.8
32	1 %	18%	24%	32%	35%	38%	40%	40%	39%
33	0.0	0.1	0.3	0.7	1.0	1.3	1.5	1.9	2.2
33	4 %	22%	32%	36%	38%	40%	39%	39%	39%
34	0.0	0.2	0.5	1.0	1.3	1.6	1.9	2.3	2.7
34	10%	31%	38%	39%	39%	39%	40%	40%	38%
35	0.0	0.4	0.9	1.3	1.8	2.1	2.4	2.7	3.1
35	21%	37%	39%	39%	38%	39%	39%	39%	38%
36	0.2	0.7	1.2	1.8	2.2	2.5	2.8	3.2	3.7
36	33%	39%	39%	39%	38%	38%	39%	38%	36%
37	0.4	1.1	1.7	2.3	2.7	3.1	3.4	3.8	4.3
37	39%	39%	39%	37%	37%	37%	36%	36%	35%
38	0.8	1.6	2.2	2.8	3.3	3.7	4.0	4.4	4.9
38	39%	39%	37%	36%	35%	35%	35%	36%	36%
39	1.3	2.2	2.8	3.4	3.9	4.3	4.6	5.0	5.5
39	40%	36%	36%	37%	39%	38%	40%	39%	38%
40	1.9	2.8	3.4	4.1	4.6	5.0	5.3	5.7	6.3
40	37%	38%	39%	42%	42%	41%	41%	44%	43%
41	2.7	3.6	4.2	4.9	5.4	5.8	6.1	6.6	7.2
41	40%	41%	42%	42%	42%	42%	42%	42%	42%
42	3.6	4.5	5.1	5.8	6.3	6.7	7.1	7.5	8.0
42	40%	42%	41%	41%	39%	40%	40%	39%	39%
43	4.6	5.5	6.1	6.7	7.2	7.5	7.9	8.3	8.9
43	41%	40%	40%	41%	40%	40%	40%	42%	38%
44	5.5	6.4	7.0	7.6	8.0	8.4	8.7	9.1	9.6
44	41%	40%	40%	40%	41%	41%	41%	43%	41%
45	6.5	7.4	7.9	8.6	9.0	9.4	9.7	10.	10.
45	42%	40%	40%	40%	41%	41%	40%	40%	39%

High Volatility

STOCK PRICE — NUMBER OF MONTHS BEFORE THE OPTIONS EXPIRE

STOCK PRICE	1	2	3	4	5	6	7	8	9
30	0.0	0.3	0.8	1.4	1.8	2.2	2.6	3.1	3.9
30	7 %	23%	30%	32%	32%	32%	33%	32%	33%
31	0.0	0.5	1.0	1.7	2.2	2.6	3.0	3.6	4.3
31	11%	25%	32%	33%	32%	33%	32%	34%	34%
32	0.1	0.6	1.3	2.0	2.6	3.1	3.6	4.1	4.8
32	16%	33%	33%	33%	32%	32%	33%	34%	34%
33	0.2	0.9	1.7	2.5	3.1	3.6	4.1	4.6	5.4
33	23%	32%	32%	32%	34%	34%	34%	35%	35%
34	0.3	1.2	2.0	3.0	3.6	4.1	4.6	5.2	6.0
34	27%	32%	33%	35%	35%	35%	35%	36%	35%
35	0.5	1.6	2.5	3.5	4.1	4.6	5.2	5.8	6.6
35	32%	32%	34%	36%	35%	35%	35%	35%	35%
36	0.8	2.1	3.1	4.0	4.7	5.3	5.8	6.4	7.3
36	34%	35%	36%	35%	36%	35%	34%	36%	37%
37	1.2	2.7	3.6	4.7	5.4	5.9	6.5	7.1	8.0
37	34%	35%	36%	37%	37%	37%	37%	39%	38%
38	1.8	3.2	4.3	5.3	6.0	6.6	7.1	7.8	8.6
38	35%	37%	38%	37%	37%	37%	38%	38%	38%
39	2.4	3.9	4.9	6.0	6.7	7.3	7.9	8.6	9.5
39	38%	40%	38%	40%	40%	40%	39%	39%	38%
40	3.1	4.6	5.7	6.8	7.5	8.1	8.7	9.3	10.
40	40%	40%	40%	40%	40%	40%	39%	39%	39%
41	3.9	5.5	6.5	7.6	8.3	8.9	9.5	10.	11.
41	41%	40%	40%	40%	40%	40%	40%	40%	40%
42	4.8	6.4	7.4	8.5	9.3	9.8	10.	11.	12.
42	42%	41%	40%	40%	40%	40%	41%	40%	40%
43	5.8	7.3	8.4	9.5	10.	10.	11.	12.	13.
43	41%	41%	40%	40%	40%	40%	40%	40%	40%
44	6.8	8.3	9.3	10.	11.	11.	12.	12.	13.
44	41%	41%	41%	40%	40%	41%	41%	40%	40%
45	7.8	9.3	10.	11.	12.	12.	13.	13.	14.
45	42%	41%	41%	40%	40%	40%	40%	40%	40%

HIGH PRICE CALL TABLE

Exercise Price is (45)

Average Volatility

STOCK PRICE — NUMBER OF MONTHS BEFORE THE OPTIONS EXPIRE

STOCK PRICE	1	2	3	4	5	6	7	8	9
35	0.0	0.0	0.2	0.4	0.7	0.9	1.1	1.3	1.8
35	1%	10%	20%	27%	30%	34%	35%	39%	39%
36	0.0	0.1	0.3	0.6	0.9	1.1	1.4	1.7	2.1
36	2%	17%	24%	31%	32%	37%	38%	40%	38%
37	0.0	0.1	0.4	0.7	1.2	1.4	1.8	2.0	2.5
37	4%	22%	31%	36%	36%	39%	39%	39%	39%
38	0.0	0.3	0.6	1.1	1.5	1.8	2.2	2.5	3.0
38	9%	26%	34%	39%	37%	39%	38%	39%	38%
39	0.0	0.4	0.9	1.4	1.9	2.2	2.6	2.9	3.4
39	20%	34%	39%	39%	37%	39%	39%	39%	37%
40	0.2	0.7	1.2	1.8	2.4	2.7	3.1	3.4	3.9
40	25%	38%	39%	39%	36%	38%	38%	38%	36%
41	0.3	1.0	1.6	2.2	2.9	3.1	3.6	3.9	4.5
41	35%	39%	39%	39%	36%	37%	35%	39%	34%
42	0.7	1.5	2.1	2.8	3.4	3.7	4.2	4.5	5.1
42	39%	38%	38%	37%	34%	34%	35%	36%	34%
43	1.1	2.0	2.6	3.3	4.1	4.4	4.8	5.1	5.7
43	38%	36%	36%	36%	35%	36%	34%	39%	36%
44	1.6	2.6	3.2	4.0	4.7	4.9	5.4	5.7	6.4
44	36%	36%	36%	37%	36%	39%	40%	40%	38%
45	2.2	3.2	3.9	4.6	5.4	5.7	6.1	6.5	7.1
45	36%	38%	38%	41%	37%	41%	40%	43%	43%
46	3.0	4.0	4.7	5.4	6.1	6.5	7.0	7.3	8.0
46	40%	40%	43%	41%	40%	41%	42%	42%	41%
47	3.9	4.9	5.6	6.3	7.1	7.4	7.9	8.1	8.8
47	40%	42%	41%	41%	38%	41%	40%	40%	39%
48	4.9	5.9	6.5	7.2	8.0	8.3	8.7	9.0	9.8
48	40%	41%	41%	40%	38%	40%	38%	41%	38%
49	5.9	6.8	7.4	8.1	8.9	9.1	9.5	9.9	10.
49	40%	40%	40%	40%	40%	40%	40%	40%	39%
50	6.8	7.7	8.3	9.0	9.8	10.	10.	10.	11.
50	40%	41%	40%	40%	38%	41%	39%	43%	39%

High Volatility

STOCK PRICE — NUMBER OF MONTHS BEFORE THE OPTIONS EXPIRE

STOCK PRICE	1	2	3	4	5	6	7	8	9
35	0.1	0.6	1.2	1.9	2.8	3.1	3.7	4.1	5.1
35	12%	26%	32%	33%	32%	32%	32%	33%	34%
36	0.1	0.8	1.5	2.3	3.2	3.5	4.2	4.6	5.5
36	14%	31%	32%	32%	32%	33%	33%	34%	34%
37	0.2	1.0	1.8	2.7	3.7	4.0	4.7	5.1	6.2
37	23%	32%	32%	32%	33%	34%	34%	35%	35%
38	0.4	1.4	2.2	3.2	4.2	4.5	5.2	5.7	6.8
38	25%	32%	32%	35%	32%	35%	35%	35%	35%
39	0.6	1.7	2.7	3.8	4.8	5.1	5.8	6.3	7.3
39	32%	32%	34%	35%	34%	35%	35%	35%	35%
40	0.9	2.2	3.2	4.3	5.4	5.7	6.4	6.9	7.9
40	33%	32%	35%	35%	35%	36%	35%	36%	36%
41	1.2	2.7	3.8	4.9	6.0	6.4	7.1	7.5	8.7
41	32%	35%	34%	37%	35%	35%	33%	38%	38%
42	1.7	3.3	4.3	5.5	6.7	7.0	7.8	8.2	9.4
42	33%	34%	37%	37%	34%	37%	38%	39%	37%
43	2.3	3.9	5.0	6.2	7.4	7.7	8.4	8.9	10.
43	31%	37%	38%	37%	37%	38%	38%	38%	38%
44	2.9	4.6	5.7	6.9	8.1	8.4	9.2	9.7	10.
44	35%	40%	39%	40%	37%	41%	38%	38%	36%
45	3.6	5.3	6.4	7.7	8.9	9.2	10.	10.	11.
45	40%	40%	40%	40%	39%	40%	38%	39%	38%
46	4.4	6.1	7.2	8.5	9.7	10.	10.	11.	12.
46	40%	40%	41%	40%	39%	41%	39%	40%	40%
47	5.4	7.0	8.1	9.4	10.	11.	11.	12.	13.
47	40%	40%	40%	40%	40%	40%	40%	40%	40%
48	6.3	8.0	9.0	10.	11.	11.	12.	13.	14.
48	40%	42%	42%	40%	40%	40%	40%	40%	40%
49	7.3	8.9	9.9	11.	12.	12.	13.	14.	15.
49	40%	41%	41%	40%	40%	40%	40%	40%	40%
50	8.3	9.9	10.	12.	13.	13.	14.	15.	16.
50	40%	42%	41%	40%	40%	40%	40%	40%	40%

HIGH PRICE CALL TABLE

Exercise Price is (50)

Average Volatility

STOCK PRICE — NUMBER OF MONTHS BEFORE THE OPTIONS EXPIRE

STOCK PRICE	1	2	3	4	5	6	7	8	9
35	0.0	0.0	0.0	0.1	0.2	0.3	0.5	0.7	0.9
35	1%	1%	4%	11%	17%	21%	24%	25%	28%
36	0.0	0.0	0.0	0.1	0.2	0.4	0.5	0.7	1.0
36	1%	4%	6%	18%	21%	25%	26%	31%	34%
37	0.0	0.0	0.0	0.2	0.4	0.5	0.7	1.0	1.3
37	1%	4%	9%	20%	25%	26%	31%	35%	34%
38	0.0	0.0	0.0	0.2	0.4	0.7	0.9	1.2	1.5
38	1%	5%	17%	25%	27%	32%	35%	37%	39%
39	0.0	0.0	0.1	0.4	0.6	0.9	1.1	1.5	1.8
39	1%	9%	19%	26%	32%	35%	37%	39%	39%
40	0.0	0.1	0.2	0.5	0.8	1.1	1.3	1.6	2.0
40	1%	14%	25%	32%	35%	39%	39%	39%	39%
41	0.0	0.1	0.4	0.8	1.1	1.4	1.8	2.2	2.6
41	3%	21%	29%	35%	38%	39%	39%	39%	40%
42	0.0	0.2	0.5	0.9	1.3	1.6	1.9	2.3	2.7
42	6%	24%	35%	39%	39%	41%	41%	41%	39%
43	0.0	0.4	0.9	1.4	1.8	2.2	2.6	3.0	3.5
43	13%	30%	37%	38%	39%	39%	39%	39%	38%
44	0.1	0.6	1.0	1.6	2.1	2.4	2.8	3.2	3.7
44	22%	38%	39%	40%	39%	40%	40%	39%	39%
45	0.2	0.9	1.5	2.2	2.7	3.1	3.5	4.0	4.6
45	29%	39%	39%	40%	38%	39%	39%	38%	35%
46	0.4	1.2	1.8	2.5	3.0	3.4	3.8	4.3	4.8
46	39%	39%	41%	39%	39%	40%	40%	41%	37%
47	0.8	1.8	2.5	3.2	3.8	4.3	4.7	5.2	5.8
47	39%	38%	38%	35%	35%	34%	34%	34%	33%
48	1.1	2.1	2.9	3.6	4.2	4.6	5.0	5.5	6.0
48	40%	39%	40%	38%	37%	37%	38%	39%	39%
49	1.7	2.8	3.6	4.4	5.0	5.5	5.9	6.4	6.9
49	39%	36%	36%	35%	38%	39%	40%	39%	38%
50	2.3	3.4	4.1	4.9	5.4	5.9	6.3	6.8	7.5
50	37%	38%	39%	44%	43%	42%	41%	43%	43%
51	3.0	4.2	4.9	5.7	6.4	6.9	7.3	7.9	8.5
51	40%	40%	43%	41%	42%	42%	43%	43%	41%
52	3.9	5.0	5.7	6.5	7.0	7.5	8.0	8.6	9.2
52	42%	43%	44%	43%	43%	43%	42%	42%	41%
53	4.9	6.0	6.7	7.5	8.1	8.6	9.1	9.5	10.
53	42%	41%	41%	40%	40%	41%	39%	40%	40%
54	5.9	6.9	7.6	8.3	8.9	9.3	9.8	10.	10.
54	41%	41%	40%	40%	40%	41%	42%	43%	41%
55	6.8	7.8	8.5	9.2	9.8	10.	10.	11.	11.
55	41%	41%	40%	41%	41%	42%	42%	44%	41%

High Volatility

STOCK PRICE — NUMBER OF MONTHS BEFORE THE OPTIONS EXPIRE

STOCK PRICE	1	2	3	4	5	6	7	8	9
35	0.0	0.2	0.5	1.1	1.5	1.9	2.3	2.8	3.4
35	3%	14%	23%	25%	31%	32%	32%	32%	33%
36	0.0	0.2	0.6	1.2	1.6	2.0	2.4	2.9	3.5
36	4%	19%	24%	30%	32%	33%	33%	33%	34%
37	0.0	0.3	0.8	1.5	2.0	2.4	2.9	3.6	4.2
37	4%	22%	27%	32%	32%	33%	33%	34%	32%
38	0.0	0.4	1.0	1.7	2.3	2.7	3.2	3.8	4.5
38	8%	24%	32%	32%	32%	33%	34%	34%	35%
39	0.0	0.6	1.2	2.0	2.7	3.2	3.7	4.5	5.2
39	10%	25%	32%	32%	32%	33%	33%	33%	33%
40	0.1	0.7	1.4	2.3	2.9	3.4	3.9	4.7	5.4
40	14%	31%	33%	34%	34%	34%	34%	35%	35%
41	0.2	1.0	1.8	2.8	3.5	4.0	4.7	5.4	6.1
41	21%	32%	34%	32%	32%	33%	33%	34%	35%
42	0.3	1.2	2.0	3.1	3.8	4.4	5.0	5.7	6.5
42	26%	34%	35%	35%	35%	37%	36%	35%	35%
43	0.5	1.7	2.6	3.7	4.6	5.1	5.7	6.5	7.4
43	29%	32%	34%	34%	35%	35%	35%	35%	36%
44	0.6	1.9	2.9	4.1	4.8	5.4	6.0	6.9	7.6
44	33%	34%	35%	35%	35%	36%	36%	36%	36%
45	1.0	2.5	3.6	4.8	5.7	6.3	7.0	7.8	8.6
45	33%	34%	35%	35%	35%	35%	35%	35%	38%
46	1.3	2.9	4.0	5.2	6.1	6.7	7.3	8.2	8.9
46	36%	36%	35%	37%	38%	38%	38%	39%	40%
47	1.9	3.7	4.8	6.1	7.0	7.7	8.3	9.1	10.
47	35%	34%	37%	37%	36%	37%	38%	38%	40%
48	2.3	4.2	5.3	6.6	7.5	8.1	8.7	9.6	10.
48	35%	37%	40%	38%	38%	40%	39%	40%	40%
49	3.0	4.9	6.1	7.4	8.3	8.9	9.6	10.	11.
49	37%	40%	39%	40%	40%	40%	40%	40%	37%
50	3.6	5.5	6.7	8.1	8.9	9.6	10.	11.	12.
50	41%	41%	41%	40%	40%	40%	40%	40%	40%
51	4.4	6.4	7.6	9.0	9.9	10.	11.	12.	13.
51	41%	41%	40%	40%	40%	40%	41%	41%	40%
52	5.3	7.1	8.3	9.7	10.	11.	11.	12.	13.
52	41%	41%	41%	41%	40%	40%	40%	40%	40%
53	6.3	8.1	9.3	10.	11.	12.	13.	13.	14.
53	41%	41%	41%	40%	40%	40%	40%	40%	40%
54	7.2	9.1	10.	11.	12.	13.	13.	14.	15.
54	41%	41%	41%	41%	41%	40%	40%	40%	40%
55	8.2	10.	11.	12.	13.	14.	14.	15.	16.
55	41%	42%	42%	41%	40%	41%	40%	40%	40%

HIGH PRICE CALL TABLE

Exercise Price is ⑥⓪

Average Volatility

STOCK PRICE

NUMBER OF MONTHS BEFORE THE OPTIONS EXPIRE

STOCK PRICE	1	2	3	4	5	6	7	8	9
45	0.0	0.0	0.1	0.4	0.6	0.8	1.1	1.4	1.8
45	1%	4%	12%	21%	24%	28%	32%	34%	36%
46	0.0	0.0	0.1	0.4	0.7	0.9	1.1	1.5	1.8
46	1%	6%	19%	25%	29%	34%	37%	39%	39%
47	0.0	0.0	0.2	0.6	0.9	1.2	1.5	1.9	2.4
47	0%	9%	21%	26%	32%	34%	37%	39%	39%
48	0.0	0.0	0.3	0.7	1.1	1.4	1.7	2.1	2.5
48	1%	17%	24%	32%	35%	38%	39%	39%	39%
49	0.0	0.1	0.4	0.9	1.3	1.7	2.1	2.6	3.1
49	4%	19%	27%	35%	38%	39%	39%	39%	39%
50	0.0	0.2	0.6	1.1	1.5	1.9	2.3	2.8	3.3
50	5%	25%	35%	38%	40%	39%	39%	39%	39%
51	0.0	0.4	0.9	1.5	2.0	2.5	2.9	3.4	4.0
51	9%	28%	35%	39%	39%	39%	39%	39%	39%
52	0.0	0.5	1.0	1.6	2.2	2.6	3.0	3.6	4.1
52	18%	35%	39%	40%	40%	39%	41%	39%	39%
53	0.2	0.9	1.5	2.2	2.9	3.4	3.8	4.4	4.9
53	25%	36%	39%	39%	38%	39%	39%	38%	36%
54	0.3	1.0	1.7	2.5	3.0	3.6	4.0	4.6	5.2
54	31%	39%	41%	39%	39%	39%	39%	39%	40%
55	0.5	1.5	2.3	3.2	3.8	4.3	4.9	5.5	6.2
55	37%	39%	39%	37%	37%	36%	36%	37%	34%
56	0.8	1.8	2.6	3.4	4.1	4.6	5.1	5.7	6.4
56	39%	40%	39%	39%	39%	39%	40%	38%	37%
57	1.2	2.4	3.3	4.3	5.0	5.6	6.1	6.7	7.3
57	39%	36%	35%	34%	35%	35%	35%	33%	35%
58	1.6	2.8	3.7	4.7	5.3	5.9	6.3	7.0	7.6
58	39%	40%	38%	37%	38%	39%	39%	40%	39%
59	2.2	3.6	4.5	5.5	6.2	6.8	7.3	7.9	8.5
59	38%	35%	36%	37%	38%	39%	39%	40%	39%
60	2.8	4.1	5.0	6.0	6.6	7.2	7.7	8.3	9.1
60	37%	38%	39%	42%	43%	41%	42%	42%	43%
61	3.5	4.9	5.8	6.8	7.5	8.2	8.7	9.4	10.
61	40%	40%	42%	41%	42%	41%	43%	42%	42%
62	4.3	5.6	6.5	7.5	8.2	8.8	9.3	10.	10.
62	42%	43%	43%	44%	44%	44%	42%	42%	42%
63	5.4	6.7	7.6	8.6	9.3	10.	10.	11.	11.
63	41%	43%	42%	41%	41%	40%	41%	40%	39%
64	6.3	7.6	8.4	9.4	10.	10.	11.	11.	12.
64	42%	40%	40%	40%	40%	40%	41%	42%	42%
65	7.3	8.6	9.5	10.	11.	11.	12.	12.	13.
65	40%	40%	40%	40%	40%	40%	41%	40%	38%

High Volatility

STOCK PRICE

NUMBER OF MONTHS BEFORE THE OPTIONS EXPIRE

STOCK PRICE	1	2	3	4	5	6	7	8	9
45	0.0	0.6	1.2	2.1	2.7	3.3	3.8	4.6	5.5
45	6%	23%	27%	32%	32%	32%	33%	32%	32%
46	0.0	0.7	1.3	2.2	2.9	3.4	3.9	4.7	5.7
46	10%	25%	32%	32%	33%	35%	34%	34%	34%
47	0.1	0.8	1.6	2.6	3.4	4.1	4.7	5.6	6.6
47	12%	26%	33%	33%	32%	32%	33%	34%	33%
48	0.1	1.0	1.9	2.9	3.7	4.3	4.9	5.8	6.7
48	16%	30%	32%	32%	33%	33%	34%	34%	34%
49	0.2	1.2	2.2	3.4	4.2	5.0	5.7	6.6	7.6
49	21%	32%	32%	32%	32%	33%	33%	33%	35%
50	0.3	1.4	2.4	3.6	4.5	5.2	5.9	6.8	7.9
50	24%	32%	34%	34%	35%	34%	36%	35%	35%
51	0.5	1.8	2.9	4.3	5.2	6.0	6.7	7.7	8.7
51	25%	33%	34%	34%	35%	35%	36%	36%	36%
52	0.6	2.1	3.3	4.7	5.6	6.3	7.0	8.0	9.0
52	32%	34%	34%	35%	35%	35%	35%	36%	35%
53	0.9	2.6	3.9	5.4	6.3	7.1	7.9	8.8	10.
53	32%	32%	34%	35%	35%	35%	35%	34%	35%
54	1.1	2.9	4.2	5.7	6.7	7.5	8.1	9.1	10.
54	34%	36%	35%	37%	37%	36%	36%	37%	38%
55	1.6	3.6	5.1	6.5	7.6	8.4	9.1	10.	11.
55	33%	36%	35%	37%	36%	36%	37%	37%	38%
56	2.0	4.0	5.4	7.0	7.9	8.8	9.5	10.	11.
56	36%	35%	38%	38%	37%	37%	38%	40%	41%
57	2.6	4.9	6.3	7.9	9.0	9.8	10.	11.	12.
57	35%	37%	37%	36%	37%	37%	38%	38%	38%
58	3.1	5.3	6.8	8.4	9.4	10.	10.	12.	13.
58	37%	38%	37%	39%	40%	41%	41%	40%	37%
59	3.8	6.1	7.6	9.2	10.	11.	11.	13.	14.
59	38%	40%	39%	40%	40%	41%	41%	38%	37%
60	4.5	6.7	8.3	9.9	10.	11.	12.	13.	14.
60	40%	40%	40%	41%	40%	40%	41%	40%	40%
61	5.2	7.6	9.1	10.	11.	12.	13.	14.	15.
61	41%	40%	40%	40%	40%	40%	40%	40%	40%
62	6.0	8.3	9.8	11.	12.	13.	14.	15.	16.
62	41%	41%	41%	40%	40%	40%	40%	40%	40%
63	7.0	9.3	10.	12.	13.	14.	15.	16.	17.
63	42%	42%	41%	40%	40%	40%	40%	40%	40%
64	8.0	10.	11.	13.	14.	15.	15.	17.	18.
64	41%	42%	41%	40%	40%	40%	41%	41%	40%
65	9.0	11.	12.	14.	15.	16.	17.	18.	19.
65	41%	41%	41%	40%	40%	40%	40%	40%	40%

HIGH PRICE CALL TABLE

Exercise Price is (70)

Average Volatility

STOCK PRICE — NUMBER OF MONTHS BEFORE THE OPTIONS EXPIRE

STOCK PRICE	1	2	3	4	5	6	7	8	9
55	0.0	0.1	0.4	0.8	1.1	1.5	1.9	2.4	2.9
55	1%	11%	22%	27%	33%	34%	37%	38%	39%
56	0.0	0.1	0.4	0.8	1.2	1.6	1.9	2.4	3.0
56	1%	17%	24%	32%	36%	39%	39%	39%	39%
57	0.0	0.2	0.6	1.1	1.6	2.0	2.5	3.1	3.6
57	3%	19%	26%	33%	36%	38%	39%	39%	39%
58	0.0	0.2	0.7	1.3	1.8	2.2	2.6	3.2	3.8
58	4%	25%	32%	36%	39%	39%	39%	39%	40%
59	0.0	0.4	0.9	1.6	2.2	2.7	3.2	3.8	4.5
59	9%	25%	35%	39%	39%	39%	39%	39%	38%
60	0.0	0.5	1.1	1.7	2.3	2.9	3.4	4.0	4.5
60	13%	32%	39%	39%	39%	39%	39%	39%	40%
61	0.1	0.7	1.5	2.3	3.0	3.6	4.1	4.7	5.4
61	19%	35%	38%	39%	39%	39%	39%	38%	38%
62	0.2	0.9	1.6	2.5	3.1	3.7	4.2	4.9	5.6
62	25%	39%	40%	41%	40%	39%	39%	39%	40%
63	0.4	1.4	2.3	3.2	3.9	4.5	5.0	5.8	6.6
63	30%	38%	39%	38%	39%	38%	38%	37%	35%
64	0.5	1.6	2.5	3.4	4.1	4.7	5.3	6.0	6.7
64	38%	41%	39%	40%	39%	40%	40%	39%	37%
65	0.9	2.1	3.2	4.1	4.9	5.6	6.2	7.0	7.7
65	39%	39%	38%	36%	37%	36%	36%	34%	34%
66	1.1	2.4	3.4	4.4	5.2	5.8	6.4	7.1	7.8
66	41%	39%	39%	40%	48%	38%	38%	38%	40%
67	1.7	3.1	4.2	5.3	6.1	6.9	7.4	8.1	8.9
67	39%	36%	35%	35%	36%	34%	34%	36%	38%
68	2.0	3.5	4.6	5.7	6.5	7.1	7.7	8.4	9.2
68	39%	39%	36%	38%	40%	39%	40%	41%	40%
69	2.7	4.3	5.4	6.6	7.3	8.0	8.6	9.3	10.
69	36%	35%	35%	38%	39%	40%	39%	38%	39%
70	3.2	4.8	5.9	7.0	7.8	8.4	9.0	9.8	10.
70	37%	38%	40%	42%	43%	41%	42%	43%	43%
71	4.0	5.7	6.7	7.9	8.7	9.5	10.	10.	11.
71	40%	41%	42%	41%	42%	41%	44%	43%	42%
72	4.8	6.3	7.4	8.5	9.3	10.	10.	11.	12.
72	41%	43%	44%	44%	45%	45%	45%	43%	42%
73	5.8	7.3	8.4	9.6	10.	11.	11.	12.	13.
73	42%	43%	43%	41%	42%	41%	42%	41%	40%
74	6.7	8.2	9.3	10.	11.	11.	11.	13.	14.
74	43%	42%	41%	40%	41%	41%	42%	42%	42%
75	7.8	9.3	10.	11.	12.	13.	13.	14.	15.
75	41%	40%	40%	40%	40%	41%	40%	39%	40%

High Volatility

STOCK PRICE — NUMBER OF MONTHS BEFORE THE OPTIONS EXPIRE

STOCK PRICE	1	2	3	4	5	6	7	8	9
55	0.1	1.1	2.0	3.2	4.1	4.8	5.6	6.7	7.9
55	12%	25%	32%	32%	32%	33%	33%	33%	33%
56	0.2	1.2	2.1	3.4	4.3	5.0	5.8	6.8	7.9
56	15%	30%	32%	34%	34%	34%	35%	35%	35%
57	0.2	1.4	2.6	4.0	5.0	5.8	6.7	7.8	9.1
57	22%	33%	32%	33%	34%	34%	34%	34%	34%
58	0.3	1.7	2.9	4.3	5.2	6.1	6.9	7.9	9.2
58	23%	32%	33%	33%	34%	34%	36%	35%	35%
59	0.5	2.0	3.3	4.9	6.0	6.9	7.7	8.8	10.
59	25%	32%	32%	33%	34%	35%	35%	35%	35%
60	0.6	2.2	3.6	5.1	6.3	7.1	7.9	9.1	10.
60	30%	34%	35%	35%	35%	35%	35%	35%	36%
61	0.9	2.7	4.2	5.9	7.0	7.9	8.8	10.	11.
61	33%	33%	34%	35%	35%	36%	35%	35%	34%
62	1.0	3.1	4.6	6.2	7.4	8.2	9.1	10.	11.
62	33%	35%	35%	36%	36%	36%	36%	36%	37%
63	1.5	3.7	5.3	7.0	8.2	9.1	10.	11.	12.
63	33%	35%	35%	35%	36%	35%	34%	35%	37%
64	1.7	4.0	5.6	7.3	8.5	9.4	10.	11.	12.
64	35%	35%	35%	37%	38%	37%	37%	38%	38%
65	2.3	4.8	6.5	8.3	9.5	10.	11.	12.	14.
65	34%	35%	37%	37%	38%	37%	37%	38%	38%
66	2.7	5.2	6.9	8.6	9.8	10.	11.	12.	14.
66	36%	38%	39%	37%	37%	40%	39%	40%	40%
67	3.4	6.1	7.8	9.7	10.	11.	12.	14.	15.
67	34%	37%	38%	37%	37%	39%	39%	38%	38%
68	3.9	6.6	8.3	10.	11.	12.	13.	14.	15.
68	36%	40%	39%	41%	41%	40%	40%	40%	37%
69	4.6	7.4	9.1	11.	12.	13.	14.	15.	16.
69	38%	39%	40%	40%	40%	40%	40%	37%	38%
70	5.3	8.0	9.7	11.	12.	13.	14.	16.	17.
70	41%	40%	40%	40%	40%	41%	41%	41%	40%
71	6.0	8.8	10.	12.	13.	14.	15.	17.	18.
71	41%	40%	40%	40%	40%	40%	41%	40%	40%
72	6.8	9.5	11.	13.	14.	15.	16.	17.	19.
72	41%	41%	41%	40%	40%	40%	40%	40%	40%
73	7.8	10.	12.	14.	15.	16.	17.	18.	20.
73	41%	41%	41%	41%	40%	40%	40%	40%	40%
74	8.7	11.	13.	15.	16.	17.	18.	19.	21.
74	42%	42%	42%	41%	41%	40%	40%	40%	40%
75	9.8	12.	14.	16.	17.	18.	19.	20.	22.
75	41%	42%	41%	40%	40%	40%	40%	41%	40%

HIGH PRICE CALL TABLE

Exercise Price is (80)

Average Volatility

STOCK PRICE — NUMBER OF MONTHS BEFORE THE OPTIONS EXPIRE

STOCK PRICE	1	2	3	4	5	6	7	8	9
65	0.0	0.3	0.7	1.3	1.9	2.4	2.9	3.5	4.2
65	4%	20%	25%	32%	35%	38%	39%	39%	38%
66	0.0	0.3	0.8	1.4	1.9	2.4	2.9	3.5	4.2
66	4%	22%	33%	36%	39%	39%	39%	39%	39%
67	0.0	0.4	1.0	1.8	2.4	3.0	3.6	4.2	5.0
67	6%	25%	34%	36%	38%	39%	39%	39%	38%
68	0.0	0.5	1.2	1.9	2.6	3.2	3.7	4.3	5.1
68	10%	28%	36%	40%	39%	39%	39%	39%	40%
69	0.1	0.7	1.5	2.4	3.2	3.8	4.4	5.1	5.9
69	17%	32%	38%	38%	38%	39%	39%	39%	38%
70	0.2	0.9	1.7	2.6	3.3	4.0	4.5	5.1	5.9
70	21%	38%	39%	39%	39%	39%	39%	39%	39%
71	0.3	1.3	2.2	3.2	4.0	4.7	5.3	6.0	7.0
71	24%	38%	39%	38%	38%	38%	39%	38%	36%
72	0.4	1.4	2.3	3.4	4.2	4.9	5.4	6.2	7.2
72	32%	39%	40%	40%	39%	39%	39%	40%	37%
73	0.7	2.0	3.0	4.1	5.0	5.7	6.4	7.2	8.2
73	35%	38%	39%	38%	36%	36%	36%	36%	35%
74	0.8	2.2	3.2	4.3	5.2	6.0	6.6	7.4	8.3
74	39%	40%	39%	39%	39%	39%	39%	38%	36%
75	1.3	2.8	4.0	5.1	6.1	6.9	7.6	8.4	9.2
75	39%	38%	36%	36%	34%	34%	34%	35%	34%
76	1.5	3.1	4.2	5.4	6.3	7.1	7.7	8.4	9.4
76	41%	39%	39%	39%	39%	38%	38%	41%	39%
77	2.2	3.9	5.1	6.4	7.4	8.2	8.7	9.6	10.
77	38%	36%	35%	36%	35%	35%	36%	38%	38%
78	2.5	4.3	5.5	6.7	7.7	8.4	9.0	9.8	10.
78	42%	36%	36%	39%	38%	39%	40%	40%	38%
79	3.2	5.1	6.3	7.6	8.6	9.4	10.	10.	11.
79	36%	35%	37%	38%	39%	39%	39%	38%	39%
80	3.7	5.6	6.8	8.1	9.0	9.8	10.	11.	12.
80	37%	39%	40%	42%	42%	41%	43%	44%	45%
81	4.5	6.4	7.6	9.0	10.	10.	11.	12.	13.
81	40%	40%	41%	40%	41%	41%	43%	44%	42%
82	5.2	7.1	8.3	9.5	10.	11.	11.	12.	13.
82	40%	42%	43%	44%	44%	45%	45%	44%	42%
83	6.2	8.0	9.2	10.	11.	12.	13.	14.	15.
83	40%	42%	43%	43%	41%	41%	42%	42%	41%
84	7.2	8.9	10.	11.	12.	13.	13.	14.	15.
84	42%	44%	42%	42%	42%	42%	42%	42%	42%
85	8.2	10.	11.	12.	13.	14.	14.	15.	16.
85	41%	40%	41%	40%	40%	40%	40%	40%	39%

High Volatility

STOCK PRICE — NUMBER OF MONTHS BEFORE THE OPTIONS EXPIRE

STOCK PRICE	1	2	3	4	5	6	7	8	9
65	0.3	1.7	2.9	4.5	5.7	6.7	7.6	8.8	10.
65	21%	32%	33%	32%	33%	33%	34%	34%	35%
66	0.4	1.8	3.1	4.7	5.8	6.8	7.7	8.9	10.
66	24%	33%	35%	35%	35%	36%	37%	35%	35%
67	0.5	2.2	3.7	5.5	6.8	7.8	8.7	10.	11.
67	24%	32%	33%	33%	34%	34%	34%	35%	36%
68	0.7	2.5	4.0	5.7	7.0	7.9	8.8	10.	11.
68	26%	32%	34%	35%	35%	35%	35%	35%	35%
69	0.8	2.9	4.6	6.5	7.8	8.8	9.8	11.	12.
69	32%	32%	32%	35%	35%	35%	35%	35%	34%
70	1.0	3.1	4.8	6.7	8.0	9.0	10.	11.	12.
70	33%	35%	36%	35%	35%	37%	36%	37%	36%
71	1.3	3.7	5.6	7.5	8.9	10.	11.	12.	13.
71	33%	32%	35%	36%	35%	35%	36%	34%	36%
72	1.6	4.1	5.9	7.9	9.2	10.	11.	13.	14.
72	34%	35%	35%	37%	35%	36%	36%	37%	38%
73	2.1	4.7	6.7	8.7	10.	11.	12.	13.	15.
73	33%	35%	34%	36%	36%	35%	37%	37%	38%
74	2.4	5.1	7.0	9.0	10.	11.	12.	13.	15.
74	36%	36%	38%	38%	37%	38%	38%	38%	40%
75	3.0	5.9	7.9	10.	11.	12.	13.	15.	16.
75	35%	35%	37%	37%	37%	37%	39%	38%	38%
76	3.4	6.3	8.2	10.	11.	12.	13.	15.	16.
76	35%	37%	40%	38%	38%	39%	41%	40%	40%
77	4.2	7.3	9.3	11.	12.	14.	15.	16.	18.
77	34%	37%	37%	37%	38%	39%	38%	38%	37%
78	4.7	7.7	9.7	11.	13.	14.	15.	16.	18.
78	38%	40%	40%	40%	41%	40%	40%	39%	38%
79	5.4	8.5	10.	12.	14.	15.	16.	18.	19.
79	39%	41%	41%	40%	40%	41%	40%	37%	39%
80	6.1	9.2	11.	13.	14.	15.	16.	18.	20.
80	40%	40%	40%	40%	40%	40%	40%	40%	40%
81	6.8	10.	12.	14.	15.	16.	17.	19.	21.
81	40%	40%	40%	40%	40%	40%	40%	40%	40%
82	7.6	10.	12.	14.	16.	17.	18.	20.	21.
82	41%	41%	41%	40%	40%	40%	40%	40%	40%
83	8.6	11.	13.	15.	17.	18.	19.	21.	22.
83	42%	41%	41%	41%	41%	41%	41%	41%	40%
84	9.5	12.	14.	16.	18.	19.	20.	21.	23.
84	41%	41%	41%	41%	41%	40%	41%	40%	40%
85	10.	13.	15.	17.	19.	20.	21.	23.	25.
85	41%	41%	41%	40%	40%	40%	40%	40%	40%

HIGH PRICE CALL TABLE

Exercise Price is (90)

Average Volatility

STOCK PRICE — NUMBER OF MONTHS BEFORE THE OPTIONS EXPIRE

STOCK PRICE	1	2	3	4	5	6	7	8	9
75	0.0	0.3	0.9	1.8	2.5	3.2	3.8	4.6	5.4
75	3%	23%	30%	38%	39%	40%	40%	42%	41%
76	0.0	0.6	1.4	2.3	3.2	3.8	4.5	5.4	6.3
76	6%	24%	28%	34%	36%	38%	38%	38%	36%
77	0.0	0.6	1.4	2.4	3.2	3.9	4.6	5.3	6.2
77	9%	27%	39%	41%	42%	42%	42%	42%	42%
78	0.1	0.9	1.9	3.0	4.0	4.8	5.4	6.3	7.1
78	13%	28%	35%	37%	39%	38%	39%	36%	37%
79	0.1	1.0	2.0	3.2	4.1	4.8	5.5	6.3	7.2
79	18%	39%	41%	42%	41%	41%	42%	42%	41%
80	0.3	1.6	2.7	3.9	4.9	5.7	6.4	7.1	8.1
80	25%	36%	39%	38%	38%	37%	36%	37%	33%
81	0.4	1.6	2.7	4.0	4.9	5.7	6.3	7.2	8.2
81	27%	43%	44%	42%	42%	42%	43%	42%	39%
82	0.7	2.3	3.5	4.8	5.9	6.5	7.3	8.2	9.3
82	33%	40%	40%	36%	33%	36%	33%	35%	34%
83	0.9	2.5	3.7	5.0	6.0	6.8	7.5	8.4	9.4
83	40%	42%	43%	40%	40%	38%	38%	38%	36%
84	1.3	3.1	4.5	5.8	6.9	7.8	8.5	9.4	10.
84	39%	41%	37%	33%	34%	33%	35%	35%	38%
85	1.6	3.4	4.7	6.0	7.1	7.9	8.6	9.5	10.
85	44%	42%	42%	37%	36%	37%	38%	39%	40%
86	2.2	4.1	5.5	7.0	8.1	9.0	9.7	10.	11.
86	41%	33%	34%	35%	36%	36%	36%	37%	37%
87	2.5	4.4	5.8	7.2	8.3	9.1	9.8	10.	11.
87	44%	40%	36%	39%	41%	41%	41%	42%	42%
88	3.1	5.2	6.7	8.1	9.3	10.	11.	11.	13.
88	34%	34%	36%	38%	40%	40%	40%	41%	43%
89	3.6	5.7	7.2	8.6	9.7	10.	11.	12.	13.
89	36%	39%	41%	42%	43%	42%	43%	43%	44%
90	4.4	6.6	8.1	9.6	10.	11.	12.	13.	14.
90	34%	40%	41%	42%	41%	41%	40%	41%	42%
91	5.0	7.2	8.6	10.	11.	12.	12.	13.	15.
91	38%	43%	44%	44%	41%	44%	47%	49%	49%
92	6.0	8.1	9.7	11.	12.	13.	14.	15.	16.
92	43%	43%	43%	40%	42%	42%	43%	46%	44%
93	6.8	8.9	10.	11.	12.	13.	14.	15.	16.
93	43%	44%	42%	43%	45%	45%	46%	44%	43%
94	7.9	10.	11.	12.	14.	15.	15.	16.	18.
94	43%	41%	41%	40%	41%	40%	41%	42%	41%
95	8.8	10.	12.	13.	14.	15.	16.	17.	18.
95	43%	43%	41%	41%	41%	41%	41%	41%	42%

High Volatility

STOCK PRICE — NUMBER OF MONTHS BEFORE THE OPTIONS EXPIRE

STOCK PRICE	1	2	3	4	5	6	7	8	9
75	0.4	2.3	4.1	6.1	7.5	8.6	9.5	11.	12.
75	19%	33%	35%	32%	32%	33%	34%	36%	35%
76	0.7	2.8	4.7	6.8	8.3	9.3	10.	12.	13.
76	24%	31%	32%	33%	31%	33%	34%	34%	33%
77	0.8	3.0	4.9	7.0	8.5	9.6	10.	12.	13.
77	27%	35%	35%	33%	34%	35%	36%	36%	36%
78	1.1	3.6	5.7	7.9	9.3	10.	11.	13.	15.
78	29%	31%	32%	31%	33%	35%	35%	33%	35%
79	1.2	3.9	5.9	8.1	9.7	10.	11.	13.	15.
79	35%	35%	32%	33%	35%	35%	36%	36%	37%
80	1.6	4.5	6.7	8.9	10.	11.	12.	14.	16.
80	34%	32%	31%	32%	35%	35%	37%	36%	33%
81	1.8	4.8	6.9	9.2	10.	12.	13.	14.	16.
81	37%	35%	34%	35%	37%	37%	39%	37%	36%
82	2.4	5.5	7.8	10.	11.	13.	14.	15.	17.
82	35%	32%	31%	37%	35%	35%	35%	34%	36%
83	2.7	5.9	8.1	10.	12.	13.	14.	16.	17.
83	36%	33%	36%	38%	40%	37%	35%	39%	38%
84	3.3	6.7	9.0	11.	13.	14.	15.	17.	19.
84	33%	33%	35%	37%	36%	35%	35%	38%	38%
85	3.7	7.0	9.3	11.	13.	14.	15.	17.	19.
85	36%	36%	39%	37%	35%	36%	39%	39%	40%
86	4.4	8.0	10.	12.	14.	15.	17.	18.	20.
86	33%	39%	39%	34%	35%	35%	38%	37%	38%
87	4.8	8.4	10.	13.	14.	16.	17.	19.	20.
87	35%	40%	41%	37%	38%	40%	40%	40%	40%
88	5.6	9.2	11.	14.	15.	17.	18.	20.	22.
88	34%	40%	35%	37%	38%	38%	40%	40%	37%
89	6.2	9.9	12.	14.	16.	17.	18.	20.	22.
89	38%	42%	37%	40%	42%	41%	42%	40%	35%
90	7.1	10.	13.	15.	17.	18.	20.	22.	23.
90	42%	36%	37%	39%	40%	40%	40%	36%	35%
91	7.8	11.	13.	16.	18.	19.	20.	22.	24.
91	43%	41%	42%	42%	42%	41%	38%	36%	37%
92	8.7	12.	14.	17.	19.	20.	21.	23.	25.
92	43%	41%	42%	42%	40%	37%	37%	35%	35%
93	9.6	13.	15.	18.	19.	21.	22.	24.	26.
93	43%	43%	43%	43%	41%	38%	40%	40%	39%
94	10.	14.	16.	19.	21.	22.	23.	25.	27.
94	43%	43%	43%	40%	37%	37%	38%	38%	39%
95	11.	15.	17.	20.	21.	22.	24.	25.	27.
95	43%	43%	43%	40%	41%	41%	42%	42%	42%

HIGH PRICE CALL TABLE

Average Volatility

STOCK PRICE — NUMBER OF MONTHS BEFORE THE OPTIONS EXPIRE

STOCK PRICE	1	2	3	4	5	6	7	8	9
85	0.0	0.6	1.5	2.5	3.4	4.2	4.9	5.8	6.7
85	8%	27%	38%	40%	42%	42%	42%	42%	42%
86	0.1	1.0	2.0	3.1	4.1	5.0	5.7	6.8	7.5
86	9%	27%	33%	36%	39%	37%	40%	36%	38%
87	0.1	1.0	2.1	3.2	4.2	5.0	5.7	6.7	7.5
87	15%	35%	40%	42%	41%	42%	42%	42%	42%
88	0.2	1.5	2.6	3.9	5.1	5.9	6.6	7.5	8.7
88	18%	33%	38%	38%	37%	37%	38%	37%	33%
89	0.3	1.5	2.8	4.1	5.2	6.0	6.6	7.7	8.7
89	26%	41%	42%	41%	41%	42%	43%	41%	38%
90	0.6	2.2	3.4	4.9	6.0	6.9	7.5	8.6	9.7
90	27%	36%	40%	38%	36%	34%	37%	33%	33%
91	0.7	2.2	3.5	4.9	6.0	6.8	7.6	8.6	9.7
91	37%	44%	42%	42%	41%	42%	43%	41%	37%
92	1.1	2.9	4.3	5.8	6.9	7.8	8.6	9.7	10.
92	37%	40%	38%	35%	35%	34%	34%	33%	35%
93	1.3	3.1	4.6	6.0	7.1	8.1	8.7	9.9	11.
93	41%	42%	42%	40%	39%	37%	38%	37%	39%
94	1.8	3.8	5.3	6.8	8.1	9.0	9.8	11.	12.
94	41%	39%	33%	33%	33%	35%	35%	38%	37%
95	2.0	4.1	5.6	7.0	8.2	9.2	9.9	11.	12.
95	43%	42%	38%	37%	36%	37%	39%	39%	40%
96	2.7	4.9	6.4	8.0	9.3	10.	11.	12.	13.
96	41%	32%	33%	36%	35%	37%	37%	38%	38%
97	3.0	5.2	6.7	8.2	9.5	10.	11.	12.	13.
97	43%	38%	36%	40%	43%	42%	42%	42%	42%
98	3.7	6.0	7.6	9.2	10.	11.	12.	13.	14.
98	36%	34%	36%	41%	41%	41%	41%	42%	41%
99	4.2	6.4	8.1	9.7	10.	11.	12.	13.	15.
99	36%	39%	41%	42%	42%	43%	45%	42%	44%
100	5.0	7.4	9.0	10.	12.	13.	13.	15.	16.
100	35%	40%	41%	41%	41%	41%	41%	41%	42%
101	5.5	7.9	9.5	11.	12.	13.	14.	15.	16.
101	35%	41%	44%	44%	41%	44%	47%	49%	49%
102	6.5	8.9	10.	12.	13.	14.	15.	16.	18.
102	42%	43%	43%	42%	41%	42%	46%	46%	44%
103	7.3	9.6	11.	12.	14.	15.	15.	17.	18.
103	43%	44%	42%	43%	45%	46%	46%	45%	44%
104	8.4	10.	12.	13.	15.	16.	17.	18.	19.
104	43%	43%	41%	41%	42%	41%	44%	41%	41%
105	9.3	11.	13.	14.	16.	16.	17.	18.	20.
105	43%	43%	41%	41%	41%	41%	41%	41%	41%

High Volatility

STOCK PRICE — NUMBER OF MONTHS BEFORE THE OPTIONS EXPIRE

STOCK PRICE	1	2	3	4	5	6	7	8	9
85	0.8	3.2	5.3	7.6	9.2	10.	11.	13.	15.
85	26%	33%	34%	33%	33%	34%	36%	35%	37%
86	1.1	3.8	5.9	8.3	10.	11.	12.	14.	16.
86	26%	31%	32%	31%	33%	34%	35%	34%	35%
87	1.2	4.0	6.2	8.6	10.	11.	12.	14.	16.
87	31%	34%	34%	34%	37%	35%	36%	36%	38%
88	1.6	4.7	7.0	9.4	11.	12.	13.	15.	17.
88	31%	32%	33%	33%	34%	35%	34%	35%	33%
89	1.8	5.0	7.3	9.7	11.	12.	14.	15.	17.
89	35%	34%	35%	36%	36%	35%	37%	38%	35%
90	2.3	5.6	8.0	10.	12.	13.	15.	16.	19.
90	35%	32%	32%	35%	34%	35%	34%	35%	34%
91	2.5	5.9	8.3	10.	12.	14.	15.	17.	19.
91	37%	34%	33%	37%	37%	39%	37%	35%	39%
92	3.1	6.8	9.2	11.	13.	15.	16.	18.	20.
92	35%	33%	34%	35%	36%	35%	35%	35%	36%
93	3.5	7.1	9.5	12.	14.	15.	16.	18.	21.
93	36%	34%	37%	40%	37%	35%	37%	38%	39%
94	4.1	7.9	10.	13.	15.	16.	17.	19.	21.
94	34%	32%	37%	39%	34%	35%	35%	38%	37%
95	4.5	8.2	10.	13.	15.	16.	18.	19.	22.
95	34%	35%	40%	38%	35%	38%	39%	40%	40%
96	5.3	9.2	11.	14.	16.	18.	19.	21.	23.
96	31%	35%	40%	35%	35%	38%	38%	39%	38%
97	5.7	9.6	12.	14.	16.	18.	19.	21.	23.
97	36%	40%	37%	38%	39%	40%	41%	41%	40%
98	6.5	10.	13.	16.	17.	19.	20.	22.	24.
98	35%	41%	35%	38%	38%	38%	40%	40%	36%
99	7.1	11.	13.	16.	18.	20.	21.	23.	25.
99	38%	41%	38%	42%	42%	41%	42%	40%	35%
100	8.0	12.	14.	17.	19.	21.	22.	24.	26.
100	41%	36%	39%	40%	40%	40%	40%	36%	35%
101	8.6	12.	15.	18.	20.	21.	22.	24.	27.
101	43%	41%	42%	42%	42%	41%	38%	36%	37%
102	9.6	13.	16.	19.	21.	22.	24.	26.	28.
102	43%	41%	42%	42%	40%	37%	36%	35%	35%
103	10.	14.	17.	19.	21.	23.	24.	26.	28.
103	43%	43%	43%	43%	41%	38%	40%	39%	39%
104	11.	15.	18.	21.	23.	24.	25.	27.	30.
104	42%	43%	43%	43%	37%	36%	37%	38%	39%
105	12.	16.	18.	21.	23.	25.	26.	28.	30.
105	43%	43%	43%	42%	40%	40%	43%	42%	42%

THE HIGH PRICE PUT TABLES

Decimal to Fraction
Conversion Chart

Table Shows		Market Fraction
.1	=	1/16
.1	=	1/8
.2	=	3/16
.2	=	1/4
.3	=	5/16
.4	=	3/8
.4	=	7/16
.5	=	1/2
.6	=	9/16
.6	=	5/8
.7	=	11/16
.8	=	3/4
.8	=	13/16
.9	=	7/8
.9	=	15/16

*The Future Value Tables are generated by computer simulation. Due to the nature of the computer simulation techniques that we used there may be slight aberrations in the option prices presented. Therefore you should allow a variance of plus or minus 10% of these option prices. In a few cases, some of the less important, peripheral option prices may vary more than 10%.

T57

HIGH PRICE PUT TABLE

Exercise Price is ⑩

Average Volatility

STOCK PRICE — NUMBER OF MONTHS BEFORE THE OPTIONS EXPIRE

	1	2	3	4	5	6	7	8	9
20	0.0	0.0	0.0	0.0	0.0	0.0	0.0	0.0	0.0
20	1 %	1 %	1 %	1 %	1 %	1 %	1 %	1 %	1 %
19	0.0	0.0	0.0	0.0	0.0	0.0	0.0	0.0	0.0
19	1 %	1 %	1 %	1 %	1 %	1 %	1 %	1 %	1 %
18	0.0	0.0	0.0	0.0	0.0	0.0	0.0	0.0	0.0
18	1 %	1 %	1 %	1 %	1 %	1 %	1 %	1 %	1 %
17	0.0	0.0	0.0	0.0	0.0	0.0	0.0	0.0	0.0
17	1 %	1 %	1 %	1 %	1 %	1 %	1 %	1 %	1 %
16	0.0	0.0	0.0	0.0	0.0	0.0	0.0	0.0	0.0
16	1 %	1 %	1 %	1 %	1 %	1 %	1 %	1 %	1 %
15	0.0	0.0	0.0	0.0	0.0	0.0	0.0	0.0	0.0
15	1 %	1 %	1 %	1 %	1 %	1 %	0 %	2 %	3 %
14	0.0	0.0	0.0	0.0	0.0	0.0	0.0	0.0	0.0
14	1 %	1 %	1 %	0 %	4 %	4 %	6 %	7 %	13%
13	0.0	0.0	0.0	0.0	0.0	0.0	0.0	0.0	0.1
13	1 %	1 %	4 %	8 %	12%	18%	21%	25%	27%
12	0.0	0.0	0.0	0.0	0.1	0.1	0.2	0.2	0.3
12	1 %	8 %	21%	27%	34%	39%	38%	39%	39%
11	0.0	0.0	0.1	0.2	0.3	0.4	0.5	0.5	0.6
11	26%	39%	41%	41%	39%	41%	39%	40%	40%
10	0.3	0.5	0.5	0.7	0.8	0.9	0.9	1.0	1.1
10	35%	36%	38%	38%	41%	41%	41%	40%	39%
9	1.2	1.3	1.4	1.5	1.6	1.6	1.7	1.7	1.9
9	26%	39%	41%	41%	39%	41%	39%	40%	40%
8	2.2	2.2	2.3	2.4	2.5	2.6	2.6	2.6	2.7
8	1 %	8 %	21%	27%	34%	39%	38%	39%	39%
7	3.1	3.2	3.3	3.4	3.5	3.5	3.5	3.6	3.7
7	1 %	1 %	4 %	8 %	12%	18%	21%	25%	27%
6	4.1	4.2	4.3	4.4	4.4	4.5	4.5	4.6	4.6
6	1 %	1 %	1 %	0 %	4 %	4 %	6 %	7 %	13%
5	5.1	5.2	5.2	5.3	5.4	5.4	5.5	5.5	5.5
5	1 %	1 %	1 %	1 %	1 %	1 %	0 %	2 %	3 %

High Volatility

STOCK PRICE — NUMBER OF MONTHS BEFORE THE OPTIONS EXPIRE

	1	2	3	4	5	6	7	8	9
20	0.0	0.0	0.0	0.0	0.0	0.0	0.0	0.0	0.0
20	1 %	1 %	1 %	1 %	1 %	1 %	1 %	1 %	1 %
19	0.0	0.0	0.0	0.0	0.0	0.0	0.0	0.0	0.0
19	1 %	1 %	1 %	1 %	1 %	1 %	1 %	1 %	0 %
18	0.0	0.0	0.0	0.0	0.0	0.0	0.0	0.0	0.0
18	1 %	1 %	1 %	1 %	1 %	1 %	1 %	1 %	1 %
17	0.0	0.0	0.0	0.0	0.0	0.0	0.0	0.0	0.0
17	1 %	1 %	1 %	1 %	0 %	1 %	1 %	2 %	2 %
16	0.0	0.0	0.0	0.0	0.0	0.0	0.0	0.0	0.0
16	1 %	1 %	1 %	1 %	1 %	2 %	3 %	7 %	9 %
15	0.0	0.0	0.0	0.0	0.0	0.0	0.0	0.0	0.1
15	1 %	1 %	1 %	2 %	5 %	9 %	9 %	13%	16%
14	0.0	0.0	0.0	0.0	0.0	0.0	0.1	0.1	0.2
14	1 %	1 %	4 %	9 %	13%	17%	19%	24%	25%
13	0.0	0.0	0.0	0.1	0.2	0.2	0.3	0.3	0.5
13	1 %	8 %	14%	23%	25%	28%	32%	37%	34%
12	0.0	0.1	0.2	0.3	0.4	0.5	0.6	0.7	0.9
12	9 %	24%	33%	36%	35%	35%	38%	38%	35%
11	0.0	0.3	0.4	0.6	0.8	0.9	1.0	1.1	1.3
11	38%	38%	38%	36%	33%	36%	35%	40%	36%
10	0.5	0.8	0.9	1.1	1.3	1.4	1.5	1.6	1.7
10	39%	41%	39%	41%	40%	40%	40%	42%	41%
9	1.3	1.6	1.7	1.9	2.0	2.2	2.3	2.3	2.5
9	38%	38%	38%	36%	33%	36%	35%	40%	36%
8	2.3	2.5	2.6	2.8	2.9	3.0	3.0	3.2	3.3
8	9 %	24%	33%	36%	35%	35%	38%	38%	35%
7	3.2	3.5	3.5	3.7	3.8	3.9	4.0	4.0	4.2
7	1 %	8 %	14%	23%	25%	28%	32%	37%	34%
6	4.2	4.4	4.5	4.6	4.7	4.8	4.9	4.9	5.1
6	1 %	1 %	1 %	9 %	13%	17%	19%	24%	25%
5	5.2	5.3	5.4	5.5	5.6	5.7	5.8	5.8	5.9
5	1 %	1 %	1 %	2 %	5 %	9 %	9 %	13%	16%

HIGH PRICE PUT TABLE

Exercise Price is

Average Volatility

STOCK PRICE — NUMBER OF MONTHS BEFORE THE OPTIONS EXPIRE

STOCK PRICE	1	2	3	4	5	6	7	8	9
25	0.0	0.0	0.0	0.0	0.0	0.0	0.0	0.0	0.0
25	1 %	1 %	1 %	1 %	1 %	1 %	1 %	1 %	1 %
24	0.0	0.0	0.0	0.0	0.0	0.0	0.0	0.0	0.0
24	1 %	1 %	1 %	1 %	1 %	1 %	1 %	1 %	1 %
23	0.0	0.0	0.0	0.0	0.0	0.0	0.0	0.0	0.0
23	1 %	1 %	1 %	1 %	1 %	1 %	0 %	1 %	4 %
22	0.0	0.0	0.0	0.0	0.0	0.0	0.0	0.0	0.0
22	1 %	1 %	1 %	1 %	1 %	1 %	4 %	4 %	7 %
21	0.0	0.0	0.0	0.0	0.0	0.0	0.0	0.0	0.0
21	1 %	1 %	1 %	1 %	4 %	4 %	8 %	10%	17%
20	0.0	0.0	0.0	0.0	0.0	0.0	0.0	0.0	0.1
20	1 %	1 %	1 %	4 %	9 %	14%	20%	21%	24%
19	0.0	0.0	0.0	0.0	0.0	0.1	0.1	0.2	0.2
19	1 %	4 %	8 %	17%	22%	26%	28%	34%	37%
18	0.0	0.0	0.0	0.1	0.2	0.3	0.3	0.4	0.5
18	1 %	12%	23%	30%	37%	38%	38%	39%	39%
17	0.0	0.0	0.1	0.3	0.4	0.5	0.6	0.7	0.9
17	15%	35%	39%	39%	39%	40%	40%	39%	39%
16	0.0	0.3	0.5	0.7	0.9	0.9	1.0	1.1	1.3
16	40%	40%	39%	39%	39%	40%	38%	37%	36%
15	0.5	0.7	1.0	1.1	1.3	1.4	1.5	1.7	1.7
15	36%	38%	38%	39%	41%	40%	41%	39%	40%
14	1.3	1.6	1.7	2.0	2.1	2.2	2.3	2.4	2.5
14	40%	40%	39%	39%	39%	40%	38%	37%	36%
13	2.3	2.5	2.7	2.8	2.9	3.1	3.1	3.2	3.3
13	15%	35%	39%	39%	39%	40%	40%	39%	39%
12	3.3	3.4	3.6	3.7	3.8	3.9	4.0	4.1	4.2
12	1 %	12%	23%	30%	37%	38%	38%	39%	39%
11	4.3	4.4	4.6	4.7	4.8	4.9	4.9	5.1	5.2
11	1 %	4.%	8 %	17%	22%	26%	28%	34%	37%
10	5.2	5.4	5.5	5.6	5.7	5.8	5.9	6.0	6.1
10	1 %	1 %	1 %	4 %	9 %	14%	20%	21%	24%

High Volatility

STOCK PRICE — NUMBER OF MONTHS BEFORE THE OPTIONS EXPIRE

STOCK PRICE	1	2	3	4	5	6	7	8	9
25	0.0	0.0	0.0	0.0	0.0	0.0	0.0	0.0	0.0
25	1 %	1 %	1 %	1 %	1 %	2 %	2 %	5 %	8 %
24	0.0	0.0	0.0	0.0	0.0	0.0	0.0	0.0	0.1
24	1 %	1 %	1 %	1 %	2 %	3 %	7 %	8 %	11%
23	0.0	0.0	0.0	0.0	0.0	0.0	0.1	0.1	0.1
23	1 %	1 %	1 %	2 %	6 %	9 %	9 %	12%	14%
22	0.0	0.0	0.0	0.0	0.0	0.0	0.1	0.2	0.3
22	1 %	1 %	2 %	7 %	10%	12%	14%	19%	21%
21	0.0	0.0	0.0	0.0	0.1	0.1	0.2	0.3	0.4
21	1 %	2 %	7 %	12%	17%	19%	24%	26%	29%
20	0.0	0.0	0.0	0.1	0.2	0.3	0.4	0.5	0.7
20	1 %	7 %	12%	19%	24%	27%	29%	30%	34%
19	0.0	0.0	0.1	0.3	0.4	0.5	0.7	0.8	1.0
19	2 %	13%	23%	29%	35%	36%	37%	38%	36%
18	0.0	0.1	0.3	0.6	0.8	0.9	1.1	1.3	1.5
18	10%	26%	35%	35%	36%	36%	36%	36%	36%
17	0.0	0.3	0.6	0.9	1.2	1.3	1.5	1.7	2.0
17	26%	36%	35%	35%	33%	33%	35%	36%	37%
16	0.3	0.8	1.0	1.4	1.6	1.8	1.9	2.1	2.4
16	38%	34%	37%	39%	40%	40%	38%	37%	38%
15	0.8	1.3	1.6	1.9	2.1	2.2	2.4	2.7	2.9
15	42%	42%	39%	43%	42%	41%	41%	41%	40%
14	1.7	2.1	2.4	2.7	2.9	3.0	3.2	3.4	3.6
14	38%	34%	37%	39%	40%	40%	38%	37%	38%
13	2.6	3.0	3.2	3.5	3.7	3.8	3.9	4.2	4.4
13	26%	36%	35%	35%	33%	33%	35%	36%	37%
12	3.6	3.9	4.1	4.4	4.6	4.7	4.8	5.0	5.2
12	10%	26%	35%	35%	36%	36%	36%	36%	36%
11	4.5	4.8	5.1	5.3	5.4	5.6	5.7	5.9	6.1
11	2 %	13%	23%	29%	35%	36%	37%	38%	36%
10	5.5	5.7	6.0	6.2	6.4	6.5	6.6	6.8	6.9
10	1 %	7 %	12%	19%	24%	27%	29%	30%	34%

HIGH PRICE PUT TABLE

Exercise Price is (20)

Average Volatility

STOCK PRICE

NUMBER OF MONTHS BEFORE THE OPTIONS EXPIRE

STOCK PRICE	1	2	3	4	5	6	7	8	9
30	0.0	0.0	0.0	0.0	0.0	0.0	0.0	0.0	0.0
30	1 %	1 %	1 %	1 %	1 %	1 %	4 %	4 %	5 %
29	0.0	0.0	1 %	0.0	0.0	0.0	0.0	0.0	0.0
29	1 %	1 %	1 %	0.0	0.0	4 %	0.0	0.0	0.0
28	0.0	0.0	0.0	1 %	1 %	4 %	4 %	6 %	9 %
28	1 %	1 %	1 %	1 %	4 %	7 %	8 %	11%	17%
27	0.0	0.0	0.0	0.0	0.0	0.0	0.0	0.1	0.1
27	1 %	1 %	1 %	4 %	8 %	12%	17%	20%	24%
26	0.0	0.0	0.0	0.0	0.0	0.0	0.1	0.1	0.2
26	1 %	1 %	4 %	8 %	18%	22%	24%	27%	32%
25	0.0	0.0	0.0	0.0	0.1	0.2	0.3	0.4	0.5
25	1 %	4 %	12%	21%	25%	28%	34%	35%	37%
24	0.0	0.0	0.0	0.2	0.3	0.4	0.5	0.6	0.8
24	1 %	13%	25%	32%	37%	39%	39%	40%	40%
23	0.0	0.0	0.1	0.3	0.5	0.6	0.8	0.9	1.1
23	8 %	26%	37%	39%	39%	39%	41%	39%	39%
22	0.0	0.2	0.4	0.7	0.9	1.1	1.2	1.4	1.5
22	30%	39%	39%	39%	39%	39%	39%	40%	39%
21	0.2	0.6	0.8	1.1	1.3	1.5	1.6	1.8	2.0
21	40%	39%	40%	37%	36%	37%	35%	35%	36%
20	0.7	1.1	1.3	1.6	1.8	2.0	2.1	2.2	2.5
20	36%	37%	38%	40%	41%	41%	39%	40%	41%
19	1.5	1.9	2.2	2.4	2.6	2.7	2.9	3.0	3.2
19	40%	39%	40%	37%	36%	37%	35%	35%	36%
18	2.5	2.8	3.0	3.2	3.4	3.5	3.6	3.8	3.9
18	30%	39%	39%	39%	39%	39%	39%	40%	39%
17	3.5	3.7	3.9	4.1	4.3	4.4	4.5	4.7	4.8
17	8 %	26%	37%	39%	39%	39%	41%	39%	39%
16	4.4	4.7	4.8	5.0	5.2	5.3	5.4	5.6	5.7
16	1 %	13%	25%	32%	37%	39%	39%	40%	40%
15	5.4	5.7	5.8	6.0	6.2	6.3	6.4	6.5	6.7
15	1 %	4 %	12%	21%	25%	28%	34%	35%	37%

High Volatility

STOCK PRICE

NUMBER OF MONTHS BEFORE THE OPTIONS EXPIRE

STOCK PRICE	1	2	3	4	5	6	7	8	9
30	0.0	0.0	0.0	0.0	0.0	0.1	0.1	0.2	0.3
30	1 %	1 %	2 %	6 %	9 %	12%	13%	17%	19%
29	0.0	0.0	0.0	0.0	0.1	0.2	0.2	0.3	0.6
29	1 %	1 %	3 %	10%	11%	14%	18%	20%	23%
28	0.0	0.0	0.0	0.1	0.2	0.3	0.4	0.5	0.8
28	1 %	2 %	8 %	12%	17%	19%	23%	25%	30%
27	0.0	0.0	0.0	0.2	0.3	0.4	0.6	0.8	1.1
27	1 %	6 %	11%	19%	22%	25%	28%	29%	31%
26	0.0	0.0	0.1	0.3	0.5	0.6	0.8	1.1	1.3
26	1 %	11%	19%	26%	29%	34%	35%	36%	35%
25	0.0	0.1	0.3	0.6	0.8	1.0	1.1	1.4	1.8
25	3 %	19%	25%	31%	35%	35%	37%	37%	35%
24	0.0	0.2	0.5	0.8	1.1	1.3	1.5	1.8	2.1
24	12%	28%	35%	36%	37%	36%	38%	36%	33%
23	0.0	0.4	0.8	1.2	1.5	1.8	2.0	2.3	2.6
23	23%	35%	35%	36%	32%	34%	33%	37%	35%
22	0.2	0.8	1.3	1.6	1.9	2.2	2.4	2.7	3.0
22	36%	36%	34%	37%	35%	37%	37%	40%	37%
21	0.7	1.3	1.7	2.2	2.4	2.7	2.9	3.2	3.5
21	37%	37%	39%	40%	35%	35%	38%	40%	41%
20	1.1	1.8	2.2	2.7	2.9	3.2	3.4	3.7	4.0
20	42%	40%	40%	42%	42%	42%	42%	40%	37%
19	2.0	2.6	3.0	3.4	3.7	3.9	4.1	4.3	4.7
19	37%	37%	39%	40%	35%	35%	38%	40%	41%
18	2.9	3.5	3.8	4.2	4.5	4.7	4.9	5.1	5.5
18	36%	36%	34%	37%	35%	37%	37%	40%	37%
17	3.9	4.4	4.7	5.1	5.3	5.6	5.7	5.9	6.3
17	23%	35%	35%	36%	32%	34%	33%	37%	35%
16	4.8	5.3	5.6	5.9	6.2	6.4	6.5	6.7	7.1
16	12%	28%	35%	36%	37%	36%	38%	36%	33%
15	5.8	6.2	6.5	6.9	7.1	7.2	7.4	7.6	7.9
15	3 %	19%	25%	31%	35%	35%	37%	37%	35%

HIGH PRICE PUT TABLE

Exercise Price is 25

Average Volatility

STOCK PRICE — NUMBER OF MONTHS BEFORE THE OPTIONS EXPIRE

STOCK PRICE	1	2	3	4	5	6	7	8	9
35	0.0	0.0	0.0	0.0	0.0	0.0	0.0	0.0	0.1
35	1 %	1 %	1 %	3 %	4 %	7 %	9 %	12%	19%
34	0.0	0.0	0.0	0.0	0.0	0.0	0.0	0.1	0.2
34	1 %	1 %	1 %	4 %	8 %	10%	16%	20%	23%
33	0.0	0.0	0.0	0.0	0.0	0.1	0.1	0.2	0.3
33	1 %	1 %	4 %	8 %	14%	20%	22%	24%	26%
32	0.0	0.0	0.0	0.0	0.1	0.1	0.2	0.3	0.5
32	1 %	4 %	6 %	17%	21%	24%	26%	31%	35%
31	0.0	0.0	0.0	0.1	0.2	0.3	0.4	0.5	0.7
31	1 %	5 %	18%	24%	29%	33%	37%	38%	39%
30	0.0	0.0	0.1	0.3	0.4	0.5	0.7	0.9	1.1
30	1 %	16%	24%	32%	35%	37%	39%	39%	39%
29	0.0	0.0	0.1	0.4	0.6	0.8	0.9	1.1	1.4
29	7 %	24%	35%	39%	39%	39%	39%	39%	40%
28	0.0	0.2	0.4	0.7	1.0	1.2	1.4	1.6	1.8
28	22%	38%	40%	40%	40%	39%	39%	39%	39%
27	0.1	0.5	0.8	1.1	1.4	1.6	1.8	2.0	2.2
27	39%	39%	39%	38%	38%	39%	38%	37%	35%
26	0.5	0.9	1.3	1.5	1.8	2.1	2.2	2.4	2.7
26	39%	38%	36%	35%	37%	35%	35%	37%	38%
25	0.9	1.4	1.7	2.1	2.3	2.5	2.7	2.9	3.2
25	36%	38%	38%	40%	43%	40%	39%	40%	41%
24	1.8	2.2	2.5	2.8	3.1	3.2	3.5	3.7	4.0
24	39%	38%	36%	35%	35%	35%	35%	37%	38%
23	2.7	3.1	3.4	3.7	3.9	4.1	4.3	4.5	4.7
23	39%	39%	39%	38%	38%	39%	38%	37%	35%
22	3.6	4.0	4.3	4.5	4.7	4.9	5.0	5.3	5.5
22	22%	38%	40%	40%	40%	39%	39%	39%	39%
21	4.6	4.9	5.2	5.4	5.7	5.8	5.9	6.2	6.4
21	7 %	24%	35%	39%	39%	39%	39%	39%	40%
20	5.6	5.9	6.1	6.4	6.6	6.7	6.9	7.0	7.3
20	1 %	16%	24%	32%	35%	37%	39%	39%	39%

High Volatility

STOCK PRICE — NUMBER OF MONTHS BEFORE THE OPTIONS EXPIRE

STOCK PRICE	1	2	3	4	5	6	7	8	9
35	0.0	0.0	0.0	0.1	0.3	0.4	0.5	0.8	1.0
35	1 %	2 %	9 %	13%	17%	19%	24%	26%	29%
34	0.0	0.0	0.1	0.3	0.4	0.6	0.8	1.0	1.3
34	1 %	6 %	12%	17%	20%	24%	28%	29%	32%
33	0.0	0.0	0.1	0.4	0.6	0.7	1.0	1.3	1.6
33	0 %	9 %	16%	20%	26%	30%	32%	36%	35%
32	0.0	0.1	0.3	0.6	0.8	1.0	1.4	1.7	2.0
32	2 %	13%	19%	27%	31%	32%	35%	36%	34%
31	0.0	0.2	0.4	0.8	1.1	1.3	1.6	2.1	2.4
31	6 %	20%	29%	33%	35%	35%	35%	35%	32%
30	0.0	0.4	0.7	1.2	1.5	1.8	2.1	2.4	2.8
30	12%	26%	34%	36%	36%	36%	36%	35%	33%
29	0.0	0.5	0.9	1.5	1.9	2.2	2.5	2.8	3.3
29	19%	35%	37%	37%	34%	33%	33%	35%	35%
28	0.2	0.9	1.4	1.9	2.3	2.6	3.0	3.4	3.8
28	36%	35%	36%	34%	37%	36%	36%	36%	36%
27	0.6	1.3	1.9	2.4	2.8	3.1	3.4	3.8	4.2
27	36%	35%	37%	37%	38%	40%	37%	36%	38%
26	1.0	1.8	2.3	2.9	3.3	3.6	3.9	4.3	4.7
26	35%	37%	41%	36%	36%	39%	39%	40%	40%
25	1.5	2.3	2.8	3.4	3.9	4.1	4.4	4.8	5.2
25	42%	41%	42%	42%	42%	41%	42%	40%	36%
24	2.3	3.1	3.6	4.1	4.5	4.8	5.1	5.4	5.8
24	35%	37%	41%	36%	36%	39%	39%	40%	40%
23	3.2	4.0	4.5	5.0	5.3	5.5	5.9	6.2	6.6
23	36%	35%	37%	37%	38%	40%	37%	36%	38%
22	4.1	4.8	5.3	5.8	6.2	6.4	6.6	7.0	7.4
22	36%	35%	36%	34%	37%	36%	36%	36%	36%
21	5.1	5.7	6.2	6.7	7.0	7.2	7.4	7.8	8.2
21	19%	35%	37%	37%	34%	33%	33%	35%	35%
20	6.0	6.7	7.1	7.5	7.9	8.1	8.3	8.4	8.4
20	12%	26%	34%	36%	36%	36%	36%	35%	33%

HIGH PRICE PUT TABLE

Exercise Price is ⟨30⟩

Average Volatility

STOCK PRICE — NUMBER OF MONTHS BEFORE THE OPTIONS EXPIRE

STOCK PRICE	1	2	3	4	5	6	7	8	9
40	0.0	0.0	0.0	0.0	0.0	0.1	0.2	0.3	
40	1 %	1 %	4 %	7 %	10%	18%	19%	25%	25%
39	0.0	0.0	0.0	0.1	0.2	0.2	0.4	0.5	
39	1 %	1 %	4 %	10%	20%	23%	25%	26%	31%
38	0.0	0.0	0.0	0.1	0.2	0.3	0.4	0.5	0.7
38	1 %	4 %	9 %	20%	25%	26%	30%	34%	35%
37	0.0	0.0	0.0	0.2	0.3	0.4	0.6	0.8	1.0
37	1 %	7 %	19%	24%	30%	34%	35%	37%	38%
36	0.0	0.0	0.1	0.3	0.5	0.6	0.8	1.0	1.3
36	1 %	17%	24%	32%	37%	39%	39%	39%	40%
35	0.0	0.0	0.2	0.5	0.7	0.9	1.1	1.4	1.6
35	5 %	24%	33%	36%	40%	39%	39%	40%	39%
34	0.0	0.1	0.4	0.8	1.0	1.3	1.5	1.8	2.0
34	18%	34%	39%	39%	39%	40%	39%	39%	39%
33	0.0	0.4	0.8	1.2	1.4	1.7	1.9	2.2	2.5
33	33%	40%	39%	39%	38%	38%	39%	38%	38%
32	0.3	0.8	1.1	1.6	1.9	2.1	2.3	2.7	2.9
32	39%	39%	39%	36%	37%	36%	36%	35%	35%
31	0.7	1.2	1.6	2.1	2.3	2.6	2.8	3.0	3.4
31	40%	40%	37%	36%	36%	35%	35%	35%	35%
30	1.1	1.7	2.1	2.5	2.8	3.1	3.3	3.5	3.9
30	37%	38%	38%	40%	43%	41%	40%	42%	41%
29	1.9	2.5	2.8	3.3	3.6	3.8	4.0	4.3	4.6
29	40%	40%	37%	36%	36%	35%	39%	39%	38%
28	2.9	3.4	3.7	4.2	4.4	4.6	4.8	5.1	5.4
28	39%	39%	39%	36%	37%	36%	36%	34%	35%
27	3.8	4.3	4.6	4.9	5.2	5.4	5.6	5.9	6.2
27	33%	40%	39%	39%	38%	38%	39%	38%	38%
26	4.8	5.2	5.5	5.9	6.1	6.3	6.5	6.7	7.0
26	18%	34%	39%	39%	39%	40%	39%	39%	39%
25	5.7	6.2	6.4	6.8	7.0	7.2	7.4	7.6	7.9
25	5 %	24%	33%	36%	40%	39%	39%	40%	39%

High Volatility

STOCK PRICE — NUMBER OF MONTHS BEFORE THE OPTIONS EXPIRE

STOCK PRICE	1	2	3	4	5	6	7	8	9
40	0.0	0.0	0.2	0.4	0.7	1.0	1.2	1.5	1.9
40	1 %	8 %	14%	20%	26%	29%	30%	32%	33%
39	0.0	0.1	0.3	0.6	0.9	1.2	1.5	1.8	2.3
39	1 %	12%	20%	26%	30%	31%	34%	35%	35%
38	0.0	0.1	0.4	0.8	1.1	1.5	1.8	2.2	2.6
38	2 %	16%	25%	31%	33%	35%	35%	35%	34%
37	0.0	0.3	0.6	1.1	1.5	1.8	2.2	2.6	3.1
37	7 %	20%	30%	31%	33%	35%	35%	36%	32%
36	0.0	0.4	0.9	1.4	1.9	2.2	2.6	3.0	3.5
36	12%	29%	34%	36%	34%	36%	35%	32%	32%
35	0.0	0.6	1.1	1.8	2.2	2.6	2.9	3.4	3.9
35	20%	33%	35%	34%	32%	32%	33%	35%	36%
34	0.2	0.9	1.6	2.3	2.7	3.0	3.4	3.9	4.4
34	30%	36%	36%	34%	35%	36%	36%	37%	38%
33	0.5	1.4	2.0	2.7	3.2	3.5	3.9	4.3	4.9
33	36%	36%	33%	36%	35%	37%	39%	36%	37%
32	0.9	1.8	2.5	3.1	3.7	4.0	4.3	4.8	5.3
32	37%	34%	37%	40%	37%	35%	38%	39%	40%
31	1.4	2.3	2.9	3.6	4.2	4.5	4.9	5.3	5.8
31	34%	38%	40%	37%	38%	41%	40%	40%	41%
30	1.8	2.8	3.5	4.2	4.6	5.0	5.3	5.8	6.3
30	42%	40%	41%	42%	42%	42%	42%	38%	37%
29	2.7	3.6	4.2	4.9	5.4	5.7	6.0	6.5	7.0
29	34%	38%	40%	38%	38%	41%	40%	40%	41%
28	3.6	4.5	5.0	5.7	6.2	6.5	6.8	7.3	7.7
28	37%	34%	37%	40%	37%	35%	38%	39%	40%
27	4.5	5.3	5.9	6.5	6.9	7.2	7.5	8.0	8.3
27	36%	36%	33%	36%	35%	37%	37%	36%	37%
26	5.4	6.2	6.7	7.3	7.8	8.1	8.4	8.4	9.1
26	30%	36%	36%	34%	35%	36%	36%	37%	38%
25	6.4	7.1	7.6	8.2	8.5	8.5	9.2	9.2	9.9
25	20%	33%	35%	34%	32%	32%	33%	35%	36%

HIGH PRICE PUT TABLE

Exercise Price is (35)

Average Volatility

STOCK PRICE — NUMBER OF MONTHS BEFORE THE OPTIONS EXPIRE

STOCK PRICE	1	2	3	4	5	6	7	8	9
45	0.0	0.0	0.0	0.1	0.1	0.2	0.4	0.5	0.7
45	1 %	4 %	7 %	16%	21%	25%	26%	31%	32%
44	0.0	0.0	0.0	0.1	0.3	0.4	0.5	0.7	0.9
44	1 %	4 %	11%	21%	25%	27%	32%	34%	35%
43	0.0	0.0	0.1	0.2	0.4	0.6	0.7	1.0	1.2
43	1 %	9 %	19%	24%	32%	34%	36%	38%	39%
42	0.0	0.0	0.2	0.4	0.6	0.8	1.0	1.3	1.6
42	2 %	17%	24%	32%	35%	38%	39%	39%	39%
41	0.0	0.0	0.2	0.5	0.8	1.0	1.2	1.5	1.9
41	4 %	25%	33%	38%	39%	39%	39%	39%	39%
40	0.0	0.1	0.5	0.8	1.1	1.4	1.7	2.0	2.3
40	12%	32%	38%	39%	40%	39%	39%	39%	38%
39	0.0	0.4	0.8	1.2	1.5	1.8	2.0	2.3	2.7
39	25%	38%	39%	40%	39%	39%	39%	39%	38%
38	0.1	0.7	1.1	1.6	2.0	2.2	2.4	2.8	3.2
38	38%	40%	39%	38%	37%	38%	37%	37%	35%
37	0.5	1.1	1.6	2.0	2.4	2.6	2.9	3.3	3.6
37	39%	38%	38%	36%	36%	35%	35%	35%	35%
36	0.8	1.5	2.0	2.5	2.8	3.1	3.4	3.7	4.1
36	39%	36%	36%	35%	37%	38%	40%	40%	39%
35	1.3	2.0	2.5	3.0	3.4	3.6	3.9	4.2	4.6
35	37%	39%	38%	40%	43%	41%	40%	43%	43%
34	2.1	2.8	3.3	3.8	4.1	4.3	4.6	5.0	5.3
34	39%	36%	36%	35%	37%	38%	40%	40%	39%
33	3.1	3.7	4.1	4.6	4.9	5.2	5.5	5.8	6.1
33	39%	38%	38%	36%	36%	35%	35%	35%	35%
32	4.0	4.6	5.0	5.4	5.7	6.0	6.2	6.5	6.8
32	38%	40%	39%	38%	37%	38%	39%	37%	35%
31	4.9	5.5	5.9	6.3	6.6	6.8	7.0	7.3	7.6
31	25%	38%	39%	40%	39%	39%	39%	39%	38%
30	5.9	6.5	6.8	7.2	7.5	7.7	7.9	8.2	8.5
30	12%	32%	38%	39%	40%	39%	39%	39%	38%

High Volatility

STOCK PRICE — NUMBER OF MONTHS BEFORE THE OPTIONS EXPIRE

STOCK PRICE	1	2	3	4	5	6	7	8	9
45	0.0	0.1	0.4	0.9	1.3	1.6	1.9	2.4	2.9
45	4 %	20%	24%	31%	32%	32%	32%	32%	32%
44	0.0	0.2	0.6	1.1	1.6	1.9	2.2	2.7	3.3
44	3 %	23%	26%	32%	32%	33%	34%	33%	32%
43	0.0	0.4	0.8	1.4	1.8	2.2	2.7	3.2	3.7
43	9 %	25%	32%	32%	32%	34%	33%	32%	33%
42	0.0	0.6	1.1	1.8	2.3	2.6	3.0	3.6	4.1
42	15%	31%	32%	32%	32%	32%	34%	35%	34%
41	0.0	0.7	1.3	2.1	2.6	3.0	3.5	4.0	4.6
41	23%	33%	32%	32%	33%	34%	34%	34%	35%
40	0.2	1.0	1.7	2.6	3.1	3.4	3.9	4.4	5.1
40	30%	32%	32%	34%	35%	35%	36%	35%	35%
39	0.4	1.4	2.1	3.0	3.5	3.9	4.4	5.0	5.5
39	33%	32%	35%	36%	35%	37%	35%	35%	36%
38	0.8	1.9	2.6	3.5	4.0	4.4	4.8	5.4	6.0
38	33%	36%	34%	37%	35%	36%	36%	37%	38%
37	1.2	2.3	3.1	3.9	4.5	4.9	5.3	5.9	6.4
37	35%	37%	37%	37%	38%	37%	38%	38%	39%
36	1.7	2.8	3.6	4.4	5.0	5.4	5.8	6.4	6.9
36	36%	39%	39%	40%	39%	40%	39%	40%	37%
35	2.2	3.4	4.1	5.0	5.5	5.9	6.3	6.8	7.4
35	40%	40%	40%	41%	40%	40%	40%	39%	39%
34	3.0	4.1	4.8	5.7	6.2	6.6	7.0	7.6	8.1
34	36%	39%	39%	40%	39%	40%	39%	40%	37%
33	3.9	5.0	5.6	6.5	7.0	7.3	7.7	8.3	8.4
33	35%	37%	37%	37%	38%	37%	37%	38%	39%
32	4.8	5.8	6.5	7.3	7.8	8.2	8.4	8.4	9.2
32	33%	36%	34%	37%	35%	36%	36%	37%	38%
31	5.8	6.7	7.3	8.1	8.5	8.5	9.2	9.2	10.
31	33%	32%	35%	36%	35%	37%	35%	35%	36%
30	6.7	7.6	8.2	8.6	9.3	9.3	10.	10.	10.
30	30%	32%	32%	34%	35%	35%	36%	35%	35%

HIGH PRICE PUT TABLE

Exercise Price is **40**

Average Volatility

STOCK PRICE — NUMBER OF MONTHS BEFORE THE OPTIONS EXPIRE

STOCK PRICE	1	2	3	4	5	6	7	8	9
50	0.0	0.0	0.0	0.2	0.3	0.5	0.7	0.9	1.2
50	1 %	4 %	13%	22%	26%	30%	33%	35%	36%
49	0.0	0.0	0.1	0.3	0.5	0.7	0.9	1.2	1.5
49	1 %	9 %	19%	25%	31%	34%	35%	38%	38%
48	0.0	0.0	0.2	0.4	0.7	0.9	1.2	1.5	1.8
48	1 %	18%	24%	32%	35%	38%	40%	40%	39%
47	0.0	0.0	0.2	0.6	0.9	1.2	1.4	1.8	2.1
47	4 %	22%	32%	36%	38%	40%	39%	39%	39%
46	0.0	0.1	0.4	0.9	1.2	1.5	1.8	2.2	2.6
46	10%	31%	38%	39%	39%	39%	40%	40%	38%
45	0.0	0.3	0.8	1.2	1.7	2.0	2.2	2.5	2.9
45	21%	37%	39%	39%	38%	39%	39%	39%	38%
44	0.1	0.6	1.1	1.6	2.0	2.3	2.6	2.9	3.4
44	33%	39%	39%	39%	38%	38%	39%	38%	36%
43	0.3	1.0	1.5	2.1	2.4	2.8	3.1	3.4	3.9
43	39%	39%	39%	37%	37%	37%	36%	36%	35%
42	0.7	1.4	1.9	2.4	2.9	3.3	3.5	3.9	4.3
42	39%	39%	37%	36%	35%	35%	35%	36%	36%
41	1.1	1.9	2.4	2.9	3.3	3.7	4.0	4.3	4.7
41	40%	36%	36%	37%	39%	38%	40%	39%	38%
40	1.6	2.3	2.8	3.4	3.9	4.2	4.5	4.8	5.3
40	37%	38%	39%	42%	42%	41%	41%	44%	43%
39	2.4	3.1	3.6	4.2	4.6	4.9	5.2	5.6	6.1
39	40%	36%	36%	37%	39%	38%	40%	39%	38%
38	3.2	4.0	4.5	5.0	5.4	5.7	6.1	6.4	6.8
38	39%	39%	37%	36%	35%	35%	35%	36%	36%
37	4.2	4.9	5.4	5.9	6.3	6.5	6.8	7.1	7.6
37	39%	39%	39%	37%	37%	37%	36%	36%	35%
36	5.1	5.8	6.2	6.7	7.0	7.3	7.5	7.9	8.2
36	33%	39%	39%	39%	38%	38%	38%	38%	36%
35	6.1	6.7	7.1	7.6	7.9	8.2	8.4	8.7	8.7
35	21%	37%	39%	39%	38%	39%	39%	39%	38%

High Volatility

STOCK PRICE — NUMBER OF MONTHS BEFORE THE OPTIONS EXPIRE

STOCK PRICE	1	2	3	4	5	6	7	8	9
50	0.0	0.3	0.8	1.4	1.9	2.3	2.7	3.2	4.1
50	7 %	23%	30%	32%	32%	32%	33%	32%	33%
49	0.0	0.5	1.0	1.7	2.2	2.7	3.1	3.7	4.4
49	11%	25%	32%	33%	32%	33%	32%	34%	34%
48	0.1	0.6	1.3	2.0	2.6	3.1	3.6	4.1	4.8
48	16%	33%	33%	33%	32%	32%	33%	34%	34%
47	0.1	0.8	1.6	2.4	3.0	3.5	4.0	4.5	5.3
47	23%	32%	32%	32%	34%	34%	34%	35%	35%
46	0.2	1.1	1.9	2.9	3.5	4.0	4.4	5.0	5.8
46	27%	32%	33%	35%	35%	35%	35%	36%	35%
45	0.4	1.5	2.3	3.3	3.9	4.3	4.9	5.5	6.3
45	32%	32%	34%	36%	35%	35%	35%	35%	35%
44	0.7	1.9	2.8	3.7	4.3	4.9	5.4	5.9	6.8
44	34%	35%	36%	35%	36%	35%	35%	36%	37%
43	1.0	2.4	3.2	4.2	4.9	5.3	5.9	6.4	7.3
43	34%	35%	36%	37%	37%	37%	37%	39%	38%
42	1.6	2.8	3.8	4.7	5.3	5.8	6.3	6.9	7.6
42	35%	37%	38%	37%	37%	37%	38%	38%	38%
41	2.0	3.3	4.2	5.2	5.8	6.3	6.8	7.4	8.2
41	38%	40%	38%	40%	40%	40%	39%	39%	38%
40	2.6	3.9	4.8	5.7	6.3	6.8	7.3	7.9	8.5
40	40%	40%	40%	40%	40%	40%	39%	39%	39%
39	3.4	4.7	5.5	6.4	7.0	7.5	8.0	8.4	9.2
39	38%	40%	38%	40%	40%	40%	39%	39%	38%
38	4.2	5.5	6.3	7.2	7.8	8.2	8.4	9.2	10.
38	35%	37%	38%	37%	37%	37%	38%	38%	38%
37	5.2	6.3	7.2	8.1	8.5	8.5	9.2	10.	10.
37	34%	35%	36%	37%	37%	37%	37%	39%	38%
36	6.1	7.2	8.0	8.5	9.3	9.3	10.	10.	10.
36	34%	35%	36%	35%	36%	35%	35%	36%	37%
35	7.0	8.1	8.7	9.4	10.	10.	10.	10.	11.
35	32%	32%	34%	36%	35%	35%	35%	35%	35%

HIGH PRICE PUT TABLE

Exercise Price is

Average Volatility

STOCK PRICE	NUMBER OF MONTHS BEFORE THE OPTIONS EXPIRE								
	1	2	3	4	5	6	7	8	9
55	0.0	0.0	0.2	0.4	0.7	0.9	1.1	1.3	1.8
55	1%	10%	20%	27%	30%	34%	35%	39%	39%
54	0.0	0.1	0.3	0.6	0.9	1.1	1.4	1.7	2.1
54	2%	17%	24%	31%	32%	37%	38%	40%	38%
53	0.0	0.1	0.4	0.7	1.2	1.4	1.8	2.0	2.5
53	4%	22%	31%	36%	36%	39%	39%	39%	39%
52	0.0	0.2	0.5	1.0	1.4	1.7	2.1	2.4	2.9
52	9%	26%	34%	39%	37%	39%	38%	39%	38%
51	0.0	0.3	0.8	1.3	1.8	2.1	2.5	2.7	3.2
51	20%	34%	39%	39%	37%	39%	39%	39%	37%
50	0.1	0.6	1.1	1.7	2.2	2.5	2.9	3.2	3.6
50	25%	38%	39%	39%	36%	38%	38%	38%	36%
49	0.2	0.9	1.4	2.0	2.6	2.8	3.3	3.6	4.1
49	35%	39%	39%	39%	36%	37%	37%	36%	34%
48	0.6	1.3	1.9	2.5	3.0	3.3	3.8	4.0	4.6
48	39%	38%	38%	37%	34%	34%	34%	36%	34%
47	0.9	1.7	2.3	2.9	3.6	3.9	4.2	4.5	5.0
47	38%	36%	36%	36%	35%	36%	34%	39%	36%
46	1.3	2.2	2.7	3.4	4.0	4.2	4.6	4.9	5.5
46	36%	36%	36%	37%	36%	39%	40%	40%	38%
45	1.8	2.7	3.3	3.9	4.5	4.8	5.1	5.5	6.0
45	36%	38%	38%	41%	37%	41%	40%	43%	43%
44	2.6	3.4	4.0	4.6	5.2	5.5	5.9	6.2	6.8
44	36%	36%	36%	37%	36%	39%	40%	40%	38%
43	3.5	4.3	4.9	5.4	6.1	6.3	6.7	6.9	7.5
43	38%	36%	36%	36%	35%	36%	34%	39%	36%
42	4.5	5.3	5.7	6.3	6.9	7.2	7.5	7.7	8.3
42	39%	38%	38%	37%	34%	34%	35%	36%	34%
41	5.4	6.1	6.6	7.1	7.7	7.9	8.2	8.5	8.6
41	35%	39%	39%	39%	36%	37%	37%	35%	39%
40	6.3	7.0	7.4	8.0	8.6	8.7	8.7	8.7	9.5
40	25%	38%	39%	39%	36%	38%	38%	38%	36%

High Volatility

STOCK PRICE	NUMBER OF MONTHS BEFORE THE OPTIONS EXPIRE								
	1	2	3	4	5	6	7	8	9
55	0.1	0.6	1.2	1.9	2.9	3.2	3.8	4.2	5.2
55	12%	26%	32%	33%	32%	32%	32%	33%	34%
54	0.1	0.8	1.5	2.3	3.2	3.5	4.2	4.6	5.6
54	14%	31%	32%	32%	32%	33%	33%	34%	34%
53	0.2	1.0	1.8	2.7	3.7	4.0	4.7	5.1	6.2
53	23%	32%	32%	32%	33%	34%	34%	35%	35%
52	0.3	1.3	2.1	3.1	4.1	4.4	5.1	5.5	6.6
52	25%	32%	32%	35%	32%	35%	35%	35%	35%
51	0.5	1.6	2.6	3.6	4.6	4.9	5.5	6.0	7.0
51	32%	32%	34%	35%	34%	35%	34%	35%	35%
50	0.8	2.0	3.0	4.0	5.1	5.3	6.0	6.5	7.4
50	33%	32%	35%	35%	35%	36%	35%	36%	36%
49	1.1	2.4	3.5	4.5	5.5	5.9	6.5	6.9	8.0
49	32%	35%	34%	37%	35%	35%	33%	38%	38%
48	1.5	2.9	3.8	4.9	6.0	6.3	7.0	7.4	8.5
48	33%	34%	37%	37%	34%	37%	38%	38%	37%
47	2.0	3.4	4.4	5.5	6.5	6.8	7.4	7.9	8.8
47	31%	37%	38%	37%	37%	38%	38%	40%	38%
46	2.5	3.9	4.9	5.9	7.0	7.2	7.9	8.4	8.6
46	35%	40%	39%	40%	37%	41%	38%	37%	36%
45	3.0	4.5	5.4	6.5	7.5	7.8	8.5	8.5	9.3
45	40%	40%	40%	40%	39%	40%	38%	39%	38%
44	3.8	5.2	6.1	7.2	8.2	8.4	8.4	9.3	10.
44	35%	40%	39%	40%	37%	41%	38%	37%	36%
43	4.7	6.0	6.9	8.0	8.4	9.3	9.3	10.	10.
43	31%	37%	38%	37%	37%	38%	38%	40%	38%
42	5.6	6.9	7.7	8.5	9.3	9.3	10.	10.	11.
42	33%	34%	37%	37%	34%	37%	38%	39%	37%
41	6.5	7.7	8.5	9.4	10.	10.	10.	11.	12.
41	32%	35%	34%	37%	35%	35%	33%	38%	38%
40	7.4	8.7	8.7	10.	11.	11.	11.	12.	13.
40	33%	32%	35%	35%	35%	36%	35%	36%	36%

HIGH PRICE PUT TABLE

Exercise Price is (50)

Average Volatility

STOCK PRICE — NUMBER OF MONTHS BEFORE THE OPTIONS EXPIRE

STOCK PRICE	1	2	3	4	5	6	7	8	9
65	0.0	0.0	0.0	0.1	0.2	0.3	0.5	0.7	0.9
65	1 %	1 %	4 %	11%	17%	21%	24%	25%	28%
64	0.0	0.0	0.0	0.1	0.2	0.4	0.5	0.7	1.0
64	1 %	4 %	6 %	18%	21%	25%	26%	31%	34%
63	0.0	0.0	0.0	0.2	0.4	0.5	0.7	1.0	1.3
63	1 %	4 %	9 %	20%	25%	26%	31%	35%	34%
62	0.0	0.0	0.0	0.2	0.4	0.7	0.9	1.2	1.5
62	1 %	5 %	17%	25%	27%	32%	35%	37%	39%
61	0.0	0.0	0.1	0.4	0.6	0.9	1.1	1.5	1.8
61	1 %	9 %	19%	26%	32%	35%	37%	39%	39%
60	0.0	0.1	0.2	0.5	0.8	1.1	1.3	1.6	2.0
60	1 %	14%	25%	32%	35%	39%	39%	39%	39%
59	0.0	0.1	0.4	0.8	1.1	1.4	1.8	2.2	2.6
59	3 %	21%	29%	35%	38%	39%	39%	39%	40%
58	0.0	0.1	0.4	0.8	1.2	1.5	1.8	2.2	2.6
58	6 %	24%	35%	39%	39%	41%	41%	41%	39%
57	0.0	0.3	0.8	1.3	1.7	2.1	2.5	2.9	3.3
57	13%	30%	37%	38%	39%	39%	39%	39%	38%
56	0.0	0.5	0.9	1.5	1.9	2.2	2.6	3.0	3.5
56	22%	38%	39%	40%	39%	40%	40%	39%	39%
55	0.1	0.8	1.4	2.0	2.5	2.8	3.2	3.7	4.3
55	29%	39%	39%	40%	38%	39%	39%	38%	35%
54	0.3	1.1	1.6	2.2	2.7	3.1	3.4	3.9	4.4
54	39%	39%	41%	39%	39%	40%	40%	41%	37%
53	0.7	1.6	2.2	2.8	3.4	3.8	4.2	4.6	5.2
53	39%	38%	38%	35%	35%	34%	34%	34%	33%
52	0.9	1.8	2.5	3.1	3.7	4.0	4.4	4.8	5.3
52	40%	39%	40%	38%	37%	37%	38%	39%	39%
51	1.4	2.4	3.1	3.6	4.3	4.7	5.1	5.5	5.9
51	39%	36%	36%	35%	38%	39%	40%	39%	38%
50	1.9	2.8	3.4	4.1	4.5	5.0	5.3	5.7	6.3
50	37%	38%	39%	44%	43%	42%	41%	43%	43%
49	2.6	3.6	4.2	4.9	5.4	5.9	6.2	6.7	7.2
49	39%	36%	36%	35%	38%	39%	40%	39%	38%
48	3.5	4.4	5.0	5.6	6.0	6.4	6.8	7.3	7.8
48	40%	39%	40%	38%	37%	37%	38%	39%	39%
47	4.5	5.3	5.9	6.5	7.0	7.4	7.8	8.1	8.5
47	39%	38%	38%	35%	35%	34%	34%	34%	33%
46	5.4	6.2	6.8	7.3	7.8	8.1	8.5	8.6	8.6
46	39%	39%	41%	39%	39%	40%	40%	41%	37%
45	6.3	7.1	7.6	8.2	8.6	8.8	8.8	9.5	9.5
45	29%	39%	39%	40%	38%	39%	39%	38%	35%

High Volatility

STOCK PRICE — NUMBER OF MONTHS BEFORE THE OPTIONS EXPIRE

STOCK PRICE	1	2	3	4	5	6	7	8	9
65	0.0	0.2	0.5	1.2	1.6	2.0	2.5	3.0	3.7
65	3 %	14%	23%	25%	31%	32%	32%	32%	33%
64	0.0	0.2	0.6	1.3	1.7	2.1	2.6	3.1	3.8
64	4 %	19%	24%	30%	32%	33%	33%	33%	34%
63	0.0	0.3	0.8	1.6	2.1	2.5	3.1	3.8	4.4
63	4 %	22%	27%	32%	32%	33%	33%	34%	32%
62	0.0	0.4	1.0	1.7	2.4	2.8	3.3	4.0	4.7
62	8 %	24%	32%	32%	32%	33%	34%	34%	35%
61	0.0	0.6	1.2	2.0	2.7	3.3	3.8	4.6	5.3
61	10%	25%	32%	32%	32%	33%	33%	33%	33%
60	0.1	0.7	1.4	2.3	2.9	3.4	3.9	4.7	5.5
60	14%	31%	33%	34%	34%	34%	34%	34%	35%
59	0.2	1.0	1.8	2.8	3.5	4.0	4.7	5.4	6.1
59	21%	32%	34%	32%	32%	33%	33%	34%	35%
58	0.2	1.1	1.9	3.0	3.7	4.3	4.9	5.6	6.4
58	26%	34%	35%	35%	35%	37%	36%	35%	35%
57	0.4	1.6	2.5	3.5	4.4	4.9	5.5	6.2	7.1
57	29%	32%	34%	34%	35%	35%	35%	35%	36%
56	0.5	1.8	2.7	3.9	4.5	5.1	5.7	6.5	7.2
56	33%	34%	35%	35%	35%	37%	36%	36%	36%
55	0.9	2.3	3.3	4.4	5.3	5.8	6.5	7.2	8.0
55	33%	34%	35%	35%	36%	35%	35%	35%	38%
54	1.1	2.6	3.6	4.7	5.5	6.1	6.7	7.5	8.1
54	36%	36%	35%	37%	38%	38%	38%	39%	40%
53	1.7	3.3	4.3	5.4	6.3	6.9	7.4	8.1	9.0
53	35%	34%	37%	37%	36%	37%	38%	38%	40%
52	2.0	3.7	4.6	5.8	6.6	7.1	7.6	8.4	8.8
52	35%	37%	40%	38%	38%	40%	39%	40%	40%
51	2.6	4.2	5.2	6.4	7.1	7.7	8.3	8.6	9.5
51	37%	40%	39%	40%	40%	40%	40%	40%	37%
50	3.0	4.6	5.6	6.8	7.5	8.1	8.5	9.3	10.
50	41%	41%	41%	40%	40%	40%	40%	40%	40%
49	3.8	5.4	6.4	7.6	8.4	8.4	9.3	10.	10.
49	37%	40%	39%	40%	40%	40%	40%	40%	37%
48	4.6	6.1	7.1	8.2	8.5	9.3	9.3	10.	10.
48	35%	37%	40%	38%	38%	40%	39%	40%	40%
47	5.6	7.0	8.0	8.5	9.3	10.	10.	10.	11.
47	35%	34%	37%	37%	36%	37%	38%	38%	40%
46	6.5	7.9	8.6	9.4	10.	11.	11.	11.	12.
46	36%	36%	35%	37%	38%	38%	38%	39%	40%
45	7.4	8.8	9.5	10.	11.	11.	11.	12.	13.
45	33%	34%	35%	35%	36%	35%	35%	35%	38%

HIGH PRICE PUT TABLE

Exercise Price is ⑥⓪

Average Volatility

STOCK PRICE — NUMBER OF MONTHS BEFORE THE OPTIONS EXPIRE

PRICE	1	2	3	4	5	6	7	8	9
75	0.0	0.0	0.1	0.4	0.6	0.8	1.1	1.4	1.9
75	1 %	4 %	12%	21%	24%	28%	32%	34%	36%
74	0.0	0.0	0.1	0.4	0.7	0.9	1.1	1.5	1.8
74	1 %	6 %	19%	25%	29%	34%	37%	39%	39%
73	0.0	0.0	0.2	0.6	0.9	1.2	1.5	1.9	2.4
73	0 %	9 %	21%	26%	32%	34%	37%	39%	39%
72	0.0	0.0	0.3	0.7	1.1	1.4	1.7	2.1	2.5
72	1 %	17%	24%	32%	35%	38%	39%	39%	39%
71	0.0	0.1	0.4	0.9	1.3	1.7	2.1	2.6	3.1
71	4 %	19%	27%	35%	38%	39%	39%	39%	39%
70	0.0	0.1	0.5	1.0	1.4	1.8	2.2	2.7	3.2
70	5 %	25%	35%	38%	40%	39%	39%	40%	39%
69	0.0	0.3	0.8	1.4	1.9	2.4	2.8	3.3	3.9
69	9 %	28%	35%	39%	39%	39%	39%	39%	39%
68	0.0	0.4	0.9	1.5	2.1	2.5	2.8	3.4	3.9
68	18%	35%	39%	40%	40%	39%	41%	39%	39%
67	0.1	0.8	1.4	2.0	2.7	3.2	3.6	4.1	4.6
67	25%	36%	39%	39%	38%	39%	39%	38%	36%
66	0.2	0.9	1.5	2.3	2.8	3.3	3.7	4.3	4.8
66	31%	39%	41%	39%	39%	39%	39%	39%	40%
65	0.4	1.3	2.1	2.9	3.4	3.9	4.5	5.0	5.7
65	37%	39%	39%	37%	37%	36%	36%	37%	34%
64	0.7	1.6	2.3	3.0	3.7	4.1	4.6	5.1	5.8
64	39%	40%	39%	39%	39%	39%	40%	38%	37%
63	1.0	2.1	2.9	3.8	4.4	4.9	5.4	5.9	6.5
63	39%	36%	35%	34%	35%	35%	35%	33%	35%
62	1.4	2.4	3.2	4.1	4.6	5.1	5.5	6.1	6.6
62	39%	40%	38%	37%	38%	39%	39%	40%	39%
61	1.9	3.1	3.8	4.7	5.3	5.8	6.3	6.8	7.3
61	38%	35%	36%	37%	38%	39%	39%	40%	39%
60	2.3	3.4	4.2	5.1	5.6	6.1	6.5	7.0	7.7
60	37%	38%	39%	42%	43%	41%	42%	42%	43%
59	3.0	4.2	5.0	5.8	6.4	7.0	7.4	8.0	8.5
59	38%	35%	36%	37%	38%	39%	39%	40%	39%
58	3.8	4.9	5.6	6.5	7.0	7.5	7.9	8.5	8.5
58	39%	40%	38%	37%	38%	39%	39%	40%	39%
57	4.9	5.9	6.7	7.5	8.0	8.6	8.6	9.4	
57	39%	36%	35%	34%	35%	35%	35%	33%	35%
56	5.8	6.8	7.4	8.2	8.7	8.7	9.5	9.5	10.
56	39%	40%	39%	39%	39%	39%	40%	38%	37%
55	6.7	7.8	8.5	8.8	9.6	9.6	10.	10.	11.
55	37%	39%	39%	37%	37%	36%	36%	37%	34%

High Volatility

STOCK PRICE — NUMBER OF MONTHS BEFORE THE OPTIONS EXPIRE

PRICE	1	2	3	4	5	6	7	8	9
75	0.0	0.6	1.2	2.2	2.8	3.5	4.0	4.8	5.8
75	6 %	23%	27%	32%	32%	32%	33%	32%	32%
74	0.0	0.7	1.3	2.3	3.0	3.5	4.0	4.9	5.9
74	10%	25%	32%	32%	33%	35%	34%	34%	34%
73	0.1	0.8	1.6	2.6	3.5	4.2	4.8	5.7	6.8
73	12%	26%	33%	33%	32%	32%	33%	34%	33%
72	0.1	1.0	1.9	2.9	3.7	4.3	4.9	5.9	6.8
72	16%	30%	32%	32%	33%	33%	34%	34%	34%
71	0.2	1.2	2.2	3.4	4.2	5.0	5.7	6.6	7.6
71	21%	32%	32%	32%	32%	33%	33%	33%	35%
70	0.2	1.3	2.3	3.5	4.4	5.1	5.8	6.7	7.8
70	24%	32%	34%	34%	35%	34%	36%	35%	35%
69	0.4	1.7	2.8	4.2	5.0	5.8	6.5	7.5	8.5
69	25%	33%	34%	34%	35%	35%	36%	36%	36%
68	0.5	2.0	3.1	4.5	5.3	6.0	6.7	7.7	8.6
68	32%	34%	34%	35%	35%	35%	35%	36%	35%
67	0.8	2.4	3.7	5.1	5.9	6.7	7.4	8.3	9.4
67	32%	34%	35%	35%	35%	35%	35%	34%	35%
66	1.0	2.7	3.9	5.3	6.2	7.0	7.5	8.5	9.3
66	34%	36%	35%	37%	36%	36%	36%	37%	38%
65	1.4	3.3	4.6	5.9	6.9	7.7	8.3	9.2	10.
65	33%	36%	35%	37%	36%	36%	37%	37%	38%
64	1.8	3.6	4.8	6.3	7.1	7.9	8.6	9.0	9.9
64	36%	35%	38%	38%	37%	37%	38%	40%	41%
63	2.3	4.3	5.6	7.0	8.0	8.7	8.9	9.8	10.
63	35%	37%	37%	36%	37%	37%	38%	38%	38%
62	2.7	4.6	5.9	7.3	8.2	8.7	8.7	10.	11.
62	37%	38%	37%	39%	40%	41%	41%	40%	37%
61	3.2	5.2	6.5	7.9	8.6	9.5	9.5	11.	12.
61	38%	40%	39%	40%	40%	41%	41%	41%	37%
60	3.8	5.6	7.0	8.4	8.5	9.3	10.	11.	11.
60	40%	40%	40%	41%	40%	40%	41%	40%	40%
59	4.5	6.5	7.7	8.5	9.3	10.	11.	11.	12.
59	38%	40%	39%	40%	41%	41%	41%	41%	37%
58	5.2	7.1	8.4	9.3	10.	11.	11.	12.	13.
58	37%	38%	37%	39%	40%	41%	41%	41%	37%
57	6.2	8.0	8.6	10.	11.	11.	12.	13.	14.
57	35%	37%	37%	36%	37%	37%	38%	38%	38%
56	7.1	8.7	9.5	11.	11.	12.	12.	14.	15.
56	36%	35%	38%	38%	37%	37%	38%	40%	41%
55	8.1	9.6	10.	12.	12.	13.	14.	15.	15.
55	33%	36%	35%	37%	36%	36%	37%	37%	38%

HIGH PRICE PUT TABLE

Exercise Price is **70**

Average Volatility

STOCK PRICE	\multicolumn{9}{c}{NUMBER OF MONTHS BEFORE THE OPTIONS EXPIRE}								
	1	2	3	4	5	6	7	8	9
85	0.0	0.1	0.4	0.8	1.1	1.5	1.9	2.4	2.9
85	1 %	11%	22%	27%	33%	34%	37%	38%	39%
84	0.0	0.1	0.4	0.8	1.2	1.6	1.9	2.4	3.0
84	1 %	17%	24%	32%	36%	39%	39%	39%	39%
83	0.0	0.2	0.6	1.1	1.6	2.0	2.5	3.1	3.6
83	3 %	19%	26%	33%	36%	38%	39%	39%	39%
82	0.0	0.1	0.6	1.2	1.7	2.1	2.5	3.1	3.7
82	4 %	25%	32%	36%	39%	39%	39%	39%	40%
81	0.0	0.3	0.8	1.5	2.1	2.6	3.1	3.7	4.4
81	9 %	25%	35%	39%	39%	39%	39%	39%	38%
80	0.0	0.4	1.0	1.6	2.2	2.8	3.3	3.8	4.3
80	13%	32%	39%	39%	39%	39%	39%	39%	40%
79	0.0	0.6	1.4	2.2	2.8	3.4	3.9	4.5	5.1
79	19%	35%	38%	39%	39%	39%	39%	38%	38%
78	0.1	0.8	1.5	2.3	2.9	3.5	3.9	4.6	5.3
78	25%	39%	40%	41%	40%	39%	39%	39%	40%
77	0.3	1.3	2.1	2.9	3.6	4.2	4.6	5.4	6.1
77	30%	38%	39%	38%	39%	38%	38%	37%	35%
76	0.4	1.4	2.3	3.1	3.7	4.3	4.8	5.5	6.1
76	38%	41%	39%	40%	39%	40%	40%	39%	37%
75	0.8	1.9	2.9	3.7	4.4	5.1	5.6	6.3	7.0
75	39%	39%	38%	36%	37%	36%	36%	34%	34%
74	0.9	2.1	3.0	3.9	4.6	5.2	5.7	6.3	7.0
74	41%	39%	39%	40%	38%	38%	38%	38%	40%
73	1.5	2.7	3.7	4.6	5.4	6.1	6.5	7.1	7.8
73	39%	36%	35%	35%	36%	34%	34%	36%	38%
72	1.7	3.0	4.0	4.9	5.6	6.2	6.7	7.3	8.0
72	39%	39%	36%	38%	40%	39%	40%	41%	40%
71	2.3	3.7	4.6	5.6	6.2	6.8	7.4	8.0	8.6
71	36%	35%	35%	38%	39%	40%	39%	38%	39%
70	2.7	4.0	5.0	5.9	6.6	7.1	7.6	8.3	8.5
70	37%	38%	40%	42%	43%	41%	42%	43%	43%
69	3.5	4.9	5.7	6.7	7.4	8.1	8.5	8.5	9.3
69	36%	35%	35%	38%	39%	40%	39%	38%	39%
68	4.3	5.5	6.4	7.3	8.0	8.6	8.6	9.4	10.
68	39%	39%	36%	38%	40%	39%	40%	41%	40%
67	5.2	6.4	7.3	8.3	8.6	9.5	9.5	10.	11.
67	39%	36%	35%	35%	36%	34%	34%	36%	38%
66	6.1	7.3	8.2	8.8	9.6	9.6	10.	11.	12.
66	41%	39%	39%	40%	38%	38%	38%	38%	40%
65	7.2	8.3	8.9	9.7	10.	11.	11.	12.	12.
65	39%	39%	38%	36%	37%	36%	36%	34%	34%

High Volatility

STOCK PRICE	\multicolumn{9}{c}{NUMBER OF MONTHS BEFORE THE OPTIONS EXPIRE}								
	1	2	3	4	5	6	7	8	9
85	0.1	1.1	2.0	3.3	4.2	4.9	5.7	6.9	8.1
85	12%	25%	32%	32%	32%	33%	33%	33%	33%
84	0.2	1.2	2.1	3.4	4.3	5.1	5.9	6.9	8.0
84	15%	30%	32%	34%	34%	34%	34%	35%	35%
83	0.2	1.4	2.6	4.0	5.0	5.8	6.7	7.8	9.1
83	22%	33%	32%	32%	32%	34%	34%	34%	34%
82	0.2	1.6	2.8	4.2	5.1	6.0	6.8	7.8	9.1
82	23%	32%	33%	33%	34%	34%	36%	35%	35%
81	0.4	1.9	3.2	4.8	5.9	6.7	7.5	8.6	9.8
81	25%	32%	32%	33%	34%	35%	35%	35%	35%
80	0.5	2.1	3.4	4.9	6.1	6.8	7.6	8.8	9.7
80	30%	34%	34%	35%	35%	35%	35%	36%	36%
79	0.8	2.5	4.0	5.6	6.7	7.5	8.4	9.5	10.
79	33%	33%	34%	35%	35%	36%	35%	35%	34%
78	0.9	2.9	4.3	5.8	7.0	7.7	8.6	9.4	10.
78	33%	35%	35%	35%	36%	36%	36%	36%	37%
77	1.4	3.4	4.9	6.5	7.6	8.5	9.3	10.	11.
77	33%	35%	35%	35%	36%	35%	34%	35%	37%
76	1.5	3.6	5.1	6.7	7.8	8.6	9.2	10.	11.
76	35%	35%	35%	37%	38%	37%	37%	38%	38%
75	2.0	4.3	5.9	7.5	8.6	9.1	10.	10.	12.
75	34%	35%	37%	37%	38%	37%	37%	38%	38%
74	2.4	4.6	6.2	7.7	8.8	8.9	9.8	10.	12.
74	36%	38%	39%	37%	37%	40%	39%	40%	40%
73	3.0	5.4	6.9	8.5	8.8	9.7	10.	12.	13.
73	34%	37%	38%	37%	37%	39%	39%	38%	38%
72	3.4	5.7	7.2	8.7	9.6	10.	11.	12.	13.
72	36%	40%	39%	40%	41%	40%	40%	40%	37%
71	3.9	6.3	7.8	9.4	10.	11.	12.	12.	13.
71	38%	39%	40%	40%	40%	40%	40%	37%	38%
70	4.5	6.8	8.2	9.3	10.	11.	11.	13.	14.
70	41%	40%	40%	40%	40%	41%	41%	41%	40%
69	5.1	7.5	8.5	10.	11.	11.	12.	14.	15.
69	38%	39%	40%	40%	40%	40%	40%	37%	38%
68	5.9	8.1	9.4	11.	11.	12.	13.	14.	16.
68	36%	40%	39%	40%	41%	40%	40%	40%	37%
67	6.9	8.6	10.	11.	12.	13.	14.	15.	16.
67	34%	37%	38%	37%	37%	39%	39%	38%	38%
66	7.7	9.6	11.	12.	13.	14.	15.	16.	17.
66	36%	38%	39%	37%	37%	40%	39%	40%	40%
65	8.7	10.	12.	13.	14.	15.	16.	16.	18.
65	34%	35%	37%	37%	38%	37%	37%	38%	38%

HIGH PRICE PUT TABLE

Exercise Price is **80**

Average Volatility

STOCK PRICE — NUMBER OF MONTHS BEFORE THE OPTIONS EXPIRE

STOCK PRICE	1	2	3	4	5	6	7	8	9
95	0.0	0.3	0.7	1.3	1.9	2.4	2.9	3.5	4.2
95	4 %	20%	25%	32%	35%	38%	39%	39%	38%
94	0.0	0.2	0.7	1.3	1.8	2.3	2.8	3.4	4.1
94	4 %	22%	33%	36%	39%	39%	39%	39%	39%
93	0.0	0.3	0.9	1.7	2.3	2.9	3.5	4.1	4.9
93	6 %	25%	34%	36%	38%	39%	39%	39%	38%
92	0.0	0.4	1.1	1.8	2.5	3.1	3.6	4.2	4.9
92	10%	28%	36%	40%	39%	39%	39%	39%	40%
91	0.0	0.6	1.4	2.3	3.0	3.6	4.2	4.9	5.7
91	17%	32%	38%	38%	38%	39%	39%	39%	38%
90	0.1	0.8	1.6	2.4	3.1	3.8	4.3	4.8	5.6
90	21%	38%	39%	39%	39%	39%	39%	39%	39%
89	0.2	1.2	2.0	3.0	3.7	4.4	5.0	5.6	6.6
89	24%	38%	39%	38%	38%	38%	39%	38%	36%
88	0.3	1.3	2.1	3.1	3.9	4.5	5.0	5.7	6.7
88	32%	39%	40%	40%	39%	39%	39%	40%	37%
87	0.6	1.8	2.7	3.7	4.6	5.2	5.9	6.6	7.5
87	35%	38%	39%	38%	36%	36%	36%	36%	35%
86	0.7	2.0	2.9	3.9	4.7	5.4	6.0	6.7	7.5
86	39%	40%	39%	39%	39%	39%	39%	38%	36%
85	1.1	2.5	3.6	4.6	5.5	6.2	6.8	7.5	8.3
85	39%	38%	36%	36%	34%	34%	34%	35%	34%
84	1.3	2.7	3.7	4.8	5.6	6.3	6.8	7.4	8.3
84	41%	39%	39%	39%	39%	38%	38%	41%	39%
83	1.9	3.4	4.4	5.6	6.5	7.2	7.6	8.4	8.8
83	38%	36%	35%	36%	35%	35%	36%	38%	38%
82	2.1	3.7	4.7	5.8	6.7	7.3	7.8	8.5	8.7
82	42%	36%	36%	39%	38%	39%	40%	40%	38%
81	2.7	4.3	5.4	6.5	7.4	8.0	8.6	8.6	9.4
81	36%	35%	37%	38%	39%	39%	39%	38%	39%
80	3.1	4.7	5.7	6.8	7.6	8.3	8.5	9.3	10.
80	37%	39%	40%	42%	42%	41%	43%	44%	45%
79	3.9	5.5	6.5	7.7	8.5	8.5	9.3	10.	11.
79	36%	35%	37%	38%	39%	39%	39%	38%	39%
78	4.6	6.2	7.2	8.2	8.6	9.4	9.4	10.	11.
78	42%	36%	36%	39%	38%	39%	40%	40%	38%
77	5.6	7.0	8.0	8.7	9.5	10.	11.	11.	12.
77	38%	36%	35%	36%	35%	35%	36%	38%	38%
76	6.5	7.9	8.8	9.6	10.	11.	11.	12.	12.
76	41%	39%	39%	39%	39%	38%	38%	41%	39%
75	7.5	8.9	9.7	10.	11.	12.	12.	12.	13.
75	39%	38%	36%	36%	34%	34%	34%	35%	34%

High Volatility

STOCK PRICE — NUMBER OF MONTHS BEFORE THE OPTIONS EXPIRE

STOCK PRICE	1	2	3	4	5	6	7	8	9
95	0.3	1.7	2.9	4.5	5.7	6.7	7.6	8.8	10.
95	21%	32%	33%	32%	33%	33%	34%	34%	35%
94	0.3	1.7	3.0	4.6	5.7	6.7	7.6	8.8	9.9
94	24%	33%	35%	35%	36%	36%	37%	35%	35%
93	0.4	2.1	3.6	5.4	6.7	7.7	8.5	9.8	10.
93	24%	32%	33%	33%	34%	34%	34%	35%	36%
92	0.6	2.4	3.9	5.5	6.8	7.7	8.6	9.7	10.
92	26%	32%	34%	35%	35%	35%	35%	35%	35%
91	0.7	2.8	4.4	6.2	7.5	8.5	9.4	10.	11.
91	32%	32%	32%	35%	35%	35%	35%	35%	34%
90	0.9	2.9	4.5	6.4	7.6	8.6	9.5	10.	11.
90	33%	35%	36%	35%	35%	37%	36%	37%	36%
89	1.2	3.4	5.2	7.0	8.4	9.4	10.	11.	12.
89	33%	32%	35%	36%	35%	35%	36%	34%	36%
88	1.4	3.8	5.5	7.3	8.6	9.3	10.	11.	13.
88	34%	35%	35%	37%	35%	36%	36%	37%	38%
87	1.9	4.3	6.1	8.0	9.2	10.	11.	12.	13.
87	33%	35%	34%	36%	36%	35%	37%	37%	38%
86	2.1	4.6	6.3	8.2	9.1	10.	10.	11.	13.
86	36%	36%	38%	38%	38%	38%	38%	38%	40%
85	2.7	5.3	7.1	9.0	9.9	10.	11.	13.	14.
85	35%	35%	37%	37%	37%	37%	39%	39%	38%
84	3.0	5.6	7.3	8.9	9.8	10.	11.	13.	14.
84	35%	37%	40%	38%	38%	39%	41%	40%	40%
83	3.7	6.4	8.2	9.7	10.	12.	13.	14.	15.
83	34%	37%	37%	37%	38%	39%	38%	38%	37%
82	4.0	6.7	8.4	9.5	11.	12.	13.	13.	15.
82	38%	40%	40%	40%	41%	40%	40%	39%	38%
81	4.6	7.3	8.6	10.	12.	12.	13.	15.	16.
81	39%	41%	41%	40%	40%	41%	40%	37%	39%
80	5.1	7.8	9.3	11.	11.	12.	13.	15.	17.
80	40%	40%	40%	40%	40%	40%	40%	40%	40%
79	5.8	8.5	10.	11.	12.	13.	14.	16.	17.
79	39%	41%	41%	40%	40%	41%	40%	37%	39%
78	6.6	8.6	10.	11.	13.	14.	15.	16.	17.
78	38%	40%	40%	40%	41%	40%	40%	39%	38%
77	7.5	9.5	11.	12.	14.	15.	16.	17.	18.
77	34%	37%	37%	37%	38%	39%	38%	38%	37%
76	8.4	10.	12.	13.	15.	16.	16.	17.	19.
76	35%	37%	40%	38%	38%	39%	41%	40%	40%
75	8.9	11.	12.	14.	16.	16.	17.	19.	20.
75	35%	35%	37%	37%	37%	37%	39%	39%	38%

HIGH PRICE PUT TABLE

Exercise Price is (90)

Average Volatility

STOCK PRICE	1	2	3	4	5	6	7	8	9
	NUMBER OF MONTHS BEFORE THE OPTIONS EXPIRE								
105	0.0	0.2	0.8	1.7	2.4	3.1	3.7	4.5	5.3
105	3 %	23%	30%	38%	39%	40%	40%	42%	41%
104	0.0	0.5	1.3	2.2	3.1	3.7	4.4	5.3	6.1
104	6 %	24%	28%	34%	36%	38%	38%	38%	36%
103	0.0	0.5	1.3	2.3	3.1	3.7	4.4	5.1	6.0
103	9 %	27%	39%	41%	42%	42%	42%	42%	42%
102	0.0	0.8	1.8	2.8	3.8	4.6	5.2	6.0	6.8
102	13%	28%	35%	37%	39%	38%	39%	36%	37%
101	0.0	0.9	1.9	3.0	3.9	4.5	5.2	6.0	6.8
101	18%	39%	41%	42%	41%	41%	41%	42%	41%
100	0.2	1.5	2.5	3.6	4.6	5.3	6.0	6.7	7.6
100	25%	36%	39%	38%	38%	37%	36%	37%	33%
99	0.3	1.4	2.5	3.7	4.5	5.3	5.8	6.7	7.6
99	27%	43%	44%	42%	42%	42%	43%	42%	39%
98	0.6	2.1	3.2	4.4	5.4	6.0	6.7	7.5	8.6
98	33%	40%	40%	36%	33%	36%	33%	35%	34%
97	0.8	2.2	3.3	4.5	5.4	6.2	6.8	7.6	8.6
97	40%	42%	43%	40%	40%	38%	38%	38%	36%
96	1.1	2.8	4.0	5.2	6.2	7.0	7.7	8.5	9.0
96	39%	41%	37%	33%	34%	33%	35%	35%	38%
95	1.4	3.0	4.2	5.3	6.3	7.0	7.7	8.5	8.9
95	44%	42%	42%	37%	36%	37%	38%	39%	40%
94	1.9	3.6	4.8	6.2	7.1	7.9	8.6	8.8	9.7
94	41%	33%	34%	35%	36%	36%	38%	37%	37%
93	2.1	3.8	5.0	6.3	7.2	7.9	8.6	8.7	9.6
93	44%	40%	36%	39%	41%	41%	41%	42%	42%
92	2.6	4.5	5.8	7.0	8.0	8.6	9.5	9.5	11.
92	34%	34%	36%	38%	40%	40%	40%	41%	43%
91	3.0	4.8	6.1	7.3	8.3	8.5	9.4	10.	11.
91	36%	39%	41%	42%	43%	42%	43%	43%	44%
90	3.7	5.6	6.8	8.1	8.5	9.3	10.	11.	11.
90	34%	40%	41%	42%	42%	41%	40%	41%	42%
89	4.3	6.2	7.3	8.5	9.4	10.	10.	11.	12.
89	36%	39%	41%	42%	43%	42%	43%	43%	44%
88	5.3	7.0	8.3	9.4	10.	11.	11.	12.	13.
88	34%	34%	36%	38%	40%	40%	40%	41%	43%
87	6.1	7.8	8.7	9.5	10.	11.	12.	12.	13.
87	44%	40%	36%	39%	41%	41%	41%	42%	42%
86	7.1	8.8	9.6	10.	12.	12.	12.	13.	15.
86	41%	33%	34%	35%	36%	36%	38%	37%	37%
85	8.0	9.0	10.	11.	12.	13.	13.	14.	15.
85	44%	42%	42%	37%	36%	37%	38%	39%	40%

High Volatility

STOCK PRICE	1	2	3	4	5	6	7	8	9
	NUMBER OF MONTHS BEFORE THE OPTIONS EXPIRE								
105	0.3	2.2	4.0	6.0	7.4	8.5	9.4	10.	11.
105	19%	33%	35%	32%	32%	33%	34%	36%	35%
104	0.6	2.7	4.6	6.6	8.1	9.1	9.8	11.	12.
104	24%	31%	32%	33%	31%	33%	34%	34%	33%
103	0.7	2.9	4.7	6.8	8.2	9.3	9.7	11.	12.
103	27%	35%	35%	33%	34%	35%	36%	36%	36%
102	1.0	3.4	5.4	7.6	8.9	9.6	10.	12.	14.
102	29%	31%	32%	31%	33%	35%	35%	33%	35%
101	1.1	3.7	5.6	7.7	9.2	9.5	10.	12.	14.
101	35%	35%	32%	33%	35%	35%	38%	36%	37%
100	1.5	4.2	6.3	8.4	9.4	10.	11.	13.	15.
100	34%	32%	31%	32%	35%	35%	37%	36%	33%
99	1.6	4.4	6.4	8.6	9.3	11.	12.	13.	14.
99	37%	35%	34%	35%	37%	37%	39%	37%	36%
98	2.2	5.0	7.2	9.2	10.	12.	12.	13.	15.
98	35%	32%	31%	37%	35%	35%	35%	34%	36%
97	2.4	5.4	7.4	9.1	10.	11.	12.	14.	15.
97	36%	33%	36%	38%	40%	37%	35%	39%	38%
96	2.9	6.0	8.1	9.9	11.	12.	13.	15.	17.
96	33%	33%	35%	37%	36%	35%	35%	38%	38%
95	3.3	6.2	8.3	9.8	11.	12.	13.	15.	17.
95	36%	36%	39%	37%	35%	36%	39%	39%	40%
94	3.9	7.1	8.8	10.	12.	13.	15.	15.	17.
94	33%	35%	39%	34%	35%	35%	38%	37%	38%
93	4.2	7.3	8.7	11.	12.	14.	14.	16.	17.
93	35%	40%	41%	37%	38%	40%	40%	40%	40%
92	4.8	7.9	9.5	12.	13.	14.	15.	17.	19.
92	34%	40%	35%	37%	38%	38%	40%	40%	37%
91	5.3	8.5	10.	12.	13.	14.	15.	17.	18.
91	38%	42%	37%	40%	42%	41%	42%	40%	35%
90	6.0	8.5	11.	12.	14.	15.	17.	18.	19.
90	42%	36%	37%	39%	40%	40%	40%	36%	35%
89	6.7	9.4	11.	13.	15.	16.	16.	18.	20.
89	38%	42%	37%	40%	42%	41%	42%	40%	35%
88	7.5	10.	11.	14.	16.	16.	17.	19.	21.
88	34%	40%	35%	37%	38%	38%	40%	40%	37%
87	8.4	11.	12.	15.	16.	17.	18.	20.	21.
87	35%	40%	41%	37%	38%	40%	40%	40%	40%
86	8.8	12.	13.	16.	17.	18.	19.	21.	22.
86	33%	35%	39%	34%	35%	35%	38%	37%	38%
85	9.8	13.	14.	17.	17.	18.	20.	21.	22.
85	36%	36%	39%	37%	35%	36%	39%	39%	40%

HIGH PRICE PUT TABLE

Exercise Price is (100)

Average Volatility

STOCK PRICE — NUMBER OF MONTHS BEFORE THE OPTIONS EXPIRE

	1	2	3	4	5	6	7	8	9
115	0.0	0.5	1.4	2.4	3.3	4.1	4.7	5.6	6.5
115	8 %	27%	38%	40%	42%	42%	42%	42%	42%
114	0.0	0.9	1.9	3.0	3.9	4.8	5.5	6.5	7.2
114	9 %	27%	33%	36%	39%	37%	40%	36%	38%
113	0.0	0.9	2.0	3.0	4.0	4.8	5.4	6.4	7.2
113	15%	35%	40%	42%	41%	42%	42%	42%	42%
112	0.1	1.4	2.4	3.7	4.8	5.6	6.2	7.1	8.2
112	18%	33%	38%	38%	37%	37%	38%	37%	33%
111	0.2	1.4	2.6	3.8	4.9	5.6	6.2	7.2	8.2
111	26%	41%	42%	41%	41%	42%	43%	41%	38%
110	0.5	2.0	3.1	4.5	5.6	6.4	7.0	8.0	9.0
110	27%	36%	40%	38%	36%	34%	37%	33%	33%
109	0.6	2.0	3.2	4.5	5.5	6.3	7.0	7.9	8.9
109	37%	44%	42%	42%	41%	42%	43%	41%	37%
108	1.0	2.6	3.9	5.3	6.3	7.1	7.8	8.9	9.1
108	37%	40%	38%	35%	35%	34%	34%	33%	35%
107	1.1	2.8	4.1	5.4	6.4	7.3	7.9	9.0	10.
107	41%	42%	42%	40%	39%	37%	38%	37%	39%
106	1.6	3.4	4.7	6.1	7.2	8.1	8.8	9.9	10.
106	41%	39%	33%	33%	33%	35%	35%	38%	37%
105	1.7	3.6	4.9	6.2	7.3	8.2	8.8	9.8	10.
105	43%	42%	38%	37%	36%	37%	37%	39%	40%
104	2.3	4.3	5.6	7.0	8.2	8.8	9.7	10.	11.
104	41%	32%	33%	36%	35%	37%	37%	38%	38%
103	2.6	4.5	5.8	7.1	8.3	8.7	9.6	10.	11.
103	43%	38%	36%	40%	43%	42%	42%	42%	42%
102	3.2	5.2	6.5	7.9	8.6	9.5	10.	11.	12.
102	36%	34%	36%	41%	41%	41%	41%	42%	41%
101	3.6	5.4	6.9	8.3	8.5	9.4	10.	11.	12.
101	36%	39%	41%	42%	42%	43%	45%	42%	44%
100	4.2	6.2	7.6	8.5	10.	11.	11.	12.	13.
100	35%	40%	41%	41%	42%	41%	41%	41%	42%
99	4.7	6.8	8.1	9.4	10.	11.	11.	12.	13.
99	36%	39%	41%	42%	42%	43%	45%	42%	44%
98	5.7	7.7	8.6	10.	11.	11.	11.	13.	15.
98	36%	34%	36%	41%	41%	41%	41%	42%	41%
97	6.5	8.4	9.5	10.	12.	12.	12.	14.	15.
97	43%	38%	36%	40%	43%	42%	42%	42%	42%
96	7.5	8.8	10.	11.	12.	13.	14.	15.	16.
96	41%	32%	33%	36%	35%	37%	37%	38%	38%
95	8.4	9.8	11.	12.	13.	13.	14.	15.	17.
95	43%	42%	38%	37%	36%	37%	37%	39%	40%

High Volatility

STOCK PRICE — NUMBER OF MONTHS BEFORE THE OPTIONS EXPIRE

	1	2	3	4	5	6	7	8	9
115	0.7	3.1	5.1	7.4	8.9	9.7	10.	12.	14.
115	26%	33%	34%	33%	33%	34%	36%	35%	37%
114	1.0	3.6	5.7	8.0	9.6	10.	11.	13.	15.
114	26%	31%	32%	31%	33%	34%	35%	34%	35%
113	1.1	3.8	5.9	8.2	9.6	10.	11.	13.	15.
113	31%	34%	34%	34%	34%	37%	35%	36%	38%
112	1.5	4.4	6.6	8.9	10.	11.	12.	14.	16.
112	31%	32%	33%	33%	34%	35%	34%	35%	33%
111	1.6	4.7	6.8	9.1	10.	11.	13.	14.	16.
111	35%	34%	35%	36%	36%	35%	37%	38%	35%
110	2.1	5.2	7.4	9.3	11.	12.	14.	14.	17.
110	35%	32%	32%	35%	34%	35%	34%	35%	34%
109	2.3	5.4	7.6	9.2	11.	12.	13.	15.	17.
109	37%	34%	33%	37%	37%	37%	37%	35%	39%
108	2.8	6.2	8.4	10.	11.	13.	14.	16.	18.
108	35%	33%	34%	35%	36%	35%	35%	36%	36%
107	3.1	6.4	8.6	10.	12.	13.	14.	16.	18.
107	36%	34%	37%	40%	37%	35%	37%	38%	39%
106	3.6	7.1	9.0	11.	13.	14.	15.	17.	18.
106	34%	32%	37%	39%	34%	35%	35%	38%	37%
105	4.0	7.3	8.9	11.	13.	14.	16.	16.	19.
105	34%	35%	40%	38%	35%	38%	39%	40%	40%
104	4.6	8.1	9.7	12.	14.	15.	16.	18.	20.
104	31%	35%	40%	35%	35%	35%	38%	39%	38%
103	4.9	8.4	10.	12.	14.	15.	16.	18.	20.
103	36%	40%	37%	38%	39%	40%	41%	41%	40%
102	5.6	8.6	11.	13.	14.	16.	17.	19.	20.
102	35%	41%	35%	38%	38%	38%	40%	40%	36%
101	6.0	9.4	11.	13.	15.	17.	18.	19.	21.
101	38%	41%	38%	42%	42%	41%	42%	40%	35%
100	6.8	10.	11.	14.	16.	18.	17.	18.	20.
100	41%	35%	39%	40%	40%	40%	40%	36%	35%
99	7.3	10.	12.	15.	16.	17.	18.	20.	22.
99	38%	41%	38%	42%	42%	41%	42%	40%	35%
98	8.3	11.	13.	16.	17.	18.	20.	21.	23.
98	35%	41%	35%	38%	38%	38%	40%	40%	36%
97	8.7	12.	14.	16.	17.	19.	20.	21.	23.
97	36%	40%	37%	38%	39%	40%	41%	41%	40%
96	9.7	12.	15.	17.	19.	20.	21.	22.	25.
96	31%	35%	40%	35%	35%	35%	38%	39%	38%
95	10.	13.	15.	17.	19.	21.	21.	23.	25.
95	34%	35%	40%	38%	35%	38%	39%	40%	40%

THE FUTURE VALUE CALENDAR SPREAD TABLES CALL OPTIONS

Decimal to Fraction
Conversion Chart

Table Shows		Market Fraction
.1	=	1/16
.1	=	1/8
.2	=	3/16
.2	=	1/4
.3	=	5/16
.4	=	3/8
.4	=	7/16
.5	=	1/2
.6	=	9/16
.6	=	5/8
.7	=	11/16
.8	=	3/4
.8	=	13/16
.9	=	7/8
.9	=	15/16

*The Future Value Tables are generated by computer simulation. Due to the nature of the computer simulation techniques that we used there may be slight aberrations in the option prices presented. Therefore you should allow a variance of plus or minus 10% of these option prices. In a few cases, some of the less important, peripheral option prices may vary more than 10%.

T72

CALENDAR SPREAD TABLE

Call Options Exercise Price is (10)

Low Volatility

STOCK PRICE

NUMBER OF MONTHS BEFORE THE LONGER TERM OPTIONS EXPIRE

NUMBER OF MONTHS BEFORE THE SHORTER TERM OPTIONS EXPIRE

| | 3 | 4 | 5 | 6 | 7 | 8 | 9 |
	0	1	2	3	4	5	6
0	0.0	0.0	0.0	0.0	0.0	0.0	0.0
1	0.0	0.0	0.0	0.0	0.0	0.0	0.0
2	0.0	0.0	0.0	0.0	0.0	0.0	0.0
3	0.0	0.0	0.0	0.0	0.0	0.0	0.0
4	0.0	0.0	0.0	0.0	0.0	0.0	0.0
5	0.0	0.0	0.0	0.0	0.0	0.0	0.0
6	0.0	0.0	0.0	0.0	0.0	0.0	0.0
7	0.0	0.0	0.0	0.0	0.0	0.0	0.0
8	0.0	0.0	0.0	0.0	0.0	0.0	0.0
9	0.1	0.1	0.1	0.1	0.2	0.2	0.1
10	0.5	0.4	0.4	0.4	0.4	0.3	0.3
11	0.2	0.2	0.2	0.3	0.2	0.2	0.2
12	0.1	0.1	0.1	0.1	0.1	0.1	0.2
13	0.1	0.1	0.1	0.1	0.1	0.2	0.2
14	0.1	0.1	0.1	0.1	0.1	0.2	0.2
15	0.1	0.1	0.1	0.1	0.1	0.1	0.1

Average Volatility

STOCK PRICE

NUMBER OF MONTHS BEFORE THE LONGER TERM OPTIONS EXPIRE

NUMBER OF MONTHS BEFORE THE SHORTER TERM OPTIONS EXPIRE

| | 3 | 4 | 5 | 6 | 7 | 8 | 9 |
	0	1	2	3	4	5	6
0	0.0	0.0	0.0	0.0	0.0	0.0	0.0
1	0.0	0.0	0.0	0.0	0.0	0.0	0.0
2	0.0	0.0	0.0	0.0	0.0	0.0	0.0
3	0.0	0.0	0.0	0.0	0.0	0.0	0.0
4	0.0	0.0	0.0	0.0	0.0	0.0	0.0
5	0.0	0.0	0.0	0.0	0.0	0.0	0.0
6	0.0	0.0	0.0	0.0	0.0	0.0	0.0
7	0.0	0.0	0.0	0.0	0.0	0.0	0.0
8	0.0	0.0	0.0	0.0	0.0	0.0	0.0
9	0.3	0.3	0.3	0.3	0.2	0.2	0.2
10	0.7	0.5	0.5	0.4	0.4	0.4	0.4
11	0.2	0.3	0.3	0.3	0.3	0.3	0.3
12	0.1	0.1	0.1	0.2	0.2	0.2	0.2
13	0.1	0.1	0.1	0.2	0.2	0.2	0.2
14	0.1	0.1	0.1	0.2	0.2	0.2	0.2
15	0.1	0.1	0.1	0.2	0.3	0.3	0.3

High Volatility

STOCK PRICE

NUMBER OF MONTHS BEFORE THE LONGER TERM OPTIONS EXPIRE

NUMBER OF MONTHS BEFORE THE SHORTER TERM OPTIONS EXPIRE

| | 3 | 4 | 5 | 6 | 7 | 8 | 9 |
	0	1	2	3	4	5	6
0	0.0	0.0	0.0	0.0	0.0	0.0	0.0
1	0.0	0.0	0.0	0.0	0.0	0.0	0.0
2	0.0	0.0	0.0	0.0	0.0	0.0	0.0
3	0.0	0.0	0.0	0.0	0.0	0.0	0.0
4	0.0	0.0	0.0	0.0	0.0	0.0	0.0
5	0.0	0.0	0.0	0.0	0.0	0.0	0.0
6	0.0	0.0	0.0	0.0	0.0	0.0	0.0
7	0.0	0.0	0.0	0.0	0.0	0.0	0.0
8	0.0	0.1	0.1	0.1	0.1	0.1	0.1
9	0.4	0.3	0.3	0.2	0.2	0.3	0.2
10	0.8	0.5	0.4	0.4	0.4	0.4	0.3
11	0.2	0.4	0.3	0.3	0.3	0.3	0.3
12	0.1	0.2	0.2	0.2	0.2	0.2	0.2
13	0.1	0.2	0.2	0.2	0.2	0.2	0.2
14	0.1	0.2	0.2	0.2	0.2	0.3	0.3
15	0.1	0.2	0.3	0.3	0.3	0.3	0.3

CALENDAR SPREAD TABLE
Call Options

Exercise Price is 15

Low Volatility

STOCK PRICE

NUMBER OF MONTHS BEFORE THE LONGER TERM OPTIONS EXPIRE

NUMBER OF MONTHS BEFORE THE SHORTER TERM OPTIONS EXPIRE

STOCK PRICE	3 / 0	4 / 1	5 / 2	6 / 3	7 / 4	8 / 5	9 / 6
5	0.0	0.0	0.0	0.0	0.0	0.0	0.0
6	0.0	0.0	0.0	0.0	0.0	0.0	0.0
7	0.0	0.0	0.0	0.0	0.0	0.0	0.0
8	0.0	0.0	0.0	0.0	0.0	0.0	0.0
9	0.0	0.0	0.0	0.0	0.0	0.0	0.0
10	0.0	0.0	0.0	0.0	0.0	0.0	0.0
11	0.0	0.0	0.0	0.0	0.0	0.0	0.0
12	0.0	0.0	0.0	0.0	0.0	0.0	0.1
13	0.0	0.1	0.1	0.1	0.1	0.1	0.1
14	0.4	0.4	0.4	0.4	0.4	0.4	0.4
15	0.8	0.7	0.6	0.6	0.5	0.5	0.5
16	0.5	0.5	0.5	0.5	0.5	0.5	0.4
17	0.3	0.3	0.3	0.3	0.3	0.3	0.3
18	0.1	0.2	0.2	0.3	0.3	0.3	0.3
19	0.1	0.2	0.2	0.2	0.2	0.2	0.3
20	0.1	0.2	0.2	0.2	0.2	0.2	0.3

Average Volatility

STOCK PRICE

NUMBER OF MONTHS BEFORE THE LONGER TERM OPTIONS EXPIRE

NUMBER OF MONTHS BEFORE THE SHORTER TERM OPTIONS EXPIRE

STOCK PRICE	3 / 0	4 / 1	5 / 2	6 / 3	7 / 4	8 / 5	9 / 6
5	0.0	0.0	0.0	0.0	0.0	0.0	0.0
6	0.0	0.0	0.0	0.0	0.0	0.0	0.0
7	0.0	0.0	0.0	0.0	0.0	0.0	0.0
8	0.0	0.0	0.0	0.0	0.0	0.0	0.0
9	0.0	0.0	0.0	0.0	0.0	0.0	0.0
10	0.0	0.0	0.0	0.0	0.0	0.0	0.0
11	0.0	0.0	0.0	0.0	0.0	0.0	0.0
12	0.0	0.0	0.0	0.1	0.1	0.1	0.1
13	0.2	0.2	0.3	0.3	0.3	0.3	0.3
14	0.6	0.6	0.5	0.5	0.5	0.5	0.5
15	1.0	0.8	0.7	0.6	0.6	0.6	0.6
16	0.6	0.6	0.6	0.5	0.5	0.5	0.5
17	0.3	0.4	0.4	0.4	0.4	0.4	0.4
18	0.1	0.3	0.3	0.3	0.3	0.3	0.3
19	0.1	0.2	0.2	0.3	0.3	0.3	0.3
20	0.1	0.2	0.3	0.3	0.3	0.3	0.3

High Volatility

STOCK PRICE

NUMBER OF MONTHS BEFORE THE LONGER TERM OPTIONS EXPIRE

NUMBER OF MONTHS BEFORE THE SHORTER TERM OPTIONS EXPIRE

STOCK PRICE	3 / 0	4 / 1	5 / 2	6 / 3	7 / 4	8 / 5	9 / 6
5	0.0	0.0	0.0	0.0	0.0	0.0	0.0
6	0.0	0.0	0.0	0.0	0.0	0.0	0.0
7	0.0	0.0	0.0	0.0	0.0	0.0	0.0
8	0.0	0.0	0.0	0.0	0.0	0.0	0.0
9	0.0	0.0	0.0	0.0	0.0	0.0	0.0
10	0.0	0.0	0.0	0.0	0.0	0.0	0.1
11	0.0	0.0	0.1	0.1	0.1	0.1	0.1
12	0.0	0.1	0.2	0.2	0.2	0.2	0.2
13	0.4	0.4	0.4	0.3	0.3	0.3	0.3
14	0.8	0.6	0.5	0.5	0.5	0.5	0.5
15	1.2	0.7	0.6	0.6	0.5	0.5	0.5
16	0.6	0.6	0.5	0.5	0.5	0.5	0.5
17	0.3	0.4	0.4	0.4	0.4	0.4	0.4
18	0.1	0.3	0.4	0.4	0.4	0.4	0.4
19	0.1	0.3	0.3	0.4	0.4	0.4	0.4
20	0.1	0.2	0.3	0.4	0.4	0.4	0.4

CALENDAR SPREAD TABLE

Call Options

Exercise Price is (20)

Low Volatility

STOCK PRICE	NUMBER OF MONTHS BEFORE THE LONGER TERM OPTIONS EXPIRE						
	3	4	5	6	7	8	9
	NUMBER OF MONTHS BEFORE THE SHORTER TERM OPTIONS EXPIRE						
	0	1	2	3	4	5	6
10	0.0	0.0	0.0	0.0	0.0	0.0	0.0
11	0.0	0.0	0.0	0.0	0.0	0.0	0.0
12	0.0	0.0	0.0	0.0	0.0	0.0	0.0
13	0.0	0.0	0.0	0.0	0.0	0.0	0.0
14	0.0	0.0	0.0	0.0	0.0	0.0	0.0
15	0.0	0.0	0.0	0.0	0.0	0.0	0.0
16	0.0	0.0	0.0	0.0	0.0	0.0	0.0
17	0.0	0.0	0.1	0.1	0.1	0.1	0.1
18	0.3	0.3	0.3	0.3	0.3	0.3	0.3
19	0.7	0.7	0.6	0.6	0.6	0.6	0.6
20	1.1	0.9	0.8	0.8	0.7	0.7	0.7
21	0.5	0.7	0.7	0.7	0.6	0.6	0.6
22	0.4	0.5	0.6	0.6	0.5	0.5	0.5
23	0.4	0.4	0.4	0.4	0.5	0.5	0.5
24	0.3	0.3	0.3	0.4	0.4	0.4	0.4
25	0.3	0.3	0.3	0.3	0.3	0.4	0.4

Average Volatility

STOCK PRICE	NUMBER OF MONTHS BEFORE THE LONGER TERM OPTIONS EXPIRE						
	3	4	5	6	7	8	9
	NUMBER OF MONTHS BEFORE THE SHORTER TERM OPTIONS EXPIRE						
	0	1	2	3	4	5	6
10	0.0	0.0	0.0	0.0	0.0	0.0	0.0
11	0.0	0.0	0.0	0.0	0.0	0.0	0.0
12	0.0	0.0	0.0	0.0	0.0	0.0	0.0
13	0.0	0.0	0.0	0.0	0.0	0.0	0.0
14	0.0	0.0	0.0	0.0	0.0	0.0	0.0
15	0.0	0.0	0.0	0.0	0.1	0.1	0.1
16	0.0	0.0	0.1	0.1	0.1	0.2	0.2
17	0.2	0.2	0.3	0.3	0.3	0.3	0.3
18	0.6	0.6	0.6	0.5	0.5	0.5	0.5
19	1.0	0.9	0.8	0.8	0.7	0.7	0.7
20	1.4	1.1	0.9	0.9	0.8	0.8	0.8
21	0.8	0.9	0.8	0.8	0.7	0.7	0.7
22	0.4	0.7	0.6	0.6	0.6	0.6	0.6
23	0.4	0.5	0.5	0.5	0.5	0.5	0.5
24	0.2	0.4	0.4	0.4	0.5	0.5	0.5
25	0.2	0.3	0.4	0.4	0.4	0.4	0.5

High Volatility

STOCK PRICE	NUMBER OF MONTHS BEFORE THE LONGER TERM OPTIONS EXPIRE						
	3	4	5	6	7	8	9
	NUMBER OF MONTHS BEFORE THE SHORTER TERM OPTIONS EXPIRE						
	0	1	2	3	4	5	6
10	0.0	0.0	0.0	0.0	0.0	0.0	0.0
11	0.0	0.0	0.0	0.0	0.0	0.0	0.0
12	0.0	0.0	0.0	0.0	0.0	0.1	0.1
13	0.0	0.0	0.0	0.1	0.1	0.1	0.1
14	0.0	0.0	0.1	0.1	0.1	0.1	0.1
15	0.0	0.1	0.1	0.2	0.2	0.2	0.2
16	0.0	0.2	0.3	0.3	0.3	0.3	0.3
17	0.4	0.4	0.4	0.4	0.4	0.4	0.4
18	0.8	0.7	0.6	0.6	0.6	0.5	0.5
19	1.2	0.9	0.8	0.7	0.7	0.6	0.6
20	1.6	1.0	0.8	0.8	0.7	0.7	0.7
21	1.0	0.9	0.7	0.7	0.7	0.6	0.6
22	0.4	0.7	0.6	0.6	0.6	0.6	0.6
23	0.5	0.6	0.6	0.5	0.5	0.5	0.5
24	0.2	0.5	0.5	0.5	0.5	0.5	0.5
25	0.2	0.4	0.5	0.5	0.5	0.5	0.5

CALENDAR SPREAD TABLE

Call Options

Exercise Price is (25)

Low Volatility

STOCK PRICE	NUMBER OF MONTHS BEFORE THE LONGER TERM OPTIONS EXPIRE						
	3	4	5	6	7	8	9
	NUMBER OF MONTHS BEFORE THE SHORTER TERM OPTIONS EXPIRE						
	0	1	2	3	4	5	6
15	0.0	0.0	0.0	0.0	0.0	0.0	0.0
16	0.0	0.0	0.0	0.0	0.0	0.0	0.0
17	0.0	0.0	0.0	0.0	0.0	0.0	0.0
18	0.0	0.0	0.0	0.0	0.0	0.0	0.0
19	0.0	0.0	0.0	0.0	0.0	0.0	0.0
20	0.0	0.0	0.0	0.0	0.0	0.1	0.1
21	0.0	0.0	0.1	0.0	0.1	0.1	0.1
22	0.2	0.2	0.3	0.3	0.3	0.3	0.3
23	0.6	0.6	0.6	0.6	0.6	0.5	0.5
24	1.0	0.9	0.9	0.8	0.8	0.8	0.7
25	1.4	1.1	1.0	0.9	0.9	0.9	0.8
26	0.8	0.9	0.9	0.9	0.8	0.8	0.8
27	0.9	0.8	0.8	0.8	0.8	0.7	0.7
28	0.5	0.6	0.6	0.6	0.6	0.6	0.6
29	0.5	0.5	0.5	0.5	0.6	0.6	0.6
30	0.3	0.4	0.4	0.5	0.5	0.5	0.5

Average Volatility

STOCK PRICE	NUMBER OF MONTHS BEFORE THE LONGER TERM OPTIONS EXPIRE						
	3	4	5	6	7	8	9
	NUMBER OF MONTHS BEFORE THE SHORTER TERM OPTIONS EXPIRE						
	0	1	2	3	4	5	6
15	0.0	0.0	0.0	0.0	0.0	0.0	0.0
16	0.0	0.0	0.0	0.0	0.0	0.0	0.0
17	0.0	0.0	0.0	0.0	0.0	0.0	0.0
18	0.0	0.0	0.0	0.0	0.0	0.1	0.1
19	0.0	0.0	0.0	0.1	0.1	0.1	0.1
20	0.0	0.1	0.1	0.2	0.2	0.2	0.2
21	0.1	0.2	0.3	0.3	0.3	0.4	0.4
22	0.5	0.6	0.6	0.6	0.5	0.6	0.5
23	0.9	0.9	0.8	0.8	0.8	0.8	0.7
24	1.3	1.2	1.1	1.0	0.9	0.9	0.9
25	1.7	1.3	1.2	1.1	1.0	1.0	1.0
26	1.1	1.1	1.1	1.0	0.9	0.9	0.9
27	1.0	0.9	0.9	0.9	0.8	0.8	0.8
28	0.5	0.7	0.7	0.7	0.7	0.7	0.7
29	0.6	0.6	0.6	0.7	0.7	0.7	0.6
30	0.3	0.5	0.5	0.6	0.6	0.6	0.6

High Volatility

STOCK PRICE	NUMBER OF MONTHS BEFORE THE LONGER TERM OPTIONS EXPIRE						
	3	4	5	6	7	8	9
	NUMBER OF MONTHS BEFORE THE SHORTER TERM OPTIONS EXPIRE						
	0	1	2	3	4	5	6
15	0.0	0.0	0.0	0.1	0.1	0.1	0.1
16	0.0	0.0	0.0	0.1	0.1	0.1	0.1
17	0.0	0.0	0.1	0.1	0.1	0.2	0.2
18	0.0	0.0	0.1	0.2	0.2	0.2	0.2
19	0.0	0.1	0.2	0.2	0.3	0.3	0.3
20	0.0	0.3	0.3	0.3	0.4	0.4	0.4
21	0.4	0.5	0.5	0.5	0.5	0.5	0.5
22	0.8	0.7	0.7	0.7	0.6	0.6	0.6
23	1.2	1.0	0.9	0.8	0.8	0.7	0.7
24	1.6	1.2	1.0	0.9	0.9	0.8	0.8
25	2.0	1.3	1.1	1.0	0.9	0.9	0.9
26	1.4	1.1	1.0	0.9	0.9	0.8	0.8
27	1.1	1.0	0.9	0.8	0.8	0.8	0.8
28	0.6	0.8	0.8	0.7	0.7	0.7	0.7
29	0.6	0.7	0.7	0.7	0.7	0.7	0.7
30	0.3	0.6	0.6	0.6	0.6	0.6	0.7

CALENDAR SPREAD TABLE

Call Options Exercise Price is (30)

Low Volatility

STOCK PRICE

NUMBER OF MONTHS BEFORE THE LONGER TERM OPTIONS EXPIRE

NUMBER OF MONTHS BEFORE THE SHORTER TERM OPTIONS EXPIRE

Longer:	3	4	5	6	7	8	9
Shorter:	0	1	2	3	4	5	6
20	0.0	0.0	0.0	0.0	0.0	0.0	0.0
21	0.0	0.0	0.0	0.0	0.0	0.0	0.0
22	0.0	0.0	0.0	0.0	0.0	0.0	0.0
23	0.0	0.0	0.0	0.0	0.0	0.0	0.0
24	0.0	0.0	0.0	0.0	0.1	0.1	0.1
25	0.0	0.0	0.1	0.1	0.1	0.2	0.2
26	0.1	0.2	0.2	0.3	0.3	0.3	0.3
27	0.5	0.5	0.5	0.5	0.5	0.5	0.5
28	0.9	0.9	0.8	0.8	0.8	0.8	0.8
29	1.3	1.2	1.1	1.0	1.0	1.0	0.9
30	1.7	1.4	1.2	1.1	1.1	1.0	1.0
31	1.1	1.2	1.1	1.1	1.0	1.0	1.0
32	1.1	1.1	1.0	1.0	0.9	0.9	0.9
33	0.6	0.8	0.9	0.9	0.8	0.8	0.8
34	0.6	0.7	0.7	0.7	0.7	0.7	0.7
35	0.6	0.6	0.6	0.6	0.7	0.7	0.7

Average Volatility

STOCK PRICE

NUMBER OF MONTHS BEFORE THE LONGER TERM OPTIONS EXPIRE

NUMBER OF MONTHS BEFORE THE SHORTER TERM OPTIONS EXPIRE

Longer:	3	4	5	6	7	8	9
Shorter:	0	1	2	3	4	5	6
20	0.0	0.0	0.0	0.0	0.0	0.0	0.0
21	0.0	0.0	0.0	0.0	0.0	0.1	0.1
22	0.0	0.0	0.0	0.1	0.1	0.1	0.1
23	0.0	0.0	0.1	0.1	0.2	0.2	0.2
24	0.0	0.1	0.2	0.2	0.3	0.3	0.3
25	0.1	0.3	0.3	0.4	0.4	0.4	0.4
26	0.5	0.6	0.6	0.6	0.6	0.6	0.6
27	0.9	0.9	0.9	0.8	0.8	0.8	0.8
28	1.3	1.2	1.1	1.1	1.0	1.0	1.0
29	1.7	1.5	1.3	1.2	1.1	1.1	1.1
30	2.1	1.6	1.4	1.3	1.2	1.2	1.1
31	1.5	1.4	1.3	1.2	1.1	1.1	1.1
32	1.2	1.2	1.2	1.1	1.0	1.0	1.0
33	0.6	1.0	1.0	1.0	0.9	0.9	0.9
34	0.6	0.8	0.9	0.9	0.8	0.8	0.8
35	0.6	0.7	0.8	0.8	0.8	0.8	0.8

High Volatility

STOCK PRICE

NUMBER OF MONTHS BEFORE THE LONGER TERM OPTIONS EXPIRE

NUMBER OF MONTHS BEFORE THE SHORTER TERM OPTIONS EXPIRE

Longer:	3	4	5	6	7	8	9
Shorter:	0	1	2	3	4	5	6
20	0.0	0.0	0.1	0.1	0.2	0.2	0.2
21	0.0	0.0	0.1	0.2	0.2	0.2	0.2
22	0.0	0.1	0.2	0.2	0.3	0.3	0.3
23	0.0	0.2	0.3	0.3	0.3	0.3	0.4
24	0.0	0.3	0.4	0.4	0.4	0.4	0.5
25	0.4	0.6	0.6	0.6	0.6	0.6	0.6
26	0.8	0.8	0.8	0.7	0.7	0.7	0.7
27	1.2	1.0	1.0	0.9	0.8	0.8	0.8
28	1.6	1.3	1.1	1.0	1.0	0.9	0.9
29	2.0	1.4	1.2	1.1	1.0	1.0	1.0
30	2.4	1.5	1.3	1.1	1.1	1.0	1.0
31	1.8	1.4	1.2	1.1	1.0	1.0	1.0
32	1.3	1.2	1.1	1.0	1.0	0.9	0.9
33	1.0	1.1	1.0	0.9	0.9	0.9	0.9
34	0.7	0.9	0.9	0.9	0.9	0.9	0.8
35	0.7	0.8	0.8	0.8	0.8	0.8	0.8

T77

CALENDAR SPREAD TABLE

Call Options

Exercise Price is 35

Low Volatility

NUMBER OF MONTHS BEFORE THE LONGER TERM OPTIONS EXPIRE

NUMBER OF MONTHS BEFORE THE SHORTER TERM OPTIONS EXPIRE

STOCK PRICE	3 / 0	4 / 1	5 / 2	6 / 3	7 / 4	8 / 5	9 / 6
25	0.0	0.0	0.0	0.0	0.0	0.0	0.0
26	0.0	0.0	0.0	0.0	0.0	0.0	0.0
27	0.0	0.0	0.0	0.0	0.0	0.0	0.1
28	0.0	0.0	0.0	0.0	0.0	0.0	0.1
29	0.0	0.0	0.0	0.0	0.1	0.1	0.1
30	0.0	0.1	0.2	0.3	0.2	0.2	0.2
31	0.4	0.4	0.5	0.5	0.5	0.5	0.5
32	0.8	0.8	0.8	0.8	0.7	0.7	0.7
33	1.2	1.1	1.1	1.0	1.0	1.0	1.0
34	1.6	1.4	1.3	1.2	1.2	1.1	1.1
35	2.0	1.6	1.4	1.3	1.2	1.2	1.2
36	1.4	1.4	1.3	1.3	1.2	1.2	1.1
37	1.3	1.3	1.2	1.2	1.1	1.1	1.1
38	1.3	1.1	1.1	1.1	1.1	1.1	1.0
39	0.7	0.9	0.9	0.9	0.9	0.9	0.9
40	0.7	0.8	0.8	0.8	0.9	0.9	0.9

Average Volatility

NUMBER OF MONTHS BEFORE THE LONGER TERM OPTIONS EXPIRE

NUMBER OF MONTHS BEFORE THE SHORTER TERM OPTIONS EXPIRE

STOCK PRICE	3 / 0	4 / 1	5 / 2	6 / 3	7 / 4	8 / 5	9 / 6
25	0.0	0.0	0.0	0.0	0.1	0.1	0.1
26	0.0	0.0	0.0	0.1	0.1	0.2	0.2
27	0.0	0.0	0.1	0.2	0.2	0.2	0.3
28	0.0	0.1	0.2	0.3	0.3	0.3	0.3
29	0.1	0.3	0.4	0.4	0.5	0.5	0.5
30	0.5	0.5	0.6	0.6	0.6	0.6	0.6
31	0.9	0.9	0.9	0.8	0.8	0.8	0.8
32	1.3	1.2	1.1	1.1	1.1	1.0	1.0
33	1.7	1.5	1.4	1.3	1.2	1.2	1.2
34	2.1	1.8	1.6	1.4	1.4	1.3	1.3
35	2.5	1.9	1.6	1.5	1.4	1.4	1.3
36	1.9	1.7	1.5	1.4	1.3	1.3	1.3
37	1.7	1.5	1.5	1.4	1.3	1.3	1.2
38	1.5	1.3	1.3	1.3	1.2	1.2	1.1
39	0.7	1.1	1.1	1.1	1.0	1.0	1.0
40	0.7	0.9	1.0	1.0	1.0	1.0	1.0

High Volatility

NUMBER OF MONTHS BEFORE THE LONGER TERM OPTIONS EXPIRE

NUMBER OF MONTHS BEFORE THE SHORTER TERM OPTIONS EXPIRE

STOCK PRICE	3 / 0	4 / 1	5 / 2	6 / 3	7 / 4	8 / 5	9 / 6
25	0.0	0.1	0.2	0.2	0.3	0.3	0.3
26	0.0	0.2	0.3	0.3	0.3	0.3	0.4
27	0.0	0.3	0.4	0.4	0.4	0.4	0.4
28	0.0	0.4	0.5	0.5	0.5	0.5	0.6
29	0.4	0.6	0.7	0.6	0.7	0.7	0.7
30	0.8	0.9	0.8	0.8	0.7	0.8	0.8
31	1.2	1.1	1.0	1.0	0.8	0.9	0.9
32	1.6	1.3	1.2	1.1	1.1	1.0	1.0
33	2.0	1.6	1.3	1.2	1.1	1.1	1.1
34	2.4	1.7	1.4	1.3	1.2	1.2	1.2
35	2.8	1.7	1.5	1.3	1.3	1.2	1.2
36	2.2	1.7	1.4	1.3	1.2	1.2	1.1
37	1.8	1.5	1.3	1.2	1.2	1.1	1.1
38	1.6	1.3	1.2	1.2	1.1	1.1	1.1
39	0.8	1.2	1.1	1.1	1.0	1.0	1.0
40	0.8	1.1	1.0	1.0	1.0	1.0	1.0

CALENDAR SPREAD TABLE

Call Options Exercise Price is (40)

Low Volatility

| STOCK PRICE | \multicolumn{7}{c}{NUMBER OF MONTHS BEFORE THE LONGER TERM OPTIONS EXPIRE} |
| | 3 | 4 | 5 | 6 | 7 | 8 | 9 |

NUMBER OF MONTHS BEFORE THE SHORTER TERM OPTIONS EXPIRE

STOCK PRICE	0	1	2	3	4	5	6
30	0.0	0.0	0.0	0.0	0.0	0.0	0.0
31	0.0	0.0	0.0	0.0	0.0	0.1	0.1
32	0.0	0.0	0.0	0.1	0.1	0.1	0.1
33	0.0	0.0	0.1	0.1	0.2	0.2	0.2
34	0.0	0.1	0.2	0.3	0.3	0.3	0.3
35	0.3	0.3	0.4	0.5	0.5	0.5	0.5
36	0.7	0.7	0.7	0.7	0.7	0.7	0.7
37	1.1	1.0	1.0	1.0	1.0	1.0	0.9
38	1.5	1.4	1.3	1.2	1.2	1.2	1.2
39	1.9	1.7	1.5	1.4	1.4	1.3	1.3
40	2.3	1.8	1.6	1.5	1.4	1.4	1.4
41	1.7	1.6	1.5	1.5	1.4	1.4	1.3
42	1.6	1.5	1.4	1.4	1.3	1.3	1.2
43	1.5	1.4	1.3	1.3	1.3	1.2	1.2
44	1.3	1.1	1.2	1.2	1.1	1.1	1.1
45	0.8	0.9	1.0	1.0	1.0	1.0	1.0

Average Volatility

| STOCK PRICE | \multicolumn{7}{c}{NUMBER OF MONTHS BEFORE THE LONGER TERM OPTIONS EXPIRE} |
| | 3 | 4 | 5 | 6 | 7 | 8 | 9 |

NUMBER OF MONTHS BEFORE THE SHORTER TERM OPTIONS EXPIRE

STOCK PRICE	0	1	2	3	4	5	6
30	0.0	0.0	0.1	0.1	0.2	0.2	0.2
31	0.0	0.0	0.1	0.2	0.3	0.3	0.3
32	0.0	0.1	0.3	0.3	0.4	0.4	0.4
33	0.0	0.3	0.4	0.5	0.5	0.5	0.5
34	0.4	0.5	0.6	0.7	0.7	0.7	0.7
35	0.8	0.9	0.9	0.9	0.9	0.9	0.9
36	1.2	1.2	1.2	1.1	1.1	1.1	1.1
37	1.6	1.5	1.4	1.4	1.3	1.3	1.2
38	2.0	1.8	1.6	1.6	1.4	1.4	1.4
39	2.4	2.1	1.8	1.6	1.5	1.5	1.5
40	2.8	2.1	1.8	1.7	1.6	1.6	1.5
41	2.2	2.0	1.8	1.7	1.5	1.5	1.5
42	1.6	1.8	1.6	1.5	1.4	1.4	1.4
43	1.6	1.6	1.5	1.4	1.4	1.3	1.3
44	0.8	1.4	1.3	1.3	1.3	1.2	1.2
45	0.7	1.1	1.2	1.2	1.2	1.1	1.1

High Volatility

| STOCK PRICE | \multicolumn{7}{c}{NUMBER OF MONTHS BEFORE THE LONGER TERM OPTIONS EXPIRE} |
| | 3 | 4 | 5 | 6 | 7 | 8 | 9 |

NUMBER OF MONTHS BEFORE THE SHORTER TERM OPTIONS EXPIRE

STOCK PRICE	0	1	2	3	4	5	6
30	0.0	0.2	0.4	0.4	0.4	0.4	0.4
31	0.0	0.3	0.5	0.5	0.5	0.5	0.5
32	0.0	0.5	0.6	0.6	0.6	0.6	0.6
33	0.4	0.7	0.7	0.7	0.8	0.8	0.8
34	0.8	0.9	0.9	0.9	0.9	0.9	0.9
35	1.2	1.2	1.1	1.1	1.0	1.0	1.0
36	1.6	1.4	1.3	1.2	1.1	1.1	1.1
37	2.0	1.6	1.4	1.3	1.3	1.2	1.2
38	2.4	1.8	1.6	1.4	1.3	1.3	1.3
39	2.8	1.9	1.6	1.5	1.4	1.4	1.3
40	3.2	2.0	1.7	1.5	1.4	1.4	1.3
41	2.6	1.9	1.6	1.5	1.4	1.3	1.3
42	2.0	1.8	1.5	1.4	1.3	1.3	1.3
43	1.7	1.6	1.4	1.4	1.3	1.2	1.2
44	0.9	1.4	1.3	1.3	1.2	1.2	1.2
45	0.9	1.3	1.2	1.2	1.2	1.2	1.1

CALENDAR SPREAD TABLE

Call Options

Exercise Price is 45

Low Volatility

STOCK PRICE	NUMBER OF MONTHS BEFORE THE LONGER TERM OPTIONS EXPIRE						
	3	4	5	6	7	8	9
	NUMBER OF MONTHS BEFORE THE SHORTER TERM OPTIONS EXPIRE						
	0	1	2	3	4	5	6
35	0.0	0.0	0.0	0.0	0.1	0.1	0.1
36	0.0	0.0	0.0	0.1	0.1	0.1	0.2
37	0.0	0.0	0.1	0.1	0.2	0.2	0.2
38	0.0	0.1	0.2	0.3	0.3	0.3	0.4
39	0.2	0.3	0.4	0.4	0.5	0.5	0.5
40	0.6	0.6	0.7	0.7	0.7	0.7	0.7
41	1.0	1.0	1.0	0.9	0.9	0.9	0.9
42	1.4	1.3	1.2	1.2	1.2	1.2	1.2
43	1.8	1.6	1.6	1.5	1.4	1.4	1.3
44	2.2	1.9	1.8	1.5	1.5	1.5	1.3
45	2.6	2.0	1.8	1.7	1.5	1.5	1.5
46	2.0	1.9	1.7	1.7	1.6	1.6	1.5
47	1.9	1.7	1.6	1.6	1.5	1.5	1.4
48	1.7	1.6	1.6	1.5	1.4	1.4	1.4
49	1.7	1.5	1.5	1.4	1.3	1.3	1.3
50	0.9	1.1	1.2	1.2	1.2	1.2	1.2

Average Volatility

STOCK PRICE	NUMBER OF MONTHS BEFORE THE LONGER TERM OPTIONS EXPIRE						
	3	4	5	6	7	8	9
	NUMBER OF MONTHS BEFORE THE SHORTER TERM OPTIONS EXPIRE						
	0	1	2	3	4	5	6
35	0.0	0.1	0.2	0.3	0.3	0.3	0.4
36	0.0	0.1	0.3	0.4	0.4	0.4	0.5
37	0.0	0.3	0.5	0.5	0.6	0.6	0.6
38	0.4	0.6	0.7	0.7	0.7	0.7	0.7
39	0.8	0.9	0.9	0.9	0.9	0.9	0.9
40	1.2	1.2	1.2	1.1	1.1	1.1	1.1
41	1.6	1.5	1.4	1.4	1.3	1.3	1.3
42	2.0	1.8	1.7	1.6	1.5	1.5	1.5
43	2.4	2.1	1.9	1.8	1.7	1.6	1.6
44	2.8	2.3	2.0	1.8	1.7	1.6	1.6
45	3.2	2.4	2.1	1.9	1.8	1.7	1.7
46	2.6	2.2	2.0	1.9	1.8	1.7	1.7
47	2.0	2.0	1.9	1.8	1.7	1.6	1.6
48	1.8	1.9	1.7	1.6	1.6	1.5	1.5
49	1.7	1.7	1.6	1.5	1.5	1.4	1.4
50	1.0	1.4	1.4	1.4	1.4	1.3	1.3

High Volatility

STOCK PRICE	NUMBER OF MONTHS BEFORE THE LONGER TERM OPTIONS EXPIRE						
	3	4	5	6	7	8	9
	NUMBER OF MONTHS BEFORE THE SHORTER TERM OPTIONS EXPIRE						
	0	1	2	3	4	5	6
35	0.0	0.4	0.5	0.6	0.6	0.6	0.6
36	0.0	0.5	0.6	0.7	0.7	0.7	0.7
37	0.4	0.8	0.8	0.8	0.8	0.8	0.8
38	0.8	1.0	1.0	1.0	1.0	1.0	1.0
39	1.2	1.2	1.1	1.2	1.1	1.1	1.1
40	1.6	1.5	1.3	1.3	1.2	1.2	1.2
41	2.0	1.7	1.5	1.4	1.3	1.3	1.3
42	2.4	1.9	1.7	1.6	1.4	1.4	1.3
43	2.8	2.1	1.8	1.7	1.5	1.5	1.4
44	3.2	2.2	1.9	1.7	1.6	1.5	1.5
45	3.6	2.2	1.9	1.7	1.6	1.6	1.5
46	3.0	2.2	1.8	1.7	1.6	1.6	1.5
47	2.4	2.0	1.7	1.6	1.5	1.5	1.5
48	2.0	1.9	1.7	1.5	1.5	1.4	1.4
49	2.0	1.7	1.6	1.5	1.4	1.4	1.4
50	1.0	1.5	1.4	1.4	1.3	1.3	1.3

CALENDAR SPREAD TABLE

Call Options

Exercise Price is 50

Low Volatility

STOCK PRICE	NUMBER OF MONTHS BEFORE THE LONGER TERM OPTIONS EXPIRE						
	3	4	5	6	7	8	9
	NUMBER OF MONTHS BEFORE THE SHORTER TERM OPTIONS EXPIRE						
	0	1	2	3	4	5	6
35	0.0	0.0	0.0	0.0	0.0	0.0	0.0
36	0.0	0.0	0.0	0.0	0.0	0.0	0.0
37	0.0	0.0	0.0	0.0	0.0	0.0	0.0
38	0.0	0.0	0.0	0.0	0.0	0.0	0.1
39	0.0	0.0	0.0	0.0	0.1	0.1	0.1
40	0.0	0.0	0.0	0.1	0.2	0.1	0.2
41	0.0	0.0	0.1	0.1	0.3	0.2	0.3
42	0.0	0.1	0.2	0.3	0.4	0.4	0.4
43	0.0	0.2	0.4	0.4	0.5	0.5	0.5
44	0.4	0.5	0.7	0.6	0.8	0.8	0.7
45	0.8	0.9	1.0	0.9	1.0	1.0	0.9
46	1.2	1.3	1.3	1.1	1.2	1.2	1.1
47	1.6	1.6	1.5	1.4	1.5	1.4	1.4
48	2.0	2.0	1.7	1.6	1.7	1.6	1.6
49	2.4	2.2	1.9	1.8	1.8	1.7	1.8
50	2.8	2.3	2.0	1.9	1.9	1.7	1.8
51	2.2	2.1	2.0	1.9	1.8	1.7	1.8
52	2.0	1.9	1.8	1.8	1.7	1.7	1.7
53	1.8	1.8	1.8	1.8	1.7	1.7	1.6
54	1.9	1.7	1.7	1.7	1.6	1.6	1.5
55	1.1	1.4	1.4	1.5	1.4	1.4	1.4

Average Volatility

STOCK PRICE	NUMBER OF MONTHS BEFORE THE LONGER TERM OPTIONS EXPIRE						
	3	4	5	6	7	8	9
	NUMBER OF MONTHS BEFORE THE SHORTER TERM OPTIONS EXPIRE						
	0	1	2	3	4	5	6
35	0.0	0.0	0.0	0.0	0.1	0.1	0.1
36	0.0	0.0	0.0	0.1	0.1	0.1	0.2
37	0.0	0.0	0.0	0.1	0.2	0.2	0.2
38	0.0	0.0	0.1	0.2	0.2	0.3	0.3
39	0.0	0.1	0.2	0.2	0.3	0.4	0.4
40	0.0	0.1	0.3	0.4	0.4	0.5	0.5
41	0.0	0.3	0.4	0.5	0.6	0.6	0.6
42	0.3	0.5	0.7	0.7	0.8	0.8	0.8
43	0.7	0.8	0.9	0.9	1.0	0.9	1.0
44	1.1	1.2	1.2	1.2	1.2	1.2	1.2
45	1.5	1.5	1.5	1.4	1.4	1.4	1.4
46	1.9	1.8	1.7	1.7	1.6	1.6	1.6
47	2.3	2.2	2.0	1.9	1.8	1.8	1.7
48	2.7	2.5	2.2	2.1	2.0	1.9	1.9
49	3.1	2.7	2.4	2.2	2.1	2.0	2.0
50	3.5	2.7	2.4	2.2	2.1	2.0	2.0
51	2.9	2.6	2.3	2.2	2.1	2.0	2.0
52	2.3	2.3	2.2	2.1	1.9	1.9	1.9
53	2.0	2.2	2.0	1.9	1.8	1.8	1.8
54	2.1	2.0	1.9	1.8	1.8	1.7	1.7
55	1.1	1.7	1.7	1.7	1.6	1.6	1.6

High Volatility

STOCK PRICE	NUMBER OF MONTHS BEFORE THE LONGER TERM OPTIONS EXPIRE						
	3	4	5	6	7	8	9
	NUMBER OF MONTHS BEFORE THE SHORTER TERM OPTIONS EXPIRE						
	0	1	2	3	4	5	6
35	0.0	0.1	0.2	0.3	0.4	0.4	0.4
36	0.0	0.1	0.3	0.4	0.4	0.4	0.4
37	0.0	0.2	0.3	0.4	0.5	0.5	0.5
38	0.0	0.3	0.4	0.5	0.6	0.6	0.6
39	0.0	0.4	0.5	0.6	0.6	0.7	0.7
40	0.0	0.6	0.7	0.7	0.8	0.8	0.8
41	0.4	0.8	0.8	0.9	0.9	0.9	0.9
42	0.8	1.0	1.0	1.1	1.1	1.1	1.1
43	1.2	1.3	1.3	1.2	1.2	1.2	1.2
44	1.6	1.6	1.5	1.4	1.4	1.3	1.3
45	2.0	1.8	1.7	1.6	1.5	1.5	1.4
46	2.4	2.1	1.9	1.7	1.7	1.6	1.6
47	2.8	2.3	2.0	1.9	1.8	1.7	1.7
48	3.2	2.5	2.2	2.0	1.9	1.8	1.7
49	3.6	2.6	2.3	2.1	1.9	1.8	1.8
50	4.0	2.7	2.3	2.1	1.9	1.9	1.8
51	3.4	2.6	2.2	2.0	1.9	1.8	1.8
52	2.8	2.4	2.1	1.9	1.8	1.8	1.7
53	2.2	2.2	2.0	1.8	1.8	1.7	1.7
54	2.2	2.0	1.9	1.8	1.7	1.6	1.6
55	1.1	1.8	1.7	1.7	1.6	1.6	1.5

CALENDAR SPREAD TABLE

Call Options

Exercise Price is 60

Low Volatility

STOCK PRICE	NUMBER OF MONTHS BEFORE THE LONGER TERM OPTIONS EXPIRE						
	3	4	5	6	7	8	9
	NUMBER OF MONTHS BEFORE THE SHORTER TERM OPTIONS EXPIRE						
	0	1	2	3	4	5	6
45	0.0	0.0	0.0	0.0	0.0	0.1	0.1
46	0.0	0.0	0.0	0.0	0.1	0.1	0.1
47	0.0	0.0	0.0	0.0	0.1	0.1	0.1
48	0.0	0.0	0.0	0.1	0.1	0.2	0.2
49	0.0	0.0	0.1	0.2	0.2	0.3	0.3
50	0.0	0.1	0.2	0.3	0.3	0.4	0.4
51	0.0	0.2	0.3	0.4	0.5	0.5	0.5
52	0.2	0.4	0.5	0.6	0.6	0.7	0.7
53	0.6	0.7	0.8	0.8	0.9	0.9	0.9
54	1.0	1.1	1.1	1.1	1.1	1.1	1.1
55	1.4	1.4	1.4	1.4	1.3	1.4	1.3
56	1.8	1.8	1.7	1.6	1.6	1.6	1.6
57	2.2	2.1	2.0	1.9	1.8	1.8	1.7
58	2.6	2.4	2.2	2.1	2.0	2.0	1.9
59	3.0	2.7	2.4	2.3	2.1	2.1	2.0
60	3.4	2.8	2.5	2.3	2.2	2.1	2.1
61	2.8	2.6	2.4	2.3	2.2	2.1	2.0
62	2.4	2.4	2.3	2.2	2.1	2.0	2.0
63	2.2	2.2	2.2	2.1	2.0	2.0	1.9
64	2.2	2.2	2.1	2.0	2.0	1.9	1.8
65	2.1	2.0	2.0	1.9	1.9	1.8	1.8

Average Volatility

STOCK PRICE	NUMBER OF MONTHS BEFORE THE LONGER TERM OPTIONS EXPIRE						
	3	4	5	6	7	8	9
	NUMBER OF MONTHS BEFORE THE SHORTER TERM OPTIONS EXPIRE						
	0	1	2	3	4	5	6
45	0.0	0.0	0.1	0.2	0.3	0.3	0.3
46	0.0	0.0	0.2	0.3	0.3	0.4	0.4
47	0.0	0.1	0.3	0.4	0.4	0.5	0.5
48	0.0	0.2	0.4	0.5	0.5	0.6	0.6
49	0.0	0.3	0.5	0.6	0.7	0.7	0.7
50	0.2	0.5	0.7	0.8	0.8	0.8	0.9
51	0.6	0.8	1.0	1.0	1.0	1.0	1.0
52	1.0	1.2	1.2	1.2	1.2	1.2	1.2
53	1.4	1.5	1.5	1.5	1.4	1.4	1.4
54	1.8	1.8	1.8	1.7	1.7	1.6	1.6
55	2.2	2.2	2.0	2.0	1.9	1.8	1.8
56	2.6	2.5	2.3	2.2	2.1	2.0	2.0
57	3.0	2.8	2.5	2.4	2.3	2.2	2.1
58	3.4	3.0	2.7	2.5	2.4	2.3	2.2
59	3.8	3.2	2.8	2.6	2.5	2.4	2.3
60	4.2	3.3	2.9	2.7	2.5	2.4	2.4
61	3.6	3.1	2.8	2.6	2.5	2.4	2.3
62	3.0	2.9	2.7	2.5	2.4	2.3	2.2
63	2.7	2.7	2.5	2.4	2.3	2.2	2.1
64	2.5	2.5	2.4	2.3	2.2	2.1	2.1
65	2.5	2.3	2.2	2.2	2.1	2.0	2.0

High Volatility

STOCK PRICE	NUMBER OF MONTHS BEFORE THE LONGER TERM OPTIONS EXPIRE						
	3	4	5	6	7	8	9
	NUMBER OF MONTHS BEFORE THE SHORTER TERM OPTIONS EXPIRE						
	0	1	2	3	4	5	6
45	0.0	0.3	0.5	0.6	0.6	0.6	0.7
46	0.0	0.4	0.6	0.7	0.7	0.7	0.7
47	0.0	0.5	0.7	0.8	0.7	0.7	0.7
48	0.0	0.7	0.9	0.9	0.8	0.8	0.8
49	0.4	0.9	1.0	1.0	0.9	0.9	0.9
50	0.8	1.1	1.2	1.2	1.1	1.1	1.1
51	1.2	1.4	1.4	1.4	1.2	1.2	1.3
52	1.6	1.7	1.6	1.5	1.4	1.4	1.3
53	2.0	1.9	1.8	1.7	1.5	1.5	1.5
54	2.4	2.2	2.0	1.9	1.7	1.6	1.6
55	2.8	2.4	2.2	2.0	1.8	1.7	1.7
56	3.2	2.7	2.4	2.2	1.9	1.9	1.8
57	3.6	2.9	2.5	2.3	2.2	2.0	1.9
58	4.0	3.0	2.6	2.4	2.2	2.1	2.1
59	4.4	3.1	2.7	2.4	2.3	2.2	2.1
60	4.8	3.2	2.7	2.5	2.3	2.2	2.2
61	4.2	3.1	2.6	2.4	2.3	2.2	2.2
62	3.6	3.0	2.5	2.3	2.2	2.2	2.1
63	3.0	2.8	2.4	2.3	2.1	2.1	2.0
64	2.6	2.6	2.3	2.2	2.1	2.0	2.0
65	2.5	2.4	2.2	2.1	2.0	2.0	1.9

CALENDAR SPREAD TABLE

Call Options

Exercise Price is 70

Low Volatility

STOCK PRICE

NUMBER OF MONTHS BEFORE THE LONGER TERM OPTIONS EXPIRE

NUMBER OF MONTHS BEFORE THE SHORTER TERM OPTIONS EXPIRE

	3	4	5	6	7	8	9
	0	1	2	3	4	5	6
55	0.0	0.0	0.0	0.1	0.1	0.2	0.2
56	0.0	0.0	0.1	0.1	0.2	0.3	0.3
57	0.0	0.0	0.1	0.2	0.3	0.3	0.4
58	0.0	0.1	0.2	0.3	0.4	0.4	0.4
59	0.0	0.2	0.3	0.4	0.5	0.5	0.6
60	0.0	0.3	0.5	0.6	0.6	0.7	0.7
61	0.4	0.6	0.7	0.8	0.8	0.9	0.9
62	0.8	0.9	1.0	1.0	1.1	1.1	1.1
63	1.2	1.2	1.3	1.3	1.3	1.3	1.3
64	1.6	1.6	1.6	1.6	1.5	1.5	1.5
65	2.0	1.9	1.9	1.8	1.8	1.8	1.7
66	2.4	2.3	2.2	2.1	2.0	2.0	2.0
67	2.8	2.6	2.4	2.3	2.2	2.2	2.1
68	3.2	2.9	2.7	2.5	2.4	2.3	2.3
69	3.6	3.1	2.8	2.7	2.5	2.4	2.4
70	4.0	3.2	2.9	2.7	2.5	2.5	2.4
71	3.4	3.1	2.8	2.7	2.5	2.4	2.4
72	2.8	2.8	2.7	2.6	2.5	2.4	2.3
73	2.7	2.6	2.6	2.5	2.4	2.3	2.3
74	2.6	2.6	2.5	2.4	2.3	2.3	2.2
75	2.5	2.5	2.4	2.3	2.2	2.2	2.1

Average Volatility

STOCK PRICE

NUMBER OF MONTHS BEFORE THE LONGER TERM OPTIONS EXPIRE

NUMBER OF MONTHS BEFORE THE SHORTER TERM OPTIONS EXPIRE

	3	4	5	6	7	8	9
	0	1	2	3	4	5	6
55	0.0	0.1	0.3	0.5	0.5	0.6	0.6
56	0.0	0.2	0.5	0.6	0.7	0.7	0.7
57	0.0	0.4	0.6	0.7	0.8	0.8	0.8
58	0.2	0.6	0.8	0.9	1.0	1.0	1.0
59	0.6	0.8	1.0	1.1	1.1	1.1	1.1
60	1.0	1.1	1.3	1.3	1.3	1.3	1.3
61	1.4	1.5	1.5	1.5	1.5	1.5	1.5
62	1.8	1.8	1.8	1.7	1.7	1.7	1.7
63	2.2	2.1	2.1	2.0	2.0	1.9	1.9
64	2.6	2.5	2.3	2.2	2.2	2.1	2.1
65	3.0	2.8	2.6	2.5	2.4	2.3	2.3
66	3.4	3.1	2.8	2.7	2.5	2.5	2.4
67	3.8	3.4	3.0	2.9	2.7	2.6	2.5
68	4.2	3.6	3.2	3.0	2.8	2.7	2.7
69	4.6	3.8	3.3	3.1	2.9	2.8	2.7
70	5.0	3.8	3.3	3.3	2.9	2.8	2.7
71	4.4	3.7	3.3	3.1	2.9	2.8	2.6
72	3.8	3.5	3.2	3.0	2.8	2.7	2.5
73	3.2	3.2	3.0	2.8	2.7	2.6	2.5
74	3.0	3.1	2.9	2.7	2.5	2.5	2.5
75	2.9	2.9	2.7	2.6	2.5	2.4	2.4

High Volatility

STOCK PRICE

NUMBER OF MONTHS BEFORE THE LONGER TERM OPTIONS EXPIRE

NUMBER OF MONTHS BEFORE THE SHORTER TERM OPTIONS EXPIRE

	3	4	5	6	7	8	9
	0	1	2	3	4	5	6
55	0.0	0.7	0.9	0.9	1.0	1.0	1.0
56	0.0	0.8	1.0	1.0	1.1	1.1	1.1
57	0.4	1.0	1.2	1.2	1.2	1.2	1.2
58	0.8	1.3	1.4	1.3	1.4	1.4	1.4
59	1.2	1.5	1.5	1.5	1.5	1.5	1.5
60	1.6	1.8	1.7	1.7	1.7	1.6	1.6
61	2.0	2.0	1.9	1.9	1.8	1.8	1.8
62	2.4	2.3	2.1	2.0	2.0	1.9	1.9
63	2.8	2.5	2.3	2.2	2.1	2.0	2.0
64	3.2	2.8	2.5	2.3	2.2	2.1	2.1
65	3.6	3.0	2.7	2.5	2.3	2.3	2.2
66	4.0	3.2	2.8	2.6	2.4	2.3	2.3
67	4.4	3.4	2.9	2.7	2.5	2.4	2.4
68	4.8	3.5	3.0	2.8	2.6	2.5	2.4
69	5.2	3.6	3.1	2.8	2.6	2.5	2.5
70	5.6	3.6	3.1	2.8	2.7	2.6	2.5
71	5.0	3.6	3.0	2.8	2.6	2.5	2.5
72	4.4	3.5	2.9	2.7	2.6	2.4	2.4
73	3.8	3.3	2.8	2.7	2.5	2.4	2.3
74	3.0	3.1	2.7	2.6	2.4	2.4	2.3
75	3.1	2.9	2.7	2.5	2.4	2.3	2.3

CALENDAR SPREAD TABLE
Call Options

Exercise Price is (80)

Low Volatility

NUMBER OF MONTHS BEFORE THE LONGER TERM OPTIONS EXPIRE

NUMBER OF MONTHS BEFORE THE SHORTER TERM OPTIONS EXPIRE

STOCK PRICE	3 / 0	4 / 1	5 / 2	6 / 3	7 / 4	8 / 5	9 / 6
65	0.0	0.0	0.1	0.2	0.3	0.4	0.4
66	0.0	0.1	0.2	0.3	0.4	0.5	0.5
67	0.0	0.1	0.3	0.4	0.5	0.6	0.6
68	0.0	0.3	0.5	0.6	0.6	0.7	0.8
69	0.2	0.5	0.7	0.8	0.8	0.9	0.9
70	0.6	0.8	0.9	1.0	1.0	1.1	1.1
71	1.0	1.1	1.2	1.2	1.2	1.3	1.3
72	1.4	1.4	1.5	1.5	1.5	1.5	1.5
73	1.8	1.8	1.8	1.8	1.7	1.8	1.7
74	2.2	2.1	2.1	2.0	1.9	2.0	1.9
75	2.6	2.5	2.4	2.3	2.2	2.2	2.1
76	3.0	2.8	2.6	2.5	2.4	2.5	2.3
77	3.4	3.1	2.9	2.7	2.6	2.6	2.5
78	3.8	3.4	3.1	2.9	2.7	2.7	2.6
79	4.2	3.6	3.3	3.0	2.8	2.8	2.7
80	4.6	3.7	3.3	3.1	2.8	2.9	2.7
81	4.0	3.5	3.2	3.1	2.9	2.9	2.7
82	3.4	3.3	3.1	3.0	2.8	2.8	2.7
83	3.2	3.1	3.0	2.9	2.8	2.7	2.6
84	3.0	3.0	2.9	2.8	2.7	2.6	2.5
85	2.9	2.9	2.8	2.7	2.6	2.6	2.5

Average Volatility

NUMBER OF MONTHS BEFORE THE LONGER TERM OPTIONS EXPIRE

NUMBER OF MONTHS BEFORE THE SHORTER TERM OPTIONS EXPIRE

STOCK PRICE	3 / 0	4 / 1	5 / 2	6 / 3	7 / 4	8 / 5	9 / 6
65	0.0	0.4	0.7	0.8	0.9	0.9	1.0
66	0.1	0.6	0.9	1.0	1.1	1.0	1.1
67	0.5	0.9	1.1	1.2	1.2	1.2	1.3
68	0.9	1.1	1.3	1.4	1.4	1.4	1.4
69	1.3	1.5	1.6	1.6	1.6	1.6	1.6
70	1.7	1.8	1.8	1.8	1.8	1.8	1.8
71	2.1	2.1	2.1	2.0	2.0	2.0	2.0
72	2.5	2.4	2.4	2.3	2.2	2.2	2.2
73	2.9	2.8	2.6	2.5	2.5	2.4	2.4
74	3.3	3.1	2.9	2.8	2.7	2.6	2.6
75	3.7	3.4	3.1	3.0	2.8	2.7	2.7
76	4.1	3.7	3.4	3.2	3.0	2.9	2.9
77	4.5	4.0	3.6	3.3	3.1	3.0	3.0
78	4.9	4.2	3.7	3.4	3.2	3.1	3.1
79	5.3	4.3	3.8	3.5	3.3	3.2	3.1
80	5.7	4.3	3.7	3.5	3.3	3.2	3.1
81	5.1	4.2	3.7	3.5	3.3	3.2	3.2
82	4.5	4.0	3.6	3.4	3.2	3.1	3.1
83	3.9	3.8	3.5	3.3	3.1	3.0	3.0
84	3.3	3.6	3.3	3.2	3.0	2.9	3.0
85	3.3	3.4	3.2	3.0	2.9	2.8	2.8

High Volatility

NUMBER OF MONTHS BEFORE THE LONGER TERM OPTIONS EXPIRE

NUMBER OF MONTHS BEFORE THE SHORTER TERM OPTIONS EXPIRE

STOCK PRICE	3 / 0	4 / 1	5 / 2	6 / 3	7 / 4	8 / 5	9 / 6
65	0.4	1.2	1.3	1.4	1.4	1.4	1.4
66	0.8	1.4	1.5	1.5	1.5	1.6	1.6
67	1.2	1.6	1.7	1.7	1.6	1.7	1.7
68	1.6	1.9	1.9	1.8	1.8	1.8	1.8
69	2.0	2.2	2.1	2.0	2.0	2.0	2.0
70	2.4	2.4	2.3	2.2	2.1	2.1	2.1
71	2.8	2.7	2.5	2.4	2.2	2.2	2.2
72	3.2	2.9	2.7	2.5	2.4	2.3	2.3
73	3.6	3.1	2.9	2.6	2.5	2.4	2.4
74	4.0	3.4	3.0	2.8	2.6	2.5	2.4
75	4.4	3.6	3.2	2.9	2.6	2.5	2.5
76	4.8	3.8	3.3	3.0	2.7	2.6	2.6
77	5.2	3.9	3.4	3.1	2.8	2.7	2.7
78	5.6	4.1	3.5	3.2	2.9	2.8	2.7
79	6.0	4.1	3.5	3.2	3.0	2.9	2.8
80	6.4	4.1	3.5	3.2	3.0	2.9	2.9
81	5.8	4.1	3.5	3.2	3.0	2.8	2.8
82	5.2	4.0	3.4	3.1	2.9	2.8	2.8
83	4.6	3.8	3.3	3.0	2.9	2.8	2.7
84	4.0	3.6	3.1	3.0	2.8	2.7	2.7
85	3.5	3.4	3.1	2.9	2.8	2.7	2.6

CALENDAR SPREAD TABLE

Call Options

Exercise Price is (90)

Low Volatility

STOCK PRICE

NUMBER OF MONTHS BEFORE THE LONGER TERM OPTIONS EXPIRE

NUMBER OF MONTHS BEFORE THE SHORTER TERM OPTIONS EXPIRE

	3	4	5	6	7	8	9
	0	1	2	3	4	5	6
75	0.0	0.1	0.3	0.4	0.6	0.6	0.6
76	0.0	0.2	0.4	0.6	0.7	0.7	0.7
77	0.0	0.4	0.6	0.7	0.8	0.9	0.9
78	0.4	0.6	0.8	0.9	1.0	1.1	1.1
79	0.8	0.9	1.1	1.2	1.3	1.3	1.3
80	1.2	1.3	1.4	1.4	1.5	1.5	1.4
81	1.6	1.6	1.7	1.7	1.7	1.7	1.6
82	2.0	1.9	2.0	2.0	1.9	1.9	1.9
83	2.4	2.3	2.2	2.2	2.2	2.2	2.1
84	2.8	2.7	2.5	2.5	2.4	2.4	2.3
85	3.2	3.0	2.8	2.7	2.6	2.6	2.5
86	3.6	3.3	3.1	3.0	2.8	2.8	2.7
87	4.0	3.6	3.3	3.2	3.0	2.9	2.8
88	4.4	3.9	3.5	3.3	3.1	3.0	3.0
89	4.8	4.1	3.7	3.4	3.2	3.1	3.1
90	5.2	4.1	3.7	3.5	3.3	3.2	3.1
91	4.6	4.0	3.7	3.4	3.2	3.2	3.1
92	4.0	3.8	3.5	3.4	3.2	3.1	3.0
93	3.4	3.6	3.4	3.3	3.1	3.0	3.0
94	3.4	3.4	3.3	3.2	3.0	2.9	2.9
95	3.3	3.3	3.3	3.1	3.0	2.9	2.9

Average Volatility

STOCK PRICE

NUMBER OF MONTHS BEFORE THE LONGER TERM OPTIONS EXPIRE

NUMBER OF MONTHS BEFORE THE SHORTER TERM OPTIONS EXPIRE

	3	4	5	6	7	8	9
	0	1	2	3	4	5	6
75	0.4	0.9	1.1	1.2	1.3	1.3	1.4
76	0.8	1.1	1.3	1.4	1.5	1.5	1.5
77	1.2	1.5	1.6	1.7	1.7	1.7	1.7
78	1.6	1.8	1.9	1.9	1.9	1.9	1.9
79	2.0	2.1	2.1	2.1	2.1	2.1	2.1
80	2.4	2.4	2.4	2.3	2.3	2.3	2.3
81	2.8	2.8	2.7	2.6	2.5	2.5	2.5
82	3.2	3.1	2.9	2.8	2.7	2.7	2.6
83	3.6	3.4	3.2	3.0	2.9	2.8	2.8
84	4.0	3.7	3.4	3.3	3.1	3.0	3.0
85	4.4	4.0	3.7	3.5	3.3	3.2	3.1
86	4.8	4.3	3.9	3.6	3.4	3.3	3.2
87	5.2	4.6	4.1	3.8	3.5	3.4	3.4
88	5.6	4.7	4.2	3.9	3.6	3.5	3.5
89	6.0	4.9	4.3	3.9	3.7	3.6	3.5
90	6.4	4.9	4.3	4.0	3.7	3.6	3.5
91	5.8	4.8	4.2	3.9	3.7	3.5	3.5
92	5.2	4.6	4.2	3.9	3.6	3.5	3.4
93	4.6	4.4	4.0	3.7	3.5	3.4	3.3
94	4.0	4.1	3.9	3.6	3.4	3.3	3.3
95	3.6	4.0	3.7	3.5	3.3	3.2	3.1

High Volatility

STOCK PRICE

NUMBER OF MONTHS BEFORE THE LONGER TERM OPTIONS EXPIRE

NUMBER OF MONTHS BEFORE THE SHORTER TERM OPTIONS EXPIRE

	3	4	5	6	7	8	9
	0	1	2	3	4	5	6
75	1.2	1.8	1.8	1.8	1.8	1.9	1.8
76	1.6	2.0	2.0	2.0	2.0	2.0	2.0
77	2.0	2.2	2.2	2.2	2.1	2.1	2.1
78	2.4	2.5	2.4	2.4	2.3	2.2	2.2
79	2.8	2.7	2.6	2.5	2.4	2.4	2.3
80	3.2	3.0	2.8	2.7	2.5	2.5	2.4
81	3.6	3.2	3.0	2.8	2.6	2.6	2.5
82	4.0	3.5	3.2	3.0	2.8	2.7	2.7
83	4.4	3.7	3.3	3.1	2.9	2.8	2.8
84	4.8	4.0	3.5	3.2	3.0	2.9	2.8
85	5.2	4.2	3.6	3.4	3.1	3.0	2.9
86	5.6	4.3	3.7	3.4	3.2	3.1	3.0
87	6.0	4.5	3.8	3.5	3.2	3.1	3.1
88	6.4	4.6	3.9	3.6	3.3	3.2	3.1
89	6.8	4.6	3.9	3.6	3.4	3.3	3.2
90	7.2	4.6	3.9	3.6	3.4	3.3	3.2
91	6.6	4.6	3.9	3.6	3.3	3.2	3.1
92	6.0	4.5	3.8	3.5	3.2	3.2	3.1
93	5.4	4.3	3.7	3.4	3.2	3.2	3.1
94	4.8	4.2	3.6	3.4	3.2	3.1	3.1
95	3.9	3.9	3.5	3.3	3.1	3.1	3.0

CALENDAR SPREAD TABLE

Call Options

Exercise Price is (100)

Low Volatility

NUMBER OF MONTHS BEFORE THE LONGER TERM OPTIONS EXPIRE

NUMBER OF MONTHS BEFORE THE SHORTER TERM OPTIONS EXPIRE

STOCK PRICE	3 / 0	4 / 1	5 / 2	6 / 3	7 / 4	8 / 5	9 / 6
85	0.0	0.4	0.6	0.7	0.8	0.9	1.0
86	0.1	0.6	0.8	0.9	1.0	1.1	1.1
87	0.5	0.8	1.0	1.1	1.2	1.3	1.3
88	0.9	1.1	1.3	1.4	1.4	1.4	1.5
89	1.3	1.4	1.6	1.6	1.7	1.7	1.7
90	1.7	1.8	1.9	1.9	1.9	1.9	1.9
91	2.1	2.1	2.2	2.2	2.1	2.1	2.1
92	2.5	2.5	2.4	2.4	2.4	2.3	2.3
93	2.9	2.9	2.7	2.7	2.6	2.6	2.5
94	3.3	3.2	3.0	2.9	2.8	2.8	2.7
95	3.7	3.5	3.3	3.2	3.1	3.0	2.9
96	4.1	3.8	3.5	3.4	3.3	3.2	3.1
97	4.5	4.1	3.8	3.6	3.4	3.3	3.2
98	4.9	4.4	4.0	3.8	3.5	3.4	3.3
99	5.3	4.5	4.1	3.9	3.6	3.5	3.4
100	5.7	4.6	4.1	3.9	3.6	3.5	3.4
101	5.1	4.5	4.1	3.8	3.6	3.5	3.4
102	4.5	4.3	3.9	3.8	3.6	3.5	3.4
103	3.9	4.1	3.8	3.7	3.5	3.4	3.3
104	3.3	3.9	3.7	3.6	3.4	3.3	3.2
105	2.7	3.7	3.7	3.5	3.4	3.3	3.2

Average Volatility

NUMBER OF MONTHS BEFORE THE LONGER TERM OPTIONS EXPIRE

NUMBER OF MONTHS BEFORE THE SHORTER TERM OPTIONS EXPIRE

STOCK PRICE	3 / 0	4 / 1	5 / 2	6 / 3	7 / 4	8 / 5	9 / 6
85	1.1	1.4	1.7	1.7	1.8	1.8	1.8
86	1.5	1.7	1.9	2.0	2.0	2.0	2.0
87	1.9	2.1	2.2	2.2	2.2	2.1	2.2
88	2.3	2.4	2.5	2.4	2.4	2.4	2.3
89	2.7	2.7	2.7	2.6	2.6	2.6	2.5
90	3.1	3.1	3.0	2.9	2.8	2.7	2.7
91	3.5	3.4	3.2	3.1	3.0	2.9	2.9
92	3.9	3.7	3.5	3.4	3.2	3.1	3.1
93	4.3	4.0	3.7	3.6	3.4	3.3	3.2
94	4.7	4.3	4.0	3.8	3.6	3.5	3.4
95	5.1	4.6	4.2	3.9	3.7	3.6	3.5
96	5.5	4.9	4.4	4.1	3.9	3.7	3.6
97	5.9	5.1	4.6	4.2	3.9	3.8	3.7
98	6.3	5.3	4.7	4.3	4.0	3.9	3.8
99	6.7	5.4	4.7	4.4	4.1	4.0	3.8
100	7.1	5.4	4.7	4.4	4.1	4.0	3.9
101	6.5	5.3	4.7	4.4	4.1	3.9	3.8
102	5.9	5.1	4.6	4.3	4.0	3.9	3.8
103	5.3	4.9	4.5	4.2	3.9	3.8	3.7
104	4.7	4.7	4.4	4.1	3.8	3.7	3.6
105	4.1	4.5	4.2	3.9	3.7	3.6	3.5

High Volatility

NUMBER OF MONTHS BEFORE THE LONGER TERM OPTIONS EXPIRE

NUMBER OF MONTHS BEFORE THE SHORTER TERM OPTIONS EXPIRE

STOCK PRICE	3 / 0	4 / 1	5 / 2	6 / 3	7 / 4	8 / 5	9 / 6
85	2.0	2.6	2.5	2.2	2.3	2.3	2.1
86	2.4	2.8	2.6	2.3	2.4	2.4	2.3
87	2.8	3.1	2.7	2.4	2.5	2.5	2.4
88	3.2	3.3	2.8	2.5	2.7	2.6	2.4
89	3.6	3.6	3.0	2.7	2.8	2.8	2.7
90	4.0	3.9	3.1	2.8	2.9	2.8	2.8
91	4.4	4.1	3.2	2.9	3.0	2.9	3.0
92	4.8	4.3	3.3	3.0	3.1	3.0	3.1
93	5.2	4.5	3.5	3.1	3.3	3.2	3.2
94	5.6	4.7	3.6	3.2	3.4	3.2	3.3
95	6.0	4.9	3.7	3.4	3.5	3.3	3.4
96	6.4	5.1	3.8	3.5	3.6	3.4	3.5
97	6.8	5.2	3.9	3.5	3.7	3.4	3.6
98	7.2	5.3	3.9	3.6	3.8	3.4	3.7
99	7.6	5.3	3.9	3.7	3.9	3.4	3.7
100	8.0	5.3	3.9	3.7	3.9	3.4	3.7
101	7.4	5.2	3.9	3.6	3.9	3.3	3.7
102	6.8	5.1	3.8	3.6	3.9	3.3	3.7
103	6.2	5.0	3.8	3.6	3.8	3.3	3.7
104	5.6	4.8	3.7	3.5	3.7	3.2	3.6
105	5.0	4.6	3.7	3.5	3.6	3.2	3.5

THE FUTURE VALUE CALENDAR SPREAD TABLES PUT OPTIONS

Decimal to Fraction Conversion Chart		
Table Shows		Market Fraction
.1	=	1/16
.1	=	1/8
.2	=	3/16
.2	=	1/4
.3	=	5/16
.4	=	3/8
.4	=	7/16
.5	=	1/2
.6	=	9/16
.6	=	5/8
.7	=	11/16
.8	=	3/4
.8	=	13/16
.9	=	7/8
.9	=	15/16

*The Future Value Tables are generated by computer simulation. Due to the nature of the computer simulation techniques that we used there may be slight aberrations in the option prices presented. Therefore you should allow a variance of plus or minus 10% of these option prices. In a few cases, some of the less important, peripheral option prices may vary more than 10%.

CALENDAR SPREAD TABLE

Put Options

  10

Low Volatility

STOCK PRICE	NUMBER OF MONTHS BEFORE THE LONGER TERM OPTIONS EXPIRE						
	3	4	5	6	7	8	9
	NUMBER OF MONTHS BEFORE THE SHORTER TERM OPTIONS EXPIRE						
	0	1	2	3	4	5	6
5	0.0	0.0	0.0	0.0	0.0	0.0	0.0
6	0.0	0.0	0.0	0.0	0.1	0.0	0.0
7	0.0	0.0	0.0	0.0	0.1	0.1	0.1
8	0.0	0.0	0.1	0.1	0.1	0.1	0.1
9	0.2	0.2	0.2	0.2	0.2	0.2	0.2
10	0.4	0.3	0.3	0.2	0.2	0.2	0.2
11	0.1	0.1	0.1	0.1	0.1	0.1	0.1
12	0.0	0.0	0.0	0.0	0.0	0.0	0.0
13	0.0	0.0	0.0	0.0	0.0	0.0	0.0
14	0.0	0.0	0.0	0.0	0.0	0.0	0.0
15	0.0	0.0	0.0	0.0	0.0	0.0	0.0
16	0.0	0.0	0.0	0.0	0.0	0.0	0.0
17	0.0	0.0	0.0	0.0	0.0	0.0	0.0
18	0.0	0.0	0.0	0.0	0.0	0.0	0.0
19	0.0	0.0	0.0	0.0	0.0	0.0	0.0
20	0.0	0.0	0.0	0.0	0.0	0.0	0.0

Average Volatility

STOCK PRICE	NUMBER OF MONTHS BEFORE THE LONGER TERM OPTIONS EXPIRE						
	3	4	5	6	7	8	9
	NUMBER OF MONTHS BEFORE THE SHORTER TERM OPTIONS EXPIRE						
	0	1	2	3	4	5	6
5	0.0	0.0	0.0	0.0	0.0	0.0	0.0
6	0.0	0.0	0.1	0.1	0.1	0.1	0.1
7	0.0	0.0	0.1	0.1	0.1	0.1	0.1
8	0.0	0.1	0.1	0.1	0.1	0.1	0.1
9	0.2	0.2	0.2	0.2	0.2	0.2	0.2
10	0.5	0.3	0.3	0.2	0.2	0.2	0.2
11	0.2	0.2	0.2	0.2	0.1	0.1	0.1
12	0.0	0.0	0.0	0.1	0.1	0.1	0.1
13	0.0	0.0	0.0	0.0	0.0	0.0	0.0
14	0.0	0.0	0.0	0.0	0.0	0.0	0.0
15	0.0	0.0	0.0	0.0	0.0	0.0	0.0
16	0.0	0.0	0.0	0.0	0.0	0.0	0.0
17	0.0	0.0	0.0	0.0	0.0	0.0	0.0
18	0.0	0.0	0.0	0.0	0.0	0.0	0.0
19	0.0	0.0	0.0	0.0	0.0	0.0	0.0
20	0.0	0.0	0.0	0.0	0.0	0.0	0.0

High Volatility

STOCK PRICE	NUMBER OF MONTHS BEFORE THE LONGER TERM OPTIONS EXPIRE						
	3	4	5	6	7	8	9
	NUMBER OF MONTHS BEFORE THE SHORTER TERM OPTIONS EXPIRE						
	0	1	2	3	4	5	6
5	0.0	0.0	0.0	0.0	0.0	0.0	0.0
6	0.0	0.0	0.0	0.0	0.0	0.0	0.0
7	0.0	0.0	0.0	0.0	0.0	0.0	0.0
8	0.0	0.1	0.1	0.1	0.1	0.1	0.1
9	0.2	0.2	0.2	0.2	0.2	0.1	0.1
10	0.6	0.3	0.2	0.2	0.2	0.2	0.1
11	0.3	0.2	0.2	0.2	0.2	0.1	0.1
12	0.0	0.1	0.1	0.1	0.1	0.1	0.1
13	0.0	0.0	0.0	0.1	0.1	0.0	0.0
14	0.0	0.0	0.0	0.0	0.0	0.0	0.0
15	0.0	0.0	0.0	0.0	0.0	0.0	0.0
16	0.0	0.0	0.0	0.0	0.0	0.0	0.0
17	0.0	0.0	0.0	0.0	0.0	0.0	0.0
18	0.0	0.0	0.0	0.0	0.0	0.0	0.0
19	0.0	0.0	0.0	0.0	0.0	0.0	0.0
20	0.0	0.0	0.0	0.0	0.0	0.0	0.0

CALENDAR SPREAD TABLE

Put Options Exercise Price is (15)

Low Volatility

STOCK PRICE	NUMBER OF MONTHS BEFORE THE LONGER TERM OPTIONS EXPIRE						
	3	4	5	6	7	8	9
	NUMBER OF MONTHS BEFORE THE SHORTER TERM OPTIONS EXPIRE						
	0	1	2	3	4	5	6
10	0.0	0.0	0.1	0.1	0.1	0.1	0.1
11	0.0	0.1	0.1	0.1	0.1	0.1	0.1
12	0.0	0.1	0.1	0.1	0.2	0.1	0.1
13	0.3	0.3	0.3	0.3	0.3	0.3	0.2
14	0.5	0.4	0.4	0.4	0.3	0.4	0.3
15	0.6	0.5	0.4	0.4	0.4	0.4	0.4
16	0.3	0.3	0.3	0.3	0.3	0.3	0.3
17	0.1	0.1	0.1	0.1	0.2	0.2	0.2
18	0.0	0.0	0.0	0.0	0.0	0.0	0.0
19	0.0	0.0	0.0	0.0	0.0	0.0	0.0
20	0.0	0.0	0.0	0.0	0.0	0.0	0.0
21	0.0	0.0	0.0	0.0	0.0	0.0	0.0
22	0.0	0.0	0.0	0.0	0.0	0.0	0.0
23	0.0	0.0	0.0	0.0	0.0	0.0	0.0
24	0.0	0.0	0.0	0.0	0.0	0.0	0.0
25	0.0	0.0	0.0	0.0	0.0	0.0	0.0

Average Volatility

STOCK PRICE	NUMBER OF MONTHS BEFORE THE LONGER TERM OPTIONS EXPIRE						
	3	4	5	6	7	8	9
	NUMBER OF MONTHS BEFORE THE SHORTER TERM OPTIONS EXPIRE						
	0	1	2	3	4	5	6
10	0.0	0.0	0.1	0.1	0.1	0.1	0.1
11	0.0	0.1	0.1	0.1	0.1	0.2	0.2
12	0.0	0.1	0.2	0.2	0.2	0.2	0.2
13	0.4	0.3	0.3	0.3	0.3	0.3	0.3
14	0.5	0.4	0.4	0.4	0.3	0.3	0.3
15	0.8	0.5	0.5	0.4	0.4	0.4	0.4
16	0.5	0.4	0.4	0.3	0.3	0.3	0.3
17	0.2	0.2	0.2	0.2	0.2	0.2	0.2
18	0.0	0.1	0.1	0.1	0.1	0.1	0.1
19	0.0	0.0	0.0	0.1	0.1	0.1	0.1
20	0.0	0.0	0.0	0.0	0.0	0.0	0.0
21	0.0	0.0	0.0	0.0	0.0	0.0	0.0
22	0.0	0.0	0.0	0.0	0.0	0.0	0.0
23	0.0	0.0	0.0	0.0	0.0	0.0	0.0
24	0.0	0.0	0.0	0.0	0.0	0.0	0.0
25	0.0	0.0	0.0	0.0	0.0	0.0	0.0

High Volatility

STOCK PRICE	NUMBER OF MONTHS BEFORE THE LONGER TERM OPTIONS EXPIRE						
	3	4	5	6	7	8	9
	NUMBER OF MONTHS BEFORE THE SHORTER TERM OPTIONS EXPIRE						
	0	1	2	3	4	5	6
10	0.0	0.1	0.2	0.2	0.1	0.0	0.0
11	0.0	0.2	0.2	0.2	0.1	0.0	0.0
12	0.0	0.2	0.2	0.2	0.2	0.1	0.2
13	0.4	0.4	0.3	0.3	0.3	0.2	0.3
14	0.5	0.4	0.4	0.3	0.3	0.3	0.3
15	0.9	0.5	0.4	0.3	0.3	0.3	0.3
16	0.6	0.4	0.3	0.3	0.3	0.3	0.3
17	0.3	0.3	0.2	0.2	0.2	0.3	0.2
18	0.1	0.2	0.1	0.2	0.2	0.2	0.1
19	0.0	0.1	0.1	0.1	0.1	0.1	0.1
20	0.0	0.0	0.1	0.1	0.1	0.1	0.1
21	0.0	0.0	0.0	0.0	0.0	0.1	0.0
22	0.0	0.0	0.0	0.0	0.0	0.0	0.0
23	0.0	0.0	0.0	0.0	0.0	0.0	0.0
24	0.0	0.0	0.0	0.0	0.0	0.0	0.0
25	0.0	0.0	0.0	0.0	0.0	0.0	0.0

T89

CALENDAR SPREAD TABLE

Put Options

Exercise Price is 20

Low Volatility

STOCK PRICE	NUMBER OF MONTHS BEFORE THE LONGER TERM OPTIONS EXPIRE						
	3	4	5	6	7	8	9
	NUMBER OF MONTHS BEFORE THE SHORTER TERM OPTIONS EXPIRE						
	0	1	2	3	4	5	6
15	0.0	0.1	0.1	0.1	0.1	0.2	0.2
16	0.0	0.1	0.2	0.2	0.2	0.2	0.2
17	0.5	0.4	0.3	0.3	0.3	0.4	0.3
18	0.5	0.5	0.4	0.5	0.4	0.4	0.4
19	0.6	0.6	0.6	0.5	0.5	0.5	0.4
20	0.9	0.7	0.6	0.6	0.5	0.5	0.5
21	0.6	0.5	0.5	0.5	0.5	0.5	0.4
22	0.3	0.3	0.3	0.3	0.3	0.3	0.3
23	0.0	0.1	0.1	0.1	0.2	0.2	0.2
24	0.0	0.0	0.0	0.0	0.1	0.1	0.1
25	0.0	0.0	0.0	0.0	0.0	0.0	0.0
26	0.0	0.0	0.0	0.0	0.0	0.0	0.0
27	0.0	0.0	0.0	0.0	0.0	0.0	0.0
28	0.0	0.0	0.0	0.0	0.0	0.0	0.0
29	0.0	0.0	0.0	0.0	0.0	0.0	0.0
30	0.0	0.0	0.0	0.0	0.0	0.0	0.0

Average Volatility

STOCK PRICE	NUMBER OF MONTHS BEFORE THE LONGER TERM OPTIONS EXPIRE						
	3	4	5	6	7	8	9
	NUMBER OF MONTHS BEFORE THE SHORTER TERM OPTIONS EXPIRE						
	0	1	2	3	4	5	6
15	0.0	0.1	0.2	0.2	0.2	0.2	0.2
16	0.0	0.2	0.2	0.3	0.3	0.3	0.3
17	0.4	0.4	0.4	0.4	0.4	0.4	0.4
18	0.5	0.5	0.5	0.5	0.4	0.4	0.4
19	0.6	0.6	0.6	0.5	0.5	0.5	0.5
20	1.1	0.8	0.6	0.6	0.5	0.5	0.5
21	0.8	0.6	0.6	0.5	0.5	0.5	0.4
22	0.5	0.5	0.4	0.4	0.4	0.4	0.4
23	0.2	0.3	0.3	0.3	0.3	0.3	0.3
24	0.0	0.1	0.2	0.2	0.2	0.2	0.2
25	0.0	0.0	0.1	0.1	0.1	0.1	0.1
26	0.0	0.0	0.0	0.1	0.1	0.1	0.1
27	0.0	0.0	0.0	0.0	0.0	0.1	0.1
28	0.0	0.0	0.0	0.0	0.0	0.0	0.0
29	0.0	0.0	0.0	0.0	0.0	0.0	0.0
30	0.0	0.0	0.0	0.0	0.0	0.0	0.0

High Volatility

STOCK PRICE	NUMBER OF MONTHS BEFORE THE LONGER TERM OPTIONS EXPIRE						
	3	4	5	6	7	8	9
	NUMBER OF MONTHS BEFORE THE SHORTER TERM OPTIONS EXPIRE						
	0	1	2	3	4	5	6
15	0.0	0.2	0.3	0.3	0.2	0.3	0.0
16	0.0	0.3	0.3	0.3	0.3	0.3	0.1
17	0.6	0.5	0.4	0.3	0.4	0.3	0.2
18	0.6	0.5	0.4	0.4	0.4	0.4	0.3
19	0.7	0.6	0.5	0.5	0.5	0.4	0.4
20	1.2	0.7	0.5	0.5	0.5	0.4	0.4
21	0.9	0.6	0.5	0.5	0.4	0.4	0.4
22	0.6	0.5	0.4	0.4	0.4	0.3	0.3
23	0.4	0.4	0.4	0.3	0.3	0.3	0.3
24	0.1	0.2	0.3	0.2	0.2	0.2	0.2
25	0.0	0.1	0.2	0.1	0.2	0.1	0.2
26	0.0	0.1	0.2	0.1	0.1	0.1	0.2
27	0.0	0.0	0.1	0.1	0.1	0.1	0.1
28	0.0	0.0	0.1	0.0	0.1	0.0	0.1
29	0.0	0.0	0.0	0.0	0.1	0.0	0.1
30	0.0	0.0	0.0	0.0	0.0	0.0	0.1

CALENDAR SPREAD TABLE

Put Options

Exercise Price is 25

Low Volatility

STOCK PRICE

NUMBER OF MONTHS BEFORE THE LONGER TERM OPTIONS EXPIRE

NUMBER OF MONTHS BEFORE THE SHORTER TERM OPTIONS EXPIRE

	3	4	5	6	7	8	9
	0	1	2	3	4	5	6
20	0.1	0.2	0.2	0.2	0.3	0.3	0.3
21	0.7	0.4	0.4	0.4	0.4	0.4	0.4
22	0.8	0.6	0.6	0.5	0.5	0.5	0.5
23	0.9	0.7	0.7	0.7	0.6	0.6	0.6
24	1.0	0.8	0.7	0.7	0.6	0.6	0.6
25	1.1	0.9	0.8	0.7	0.7	0.6	0.6
26	0.8	0.7	0.7	0.6	0.6	0.6	0.5
27	0.5	0.5	0.5	0.5	0.5	0.4	0.4
28	0.2	0.3	0.3	0.3	0.4	0.3	0.3
29	0.0	0.1	0.1	0.2	0.2	0.2	0.2
30	0.0	0.0	0.0	0.1	0.1	0.1	0.1
31	0.0	0.0	0.0	0.0	0.0	0.0	0.0
32	0.0	0.0	0.0	0.0	0.0	0.0	0.0
33	0.0	0.0	0.0	0.0	0.0	0.0	0.0
34	0.0	0.0	0.0	0.0	0.0	0.0	0.0
35	0.0	0.0	0.0	0.0	0.0	0.0	0.0

Average Volatility

STOCK PRICE

NUMBER OF MONTHS BEFORE THE LONGER TERM OPTIONS EXPIRE

NUMBER OF MONTHS BEFORE THE SHORTER TERM OPTIONS EXPIRE

	3	4	5	6	7	8	9
	0	1	2	3	4	5	6
20	0.1	0.2	0.3	0.3	0.3	0.3	0.3
21	0.5	0.5	0.5	0.5	0.5	0.4	0.4
22	0.6	0.6	0.6	0.5	0.5	0.5	0.5
23	0.8	0.7	0.7	0.7	0.6	0.6	0.6
24	0.9	0.9	0.8	0.7	0.7	0.7	0.6
25	1.3	1.0	0.8	0.8	0.7	0.7	0.7
26	1.0	0.9	0.8	0.7	0.6	0.6	0.6
27	0.7	0.7	0.6	0.6	0.5	0.5	0.5
28	0.5	0.5	0.5	0.5	0.4	0.4	0.4
29	0.2	0.3	0.3	0.3	0.3	0.3	0.3
30	0.0	0.1	0.2	0.2	0.2	0.2	0.2
31	0.0	0.0	0.1	0.1	0.2	0.2	0.2
32	0.0	0.0	0.1	0.1	0.1	0.1	0.1
33	0.0	0.0	0.0	0.0	0.1	0.1	0.1
34	0.0	0.0	0.0	0.0	0.0	0.1	0.1
35	0.0	0.0	0.0	0.0	0.0	0.0	0.0

High Volatility

STOCK PRICE

NUMBER OF MONTHS BEFORE THE LONGER TERM OPTIONS EXPIRE

NUMBER OF MONTHS BEFORE THE SHORTER TERM OPTIONS EXPIRE

	3	4	5	6	7	8	9
	0	1	2	3	4	5	6
20	0.1	0.4	0.4	0.4	0.4	0.4	0.3
21	0.8	0.5	0.5	0.4	0.4	0.4	0.3
22	0.9	0.6	0.6	0.5	0.5	0.4	0.5
23	1.0	0.7	0.6	0.6	0.5	0.5	0.5
24	1.1	0.8	0.7	0.6	0.5	0.5	0.5
25	1.5	0.9	0.7	0.6	0.5	0.6	0.5
26	1.2	0.8	0.7	0.6	0.5	0.5	0.5
27	0.9	0.7	0.6	0.6	0.4	0.5	0.4
28	0.7	0.6	0.5	0.5	0.4	0.5	0.4
29	0.4	0.5	0.4	0.4	0.3	0.4	0.3
30	0.2	0.4	0.4	0.3	0.3	0.3	0.3
31	0.0	0.2	0.3	0.3	0.3	0.3	0.3
32	0.0	0.2	0.2	0.2	0.3	0.2	0.2
33	0.0	0.1	0.2	0.2	0.2	0.2	0.2
34	0.0	0.0	0.1	0.1	0.2	0.1	0.2
35	0.0	0.0	0.1	0.1	0.2	0.1	0.1

CALENDAR SPREAD TABLE

Put Options

Exercise Price is (30)

Low Volatility

STOCK PRICE

NUMBER OF MONTHS BEFORE THE LONGER TERM OPTIONS EXPIRE

| | 3 | 4 | 5 | 6 | 7 | 8 | 9 |

NUMBER OF MONTHS BEFORE THE SHORTER TERM OPTIONS EXPIRE

Stock Price	0	1	2	3	4	5	6
25	0.1	0.4	0.4	0.4	0.5	0.5	0.5
26	0.7	0.6	0.6	0.6	0.6	0.5	0.6
27	0.9	0.8	0.7	0.7	0.7	0.6	0.7
28	1.0	0.9	0.9	0.8	0.8	0.7	0.7
29	1.1	1.0	0.9	0.9	0.8	0.8	0.7
30	1.3	1.0	1.0	0.9	0.8	0.8	0.8
31	1.0	0.9	0.9	0.8	0.7	0.8	0.7
32	0.7	0.7	0.7	0.7	0.6	0.6	0.6
33	0.5	0.5	0.5	0.6	0.5	0.5	0.5
34	0.2	0.3	0.3	0.4	0.3	0.4	0.3
35	0.0	0.1	0.1	0.2	0.2	0.2	0.2
36	0.0	0.0	0.0	0.1	0.1	0.1	0.1
37	0.0	0.0	0.0	0.0	0.0	0.1	0.1
38	0.0	0.0	0.0	0.0	0.0	0.0	0.0
39	0.0	0.0	0.0	0.0	0.0	0.0	0.0
40	0.0	0.0	0.0	0.0	0.0	0.0	0.0

Average Volatility

STOCK PRICE

NUMBER OF MONTHS BEFORE THE LONGER TERM OPTIONS EXPIRE

| | 3 | 4 | 5 | 6 | 7 | 8 | 9 |

NUMBER OF MONTHS BEFORE THE SHORTER TERM OPTIONS EXPIRE

Stock Price	0	1	2	3	4	5	6
25	0.1	0.5	0.5	0.5	0.5	0.5	0.5
26	0.8	0.7	0.7	0.6	0.6	0.6	0.6
27	0.9	0.8	0.8	0.7	0.7	0.7	0.7
28	1.1	1.0	0.9	0.8	0.8	0.8	0.7
29	1.1	1.1	1.0	0.9	0.8	0.8	0.8
30	1.6	1.2	1.0	0.9	0.8	0.8	0.8
31	1.3	1.1	0.9	0.9	0.8	0.8	0.8
32	1.0	0.9	0.8	0.8	0.7	0.7	0.7
33	0.7	0.7	0.7	0.6	0.6	0.6	0.6
34	0.5	0.5	0.5	0.5	0.5	0.5	0.5
35	0.2	0.3	0.4	0.4	0.4	0.4	0.4
36	0.0	0.2	0.2	0.3	0.3	0.3	0.3
37	0.0	0.1	0.2	0.2	0.2	0.2	0.2
38	0.0	0.0	0.1	0.1	0.2	0.2	0.2
39	0.0	0.0	0.0	0.1	0.1	0.1	0.1
40	0.0	0.0	0.0	0.0	0.1	0.1	0.1

High Volatility

STOCK PRICE

NUMBER OF MONTHS BEFORE THE LONGER TERM OPTIONS EXPIRE

| | 3 | 4 | 5 | 6 | 7 | 8 | 9 |

NUMBER OF MONTHS BEFORE THE SHORTER TERM OPTIONS EXPIRE

Stock Price	0	1	2	3	4	5	6
25	0.1	0.6	0.6	0.6	0.5	0.5	0.5
26	0.8	0.7	0.7	0.6	0.5	0.5	0.5
27	0.9	0.8	0.7	0.6	0.6	0.6	0.6
28	1.1	0.9	0.8	0.7	0.6	0.6	0.6
29	1.4	1.1	0.8	0.8	0.7	0.7	0.6
30	1.8	1.1	0.9	0.9	0.7	0.7	0.7
31	1.5	1.1	0.8	0.8	0.7	0.7	0.6
32	1.2	1.0	0.8	0.7	0.6	0.7	0.6
33	1.0	0.9	0.7	0.6	0.6	0.6	0.6
34	0.7	0.7	0.6	0.6	0.5	0.6	0.5
35	0.5	0.6	0.5	0.5	0.5	0.5	0.5
36	0.2	0.4	0.4	0.4	0.4	0.4	0.4
37	0.0	0.3	0.3	0.3	0.3	0.3	0.3
38	0.0	0.2	0.2	0.2	0.3	0.2	0.3
39	0.0	0.1	0.2	0.2	0.3	0.2	0.2
40	0.0	0.0	0.2	0.2	0.2	0.2	0.2

CALENDAR SPREAD TABLE

Put Options

Exercise Price is 35

Low Volatility

STOCK PRICE

NUMBER OF MONTHS BEFORE THE LONGER TERM OPTIONS EXPIRE

NUMBER OF MONTHS BEFORE THE SHORTER TERM OPTIONS EXPIRE

	3	4	5	6	7	8	9
	0	1	2	3	4	5	6
30	0.8	0.7	0.7	0.7	0.6	0.7	0.6
31	0.9	0.8	0.8	0.8	0.7	0.8	0.7
32	1.0	1.0	1.0	0.9	0.9	0.9	0.8
33	1.1	1.1	1.0	1.0	0.9	0.9	0.9
34	1.2	1.1	1.1	1.0	1.0	1.0	0.9
35	1.6	1.2	1.1	1.1	1.0	1.0	1.0
36	1.3	1.1	1.0	1.0	0.9	0.9	0.9
37	1.0	0.9	0.9	0.9	0.8	0.8	0.8
38	0.7	0.7	0.7	0.7	0.7	0.6	0.7
39	0.4	0.4	0.5	0.5	0.5	0.5	0.5
40	0.2	0.2	0.3	0.3	0.4	0.3	0.4
41	0.0	0.1	0.1	0.2	0.3	0.2	0.3
42	0.0	0.0	0.0	0.1	0.2	0.1	0.2
43	0.0	0.0	0.0	0.0	0.1	0.1	0.1
44	0.0	0.0	0.0	0.0	0.0	0.0	0.0
45	0.0	0.0	0.0	0.0	0.0	0.0	0.0

Average Volatility

STOCK PRICE

NUMBER OF MONTHS BEFORE THE LONGER TERM OPTIONS EXPIRE

NUMBER OF MONTHS BEFORE THE SHORTER TERM OPTIONS EXPIRE

	3	4	5	6	7	8	9
	0	1	2	3	4	5	6
30	1.0	0.7	0.7	0.7	0.7	0.7	0.7
31	1.2	0.9	0.8	0.8	0.8	0.8	0.8
32	1.4	1.0	1.0	0.9	0.9	0.9	0.8
33	1.5	1.2	1.1	1.0	1.0	0.9	0.9
34	1.7	1.3	1.1	1.1	1.0	1.0	0.9
35	1.9	1.4	1.2	1.1	1.0	1.0	0.9
36	1.6	1.3	1.1	1.0	1.0	1.0	0.9
37	1.3	1.2	1.0	1.0	0.9	0.9	0.9
38	1.0	1.0	0.9	0.8	0.8	0.7	0.8
39	0.7	0.8	0.7	0.7	0.7	0.6	0.7
40	0.5	0.6	0.6	0.6	0.6	0.5	0.6
41	0.3	0.4	0.4	0.4	0.4	0.4	0.4
42	0.0	0.2	0.3	0.3	0.3	0.3	0.3
43	0.0	0.1	0.2	0.2	0.3	0.3	0.3
44	0.0	0.0	0.1	0.2	0.2	0.2	0.2
45	0.0	0.0	0.1	0.1	0.2	0.2	0.2

High Volatility

STOCK PRICE

NUMBER OF MONTHS BEFORE THE LONGER TERM OPTIONS EXPIRE

NUMBER OF MONTHS BEFORE THE SHORTER TERM OPTIONS EXPIRE

	3	4	5	6	7	8	9
	0	1	2	3	4	5	6
30	1.0	0.9	0.7	0.8	0.7	0.7	0.7
31	1.1	1.0	0.8	0.8	0.8	0.7	0.7
32	1.3	1.1	0.9	0.9	0.8	0.7	0.8
33	1.5	1.2	1.0	0.9	0.8	0.7	0.8
34	1.7	1.3	1.1	1.0	0.9	0.7	0.8
35	2.2	1.4	1.1	1.0	0.9	0.7	0.8
36	1.8	1.3	1.1	0.9	0.9	0.7	0.8
37	1.5	1.2	1.1	0.9	0.8	0.6	0.8
38	1.3	1.1	1.0	0.8	0.7	0.6	0.7
39	1.0	0.9	0.9	0.7	0.7	0.5	0.6
40	0.8	0.7	0.8	0.6	0.6	0.5	0.5
41	0.5	0.6	0.6	0.5	0.5	0.4	0.5
42	0.3	0.4	0.5	0.4	0.4	0.4	0.4
43	0.1	0.3	0.4	0.3	0.4	0.4	0.3
44	0.0	0.2	0.3	0.3	0.3	0.3	0.3
45	0.0	0.1	0.2	0.2	0.3	0.3	0.2

CALENDAR SPREAD TABLE

Put Options

Low Volatility

STOCK PRICE	NUMBER OF MONTHS BEFORE THE LONGER TERM OPTIONS EXPIRE						
	3	4	5	6	7	8	9
	NUMBER OF MONTHS BEFORE THE SHORTER TERM OPTIONS EXPIRE						
	0	1	2	3	4	5	6
35	0.9	0.9	0.8	0.9	0.8	0.8	0.9
36	1.0	1.0	1.0	1.0	0.9	0.9	0.9
37	1.2	1.2	1.1	1.1	1.0	1.0	1.0
38	1.2	1.2	1.1	1.1	1.1	1.0	1.0
39	1.3	1.3	1.3	1.2	1.1	1.1	1.1
40	1.8	1.4	1.3	1.3	1.2	1.1	1.0
41	1.5	1.3	1.2	1.1	1.1	1.0	1.0
42	1.2	1.1	1.1	1.0	1.0	1.0	0.9
43	0.9	0.9	0.9	0.8	0.9	0.8	0.8
44	0.6	0.6	0.7	0.6	0.7	0.7	0.6
45	0.4	0.4	0.5	0.5	0.5	0.6	0.5
46	0.1	0.2	0.3	0.3	0.4	0.4	0.4
47	0.0	0.1	0.2	0.2	0.2	0.3	0.3
48	0.0	0.0	0.1	0.1	0.1	0.2	0.2
49	0.0	0.0	0.0	0.0	0.1	0.2	0.1
50	0.0	0.0	0.0	0.0	0.0	0.1	0.1

Average Volatility

STOCK PRICE	NUMBER OF MONTHS BEFORE THE LONGER TERM OPTIONS EXPIRE						
	3	4	5	6	7	8	9
	NUMBER OF MONTHS BEFORE THE SHORTER TERM OPTIONS EXPIRE						
	0	1	2	3	4	5	6
35	1.0	0.9	0.9	0.9	0.9	0.9	0.8
36	1.2	1.1	1.0	1.0	1.0	0.9	0.9
37	1.5	1.3	1.2	1.1	1.0	1.0	1.0
38	1.6	1.4	1.2	1.2	1.1	1.1	1.0
39	1.7	1.5	1.3	1.2	1.2	1.1	1.1
40	2.2	1.6	1.4	1.3	1.2	1.1	1.1
41	1.9	1.5	1.3	1.2	1.1	1.1	1.1
42	1.6	1.4	1.3	1.1	1.1	1.0	1.0
43	1.3	1.2	1.1	1.0	1.0	0.9	0.9
44	1.0	1.0	0.9	0.9	0.8	0.8	0.8
45	0.7	0.8	0.8	0.8	0.7	0.7	0.7
46	0.5	0.6	0.6	0.6	0.6	0.6	0.6
47	0.3	0.4	0.5	0.5	0.5	0.5	0.5
48	0.0	0.2	0.4	0.4	0.4	0.4	0.4
49	0.0	0.1	0.2	0.3	0.3	0.3	0.3
50	0.0	0.1	0.2	0.2	0.3	0.3	0.3

High Volatility

STOCK PRICE	NUMBER OF MONTHS BEFORE THE LONGER TERM OPTIONS EXPIRE						
	3	4	5	6	7	8	9
	NUMBER OF MONTHS BEFORE THE SHORTER TERM OPTIONS EXPIRE						
	0	1	2	3	4	5	6
35	1.0	1.0	1.0	0.8	0.8	0.8	0.8
36	1.2	1.1	1.0	0.9	0.9	0.8	0.8
37	1.4	1.3	1.1	0.9	0.9	0.9	0.8
38	1.7	1.3	1.1	1.0	0.9	0.9	0.8
39	2.0	1.4	1.1	1.0	1.0	1.0	0.9
40	2.5	1.5	1.2	1.1	1.0	1.0	0.9
41	2.2	1.4	1.1	1.1	1.0	0.9	0.9
42	1.9	1.3	1.1	1.0	0.9	0.8	0.9
43	1.6	1.3	1.0	1.0	0.9	0.8	0.8
44	1.3	1.1	0.9	0.9	0.8	0.8	0.8
45	1.0	1.0	0.8	0.9	0.7	0.7	0.7
46	0.8	0.8	0.7	0.8	0.7	0.7	0.7
47	0.6	0.6	0.6	0.7	0.6	0.6	0.6
48	0.3	0.5	0.5	0.6	0.5	0.5	0.6
49	0.1	0.4	0.4	0.5	0.4	0.4	0.5
50	0.0	0.3	0.3	0.5	0.4	0.4	0.4

CALENDAR SPREAD TABLE

Put Options

Exercise Price is **45**

Low Volatility

STOCK PRICE	NUMBER OF MONTHS BEFORE THE LONGER TERM OPTIONS EXPIRE						
	3	4	5	6	7	8	9
	NUMBER OF MONTHS BEFORE THE SHORTER TERM OPTIONS EXPIRE						
	0	1	2	3	4	5	6
40	1.0	1.1	1.0	1.1	1.0	1.0	1.0
41	1.3	1.3	1.3	1.2	1.2	1.1	1.1
42	1.5	1.4	1.3	1.3	1.2	1.2	1.2
43	1.6	1.4	1.3	1.3	1.2	1.2	1.2
44	1.6	1.6	1.4	1.4	1.2	1.2	1.2
45	2.0	1.6	1.5	1.4	1.3	1.2	1.2
46	1.7	1.5	1.4	1.4	1.2	1.2	1.2
47	1.4	1.3	1.2	1.2	1.1	1.1	1.1
48	1.1	1.1	1.1	1.0	0.9	0.9	0.9
49	0.9	0.8	0.9	0.8	0.8	0.8	0.8
50	0.6	0.6	0.7	0.6	0.6	0.6	0.6
51	0.3	0.4	0.5	0.4	0.5	0.5	0.5
52	0.1	0.2	0.3	0.3	0.3	0.3	0.4
53	0.0	0.1	0.2	0.1	0.2	0.2	0.3
54	0.0	0.0	0.1	0.1	0.2	0.2	0.2
55	0.0	0.0	0.0	0.0	0.1	0.1	0.1

Average Volatility

STOCK PRICE	NUMBER OF MONTHS BEFORE THE LONGER TERM OPTIONS EXPIRE						
	3	4	5	6	7	8	9
	NUMBER OF MONTHS BEFORE THE SHORTER TERM OPTIONS EXPIRE						
	0	1	2	3	4	5	6
40	1.0	1.1	1.1	1.1	1.0	1.0	1.0
41	1.3	1.3	1.2	1.2	1.1	1.1	1.1
42	1.4	1.5	1.3	1.3	1.2	1.2	1.1
43	1.8	1.6	1.4	1.3	1.3	1.2	1.2
44	2.0	1.8	1.5	1.4	1.3	1.3	1.2
45	2.4	1.8	1.6	1.5	1.3	1.3	1.2
46	2.1	1.8	1.5	1.4	1.3	1.3	1.2
47	1.8	1.6	1.4	1.3	1.2	1.2	1.1
48	1.5	1.4	1.3	1.2	1.1	1.1	1.1
49	1.3	1.2	1.1	1.1	1.0	1.0	0.9
50	1.0	1.0	1.0	1.0	0.9	0.9	0.8
51	0.8	0.8	0.8	0.8	0.8	0.7	0.7
52	0.5	0.6	0.7	0.7	0.7	0.6	0.6
53	0.3	0.4	0.5	0.5	0.5	0.5	0.5
54	0.0	0.3	0.4	0.4	0.4	0.5	0.5
55	0.0	0.2	0.3	0.3	0.4	0.4	0.4

High Volatility

STOCK PRICE	NUMBER OF MONTHS BEFORE THE LONGER TERM OPTIONS EXPIRE						
	3	4	5	6	7	8	9
	NUMBER OF MONTHS BEFORE THE SHORTER TERM OPTIONS EXPIRE						
	0	1	2	3	4	5	6
40	1.1	1.2	1.0	1.1	0.8	0.9	1.0
41	1.4	1.3	1.1	1.2	0.9	1.0	1.0
42	1.7	1.4	1.2	1.2	0.9	1.1	1.0
43	1.8	1.5	1.3	1.2	1.0	1.1	1.0
44	2.3	1.6	1.3	1.3	1.0	1.1	1.1
45	2.8	1.6	1.4	1.2	1.1	1.1	1.1
46	2.5	1.6	1.4	1.2	1.1	1.1	1.0
47	2.2	1.5	1.4	1.2	1.0	1.1	1.0
48	1.9	1.4	1.3	1.1	1.1	1.0	0.9
49	1.6	1.3	1.2	1.0	1.0	0.9	0.8
50	1.3	1.2	1.1	0.9	0.9	0.8	0.8
51	1.1	1.1	1.0	0.9	0.9	0.8	0.7
52	0.8	1.0	0.9	0.8	0.8	0.7	0.7
53	0.6	0.8	0.8	0.7	0.8	0.6	0.6
54	0.4	0.7	0.7	0.7	0.7	0.6	0.6
55	0.2	0.6	0.6	0.6	0.7	0.5	0.5

CALENDAR SPREAD TABLE
Put Options Exercise Price is 50

Low Volatility

STOCK PRICE	NUMBER OF MONTHS BEFORE THE LONGER TERM OPTIONS EXPIRE						
	3	4	5	6	7	8	9
	NUMBER OF MONTHS BEFORE THE SHORTER TERM OPTIONS EXPIRE						
	0	1	2	3	4	5	6
45	1.0	1.2	1.2	1.2	1.2	1.2	1.2
46	1.5	1.5	1.4	1.3	1.3	1.3	1.2
47	1.6	1.6	1.4	1.5	1.3	1.3	1.2
48	1.7	1.6	1.5	1.5	1.3	1.3	1.3
49	1.8	1.7	1.6	1.5	1.3	1.3	1.3
50	2.3	1.8	1.7	1.6	1.4	1.4	1.3
51	1.9	1.7	1.6	1.5	1.4	1.3	1.3
52	1.6	1.5	1.5	1.4	1.3	1.2	1.2
53	1.4	1.3	1.3	1.3	1.2	1.1	1.0
54	1.1	1.1	1.1	1.1	1.0	0.9	0.9
55	0.8	0.8	0.9	0.9	0.9	0.8	0.8
56	0.5	0.6	0.7	0.7	0.7	0.7	0.6
57	0.3	0.4	0.5	0.5	0.5	0.5	0.5
58	0.1	0.2	0.3	0.4	0.4	0.4	0.4
59	0.0	0.1	0.2	0.2	0.3	0.4	0.3
60	0.0	0.0	0.1	0.2	0.2	0.2	0.2
61	0.0	0.0	0.1	0.1	0.1	0.2	0.2
62	0.0	0.0	0.0	0.0	0.1	0.1	0.1
63	0.0	0.0	0.0	0.0	0.0	0.1	0.1
64	0.0	0.0	0.0	0.0	0.0	0.0	0.1
65	0.0	0.0	0.0	0.0	0.0	0.0	0.0

Average Volatility

STOCK PRICE	NUMBER OF MONTHS BEFORE THE LONGER TERM OPTIONS EXPIRE						
	3	4	5	6	7	8	9
	NUMBER OF MONTHS BEFORE THE SHORTER TERM OPTIONS EXPIRE						
	0	1	2	3	4	5	6
45	1.2	1.4	1.3	1.2	1.2	1.2	1.2
46	1.5	1.5	1.4	1.4	1.3	1.3	1.3
47	1.7	1.6	1.5	1.4	1.4	1.3	1.3
48	1.8	1.8	1.6	1.5	1.4	1.4	1.4
49	2.3	1.9	1.7	1.6	1.4	1.4	1.4
50	2.7	2.0	1.7	1.6	1.5	1.4	1.4
51	2.4	1.9	1.7	1.5	1.5	1.4	1.3
52	2.1	1.8	1.6	1.5	1.4	1.3	1.3
53	1.8	1.7	1.5	1.4	1.3	1.2	1.2
54	1.5	1.5	1.3	1.3	1.2	1.1	1.1
55	1.3	1.3	1.2	1.1	1.1	1.0	1.0
56	1.0	1.1	1.0	1.0	0.9	0.9	0.9
57	0.8	0.9	0.9	0.9	0.8	0.8	0.8
58	0.5	0.7	0.7	0.7	0.7	0.7	0.6
59	0.3	0.5	0.6	0.6	0.6	0.6	0.6
60	0.1	0.3	0.5	0.5	0.5	0.5	0.5
61	0.0	0.2	0.4	0.4	0.4	0.4	0.4
62	0.0	0.1	0.3	0.3	0.4	0.4	0.4
63	0.0	0.1	0.2	0.3	0.3	0.3	0.3
64	0.0	0.0	0.1	0.2	0.3	0.3	0.3
65	0.0	0.0	0.1	0.2	0.2	0.2	0.3

High Volatility

STOCK PRICE	NUMBER OF MONTHS BEFORE THE LONGER TERM OPTIONS EXPIRE						
	3	4	5	6	7	8	9
	NUMBER OF MONTHS BEFORE THE SHORTER TERM OPTIONS EXPIRE						
	0	1	2	3	4	5	6
45	1.3	1.3	1.2	1.1	1.1	1.1	1.0
46	1.7	1.5	1.3	1.2	1.1	1.2	1.0
47	2.0	1.6	1.3	1.2	1.0	1.2	1.1
48	2.2	1.6	1.4	1.2	1.1	1.3	1.1
49	2.6	1.7	1.5	1.3	1.2	1.3	1.1
50	3.1	1.8	1.5	1.3	1.2	1.3	1.1
51	2.8	1.8	1.5	1.3	1.2	1.2	1.1
52	2.5	1.7	1.4	1.2	1.2	1.2	1.1
53	2.2	1.6	1.4	1.2	1.1	1.1	1.0
54	1.9	1.5	1.3	1.1	1.0	1.1	1.0
55	1.6	1.4	1.2	1.1	1.0	1.0	0.9
56	1.4	1.3	1.1	1.0	1.0	0.9	0.9
57	1.1	1.2	1.1	1.0	1.0	0.9	0.8
58	0.9	1.1	1.0	0.9	0.9	0.9	0.7
59	0.7	0.9	0.8	0.8	0.8	0.7	0.7
60	0.4	0.8	0.7	0.7	0.8	0.7	0.6
61	0.2	0.6	0.6	0.6	0.7	0.6	0.5
62	0.0	0.5	0.5	0.5	0.6	0.6	0.5
63	0.0	0.5	0.4	0.5	0.6	0.6	0.4
64	0.0	0.4	0.4	0.4	0.5	0.5	0.4
65	0.0	0.3	0.3	0.4	0.5	0.5	0.4

CALENDAR SPREAD TABLE

Put Options Exercise Price is 60

Low Volatility

STOCK PRICE	NUMBER OF MONTHS BEFORE THE LONGER TERM OPTIONS EXPIRE						
	3	4	5	6	7	8	9
	NUMBER OF MONTHS BEFORE THE SHORTER TERM OPTIONS EXPIRE						
	0	1	2	3	4	5	6
55	2.0	1.8	1.7	1.6	1.5	1.5	1.3
56	2.0	1.8	1.8	1.7	1.6	1.6	1.4
57	2.1	1.9	1.8	1.8	1.7	1.6	1.5
58	2.1	1.9	1.8	1.8	1.7	1.6	1.6
59	2.2	2.1	1.9	1.8	1.8	1.7	1.6
60	2.7	2.2	2.0	1.8	1.7	1.7	1.6
61	2.4	2.1	1.9	1.8	1.7	1.6	1.6
62	2.1	2.0	1.8	1.6	1.6	1.5	1.6
63	1.8	1.8	1.6	1.5	1.5	1.4	1.5
64	1.5	1.6	1.4	1.4	1.3	1.3	1.3
65	1.2	1.3	1.3	1.2	1.1	1.1	1.2
66	1.0	1.1	1.1	1.0	1.0	1.0	1.1
67	0.7	0.8	0.9	0.8	0.9	0.8	1.0
68	0.5	0.6	0.7	0.7	0.7	0.7	0.9
69	0.2	0.4	0.5	0.5	0.6	0.6	0.7
70	0.0	0.2	0.3	0.4	0.4	0.5	0.6
71	0.0	0.1	0.2	0.3	0.3	0.4	0.5
72	0.0	0.0	0.1	0.2	0.2	0.3	0.4
73	0.0	0.0	0.1	0.1	0.2	0.2	0.3
74	0.0	0.0	0.0	0.1	0.1	0.2	0.2
75	0.0	0.0	0.0	0.0	0.1	0.1	0.2

Average Volatility

STOCK PRICE	NUMBER OF MONTHS BEFORE THE LONGER TERM OPTIONS EXPIRE						
	3	4	5	6	7	8	9
	NUMBER OF MONTHS BEFORE THE SHORTER TERM OPTIONS EXPIRE						
	0	1	2	3	4	5	6
55	2.0	1.8	1.7	1.7	1.6	1.6	1.5
56	2.2	2.0	1.8	1.7	1.7	1.6	1.5
57	2.3	2.1	1.9	1.8	1.7	1.6	1.6
58	2.3	2.2	2.0	1.8	1.7	1.7	1.6
59	2.8	2.4	2.1	1.9	1.8	1.7	1.7
60	3.3	2.4	2.1	2.0	1.8	1.7	1.7
61	3.0	2.4	2.1	1.9	1.8	1.7	1.6
62	2.7	2.2	2.0	1.8	1.7	1.6	1.6
63	2.4	2.1	1.9	1.7	1.6	1.5	1.5
64	2.1	1.9	1.8	1.6	1.5	1.4	1.4
65	1.8	1.7	1.6	1.5	1.4	1.3	1.3
66	1.5	1.5	1.4	1.4	1.3	1.2	1.2
67	1.3	1.3	1.3	1.2	1.1	1.1	1.1
68	1.0	1.1	1.1	1.1	1.0	1.0	1.0
69	0.8	0.9	1.0	0.9	0.9	0.9	0.9
70	0.5	0.7	0.8	0.8	0.8	0.8	0.8
71	0.3	0.5	0.7	0.7	0.7	0.7	0.7
72	0.1	0.4	0.6	0.6	0.6	0.6	0.6
73	0.0	0.3	0.4	0.5	0.5	0.5	0.6
74	0.0	0.2	0.4	0.4	0.5	0.5	0.5
75	0.0	0.1	0.3	0.4	0.4	0.4	0.4

High Volatility

STOCK PRICE	NUMBER OF MONTHS BEFORE THE LONGER TERM OPTIONS EXPIRE						
	3	4	5	6	7	8	9
	NUMBER OF MONTHS BEFORE THE SHORTER TERM OPTIONS EXPIRE						
	0	1	2	3	4	5	6
55	2.1	1.8	1.6	1.5	1.3	1.2	1.2
56	2.3	1.9	1.7	1.5	1.3	1.3	1.2
57	2.5	2.0	1.7	1.5	1.4	1.3	1.2
58	2.8	2.1	1.7	1.6	1.5	1.3	1.3
59	3.2	2.1	1.8	1.7	1.5	1.3	1.4
60	3.7	2.2	1.8	1.7	1.5	1.4	1.4
61	3.4	2.2	1.7	1.6	1.5	1.4	1.4
62	3.1	2.1	1.6	1.6	1.5	1.4	1.3
63	2.8	2.0	1.6	1.5	1.4	1.3	1.3
64	2.5	1.9	1.5	1.5	1.4	1.2	1.3
65	2.2	1.8	1.4	1.4	1.3	1.3	1.3
66	2.0	1.6	1.4	1.3	1.3	1.2	1.2
67	1.7	1.5	1.3	1.3	1.2	1.1	1.1
68	1.5	1.4	1.2	1.2	1.1	1.1	1.1
69	1.2	1.2	1.1	1.1	1.0	1.0	1.0
70	1.0	1.1	1.0	1.0	0.9	0.9	1.0
71	0.7	1.0	0.9	1.0	0.8	0.9	0.9
72	0.5	0.8	0.8	0.9	0.8	0.8	0.8
73	0.3	0.7	0.7	0.8	0.7	0.8	0.7
74	0.1	0.6	0.7	0.7	0.6	0.7	0.6
75	0.0	0.5	0.6	0.7	0.6	0.6	0.5

CALENDAR SPREAD TABLE
Put Options
Exercise Price is 70

Low Volatility

STOCK PRICE	NUMBER OF MONTHS BEFORE THE LONGER TERM OPTIONS EXPIRE						
	3	4	5	6	7	8	9
	NUMBER OF MONTHS BEFORE THE SHORTER TERM OPTIONS EXPIRE						
	0	1	2	3	4	5	6
65	2.1	2.1	2.1	2.0	1.9	1.9	1.7
66	2.2	2.2	2.1	2.1	2.0	1.9	1.7
67	2.3	2.2	2.2	2.1	2.0	1.9	1.8
68	2.4	2.3	2.2	2.1	2.1	2.0	1.9
69	2.7	2.4	2.3	2.1	2.1	2.0	1.9
70	3.2	2.5	2.4	2.2	2.1	2.0	1.9
71	2.9	2.5	2.3	2.1	2.1	2.0	1.9
72	2.6	2.3	2.2	2.0	2.0	1.9	1.8
73	2.3	2.1	2.0	1.8	1.8	1.8	1.7
74	2.0	1.9	1.8	1.6	1.6	1.7	1.7
75	1.7	1.7	1.6	1.5	1.5	1.5	1.5
76	1.4	1.5	1.4	1.3	1.3	1.3	1.4
77	1.2	1.2	1.2	1.1	1.2	1.2	1.2
78	0.9	1.0	1.0	1.0	1.0	1.0	1.1
79	0.6	0.7	0.7	0.8	0.8	0.8	1.0
80	0.4	0.5	0.6	0.6	0.6	0.7	0.8
81	0.1	0.4	0.4	0.5	0.5	0.5	0.7
82	0.0	0.2	0.3	0.4	0.4	0.4	0.6
83	0.0	0.1	0.2	0.3	0.3	0.3	0.5
84	0.0	0.0	0.1	0.2	0.2	0.2	0.4
85	0.0	0.0	0.1	0.1	0.2	0.2	0.4

Average Volatility

STOCK PRICE	NUMBER OF MONTHS BEFORE THE LONGER TERM OPTIONS EXPIRE						
	3	4	5	6	7	8	9
	NUMBER OF MONTHS BEFORE THE SHORTER TERM OPTIONS EXPIRE						
	0	1	2	3	4	5	6
65	2.6	2.3	2.1	2.0	1.9	1.9	1.8
66	2.6	2.4	2.2	2.1	2.0	1.9	1.9
67	2.7	2.5	2.3	2.1	2.0	2.0	1.9
68	2.9	2.7	2.4	2.2	2.1	2.0	1.9
69	3.4	2.8	2.4	2.3	2.1	2.0	2.0
70	3.8	2.9	2.5	2.3	2.1	2.1	2.0
71	3.5	2.8	2.4	2.2	2.1	2.0	1.9
72	3.2	2.7	2.4	2.2	2.0	2.0	1.9
73	2.9	2.5	2.3	2.1	2.0	1.9	1.8
74	2.6	2.4	2.1	2.0	1.8	1.8	1.7
75	2.3	2.2	2.0	1.9	1.7	1.7	1.6
76	2.1	2.0	1.8	1.8	1.7	1.5	1.5
77	1.8	1.8	1.7	1.6	1.5	1.4	1.4
78	1.5	1.6	1.5	1.5	1.4	1.3	1.3
79	1.3	1.4	1.4	1.3	1.3	1.2	1.2
80	1.0	1.2	1.2	1.2	1.2	1.1	1.1
81	0.8	1.0	1.0	1.0	1.0	1.0	1.0
82	0.6	0.8	0.9	0.9	0.9	0.9	0.9
83	0.3	0.6	0.8	0.8	0.8	0.8	0.8
84	0.1	0.4	0.7	0.7	0.7	0.7	0.8
85	0.0	0.3	0.5	0.6	0.6	0.6	0.7

High Volatility

STOCK PRICE	NUMBER OF MONTHS BEFORE THE LONGER TERM OPTIONS EXPIRE						
	3	4	5	6	7	8	9
	NUMBER OF MONTHS BEFORE THE SHORTER TERM OPTIONS EXPIRE						
	0	1	2	3	4	5	6
65	2.7	2.2	2.0	1.9	1.7	1.6	1.5
66	2.6	2.3	2.0	1.9	1.7	1.7	1.5
67	3.0	2.3	2.1	1.9	1.8	1.7	1.6
68	3.4	2.4	2.2	2.0	1.8	1.7	1.6
69	3.9	2.5	2.2	2.0	1.9	1.7	1.7
70	4.4	2.6	2.2	2.0	1.9	1.8	1.7
71	4.0	2.6	2.2	2.0	1.9	1.7	1.7
72	3.7	2.5	2.2	2.0	1.9	1.7	1.6
73	3.4	2.4	2.1	2.0	1.8	1.7	1.6
74	3.1	2.3	2.0	1.9	1.7	1.6	1.6
75	2.9	2.3	1.9	1.8	1.7	1.6	1.5
76	2.6	2.1	1.8	1.8	1.6	1.5	1.5
77	2.3	2.0	1.7	1.7	1.6	1.4	1.4
78	2.1	1.9	1.6	1.6	1.5	1.3	1.4
79	1.8	1.8	1.5	1.4	1.4	1.3	1.3
80	1.6	1.6	1.4	1.4	1.3	1.3	1.2
81	1.3	1.5	1.3	1.3	1.3	1.2	1.2
82	1.1	1.3	1.2	1.2	1.2	1.1	1.1
83	0.8	1.2	1.1	1.1	1.1	1.1	1.0
84	0.6	1.1	1.0	1.0	1.0	1.0	1.0
85	0.4	0.9	0.9	0.9	0.9	0.9	0.9

CALENDAR SPREAD TABLE
Put Options   Exercise Price is 80

Low Volatility

STOCK PRICE	NUMBER OF MONTHS BEFORE THE LONGER TERM OPTIONS EXPIRE						
	3	4	5	6	7	8	9
	NUMBER OF MONTHS BEFORE THE SHORTER TERM OPTIONS EXPIRE						
	0	1	2	3	4	5	6
75	2.6	2.5	2.4	2.2	2.2	2.1	2.0
76	2.6	2.5	2.4	2.2	2.2	2.2	2.0
77	2.6	2.6	2.5	2.3	2.3	2.2	2.1
78	2.7	2.8	2.6	2.4	2.3	2.3	2.2
79	3.2	2.9	2.7	2.5	2.4	2.3	2.2
80	3.6	2.9	2.7	2.5	2.4	2.4	2.2
81	3.3	2.9	2.6	2.5	2.3	2.3	2.1
82	3.0	2.7	2.5	2.4	2.2	2.2	2.0
83	2.7	2.6	2.3	2.2	2.0	2.2	2.0
84	2.4	2.4	2.1	2.1	2.0	2.1	2.0
85	2.1	2.1	2.0	2.1	1.9	2.0	1.9
86	1.9	1.9	1.8	1.9	1.9	1.8	1.6
87	1.6	1.6	1.6	1.7	1.6	1.6	1.4
88	1.3	1.4	1.4	1.6	1.5	1.5	1.3
89	1.1	1.1	1.1	1.4	1.2	1.3	1.2
90	0.8	0.9	0.9	1.2	1.0	1.1	1.1
91	0.6	0.7	0.7	1.0	1.0	1.0	1.0
92	0.3	0.5	0.6	0.8	0.8	0.9	0.8
93	0.1	0.3	0.4	0.7	0.7	0.7	0.7
94	0.0	0.2	0.3	0.6	0.6	0.6	0.6
95	0.0	0.1	0.2	0.4	0.4	0.5	0.5

Average Volatility

STOCK PRICE	NUMBER OF MONTHS BEFORE THE LONGER TERM OPTIONS EXPIRE						
	3	4	5	6	7	8	9
	NUMBER OF MONTHS BEFORE THE SHORTER TERM OPTIONS EXPIRE						
	0	1	2	3	4	5	6
75	2.7	2.7	2.5	2.3	2.3	2.2	2.1
76	2.8	2.8	2.6	2.4	2.3	2.2	2.2
77	3.0	3.0	2.7	2.5	2.3	2.3	2.2
78	3.4	3.1	2.8	2.6	2.4	2.3	2.2
79	3.9	3.2	2.8	2.6	2.4	2.3	2.3
80	4.4	3.3	2.8	2.6	2.4	2.3	2.3
81	4.1	3.2	2.8	2.6	2.4	2.3	2.2
82	3.8	3.1	2.7	2.5	2.4	2.3	2.2
83	3.5	3.0	2.7	2.4	2.3	2.2	2.2
84	3.2	2.9	2.6	2.3	2.1	2.1	2.0
85	2.9	2.7	2.4	2.2	2.1	2.0	2.0
86	2.6	2.5	2.2	2.1	2.0	1.9	1.8
87	2.3	2.3	2.1	2.0	1.9	1.8	1.7
88	2.1	2.1	1.9	1.8	1.7	1.7	1.6
89	1.8	1.9	1.8	1.7	1.6	1.6	1.5
90	1.5	1.7	1.6	1.6	1.6	1.6	1.5
91	1.3	1.5	1.4	1.4	1.4	1.3	1.3
92	1.0	1.3	1.3	1.3	1.2	1.2	1.2
93	0.8	1.1	1.1	1.2	1.1	1.1	1.1
94	0.6	0.9	1.0	1.0	1.0	1.0	1.0
95	0.3	0.7	0.9	0.9	0.9	0.9	0.9

High Volatility

STOCK PRICE	NUMBER OF MONTHS BEFORE THE LONGER TERM OPTIONS EXPIRE						
	3	4	5	6	7	8	9
	NUMBER OF MONTHS BEFORE THE SHORTER TERM OPTIONS EXPIRE						
	0	1	2	3	4	5	6
75	3.0	2.6	2.3	2.1	2.0	1.9	1.9
76	2.9	2.7	2.3	2.2	2.0	1.9	1.9
77	3.6	2.8	2.4	2.2	2.1	2.0	1.9
78	4.0	2.9	2.5	2.2	2.1	2.0	2.0
79	4.5	3.0	2.5	2.3	2.1	2.0	1.9
80	5.0	3.0	2.5	2.3	2.1	2.0	2.0
81	4.7	3.0	2.5	2.2	2.1	2.0	1.9
82	4.4	2.9	2.4	2.2	2.1	1.9	1.9
83	4.1	2.8	2.4	2.1	2.0	1.9	1.8
84	3.8	2.8	2.3	2.1	1.9	1.9	1.9
85	3.5	2.7	2.2	2.0	1.8	1.8	1.8
86	3.2	2.5	2.1	2.0	1.8	1.7	1.7
87	2.9	2.4	2.1	1.8	1.7	1.6	1.6
88	2.7	2.3	2.0	1.8	1.6	1.6	1.6
89	2.4	2.1	1.8	1.7	1.6	1.5	1.5
90	2.1	2.0	1.7	1.6	1.5	1.5	1.5
91	1.9	1.9	1.6	1.5	1.4	1.4	1.4
92	1.6	1.7	1.5	1.4	1.3	1.3	1.3
93	1.4	1.6	1.4	1.3	1.3	1.2	1.2
94	1.2	1.4	1.3	1.2	1.2	1.2	1.2
95	0.9	1.3	1.2	1.1	1.1	1.1	1.1

CALENDAR SPREAD TABLE
Put Options
Exercise Price is (90)

Low Volatility

STOCK PRICE	NUMBER OF MONTHS BEFORE THE LONGER TERM OPTIONS EXPIRE						
	3	4	5	6	7	8	9
	NUMBER OF MONTHS BEFORE THE SHORTER TERM OPTIONS EXPIRE						
	0	1	2	3	4	5	6
85	2.9	2.8	2.8	2.5	2.6	2.2	2.5
86	3.0	2.9	2.8	2.6	2.6	2.2	2.5
87	3.1	3.0	2.9	2.7	2.6	2.3	2.5
88	3.2	3.1	2.9	2.7	2.6	2.3	2.5
89	3.6	3.3	3.0	2.8	2.8	2.4	2.6
90	4.1	3.3	3.0	2.8	2.8	2.5	2.6
91	3.8	3.3	3.0	2.8	2.8	2.4	2.6
92	3.5	3.2	2.9	2.7	2.7	2.4	2.5
93	3.2	3.0	2.7	2.6	2.6	2.3	2.4
94	2.9	2.8	2.5	2.4	2.4	2.2	2.2
95	2.6	2.6	2.4	2.3	2.3	2.1	2.1
96	2.3	2.3	2.1	2.1	2.1	2.0	1.9
97	2.0	2.1	1.9	1.9	2.0	1.9	1.8
98	1.8	1.8	1.7	1.8	1.8	1.7	1.6
99	1.5	1.5	1.5	1.6	1.6	1.6	1.5
100	1.2	1.3	1.3	1.4	1.4	1.5	1.3
101	1.0	1.0	1.1	1.2	1.3	1.3	1.2
102	0.7	0.8	0.9	1.0	1.1	1.2	1.0
103	0.5	0.6	0.7	0.9	0.9	1.0	0.9
104	0.2	0.4	0.5	0.8	0.8	0.9	0.7
105	0.0	0.3	0.4	0.6	0.6	0.8	0.6

Average Volatility

STOCK PRICE	NUMBER OF MONTHS BEFORE THE LONGER TERM OPTIONS EXPIRE						
	3	4	5	6	7	8	9
	NUMBER OF MONTHS BEFORE THE SHORTER TERM OPTIONS EXPIRE						
	0	1	2	3	4	5	6
85	3.1	3.1	2.9	2.7	2.6	2.5	2.4
86	3.1	3.3	3.0	2.8	2.6	2.5	2.5
87	3.5	3.4	3.1	2.8	2.7	2.5	2.5
88	4.0	3.6	3.2	2.9	2.7	2.6	2.5
89	4.5	3.7	3.2	3.0	2.8	2.6	2.6
90	4.9	3.7	3.2	3.0	2.8	2.6	2.6
91	4.6	3.6	3.2	2.9	2.8	2.6	2.5
92	4.3	3.6	3.1	2.9	2.7	2.6	2.5
93	4.0	3.4	3.1	2.8	2.6	2.5	2.5
94	3.7	3.3	3.0	2.7	2.5	2.4	2.4
95	3.4	3.1	2.8	2.6	2.4	2.3	2.3
96	3.1	2.9	2.7	2.5	2.3	2.2	2.2
97	2.9	2.7	2.5	2.4	2.2	2.1	2.1
98	2.6	2.5	2.4	2.2	2.1	2.0	2.0
99	2.3	2.3	2.2	2.1	2.0	1.9	1.9
100	2.1	2.1	2.0	1.9	1.8	1.8	1.8
101	1.8	1.9	1.9	1.8	1.7	1.6	1.6
102	1.6	1.7	1.7	1.6	1.6	1.6	1.5
103	1.3	1.5	1.5	1.5	1.5	1.4	1.4
104	1.1	1.3	1.4	1.4	1.4	1.4	1.3
105	0.8	1.1	1.2	1.3	1.2	1.3	1.2

High Volatility

STOCK PRICE	NUMBER OF MONTHS BEFORE THE LONGER TERM OPTIONS EXPIRE						
	3	4	5	6	7	8	9
	NUMBER OF MONTHS BEFORE THE SHORTER TERM OPTIONS EXPIRE						
	0	1	2	3	4	5	6
85	3.3	3.0	2.6	2.4	2.2	2.2	2.1
86	3.7	3.1	2.6	2.5	2.3	2.2	2.1
87	4.2	3.2	2.8	2.5	2.4	2.3	2.2
88	4.7	3.3	2.8	2.5	2.4	2.3	2.2
89	5.1	3.4	2.8	2.6	2.4	2.3	2.2
90	5.6	3.4	2.8	2.6	2.4	2.3	2.2
91	5.3	3.4	2.8	2.6	2.3	2.2	2.2
92	5.0	3.3	2.8	2.5	2.3	2.2	2.1
93	4.7	3.2	2.7	2.5	2.3	2.2	2.1
94	4.4	3.2	2.7	2.4	2.2	2.2	2.1
95	4.1	3.1	2.6	2.3	2.2	2.1	2.0
96	3.8	3.0	2.5	2.3	2.1	2.0	2.0
97	3.5	2.9	2.4	2.2	2.0	1.9	1.9
98	3.3	2.8	2.3	2.1	2.0	1.8	1.8
99	3.0	2.6	2.2	2.0	1.9	1.8	1.7
100	2.7	2.5	2.1	2.0	1.8	1.8	1.7
101	2.5	2.3	2.0	1.9	1.7	1.7	1.7
102	2.2	2.2	1.9	1.8	1.6	1.6	1.6
103	2.0	2.0	1.8	1.7	1.6	1.5	1.5
104	1.7	1.9	1.7	1.6	1.5	1.4	1.4
105	1.5	1.7	1.6	1.5	1.5	1.4	1.4

CALENDAR SPREAD TABLE
Put Options

Exercise Price is (100)

Low Volatility

STOCK PRICE	NUMBER OF MONTHS BEFORE THE LONGER TERM OPTIONS EXPIRE						
	3	4	5	6	7	8	9
	NUMBER OF MONTHS BEFORE THE SHORTER TERM OPTIONS EXPIRE						
	0	1	2	3	4	5	6
95	3.1	3.2	3.1	3.0	2.8	2.7	2.7
96	2.7	3.2	3.2	3.0	2.8	2.8	2.7
97	3.2	3.4	3.3	3.0	2.8	2.9	2.8
98	3.6	3.6	3.3	3.1	2.8	2.9	2.8
99	4.1	3.7	3.3	3.1	2.8	3.0	2.8
100	4.6	3.7	3.4	3.2	2.9	3.0	2.9
101	4.3	3.6	3.4	3.2	2.9	2.9	2.8
102	3.9	3.4	3.3	3.1	2.8	2.9	2.7
103	3.6	3.2	3.2	2.9	2.7	2.8	2.5
104	3.3	3.0	3.0	2.7	2.6	2.7	2.4
105	0.0	2.8	2.9	2.5	2.4	2.6	2.3
106	2.8	2.6	2.7	2.4	2.3	2.5	2.2
107	2.5	2.4	2.5	2.2	2.1	2.3	2.1
108	2.2	2.1	2.3	2.1	2.0	2.1	1.9
109	1.9	1.9	2.1	1.9	1.9	2.0	1.8
110	1.7	1.6	1.9	1.8	1.7	1.8	1.6
111	1.4	1.4	1.6	1.6	1.6	1.6	1.5
112	1.1	1.1	1.4	1.4	1.4	1.5	1.3
113	0.9	0.9	1.2	1.2	1.2	1.3	1.2
114	0.6	0.7	1.0	1.1	1.1	1.2	1.1
115	0.4	0.5	0.8	0.9	1.0	1.0	0.9

Average Volatility

STOCK PRICE	NUMBER OF MONTHS BEFORE THE LONGER TERM OPTIONS EXPIRE						
	3	4	5	6	7	8	9
	NUMBER OF MONTHS BEFORE THE SHORTER TERM OPTIONS EXPIRE						
	0	1	2	3	4	5	6
95	3.4	3.5	3.3	3.0	2.9	2.8	2.8
96	3.6	3.7	3.4	3.1	2.9	2.9	2.8
97	4.1	3.9	3.4	3.2	3.0	2.9	2.8
98	4.6	4.0	3.5	3.3	3.1	2.9	2.9
99	5.0	4.1	3.6	3.3	3.0	2.9	2.9
100	5.5	4.1	3.6	3.3	3.1	2.9	2.9
101	5.2	4.1	3.6	3.3	3.1	2.9	2.8
102	4.9	4.0	3.5	3.2	3.0	2.9	2.8
103	4.6	3.9	3.4	3.1	2.9	2.8	2.8
104	4.3	3.7	3.4	3.1	2.8	2.7	2.7
105	4.0	3.6	3.2	3.0	2.7	2.7	2.6
106	3.7	3.5	3.1	2.9	2.6	2.5	2.5
107	3.4	3.2	2.9	2.8	2.5	2.4	2.4
108	3.1	3.0	2.8	2.7	2.4	2.3	2.3
109	2.9	2.8	2.6	2.5	2.3	2.2	2.1
110	2.6	2.6	2.4	2.4	2.2	2.1	2.1
111	2.3	2.4	2.3	2.2	2.1	2.0	2.0
112	2.1	2.2	2.1	2.1	1.9	1.9	1.9
113	1.8	2.0	1.9	1.9	1.8	1.7	1.7
114	1.6	1.8	1.8	1.8	1.7	1.6	1.6
115	1.4	1.6	1.6	1.6	1.6	1.6	1.5

High Volatility

STOCK PRICE	NUMBER OF MONTHS BEFORE THE LONGER TERM OPTIONS EXPIRE						
	3	4	5	6	7	8	9
	NUMBER OF MONTHS BEFORE THE SHORTER TERM OPTIONS EXPIRE						
	0	1	2	3	4	5	6
95	3.6	3.5	2.9	2.8	2.5	2.4	2.4
96	4.4	3.5	3.1	2.8	2.6	2.5	2.4
97	4.8	3.6	3.1	2.9	2.6	2.5	2.5
98	5.3	3.7	3.1	2.9	2.7	2.6	2.4
99	5.8	3.8	3.1	2.9	2.7	2.6	2.5
100	6.2	3.8	3.1	2.9	2.7	2.6	2.5
101	5.9	3.8	3.1	2.9	2.6	2.5	2.4
102	5.6	3.7	3.0	2.8	2.6	2.5	2.4
103	5.3	3.6	3.0	2.8	2.6	2.5	2.3
104	5.0	3.6	3.0	2.7	2.5	2.5	2.3
105	4.7	3.5	2.9	2.6	2.5	2.4	2.3
106	4.4	3.4	2.8	2.6	2.4	2.3	2.2
107	4.1	3.3	2.7	2.6	2.3	2.3	2.2
108	3.9	3.2	2.7	2.4	2.3	2.2	2.1
109	3.6	3.1	2.6	2.4	2.2	2.1	2.0
110	3.3	2.9	2.5	2.3	2.1	2.0	1.9
111	3.1	2.8	2.3	2.2	2.1	2.0	1.9
112	2.8	2.6	2.2	2.1	2.0	1.9	1.9
113	2.6	2.5	2.1	2.0	1.9	1.8	1.8
114	2.3	2.3	2.0	1.9	1.8	1.8	1.7
115	2.1	2.2	1.9	1.8	1.8	1.7	1.6

T101

THE FUTURE VALUE STRADDLE TABLES

*The Future Value Tables are generated by computer simulations. Due to the nature of the computer simulation techniques that we used there may be slight aberrations in the option prices presented. Therefore you should allow a variance of plus or minus 10% of these option prices. In a few cases, some of the less important, peripheral option prices may vary more than 10%.

STRADDLE TABLE

Exercise Price is (10)

Low Volatility

STOCK PRICE — NUMBER OF MONTHS BEFORE THE OPTIONS EXPIRE

STOCK PRICE	1	2	3	4	5	6	7	8	9
1	9.0	9.0	8.9	8.9	9.0	9.0	9.1	8.9	8.9
2	8.0	8.0	7.9	7.9	8.0	8.0	8.1	7.9	7.9
3	7.0	7.0	6.9	6.9	7.0	7.0	7.1	6.9	6.9
4	6.0	6.0	5.9	5.9	6.0	6.0	6.1	5.9	5.9
5	5.0	5.0	4.9	4.9	5.0	5.0	5.1	4.9	4.9
6	4.0	4.0	3.9	3.9	4.0	4.0	4.1	3.9	3.9
7	3.0	3.0	2.9	2.9	3.0	3.0	3.1	2.9	2.9
8	2.0	2.0	1.9	1.9	2.0	2.0	2.1	2.0	2.0
9	1.0	1.0	1.0	1.0	1.1	1.2	1.2	1.1	1.2
10	0.3	0.3	0.4	0.5	0.7	0.7	0.7	0.7	0.9
11	0.9	0.9	1.0	1.1	1.1	1.2	1.0	1.1	1.3
12	1.9	1.9	2.0	2.0	2.0	1.9	1.8	2.0	2.1
13	2.9	2.9	3.0	3.0	2.9	2.9	2.8	3.0	3.0
14	3.9	3.9	4.0	4.0	3.9	3.9	3.8	4.0	4.0
15	4.9	4.9	5.0	5.0	4.9	4.9	4.8	5.0	5.0
16	5.9	5.9	6.0	6.0	5.9	5.9	5.8	6.0	6.0
17	6.9	6.9	7.0	7.0	6.9	6.9	6.8	7.0	7.0
18	7.9	7.9	8.0	8.0	7.9	7.9	7.8	8.0	8.0
19	8.9	8.9	9.0	9.0	8.9	8.9	8.8	9.0	9.0
20	9.9	9.9	10.	10.	9.9	9.9	9.8	10.	10.

Average Volatility

STOCK PRICE — NUMBER OF MONTHS BEFORE THE OPTIONS EXPIRE

STOCK PRICE	1	2	3	4	5	6	7	8	9
1	8.9	9.0	9.0	8.9	8.9	9.0	9.1	8.9	8.5
2	7.9	8.0	8.0	7.9	7.9	8.0	8.1	7.9	7.5
3	6.9	7.0	7.0	6.9	6.9	7.0	7.1	6.9	6.5
4	5.9	6.0	6.0	5.9	5.9	6.0	6.1	5.9	5.5
5	4.9	5.0	5.0	4.9	4.9	5.0	5.1	4.9	4.5
6	3.9	4.0	4.0	3.9	3.9	4.0	4.1	3.9	3.5
7	2.9	3.0	3.0	2.9	2.9	3.0	3.1	3.0	2.6
8	1.9	2.0	2.0	2.0	2.0	2.1	2.2	2.1	1.8
9	0.9	1.1	1.1	1.2	1.3	1.4	1.5	1.4	1.2
10	0.4	0.6	0.6	0.8	0.9	1.1	1.0	1.1	1.1
11	1.0	1.0	1.0	1.2	1.3	1.4	1.3	1.4	1.7
12	2.0	1.9	1.9	2.0	2.0	2.1	1.9	2.1	2.5
13	3.0	2.9	2.9	3.0	3.0	2.9	2.8	3.0	3.4
14	4.0	3.9	3.9	4.0	4.0	3.9	3.8	4.0	4.4
15	5.0	4.9	4.9	5.0	5.0	4.9	4.8	5.0	5.4
16	6.0	5.9	5.9	6.0	6.0	5.9	5.8	6.0	6.4
17	7.0	6.9	6.9	7.0	7.0	6.9	6.8	7.0	7.4
18	8.0	7.9	7.9	8.0	8.0	7.9	7.8	8.0	8.4
19	9.0	8.9	8.9	9.0	9.0	8.9	8.8	9.0	9.4
20	10.	9.9	9.9	10.	10.	9.9	9.8	10.	10.

High Volatility

STOCK PRICE — NUMBER OF MONTHS BEFORE THE OPTIONS EXPIRE

STOCK PRICE	1	2	3	4	5	6	7	8	9
1	8.8	9.1	9.1	8.9	8.9	9.0	9.3	8.9	8.1
2	7.8	8.1	8.1	7.9	7.9	8.0	8.3	7.9	7.1
3	6.8	7.1	7.1	6.9	6.9	7.0	7.3	6.9	6.1
4	5.8	6.1	6.1	5.9	5.9	6.1	6.3	6.0	5.2
5	4.8	5.1	5.1	4.9	4.9	5.1	5.3	5.0	4.3
6	3.8	4.1	4.1	4.0	4.0	4.2	4.4	4.2	3.5
7	2.8	3.1	3.1	3.1	3.2	3.5	3.6	3.4	2.9
8	1.9	2.3	2.2	2.3	2.5	2.8	2.9	2.8	2.4
9	1.1	1.5	1.5	1.7	2.0	2.3	2.3	2.2	2.1
10	0.8	1.1	1.2	1.5	1.8	2.1	2.0	2.0	2.1
11	1.3	1.4	1.5	1.8	2.0	2.3	2.1	2.2	2.6
12	2.1	2.1	2.1	2.4	2.6	2.8	2.5	2.7	3.2
13	3.1	2.9	2.9	3.2	3.2	3.4	3.1	3.4	4.1
14	4.1	3.8	3.8	4.1	4.1	4.2	3.8	4.2	5.0
15	5.1	4.8	4.8	5.0	5.0	5.0	4.7	5.1	5.9
16	6.1	5.8	5.8	6.0	6.0	5.9	5.7	6.0	6.9
17	7.1	6.8	6.8	7.0	7.0	6.9	6.6	7.0	7.8
18	8.1	7.8	7.8	8.0	8.0	7.9	7.6	8.0	8.8
19	9.1	8.8	8.8	9.0	9.0	8.9	8.6	9.0	9.8
20	10.	9.8	9.8	10.	10.	9.9	9.6	10.	10.

STRADDLE TABLE

Exercise
Price is (15)

Low Volatility

STOCK PRICE — NUMBER OF MONTHS BEFORE THE OPTIONS EXPIRE

STOCK PRICE	1	2	3	4	5	6	7	8	9
10	5.0	5.0	5.0	5.0	5.0	5.0	5.0	5.0	5.0
11	4.0	4.0	4.0	4.0	4.0	4.0	4.0	4.0	4.0
12	3.0	3.0	3.0	3.0	3.0	3.0	3.0	3.1	3.1
13	2.0	2.0	2.0	2.1	2.1	2.1	2.2	2.2	2.3
14	1.0	1.1	1.2	1.3	1.3	1.4	1.4	1.5	1.6
15	0.4	0.6	0.7	0.9	0.9	1.0	1.1	1.2	1.2
16	0.9	1.1	1.1	1.2	1.3	1.4	1.4	1.5	1.5
17	1.9	1.9	1.9	2.0	2.0	2.1	2.1	2.1	2.2
18	2.9	2.9	2.9	2.9	2.9	2.9	2.9	2.9	3.0
19	3.9	3.9	3.9	3.9	3.9	3.9	3.9	3.9	3.9
20	4.9	4.9	4.9	4.9	4.9	4.9	4.9	4.9	4.9
21	5.9	5.9	5.9	5.9	5.9	5.9	5.9	5.9	5.9
22	6.9	6.9	6.9	6.9	6.9	6.9	6.9	6.9	6.9
23	7.9	7.9	7.9	7.9	7.9	7.9	7.9	7.9	7.9
24	8.9	8.9	8.9	8.9	8.9	8.9	8.9	8.9	8.9
25	9.9	9.9	9.9	9.9	9.9	9.9	9.9	9.9	9.9

Average Volatility

STOCK PRICE — NUMBER OF MONTHS BEFORE THE OPTIONS EXPIRE

STOCK PRICE	1	2	3	4	5	6	7	8	9
10	5.0	5.0	5.0	5.0	5.1	5.1	5.1	5.1	5.1
11	4.0	4.0	4.0	4.1	4.1	4.1	4.1	4.1	4.2
12	3.0	3.0	3.1	3.1	3.2	3.2	3.3	3.3	3.4
13	2.0	2.1	2.2	2.3	2.4	2.4	2.5	2.5	2.7
14	1.1	1.3	1.4	1.6	1.7	1.8	1.9	2.0	2.1
15	0.6	0.9	1.1	1.3	1.4	1.5	1.6	1.7	1.9
16	1.1	1.3	1.4	1.6	1.7	1.8	1.9	2.0	2.1
17	1.9	2.0	2.1	2.2	2.3	2.4	2.4	2.5	2.6
18	2.9	2.9	2.9	3.0	3.0	3.1	3.1	3.2	3.3
19	3.9	3.9	3.9	3.9	3.9	3.9	3.9	4.0	4.1
20	4.9	4.9	4.9	4.9	4.8	4.9	4.9	4.9	4.9
21	5.9	5.9	5.9	5.9	5.8	5.9	5.8	5.9	5.9
22	6.9	6.9	6.9	6.9	6.8	6.9	6.8	6.9	6.8
23	7.9	7.9	7.9	7.9	7.8	7.9	7.8	7.9	7.8
24	8.9	8.9	8.9	8.9	8.8	8.9	8.8	8.9	8.8
25	9.9	9.9	9.9	9.9	9.8	9.9	9.8	9.9	9.8

High Volatility

STOCK PRICE — NUMBER OF MONTHS BEFORE THE OPTIONS EXPIRE

STOCK PRICE	1	2	3	4	5	6	7	8	9
10	5.0	5.1	5.2	5.4	5.5	5.6	5.7	5.7	6.0
11	4.0	4.1	4.3	4.5	4.7	4.8	4.9	5.0	5.2
12	3.1	3.3	3.5	3.8	4.0	4.2	4.3	4.4	4.6
13	2.2	2.5	2.8	3.1	3.3	3.5	3.6	3.8	4.1
14	1.5	1.9	2.3	2.7	2.9	3.0	3.2	3.4	3.7
15	1.1	1.7	2.1	2.5	2.7	2.9	3.0	3.3	3.6
16	1.4	2.0	2.3	2.7	2.9	3.0	3.2	3.4	3.8
17	2.1	2.5	2.8	3.1	3.3	3.4	3.6	3.8	4.1
18	2.9	3.2	3.4	3.7	3.8	4.0	4.1	4.3	4.6
19	3.9	4.0	4.1	4.4	4.5	4.6	4.7	4.9	5.1
20	4.9	4.9	5.0	5.1	5.2	5.4	5.4	5.6	5.8
21	5.9	5.9	5.9	6.0	6.0	6.2	6.2	6.4	6.5
22	6.9	6.9	6.8	6.9	6.9	7.0	7.0	7.2	7.3
23	7.9	7.9	7.8	7.8	7.8	7.9	7.9	8.0	8.1
24	8.9	8.9	8.8	8.8	8.8	8.8	8.8	8.9	8.9
25	9.9	9.9	9.8	9.8	9.7	9.8	9.8	9.8	9.8

STRADDLE TABLE

Exercise Price is 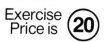 (20)

Low Volatility

STOCK PRICE	NUMBER OF MONTHS BEFORE THE OPTIONS EXPIRE								
	1	2	3	4	5	6	7	8	9
10	10.	10.	10.	10.	10.	10.	10.	10.	10.
11	9.0	9.0	9.0	9.0	9.0	9.1	9.0	9.1	9.0
12	8.0	8.0	8.0	8.0	8.0	8.1	8.0	8.1	8.0
13	7.0	7.0	7.0	7.0	7.0	7.1	7.0	7.1	7.0
14	6.0	6.0	6.0	6.0	6.0	6.1	6.0	6.1	6.0
15	5.0	5.0	5.0	5.0	5.0	5.1	5.1	5.1	5.1
16	4.0	4.0	4.0	4.0	4.0	4.1	4.1	4.1	4.1
17	3.0	3.0	3.0	3.1	3.1	3.2	3.2	3.2	3.3
18	2.0	2.0	2.1	2.2	2.3	2.3	2.4	2.4	2.5
19	1.1	1.2	1.3	1.5	1.6	1.7	1.7	1.8	1.9
20	0.5	0.8	1.0	1.2	1.3	1.4	1.4	1.6	1.7
21	1.0	1.2	1.3	1.5	1.6	1.6	1.7	1.8	1.9
22	1.9	2.0	2.0	2.1	2.2	2.2	2.3	2.4	2.5
23	2.9	2.9	2.9	3.0	3.0	3.0	3.1	3.1	3.2
24	3.9	3.9	3.9	3.9	3.9	3.9	3.9	3.9	4.0
25	4.9	4.9	4.9	4.9	4.9	4.8	4.9	4.9	4.9
26	5.9	5.9	5.9	5.9	5.9	5.8	5.9	5.8	5.9
27	6.9	6.9	6.9	6.9	6.9	6.8	6.9	6.8	6.9
28	7.9	7.9	7.9	7.9	7.9	7.8	7.9	7.8	7.9
29	8.9	8.9	8.9	8.9	8.9	8.8	8.9	8.8	8.9
30	9.9	9.9	9.9	9.9	9.9	9.8	9.9	9.8	9.9

Average Volatility

STOCK PRICE	NUMBER OF MONTHS BEFORE THE OPTIONS EXPIRE								
	1	2	3	4	5	6	7	8	9
10	10.	10.	10.	10.	10.	10.	10.	10.	10.
11	9.0	9.0	9.1	9.1	9.1	9.0	9.1	9.1	9.1
12	8.0	8.0	8.1	8.1	8.1	8.0	8.1	8.1	8.1
13	7.0	7.0	7.1	7.1	7.1	7.1	7.1	7.1	7.2
14	6.0	6.0	6.1	6.1	6.1	6.1	6.1	6.2	6.2
15	5.0	5.0	5.1	5.1	5.1	5.1	5.2	5.3	5.4
16	4.0	4.0	4.1	4.2	4.3	4.3	4.4	4.5	4.6
17	3.0	3.1	3.2	3.3	3.4	3.5	3.6	3.7	3.8
18	2.0	2.2	2.4	2.6	2.7	2.8	2.9	3.0	3.2
19	1.2	1.5	1.7	2.0	2.2	2.2	2.4	2.5	2.7
20	0.8	1.2	1.4	1.8	1.9	2.0	2.2	2.5	2.7
21	1.2	1.5	1.7	2.0	2.2	2.3	2.4	2.5	2.7
22	2.0	2.2	2.3	2.5	2.7	2.7	2.9	3.0	3.2
23	2.9	3.0	3.1	3.2	3.3	3.4	3.5	3.6	3.7
24	3.9	3.9	3.9	4.0	4.1	4.2	4.2	4.3	4.4
25	4.9	4.9	4.9	4.9	4.9	5.0	5.0	5.1	5.2
26	5.9	5.9	5.8	5.9	5.8	5.9	5.9	5.9	6.0
27	6.9	6.9	6.8	6.8	6.8	6.8	6.8	6.8	6.9
28	7.9	7.9	7.8	7.8	7.8	7.9	7.8	7.8	7.8
29	8.9	8.9	8.8	8.8	8.8	8.9	8.8	8.8	8.8
30	9.9	9.9	9.8	9.8	9.8	9.9	9.8	9.8	9.8

High Volatility

STOCK PRICE	NUMBER OF MONTHS BEFORE THE OPTIONS EXPIRE								
	1	2	3	4	5	6	7	8	9
10	10.	10.	10.	10.	10.	10.	10.	10.	10.
11	9.0	9.1	9.2	9.2	9.3	9.4	9.5	9.7	9.8
12	8.0	8.1	8.2	8.3	8.4	8.5	8.6	8.8	9.0
13	7.0	7.1	7.3	7.4	7.6	7.6	7.8	8.0	8.2
14	6.0	6.2	6.4	6.6	6.8	6.8	7.0	7.3	7.4
15	5.1	5.2	5.5	5.8	6.0	6.1	6.3	6.5	6.7
16	4.1	4.4	4.7	5.1	5.3	5.4	5.6	5.9	6.1
17	3.2	3.6	4.0	4.4	4.7	4.8	5.0	5.3	5.6
18	2.4	3.0	3.4	3.9	4.2	4.3	4.5	4.9	5.2
19	1.8	2.5	3.0	3.5	3.8	4.0	4.2	4.6	4.9
20	1.5	2.3	2.8	3.3	3.7	3.8	4.1	4.4	4.8
21	1.8	2.5	3.0	3.5	3.8	4.0	4.2	4.6	4.9
22	2.3	3.0	3.3	3.8	4.1	4.3	4.6	4.8	5.2
23	3.1	3.6	3.9	4.3	4.6	4.8	5.0	5.2	5.6
24	3.9	4.3	4.6	5.0	5.2	5.3	5.5	5.7	6.1
25	4.9	5.1	5.3	5.6	5.8	6.0	6.2	6.4	6.7
26	5.9	5.9	6.1	6.4	6.5	6.7	6.8	7.0	7.3
27	6.9	6.9	6.9	7.2	7.3	7.4	7.6	7.7	8.0
28	7.9	7.8	7.8	8.0	8.1	8.2	8.3	8.5	8.7
29	8.9	8.8	8.8	8.9	9.0	9.1	9.2	9.3	9.5
30	9.9	9.8	9.8	9.8	9.8	10.	10.	10.	10.

STRADDLE TABLE

Exercise Price is (25)

Low Volatility

STOCK PRICE	NUMBER OF MONTHS BEFORE THE OPTIONS EXPIRE								
	1	2	3	4	5	6	7	8	9
15	10.	10.	10.	10.	10.	10.	10.	10.	10.
16	9.0	9.0	9.0	9.1	9.0	9.1	9.1	9.1	9.0
17	8.0	8.0	8.0	8.1	8.0	8.1	8.1	8.1	8.0
18	7.0	7.0	7.0	7.1	7.0	7.1	7.1	7.1	7.1
19	6.0	6.0	6.0	6.1	6.0	6.1	6.1	6.1	6.1
20	5.0	5.0	5.0	5.1	5.1	5.1	5.1	5.1	5.2
21	4.0	4.0	4.0	4.1	4.1	4.2	4.2	4.3	4.3
22	3.0	3.0	3.1	3.2	3.3	3.3	3.4	3.4	3.5
23	2.0	2.1	2.2	2.4	2.5	2.6	2.6	2.7	2.8
24	1.1	1.4	1.5	1.7	1.9	2.0	2.1	2.2	2.3
25	0.6	1.0	1.2	1.5	1.6	1.7	1.8	2.0	2.1
26	1.1	1.4	1.5	1.7	1.9	2.0	2.1	2.2	2.3
27	1.9	2.1	2.2	2.3	2.4	2.5	2.6	2.7	2.8
28	2.9	2.9	3.0	3.0	3.1	3.2	3.3	3.3	3.4
29	3.9	3.9	3.9	3.9	4.0	4.0	4.0	4.1	4.2
30	4.9	4.9	4.9	4.8	4.9	4.9	4.9	4.9	5.0
31	5.9	5.9	5.9	5.8	5.9	5.9	5.9	5.9	5.9
32	6.9	6.9	6.9	6.8	6.9	6.8	6.8	6.8	6.9
33	7.9	7.9	7.9	7.8	7.9	7.8	7.8	7.8	7.9
34	8.9	8.9	8.9	8.8	8.9	8.8	8.8	8.8	8.9
35	9.9	9.9	9.9	9.8	9.9	9.8	9.8	9.8	9.9

Average Volatility

STOCK PRICE	NUMBER OF MONTHS BEFORE THE OPTIONS EXPIRE								
	1	2	3	4	5	6	7	8	9
15	10.	10.	10.	10.	10.	10.	10.	10.	10.
16	9.0	9.0	9.1	9.1	9.1	9.1	9.1	9.1	9.2
17	8.0	8.0	8.1	8.1	8.1	8.1	8.1	8.2	8.3
18	7.0	7.0	7.1	7.1	7.2	7.1	7.2	7.3	7.4
19	6.0	6.0	6.1	6.2	6.2	6.2	6.3	6.4	6.5
20	5.0	5.0	5.1	5.3	5.3	5.4	5.5	5.6	5.7
21	4.0	4.1	4.2	4.4	4.5	4.5	4.7	4.8	5.0
22	3.1	3.2	3.4	3.6	3.7	3.8	3.9	4.1	4.3
23	2.1	2.4	2.6	2.9	3.0	3.2	3.3	3.5	3.7
24	1.4	1.8	2.1	2.4	2.6	2.7	2.9	3.1	3.4
25	1.0	1.5	1.8	2.2	2.4	2.6	2.7	2.9	3.2
26	1.3	1.8	2.1	2.4	2.6	2.7	2.9	3.1	3.3
27	2.0	2.4	2.6	2.9	3.0	3.2	3.3	3.5	3.7
28	2.9	3.1	3.3	3.5	3.6	3.8	3.9	4.0	4.2
29	3.9	3.9	4.0	4.2	4.3	4.4	4.5	4.7	4.8
30	4.9	4.9	4.9	5.0	5.1	5.2	5.3	5.4	5.5
31	5.9	5.9	5.8	5.9	5.9	6.0	6.1	6.2	6.3
32	6.9	6.9	6.8	6.8	6.8	6.9	6.9	7.0	7.1
33	7.9	7.9	7.8	7.8	7.8	7.9	7.8	7.9	7.9
34	8.9	8.9	8.8	8.8	8.8	8.8	8.8	8.8	8.8
35	9.9	9.9	9.8	9.8	9.8	9.8	9.8	9.8	9.8

High Volatility

STOCK PRICE	NUMBER OF MONTHS BEFORE THE OPTIONS EXPIRE								
	1	2	3	4	5	6	7	8	9
15	10.	10.	10.	10.	10.	10.	10.	11.	11.
16	9.1	9.1	9.3	9.6	9.7	9.8	10.	10.	10.
17	8.1	8.2	8.4	8.7	8.9	9.0	9.2	9.4	9.7
18	7.1	7.3	7.5	7.9	8.1	8.2	8.4	8.6	9.0
19	6.1	6.4	6.7	7.1	7.3	7.4	7.7	7.9	8.3
20	5.2	5.5	5.9	6.4	6.6	6.7	7.0	7.3	7.7
21	4.3	4.8	5.2	5.7	5.9	6.1	6.4	6.7	7.2
22	3.4	4.0	4.5	5.1	5.4	5.6	5.9	6.2	6.7
23	2.7	3.5	4.0	4.6	4.9	5.2	5.5	5.9	6.4
24	2.1	2.9	3.7	4.3	4.6	4.9	5.2	5.6	6.2
25	1.9	2.9	3.5	4.2	4.5	4.8	5.1	5.5	6.1
26	2.1	3.1	3.7	4.3	4.6	4.9	5.3	5.7	6.1
27	2.6	3.5	4.0	4.6	4.9	5.2	5.5	5.9	6.4
28	3.3	4.0	4.5	5.0	5.3	5.6	5.9	6.3	6.7
29	4.0	4.6	5.1	5.6	5.8	6.1	6.4	6.7	7.1
30	4.9	5.4	5.7	6.2	6.4	6.7	6.9	7.3	7.6
31	5.8	6.2	6.4	6.8	7.1	7.3	7.5	7.9	8.2
32	6.8	7.0	7.2	7.6	7.8	8.0	8.2	8.5	8.8
33	7.8	7.9	8.1	8.3	8.5	8.7	8.9	9.2	9.4
34	8.8	8.8	8.9	9.2	9.3	9.5	9.6	9.9	10.
35	9.8	9.8	9.8	10.	10.	10.	10.	10.	10.

STRADDLE TABLE

Exercise Price is (30)

Low Volatility

STOCK PRICE	NUMBER OF MONTHS BEFORE THE OPTIONS EXPIRE								
	1	2	3	4	5	6	7	8	9
20	10.	10.	10.	10.	10.	10.	10.	10.	10.
21	9.0	9.0	9.0	9.0	9.1	9.1	9.1	9.1	9.1
22	8.0	8.0	8.0	8.0	8.1	8.1	8.1	8.1	8.1
23	7.0	7.0	7.0	7.0	7.1	7.1	7.1	7.2	7.1
24	6.0	6.0	6.0	6.0	6.1	6.1	6.2	6.2	6.2
25	5.0	5.0	5.0	5.1	5.2	5.2	5.2	5.3	5.3
26	4.0	4.0	4.1	4.2	4.3	4.3	4.4	4.5	4.5
27	3.0	3.1	3.2	3.3	3.4	3.5	3.6	3.7	3.8
28	2.0	2.2	2.4	2.6	2.7	2.8	2.9	3.0	3.1
29	1.2	1.5	1.7	2.0	2.2	2.3	2.4	2.5	2.7
30	0.8	1.2	1.5	1.8	2.0	2.1	2.2	2.3	2.5
31	1.2	1.5	1.7	2.0	2.2	2.3	2.4	2.5	2.7
32	2.0	2.2	2.3	2.5	2.7	2.8	2.9	3.0	3.1
33	2.9	3.0	3.1	3.2	3.3	3.4	3.5	3.6	3.7
34	3.9	3.9	3.9	4.0	4.1	4.2	4.2	4.3	4.4
35	4.9	4.9	4.9	4.9	4.9	5.0	5.0	5.1	5.2
36	5.9	5.9	5.9	5.9	5.8	5.9	5.9	5.9	6.0
37	6.9	6.9	6.9	6.9	6.8	6.9	6.8	6.8	6.9
38	7.9	7.9	7.9	7.9	7.8	7.8	7.8	7.8	7.8
39	8.9	8.9	8.9	8.9	8.8	8.8	8.8	8.8	8.8
40	9.9	9.9	9.9	9.9	9.8	9.8	9.8	9.8	9.8

Average Volatility

STOCK PRICE	NUMBER OF MONTHS BEFORE THE OPTIONS EXPIRE								
	1	2	3	4	5	6	7	8	9
20	10.	10.	10.	10.	10.	10.	10.	10.	10.
21	9.0	9.1	9.1	9.1	9.1	9.1	9.2	9.3	9.4
22	8.0	8.1	8.1	8.2	8.2	8.2	8.3	8.4	8.5
23	7.0	7.1	7.1	7.2	7.2	7.3	7.4	7.5	7.6
24	6.0	6.1	6.1	6.3	6.4	6.4	6.5	6.7	6.8
25	5.0	5.1	5.2	5.5	5.5	5.6	5.7	5.9	6.1
26	4.0	4.2	4.4	4.7	4.8	4.8	5.0	5.2	5.4
27	3.1	3.4	3.6	3.9	4.0	4.1	4.3	4.5	4.7
28	2.2	2.6	2.9	3.3	3.5	3.6	3.8	4.0	4.3
29	1.5	2.1	2.4	2.8	3.1	3.2	3.4	3.7	3.9
30	1.2	1.8	2.2	2.7	2.9	3.1	3.3	3.6	3.8
31	1.5	2.1	2.4	2.8	3.1	3.2	3.4	3.7	4.0
32	2.2	2.6	2.9	3.2	3.5	3.6	3.8	4.0	4.3
33	3.0	3.3	3.5	3.8	4.0	4.1	4.3	4.5	4.7
34	3.9	4.0	4.2	4.5	4.7	4.8	4.9	5.1	5.3
35	4.9	4.9	5.1	5.2	5.4	5.5	5.6	5.8	6.0
36	5.9	5.8	5.9	6.0	6.2	6.3	6.4	6.5	6.7
37	6.9	6.8	6.8	6.9	7.0	7.1	7.2	7.3	7.4
38	7.9	7.8	7.8	7.8	7.9	8.0	8.0	8.1	8.2
39	8.9	8.8	8.8	8.8	8.8	8.9	8.9	8.9	9.1
40	9.9	9.8	9.8	9.8	9.8	9.8	9.8	9.8	9.9

High Volatility

STOCK PRICE	NUMBER OF MONTHS BEFORE THE OPTIONS EXPIRE								
	1	2	3	4	5	6	7	8	9
20	10.	10.	10.	10.	10.	11.	11.	11.	11.
21	9.0	9.3	9.5	10.	10.	10.	10.	10.	11.
22	8.0	8.4	8.7	9.2	9.4	9.5	9.8	10.	10.
23	7.1	7.5	7.8	8.4	8.6	8.7	9.1	9.4	9.8
24	6.1	6.7	7.1	7.6	7.9	8.0	8.4	8.8	9.2
25	5.2	5.9	6.3	6.9	7.2	7.4	7.8	8.2	8.6
26	4.4	5.2	5.6	6.3	6.7	6.9	7.3	7.7	8.2
27	3.6	4.5	5.1	5.8	6.2	6.4	6.8	7.3	7.8
28	2.9	4.0	4.6	5.4	5.8	6.1	6.5	7.0	7.5
29	2.4	3.6	4.3	5.1	5.6	5.8	6.3	6.8	7.3
30	2.2	3.5	4.2	5.0	5.5	5.8	6.2	6.7	7.2
31	2.5	3.6	4.3	5.1	5.6	5.9	6.3	6.8	7.3
32	2.9	4.0	4.6	5.4	5.9	6.1	6.5	7.0	7.5
33	3.6	4.4	5.1	5.8	6.2	6.5	6.9	7.3	7.8
34	4.3	5.0	5.6	6.2	6.7	6.9	7.3	7.7	8.2
35	5.1	5.7	6.2	6.8	7.2	7.4	7.8	8.2	8.6
36	6.0	6.4	6.9	7.4	7.8	8.0	8.3	8.7	9.2
37	6.9	7.2	7.6	8.1	8.5	8.7	9.0	9.3	9.7
38	7.9	8.0	8.4	8.8	9.2	9.3	9.6	9.9	10.
39	8.9	8.9	9.2	9.5	9.9	9.9	10.	10.	11.
40	9.9	9.8	10.	10.	10.	10.	11.	11.	11.

STRADDLE TABLE

Exercise Price is (35)

Low Volatility

STOCK PRICE — NUMBER OF MONTHS BEFORE THE OPTIONS EXPIRE

STOCK PRICE	1	2	3	4	5	6	7	8	9
25	10.	10.	10.	10.	10.	10.	10.	10.	10.
26	9.0	9.0	9.1	9.1	9.1	9.1	9.1	9.1	9.2
27	8.0	8.0	8.1	8.1	8.1	8.1	8.2	8.1	8.2
28	7.0	7.0	7.1	7.1	7.1	7.2	7.2	7.2	7.3
29	6.0	6.0	6.1	6.1	6.1	6.2	6.3	6.3	6.4
30	5.0	5.1	5.1	5.2	5.2	5.3	5.4	5.5	5.6
31	4.0	4.1	4.2	4.3	4.4	4.5	4.6	4.7	4.8
32	3.0	3.2	3.3	3.5	3.6	3.7	3.8	3.9	4.1
33	2.1	2.4	2.5	2.8	2.9	3.1	3.2	3.3	3.5
34	1.3	1.7	2.0	2.3	2.5	2.6	2.8	2.9	3.2
35	0.9	1.4	1.7	2.1	2.3	2.4	2.6	2.8	3.0
36	1.3	1.7	2.0	2.3	2.5	2.6	2.7	2.9	3.2
37	2.0	2.3	2.5	2.8	2.9	3.0	3.1	3.3	3.6
38	2.9	3.0	3.2	3.4	3.5	3.6	3.7	3.9	4.1
39	3.9	3.9	4.0	4.2	4.3	4.3	4.4	4.6	4.7
40	4.9	4.9	4.9	5.0	5.1	5.1	5.2	5.3	5.4
41	5.9	5.9	5.9	5.9	5.9	6.0	6.0	6.1	6.2
42	6.9	6.9	6.8	6.8	6.9	6.8	6.9	7.0	7.0
43	7.9	7.9	7.8	7.8	7.8	7.8	7.8	7.9	7.9
44	8.9	8.9	8.8	8.8	8.8	8.8	8.8	8.8	8.8
45	9.9	9.9	9.8	9.8	9.8	9.8	9.8	9.8	9.8

Average Volatility

STOCK PRICE — NUMBER OF MONTHS BEFORE THE OPTIONS EXPIRE

STOCK PRICE	1	2	3	4	5	6	7	8	9
25	10.	10.	10.	10.	10.	10.	10.	10.	10.
26	9.1	9.0	9.1	9.2	9.2	9.3	9.4	9.5	9.6
27	8.1	8.0	8.1	8.3	8.3	8.4	8.5	8.7	8.8
28	7.1	7.0	7.2	7.4	7.4	7.5	7.6	7.9	8.0
29	6.1	6.1	6.3	6.5	6.6	6.7	6.8	7.1	7.2
30	5.1	5.2	5.4	5.7	5.8	5.9	6.1	6.3	6.5
31	4.1	4.3	4.6	4.9	5.1	5.2	5.4	5.6	5.9
32	3.2	3.5	3.9	4.2	4.4	4.5	4.7	5.0	5.3
33	2.4	2.8	3.2	3.7	3.9	4.0	4.2	4.6	4.9
34	1.7	2.3	2.8	3.3	3.5	3.7	3.9	4.2	4.6
35	1.4	2.1	2.6	3.1	3.4	3.6	3.8	4.1	4.5
36	1.7	2.3	2.8	3.3	3.6	3.7	3.9	4.3	4.6
37	2.3	2.8	3.2	3.6	3.9	4.1	4.2	4.6	4.9
38	3.0	3.5	3.8	4.1	4.4	4.6	4.7	5.0	5.3
39	3.9	4.2	4.4	4.8	5.0	5.2	5.3	5.5	5.8
40	4.9	5.1	5.2	5.5	5.7	5.8	5.9	6.1	6.4
41	5.8	5.9	6.0	6.2	6.4	6.5	6.6	6.8	7.1
42	6.8	6.9	6.9	7.1	7.2	7.3	7.4	7.5	7.8
43	7.8	7.9	7.8	7.9	8.1	8.2	8.2	8.3	8.5
44	8.8	8.9	8.8	8.8	8.9	9.0	9.0	9.1	9.3
45	9.8	9.9	9.8	9.8	9.8	9.9	9.9	10.	10.

High Volatility

STOCK PRICE — NUMBER OF MONTHS BEFORE THE OPTIONS EXPIRE

STOCK PRICE	1	2	3	4	5	6	7	8	9
25	10.	10.	10.	11.	11.	11.	11.	12.	12.
26	9.1	9.4	9.9	10.	10.	10.	11.	11.	12.
27	8.2	8.5	9.1	9.7	9.9	10.	10.	10.	11.
28	7.2	7.7	8.3	8.9	9.2	9.4	9.7	10.	10.
29	6.3	6.9	7.6	8.2	8.6	8.8	9.1	9.7	10.
30	5.5	6.2	6.9	7.6	8.0	8.2	8.6	9.2	9.7
31	4.6	5.5	6.2	7.1	7.5	7.7	8.1	8.7	9.3
32	3.9	4.9	5.7	6.6	7.1	7.3	7.7	8.3	9.0
33	3.3	4.4	5.3	6.2	6.7	7.0	7.4	8.0	8.7
34	2.8	4.1	5.0	6.0	6.5	6.8	7.2	7.9	8.6
35	2.6	4.0	4.9	5.9	6.4	6.7	7.1	7.8	8.5
36	2.8	4.1	5.1	6.0	6.5	6.9	7.2	7.9	8.6
37	3.2	4.5	5.3	6.2	6.8	7.1	7.4	8.0	8.8
38	3.8	4.9	5.7	6.5	7.1	7.4	7.7	8.3	9.0
39	4.5	5.5	6.2	7.0	7.5	7.8	8.1	8.7	9.4
40	5.2	6.1	6.7	7.5	8.0	8.3	8.5	9.1	9.8
41	6.0	6.8	7.4	8.0	8.5	8.8	9.1	9.6	10.
42	6.9	7.6	8.0	8.7	9.1	9.4	9.6	10.	10.
43	7.8	8.4	8.7	9.3	9.8	10.	10.	10.	11.
44	8.8	9.2	9.5	10.	10.	10.	10.	11.	11.
45	9.8	10.	10.	10.	11.	11.	11.	11.	12.

STRADDLE TABLE

Exercise Price is (40)

Low Volatility

STOCK PRICE — NUMBER OF MONTHS BEFORE THE OPTIONS EXPIRE

	1	2	3	4	5	6	7	8	9
30	10.	10.	10.	10.	10.	10.	10.	10.	10.
31	9.0	9.1	9.1	9.1	9.1	9.1	9.2	9.2	9.2
32	8.0	8.1	8.1	8.1	8.1	8.2	8.2	8.2	8.3
33	7.0	7.1	7.1	7.1	7.2	7.2	7.3	7.3	7.4
34	6.0	6.1	6.1	6.2	6.3	6.3	6.4	6.5	6.5
35	5.0	5.1	5.2	5.3	5.4	5.5	5.6	5.6	5.8
36	4.0	4.1	4.3	4.5	4.6	4.7	4.8	4.9	5.0
37	3.0	3.3	3.5	3.7	3.8	4.0	4.1	4.2	4.4
38	2.1	2.5	2.7	3.0	3.2	3.4	3.5	3.7	3.8
39	1.4	1.9	2.2	2.6	2.8	3.0	3.1	3.3	3.5
40	1.1	1.6	2.0	2.4	2.6	2.8	2.9	3.1	3.4
41	1.4	1.9	2.2	2.6	2.8	3.0	3.1	3.3	3.5
42	2.1	2.4	2.7	3.0	3.2	3.3	3.5	3.7	3.9
43	2.9	3.1	3.3	3.6	3.8	3.9	4.0	4.2	4.4
44	3.9	4.0	4.1	4.3	4.4	4.6	4.7	4.9	5.0
45	4.9	4.9	4.9	5.1	5.2	5.3	5.4	5.6	5.7
46	5.9	5.9	5.8	5.9	6.0	6.1	6.2	6.3	6.4
47	6.9	6.8	6.8	6.8	6.9	6.9	7.0	7.1	7.2
48	7.9	7.8	7.8	7.8	7.8	7.8	7.9	8.0	8.1
49	8.9	8.8	8.8	8.8	8.8	8.8	8.8	8.9	9.0
50	9.9	9.8	9.8	9.8	9.8	9.8	9.8	9.8	9.9

Average Volatility

STOCK PRICE — NUMBER OF MONTHS BEFORE THE OPTIONS EXPIRE

	1	2	3	4	5	6	7	8	9
30	10.	10.	10.	10.	10.	10.	10.	10.	10.
31	9.1	9.1	9.2	9.3	9.4	9.5	9.6	9.8	10.
32	8.1	8.1	8.2	8.4	8.5	8.6	8.7	9.0	9.2
33	7.1	7.2	7.3	7.5	7.7	7.8	7.9	8.2	8.4
34	6.1	6.2	6.4	6.7	6.9	7.0	7.1	7.4	7.7
35	5.1	5.4	5.6	5.9	6.1	6.3	6.4	6.7	7.0
36	4.1	4.5	4.8	5.2	5.4	5.6	5.7	6.1	6.4
37	3.3	3.8	4.1	4.6	4.8	5.0	5.2	5.5	5.9
38	2.5	3.1	3.5	4.1	4.4	4.5	4.8	5.1	5.5
39	1.9	2.7	3.1	3.7	4.0	4.2	4.5	4.8	5.2
40	1.6	2.5	3.0	3.6	3.9	4.1	4.4	4.7	5.1
41	1.9	2.6	3.1	3.7	4.0	4.2	4.5	4.9	5.2
42	2.4	3.1	3.5	4.1	4.4	4.5	4.8	5.1	5.5
43	3.1	3.7	4.0	4.5	4.8	5.0	5.2	5.5	5.8
44	3.9	4.4	4.7	5.1	5.4	5.5	5.7	6.0	6.3
45	4.8	5.1	5.4	5.8	6.0	6.1	6.3	6.6	6.8
46	5.8	6.0	6.2	6.5	6.7	6.8	7.0	7.2	7.5
47	6.8	6.8	7.0	7.3	7.5	7.5	7.7	7.9	8.1
48	7.8	7.8	7.9	8.1	8.3	8.3	8.5	8.6	8.8
49	8.8	8.8	8.8	8.9	9.1	9.1	9.3	9.4	9.6
50	9.8	9.8	9.8	9.8	9.9	10.	10.	10.	10.

High Volatility

STOCK PRICE — NUMBER OF MONTHS BEFORE THE OPTIONS EXPIRE

	1	2	3	4	5	6	7	8	9
30	10.	10.	11.	11.	12.	12.	12.	13.	13.
31	9.2	9.8	10.	10.	11.	11.	11.	12.	12.
32	8.3	8.9	9.5	10.	10.	10.	11.	11.	12.
33	7.3	8.2	8.7	9.5	9.9	10.	10.	11.	11.
34	6.5	7.4	8.0	8.8	9.3	9.6	10.	10.	11.
35	5.6	6.7	7.4	8.3	8.8	9.0	9.5	10.	10.
36	4.9	6.0	6.8	7.8	8.3	8.6	9.1	9.8	10.
37	4.1	5.5	6.4	7.4	7.9	8.2	8.7	9.4	10.
38	3.6	5.1	6.0	7.0	7.6	7.9	8.4	9.1	9.8
39	3.2	4.8	5.7	6.8	7.4	7.7	8.3	9.0	9.7
40	3.0	4.6	5.6	6.7	7.4	7.7	8.2	8.9	9.6
41	3.2	4.8	5.8	6.8	7.5	7.8	8.3	9.0	9.7
42	3.5	5.0	6.0	7.0	7.7	7.9	8.5	9.2	9.8
43	4.1	5.4	6.3	7.4	8.0	8.2	8.8	9.4	10.
44	4.7	5.9	6.8	7.8	8.3	8.6	9.1	9.8	10.
45	5.4	6.5	7.3	8.2	8.8	9.0	9.5	10.	10.
46	6.2	7.1	7.9	8.7	9.3	9.5	10.	10.	11.
47	7.0	7.8	8.5	9.3	9.8	10.	10.	11.	11.
48	7.9	8.6	9.2	10.	10.	10.	11.	11.	12.
49	8.8	9.3	9.9	10.	11.	11.	11.	12.	12.
50	9.7	10.	10.	11.	11.	11.	12.	12.	13.

STRADDLE TABLE

Exercise Price is (45)

Low Volatility

STOCK PRICE — NUMBER OF MONTHS BEFORE THE OPTIONS EXPIRE

STOCK PRICE	1	2	3	4	5	6	7	8	9
35	10.	10.	10.	10.	10.	10.	10.	10.	10.
36	9.0	9.1	9.1	9.2	9.1	9.2	9.3	9.3	9.5
37	8.0	8.1	8.1	8.2	8.2	8.3	8.3	8.4	8.6
38	7.0	7.1	7.1	7.2	7.3	7.4	7.4	7.6	7.7
39	6.0	6.1	6.2	6.3	6.4	6.5	6.6	6.7	6.9
40	5.0	5.1	5.3	5.4	5.6	5.7	5.8	6.0	6.1
41	4.0	4.2	4.4	4.6	4.8	4.9	5.1	5.2	5.4
42	3.1	3.4	3.6	3.9	4.1	4.2	4.4	4.6	4.8
43	2.2	2.6	2.9	3.3	3.5	3.7	3.9	4.1	4.3
44	1.5	2.0	2.4	2.8	3.1	3.3	3.5	3.7	4.0
45	1.2	1.8	2.2	2.7	2.9	3.1	3.3	3.6	3.9
46	1.5	2.0	2.4	2.8	3.1	3.3	3.5	3.7	4.0
47	2.2	2.6	2.9	3.2	3.5	3.7	3.8	4.0	4.3
48	3.0	3.3	3.5	3.8	4.0	4.2	4.3	4.5	4.7
49	3.9	4.0	4.2	4.5	4.7	4.8	4.9	5.1	5.3
50	4.9	4.9	5.0	5.2	5.4	5.5	5.6	5.7	5.9
51	5.9	5.8	5.9	6.0	6.2	6.3	6.3	6.5	6.6
52	6.9	6.8	6.8	6.9	7.0	7.1	7.1	7.2	7.4
53	7.9	7.8	7.8	7.8	7.9	7.9	8.0	8.1	8.2
54	8.9	8.8	8.8	8.8	8.8	8.8	8.9	8.9	9.0
55	9.9	9.8	9.8	9.7	9.8	9.8	9.8	9.8	9.9

Average Volatility

STOCK PRICE — NUMBER OF MONTHS BEFORE THE OPTIONS EXPIRE

STOCK PRICE	1	2	3	4	5	6	7	8	9
35	10.	10.	10.	10.	10.	10.	10.	10.	11.
36	9.1	9.1	9.3	9.5	9.7	9.7	9.9	10.	10.
37	8.1	8.2	8.3	8.6	8.8	8.9	9.1	9.3	9.6
38	7.1	7.2	7.5	7.8	8.0	8.1	8.3	8.5	8.9
39	6.1	6.3	6.6	7.0	7.3	7.3	7.5	7.8	8.2
40	5.1	5.5	5.8	6.3	6.5	6.6	6.8	7.1	7.5
41	4.2	4.7	5.1	5.6	5.8	6.0	6.2	6.5	7.0
42	3.4	4.0	4.4	5.0	5.3	5.5	5.7	6.0	6.5
43	2.6	3.4	3.9	4.5	4.8	5.0	5.3	5.6	6.1
44	2.1	2.9	3.5	4.2	4.5	4.8	5.0	5.4	5.9
45	1.9	2.8	3.3	4.0	4.4	4.7	4.9	5.3	5.8
46	2.1	3.0	3.5	4.2	4.5	4.8	5.0	5.4	5.9
47	2.6	3.4	3.8	4.5	4.8	5.1	5.3	5.6	6.1
48	3.3	3.9	4.3	4.9	5.2	5.5	5.7	6.0	6.4
49	4.1	4.6	4.9	5.4	5.7	6.0	6.2	6.5	6.8
50	4.9	5.3	5.6	6.1	6.3	6.6	6.7	7.0	7.4
51	5.9	6.1	6.3	6.8	7.0	7.2	7.4	7.6	7.9
52	6.8	7.0	7.2	7.5	7.7	7.9	8.0	8.3	8.6
53	7.8	7.9	8.0	8.3	8.4	8.6	8.7	9.0	9.2
54	8.8	8.8	8.9	9.1	9.2	9.4	9.5	9.7	9.9
55	9.8	9.8	9.8	9.9	10.	10.	10.	10.	10.

High Volatility

STOCK PRICE — NUMBER OF MONTHS BEFORE THE OPTIONS EXPIRE

STOCK PRICE	1	2	3	4	5	6	7	8	9
35	10.	10.	11.	12.	12.	12.	13.	13.	14.
36	9.3	10.	10.	11.	12.	12.	12.	13.	13.
37	8.4	9.2	9.9	10.	11.	11.	12.	12.	13.
38	7.5	8.4	9.2	10.	10.	11.	11.	12.	12.
39	6.6	7.7	8.6	9.5	10.	10.	10.	11.	12.
40	5.9	7.0	8.0	9.0	9.6	10.	10.	11.	12.
41	5.1	6.4	7.5	8.6	9.2	9.6	10.	10.	11.
42	4.5	6.0	7.0	8.2	8.8	9.2	9.7	10.	11.
43	3.9	5.6	6.7	7.9	8.5	9.0	9.5	10.	11.
44	3.6	5.3	6.5	7.7	8.4	8.8	9.3	10.	10.
45	3.4	5.2	6.4	7.6	8.3	8.8	9.2	9.9	10.
46	3.6	5.4	6.5	7.7	8.4	8.8	9.3	10.	10.
47	3.9	5.6	6.7	7.9	8.5	9.0	9.5	10.	11.
48	4.4	6.0	7.0	8.1	8.8	9.3	9.7	10.	11.
49	5.0	6.5	7.4	8.5	9.1	9.6	10.	10.	11.
50	5.7	7.0	7.9	8.9	9.5	10.	10.	11.	11.
51	6.4	7.6	8.4	9.4	10.	10.	10.	11.	12.
52	7.2	8.3	9.0	9.9	10.	11.	11.	11.	12.
53	8.0	9.0	9.6	10.	11.	11.	11.	12.	13.
54	8.9	9.7	10.	11.	11.	11.	12.	13.	13.
55	9.8	10.	11.	11.	12.	12.	13.	13.	14.

STRADDLE TABLE

Exercise Price is (50)

Low Volatility

STOCK PRICE — NUMBER OF MONTHS BEFORE THE OPTIONS EXPIRE

STOCK PRICE	1	2	3	4	5	6	7	8	9
40	10.	10.	10.	10.	10.	10.	10.	10.	10.
41	9.0	9.1	9.1	9.2	9.3	9.3	9.4	9.5	9.5
42	8.0	8.1	8.1	8.2	8.3	8.4	8.5	8.6	8.7
43	7.0	7.1	7.2	7.3	7.4	7.5	7.6	7.8	7.9
44	6.0	6.1	6.2	6.4	6.6	6.7	6.8	7.0	7.1
45	5.0	5.2	5.3	5.6	5.8	5.9	6.0	6.2	6.3
46	4.1	4.3	4.5	4.8	5.0	5.1	5.3	5.5	5.7
47	3.1	3.5	3.8	4.1	4.3	4.5	4.7	4.9	5.1
48	2.3	2.8	3.1	3.6	3.8	4.0	4.2	4.4	4.6
49	1.6	2.3	2.7	3.2	3.4	3.6	3.8	4.1	4.3
50	1.3	2.0	2.5	3.0	3.2	3.5	3.7	4.0	4.2
51	1.6	2.3	2.7	3.2	3.4	3.6	3.8	4.1	4.3
52	2.2	2.7	3.1	3.5	3.8	4.0	4.2	4.4	4.6
53	3.0	3.4	3.7	4.1	4.3	4.5	4.6	4.9	5.1
54	3.9	4.1	4.4	4.7	4.7	5.1	5.2	5.4	5.6
55	4.9	5.0	5.2	5.4	5.6	5.7	5.8	6.0	6.2
56	5.9	5.9	6.0	6.2	6.3	6.4	6.5	6.7	6.9
57	6.9	6.8	6.9	7.0	7.1	7.2	7.3	7.5	7.6
58	7.9	7.8	7.8	7.9	7.9	7.9	8.1	8.3	8.4
59	8.9	8.8	8.8	8.8	8.8	8.9	9.0	9.1	9.2
60	9.9	9.8	9.8	9.8	9.8	9.8	9.8	9.9	10.

Average Volatility

STOCK PRICE — NUMBER OF MONTHS BEFORE THE OPTIONS EXPIRE

STOCK PRICE	1	2	3	4	5	6	7	8	9
40	10.	10.	10.	10.	10.	10.	11.	11.	11.
41	9.0	9.2	9.4	9.7	9.9	10.	10.	10.	10.
42	8.0	8.3	8.5	8.8	9.1	9.2	9.4	9.7	10.
43	7.0	7.4	7.6	8.0	8.3	8.5	8.7	8.9	9.3
44	6.1	6.5	6.8	7.3	7.5	7.7	7.9	8.2	8.6
45	5.1	5.7	6.0	6.5	6.8	7.0	7.3	7.6	8.0
46	4.3	4.9	5.3	5.9	6.2	6.4	6.7	7.1	7.5
47	3.5	4.2	4.7	5.3	5.7	5.9	6.2	6.6	7.1
48	2.8	3.6	4.2	4.9	5.3	5.5	5.9	6.3	6.8
49	2.2	3.2	3.8	4.6	5.0	5.2	5.5	6.0	6.5
50	2.0	3.1	3.7	4.5	4.9	5.2	5.5	5.9	6.5
51	2.3	3.2	3.8	4.6	5.0	5.3	5.6	6.0	6.6
52	2.8	3.6	4.2	4.9	5.3	5.5	5.9	6.3	6.8
53	3.4	4.1	4.6	5.3	5.7	5.9	6.2	6.6	7.1
54	4.2	4.7	5.2	5.8	6.1	6.3	6.6	7.0	7.5
55	5.0	5.4	5.9	6.4	6.7	6.9	7.2	7.5	8.0
56	5.9	6.2	6.6	7.1	7.3	7.5	7.8	8.1	8.5
57	6.9	7.0	7.3	7.8	8.0	8.1	8.4	8.7	9.1
58	7.9	7.9	8.1	8.5	8.7	8.8	9.1	9.4	9.7
59	8.9	8.8	9.0	9.3	9.5	9.6	9.8	10.	10.
60	9.9	9.7	9.9	10.	10.	10.	10.	10.	11.

High Volatility

STOCK PRICE — NUMBER OF MONTHS BEFORE THE OPTIONS EXPIRE

STOCK PRICE	1	2	3	4	5	6	7	8	9
40	10.	11.	11.	12.	13.	13.	14.	14.	15.
41	9.3	10.	11.	12.	12.	13.	13.	14.	14.
42	8.4	9.6	10.	11.	12.	12.	12.	13.	14.
43	7.6	8.8	9.7	10.	11.	11.	12.	13.	13.
44	6.8	8.1	9.1	10.	10.	11.	11.	12.	13.
45	6.0	7.5	8.5	9.7	10.	10.	11.	12.	13.
46	5.3	6.9	8.0	9.3	10.	10.	11.	11.	12.
47	4.7	6.5	7.6	9.0	9.7	10.	10.	11.	12.
48	4.2	6.1	7.3	8.7	9.5	9.9	10.	11.	12.
49	3.9	5.9	7.1	8.5	9.3	9.8	10.	11.	12.
50	3.8	5.8	7.0	8.4	9.3	9.7	10.	11.	12.
51	3.9	5.9	7.1	8.5	9.3	9.8	10.	11.	12.
52	4.3	6.1	7.3	8.7	9.5	9.9	10.	11.	12.
53	4.7	6.5	7.6	9.0	9.7	10.	10.	11.	12.
54	5.3	6.9	8.0	9.3	10.	10.	11.	11.	12.
55	5.9	7.4	8.5	9.7	10.	10.	11.	12.	13.
56	6.6	8.0	9.0	10.	10.	11.	11.	12.	13.
57	7.4	8.6	9.6	10.	11.	11.	12.	13.	13.
58	8.2	9.3	10.	11.	11.	12.	12.	13.	14.
59	9.1	10.	10.	11.	12.	12.	13.	14.	14.
60	9.9	10.	11.	12.	13.	13.	13.	14.	15.

STRADDLE TABLE

Exercise Price is ⑥⓪

Low Volatility

STOCK PRICE — NUMBER OF MONTHS BEFORE THE OPTIONS EXPIRE

STOCK PRICE	1	2	3	4	5	6	7	8	9
50	10.	10.	10.	10.	10.	10.	10.	10.	10.
51	9.0	9.1	9.2	9.3	9.4	9.5	9.6	9.8	10.
52	8.0	8.1	8.2	8.4	8.5	8.6	8.8	9.0	9.2
53	7.0	7.2	7.3	7.6	7.7	7.8	8.0	8.2	8.4
54	6.0	6.2	6.4	6.8	6.9	7.0	7.2	7.4	7.7
55	5.0	5.4	5.6	6.0	6.1	6.3	6.5	6.7	7.0
56	4.1	4.5	4.8	5.2	5.4	5.6	5.8	6.1	6.4
57	3.2	3.8	4.1	4.6	4.8	5.0	5.3	5.6	5.9
58	2.5	3.1	3.5	4.1	4.4	4.6	4.8	5.2	5.6
59	1.9	2.6	3.1	3.7	4.0	4.3	4.5	4.9	5.3
60	1.6	2.5	2.9	3.6	3.9	4.2	4.4	4.8	5.2
61	1.9	2.6	3.1	3.7	4.1	4.3	4.6	4.8	5.3
62	2.4	3.1	3.5	4.1	4.4	4.6	4.8	5.2	5.6
63	3.2	3.7	4.0	4.5	4.8	5.1	5.3	5.6	5.9
64	4.0	4.3	4.7	5.1	5.4	5.6	5.8	6.1	6.4
65	4.9	5.1	5.4	5.8	6.0	6.2	6.4	6.7	6.9
66	5.9	6.0	6.2	6.5	6.7	6.9	7.0	7.3	7.5
67	6.9	6.8	7.0	7.3	7.5	7.6	7.7	8.0	8.2
68	7.9	7.8	7.9	8.1	8.3	8.4	8.5	8.7	8.9
69	8.9	8.8	8.8	8.9	9.1	9.2	9.3	9.5	9.6
70	9.9	9.8	9.8	9.8	10.	10.	10.	10.	10.

Average Volatility

STOCK PRICE — NUMBER OF MONTHS BEFORE THE OPTIONS EXPIRE

STOCK PRICE	1	2	3	4	5	6	7	8	9
50	10.	10.	10.	10.	11.	11.	11.	11.	12.
51	9.2	9.3	9.6	10.	10.	10.	10.	11.	11.
52	8.2	8.4	8.8	9.3	9.6	9.9	10.	10.	10.
53	7.2	7.6	8.0	8.5	8.9	9.1	9.3	9.8	10.
54	6.3	6.8	7.2	7.8	8.2	8.5	8.6	9.1	9.5
55	5.4	6.0	6.5	7.1	7.5	7.9	8.1	8.6	9.0
56	4.5	5.3	5.8	6.6	7.0	7.4	7.6	8.1	8.5
57	3.8	4.7	5.3	6.1	6.6	6.9	7.2	7.7	8.1
58	3.1	4.2	4.8	5.7	6.2	6.6	6.8	7.4	7.8
59	2.6	3.8	4.5	5.5	6.0	6.4	6.6	7.2	7.7
60	2.4	3.7	4.4	5.4	5.9	6.3	6.6	7.1	7.6
61	2.6	3.9	4.6	5.5	6.0	6.4	6.7	7.2	7.7
62	3.0	4.2	4.9	5.8	6.2	6.6	6.9	7.4	7.9
63	3.6	4.7	5.3	6.1	6.6	6.9	7.2	7.7	8.1
64	4.3	5.2	5.8	6.6	7.0	7.3	7.6	8.1	8.5
65	5.1	5.9	6.4	7.1	7.5	7.8	8.1	8.5	8.9
66	5.9	6.6	7.1	7.8	8.1	8.4	8.7	9.0	9.4
67	6.8	7.4	7.8	8.4	8.7	9.0	9.3	9.6	10.
68	7.8	8.2	8.6	9.1	9.4	9.6	9.9	10.	10.
69	8.7	9.0	9.4	9.8	10.	10.	10.	10.	11.
70	9.7	9.9	10.	10.	10.	11.	11.	11.	11.

High Volatility

STOCK PRICE — NUMBER OF MONTHS BEFORE THE OPTIONS EXPIRE

STOCK PRICE	1	2	3	4	5	6	7	8	9
50	10.	11.	12.	13.	14.	15.	15.	16.	17.
51	9.8	11.	11.	13.	14.	14.	15.	15.	16.
52	8.9	10.	11.	12.	13.	14.	14.	15.	16.
53	8.1	9.6	10.	12.	12.	13.	14.	15.	15.
54	7.3	9.0	10.	11.	12.	13.	13.	14.	15.
55	6.6	8.4	9.7	11.	12.	12.	13.	14.	15.
56	5.9	7.9	9.3	10.	11.	12.	12.	14.	14.
57	5.4	7.6	8.9	10.	11.	12.	12.	13.	14.
58	4.9	7.2	8.6	10.	11.	12.	12.	13.	14.
59	4.6	7.1	8.5	10.	11.	11.	12.	13.	14.
60	4.5	7.0	8.4	10.	11.	11.	12.	13.	14.
61	4.6	7.1	8.5	10.	11.	11.	12.	13.	14.
62	4.9	7.3	8.7	10.	11.	12.	12.	13.	14.
63	5.3	7.6	9.0	10.	11.	12.	12.	13.	14.
64	5.8	8.0	9.3	10.	11.	12.	13.	14.	14.
65	6.4	8.4	9.7	11.	12.	12.	13.	14.	15.
66	7.0	8.9	10.	11.	12.	13.	13.	14.	15.
67	7.7	9.5	10.	12.	13.	13.	14.	15.	15.
68	8.5	10.	11.	12.	13.	14.	14.	15.	16.
69	9.2	10.	11.	13.	14.	14.	15.	15.	16.
70	10.	11.	12.	13.	14.	15.	15.	16.	17.

STRADDLE TABLE

Exercise Price is (70)

Low Volatility

STOCK PRICE	NUMBER OF MONTHS BEFORE THE OPTIONS EXPIRE								
	1	2	3	4	5	6	7	8	9
60	10.	10.	10.	10.	10.	10.	10.	11.	11.
61	9.1	9.2	9.3	9.6	9.7	9.9	9.9	10.	10.
62	8.1	8.2	8.4	8.7	8.9	9.1	9.1	9.4	9.8
63	7.1	7.3	7.5	7.9	8.1	8.3	8.4	8.7	9.0
64	6.1	6.4	6.7	7.1	7.3	7.5	7.7	8.0	8.3
65	5.1	5.5	5.9	6.4	6.6	6.8	7.0	7.3	7.7
66	4.2	4.8	5.2	5.7	5.9	6.2	6.4	6.8	7.1
67	3.4	4.0	4.5	5.1	5.4	5.7	5.9	6.3	6.7
68	2.7	3.5	4.0	4.7	5.0	5.3	5.5	6.0	6.3
69	2.1	3.0	3.6	4.3	4.7	5.0	5.2	5.7	6.1
70	1.9	2.9	3.5	4.2	4.6	4.9	5.1	5.6	6.0
71	2.1	3.0	3.6	4.3	4.7	5.0	5.3	5.7	6.1
72	2.6	3.4	4.0	4.6	5.0	5.3	5.5	5.9	6.3
73	3.3	4.0	4.5	5.0	5.4	5.6	5.9	6.3	6.6
74	4.1	4.6	5.1	5.6	5.9	6.1	6.4	6.7	7.0
75	4.9	5.3	5.7	6.2	6.5	6.7	6.9	7.2	7.5
76	5.9	6.1	6.4	6.8	7.1	7.3	7.5	7.8	8.1
77	6.8	7.0	7.2	7.6	7.8	8.0	8.2	8.5	8.7
78	7.8	7.9	8.1	8.3	8.6	8.7	8.9	9.2	9.3
79	8.8	8.8	8.9	9.1	9.3	9.5	9.7	9.9	10.
80	9.8	9.8	9.8	10.	10.	10.	10.	10.	10.

Average Volatility

STOCK PRICE	NUMBER OF MONTHS BEFORE THE OPTIONS EXPIRE								
	1	2	3	4	5	6	7	8	9
60	10.	10.	10.	11.	11.	11.	12.	12.	13.
61	9.2	9.6	10.	10.	11.	11.	11.	11.	12.
62	8.2	8.7	9.2	9.8	10.	10.	10.	11.	11.
63	7.3	7.9	8.4	9.1	9.5	9.8	10.	10.	11.
64	6.4	7.2	7.7	8.4	8.9	9.2	9.6	10.	10.
65	5.6	6.4	7.0	7.8	8.4	8.6	9.1	9.6	10.
66	4.8	5.8	6.4	7.3	7.9	8.2	8.6	9.2	9.9
67	4.1	5.2	5.9	6.9	7.5	7.8	8.3	8.8	9.5
68	3.5	4.8	5.5	6.6	7.2	7.5	8.0	8.5	9.2
69	3.1	4.5	5.3	6.4	7.0	7.3	7.8	8.4	9.1
70	2.9	4.4	5.2	6.3	6.9	7.2	7.7	8.3	9.0
71	3.1	4.5	5.3	6.4	7.0	7.3	7.8	8.4	9.1
72	3.5	4.8	5.5	6.6	7.2	7.5	8.0	8.5	9.3
73	4.0	5.2	5.9	7.0	7.5	7.8	8.3	8.8	9.5
74	4.7	5.7	6.4	7.4	7.9	8.2	8.7	9.2	9.8
75	5.4	6.3	6.9	7.9	8.4	8.7	9.1	9.6	10.
76	6.2	7.0	7.6	8.4	8.9	9.2	9.6	10.	10.
77	7.0	7.7	8.2	9.0	9.5	9.7	10.	10.	11.
78	7.9	8.5	8.9	9.7	10.	10.	10.	11.	11.
79	8.8	9.3	9.7	10.	10.	11.	11.	11.	12.
80	9.8	10.	10.	11.	11.	11.	12.	12.	12.

High Volatility

STOCK PRICE	NUMBER OF MONTHS BEFORE THE OPTIONS EXPIRE								
	1	2	3	4	5	6	7	8	9
60	11.	12.	13.	15.	16.	16.	17.	18.	19.
61	10.	11.	13.	14.	15.	16.	16.	17.	19.
62	9.4	11.	12.	13.	15.	15.	16.	17.	18.
63	8.6	10.	11.	13.	14.	15.	16.	17.	18.
64	7.9	9.9	11.	13.	14.	14.	15.	16.	18.
65	7.2	9.4	11.	12.	13.	14.	15.	16.	17.
66	6.6	9.0	10.	12.	13.	14.	15.	16.	17.
67	6.1	8.7	10.	12.	13.	14.	14.	16.	17.
68	5.7	8.4	10.	11.	13.	13.	14.	15.	17.
69	5.4	8.2	9.9	11.	13.	13.	14.	15.	17.
70	5.3	8.1	9.8	11.	13.	13.	14.	15.	17.
71	5.4	8.2	9.9	11.	13.	13.	14.	15.	17.
72	5.7	8.4	10.	11.	13.	13.	14.	15.	17.
73	6.0	8.7	10.	12.	13.	14.	14.	16.	17.
74	6.5	9.0	10.	12.	13.	14.	15.	16.	17.
75	7.0	9.4	11.	12.	13.	14.	15.	16.	17.
76	7.6	9.9	11.	13.	14.	14.	15.	16.	18.
77	8.3	10.	11.	13.	14.	15.	15.	17.	18.
78	8.9	11.	12.	14.	15.	15.	16.	17.	18.
79	9.7	11.	12.	14.	15.	16.	16.	17.	19.
80	10.	12.	13.	15.	16.	16.	17.	18.	19.

STRADDLE TABLE

Exercise Price is (80)

Low Volatility

STOCK PRICE — NUMBER OF MONTHS BEFORE THE OPTIONS EXPIRE

	1	2	3	4	5	6	7	8	9
70	10.	10.	10.	10.	10.	11.	11.	11.	11.
71	9.1	9.2	9.4	9.8	10.	10.	10.	10.	11.
72	8.1	8.3	8.6	9.0	9.2	9.4	9.6	10.	10.
73	7.1	7.4	7.7	8.2	8.4	8.6	8.9	9.2	9.6
74	6.1	6.6	7.0	7.5	7.7	7.9	8.2	8.6	9.0
75	5.2	5.8	6.2	6.8	7.0	7.3	7.6	8.0	8.4
76	4.4	5.0	5.5	6.1	6.4	6.7	7.0	7.5	7.9
77	3.6	4.4	4.9	5.6	6.0	6.3	6.6	7.1	7.5
78	2.9	3.8	4.4	5.2	5.6	5.9	6.3	6.7	7.2
79	2.4	3.5	4.1	4.9	5.3	5.7	6.0	6.5	7.0
80	2.2	3.3	4.0	4.8	5.2	5.6	5.9	6.4	6.9
81	2.4	3.5	4.1	4.9	5.3	5.7	6.0	6.5	7.0
82	2.9	3.8	4.4	5.2	5.6	6.0	6.3	6.7	7.2
83	3.5	4.3	4.9	5.6	6.0	6.3	6.6	7.0	7.5
84	4.2	4.9	5.4	6.1	6.4	6.8	7.0	7.4	7.9
85	5.0	5.6	6.1	6.7	7.0	7.3	7.6	7.9	8.4
86	5.9	6.3	6.8	7.3	7.6	7.9	8.1	8.4	8.9
87	6.8	7.1	7.5	8.0	8.3	8.6	8.8	9.1	9.4
88	7.8	8.0	8.3	8.7	9.0	9.2	9.4	9.7	10.
89	8.8	8.9	9.1	9.5	9.7	9.9	10.	10.	10.
90	9.8	9.8	10.	10.	10.	10.	10.	11.	11.

Average Volatility

STOCK PRICE — NUMBER OF MONTHS BEFORE THE OPTIONS EXPIRE

	1	2	3	4	5	6	7	8	9
70	10.	10.	11.	11.	12.	12.	12.	13.	13.
71	9.3	9.9	10.	11.	11.	11.	12.	12.	13.
72	8.3	9.1	9.7	10.	11.	11.	11.	12.	12.
73	7.4	8.3	9.0	9.8	10.	10.	10.	11.	12.
74	6.6	7.6	8.3	9.2	9.8	10.	10.	11.	11.
75	5.8	6.8	7.7	8.6	9.3	9.5	9.9	10.	11.
76	5.1	6.2	7.1	8.2	8.8	9.1	9.5	10.	10.
77	4.4	5.7	6.7	7.8	8.5	8.7	9.2	10.	10.
78	3.9	5.3	6.3	7.5	8.2	8.4	8.9	9.7	10.
79	3.5	5.0	6.1	7.3	8.0	8.2	8.7	9.6	10.
80	3.3	4.9	6.0	7.2	7.9	8.2	8.7	9.5	10.
81	3.5	5.1	6.1	7.3	8.0	8.2	8.8	9.6	10.
82	3.8	5.3	6.3	7.5	8.1	8.4	9.0	9.8	10.
83	4.3	5.7	6.6	7.8	8.4	8.7	9.2	10.	10.
84	4.9	6.2	7.0	8.2	8.8	9.0	9.6	10.	11.
85	5.6	6.8	7.5	8.7	9.2	9.4	10.	10.	11.
86	6.4	7.4	8.1	9.2	9.6	9.8	10.	11.	11.
87	7.2	8.1	8.7	9.7	10.	10.	10.	11.	12.
88	8.0	8.8	9.4	10.	10.	10.	11.	12.	12.
89	8.9	9.5	10.	11.	11.	11.	11.	12.	13.
90	9.8	10.	10.	11.	12.	12.	12.	13.	13.

High Volatility

STOCK PRICE — NUMBER OF MONTHS BEFORE THE OPTIONS EXPIRE

	1	2	3	4	5	6	7	8	9
70	11.	13.	14.	16.	17.	18.	19.	20.	21.
71	10.	12.	14.	16.	17.	17.	18.	20.	21.
72	9.7	11.	13.	15.	16.	17.	18.	19.	21.
73	9.0	11.	13.	15.	16.	17.	18.	19.	20.
74	8.3	10.	12.	14.	16.	16.	17.	18.	20.
75	7.7	10.	12.	14.	15.	16.	17.	18.	20.
76	7.1	10.	12.	14.	15.	16.	17.	18.	19.
77	6.7	9.7	11.	13.	15.	15.	16.	18.	19.
78	6.4	9.5	11.	13.	15.	15.	16.	18.	19.
79	6.1	9.3	11.	13.	14.	15.	16.	18.	19.
80	6.0	9.3	11.	13.	14.	15.	16.	17.	19.
81	6.1	9.4	11.	13.	14.	15.	16.	18.	19.
82	6.4	9.5	11.	13.	15.	15.	16.	18.	19.
83	6.7	9.8	11.	13.	15.	15.	17.	18.	19.
84	7.1	10.	12.	14.	15.	16.	17.	18.	19.
85	7.6	10.	12.	14.	15.	16.	17.	18.	20.
86	8.2	10.	12.	14.	16.	16.	17.	18.	20.
87	8.8	11.	13.	15.	16.	16.	18.	19.	20.
88	9.5	11.	13.	15.	16.	17.	18.	19.	21.
89	10.	12.	14.	16.	17.	17.	18.	20.	21.
90	10.	13.	14.	16.	17.	18.	19.	20.	21.

STRADDLE TABLE

Low Volatility

STOCK PRICE — NUMBER OF MONTHS BEFORE THE OPTIONS EXPIRE

	1	2	3	4	5	6	7	8	9
80	10.	10.	10.	10.	11.	11.	11.	11.	12.
81	9.1	9.3	9.6	10.	10.	10.	10.	11.	11.
82	8.1	8.4	8.8	9.3	9.7	9.9	10.	10.	10.
83	7.1	7.6	8.0	8.6	8.9	9.2	9.5	9.8	10.
84	6.2	6.8	7.2	7.9	8.2	8.5	8.8	9.2	9.7
85	5.3	6.0	6.5	7.2	7.6	7.9	8.3	8.6	9.2
86	4.5	5.3	5.8	6.6	7.0	7.4	7.7	8.2	8.8
87	3.7	4.7	5.3	6.1	6.6	7.0	7.3	7.8	8.4
88	3.1	4.2	4.8	5.8	6.2	6.6	7.0	7.5	8.1
89	2.6	3.8	4.6	5.5	6.0	6.4	6.8	7.3	7.9
90	2.4	3.7	4.4	5.4	5.9	6.3	6.7	7.2	7.8
91	2.6	3.9	4.6	5.6	6.0	6.4	6.8	7.3	7.9
92	3.1	4.2	4.9	5.8	6.2	6.6	7.0	7.5	8.1
93	3.7	4.7	5.3	6.2	6.6	7.0	7.3	7.8	8.3
94	4.4	5.2	5.8	6.6	7.0	7.4	7.6	8.2	8.7
95	5.2	5.9	6.4	7.2	7.5	7.8	8.1	8.6	9.1
96	6.0	6.6	7.1	7.8	8.1	8.4	8.6	9.1	9.6
97	6.9	7.4	7.8	8.4	8.7	9.0	9.2	9.7	10.
98	7.8	8.2	8.5	9.1	9.4	9.6	9.9	10.	10.
99	8.8	9.0	9.3	9.8	10.	10.	10.	10.	11.

Average Volatility

STOCK PRICE — NUMBER OF MONTHS BEFORE THE OPTIONS EXPIRE

	1	2	3	4	5	6	7	8	9
80	10.	11.	11.	12.	13.	13.	13.	14.	15.
81	9.4	10.	10.	11.	12.	12.	13.	13.	14.
82	8.5	9.4	10.	11.	11.	12.	12.	13.	13.
83	7.6	8.7	9.3	10.	11.	11.	11.	12.	13.
84	6.8	8.0	8.7	10.	10.	11.	11.	12.	13.
85	6.0	7.3	8.1	9.4	10.	10.	10.	11.	12.
86	5.3	6.8	7.7	9.0	9.7	10.	10.	11.	12.
87	4.7	6.3	7.3	8.6	9.4	9.9	10.	11.	12.
88	4.2	6.0	6.9	8.3	9.1	9.6	10.	10.	11.
89	3.9	5.7	6.7	8.1	8.9	9.4	9.8	10.	11.
90	3.8	5.6	6.7	8.1	8.9	9.4	9.8	10.	11.
91	3.9	5.7	6.8	8.1	8.9	9.5	9.8	10.	11.
92	4.2	6.0	7.0	8.3	9.1	9.6	10.	11.	11.
93	4.7	6.3	7.3	8.6	9.3	9.9	10.	11.	12.
94	5.3	6.8	7.7	8.9	9.7	10.	10.	11.	12.
95	5.9	7.3	8.2	9.3	10.	10.	10.	11.	12.
96	6.6	7.9	8.7	9.8	10.	10.	11.	12.	13.
97	7.4	8.5	9.3	10.	11.	11.	11.	12.	13.
98	8.2	9.2	10.	10.	11.	11.	12.	13.	13.
99	9.0	9.9	10.	11.	12.	12.	12.	13.	14.

High Volatility

STOCK PRICE — NUMBER OF MONTHS BEFORE THE OPTIONS EXPIRE

	1	2	3	4	5	6	7	8	9
80	11.	14.	15.	18.	19.	20.	20.	22.	24.
81	11.	13.	15.	17.	18.	19.	20.	22.	23.
82	10.	12.	14.	17.	18.	19.	20.	21.	23.
83	9.5	12.	14.	16.	18.	18.	19.	21.	22.
84	8.9	11.	13.	16.	17.	18.	19.	21.	22.
85	8.4	11.	13.	16.	17.	18.	19.	20.	22.
86	7.9	11.	13.	15.	17.	17.	18.	20.	22.
87	7.5	10.	12.	15.	17.	17.	18.	20.	22.
88	7.2	10.	12.	15.	16.	17.	18.	20.	21.
89	7.0	10.	12.	15.	16.	17.	18.	20.	21.
90	6.9	10.	12.	15.	16.	17.	18.	20.	21.
91	7.0	10.	12.	15.	16.	17.	18.	20.	21.
92	7.2	10.	12.	15.	16.	17.	18.	20.	21.
93	7.5	10.	13.	15.	17.	17.	18.	20.	22.
94	7.9	11.	13.	15.	17.	18.	19.	20.	22.
95	8.3	11.	13.	16.	17.	18.	19.	20.	22.
96	8.9	11.	13.	16.	17.	18.	19.	21.	22.
97	9.5	12.	14.	16.	18.	18.	19.	21.	22.
98	10.	12.	14.	17.	18.	19.	20.	21.	23.
99	10.	13.	15.	17.	18.	19.	20.	22.	23.

STRADDLE TABLE

Exercise Price is (100)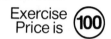

Low Volatility

STOCK PRICE	NUMBER OF MONTHS BEFORE THE OPTIONS EXPIRE								
	1	2	3	4	5	6	7	8	9
90	10.	10.	10.	11.	11.	11.	12.	12.	12.
91	9.1	9.5	9.9	10.	10.	10.	11.	11.	12.
92	8.2	8.7	9.1	9.6	10.	10.	10.	11.	11.
93	7.2	7.8	8.3	8.9	9.4	9.5	9.9	10.	10.
94	6.3	7.1	7.6	8.2	8.7	8.9	9.3	9.8	10.
95	5.5	6.3	6.8	7.6	8.1	8.4	8.8	9.3	9.9
96	4.7	5.6	6.2	7.0	7.6	7.9	8.4	8.9	9.5
97	3.9	5.0	5.7	6.6	7.2	7.5	8.0	8.5	9.1
98	3.3	4.6	5.3	6.3	6.9	7.2	7.7	8.2	8.9
99	2.9	4.3	5.0	6.0	6.7	7.0	7.5	8.1	8.7
100	2.7	4.1	4.9	5.9	6.6	6.9	7.4	8.0	8.6
101	2.9	4.3	5.0	6.1	6.7	7.0	7.5	8.1	8.7
102	3.3	4.6	5.2	6.3	6.9	7.3	7.7	8.3	8.9
103	3.9	5.0	5.6	6.7	7.2	7.6	8.0	8.5	9.1
104	4.6	5.5	6.1	7.1	7.6	8.0	8.4	8.9	9.5
105	5.3	6.1	6.6	7.6	8.1	8.4	8.8	9.3	9.9
106	6.1	6.8	7.3	8.2	8.6	9.0	9.3	9.8	10.
107	6.9	7.5	7.9	8.8	9.2	9.5	9.9	10.	10.
108	7.8	8.3	8.6	9.5	9.9	10.	10.	10.	11.
109	8.8	9.1	9.4	10.	10.	10.	11.	11.	12.
110	9.8	10.	10.	10.	11.	11.	11.	12.	12.

Average Volatility

STOCK PRICE	NUMBER OF MONTHS BEFORE THE OPTIONS EXPIRE								
	1	2	3	4	5	6	7	8	9
90	10.	11.	12.	13.	13.	14.	14.	15.	16.
91	9.5	10.	11.	12.	13.	13.	13.	14.	15.
92	8.6	9.8	10.	11.	12.	12.	13.	14.	15.
93	7.8	9.1	10.	11.	12.	12.	12.	13.	14.
94	7.0	8.4	9.4	10.	11.	11.	12.	13.	14.
95	6.3	7.8	8.9	10.	11.	11.	11.	13.	13.
96	5.6	7.3	8.5	9.8	10.	11.	11.	12.	13.
97	5.0	6.8	8.1	9.5	10.	10.	11.	12.	13.
98	4.6	6.5	7.8	9.2	10.	10.	11.	12.	13.
99	4.3	6.2	7.6	9.1	9.9	10.	11.	12.	13.
100	4.2	6.2	7.5	9.0	9.9	10.	10.	12.	13.
101	4.3	6.3	7.6	9.1	9.9	10.	11.	12.	13.
102	4.6	6.5	7.8	9.3	10.	10.	11.	12.	13.
103	5.0	6.8	8.1	9.5	10.	10.	11.	12.	13.
104	5.6	7.2	8.4	9.9	10.	11.	11.	12.	13.
105	6.2	7.7	8.8	10.	11.	11.	12.	12.	13.
106	6.9	8.3	9.3	10.	11.	11.	12.	13.	14.
107	7.6	8.9	9.9	11.	11.	12.	12.	13.	14.
108	8.4	9.6	10.	11.	12.	12.	13.	14.	15.
109	9.2	10.	11.	12.	12.	13.	13.	14.	15.
110	10.	11.	11.	12.	13.	13.	14.	15.	16.

High Volatility

STOCK PRICE	NUMBER OF MONTHS BEFORE THE OPTIONS EXPIRE								
	1	2	3	4	5	6	7	8	9
90	12.	15.	17.	19.	21.	21.	22.	24.	26.
91	11.	14.	16.	18.	20.	21.	22.	24.	26.
92	10.	13.	16.	18.	20.	21.	22.	23.	25.
93	10.	13.	15.	18.	19.	20.	21.	23.	25.
94	9.6	13.	15.	17.	19.	20.	21.	23.	25.
95	9.1	12.	15.	17.	19.	20.	21.	23.	24.
96	8.6	12.	14.	17.	18.	19.	21.	22.	24.
97	8.3	12.	14.	17.	18.	19.	21.	22.	24.
98	7.9	11.	14.	16.	18.	19.	20.	22.	24.
99	7.7	11.	14.	16.	18.	19.	20.	22.	24.
100	7.7	11.	14.	16.	18.	19.	20.	22.	24.
101	7.7	11.	14.	16.	18.	19.	20.	22.	24.
102	7.9	11.	14.	16.	18.	19.	20.	22.	24.
103	8.2	12.	14.	17.	18.	19.	21.	22.	24.
104	8.6	12.	14.	17.	18.	19.	21.	22.	24.
105	9.0	12.	15.	17.	19.	20.	21.	23.	24.
106	9.4	13.	15.	17.	19.	20.	21.	23.	25.
107	10.	13.	15.	18.	19.	20.	21.	23.	25.
108	10.	13.	16.	18.	20.	21.	22.	23.	25.
109	11.	14.	16.	18.	20.	21.	22.	24.	25.
110	11.	14.	17.	19.	20.	21.	22.	24.	26.

THE FUTURE VALUE COMBINATION TABLES

```
Decimal to Fraction
Conversion Chart
Table          Market
Shows          Fraction
  .1     =     1/16
  .1     =     1/8
  .2     =     3/16
  .2     =     1/4
  .3     =     5/16
  .4     =     3/8
  .4     =     7/16
  .5     =     1/2
  .6     =     9/16
  .6     =     5/8
  .7     =     11/16
  .8     =     3/4
  .8     =     13/16
  .9     =     7/8
  .9     =     15/16
```

*The Future Value Tables are generated by computer simulations. Due to the nature of the computer simulation techniques that we used there may be slight aberrations in the option prices presented. Therefore you should allow a variance of plus or minus 10% of these option prices. In a few cases, some of the less important, peripheral option prices may vary more than 10%.

COMBINATION TABLE

Exercise Price of the Call is

Exercise Price of the Put is

Low Volatility

STOCK PRICE — NUMBER OF MONTHS BEFORE THE OPTIONS EXPIRE

	1	2	3	4	5	6	7	8	9
2	8.0	7.9	8.0	8.0	8.0	8.0	7.9	7.9	8.1
3	6.9	6.9	6.9	6.9	7.0	6.9	6.9	6.8	6.9
4	6.0	5.9	6.0	6.0	6.1	6.0	6.0	6.0	6.0
5	5.0	5.0	5.0	4.9	4.9	5.1	4.9	5.0	5.0
6	4.0	4.0	4.0	4.0	4.1	4.1	4.1	4.1	4.1
7	3.0	3.0	3.0	3.1	3.0	3.1	2.9	3.1	3.0
8	2.0	2.0	1.9	2.0	2.0	2.0	2.1	2.0	2.0
9	0.9	1.0	1.0	1.0	1.0	1.1	1.0	1.0	1.2
10	0.1	0.2	0.3	0.3	0.4	0.4	0.5	0.5	0.5
11	0.0	0.0	0.0	0.0	0.1	0.1	0.1	0.1	0.2
12	0.0	0.0	0.0	0.0	0.0	0.0	0.0	0.0	0.1
13	0.0	0.0	0.0	0.0	0.0	0.0	0.0	0.0	0.1
14	0.0	0.0	0.0	0.0	0.1	0.1	0.1	0.1	0.2
15	0.1	0.2	0.3	0.3	0.4	0.4	0.4	0.4	0.5
16	0.8	0.8	0.9	0.9	0.9	1.0	1.0	1.0	1.0
17	1.9	1.9	1.8	1.8	1.8	1.9	1.9	1.9	1.9
18	3.0	3.0	3.0	3.0	3.0	3.0	2.9	3.1	3.0
19	3.9	3.9	4.0	3.9	4.0	4.0	4.0	4.1	3.9
20	4.9	5.0	4.9	4.9	5.0	4.9	5.0	5.0	4.9
21	5.9	5.9	6.0	6.1	6.0	5.9	6.0	6.1	6.0
22	7.0	7.0	7.0	7.0	7.1	7.1	7.0	7.0	6.9
23	8.0	8.0	8.0	8.0	8.1	8.0	8.0	8.0	7.9

Average Volatility

STOCK PRICE — NUMBER OF MONTHS BEFORE THE OPTIONS EXPIRE

	1	2	3	4	5	6	7	8	9
2	8.0	7.9	8.0	8.0	8.1	8.0	7.9	7.9	8.1
3	6.9	6.9	6.9	6.8	7.0	6.8	6.9	6.8	6.8
4	6.0	5.9	6.0	6.0	6.1	6.0	6.1	6.0	6.1
5	5.0	5.0	5.1	4.9	4.9	5.2	4.9	5.0	5.0
6	4.0	4.0	4.0	4.0	4.2	4.1	4.2	4.2	4.2
7	3.0	3.0	3.0	3.1	3.0	3.2	3.0	3.2	3.2
8	2.0	2.0	2.0	2.1	2.2	2.1	2.2	2.1	2.1
9	0.9	1.1	1.1	1.1	1.2	1.3	1.2	1.2	1.4
10	0.2	0.3	0.5	0.5	0.6	0.6	0.7	0.7	0.7
11	0.0	0.0	0.1	0.1	0.3	0.3	0.3	0.3	0.4
12	0.0	0.0	0.0	0.0	0.1	0.2	0.2	0.2	0.4
13	0.0	0.0	0.0	0.0	0.1	0.2	0.2	0.2	0.3
14	0.0	0.0	0.1	0.1	0.3	0.3	0.3	0.3	0.4
15	0.2	0.3	0.4	0.4	0.6	0.6	0.6	0.6	0.8
16	0.8	0.8	1.0	1.0	1.1	1.1	1.2	1.1	1.2
17	1.8	1.9	1.8	1.8	1.8	2.0	1.9	1.9	2.0
18	3.0	3.0	3.1	3.0	3.1	3.0	2.9	3.2	3.1
19	3.9	3.9	4.1	3.9	4.0	4.0	4.1	4.1	4.0
20	4.9	5.0	4.9	4.9	5.0	4.9	5.0	5.0	4.9
21	5.9	5.9	6.0	6.1	6.0	5.9	6.0	6.2	6.1
22	7.0	7.0	7.0	7.0	7.2	7.1	7.0	7.1	6.9
23	8.0	8.0	8.0	8.0	8.1	8.0	8.0	8.0	7.9

High Volatility

STOCK PRICE — NUMBER OF MONTHS BEFORE THE OPTIONS EXPIRE

	1	2	3	4	5	6	7	8	9
2	8.0	7.9	8.0	8.0	8.2	8.0	7.8	7.8	8.4
3	6.9	6.8	6.8	6.8	7.1	6.8	6.8	6.6	6.9
4	6.0	5.9	6.1	6.1	6.3	6.1	6.3	6.1	6.4
5	5.0	5.1	5.2	5.1	5.1	5.5	5.1	5.3	5.4
6	4.1	4.1	4.2	4.1	4.5	4.4	4.5	4.6	4.7
7	3.0	3.1	3.2	3.4	3.4	3.6	3.3	3.6	3.7
8	2.1	2.1	2.2	2.4	2.6	2.6	2.7	2.7	2.7
9	1.0	1.4	1.4	1.4	1.5	1.7	1.9	1.8	2.2
10	0.4	0.7	0.9	0.9	0.9	1.2	1.2	1.5	1.7
11	0.1	0.3	0.5	0.6	1.0	1.0	1.1	1.1	1.4
12	0.0	0.2	0.4	0.5	0.8	0.9	1.0	1.0	1.4
13	0.0	0.2	0.4	0.5	0.8	0.9	1.0	1.0	1.4
14	0.1	0.3	0.5	0.6	1.0	1.0	1.1	1.1	1.4
15	0.4	0.6	0.8	0.8	1.3	1.4	1.4	1.4	1.7
16	0.9	1.0	1.3	1.3	1.5	1.7	1.8	1.7	2.0
17	1.8	2.0	2.0	2.0	2.2	2.4	2.3	2.3	2.5
18	3.0	3.1	3.3	3.1	3.5	3.4	3.3	3.7	3.7
19	3.9	4.0	4.3	4.0	4.2	4.3	4.4	4.6	4.4
20	4.9	5.0	4.9	4.9	5.1	5.0	5.2	5.2	5.2
21	5.9	5.9	6.1	6.2	6.0	6.0	6.1	6.5	6.3
22	7.0	7.1	7.1	7.1	7.4	7.3	7.2	7.2	7.1
23	8.1	8.1	8.1	8.0	8.3	8.0	8.1	8.0	7.9

COMBINATION TABLE

Exercise Price of the Call is

Exercise Price of the Put is

Low Volatility

STOCK PRICE	NUMBER OF MONTHS BEFORE THE OPTIONS EXPIRE								
	1	2	3	4	5	6	7	8	9
10	5.0	5.0	5.0	5.0	5.0	5.0	5.0	5.0	5.0
11	4.0	4.0	4.0	4.1	4.1	4.1	4.1	4.1	4.1
12	3.0	3.0	3.0	3.1	3.1	3.1	3.1	3.2	3.2
13	2.0	2.0	2.0	2.1	2.1	2.1	2.1	2.2	2.2
14	1.0	1.0	1.1	1.1	1.2	1.2	1.2	1.3	1.3
15	0.2	0.3	0.4	0.5	0.5	0.5	0.6	0.6	0.7
16	0.0	0.0	0.1	0.1	0.2	0.2	0.2	0.3	0.3
17	0.0	0.0	0.0	0.1	0.1	0.1	0.2	0.2	0.3
18	0.0	0.0	0.0	0.1	0.1	0.1	0.2	0.2	0.3
19	0.0	0.0	0.1	0.2	0.2	0.2	0.3	0.3	0.4
20	0.2	0.3	0.4	0.5	0.5	0.5	0.6	0.6	0.7
21	0.9	0.9	0.9	1.0	1.0	1.0	1.0	1.1	1.1
22	1.9	1.8	1.8	1.8	1.8	1.8	1.9	1.9	1.9
23	3.0	3.0	3.0	3.1	3.1	3.1	3.1	3.1	3.2
24	4.0	4.0	4.0	4.0	4.0	4.0	4.0	4.0	4.0
25	4.9	4.9	4.9	4.9	4.9	4.9	4.9	4.9	4.9
26	6.0	6.0	6.0	6.0	6.0	6.0	6.0	6.0	6.0
27	7.0	7.0	7.1	7.1	7.1	7.1	7.1	7.1	7.1
28	8.0	8.0	8.1	8.1	8.1	8.1	8.1	8.1	8.1

Average Volatility

STOCK PRICE	NUMBER OF MONTHS BEFORE THE OPTIONS EXPIRE								
	1	2	3	4	5	6	7	8	9
10	5.0	5.0	5.0	5.1	5.1	5.1	5.1	5.1	5.2
11	4.0	4.1	4.1	4.2	4.2	4.2	4.3	4.3	4.3
12	3.0	3.1	3.1	3.2	3.3	3.3	3.3	3.4	3.4
13	2.0	2.1	2.2	2.3	2.3	2.4	2.4	2.5	2.6
14	1.0	1.1	1.2	1.4	1.4	1.5	1.5	1.6	1.7
15	0.3	0.5	0.6	0.7	0.8	0.9	0.9	1.0	1.1
16	0.0	0.2	0.3	0.4	0.5	0.5	0.6	0.7	0.8
17	0.0	0.1	0.2	0.3	0.4	0.5	0.5	0.6	0.7
18	0.0	0.1	0.2	0.3	0.4	0.4	0.5	0.6	0.7
19	0.0	0.2	0.2	0.4	0.5	0.6	0.6	0.7	0.9
20	0.3	0.5	0.6	0.7	0.8	0.8	0.9	1.0	1.1
21	0.9	1.0	1.0	1.1	1.2	1.2	1.2	1.3	1.4
22	1.8	1.8	1.8	1.9	1.9	1.9	2.0	2.0	2.1
23	3.0	3.1	3.1	3.2	3.2	3.3	3.3	3.4	3.4
24	4.0	4.0	4.0	4.0	4.1	4.1	4.1	4.2	4.2
25	4.9	4.9	4.9	4.9	4.9	4.9	4.9	5.0	5.0
26	6.0	6.0	6.0	6.0	6.0	6.0	6.0	6.0	6.1
27	7.0	7.1	7.1	7.1	7.2	7.1	7.2	7.2	7.2
28	8.0	8.1	8.1	8.1	8.1	8.2	8.2	8.2	8.2

High Volatility

STOCK PRICE	NUMBER OF MONTHS BEFORE THE OPTIONS EXPIRE								
	1	2	3	4	5	6	7	8	9
10	5.0	5.1	5.3	5.4	5.5	5.6	5.7	5.8	6.0
11	4.1	4.3	4.4	4.6	4.8	4.9	5.0	5.1	5.3
12	3.1	3.4	3.5	3.7	3.9	4.0	4.2	4.3	4.5
13	2.2	2.4	2.7	2.9	3.1	3.2	3.3	3.6	3.8
14	1.2	1.6	1.8	2.1	2.3	2.4	2.6	2.8	3.0
15	0.6	1.0	1.3	1.6	1.9	2.0	2.1	2.4	2.6
16	0.3	0.7	1.0	1.3	1.6	1.7	1.8	2.1	2.3
17	0.2	0.6	0.9	1.3	1.5	1.5	1.8	2.1	2.3
18	0.2	0.6	0.9	1.4	1.5	1.6	1.8	2.2	2.3
19	0.6	0.7	1.0	1.4	1.6	1.9	2.0	2.2	2.5
20	0.6	1.0	1.3	1.6	1.9	2.0	2.2	2.4	2.7
21	1.0	1.3	1.5	1.8	2.0	2.1	2.3	2.5	2.7
22	1.9	2.0	2.1	2.3	2.5	2.6	2.8	3.0	3.2
23	3.1	3.3	3.5	3.7	3.9	4.0	4.1	4.3	4.5
24	4.0	4.1	4.3	4.4	4.6	4.7	4.8	5.0	5.1
25	4.9	4.9	5.0	5.1	5.2	5.2	5.3	5.4	5.6
26	6.0	6.0	6.0	6.2	6.3	6.3	6.4	6.5	6.7
27	7.1	7.2	7.3	7.4	7.5	7.5	7.7	7.7	7.9
28	8.1	8.2	8.3	8.3	8.4	8.4	8.5	8.6	8.7

COMBINATION TABLE

Exercise Price of the Call is 25
Exercise Price of the Put is 20

Low Volatility

STOCK PRICE	\multicolumn{9}{c}{NUMBER OF MONTHS BEFORE THE OPTIONS EXPIRE}								
	1	2	3	4	5	6	7	8	9
14	6.0	6.0	6.0	6.0	6.0	6.0	6.0	6.0	6.0
15	5.0	5.0	5.0	5.0	5.0	5.0	5.0	5.1	5.1
16	4.0	4.0	4.1	4.1	4.1	4.2	4.2	4.2	4.3
17	3.0	3.1	3.1	3.2	3.2	3.2	3.2	3.3	3.4
18	2.0	2.1	2.1	2.2	2.2	2.3	2.3	2.3	2.4
19	1.0	1.1	1.1	1.2	1.3	1.3	1.4	1.5	1.5
20	0.3	0.4	0.5	0.6	0.7	0.7	0.8	0.8	0.9
21	0.0	0.1	0.2	0.3	0.3	0.4	0.4	0.5	0.6
22	0.0	0.0	0.1	0.2	0.3	0.3	0.4	0.5	0.5
23	0.0	0.0	0.1	0.2	0.2	0.3	0.3	0.4	0.5
24	0.0	0.1	0.2	0.3	0.4	0.4	0.5	0.6	0.6
25	0.3	0.4	0.5	0.6	0.7	0.7	0.8	0.8	0.9
26	0.9	0.9	1.0	1.0	1.1	1.1	1.2	1.2	1.3
27	1.8	1.8	1.8	1.9	1.9	1.9	1.9	1.9	2.0
28	3.0	3.0	3.1	3.1	3.2	3.2	3.2	3.3	3.3
29	4.0	4.0	4.0	4.0	4.0	4.0	4.1	4.1	4.2
30	4.9	4.9	4.9	4.9	4.9	4.9	4.9	4.9	4.9
31	6.0	6.0	6.0	6.0	6.0	6.0	6.0	6.0	6.0
32	7.0	7.1	7.1	7.1	7.1	7.1	7.1	7.1	7.1
33	8.0	8.0	8.1	8.1	8.1	8.1	8.1	8.1	8.2

Average Volatility

STOCK PRICE	\multicolumn{9}{c}{NUMBER OF MONTHS BEFORE THE OPTIONS EXPIRE}								
	1	2	3	4	5	6	7	8	9
14	6.0	6.0	6.0	6.0	6.0	6.0	6.1	6.1	6.2
15	5.0	5.0	5.0	5.1	5.2	5.2	5.2	5.3	5.3
16	4.0	4.1	4.2	4.2	4.3	4.4	4.4	4.5	4.6
17	3.1	3.2	3.3	3.4	3.4	3.5	3.5	3.6	3.8
18	2.1	2.2	2.3	2.4	2.5	2.6	2.6	2.7	2.9
19	1.1	1.3	1.4	1.5	1.6	1.7	1.8	1.9	2.1
20	0.4	0.6	0.8	1.0	1.1	1.2	1.3	1.4	1.6
21	0.1	0.3	0.4	0.7	0.8	0.9	1.0	1.1	1.3
22	0.0	0.2	0.4	0.6	0.7	0.8	0.9	1.1	1.2
23	0.0	0.2	0.3	0.6	0.7	0.8	0.9	1.0	1.2
24	0.1	0.3	0.5	0.8	0.8	1.0	1.0	1.2	1.3
25	0.4	0.6	0.8	1.0	1.1	1.2	1.3	1.4	1.6
26	0.9	1.1	1.1	1.3	1.4	1.5	1.5	1.6	1.8
27	1.8	1.9	1.9	2.0	2.1	2.1	2.2	2.2	2.3
28	3.1	3.1	3.2	3.3	3.4	3.5	3.5	3.6	3.7
29	4.0	4.0	4.0	4.2	4.2	4.2	4.3	4.4	4.5
30	4.9	4.9	4.9	4.9	5.0	5.0	5.0	5.0	5.1
31	6.0	6.0	6.0	6.1	6.1	6.1	6.1	6.2	6.2
32	7.1	7.1	7.2	7.2	7.2	7.3	7.3	7.3	7.3
33	8.1	8.1	8.2	8.1	8.2	8.2	8.2	8.2	8.3

High Volatility

STOCK PRICE	\multicolumn{9}{c}{NUMBER OF MONTHS BEFORE THE OPTIONS EXPIRE}								
	1	2	3	4	5	6	7	8	9
12	8.0	8.0	8.0	8.2	8.3	8.4	8.5	8.6	8.8
13	6.8	6.8	6.9	6.9	7.0	7.1	7.2	7.4	7.7
14	6.0	6.1	6.2	6.3	6.6	6.6	6.8	7.0	7.2
15	5.1	5.3	5.4	5.8	6.0	6.1	6.3	6.6	6.7
16	4.2	4.5	4.7	5.0	5.3	5.5	5.6	5.8	6.1
17	3.3	3.6	3.9	4.3	4.5	4.7	4.8	5.1	5.4
18	2.3	2.7	3.0	3.4	3.7	3.9	4.1	4.3	4.7
19	1.4	1.9	2.2	2.6	3.0	3.2	3.4	3.7	4.0
20	0.8	1.4	1.8	2.3	2.6	2.8	3.0	3.3	3.7
21	0.5	1.1	1.5	2.0	2.3	2.5	2.8	3.1	3.4
22	0.4	1.0	1.4	1.9	2.3	2.5	2.7	3.1	3.4
23	0.4	1.0	1.4	1.9	2.3	2.5	2.7	3.0	3.4
24	0.5	1.2	1.6	2.1	2.4	2.7	2.9	3.2	3.5
25	0.8	1.4	1.8	2.3	2.6	2.8	3.1	3.3	3.7
26	1.2	1.6	1.9	2.4	2.7	2.9	3.1	3.4	3.7
27	1.9	2.2	2.5	2.9	3.1	3.3	3.5	3.7	4.0
28	3.2	3.6	3.8	4.2	4.4	4.6	4.8	5.1	5.3
29	4.1	4.3	4.5	4.9	5.1	5.3	5.5	5.7	6.1
30	4.9	5.1	5.1	5.3	5.5	5.7	5.8	5.9	6.2
31	6.0	6.1	6.2	6.6	6.6	6.7	6.9	7.1	7.3
32	7.2	7.3	7.5	7.7	7.8	8.0	8.1	8.3	8.5
33	8.1	8.2	8.4	8.5	8.7	8.7	8.8	8.9	9.2

COMBINATION TABLE

Exercise Price of the Call is 30

Exercise Price of the Put is 25

Low Volatility

STOCK PRICE — NUMBER OF MONTHS BEFORE THE OPTIONS EXPIRE

	1	2	3	4	5	6	7	8	9
19	6.0	5.9	6.1	6.0	6.2	6.1	6.2	6.1	6.2
20	5.0	5.1	5.1	4.9	5.0	5.3	5.0	5.1	5.2
21	4.1	4.1	4.1	4.0	4.4	4.3	4.3	4.4	4.4
22	3.0	3.0	3.1	3.3	3.2	3.4	3.1	3.4	3.4
23	2.0	2.0	2.1	2.2	2.4	2.4	2.5	2.4	2.4
24	1.0	1.2	1.2	1.3	1.5	1.6	1.5	1.5	1.8
25	0.3	0.5	0.7	0.7	0.9	0.9	1.1	1.1	1.2
26	0.1	0.1	0.3	0.3	0.6	0.7	0.7	0.7	0.9
27	0.0	0.1	0.2	0.3	0.5	0.6	0.6	0.6	0.9
28	0.0	0.1	0.2	0.3	0.5	0.6	0.6	0.6	0.9
29	0.1	0.2	0.3	0.3	0.7	0.7	0.7	0.7	0.9
30	0.3	0.5	0.6	0.6	0.9	1.0	1.0	1.0	1.3
31	0.9	0.9	1.1	1.2	1.3	1.4	1.5	1.4	1.6
32	1.8	1.9	1.9	1.9	2.0	2.2	2.1	2.1	2.2
33	3.0	3.0	3.1	3.0	3.3	3.2	3.1	3.5	3.4
34	3.9	3.9	4.2	4.0	4.1	4.2	4.2	4.3	4.2
35	4.9	5.0	4.9	4.9	5.0	4.9	5.1	5.1	5.0
36	5.9	5.9	6.1	6.2	6.0	5.9	6.0	6.3	6.2
37	7.0	7.1	7.1	7.1	7.3	7.2	7.1	7.1	7.0
38	8.0	8.0	8.0	8.0	8.2	8.0	8.1	8.0	7.9

Average Volatility

STOCK PRICE — NUMBER OF MONTHS BEFORE THE OPTIONS EXPIRE

	1	2	3	4	5	6	7	8	9
19	6.0	6.0	6.0	6.0	6.2	6.2	6.2	6.2	6.3
20	5.0	5.1	5.1	5.2	5.4	5.3	5.5	5.5	5.6
21	4.1	4.2	4.3	4.4	4.5	4.6	4.6	4.8	4.9
22	3.1	3.3	3.4	3.6	3.6	3.7	3.8	3.9	4.1
23	2.1	2.3	2.4	2.6	2.7	2.9	2.9	3.1	3.3
24	1.2	1.4	1.6	1.8	1.9	2.0	2.1	2.3	2.5
25	0.5	0.8	1.0	1.3	1.5	1.6	1.7	1.9	2.1
26	0.2	0.5	0.7	0.9	1.1	1.3	1.4	1.6	1.8
27	0.1	0.4	0.6	0.9	1.1	1.2	1.3	1.5	1.8
28	0.1	0.4	0.6	0.9	1.0	1.2	1.3	1.5	1.7
29	0.2	0.5	0.7	1.0	1.2	1.4	1.5	1.7	1.9
30	0.5	0.8	1.0	1.3	1.4	1.6	1.7	1.9	2.1
31	1.0	1.2	1.3	1.5	1.7	1.8	1.9	2.0	2.2
32	1.8	2.0	2.0	2.2	2.3	2.3	2.4	2.6	2.7
33	3.1	3.2	3.4	3.5	3.6	3.7	3.7	3.9	4.1
34	4.0	4.1	4.2	4.3	4.3	4.4	4.5	4.6	4.7
35	4.9	4.9	4.9	5.0	5.0	5.1	5.1	5.2	5.3
36	6.0	6.0	6.0	6.1	6.1	6.2	6.2	6.3	6.4
37	7.1	7.1	7.2	7.3	7.3	7.4	7.4	7.5	7.6
38	8.1	8.1	8.2	8.2	8.2	8.3	8.3	8.4	8.4

High Volatility

STOCK PRICE — NUMBER OF MONTHS BEFORE THE OPTIONS EXPIRE

	1	2	3	4	5	6	7	8	9
17	8.0	8.1	8.2	8.4	8.6	8.8	9.0	9.2	9.5
18	6.8	6.9	7.0	7.2	7.4	7.6	7.7	8.0	8.3
19	6.0	6.3	6.4	6.7	7.1	7.2	7.3	7.6	8.0
20	5.1	5.5	5.8	6.2	6.6	6.7	7.0	7.4	7.7
21	4.3	4.7	5.1	5.5	5.8	6.1	6.3	6.7	7.1
22	3.4	3.9	4.3	4.8	5.1	5.3	5.5	6.0	6.3
23	2.5	3.0	3.5	4.0	4.4	4.7	4.9	5.3	5.7
24	1.6	2.2	2.7	3.3	3.7	3.9	4.2	4.6	5.1
25	1.0	1.8	2.4	3.0	3.4	3.7	3.9	4.4	4.5
26	0.7	1.5	2.1	2.7	3.1	3.4	3.6	4.1	4.5
27	0.7	1.5	2.1	2.7	3.1	3.4	3.6	4.1	4.6
28	0.6	1.4	2.0	2.7	3.1	3.4	3.6	4.1	4.6
29	0.8	1.6	2.2	2.8	3.2	3.5	3.7	4.2	4.7
30	1.0	1.8	2.4	3.0	3.4	3.7	3.9	4.4	4.8
31	1.3	2.0	2.5	3.0	3.5	3.7	3.9	4.4	4.8
32	2.0	2.5	2.9	3.5	3.8	4.0	4.3	4.6	5.1
33	3.4	3.9	4.3	4.7	5.1	5.4	5.5	5.9	6.4
34	4.2	4.6	5.0	5.4	5.7	6.0	6.1	6.6	6.9
35	5.0	5.2	5.4	5.8	6.0	6.2	6.3	6.7	7.0
36	6.0	6.2	6.5	6.8	7.0	7.2	7.4	7.8	8.1
37	7.2	7.4	7.7	8.1	8.3	8.5	8.6	9.0	9.3
38	8.2	8.3	8.6	8.7	9.0	9.2	9.2	9.5	9.8

COMBINATION TABLE

Exercise Price of the Call is

Exercise Price of the Put is

Low Volatility

STOCK PRICE — NUMBER OF MONTHS BEFORE THE OPTIONS EXPIRE

STOCK PRICE	1	2	3	4	5	6	7	8	9
24	6.0	6.0	6.0	6.0	6.0	6.0	6.0	6.1	6.1
25	5.0	5.0	5.1	5.1	5.1	5.2	5.2	5.3	5.4
26	4.0	4.1	4.2	4.3	4.3	4.4	4.4	4.5	4.5
27	3.1	3.1	3.2	3.3	3.4	3.4	3.5	3.6	3.7
28	2.0	2.2	2.3	2.4	2.5	2.6	2.6	2.7	2.8
29	1.1	1.3	1.4	1.5	1.6	1.7	1.8	1.9	2.0
30	0.4	0.6	0.8	0.9	1.1	1.2	1.2	1.4	1.5
31	0.1	0.3	0.4	0.6	0.7	0.8	0.9	1.1	1.2
32	0.0	0.2	0.3	0.6	0.7	0.8	0.9	1.0	1.1
33	0.0	0.2	0.3	0.5	0.7	0.7	0.8	1.0	1.1
34	0.1	0.3	0.4	0.7	0.8	0.9	1.0	1.1	1.3
35	0.4	0.6	0.7	0.9	1.1	1.1	1.3	1.4	1.5
36	0.9	1.1	1.2	1.2	1.4	1.4	1.5	1.6	1.7
37	1.8	1.9	1.9	2.0	2.0	2.1	2.1	2.2	2.3
38	3.0	3.1	3.2	3.3	3.4	3.4	3.5	3.6	3.7
39	4.0	4.0	4.1	4.1	4.2	4.2	4.3	4.3	4.4
40	4.9	4.9	4.9	4.9	5.0	4.9	5.0	5.0	5.1
41	6.0	6.0	6.0	6.0	6.0	6.0	6.1	6.1	6.2
42	7.1	7.1	7.2	7.2	7.2	7.2	7.3	7.3	7.4
43	8.0	8.1	8.2	8.2	8.2	8.2	8.2	8.3	8.3

Average Volatility

STOCK PRICE — NUMBER OF MONTHS BEFORE THE OPTIONS EXPIRE

STOCK PRICE	1	2	3	4	5	6	7	8	9
24	6.0	6.0	6.0	6.1	6.2	6.2	6.3	6.3	6.6
25	5.0	5.1	5.2	5.4	5.5	5.5	5.6	5.8	6.0
26	4.1	4.3	4.4	4.6	4.7	4.8	4.9	5.1	5.3
27	3.2	3.4	3.5	3.7	3.9	4.0	4.2	4.3	4.5
28	2.2	2.4	2.6	2.9	3.1	3.2	3.3	3.5	3.8
29	1.3	1.6	1.7	2.0	2.3	2.3	2.5	2.7	3.0
30	0.6	1.0	1.2	1.6	1.8	2.0	2.1	2.3	2.6
31	0.3	0.7	0.9	1.3	1.5	1.7	1.8	2.0	2.3
32	0.2	0.6	0.9	1.3	1.5	1.6	1.8	2.0	2.3
33	0.2	0.6	0.8	1.2	1.5	1.6	1.8	2.0	2.3
34	0.3	0.7	1.0	1.4	1.6	1.8	1.9	2.1	2.4
35	0.6	1.0	1.2	1.6	1.9	2.0	2.2	2.4	2.7
36	1.1	1.3	1.5	1.8	2.0	2.1	2.2	2.5	2.7
37	1.9	2.0	2.1	2.4	2.5	2.7	2.7	2.9	3.1
38	3.1	3.4	3.4	3.7	3.9	3.9	4.1	4.2	4.4
39	4.0	4.1	4.2	4.5	4.6	4.6	4.8	5.0	5.1
40	4.9	4.9	5.0	5.1	5.2	5.2	5.3	5.4	5.6
41	6.0	6.0	6.0	6.2	6.3	6.3	6.4	6.5	6.7
42	7.1	7.2	7.3	7.4	7.5	7.6	7.6	7.7	7.9
43	8.1	8.2	8.2	8.3	8.3	8.5	8.5	8.5	8.7

High Volatility

STOCK PRICE — NUMBER OF MONTHS BEFORE THE OPTIONS EXPIRE

STOCK PRICE	1	2	3	4	5	6	7	8	9
22	8.0	8.2	8.3	8.9	9.1	9.2	9.5	9.9	10.
23	6.8	6.9	7.1	7.6	7.9	8.1	8.3	8.6	9.0
24	6.1	6.4	6.6	7.2	7.5	7.7	8.0	8.2	8.8
25	5.2	5.8	6.2	6.8	7.2	7.4	7.7	8.1	8.7
26	4.4	5.0	5.5	6.2	6.6	6.8	7.1	7.5	8.0
27	3.5	4.2	4.7	5.4	5.9	6.1	6.5	6.8	7.3
28	2.7	3.5	4.0	4.7	5.2	5.5	5.8	6.1	6.8
29	1.8	2.7	3.3	4.0	4.5	4.8	5.2	5.6	6.2
30	1.3	2.3	2.9	3.7	4.3	4.5	4.9	5.3	5.9
31	1.0	2.0	2.6	3.5	4.0	4.3	4.6	5.0	5.7
32	0.9	2.0	2.6	3.5	4.0	4.3	4.7	5.1	5.7
33	0.9	2.0	2.6	3.4	4.0	4.2	4.6	5.1	5.7
34	1.1	2.1	2.8	3.6	4.1	4.4	4.8	5.2	5.8
35	1.3	2.3	2.9	3.7	4.3	4.5	4.9	5.3	6.0
36	1.5	2.4	3.0	3.8	4.3	4.5	4.8	5.3	5.9
37	2.2	2.9	3.4	4.1	4.6	4.8	5.1	5.4	6.0
38	3.5	4.3	4.7	5.4	5.8	6.0	6.4	6.7	7.3
39	4.3	4.9	5.4	6.1	6.5	6.6	7.0	7.4	7.9
40	5.0	5.4	5.7	6.2	6.6	6.8	7.1	7.4	7.9
41	6.1	6.5	6.7	7.3	7.7	7.9	8.1	8.5	9.1
42	7.3	7.7	8.1	8.6	8.9	9.1	9.4	9.6	10.
43	8.2	8.5	8.7	9.2	9.5	9.7	9.9	10.	10.

COMBINATION TABLE

Exercise Price of the Call is

Exercise Price of the Put is

Low Volatility

STOCK PRICE	NUMBER OF MONTHS BEFORE THE OPTIONS EXPIRE								
	1	2	3	4	5	6	7	8	9
29	6.0	6.0	6.0	6.0	6.1	6.1	6.1	6.2	6.2
30	5.0	5.0	5.1	5.2	5.2	5.3	5.3	5.4	5.5
31	4.1	4.1	4.2	4.3	4.4	4.5	4.5	4.6	4.8
32	3.1	3.2	3.3	3.5	3.5	3.6	3.7	3.8	4.0
33	2.1	2.3	2.3	2.5	2.6	2.7	2.8	2.9	3.1
34	1.1	1.3	1.5	1.6	1.8	1.9	2.0	2.1	2.3
35	0.5	0.7	0.9	1.1	1.3	1.4	1.5	1.7	1.8
36	0.1	0.4	0.6	0.8	1.0	1.1	1.2	1.4	1.6
37	0.0	0.3	0.5	0.7	0.9	1.0	1.2	1.3	1.5
38	0.0	0.3	0.5	0.7	0.9	1.0	1.1	1.3	1.5
39	0.1	0.4	0.6	0.9	1.0	1.2	1.3	1.5	1.6
40	0.5	0.7	0.9	1.1	1.3	1.4	1.5	1.7	1.9
41	1.0	1.1	1.2	1.4	1.5	1.6	1.7	1.8	2.0
42	1.8	1.9	1.9	2.1	2.2	2.2	2.3	2.4	2.5
43	3.1	3.2	3.3	3.4	3.5	3.6	3.6	3.8	3.9
44	4.0	4.0	4.1	4.2	4.3	4.3	4.4	4.5	4.7
45	4.9	4.9	4.9	4.9	5.0	5.0	5.1	5.1	5.2
46	6.0	6.0	6.0	6.1	6.1	6.1	6.2	6.2	6.3
47	7.1	7.1	7.2	7.2	7.3	7.3	7.3	7.4	7.4
48	8.1	8.1	8.2	8.2	8.2	8.2	8.3	8.3	8.4

Average Volatility

STOCK PRICE	NUMBER OF MONTHS BEFORE THE OPTIONS EXPIRE								
	1	2	3	4	5	6	7	8	9
29	6.0	6.1	6.1	6.3	6.3	6.4	6.5	6.7	6.8
30	5.1	5.2	5.3	5.6	5.7	5.8	6.0	6.2	6.3
31	4.2	4.3	4.6	4.8	5.0	5.1	5.3	5.5	5.6
32	3.2	3.5	3.7	4.0	4.2	4.3	4.5	4.7	4.9
33	2.3	2.6	2.8	3.2	3.4	3.6	3.7	4.0	4.2
34	1.3	1.7	2.0	2.4	2.6	2.7	2.9	3.2	3.4
35	0.7	1.2	1.5	2.0	2.2	2.4	2.6	2.9	3.1
36	0.4	0.9	1.2	1.7	1.9	2.1	2.3	2.6	2.8
37	0.3	0.8	1.2	1.6	1.9	2.1	2.3	2.6	2.8
38	0.3	0.8	1.1	1.6	1.9	2.1	2.3	2.6	2.8
39	0.4	0.9	1.3	1.8	2.0	2.2	2.4	2.7	3.0
40	0.7	1.2	1.5	2.0	2.2	2.5	2.6	2.9	3.1
41	1.1	1.5	1.7	2.1	2.3	2.5	2.7	2.9	3.2
42	1.9	2.1	2.3	2.7	2.8	3.0	3.1	3.3	3.6
43	3.2	3.5	3.7	4.0	4.1	4.3	4.4	4.7	4.9
44	4.0	4.2	4.4	4.7	4.9	5.0	5.2	5.3	5.6
45	4.9	5.0	5.1	5.2	5.3	5.4	5.5	5.7	5.9
46	6.0	6.0	6.2	6.4	6.4	6.5	6.7	6.8	6.9
47	7.2	7.2	7.4	7.5	7.7	7.8	7.9	8.0	8.2
48	8.1	8.2	8.3	8.4	8.5	8.5	8.6	8.7	8.9

High Volatility

STOCK PRICE	NUMBER OF MONTHS BEFORE THE OPTIONS EXPIRE								
	1	2	3	4	5	6	7	8	9
27	8.0	8.3	8.7	9.3	9.7	9.9	10.	10.	11.
28	6.8	7.2	7.5	8.1	8.4	8.8	9.0	9.4	9.9
29	6.2	6.7	7.1	7.7	8.0	8.4	8.7	9.1	9.5
30	5.4	6.1	6.7	7.5	8.0	8.2	8.6	9.1	9.6
31	4.6	5.3	6.1	6.8	7.4	7.6	8.0	8.5	9.0
32	3.7	4.6	5.3	6.1	6.6	6.9	7.2	7.8	8.3
33	2.9	3.9	4.6	5.4	6.0	6.3	6.7	7.3	7.8
34	2.0	3.1	3.9	4.8	5.4	5.7	6.1	6.7	7.2
35	1.6	2.7	3.6	4.5	5.1	5.4	5.8	6.5	7.0
36	1.3	2.5	3.3	4.2	4.8	5.2	5.6	6.2	6.8
37	1.2	2.5	3.4	4.3	4.9	5.3	5.7	6.3	6.8
38	1.2	2.4	3.3	4.2	4.8	5.2	5.6	6.2	6.8
39	1.3	2.6	3.5	4.4	5.0	5.3	5.8	6.4	6.9
40	1.6	2.8	3.6	4.6	5.1	5.5	5.9	6.5	7.0
41	1.8	2.8	3.6	4.5	5.1	5.4	5.8	6.4	6.9
42	2.4	3.3	4.0	4.8	5.3	5.6	6.0	6.5	7.0
43	3.7	4.6	5.3	6.1	6.5	7.0	7.2	7.8	8.3
44	4.4	5.2	5.9	6.7	7.2	7.6	7.9	8.4	8.9
45	5.1	5.7	6.2	6.7	7.2	7.5	7.9	8.3	8.8
46	6.2	6.7	7.3	8.0	8.3	8.6	9.0	9.4	9.8
47	7.4	7.9	8.5	9.1	9.5	9.8	10.	10.	11.
48	8.3	8.8	9.1	9.6	10.	10.	10.	11.	11.

COMBINATION TABLE

Exercise Price of the Call is (45)

Exercise Price of the Put is (40)

Low Volatility

STOCK PRICE	NUMBER OF MONTHS BEFORE THE OPTIONS EXPIRE								
	1	2	3	4	5	6	7	8	9
34	6.0	6.0	6.0	6.1	6.2	6.2	6.2	6.3	6.4
35	5.0	5.1	5.1	5.2	5.4	5.4	5.5	5.6	5.7
36	4.1	4.2	4.3	4.4	4.5	4.6	4.7	4.8	5.0
37	3.1	3.3	3.4	3.6	3.6	3.7	3.8	4.0	4.1
38	2.1	2.3	2.5	2.7	2.8	2.9	3.0	3.2	3.4
39	1.2	1.4	1.6	1.8	2.0	2.1	2.2	2.4	2.6
40	0.5	0.8	1.0	1.3	1.5	1.6	1.8	2.0	2.2
41	0.2	0.5	0.7	1.0	1.2	1.4	1.5	1.7	1.9
42	0.1	0.4	0.7	1.0	1.2	1.3	1.4	1.7	1.9
43	0.1	0.4	0.7	0.9	1.1	1.3	1.4	1.6	1.9
44	0.2	0.5	0.8	1.1	1.3	1.4	1.6	1.8	2.0
45	0.5	0.8	1.0	1.3	1.5	1.7	1.8	2.0	2.2
46	1.0	1.2	1.4	1.6	1.7	1.8	1.9	2.1	2.3
47	1.8	2.0	2.0	2.2	2.3	2.4	2.5	2.6	2.8
48	3.1	3.2	3.4	3.5	3.7	3.8	3.8	4.0	4.2
49	4.0	4.1	4.2	4.3	4.4	4.5	4.5	4.7	4.8
50	4.9	4.9	5.0	5.0	5.1	5.1	5.1	5.2	5.3
51	6.0	6.0	6.0	6.1	6.1	6.2	6.2	6.3	6.4
52	7.1	7.1	7.2	7.3	7.3	7.4	7.4	7.6	7.6
53	8.1	8.1	8.2	8.2	8.3	8.3	8.3	8.4	8.4

Average Volatility

STOCK PRICE	NUMBER OF MONTHS BEFORE THE OPTIONS EXPIRE								
	1	2	3	4	5	6	7	8	9
32	8.0	8.0	8.1	8.3	8.3	8.4	8.5	8.6	8.9
33	6.8	6.7	6.8	7.0	7.1	7.2	7.2	7.5	7.6
34	6.0	6.1	6.2	6.4	6.6	6.7	6.8	6.9	7.2
35	5.0	5.3	5.5	5.5	5.9	6.2	6.3	6.5	6.9
36	4.2	4.5	4.7	5.0	5.2	5.5	5.6	5.9	6.1
37	3.3	3.6	3.9	4.2	4.5	4.7	4.9	5.1	5.5
38	2.3	2.7	3.1	3.4	3.7	3.9	4.1	4.5	4.8
39	1.5	1.9	2.2	2.7	2.9	3.2	3.4	3.7	4.0
40	0.8	1.4	1.8	2.3	2.6	2.9	3.1	3.4	3.7
41	0.5	1.1	1.5	2.0	2.3	2.6	2.8	3.1	3.5
42	0.4	1.0	1.5	2.0	2.3	2.6	2.8	3.1	3.5
43	0.4	1.0	1.4	2.0	2.3	2.5	2.8	3.1	3.5
44	0.5	1.2	1.6	2.1	2.4	2.7	2.9	3.2	3.6
45	0.8	1.4	1.8	2.3	2.6	2.9	3.1	3.4	3.8
46	1.2	1.6	2.0	2.4	2.7	2.9	3.1	3.4	4.1
47	1.9	2.3	2.5	2.9	3.1	3.3	3.5	3.8	4.1
48	3.3	3.6	3.9	4.2	4.4	4.7	4.8	5.1	5.4
49	4.1	4.4	4.6	5.0	5.1	5.4	5.5	5.7	6.1
50	4.9	5.0	5.2	5.4	5.5	5.7	5.8	6.0	6.2
51	6.0	6.2	6.3	6.5	6.7	6.8	6.9	7.1	7.4
52	7.2	7.3	7.5	7.8	7.8	8.0	8.1	8.3	8.5
53	8.1	8.3	8.3	8.5	8.6	8.7	8.8	9.0	9.2

High Volatility

STOCK PRICE	NUMBER OF MONTHS BEFORE THE OPTIONS EXPIRE								
	1	2	3	4	5	6	7	8	9
32	8.1	8.7	9.1	9.8	10.	10.	10.	11.	12.
33	6.9	7.3	7.9	8.6	9.1	9.4	9.7	10.	10.
34	6.3	6.9	7.5	8.2	8.7	9.1	9.5	9.9	10.
35	5.5	6.5	7.2	8.1	8.6	9.1	9.5	10.	10.
36	4.7	5.8	6.6	7.4	8.0	8.5	8.9	9.5	10.
37	4.0	5.1	5.9	6.7	7.3	7.8	8.2	8.8	9.5
38	3.1	4.4	5.2	6.1	6.7	7.2	7.6	8.3	9.0
39	2.3	3.6	4.6	5.5	6.1	6.6	7.1	7.7	8.4
40	1.8	3.3	4.2	5.2	5.9	6.4	6.9	7.5	8.2
41	1.6	3.0	4.0	5.0	5.6	6.2	6.6	7.3	8.1
42	1.5	3.0	4.0	5.0	5.7	6.2	6.7	7.3	8.1
43	1.5	3.0	4.0	5.0	5.7	6.2	6.7	7.3	8.1
44	1.7	3.1	4.1	5.1	5.8	6.3	6.8	7.4	8.2
45	1.9	3.3	4.3	5.2	5.9	6.4	6.9	7.5	8.2
46	2.0	3.4	4.3	5.2	5.9	6.3	6.8	7.4	8.2
47	2.5	3.7	4.6	5.4	6.0	6.4	6.9	7.5	8.2
48	3.9	5.0	5.8	6.7	7.3	7.7	8.2	8.8	9.5
49	4.6	5.7	6.5	7.3	7.9	8.4	8.8	9.4	10.
50	5.2	5.9	6.6	7.4	7.8	8.3	8.6	9.2	9.8
51	6.3	7.1	7.7	8.5	9.0	9.4	9.7	10.	10.
52	7.6	8.3	8.9	9.7	10.	10.	10.	11.	12.
53	8.3	9.0	9.5	10.	10.	11.	11.	11.	12.

COMBINATION TABLE

Exercise Price of the Call is 50

Exercise Price of the Put is 45

Low Volatility

STOCK PRICE — NUMBER OF MONTHS BEFORE THE OPTIONS EXPIRE

STOCK PRICE	1	2	3	4	5	6	7	8	9
39	6.0	6.0	6.0	6.1	6.2	6.2	6.3	6.3	6.5
40	5.0	5.1	5.2	5.3	5.5	5.5	5.6	5.8	5.9
41	4.1	4.2	4.4	4.6	4.7	4.8	4.9	5.0	5.2
42	3.1	3.3	3.4	3.7	3.9	4.0	4.1	4.2	4.4
43	2.2	2.4	2.6	2.8	3.0	3.2	3.3	3.4	3.7
44	1.2	1.5	1.7	2.0	2.2	2.3	2.5	2.7	2.9
45	0.6	1.0	1.2	1.6	1.8	1.9	2.1	2.3	2.6
46	0.3	0.6	0.9	1.3	1.5	1.6	1.8	2.0	2.3
47	0.2	0.6	0.8	1.2	1.4	1.6	1.8	1.9	2.2
48	0.2	0.5	0.8	1.2	1.4	1.6	1.7	1.9	2.2
49	0.3	0.7	1.0	1.3	1.6	1.7	1.9	2.1	2.4
50	0.6	1.0	1.2	1.6	1.8	1.9	2.1	2.3	2.6
51	1.0	1.3	1.5	1.8	1.9	2.1	2.2	2.4	2.7
52	1.9	2.0	2.1	2.4	2.5	2.6	2.7	2.9	3.1
53	3.1	3.3	3.4	3.7	3.8	3.9	4.1	4.2	4.4
54	4.0	4.1	4.2	4.5	4.6	4.6	4.8	5.0	5.1
55	4.9	4.9	5.0	5.1	5.2	5.3	5.3	5.4	5.5
56	6.0	6.0	6.0	6.2	6.3	6.3	6.4	6.5	6.7
57	7.1	7.2	7.3	7.4	7.5	7.5	7.6	7.6	7.9
58	8.1	8.2	8.2	8.3	8.3	8.4	8.4	8.5	8.7

Average Volatility

STOCK PRICE — NUMBER OF MONTHS BEFORE THE OPTIONS EXPIRE

STOCK PRICE	1	2	3	4	5	6	7	8	9
37	8.0	8.1	8.1	8.4	8.5	8.6	8.7	8.9	9.2
38	6.8	6.8	6.8	7.1	7.2	7.4	7.5	7.7	8.0
39	6.0	6.1	6.3	6.6	6.7	6.9	7.1	7.3	7.5
40	5.1	5.4	5.6	6.0	6.2	6.5	6.7	7.0	7.3
41	4.3	4.6	4.9	5.4	5.6	5.9	6.0	6.3	6.6
42	3.4	3.8	4.1	4.6	4.8	5.0	5.3	5.6	5.9
43	2.4	2.9	3.3	3.8	4.1	4.3	4.6	4.9	5.3
44	1.5	2.1	2.4	3.1	3.3	3.6	3.8	4.2	4.6
45	1.0	1.7	2.1	2.7	3.0	3.3	3.6	3.9	4.3
46	0.6	1.3	1.8	2.4	2.7	3.0	3.3	3.7	4.1
47	0.6	1.3	1.7	2.4	2.7	3.0	3.3	3.7	4.1
48	0.6	1.3	1.7	2.4	2.7	3.0	3.3	3.7	4.0
49	0.7	1.4	1.9	2.5	2.8	3.1	3.4	3.8	4.2
50	1.0	1.7	2.1	2.8	3.0	3.3	3.6	4.0	4.3
51	1.3	1.8	2.2	2.8	3.1	3.3	3.6	4.0	4.3
52	2.0	2.4	2.7	3.2	3.5	3.8	3.9	4.3	4.6
53	3.3	3.7	4.0	4.5	4.7	5.0	5.2	5.5	5.9
54	4.1	4.5	4.8	5.2	5.4	5.7	5.9	6.2	6.5
55	4.9	5.1	5.3	5.6	5.7	6.0	6.1	6.4	6.7
56	6.0	6.2	6.4	6.7	6.9	7.0	7.2	7.5	7.7
57	7.2	7.4	7.6	7.9	8.0	8.3	8.5	8.7	9.1
58	8.2	8.3	8.4	8.7	8.7	8.9	9.1	9.3	9.5

High Volatility

STOCK PRICE — NUMBER OF MONTHS BEFORE THE OPTIONS EXPIRE

STOCK PRICE	1	2	3	4	5	6	7	8	9
37	8.2	8.9	9.4	10.	10.	11.	11.	12.	12.
38	6.9	7.6	8.2	9.2	9.6	10.	10.	11.	11.
39	6.3	7.2	7.9	8.9	9.3	9.8	10.	10.	11.
40	5.7	6.9	7.7	8.8	9.3	9.9	10.	11.	11.
41	5.0	6.2	7.0	8.2	8.8	9.4	9.8	10.	11.
42	4.2	5.5	6.3	7.5	8.1	8.6	9.1	9.8	10.
43	3.4	4.8	5.7	6.9	7.5	8.0	8.6	9.3	10.
44	2.6	4.1	5.1	6.4	7.0	7.5	8.0	8.8	9.6
45	2.2	3.8	4.8	6.1	6.7	7.3	7.8	8.6	9.4
46	1.9	3.5	4.6	5.9	6.5	7.1	7.6	8.4	9.2
47	1.9	3.5	4.6	5.9	6.6	7.2	7.7	8.5	9.2
48	1.8	3.5	4.6	5.9	6.5	7.1	7.7	8.4	9.2
49	2.0	3.7	4.7	6.0	6.6	7.2	7.7	8.5	9.3
50	2.2	3.9	4.8	6.1	6.7	7.3	7.8	8.6	9.4
51	2.3	3.8	4.8	6.0	6.7	7.2	7.8	8.5	9.3
52	2.8	4.2	5.1	6.2	6.8	7.4	7.8	8.5	9.3
53	4.1	5.4	6.3	7.4	8.0	8.6	9.1	9.8	10.
54	4.8	6.1	7.0	8.1	8.7	9.2	9.6	10.	11.
55	5.3	6.3	7.1	8.1	8.5	9.1	9.5	10.	10.
56	6.4	7.4	8.2	9.2	9.7	10.	10.	11.	11.
57	7.7	8.7	9.3	10.	10.	11.	11.	12.	13.
58	8.5	9.2	9.8	10.	11.	11.	12.	12.	13.

COMBINATION TABLE

Exercise Price of the Call is 60

Exercise Price of the Put is 50

Low Volatility

STOCK PRICE	NUMBER OF MONTHS BEFORE THE OPTIONS EXPIRE								
	1	2	3	4	5	6	7	8	9
45	5.0	5.2	5.3	5.5	5.6	5.6	5.7	5.9	6.0
46	4.1	4.4	4.6	4.8	4.9	5.0	5.2	5.3	5.5
47	3.1	3.4	3.6	3.8	3.9	4.0	4.2	4.4	4.6
48	2.1	2.4	2.6	2.8	3.0	3.0	3.2	3.4	3.7
49	1.2	1.6	1.8	2.1	2.3	2.3	2.5	2.8	3.0
50	0.9	1.4	1.7	2.1	2.2	2.4	2.6	2.9	3.1
51	0.3	0.6	0.9	1.3	1.5	1.7	1.9	2.2	2.5
52	0.2	0.5	0.7	1.1	1.3	1.5	1.7	1.9	2.2
53	0.1	0.3	0.6	1.0	1.1	1.3	1.5	1.7	2.0
54	0.0	0.3	0.6	1.0	1.2	1.4	1.6	1.8	2.1
55	0.0	0.2	0.5	0.9	1.0	1.2	1.4	1.6	1.9
56	0.0	0.3	0.5	0.9	1.1	1.2	1.4	1.7	1.9
57	0.0	0.2	0.5	0.9	1.1	1.2	1.4	1.7	2.0
58	0.2	0.5	0.7	1.1	1.2	1.4	1.6	1.9	2.1
59	0.4	0.8	1.1	1.5	1.7	1.9	2.1	2.3	2.6
60	0.8	1.2	1.5	1.9	2.0	2.3	2.4	2.7	3.0
61	1.5	2.0	2.3	2.6	2.9	3.0	3.2	3.4	3.7
62	2.2	2.5	2.7	3.0	3.1	3.3	3.5	3.7	3.9
63	3.0	3.2	3.3	3.6	3.7	3.8	3.9	4.1	4.3
64	4.0	4.2	4.4	4.6	4.7	4.7	4.9	5.1	5.2

Average Volatility

STOCK PRICE	NUMBER OF MONTHS BEFORE THE OPTIONS EXPIRE								
	1	2	3	4	5	6	7	8	9
45	5.1	5.5	5.8	6.1	6.4	6.6	6.7	7.1	7.4
46	4.4	4.9	5.2	5.6	5.9	6.2	6.4	6.8	7.1
47	3.4	3.9	4.2	4.7	4.9	5.2	5.4	5.8	6.1
48	2.4	2.8	3.3	3.8	4.1	4.4	4.7	5.0	5.4
49	1.6	2.1	2.5	3.2	3.4	3.7	4.0	4.4	4.8
50	1.4	2.1	2.6	3.3	3.7	4.0	4.3	4.7	5.0
51	0.7	1.4	1.9	2.7	3.0	3.4	3.7	4.1	4.6
52	0.5	1.2	1.7	2.4	2.7	3.1	3.3	3.8	4.2
53	0.4	1.1	1.5	2.2	2.5	2.8	3.1	3.5	3.9
54	0.3	1.1	1.6	2.3	2.6	3.0	3.3	3.7	4.1
55	0.2	0.9	1.4	2.1	2.4	2.8	3.1	3.5	3.9
56	0.3	0.9	1.4	2.1	2.4	2.8	3.1	3.5	3.9
57	0.2	0.9	1.5	2.2	2.5	2.9	3.2	3.7	4.1
58	0.5	1.1	1.6	2.4	2.6	3.0	3.3	3.7	4.1
59	0.9	1.6	2.1	2.8	3.1	3.5	3.7	4.2	4.6
60	1.2	1.9	2.4	3.2	3.6	3.9	4.2	4.6	5.0
61	2.0	2.7	3.2	3.9	4.1	4.5	4.8	5.2	5.6
62	2.5	3.1	3.5	4.1	4.4	4.7	4.9	5.3	5.7
63	3.2	3.6	3.9	4.5	4.8	5.0	5.3	5.7	6.0
64	4.2	4.6	4.9	5.4	5.6	5.9	6.1	6.4	6.8

High Volatility

STOCK PRICE	NUMBER OF MONTHS BEFORE THE OPTIONS EXPIRE								
	1	2	3	4	5	6	7	8	9
45	5.5	6.6	7.5	8.6	9.5	9.8	10.	11.	12.
46	4.8	6.2	7.2	8.5	9.2	9.6	10.	11.	12.
47	4.0	5.5	6.5	7.8	8.6	9.0	9.7	10.	11.
48	3.6	5.4	6.6	7.9	8.8	9.2	10.	10.	11.
49	3.5	5.4	6.5	7.9	8.7	9.2	9.9	10.	11.
50	2.5	4.3	5.4	6.7	7.6	8.0	8.7	9.6	10.
51	2.3	4.1	5.3	6.7	7.6	8.1	8.8	9.7	10.
52	1.8	3.7	4.9	6.4	7.2	7.7	8.4	9.3	10.
53	1.6	3.4	4.6	6.0	6.9	7.4	8.1	9.0	10.
54	1.5	3.4	4.6	6.0	6.9	7.4	8.2	9.1	10.
55	1.5	3.4	4.6	6.1	7.0	7.5	8.2	9.1	10.
56	1.6	3.4	4.6	6.1	7.0	7.4	8.2	9.1	10.
57	1.7	3.6	4.8	6.3	7.2	7.7	8.4	9.3	10.
58	1.9	3.9	5.1	6.5	7.4	7.8	8.6	9.5	10.
59	1.5	3.3	4.4	5.8	6.7	7.2	7.9	8.8	9.9
60	2.1	3.9	5.1	6.4	7.2	7.6	8.4	9.2	10.
61	2.9	4.6	5.8	7.1	8.0	8.4	9.1	10.	11.
62	3.5	5.2	6.4	7.8	8.7	9.2	9.9	10.	11.
63	4.1	5.6	6.6	7.9	8.7	9.1	9.8	10.	11.
64	5.1	6.6	7.6	8.8	9.6	10.	10.	11.	12.
65	5.9	7.3	8.3	9.5	10.	10.	11.	12.	13.

COMBINATION TABLE

Exercise Price of the Call is 70

Exercise Price of the Put is 60

Low Volatility

STOCK PRICE — NUMBER OF MONTHS BEFORE THE OPTIONS EXPIRE

STOCK PRICE	1	2	3	4	5	6	7	8	9
55	5.0	5.3	5.4	5.7	5.7	5.9	6.1	6.2	6.4
56	4.2	4.6	4.8	5.1	5.3	5.4	5.5	5.8	6.1
57	3.2	3.5	3.7	4.1	4.3	4.5	4.6	4.8	5.0
58	2.2	2.5	2.7	3.2	3.4	3.6	3.8	3.9	4.3
59	1.4	1.8	2.1	2.5	2.6	2.9	3.1	3.3	3.7
60	1.1	1.6	2.0	2.5	2.8	3.0	3.2	3.4	3.8
61	0.4	0.9	1.2	1.8	2.1	2.3	2.6	2.9	3.2
62	0.3	0.7	1.0	1.6	1.8	2.1	2.3	2.5	2.9
63	0.2	0.6	0.9	1.4	1.6	1.8	2.1	2.3	2.7
64	0.1	0.6	0.9	1.5	1.7	2.0	2.2	2.4	2.8
65	0.0	0.5	0.8	1.3	1.5	1.7	2.0	2.2	2.6
66	0.1	0.5	0.8	1.3	1.5	1.7	2.0	2.3	2.6
67	0.1	0.5	0.8	1.3	1.6	1.8	2.1	2.3	2.7
68	0.3	0.7	1.0	1.5	1.7	2.0	2.2	2.5	2.9
69	0.6	1.1	1.4	1.9	2.2	2.4	2.7	2.9	3.3
70	0.9	1.4	1.8	2.3	2.6	2.8	3.1	3.3	3.8
71	1.7	2.3	2.6	3.1	3.3	3.6	3.8	4.0	4.4
72	2.3	2.7	2.9	3.3	3.5	3.8	3.9	4.1	4.5
73	3.0	3.3	3.6	3.9	4.0	4.2	4.4	4.7	5.0
74	4.1	4.4	4.6	4.8	4.9	5.2	5.3	5.4	5.7

Average Volatility

STOCK PRICE — NUMBER OF MONTHS BEFORE THE OPTIONS EXPIRE

STOCK PRICE	1	2	3	4	5	6	7	8	9
55	5.2	5.7	6.0	6.6	6.9	7.2	7.4	7.9	8.2
56	4.5	5.1	5.6	6.3	6.3	7.0	7.3	7.8	8.2
57	3.6	4.2	4.7	5.3	5.6	6.0	6.1	6.7	7.1
58	2.6	3.2	3.8	4.4	4.4	5.2	5.4	6.0	6.5
59	1.8	2.5	3.1	3.8	4.3	4.7	4.9	5.4	5.8
60	1.7	2.6	3.2	4.1	4.9	4.9	5.1	5.7	6.2
61	0.9	1.9	2.6	3.5	4.0	4.4	4.7	5.3	5.8
62	0.7	1.7	2.3	3.1	3.6	4.0	4.2	4.8	5.3
63	0.6	1.5	2.1	2.9	3.4	3.8	4.0	4.6	5.1
64	0.6	1.6	2.2	3.1	3.5	4.0	4.2	4.8	5.3
65	0.5	1.4	2.0	2.8	3.3	3.7	4.0	4.6	5.1
66	0.5	1.4	2.0	2.9	3.3	3.8	4.0	4.6	5.1
67	0.5	1.4	2.1	3.0	3.5	3.9	4.2	4.8	5.3
68	0.7	1.6	2.3	3.1	3.5	3.9	4.2	4.8	5.3
69	1.1	2.1	2.7	3.5	4.0	4.4	4.7	5.3	5.7
70	1.4	2.4	3.1	4.0	4.4	4.8	5.1	5.7	6.2
71	2.3	3.2	3.8	4.5	4.9	5.4	5.6	6.2	6.6
72	2.7	3.4	4.0	4.7	5.1	5.5	5.7	6.3	6.8
73	3.3	3.9	4.4	5.2	5.5	5.8	6.1	6.6	7.0
74	4.4	4.9	5.3	6.0	6.2	6.6	6.9	7.4	7.7

High Volatility

STOCK PRICE — NUMBER OF MONTHS BEFORE THE OPTIONS EXPIRE

STOCK PRICE	1	2	3	4	5	6	7	8	9
55	5.8	7.4	8.7	10.	11.	11.	12.	13.	14.
56	5.2	7.1	8.4	9.7	10.	11.	12.	13.	14.
57	4.5	6.4	7.7	9.2	10.	10.	11.	12.	13.
58	4.2	6.4	7.9	9.4	10.	11.	12.	13.	14.
59	4.2	6.4	7.8	9.3	10.	11.	12.	13.	14.
60	3.1	5.3	6.6	8.1	9.4	10.	10.	11.	13.
61	2.9	5.2	6.7	8.2	9.5	10.	10.	12.	13.
62	2.5	4.8	6.3	7.8	9.1	9.7	9.7	11.	12.
63	2.2	4.5	6.0	7.6	8.9	9.4	10.	11.	12.
64	2.1	4.4	6.0	7.6	8.9	9.4	10.	11.	12.
65	2.1	4.5	6.0	7.6	9.0	9.5	10.	11.	12.
66	2.2	4.5	6.0	7.6	8.9	9.5	10.	11.	12.
67	2.3	4.7	6.2	7.8	9.2	9.7	10.	11.	12.
68	2.6	4.9	6.4	8.0	9.3	9.9	10.	11.	12.
69	2.1	4.3	5.8	7.4	8.6	9.2	10.	11.	12.
70	2.7	4.9	6.3	7.8	9.1	9.6	10.	11.	12.
71	3.5	5.6	7.1	8.5	9.8	10.	11.	12.	13.
72	4.1	6.3	7.7	9.3	10.	11.	11.	13.	14.
73	4.5	6.5	7.9	9.3	10.	11.	11.	12.	13.
74	5.6	7.5	8.8	10.	11.	11.	12.	13.	14.
75	6.3	8.2	9.5	10.	12.	12.	13.	14.	15.

COMBINATION TABLE

Exercise Price of the Call is 80

Exercise Price of the Put is 70

Low Volatility

STOCK PRICE — NUMBER OF MONTHS BEFORE THE OPTIONS EXPIRE

STOCK PRICE	1	2	3	4	5	6	7	8	9
65	5.1	5.4	5.6	5.9	6.1	6.3	6.5	6.7	7.0
66	4.3	4.7	5.0	5.4	5.7	5.8	6.0	6.4	6.8
67	3.3	3.7	4.0	4.4	4.7	4.8	4.9	5.4	5.7
68	2.3	2.7	3.0	3.5	3.8	4.0	4.2	4.6	4.9
69	1.5	2.0	2.4	2.9	3.2	3.4	3.6	4.0	4.4
70	1.2	1.9	2.4	3.0	3.3	3.6	3.8	4.2	4.6
71	0.6	1.1	1.6	2.3	2.7	3.0	3.2	3.6	4.0
72	0.4	1.0	1.4	2.0	2.4	2.6	2.8	3.2	3.7
73	0.3	0.8	1.3	1.8	2.2	2.4	2.6	3.0	3.5
74	0.2	0.9	1.3	2.0	2.3	2.6	2.8	3.2	3.6
75	0.1	0.7	1.2	1.8	2.1	2.3	2.6	3.0	3.4
76	0.2	0.7	1.2	1.8	2.1	2.4	2.6	3.0	3.4
77	0.2	0.7	1.2	1.8	2.2	2.5	2.7	3.1	3.6
78	0.4	0.9	1.4	2.0	2.3	2.6	2.8	3.2	3.6
79	0.7	1.3	1.8	2.4	2.8	3.1	3.3	3.7	4.1
80	1.1	1.7	2.2	2.8	3.2	3.4	3.7	4.1	4.5
81	1.9	2.5	2.9	3.5	3.8	4.1	4.2	4.7	5.1
82	2.4	2.9	3.2	3.7	4.0	4.3	4.5	4.8	5.3
83	3.1	3.5	3.8	4.2	4.5	4.7	4.8	5.3	5.6
84	4.2	4.5	4.8	5.1	5.4	5.5	5.6	6.0	6.3

Average Volatility

STOCK PRICE — NUMBER OF MONTHS BEFORE THE OPTIONS EXPIRE

STOCK PRICE	1	2	3	4	5	6	7	8	9
65	5.4	6.0	6.5	7.2	7.7	7.9	8.3	8.8	9.3
66	4.7	5.5	6.1	7.0	7.5	7.8	8.1	8.7	9.4
67	3.8	4.6	5.1	6.3	6.7	6.7	7.2	7.7	8.3
68	2.8	3.6	4.3	5.2	5.7	6.1	6.4	7.0	7.5
69	2.0	3.0	3.7	4.6	5.1	5.5	5.8	6.5	7.0
70	1.9	3.0	3.8	4.9	5.3	5.7	6.1	6.7	7.4
71	1.2	2.4	3.2	4.4	4.9	5.3	5.8	6.4	7.1
72	1.0	2.1	2.9	4.0	4.5	4.9	5.3	5.9	6.6
73	0.9	1.9	2.7	3.7	4.3	4.7	5.1	5.8	6.4
74	0.9	2.1	2.8	3.9	4.5	4.9	5.4	6.0	6.7
75	0.7	1.8	2.6	3.7	4.3	4.7	5.1	5.8	6.5
76	0.8	1.8	2.6	3.7	4.3	4.7	5.2	5.8	6.5
77	0.7	1.9	2.7	3.9	4.4	4.9	5.3	6.0	6.7
78	0.9	2.1	2.9	3.9	4.5	4.9	5.3	6.0	6.7
79	1.4	2.5	3.3	4.4	4.9	5.3	5.8	6.3	7.0
80	1.7	2.9	3.7	4.8	5.3	5.7	6.2	6.7	7.4
81	2.5	3.6	4.3	5.4	5.9	6.2	6.7	7.2	7.8
82	2.9	3.8	4.6	5.5	6.0	6.4	6.7	7.3	7.9
83	3.5	4.2	5.0	5.9	6.3	6.7	7.1	7.7	8.2
84	4.5	5.2	5.8	6.6	7.0	7.5	7.8	8.4	8.9

High Volatility

STOCK PRICE — NUMBER OF MONTHS BEFORE THE OPTIONS EXPIRE

STOCK PRICE	1	2	3	4	5	6	7	8	9
65	6.2	8.2	9.9	11.	12.	13.	14.	15.	17.
66	5.7	8.1	9.6	11.	12.	13.	14.	15.	16.
67	5.0	7.4	9.0	10.	12.	12.	13.	14.	16.
68	4.8	7.5	9.2	11.	12.	13.	14.	15.	16.
69	4.8	7.4	9.1	11.	11.	13.	14.	15.	16.
70	3.7	6.3	8.0	9.8	11.	12.	12.	14.	15.
71	3.5	6.3	8.0	9.9	11.	12.	13.	14.	15.
72	3.1	5.9	7.7	9.5	11.	11.	12.	13.	15.
73	2.8	5.6	7.4	9.3	10.	11.	12.	13.	15.
74	2.8	5.6	7.4	9.3	10.	11.	12.	13.	15.
75	2.8	5.6	7.4	9.4	10.	11.	12.	13.	15.
76	2.8	5.6	7.4	9.3	10.	11.	12.	13.	15.
77	2.9	5.8	7.6	9.6	11.	11.	12.	14.	15.
78	3.2	6.0	7.8	9.7	11.	12.	12.	14.	15.
79	2.7	5.4	7.2	9.1	10.	11.	12.	13.	15.
80	3.3	6.0	7.6	9.5	10.	11.	12.	13.	15.
81	4.1	6.7	8.4	10.	11.	12.	13.	14.	16.
82	4.7	7.3	9.1	11.	12.	13.	14.	15.	16.
83	5.0	7.5	9.1	10.	12.	13.	13.	15.	16.
84	6.1	8.4	10.	11.	13.	13.	14.	15.	17.
85	6.8	9.1	10.	12.	13.	14.	15.	16.	17.

COMBINATION TABLE

Exercise Price of the Call is (90)

Exercise Price of the Put is (80)

Low Volatility

STOCK PRICE	NUMBER OF MONTHS BEFORE THE OPTIONS EXPIRE								
	1	2	3	4	5	6	7	8	9
75	5.2	5.5	5.8	6.2	6.5	6.6	6.9	7.2	7.6
76	4.4	4.9	5.3	5.8	6.1	6.3	6.6	6.9	7.5
77	3.4	3.9	4.3	4.8	5.0	5.3	5.6	6.0	6.4
78	2.4	2.9	3.4	4.0	4.3	4.6	4.8	5.2	5.6
79	1.6	2.2	2.7	3.3	3.7	4.0	4.2	4.7	5.0
80	1.4	2.1	2.7	3.5	3.8	4.1	4.4	4.8	5.3
81	0.7	1.4	2.0	2.9	3.3	3.6	3.9	4.4	4.9
82	0.5	1.2	1.8	2.5	2.9	3.2	3.5	4.0	4.4
83	0.4	1.1	1.6	2.3	2.7	3.0	3.3	3.7	4.2
84	0.4	1.1	1.7	2.5	2.9	3.1	3.5	3.9	4.4
85	0.3	1.0	1.5	2.2	2.7	2.9	3.3	3.7	4.2
86	0.3	1.0	1.5	2.3	2.7	2.9	3.3	3.7	4.2
87	0.3	1.0	1.6	2.4	2.8	3.1	3.4	3.9	4.4
88	0.5	1.2	1.8	2.5	2.9	3.2	3.5	3.9	4.4
89	0.9	1.6	2.2	2.9	3.3	3.6	4.0	4.3	4.8
90	1.3	2.0	2.6	3.3	3.7	4.0	4.4	4.8	5.3
91	2.0	2.8	3.3	4.0	4.4	4.7	5.0	5.4	5.8
92	2.5	3.1	3.6	4.2	4.6	4.8	5.1	5.5	5.9
93	3.2	3.6	4.0	4.6	4.9	5.2	5.5	5.9	6.3
94	4.2	4.7	5.0	5.5	5.8	6.0	6.2	6.7	7.1

Average Volatility

STOCK PRICE	NUMBER OF MONTHS BEFORE THE OPTIONS EXPIRE								
	1	2	3	4	5	6	7	8	9
75	5.5	6.2	6.9	7.9	8.4	8.8	9.2	9.7	10.
76	4.9	5.8	6.6	7.6	8.3	8.6	9.1	9.8	10.
77	3.9	4.8	5.6	6.6	7.1	7.6	8.0	8.7	9.4
78	3.0	4.0	4.9	5.9	6.5	6.9	7.4	8.1	8.8
79	2.2	3.4	4.3	5.4	5.9	6.4	6.8	7.5	8.3
80	2.2	3.5	4.5	5.6	6.2	6.7	7.2	7.8	8.7
81	1.5	3.0	4.0	5.1	5.8	6.4	6.8	7.6	8.5
82	1.3	2.6	3.6	4.8	5.4	5.9	6.3	7.1	8.0
83	1.1	2.4	3.4	4.5	5.3	5.7	6.2	7.0	7.9
84	1.2	2.5	3.5	4.7	5.4	5.9	6.4	7.2	8.1
85	1.0	2.3	3.3	4.5	5.2	5.7	6.2	7.0	7.9
86	1.0	2.3	3.3	4.6	5.3	5.7	6.3	7.0	7.9
87	1.0	2.4	3.5	4.7	5.4	5.9	6.4	7.2	8.1
88	1.2	2.6	3.5	4.7	5.4	5.9	6.4	7.1	8.0
89	1.6	3.0	4.0	5.1	5.9	6.3	6.8	7.5	8.4
90	2.0	3.5	4.4	5.6	6.2	6.6	7.2	7.9	8.7
91	2.8	4.1	5.0	6.1	6.7	7.1	7.6	8.3	9.1
92	3.1	4.2	5.1	6.3	6.8	7.3	7.7	8.4	9.2
93	3.7	4.6	5.5	6.6	7.1	7.5	8.0	8.6	9.4
94	4.6	5.5	6.3	7.2	7.8	8.3	8.7	9.3	10.

High Volatility

STOCK PRICE	NUMBER OF MONTHS BEFORE THE OPTIONS EXPIRE								
	1	2	3	4	5	6	7	8	9
75	6.7	9.0	11.	13.	14.	15.	16.	17.	19.
76	6.3	8.8	10.	12.	14.	15.	16.	17.	19.
77	5.6	8.2	10.	12.	13.	14.	15.	17.	18.
78	5.5	8.4	10.	12.	14.	15.	16.	17.	19.
79	5.4	8.3	10.	12.	14.	15.	16.	17.	19.
80	4.3	7.1	9.4	11.	13.	14.	14.	16.	18.
81	4.2	7.2	9.5	11.	13.	14.	15.	16.	18.
82	3.8	6.8	9.1	11.	12.	13.	14.	16.	18.
83	3.5	6.5	8.8	11.	12.	13.	14.	16.	17.
84	3.4	6.5	8.9	11.	12.	13.	14.	16.	17.
85	3.5	6.6	8.9	11.	12.	13.	14.	16.	18.
86	3.5	6.6	8.9	11.	12.	13.	14.	16.	17.
87	3.6	6.8	9.1	11.	13.	13.	14.	16.	18.
88	3.9	7.0	9.3	11.	13.	14.	14.	16.	18.
89	3.3	6.3	8.6	10.	12.	13.	14.	16.	17.
90	4.0	6.8	9.1	11.	12.	13.	14.	16.	17.
91	4.7	7.5	9.8	11.	13.	14.	15.	16.	18.
92	5.3	8.3	10.	12.	14.	15.	16.	17.	19.
93	5.7	8.4	10.	12.	14.	15.	15.	17.	19.
94	6.6	9.2	11.	13.	14.	15.	16.	18.	19.
95	7.4	10.	12.	13.	15.	16.	17.	18.	20.

T129

COMBINATION TABLE

Exercise Price of the Call is

Exercise Price of the Put is

Low Volatility

STOCK PRICE

NUMBER OF MONTHS BEFORE THE OPTIONS EXPIRE

	1	2	3	4	5	6	7	8	9
85	5.2	5.6	6.0	6.6	6.9	7.2	7.4	7.8	8.3
86	4.5	5.0	5.5	6.1	6.6	6.8	7.2	7.7	8.2
87	3.5	4.0	4.5	5.2	5.5	5.8	6.1	6.6	7.1
88	2.5	3.1	3.7	4.4	4.8	5.0	5.4	5.9	6.4
89	1.8	2.4	3.0	3.8	4.2	4.5	4.8	5.3	5.9
90	1.6	2.4	3.2	3.9	4.4	4.8	5.1	5.5	6.1
91	0.8	1.8	2.5	3.4	3.9	4.2	4.6	5.1	5.8
92	0.7	1.5	2.2	3.0	3.5	3.8	4.2	4.7	5.3
93	0.5	1.4	2.0	2.8	3.3	3.6	4.0	4.5	5.1
94	0.6	1.4	2.2	3.0	3.5	3.8	4.2	4.7	5.3
95	0.4	1.2	1.9	2.8	3.3	3.6	4.0	4.5	5.1
96	0.4	1.3	1.9	2.8	3.3	3.6	4.0	4.5	5.2
97	0.4	1.3	2.0	2.9	3.4	3.7	4.1	4.7	5.3
98	0.6	1.5	2.2	3.0	3.4	3.8	4.2	4.7	5.3
99	1.0	1.9	2.6	3.4	3.9	4.3	4.6	5.1	5.7
100	1.4	2.3	3.0	3.9	4.3	4.6	5.1	5.5	6.1
101	2.2	3.0	3.7	4.5	4.9	5.2	5.6	6.1	6.6
102	2.6	3.3	3.9	4.7	5.1	5.4	5.7	6.2	6.8
103	3.3	3.8	4.3	5.1	5.4	5.7	6.1	6.5	7.1
104	4.3	4.8	5.2	5.8	6.2	6.5	6.8	7.3	7.7

Average Volatility

STOCK PRICE

NUMBER OF MONTHS BEFORE THE OPTIONS EXPIRE

	1	2	3	4	5	6	7	8	9
85	5.6	6.5	7.5	8.6	9.1	9.7	10.	10.	11.
86	5.1	6.2	7.3	8.5	9.1	9.5	9.9	10.	11.
87	4.2	5.2	6.2	7.4	8.1	8.5	9.0	9.8	10.
88	3.1	4.5	5.4	6.7	7.3	7.9	8.3	9.1	10.
89	2.4	3.8	4.9	6.1	6.8	7.3	7.8	8.6	9.4
90	2.5	4.0	5.2	6.5	7.2	7.6	8.1	9.0	9.9
91	1.8	3.5	4.6	6.1	6.9	7.4	7.9	8.8	9.7
92	1.6	3.1	4.3	5.6	6.3	6.9	7.4	8.2	9.2
93	1.4	2.9	4.1	5.5	6.2	6.8	7.3	8.2	9.1
94	1.5	3.1	4.2	5.7	6.4	7.0	7.5	8.4	9.3
95	1.3	2.9	4.0	5.5	6.2	6.8	7.3	8.2	9.1
96	1.3	2.9	4.0	5.5	6.3	6.8	7.3	8.2	9.2
97	1.3	3.0	4.2	5.7	6.4	7.0	7.5	8.4	9.3
98	1.5	3.1	4.2	5.6	6.4	6.9	7.5	8.4	9.3
99	2.0	3.5	4.7	6.0	6.8	7.3	7.8	8.7	9.6
100	2.3	3.9	5.1	6.5	7.1	7.7	8.1	9.0	10.
101	3.0	4.5	5.6	6.9	7.6	8.1	8.6	9.5	10.
102	3.4	4.7	5.8	7.1	7.7	8.3	8.7	9.6	10.
103	3.8	5.1	6.1	7.3	8.0	8.4	9.0	9.6	10.
104	4.9	5.8	6.8	8.0	8.6	9.2	9.7	10.	11.

High Volatility

STOCK PRICE

NUMBER OF MONTHS BEFORE THE OPTIONS EXPIRE

	1	2	3	4	5	6	7	8	9
85	7.2	10.	12.	14.	16.	17.	18.	20.	21.
86	6.8	10.	12.	14.	16.	17.	18.	19.	21.
87	6.2	9.4	11.	14.	15.	16.	17.	19.	21.
88	6.2	9.7	12.	14.	16.	17.	18.	19.	21.
89	6.1	9.6	11.	14.	16.	17.	18.	19.	21.
90	5.0	8.4	10.	13.	15.	16.	17.	18.	20.
91	4.9	8.5	10.	13.	15.	16.	17.	19.	20.
92	4.5	8.1	10.	13.	14.	15.	17.	18.	20.
93	4.2	7.8	10.	13.	14.	15.	16.	18.	20.
94	4.1	7.8	10.	13.	14.	15.	16.	18.	20.
95	4.2	7.9	10.	13.	14.	15.	16.	18.	20.
96	4.2	7.9	10.	13.	14.	15.	16.	18.	20.
97	4.4	8.1	10.	13.	14.	15.	17.	18.	20.
98	4.6	8.2	10.	13.	15.	16.	17.	18.	20.
99	4.0	7.6	10.	12.	14.	15.	16.	18.	20.
100	4.6	8.1	10.	13.	14.	15.	16.	18.	21.
101	5.4	8.8	11.	13.	15.	16.	17.	19.	21.
102	6.0	9.6	11.	14.	16.	17.	18.	19.	21.
103	6.3	9.5	11.	14.	16.	16.	18.	19.	21.
104	7.2	10.	12.	15.	16.	17.	18.	20.	22.
105	7.9	11.	13.	15.	17.	18.	19.	20.	22.

COMBINATION TABLE

Exercise Price of the Call is (110)
Exercise Price of the Put is (100)

Low Volatility

STOCK PRICE — NUMBER OF MONTHS BEFORE THE OPTIONS EXPIRE

STOCK PRICE	1	2	3	4	5	6	7	8	9
95	5.3	5.7	6.3	7.0	7.3	7.7	7.9	8.4	9.0
96	4.6	5.2	5.9	6.7	7.1	7.4	7.7	8.3	8.9
97	3.7	4.3	4.8	5.7	6.1	6.4	6.7	7.3	7.8
98	2.6	3.4	4.0	4.9	5.3	5.7	6.0	6.5	7.2
99	1.9	2.6	3.4	4.3	4.7	5.1	5.4	6.0	6.5
100	1.8	2.7	3.6	4.5	5.0	5.3	5.7	6.2	6.9
101	0.9	2.1	3.0	3.9	4.5	4.9	5.3	5.9	6.6
102	0.8	1.8	2.7	3.6	4.1	4.5	4.9	5.4	6.1
103	0.7	1.6	2.4	3.4	3.9	4.3	4.6	5.3	6.0
104	0.7	1.8	2.6	3.5	4.1	4.5	4.9	5.5	6.1
105	0.6	1.6	2.3	3.3	3.9	4.3	4.7	5.2	5.9
106	0.6	1.6	2.4	3.3	3.9	4.3	4.7	5.3	6.0
107	0.6	1.6	2.5	3.5	4.0	4.4	4.8	5.5	6.1
108	0.8	1.8	2.6	3.5	4.1	4.4	4.8	5.4	6.1
109	1.2	2.2	3.1	4.0	4.5	4.9	5.2	5.8	6.5
110	1.5	2.6	3.4	4.4	4.9	5.3	5.7	6.3	7.0
111	2.3	3.3	4.1	5.0	5.5	5.8	6.2	6.8	7.3
112	2.8	3.5	4.3	5.2	5.6	6.0	6.3	6.9	7.5
113	3.4	4.0	4.7	5.5	6.0	6.3	6.7	7.1	7.7
114	4.5	4.9	5.5	6.3	6.7	7.1	7.5	7.9	8.5

Average Volatility

STOCK PRICE — NUMBER OF MONTHS BEFORE THE OPTIONS EXPIRE

STOCK PRICE	1	2	3	4	5	6	7	8	9
95	5.9	7.1	8.0	9.2	9.9	10.	10.	11.	12.
96	5.4	6.8	7.9	9.2	9.9	10.	11.	11.	12.
97	4.4	5.8	6.8	8.0	8.9	9.5	10.	10.	11.
98	3.4	5.0	6.1	7.5	8.2	8.9	9.3	10.	11.
99	2.8	4.4	5.5	6.9	7.7	8.3	8.8	9.7	10.
100	2.8	4.7	5.8	7.2	8.0	8.7	9.2	10.	11.
101	2.1	4.1	5.4	6.9	7.9	8.5	9.0	10.	11.
102	1.9	3.8	4.9	6.5	7.3	8.0	8.4	9.5	10.
103	1.7	3.6	4.7	6.3	7.2	7.9	8.4	9.4	10.
104	1.8	3.7	4.9	6.5	7.4	8.1	8.6	9.7	10.
105	1.6	3.5	4.7	6.3	7.2	7.9	8.4	9.5	10.
106	1.6	3.5	4.7	6.4	7.3	7.9	8.4	9.5	10.
107	1.6	3.7	4.9	6.5	7.4	8.1	8.6	9.7	10.
108	1.9	3.7	4.9	6.5	7.4	8.1	8.6	9.6	10.
109	2.3	4.1	5.4	6.8	7.8	8.4	8.9	10.	10.
110	2.7	4.6	5.8	7.3	8.1	8.7	9.3	10.	11.
111	3.3	5.2	6.3	7.6	8.6	9.1	9.6	10.	11.
112	3.7	5.4	6.4	7.7	8.6	9.3	9.6	10.	11.
113	4.1	5.6	6.7	8.0	8.9	9.4	9.9	10.	11.
114	5.0	6.5	7.4	8.7	9.5	10.	10.	11.	12.

High Volatility

STOCK PRICE — NUMBER OF MONTHS BEFORE THE OPTIONS EXPIRE

STOCK PRICE	1	2	3	4	5	6	7	8	9
95	7.8	11.	13.	16.	18.	19.	20.	22.	24.
96	7.5	10.	13.	16.	17.	19.	20.	22.	23.
97	6.8	10.	13.	15.	17.	18.	20.	21.	23.
98	6.9	10.	13.	16.	18.	19.	20.	22.	24.
99	6.8	10.	13.	16.	17.	19.	20.	22.	24.
100	5.7	9.4	12.	15.	16.	18.	19.	21.	22.
101	5.6	9.5	12.	15.	17.	18.	19.	21.	23.
102	5.2	9.1	12.	14.	16.	18.	19.	20.	22.
103	4.9	8.8	11.	14.	16.	17.	19.	20.	22.
104	4.9	8.9	11.	14.	16.	17.	19.	20.	22.
105	4.9	9.0	11.	14.	16.	18.	19.	20.	22.
106	5.0	8.9	11.	14.	16.	17.	19.	20.	22.
107	5.2	9.1	12.	15.	16.	18.	19.	20.	22.
108	5.4	9.3	12.	15.	16.	18.	19.	20.	22.
109	4.8	8.7	11.	14.	16.	17.	19.	20.	22.
110	5.3	9.0	11.	14.	16.	17.	18.	19.	22.
111	6.1	9.8	12.	15.	17.	18.	19.	21.	23.
112	6.7	10.	13.	16.	17.	19.	20.	22.	24.
113	6.9	10.	13.	16.	17.	19.	20.	21.	23.
114	7.9	11.	14.	16.	18.	19.	19.	22.	24.
115	8.5	12.	14.	17.	18.	20.	21.	22.	24.

THE TRUE COST
COVERED OPTION
WRITING
TABLES

Decimal to Fraction Conversion Chart		
Table Shows		Market Fraction
.1	=	1/16
.1	=	1/8
.2	=	3/16
.2	=	1/4
.3	=	5/16
.4	=	3/8
.4	=	7/16
.5	=	1/2
.6	=	9/16
.6	=	5/8
.7	=	11/16
.8	=	3/4
.8	=	13/16
.9	=	7/8
.9	=	15/16

*The Future Value Tables are generated by computer simulations. Due to the nature of the computer simulation techniques that we used there may be slight aberrations in the option prices presented. Therefore you should allow a variance of plus or minus 10% of these option prices. In a few cases, some of the less important, peripheral option prices may vary more than 10%.

COVERED OPTION
WRITING TABLE   Exercise Price is 10

Low Volatility

STOCK PRICE — NUMBER OF MONTHS BEFORE THE OPTIONS EXPIRE

STOCK PRICE	1	2	3	4	5	6	7	8	9
0	0.0	0.0	0.0	0.0	0.0	0.0	0.0	0.0	0.0
1	0.0	0.0	0.0	0.0	0.0	0.0	0.0	0.0	0.0
2	0.0	0.0	0.0	0.0	0.0	0.0	0.0	0.0	0.0
3	0.0	0.0	0.0	0.0	0.0	0.0	0.0	0.0	0.0
4	0.0	0.0	0.0	0.0	0.0	0.0	0.0	0.0	0.0
5	0.0	0.0	0.0	0.0	0.0	0.0	0.0	0.0	0.0
6	0.0	0.0	0.0	0.0	0.0	0.0	0.0	0.0	0.0
7	0.0	0.0	0.0	0.0	0.0	0.0	0.0	0.0	0.1
8	0.0	0.0	0.0	0.0	0.0	0.0	0.0	0.1	0.1
9	0.0	0.0	0.0	0.0	0.1	0.1	0.1	0.1	0.1
10	0.1	0.2	0.2	0.3	0.3	0.3	0.3	0.4	0.4
11	1.0	1.0	1.0	1.0	1.0	1.0	1.1	1.1	1.1
12	2.0	2.0	2.0	2.0	2.0	2.0	2.0	2.0	2.0
13	3.0	3.0	3.0	3.0	3.0	3.0	3.0	3.0	3.0
14	4.0	4.0	4.0	4.0	4.0	4.0	4.0	4.0	4.0
15	5.0	5.0	5.0	5.0	5.0	5.0	5.0	5.0	5.0
16	6.0	6.0	6.0	6.0	6.0	6.0	6.0	6.0	6.0
17	7.0	7.0	7.0	7.0	7.0	7.0	7.0	7.0	7.0
18	8.0	8.0	8.0	8.0	8.0	8.0	8.0	8.0	8.0
19	9.0	9.0	9.0	9.0	9.0	9.0	9.0	9.0	9.0
20	10.	10.	10.	10.	10.	10.	10.	10.	10.

Average Volatility

STOCK PRICE — NUMBER OF MONTHS BEFORE THE OPTIONS EXPIRE

STOCK PRICE	1	2	3	4	5	6	7	8	9
0	0.0	0.0	0.0	0.0	0.0	0.0	0.0	0.0	0.0
1	0.0	0.0	0.0	0.0	0.0	0.0	0.0	0.0	0.0
2	0.0	0.0	0.0	0.0	0.0	0.0	0.0	0.0	0.0
3	0.0	0.0	0.0	0.0	0.0	0.0	0.0	0.0	0.0
4	0.0	0.0	0.0	0.0	0.0	0.0	0.0	0.0	0.0
5	0.0	0.0	0.0	0.0	0.0	0.0	0.0	0.0	0.0
6	0.0	0.0	0.0	0.0	0.0	0.0	0.0	0.0	0.0
7	0.0	0.0	0.0	0.0	0.0	0.0	0.0	0.1	0.1
8	0.0	0.0	0.0	0.0	0.0	0.1	0.1	0.1	0.1
9	0.0	0.0	0.1	0.1	0.2	0.2	0.2	0.3	0.3
10	0.2	0.3	0.4	0.4	0.5	0.5	0.5	0.6	0.6
11	1.0	1.0	1.1	1.1	1.2	1.2	1.2	1.2	1.3
12	2.0	2.0	2.0	2.0	2.0	2.0	2.0	2.1	2.1
13	3.0	3.0	3.0	3.0	3.0	3.0	3.0	3.0	3.0
14	4.0	4.0	4.0	4.0	4.0	4.0	4.0	4.0	4.0
15	5.0	5.0	5.0	5.0	5.0	5.0	5.0	5.0	5.0
16	6.0	6.0	6.0	6.0	6.0	6.0	6.0	6.0	6.0
17	7.0	7.0	7.0	7.0	7.0	7.0	7.0	7.0	7.0
18	8.0	8.0	8.0	8.0	8.0	8.0	8.0	8.0	8.0
19	9.0	9.0	9.0	9.0	9.0	9.0	9.0	9.0	9.0
20	10.	10.	10.	10.	10.	10.	10.	10.	10.

High Volatility

STOCK PRICE — NUMBER OF MONTHS BEFORE THE OPTIONS EXPIRE

STOCK PRICE	1	2	3	4	5	6	7	8	9
0	0.0	0.0	0.0	0.0	0.0	0.0	0.1	0.0	0.0
1	0.0	0.0	0.0	0.0	0.0	0.0	0.1	0.0	0.0
2	0.0	0.0	0.0	0.0	0.0	0.0	0.1	0.0	0.0
3	0.0	0.0	0.0	0.0	0.0	0.0	0.1	0.1	0.0
4	0.0	0.0	0.0	0.0	0.0	0.1	0.1	0.1	0.0
5	0.0	0.0	0.0	0.0	0.1	0.1	0.2	0.1	0.1
6	0.0	0.0	0.1	0.1	0.1	0.2	0.2	0.2	0.2
7	0.0	0.1	0.1	0.1	0.2	0.3	0.3	0.3	0.4
8	0.0	0.1	0.2	0.2	0.3	0.4	0.5	0.4	0.4
9	0.1	0.3	0.3	0.4	0.5	0.6	0.7	0.7	0.7
10	0.3	0.6	0.7	0.8	0.9	1.0	1.1	1.1	1.1
11	1.1	1.2	1.3	1.5	1.5	1.6	1.7	1.7	1.7
12	2.0	2.1	2.1	2.2	2.3	2.4	2.4	2.4	2.5
13	3.0	3.0	3.0	3.1	3.1	3.2	3.2	3.3	3.3
14	4.0	4.0	4.0	4.0	4.0	4.1	4.1	4.1	4.2
15	5.0	5.0	5.0	5.0	5.0	5.0	5.0	5.0	5.1
16	6.0	6.0	6.0	6.0	6.0	6.0	6.0	6.0	6.0
17	7.0	7.0	7.0	7.0	7.0	7.0	7.0	7.0	7.0
18	8.0	8.0	8.0	8.0	8.0	8.0	8.0	8.0	8.0
19	9.0	9.0	9.0	9.0	9.0	9.0	9.0	9.0	9.0
20	10.	10.	10.	10.	10.	10.	10.	10.	10.

COVERED OPTION

WRITING TABLE Exercise Price is (15)

Low Volatility

STOCK PRICE — NUMBER OF MONTHS BEFORE THE OPTIONS EXPIRE

	1	2	3	4	5	6	7	8	9
5	0.0	0.0	0.0	0.0	0.0	0.0	0.0	0.0	0.0
6	0.0	0.0	0.0	0.0	0.0	0.0	0.0	0.0	0.0
7	0.0	0.0	0.0	0.0	0.0	0.0	0.0	0.0	0.0
8	0.0	0.0	0.0	0.0	0.0	0.0	0.0	0.0	0.0
9	0.0	0.0	0.0	0.0	0.0	0.0	0.0	0.0	0.0
10	0.0	0.0	0.0	0.0	0.0	0.0	0.0	0.0	0.0
11	0.0	0.0	0.0	0.0	0.0	0.0	0.0	0.0	0.0
12	0.0	0.0	0.0	0.0	0.0	0.0	0.0	0.0	0.1
13	0.0	0.0	0.0	0.0	0.1	0.1	0.1	0.1	0.1
14	0.0	0.0	0.1	0.1	0.2	0.2	0.2	0.3	0.3
15	0.2	0.3	0.3	0.4	0.5	0.5	0.5	0.6	0.6
16	1.0	1.0	1.1	1.1	1.2	1.2	1.2	1.2	1.3
17	2.0	2.0	2.0	2.0	2.0	2.0	2.0	2.1	2.1
18	3.0	3.0	3.0	3.0	3.0	3.0	3.0	3.0	3.0
19	4.0	4.0	4.0	4.0	4.0	4.0	4.0	4.0	4.0
20	5.0	5.0	5.0	5.0	5.0	5.0	5.0	5.0	5.0
21	6.0	6.0	6.0	6.0	6.0	6.0	6.0	6.0	6.0
22	7.0	7.0	7.0	7.0	7.0	7.0	7.0	7.0	7.0
23	8.0	8.0	8.0	8.0	8.0	8.0	8.0	8.0	8.0
24	9.0	9.0	9.0	9.0	9.0	9.0	9.0	9.0	9.0
25	10.	10.	10.	10.	10.	10.	10.	10.	10.

Average Volatility

STOCK PRICE — NUMBER OF MONTHS BEFORE THE OPTIONS EXPIRE

	1	2	3	4	5	6	7	8	9
5	0.0	0.0	0.0	0.0	0.0	0.0	0.1	0.1	0.1
6	0.0	0.0	0.0	0.0	0.0	0.0	0.1	0.1	0.1
7	0.0	0.0	0.0	0.0	0.0	0.0	0.1	0.1	0.1
8	0.0	0.0	0.0	0.0	0.0	0.0	0.1	0.1	0.1
9	0.0	0.0	0.0	0.0	0.0	0.0	0.1	0.1	0.1
10	0.0	0.0	0.0	0.0	0.0	0.0	0.1	0.1	0.1
11	0.0	0.0	0.0	0.0	0.1	0.1	0.1	0.1	0.2
12	0.0	0.0	0.0	0.1	0.1	0.1	0.2	0.2	0.3
13	0.0	0.0	0.1	0.2	0.2	0.2	0.3	0.3	0.4
14	0.0	0.1	0.2	0.3	0.4	0.4	0.5	0.5	0.6
15	0.3	0.4	0.6	0.7	0.7	0.8	0.8	0.9	1.0
16	1.0	1.1	1.2	1.3	1.4	1.4	1.5	1.5	1.6
17	2.0	2.0	2.1	2.1	2.2	2.2	2.2	2.3	2.3
18	3.0	3.0	3.0	3.0	3.0	3.1	3.1	3.1	3.2
19	4.0	4.0	4.0	4.0	4.0	4.0	4.0	4.0	4.1
20	5.0	5.0	5.0	5.0	5.0	5.0	5.0	5.0	5.0
21	6.0	6.0	6.0	6.0	6.0	6.0	6.0	6.0	6.0
22	7.0	7.0	7.0	7.0	7.0	7.0	7.0	7.0	7.0
23	8.0	8.0	8.0	8.0	8.0	8.0	8.0	8.0	8.0
24	9.0	9.0	9.0	9.0	9.0	9.0	9.0	9.0	9.0
25	10.	10.	10.	10.	10.	10.	10.	10.	10.

High Volatility

STOCK PRICE — NUMBER OF MONTHS BEFORE THE OPTIONS EXPIRE

	1	2	3	4	5	6	7	8	9
5	0.0	0.0	0.1	0.1	0.1	0.1	0.1	0.2	0.2
6	0.0	0.0	0.0	0.1	0.1	0.1	0.1	0.2	0.3
7	0.0	0.0	0.0	0.1	0.1	0.2	0.2	0.2	0.3
8	0.0	0.0	0.0	0.1	0.2	0.2	0.2	0.3	0.4
9	0.0	0.0	0.0	0.1	0.2	0.2	0.2	0.3	0.5
10	0.0	0.0	0.1	0.1	0.2	0.3	0.4	0.5	0.6
11	0.0	0.1	0.2	0.3	0.3	0.4	0.5	0.6	0.7
12	0.0	0.2	0.3	0.4	0.5	0.6	0.6	0.8	0.9
13	0.1	0.3	0.4	0.6	0.7	0.8	0.9	1.0	1.1
14	0.2	0.5	0.7	0.9	1.0	1.1	1.2	1.3	1.5
15	0.6	0.9	1.1	1.3	1.4	1.5	1.6	1.7	1.9
16	1.2	1.5	1.7	1.9	2.0	2.1	2.2	2.3	2.5
17	2.1	2.3	2.4	2.6	2.7	2.8	2.9	3.0	3.1
18	3.0	3.1	3.2	3.4	3.5	3.5	3.6	3.7	3.9
19	4.0	4.0	4.1	4.2	4.3	4.4	4.4	4.5	4.7
20	5.0	5.0	5.0	5.1	5.2	5.2	5.3	5.4	5.5
21	6.0	6.0	6.0	6.0	6.1	6.1	6.2	6.2	6.3
22	7.0	7.0	7.0	7.0	7.0	7.1	7.1	7.2	7.2
23	8.0	8.0	8.0	8.0	8.0	8.0	8.0	8.1	8.1
24	9.0	9.0	9.0	9.0	9.0	9.0	9.0	9.0	9.1
25	10.	10.	10.	10.	10.	10.	10.	10.	10.

COVERED OPTION
WRITING TABLE   Exercise Price is 20

Low Volatility

STOCK PRICE — NUMBER OF MONTHS BEFORE THE OPTIONS EXPIRE

STOCK PRICE	1	2	3	4	5	6	7	8	9
10	0.0	0.0	0.0	0.0	0.0	0.0	0.0	0.0	0.1
11	0.0	0.0	0.0	0.0	0.0	0.0	0.0	0.0	0.1
12	0.0	0.0	0.0	0.0	0.0	0.0	0.0	0.0	0.1
13	0.0	0.0	0.0	0.0	0.0	0.0	0.0	0.0	0.1
14	0.0	0.0	0.0	0.0	0.0	0.0	0.0	0.0	0.1
15	0.0	0.0	0.0	0.0	0.0	0.0	0.0	0.0	0.1
16	0.0	0.0	0.0	0.0	0.0	0.0	0.0	0.1	0.1
17	0.0	0.0	0.0	0.0	0.1	0.1	0.1	0.1	0.2
18	0.0	0.0	0.1	0.1	0.2	0.2	0.2	0.2	0.3
19	0.0	0.1	0.2	0.3	0.3	0.3	0.4	0.4	0.5
20	0.2	0.4	0.5	0.6	0.7	0.7	0.7	0.8	0.9
21	1.0	1.1	1.2	1.3	1.3	1.3	1.4	1.4	1.5
22	2.0	2.0	2.0	2.1	2.1	2.1	2.2	2.2	2.3
23	3.0	3.0	3.0	3.0	3.0	3.0	3.0	3.1	3.1
24	4.0	4.0	4.0	4.0	4.0	4.0	4.0	4.0	4.0
25	5.0	5.0	5.0	5.0	5.0	5.0	5.0	5.0	5.0
26	6.0	6.0	6.0	6.0	6.0	6.0	6.0	6.0	6.0
27	7.0	7.0	7.0	7.0	7.0	7.0	7.0	7.0	7.0
28	8.0	8.0	8.0	8.0	8.0	8.0	8.0	8.0	8.0
29	9.0	9.0	9.0	9.0	9.0	9.0	9.0	9.0	9.0
30	10.	10.	10.	10.	10.	10.	10.	10.	10.

Average Volatility

STOCK PRICE — NUMBER OF MONTHS BEFORE THE OPTIONS EXPIRE

STOCK PRICE	1	2	3	4	5	6	7	8	9
10	0.0	0.0	0.0	0.1	0.1	0.1	0.1	0.1	0.1
11	0.0	0.0	0.0	0.1	0.1	0.1	0.1	0.1	0.1
12	0.0	0.0	0.0	0.1	0.1	0.1	0.1	0.1	0.1
13	0.0	0.0	0.0	0.1	0.1	0.1	0.1	0.1	0.2
14	0.0	0.0	0.0	0.1	0.1	0.1	0.1	0.2	0.2
15	0.0	0.0	0.0	0.1	0.1	0.1	0.2	0.2	0.3
16	0.0	0.0	0.1	0.1	0.1	0.2	0.2	0.3	0.3
17	0.0	0.0	0.1	0.2	0.2	0.3	0.3	0.4	0.5
18	0.0	0.1	0.2	0.3	0.4	0.4	0.5	0.6	0.6
19	0.1	0.3	0.4	0.5	0.6	0.7	0.7	0.8	0.9
20	0.4	0.6	0.8	0.9	1.0	1.1	1.1	1.2	1.3
21	1.1	1.3	1.4	1.5	1.6	1.7	1.7	1.8	1.9
22	2.0	2.1	2.2	2.3	2.4	2.4	2.5	2.5	2.6
23	3.0	3.0	3.1	3.1	3.2	3.2	3.3	3.3	3.4
24	4.0	4.0	4.0	4.1	4.1	4.1	4.1	4.2	4.3
25	5.0	5.0	5.0	5.0	5.0	5.0	5.0	5.1	5.1
26	6.0	6.0	6.0	6.0	6.0	6.0	6.0	6.0	6.1
27	7.0	7.0	7.0	7.0	7.0	7.0	7.0	7.0	7.0
28	8.0	8.0	8.0	8.0	8.0	8.0	8.0	8.0	8.0
29	9.0	9.0	9.0	9.0	9.0	9.0	9.0	9.0	9.0
30	10.	10.	10.	10.	10.	10.	10.	10.	10.

High Volatility

STOCK PRICE — NUMBER OF MONTHS BEFORE THE OPTIONS EXPIRE

STOCK PRICE	1	2	3	4	5	6	7	8	9
10	0.1	0.1	0.1	0.1	0.2	0.3	0.3	0.4	0.5
11	0.1	0.1	0.1	0.2	0.3	0.3	0.3	0.4	0.5
12	0.1	0.1	0.1	0.2	0.3	0.4	0.4	0.5	0.6
13	0.1	0.1	0.2	0.2	0.4	0.5	0.5	0.6	0.7
14	0.1	0.1	0.2	0.3	0.4	0.5	0.6	0.7	0.9
15	0.1	0.2	0.3	0.5	0.6	0.7	0.7	0.9	1.0
16	0.1	0.2	0.4	0.6	0.7	0.8	0.9	1.0	1.2
17	0.1	0.4	0.5	0.7	0.9	1.0	1.1	1.3	1.4
18	0.2	0.5	0.7	1.0	1.2	1.3	1.3	1.5	1.7
19	0.4	0.8	1.0	1.3	1.5	1.6	1.7	1.9	2.1
20	0.8	1.2	1.4	1.7	1.9	2.0	2.1	2.3	2.5
21	1.4	1.8	2.0	2.3	2.5	2.6	2.7	2.9	3.1
22	2.2	2.5	2.7	3.0	3.2	3.3	3.4	3.5	3.7
23	3.1	3.3	3.5	3.7	3.9	4.0	4.1	4.2	4.4
24	4.0	4.2	4.3	4.5	4.7	4.8	4.8	5.0	5.2
25	5.0	5.1	5.2	5.4	5.5	5.6	5.7	5.8	5.9
26	6.0	6.0	6.1	6.3	6.4	6.4	6.5	6.6	6.8
27	7.0	7.0	7.0	7.2	7.2	7.3	7.4	7.5	7.6
28	8.0	8.0	8.0	8.1	8.2	8.2	8.3	8.3	8.5
29	9.0	9.0	9.0	9.0	9.1	9.1	9.2	9.2	9.3
30	10.	10.	10.	10.	10.	10.	10.	10.	10.

COVERED OPTION
WRITING TABLE Exercise Price is (25)

Low Volatility

STOCK PRICE — NUMBER OF MONTHS BEFORE THE OPTIONS EXPIRE

STOCK PRICE	1	2	3	4	5	6	7	8	9
15	0.0	0.0	0.0	0.0	0.0	0.1	0.1	0.1	0.1
16	0.0	0.0	0.0	0.0	0.0	0.1	0.1	0.1	0.1
17	0.0	0.0	0.0	0.0	0.0	0.1	0.1	0.1	0.1
18	0.0	0.0	0.0	0.0	0.0	0.1	0.1	0.1	0.1
19	0.0	0.0	0.0	0.0	0.0	0.1	0.1	0.1	0.1
20	0.0	0.0	0.0	0.0	0.0	0.1	0.1	0.1	0.1
21	0.0	0.0	0.0	0.1	0.1	0.1	0.1	0.2	0.2
22	0.0	0.0	0.1	0.1	0.1	0.2	0.2	0.3	0.3
23	0.0	0.1	0.1	0.2	0.3	0.3	0.3	0.4	0.5
24	0.1	0.2	0.3	0.4	0.5	0.5	0.6	0.6	0.7
25	0.3	0.5	0.6	0.8	0.8	0.9	0.9	1.0	1.1
26	1.0	1.2	1.3	1.4	1.5	1.5	1.6	1.6	1.7
27	2.0	2.0	2.1	2.2	2.2	2.3	2.3	2.4	2.4
28	3.0	3.0	3.0	3.1	3.1	3.1	3.2	3.2	3.3
29	4.0	4.0	4.0	4.0	4.0	4.0	4.1	4.1	4.1
30	5.0	5.0	5.0	5.0	5.0	5.0	5.0	5.0	5.0
31	6.0	6.0	6.0	6.0	6.0	6.0	6.0	6.0	6.0
32	7.0	7.0	7.0	7.0	7.0	7.0	7.0	7.0	7.0
33	8.0	8.0	8.0	8.0	8.0	8.0	8.0	8.0	8.0
34	9.0	9.0	9.0	9.0	9.0	9.0	9.0	9.0	9.0
35	10.	10.	10.	10.	10.	10.	10.	10.	10.

Average Volatility

STOCK PRICE — NUMBER OF MONTHS BEFORE THE OPTIONS EXPIRE

STOCK PRICE	1	2	3	4	5	6	7	8	9
15	0.0	0.0	0.1	0.1	0.1	0.1	0.1	0.1	0.1
16	0.0	0.0	0.1	0.1	0.1	0.1	0.1	0.1	0.2
17	0.0	0.0	0.1	0.1	0.1	0.1	0.1	0.2	0.2
18	0.0	0.0	0.1	0.1	0.1	0.1	0.2	0.2	0.3
19	0.0	0.0	0.1	0.1	0.2	0.2	0.2	0.3	0.3
20	0.0	0.0	0.1	0.2	0.2	0.2	0.3	0.3	0.4
21	0.0	0.1	0.1	0.2	0.3	0.3	0.4	0.5	0.5
22	0.0	0.1	0.2	0.3	0.4	0.4	0.5	0.6	0.7
23	0.1	0.2	0.4	0.5	0.6	0.6	0.7	0.8	0.9
24	0.2	0.4	0.6	0.7	0.9	0.9	1.0	1.1	1.2
25	0.5	0.8	1.0	1.1	1.3	1.3	1.4	1.5	1.7
26	1.2	1.4	1.6	1.7	1.9	1.9	2.0	2.1	2.2
27	2.0	2.2	2.3	2.5	2.6	2.6	2.7	2.8	2.9
28	3.0	3.1	3.2	3.3	3.4	3.4	3.5	3.6	3.7
29	4.0	4.0	4.1	4.1	4.2	4.3	4.3	4.4	4.5
30	5.0	5.0	5.0	5.1	5.1	5.1	5.2	5.2	5.3
31	6.0	6.0	6.0	6.0	6.0	6.1	6.1	6.1	6.2
32	7.0	7.0	7.0	7.0	7.0	7.0	7.0	7.1	7.1
33	8.0	8.0	8.0	8.0	8.0	8.0	8.0	8.0	8.0
34	9.0	9.0	9.0	9.0	9.0	9.0	9.0	9.0	9.0
35	10.	10.	10.	10.	10.	10.	10.	10.	10.

High Volatility

STOCK PRICE — NUMBER OF MONTHS BEFORE THE OPTIONS EXPIRE

STOCK PRICE	1	2	3	4	5	6	7	8	9
15	0.1	0.1	0.2	0.3	0.4	0.5	0.5	0.6	0.8
16	0.1	0.1	0.2	0.4	0.5	0.5	0.6	0.7	0.9
17	0.1	0.1	0.3	0.4	0.6	0.6	0.7	0.9	1.0
18	0.1	0.2	0.3	0.5	0.7	0.7	0.8	1.0	1.2
19	0.1	0.2	0.4	0.6	0.8	0.9	1.0	1.1	1.3
20	0.1	0.3	0.5	0.8	0.9	1.0	1.1	1.3	1.5
21	0.1	0.4	0.6	0.9	1.1	1.2	1.3	1.5	1.8
22	0.2	0.6	0.8	1.1	1.3	1.4	1.6	1.8	2.0
23	0.4	0.8	1.1	1.4	1.6	1.7	1.9	2.1	2.4
24	0.6	1.1	1.4	1.8	2.0	2.1	2.2	2.5	2.7
25	1.0	1.5	1.8	2.2	2.4	2.5	2.7	2.9	3.2
26	1.6	2.1	2.4	2.8	3.0	3.1	3.2	3.5	3.7
27	2.3	2.8	3.1	3.4	3.6	3.7	3.9	4.1	4.3
28	3.2	3.5	3.8	4.1	4.3	4.4	4.6	4.8	5.0
29	4.1	4.4	4.6	4.9	5.1	5.2	5.3	5.5	5.7
30	5.0	5.2	5.4	5.7	5.9	6.0	6.1	6.3	6.5
31	6.0	6.1	6.3	6.5	6.7	6.8	6.9	7.1	7.2
32	7.0	7.0	7.2	7.4	7.5	7.6	7.7	7.9	8.1
33	8.0	8.0	8.1	8.3	8.4	8.5	8.6	8.7	8.9
34	9.0	9.0	9.0	9.2	9.3	9.4	9.4	9.6	9.7
35	10.	10.	10.	10.	10.	10.	10.	10.	10.

COVERED OPTION

WRITING TABLE Exercise Price is (30)

Low Volatility

STOCK PRICE	1	2	3	4	5	6	7	8	9
20	0.0	0.0	0.0	0.0	0.1	0.1	0.1	0.1	0.1
21	0.0	0.0	0.0	0.0	0.1	0.1	0.1	0.1	0.1
22	0.0	0.0	0.0	0.0	0.1	0.1	0.1	0.1	0.1
23	0.0	0.0	0.0	0.0	0.1	0.1	0.1	0.1	0.1
24	0.0	0.0	0.0	0.0	0.1	0.1	0.1	0.1	0.2
25	0.0	0.0	0.0	0.1	0.1	0.1	0.2	0.2	0.3
26	0.0	0.0	0.0	0.1	0.2	0.2	0.2	0.3	0.3
27	0.0	0.1	0.1	0.2	0.3	0.3	0.3	0.4	0.5
28	0.0	0.1	0.2	0.3	0.4	0.4	0.5	0.5	0.7
29	0.1	0.3	0.4	0.5	0.6	0.7	0.7	0.8	0.9
30	0.4	0.6	0.7	0.9	1.0	1.1	1.1	1.2	1.3
31	1.1	1.3	1.4	1.5	1.6	1.7	1.7	1.8	1.9
32	2.0	2.1	2.2	2.3	2.4	2.4	2.5	2.5	2.6
33	3.0	3.0	3.0	3.1	3.2	3.2	3.3	3.3	3.4
34	4.0	4.0	4.0	4.0	4.1	4.1	4.1	4.2	4.3
35	5.0	5.0	5.0	5.0	5.0	5.0	5.1	5.1	5.1
36	6.0	6.0	6.0	6.0	6.0	6.0	6.0	6.0	6.1
37	7.0	7.0	7.0	7.0	7.0	7.0	7.0	7.0	7.0
38	8.0	8.0	8.0	8.0	8.0	8.0	8.0	8.0	8.0
39	9.0	9.0	9.0	9.0	9.0	9.0	9.0	9.0	9.0
40	10.	10.	10.	10.	10.	10.	10.	10.	10.

NUMBER OF MONTHS BEFORE THE OPTIONS EXPIRE

Average Volatility

STOCK PRICE	1	2	3	4	5	6	7	8	9
20	0.0	0.1	0.1	0.1	0.1	0.1	0.1	0.2	0.3
21	0.0	0.1	0.1	0.1	0.1	0.1	0.2	0.2	0.3
22	0.0	0.1	0.1	0.1	0.2	0.2	0.2	0.3	0.4
23	0.0	0.1	0.1	0.2	0.2	0.2	0.3	0.3	0.4
24	0.0	0.1	0.1	0.2	0.3	0.3	0.3	0.4	0.5
25	0.0	0.1	0.2	0.3	0.3	0.4	0.4	0.5	0.6
26	0.0	0.1	0.2	0.2	0.4	0.4	0.5	0.6	0.8
27	0.1	0.2	0.4	0.5	0.6	0.6	0.7	0.8	1.0
28	0.1	0.3	0.5	0.7	0.8	0.8	1.0	1.1	1.2
29	0.3	0.6	0.8	1.0	1.1	1.2	1.3	1.4	1.6
30	0.6	0.9	1.2	1.4	1.5	1.6	1.7	1.8	2.0
31	1.3	1.6	1.8	2.0	2.1	2.2	2.3	2.4	2.6
32	2.1	2.3	2.5	2.7	2.8	2.9	3.0	3.1	3.2
33	3.0	3.2	3.3	3.5	3.6	3.6	3.7	3.8	4.0
34	4.0	4.1	4.2	4.3	4.4	4.4	4.5	4.6	4.7
35	5.0	5.0	5.1	5.2	5.2	5.3	5.4	5.5	5.6
36	6.0	6.0	6.0	6.1	6.1	6.2	6.2	6.3	6.4
37	7.0	7.0	7.0	7.0	7.1	7.1	7.1	7.2	7.3
38	8.0	8.0	8.0	8.0	8.0	8.0	8.1	8.1	8.2
39	9.0	9.0	9.0	9.0	9.0	9.0	9.0	9.0	9.1
40	10.	10.	10.	10.	10.	10.	10.	10.	10.

NUMBER OF MONTHS BEFORE THE OPTIONS EXPIRE

High Volatility

STOCK PRICE	1	2	3	4	5	6	7	8	9
20	0.1	0.2	0.3	0.5	0.6	0.8	0.8	1.0	1.1
21	0.1	0.2	0.3	0.6	0.7	0.9	0.9	1.1	1.3
22	0.1	0.3	0.4	0.7	0.8	1.0	1.0	1.2	1.4
23	0.1	0.3	0.5	0.8	1.0	1.1	1.1	1.4	1.6
24	0.1	0.4	0.6	0.9	1.1	1.2	1.3	1.6	1.8
25	0.2	0.5	0.7	1.1	1.3	1.4	1.5	1.8	2.0
26	0.2	0.7	0.9	1.3	1.5	1.7	1.7	2.0	2.3
27	0.4	0.8	1.1	1.5	1.8	1.9	2.0	2.3	2.6
28	0.5	1.1	1.4	1.8	2.1	2.4	2.4	2.6	2.9
29	0.8	1.4	1.7	2.2	2.4	2.6	2.7	3.0	3.3
30	1.2	1.8	2.2	2.6	2.9	3.1	3.2	3.5	3.8
31	1.8	2.4	2.7	3.2	3.5	3.6	3.8	4.1	4.3
32	2.5	3.1	3.4	3.8	4.1	4.2	4.4	4.7	4.9
33	3.3	3.8	4.1	4.5	4.8	4.9	5.0	5.3	5.6
34	4.2	4.6	4.9	5.3	5.5	5.6	5.7	6.0	6.3
35	5.1	5.4	5.7	6.0	6.2	6.4	6.5	6.7	7.0
36	6.0	6.3	6.5	6.8	7.0	7.2	7.3	7.5	7.7
37	7.0	7.2	7.4	7.7	7.9	8.0	8.1	8.3	8.5
38	8.0	8.1	8.3	8.5	8.7	8.8	8.9	9.1	9.3
39	9.0	9.0	9.2	9.4	9.6	9.7	9.8	10.	10.
40	10.	10.	10.	10.	10.	10.	10.	10.	11.

NUMBER OF MONTHS BEFORE THE OPTIONS EXPIRE

COVERED OPTION
WRITING TABLE   Exercise Price is (35)

Low Volatility

STOCK PRICE — NUMBER OF MONTHS BEFORE THE OPTIONS EXPIRE

	1	2	3	4	5	6	7	8	9
25	0.0	0.0	0.1	0.1	0.1	0.1	0.1	0.1	0.1
26	0.0	0.0	0.1	0.1	0.1	0.1	0.1	0.1	0.1
27	0.0	0.0	0.1	0.1	0.1	0.1	0.1	0.1	0.2
28	0.0	0.0	0.1	0.1	0.1	0.1	0.1	0.2	0.2
29	0.0	0.0	0.1	0.1	0.1	0.2	0.2	0.2	0.3
30	0.0	0.0	0.1	0.1	0.2	0.2	0.2	0.3	0.4
31	0.0	0.1	0.1	0.2	0.3	0.3	0.3	0.4	0.5
32	0.0	0.1	0.2	0.3	0.4	0.4	0.5	0.5	0.6
33	0.0	0.2	0.3	0.4	0.5	0.6	0.6	0.7	0.8
34	0.2	0.4	0.5	0.7	0.8	0.9	0.9	1.0	1.1
35	0.5	0.7	0.9	1.1	1.2	1.3	1.3	1.4	1.6
36	1.1	1.4	1.5	1.7	1.8	1.9	1.9	2.0	2.1
37	2.0	2.2	2.3	2.4	2.5	2.6	2.6	2.7	2.8
38	3.0	3.0	3.1	3.2	3.3	3.3	3.4	3.5	3.6
39	4.0	4.0	4.0	4.1	4.2	4.2	4.3	4.3	4.4
40	5.0	5.0	5.0	5.0	5.1	5.1	5.1	5.2	5.3
41	6.0	6.0	6.0	6.0	6.0	6.0	6.1	6.1	6.2
42	7.0	7.0	7.0	7.0	7.0	7.0	7.0	7.0	7.1
43	8.0	8.0	8.0	8.0	8.0	8.0	8.0	8.0	8.0
44	9.0	9.0	9.0	9.0	9.0	9.0	9.0	9.0	9.0
45	10.	10.	10.	10.	10.	10.	10.	10.	10.

Average Volatility

STOCK PRICE — NUMBER OF MONTHS BEFORE THE OPTIONS EXPIRE

	1	2	3	4	5	6	7	8	9
25	0.0	0.1	0.1	0.1	0.2	0.2	0.2	0.3	0.4
26	0.0	0.1	0.1	0.1	0.2	0.2	0.3	0.3	0.4
27	0.0	0.1	0.1	0.2	0.3	0.3	0.3	0.4	0.5
28	0.0	0.1	0.1	0.2	0.3	0.4	0.4	0.5	0.6
29	0.0	0.1	0.2	0.3	0.4	0.5	0.5	0.6	0.7
30	0.1	0.1	0.3	0.4	0.5	0.6	0.6	0.7	0.9
31	0.1	0.2	0.4	0.5	0.6	0.7	0.8	0.9	1.0
32	0.1	0.3	0.5	0.6	0.8	0.9	1.0	1.1	1.3
33	0.2	0.5	0.7	0.9	1.0	1.1	1.2	1.4	1.6
34	0.4	0.7	0.9	1.2	1.4	1.5	1.6	1.7	1.9
35	0.7	1.1	1.4	1.6	1.8	1.9	2.0	2.2	2.3
36	1.4	1.7	2.0	2.2	2.4	2.5	2.6	2.7	2.9
37	2.2	2.4	2.7	2.9	3.0	3.1	3.2	3.4	3.6
38	3.0	3.3	3.4	3.6	3.8	3.9	3.9	4.1	4.3
39	4.0	4.1	4.3	4.4	4.6	4.7	4.7	4.9	5.0
40	5.0	5.0	5.2	5.3	5.4	5.5	5.6	5.7	5.8
41	6.0	6.0	6.1	6.2	6.3	6.3	6.4	6.5	6.6
42	7.0	7.0	7.0	7.1	7.2	7.2	7.3	7.4	7.5
43	8.0	8.0	8.0	8.0	8.1	8.1	8.2	8.3	8.4
44	9.0	9.0	9.0	9.0	9.0	9.1	9.1	9.2	9.3
45	10.	10.	10.	10.	10.	10.	10.	10.	10.

High Volatility

STOCK PRICE — NUMBER OF MONTHS BEFORE THE OPTIONS EXPIRE

	1	2	3	4	5	6	7	8	9
25	0.1	0.3	0.5	0.7	0.9	1.0	1.1	1.3	1.6
26	0.1	0.4	0.5	0.8	1.1	1.1	1.2	1.5	1.8
27	0.1	0.4	0.6	1.0	1.2	1.3	1.3	1.6	1.9
28	0.2	0.5	0.7	1.1	1.1	1.4	1.4	1.8	2.1
29	0.2	0.6	0.9	1.2	1.5	1.6	1.7	2.0	2.3
30	0.3	0.7	1.0	1.4	1.7	1.8	1.9	2.2	2.6
31	0.4	0.9	1.2	1.7	1.9	2.1	2.2	2.5	2.9
32	0.5	1.1	1.5	1.9	2.2	2.4	2.5	2.8	3.2
33	0.7	1.3	1.8	2.3	2.6	2.7	2.9	3.2	3.6
34	1.0	1.7	2.1	2.6	2.9	3.1	3.3	3.6	4.0
35	1.4	2.1	2.6	3.1	3.4	3.6	3.7	4.1	4.5
36	2.0	2.7	3.1	3.6	4.0	4.1	4.3	4.6	5.0
37	2.7	3.3	3.8	4.3	4.6	4.7	4.9	5.2	5.6
38	3.5	4.1	4.5	4.9	5.2	5.4	5.5	5.8	6.2
39	4.3	4.8	5.2	5.6	5.9	6.1	6.2	6.5	6.9
40	5.2	5.6	6.0	6.4	6.7	6.8	6.9	7.2	7.6
41	6.1	6.5	6.8	7.2	7.4	7.6	7.7	8.0	8.3
42	7.0	7.3	7.6	8.0	8.2	8.4	8.5	8.8	9.1
43	8.0	8.2	8.5	8.8	9.0	9.2	9.3	9.5	9.8
44	9.0	9.2	9.4	9.7	9.9	10.	10.	10.	10.
45	10.	10.	10.	10.	10.	10.	10.	11.	11.

COVERED OPTION
WRITING TABLE Exercise Price is 40

Low Volatility

STOCK PRICE — NUMBER OF MONTHS BEFORE THE OPTIONS EXPIRE

STOCK PRICE	1	2	3	4	5	6	7	8	9
30	0.0	0.0	0.1	0.1	0.1	0.1	0.2	0.1	0.2
31	0.0	0.0	0.1	0.1	0.1	0.1	0.2	0.1	0.2
32	0.0	0.0	0.1	0.1	0.1	0.2	0.2	0.2	0.3
33	0.0	0.0	0.1	0.1	0.2	0.2	0.2	0.2	0.3
34	0.0	0.0	0.1	0.1	0.2	0.2	0.3	0.3	0.4
35	0.0	0.1	0.1	0.2	0.3	0.3	0.4	0.4	0.5
36	0.0	0.1	0.2	0.3	0.4	0.4	0.5	0.5	0.6
37	0.0	0.2	0.3	0.4	0.5	0.6	0.6	0.7	0.8
38	0.1	0.3	0.4	0.6	0.7	0.8	0.8	0.9	1.0
39	0.2	0.5	0.6	0.8	1.0	1.0	1.1	1.2	1.4
40	0.5	0.8	1.0	1.2	1.4	1.5	1.5	1.6	1.8
41	1.2	1.5	1.6	1.8	2.0	2.0	2.1	2.2	2.4
42	2.0	2.2	2.4	2.6	2.7	2.7	2.8	2.9	3.0
43	3.0	3.1	3.2	3.4	3.4	3.5	3.6	3.6	3.8
44	4.0	4.0	4.1	4.2	4.3	4.3	4.4	4.5	4.6
45	5.0	5.0	5.0	5.1	5.2	5.2	5.3	5.3	5.4
46	6.0	6.0	6.0	6.0	6.1	6.1	6.2	6.2	6.3
47	7.0	7.0	7.0	7.0	7.0	7.0	7.1	7.1	7.2
48	8.0	8.0	8.0	8.0	8.0	8.0	8.0	8.0	8.1
49	9.0	9.0	9.0	9.0	9.0	9.0	9.0	9.0	9.0
50	10.	10.	10.	10.	10.	10.	10.	10.	10.

Average Volatility

STOCK PRICE — NUMBER OF MONTHS BEFORE THE OPTIONS EXPIRE

STOCK PRICE	1	2	3	4	5	6	7	8	9
30	0.0	0.1	0.2	0.2	0.2	0.2	0.4	0.3	0.1
31	0.0	0.1	0.2	0.2	0.2	0.3	0.5	0.4	0.2
32	0.0	0.1	0.2	0.2	0.4	0.4	0.5	0.5	0.3
33	0.0	0.1	0.2	0.3	0.4	0.5	0.6	0.6	0.4
34	0.0	0.2	0.3	0.4	0.5	0.6	0.8	0.7	0.6
35	0.0	0.2	0.4	0.5	0.6	0.7	0.9	0.9	0.7
36	0.0	0.3	0.5	0.6	0.8	0.9	1.1	1.1	1.0
37	0.1	0.5	0.6	0.8	1.0	1.1	1.3	1.3	1.2
38	0.2	0.6	0.8	1.0	1.2	1.4	1.6	1.6	1.6
39	0.4	0.9	1.1	1.4	1.6	1.7	1.9	2.0	2.0
40	0.8	1.3	1.5	1.8	2.0	2.2	2.3	2.4	2.4
41	1.5	1.9	2.1	2.4	2.6	2.7	2.9	3.0	3.0
42	2.2	2.6	2.8	3.0	3.2	3.4	3.5	3.6	3.7
43	3.1	3.4	3.6	3.8	4.0	4.1	4.2	4.3	4.4
44	4.0	4.2	4.4	4.6	4.7	4.9	5.0	5.0	5.1
45	5.0	5.1	5.2	5.4	5.6	5.7	5.8	5.8	5.9
46	6.0	6.0	6.1	6.3	6.4	6.5	6.6	6.7	6.8
47	7.0	7.0	7.1	7.2	7.3	7.4	7.4	7.5	7.6
48	8.0	8.0	8.0	8.1	8.2	8.3	8.3	8.4	8.5
49	9.0	9.0	9.0	9.0	9.1	9.2	9.2	9.3	9.4
50	10.	10.	10.	10.	10.	10.	10.	10.	10.

High Volatility

STOCK PRICE — NUMBER OF MONTHS BEFORE THE OPTIONS EXPIRE

STOCK PRICE	1	2	3	4	5	6	7	8	9
30	0.1	0.4	0.6	1.0	1.2	1.4	1.5	1.7	2.0
31	0.2	0.5	0.7	1.1	1.3	1.5	1.7	1.9	2.2
32	0.2	0.6	0.8	1.2	1.5	1.7	1.8	2.1	2.4
33	0.2	0.7	1.0	1.4	1.6	1.9	2.0	2.3	2.6
34	0.3	0.8	1.1	1.6	1.8	2.1	2.2	2.5	2.9
35	0.4	0.9	1.3	1.8	2.1	2.3	2.5	2.8	3.1
36	0.5	1.1	1.5	2.0	2.3	2.6	2.8	3.1	3.5
37	0.6	1.3	1.8	2.3	2.6	2.9	3.1	3.4	3.8
38	0.9	1.6	2.1	2.7	3.0	3.3	3.5	3.8	4.2
39	1.2	2.0	2.5	3.1	3.4	3.7	3.9	4.2	4.6
40	1.6	2.4	2.9	3.5	3.9	4.1	4.3	4.7	5.1
41	2.2	3.0	3.5	4.1	4.4	4.7	4.9	5.2	5.6
42	2.9	3.6	4.1	4.7	5.0	5.3	5.5	5.8	6.2
43	3.6	4.3	4.8	5.3	5.6	5.9	6.1	6.4	6.8
44	4.4	5.1	5.5	6.0	6.3	6.6	6.8	7.1	7.5
45	5.3	5.9	6.3	6.8	7.1	7.3	7.5	7.8	8.2
46	6.2	6.7	7.1	7.5	7.8	8.0	8.2	8.5	8.9
47	7.1	7.5	7.9	8.3	8.6	8.8	9.0	9.2	9.6
48	8.0	8.4	8.7	9.1	9.4	9.6	9.7	10.	10.
49	9.0	9.3	9.6	10.	10.	10.	10.	10.	11.
50	10.	10.	10.	11.	11.	11.	11.	11.	11.

COVERED OPTION
WRITING TABLE Exercise Price is

Low Volatility

STOCK PRICE	NUMBER OF MONTHS BEFORE THE OPTIONS EXPIRE								
	1	2	3	4	5	6	7	8	9
35	0.0	0.1	0.1	0.1	0.1	0.2	0.2	0.2	0.2
36	0.0	0.1	0.1	0.1	0.1	0.2	0.2	0.2	0.3
37	0.0	0.1	0.1	0.1	0.2	0.2	0.2	0.3	0.3
38	0.0	0.1	0.1	0.1	0.2	0.3	0.3	0.3	0.4
39	0.0	0.1	0.1	0.2	0.3	0.3	0.4	0.4	0.5
40	0.0	0.1	0.2	0.3	0.4	0.4	0.5	0.5	0.6
41	0.0	0.1	0.2	0.4	0.5	0.5	0.6	0.7	0.8
42	0.1	0.2	0.3	0.5	0.6	0.7	0.8	0.8	1.0
43	0.1	0.3	0.5	0.7	0.8	0.9	1.0	1.1	1.2
44	0.3	0.6	0.8	1.0	1.1	1.2	1.3	1.4	1.6
45	0.6	0.9	1.2	1.4	1.5	1.6	1.7	1.8	2.0
46	1.3	1.6	1.8	2.0	2.1	2.2	2.3	2.4	2.6
47	2.1	2.3	2.5	2.7	2.8	2.9	3.0	3.1	3.2
48	3.0	3.2	3.3	3.5	3.6	3.7	3.7	3.8	4.0
49	4.0	4.1	4.2	4.3	4.4	4.5	4.5	4.6	4.7
50	5.0	5.0	5.1	5.2	5.3	5.3	5.4	5.5	5.6
51	6.0	6.0	6.0	6.1	6.2	6.2	6.3	6.3	6.4
52	7.0	7.0	7.0	7.0	7.1	7.1	7.2	7.2	7.3
53	8.0	8.0	8.0	8.0	8.0	8.0	8.1	8.1	8.2
54	9.0	9.0	9.0	9.0	9.0	9.0	9.0	9.0	9.1
55	10.	10.	10.	10.	10.	10.	10.	10.	10.

Average Volatility

STOCK PRICE	NUMBER OF MONTHS BEFORE THE OPTIONS EXPIRE								
	1	2	3	4	5	6	7	8	9
35	0.1	0.1	0.2	0.2	0.3	0.4	0.5	0.6	0.7
36	0.1	0.1	0.2	0.3	0.4	0.5	0.5	0.7	0.8
37	0.1	0.1	0.2	0.4	0.5	0.6	0.6	0.8	0.9
38	0.1	0.2	0.3	0.4	0.6	0.7	0.7	0.9	1.1
39	0.1	0.2	0.4	0.5	0.7	0.8	0.9	1.1	1.2
40	0.1	0.3	0.5	0.7	0.8	1.0	1.0	1.2	1.4
41	0.2	0.4	0.6	0.8	1.0	1.1	1.2	1.4	1.6
42	0.2	0.5	0.8	1.0	1.2	1.4	1.5	1.7	1.9
43	0.4	0.7	1.0	1.3	1.5	1.7	1.8	2.0	2.2
44	0.6	1.0	1.3	1.6	1.9	2.0	2.1	2.4	2.6
45	1.0	1.4	1.8	2.1	2.3	2.5	2.6	2.8	3.0
46	1.6	2.0	2.3	2.6	2.9	3.0	3.1	3.4	3.6
47	2.3	2.7	3.0	3.3	3.5	3.7	3.8	4.0	4.2
48	3.2	3.5	3.8	4.0	4.2	4.4	4.5	4.7	4.9
49	4.1	4.3	4.6	4.8	5.0	5.1	5.2	5.4	5.6
50	5.0	5.2	5.4	5.6	5.8	5.9	6.0	6.2	6.3
51	6.0	6.1	6.3	6.5	6.6	6.7	6.8	7.0	7.1
52	7.0	7.0	7.2	7.3	7.5	7.6	7.6	7.8	8.0
53	8.0	8.0	8.1	8.2	8.3	8.4	8.5	8.6	8.8
54	9.0	9.0	9.0	9.1	9.2	9.3	9.4	9.5	9.6
55	10.	10.	10.	10.	10.	10.	10.	10.	10.

High Volatility

STOCK PRICE	NUMBER OF MONTHS BEFORE THE OPTIONS EXPIRE								
	1	2	3	4	5	6	7	8	9
35	0.2	0.5	0.8	1.2	1.5	1.7	1.9	2.1	2.6
36	0.2	0.6	0.9	1.4	1.7	1.8	2.1	2.3	2.8
37	0.3	0.7	1.0	1.5	1.9	2.0	2.3	2.5	3.0
38	0.3	0.9	1.2	1.7	2.1	2.2	2.5	2.7	3.2
39	0.4	1.0	1.3	1.9	2.3	2.5	2.7	3.0	3.5
40	0.5	1.1	1.5	2.1	2.5	2.7	3.0	3.3	3.8
41	0.6	1.3	1.8	2.4	2.8	3.0	3.3	3.6	4.1
42	0.8	1.6	2.1	2.7	3.1	3.4	3.6	3.9	4.5
43	1.1	1.9	2.4	3.1	3.5	3.7	4.0	4.3	4.9
44	1.4	2.3	2.8	3.5	3.9	4.2	4.4	4.8	5.3
45	1.8	2.7	3.2	3.9	4.4	4.6	4.9	5.2	5.8
46	2.4	3.3	3.8	4.5	4.9	5.2	5.4	5.8	6.3
47	3.0	3.9	4.4	5.1	5.5	5.8	6.0	6.3	6.9
48	3.8	4.6	5.1	5.7	6.1	6.4	6.6	7.0	7.5
49	4.6	5.3	5.8	6.4	6.8	7.1	7.3	7.6	8.1
50	5.4	6.1	6.5	7.1	7.5	7.7	8.0	8.3	8.8
51	6.3	6.9	7.3	7.9	8.2	8.5	8.7	9.0	9.5
52	7.2	7.8	8.1	8.7	9.0	9.2	9.4	9.7	10.
53	8.1	8.6	8.9	9.5	9.8	10.	10.	10.	10.
54	9.0	9.5	9.8	10.	10.	10.	11.	11.	11.
55	10.	10.	10.	11.	11.	11.	11.	12.	12.

COVERED OPTION
WRITING TABLE Exercise Price is (50)

Low Volatility

STOCK PRICE — NUMBER OF MONTHS BEFORE THE OPTIONS EXPIRE

STOCK PRICE	1	2	3	4	5	6	7	8	9
40	0.1	0.1	0.1	0.1	0.2	0.2	0.2	0.3	0.3
41	0.0	0.1	0.1	0.1	0.2	0.2	0.3	0.3	0.4
42	0.0	0.1	0.1	0.2	0.2	0.2	0.3	0.4	0.4
43	0.0	0.1	0.2	0.2	0.3	0.3	0.4	0.5	0.5
44	0.0	0.1	0.2	0.3	0.3	0.4	0.5	0.6	0.7
45	0.0	0.1	0.2	0.3	0.4	0.5	0.6	0.7	0.8
46	0.1	0.2	0.3	0.5	0.6	0.6	0.7	0.8	1.0
47	0.1	0.3	0.5	0.6	0.7	0.8	0.9	1.0	1.2
48	0.2	0.4	0.6	0.8	1.0	1.0	1.2	1.3	1.4
49	0.3	0.7	0.9	1.1	1.3	1.4	1.5	1.6	1.8
50	0.7	1.1	1.3	1.5	1.7	1.8	1.9	2.1	2.2
51	1.3	1.7	1.9	2.1	2.3	2.4	2.5	2.6	2.8
52	2.1	2.4	2.6	2.8	3.0	3.1	3.2	3.3	3.5
53	3.0	3.2	3.4	3.6	3.7	3.8	3.9	4.0	4.2
54	4.0	4.1	4.2	4.4	4.5	4.6	4.7	4.8	4.9
55	5.0	5.0	5.1	5.3	5.4	5.4	5.5	5.6	5.7
56	6.0	6.0	6.0	6.2	6.2	6.3	6.4	6.5	6.6
57	7.0	7.0	7.0	7.1	7.1	7.2	7.2	7.3	7.4
58	8.0	8.0	8.0	8.0	8.1	8.1	8.2	8.2	8.3
59	9.0	9.0	9.0	9.0	9.0	9.0	9.1	9.1	9.2
60	10.	10.	10.	10.	10.	10.	10.	10.	10.

Average Volatility

STOCK PRICE — NUMBER OF MONTHS BEFORE THE OPTIONS EXPIRE

STOCK PRICE	1	2	3	4	5	6	7	8	9
40	0.1	0.0	0.2	0.3	0.3	0.4	0.5	0.9	0.9
41	0.0	0.0	0.2	0.3	0.4	0.5	0.6	1.0	1.0
42	0.0	0.1	0.3	0.4	0.5	0.6	0.7	1.2	1.1
43	0.0	0.1	0.4	0.5	0.6	0.7	0.9	1.3	1.3
44	0.1	0.2	0.5	0.6	0.7	0.8	1.0	1.4	1.4
45	0.1	0.3	0.6	0.8	0.9	1.0	1.2	1.6	1.6
46	0.1	0.4	0.7	1.0	1.1	1.2	1.4	1.8	1.9
47	0.2	0.6	0.9	1.2	1.3	1.5	1.7	2.1	2.2
48	0.4	0.8	1.2	1.5	1.6	1.8	2.0	2.4	2.5
49	0.6	1.1	1.5	1.8	2.0	2.2	2.4	2.8	2.9
50	1.0	1.5	1.9	2.3	2.4	2.6	2.9	3.2	3.3
51	1.6	2.1	2.5	2.8	3.0	3.2	3.4	3.8	3.9
52	2.4	2.8	3.2	3.5	3.6	3.8	4.1	4.4	4.5
53	3.2	3.6	3.9	4.2	4.3	4.5	4.7	5.0	5.1
54	4.1	4.4	4.7	4.9	5.1	5.3	5.5	5.7	5.8
55	5.0	5.3	5.5	5.7	5.9	6.0	6.2	6.4	6.6
56	6.0	6.2	6.4	6.6	6.7	6.8	7.0	7.2	7.3
57	7.0	7.1	7.3	7.4	7.6	7.7	7.8	8.0	8.1
58	8.0	8.0	8.2	8.3	8.4	8.5	8.7	8.9	9.0
59	9.0	9.0	9.1	9.2	9.3	9.4	9.5	9.7	9.8
60	10.	10.	10.	10.	10.	10.	10.	10.	10.

High Volatility

STOCK PRICE — NUMBER OF MONTHS BEFORE THE OPTIONS EXPIRE

STOCK PRICE	1	2	3	4	5	6	7	8	9
40	0.3	0.7	1.1	1.5	1.9	2.1	2.3	2.6	3.0
41	0.3	0.8	1.2	1.7	2.0	2.3	2.5	2.8	3.2
42	0.3	1.0	1.4	1.9	2.2	2.5	2.7	3.0	3.5
43	0.4	1.1	1.5	2.1	2.4	2.7	2.9	3.3	3.7
44	0.5	1.2	1.7	2.3	2.7	3.0	3.2	3.6	4.0
45	0.6	1.4	1.9	2.5	2.9	3.2	3.5	3.9	4.4
46	0.8	1.6	2.2	2.8	3.3	3.5	3.8	4.2	4.7
47	1.0	1.9	2.5	3.2	3.6	3.9	4.2	4.5	5.1
48	1.2	2.2	2.8	3.5	4.0	4.3	4.5	4.9	5.5
49	1.6	2.6	3.2	3.9	4.4	4.7	5.0	5.4	5.9
50	2.0	3.1	3.7	4.4	4.9	5.2	5.4	5.8	6.4
51	2.6	3.6	4.3	5.0	5.4	5.7	6.0	6.4	6.9
52	3.2	4.2	4.9	5.5	6.0	6.3	6.6	7.0	7.5
53	3.9	4.9	5.5	6.2	6.6	6.9	7.2	7.6	8.1
54	4.7	5.6	6.2	6.8	7.3	7.5	7.8	8.2	8.7
55	5.6	6.4	6.9	7.5	8.0	8.2	8.5	8.9	9.4
56	6.4	7.2	7.7	8.3	8.7	8.9	9.2	9.6	10.
57	7.3	8.0	8.5	9.0	9.4	9.7	9.9	10.	10.
58	8.2	8.8	9.3	9.8	10.	10.	10.	11.	11.
59	9.1	9.7	10.	10.	11.	11.	11.	11.	12.
60	10.	10.	10.	11.	11.	12.	12.	12.	13.

COVERED OPTION
WRITING TABLE   Exercise Price is ⑥⓪

Low Volatility

STOCK PRICE	NUMBER OF MONTHS BEFORE THE OPTIONS EXPIRE								
	1	2	3	4	5	6	7	8	9
50	0.1	0.1	0.1	0.2	0.2	0.3	0.4	0.4	0.5
51	0.1	0.1	0.1	0.2	0.3	0.4	0.4	0.5	0.6
52	0.1	0.1	0.2	0.3	0.4	0.4	0.5	0.6	0.7
53	0.1	0.1	0.2	0.3	0.4	0.5	0.6	0.7	0.8
54	0.1	0.2	0.3	0.4	0.5	0.6	0.7	0.8	1.0
55	0.1	0.2	0.4	0.5	0.7	0.8	0.9	1.0	1.1
56	0.1	0.3	0.5	0.7	0.8	0.9	1.0	1.2	1.3
57	0.2	0.4	0.6	0.8	1.0	1.1	1.3	1.4	1.6
58	0.3	0.6	0.8	1.1	1.3	1.4	1.5	1.7	1.9
59	0.5	0.9	1.1	1.4	1.6	1.8	1.9	2.1	2.3
60	0.8	1.3	1.5	1.8	2.0	2.2	2.3	2.5	2.7
61	1.5	1.9	2.1	2.4	2.6	2.8	2.9	3.1	3.3
62	2.2	2.6	2.8	3.1	3.3	3.4	3.5	3.7	3.9
63	3.1	3.4	3.6	3.8	4.0	4.1	4.2	4.4	4.6
64	4.0	4.2	4.4	4.6	4.8	4.9	5.0	5.1	5.3
65	5.0	5.1	5.3	5.5	5.6	5.7	5.8	5.9	6.1
66	6.0	6.0	6.2	6.3	6.4	6.5	6.6	6.7	6.9
67	7.0	7.0	7.1	7.2	7.3	7.4	7.5	7.6	7.7
68	8.0	8.0	8.0	8.1	8.2	8.3	8.4	8.4	8.6
69	9.0	9.0	9.0	9.0	9.1	9.2	9.3	9.3	9.4
70	10.	10.	10.	10.	10.	10.	10.	10.	10.

Average Volatility

STOCK PRICE	NUMBER OF MONTHS BEFORE THE OPTIONS EXPIRE								
	1	2	3	4	5	6	7	8	9
50	0.0	0.2	0.4	0.5	0.6	0.8	1.1	1.0	0.7
51	0.0	0.3	0.5	0.6	0.8	0.9	1.2	1.1	0.9
52	0.0	0.3	0.5	0.7	0.9	1.0	1.3	1.3	1.0
53	0.0	0.4	0.6	0.8	1.0	1.2	1.5	1.4	1.2
54	0.1	0.5	0.7	0.9	1.2	1.4	1.6	1.6	1.5
55	0.1	0.6	0.9	1.1	1.4	1.6	1.8	1.9	1.7
56	0.2	0.8	1.0	1.3	1.6	1.8	2.1	2.1	2.0
57	0.4	1.0	1.3	1.6	1.9	2.1	2.4	2.4	2.4
58	0.5	1.2	1.6	1.9	2.2	2.4	2.7	2.8	2.7
59	0.8	1.5	1.9	2.3	2.6	2.8	3.1	3.2	3.2
60	1.2	2.0	2.3	2.7	3.0	3.3	3.5	3.5	3.7
61	1.9	2.5	2.9	3.3	3.6	3.9	4.0	4.2	4.2
62	2.6	3.2	3.5	3.9	4.2	4.5	4.6	4.8	4.8
63	3.4	3.9	4.2	4.6	4.9	5.1	5.3	5.4	5.5
64	4.2	4.7	5.0	5.3	5.6	5.8	6.0	6.1	6.2
65	5.1	5.5	5.8	6.1	6.3	6.6	6.7	6.8	6.9
66	6.0	6.4	6.6	6.9	7.1	7.3	7.5	7.6	7.7
67	7.0	7.3	7.5	7.7	7.9	8.1	8.3	8.4	8.5
68	8.0	8.2	8.3	8.6	8.8	9.0	9.1	9.2	9.3
69	9.0	9.1	9.2	9.5	9.6	9.8	9.9	10.	10.
70	10.	10.	10.	10.	10.	10.	10.	10.	11.

High Volatility

STOCK PRICE	NUMBER OF MONTHS BEFORE THE OPTIONS EXPIRE								
	1	2	3	4	5	6	7	8	9
50	0.4	1.1	1.6	2.2	2.6	2.9	3.2	3.4	4.1
51	0.5	1.2	1.8	2.4	2.8	3.1	3.4	3.7	4.4
52	0.5	1.3	1.9	2.6	3.1	3.4	3.7	4.0	4.6
53	0.6	1.5	2.1	2.8	3.3	3.6	3.9	4.2	4.9
54	0.8	1.7	2.3	3.1	3.6	3.9	4.2	4.5	5.3
55	0.9	1.9	2.6	3.4	3.9	4.2	4.5	4.9	5.6
56	1.1	2.2	2.9	3.7	4.2	4.6	4.9	5.2	5.9
57	1.3	2.5	3.2	4.0	4.6	4.9	5.2	5.6	6.3
58	1.6	2.8	3.6	4.4	5.0	5.3	5.6	6.0	6.7
59	2.0	3.2	4.0	4.8	5.4	5.8	6.1	6.5	7.2
60	2.4	3.7	4.5	5.3	5.9	6.2	6.5	6.9	7.7
61	3.0	4.2	5.0	5.9	6.4	6.8	7.1	7.5	8.2
62	3.6	4.8	5.6	6.4	7.0	7.3	7.7	8.0	8.8
63	4.3	5.5	6.2	7.0	7.6	7.9	8.2	8.6	9.4
64	5.1	6.2	6.9	7.7	8.2	8.6	8.9	9.2	10.
65	5.9	6.9	7.6	8.4	8.9	9.2	9.5	9.9	10.
66	6.7	7.7	8.3	9.1	9.6	9.9	10.	10.	11.
67	7.5	8.4	9.1	9.8	10.	10.	10.	11.	11.
68	8.4	9.3	9.8	10.	11.	11.	11.	12.	11.
69	9.3	10.	10.	11.	11.	12.	12.	12.	13.
70	10.	10.	11.	12.	12.	12.	13.	13.	14.

T142

COVERED OPTION

WRITING TABLE   Exercise Price is 70

Low Volatility

STOCK PRICE	NUMBER OF MONTHS BEFORE THE OPTIONS EXPIRE								
	1	2	3	4	5	6	7	8	9
60	0.0	0.1	0.2	0.3	0.3	0.4	0.6	0.5	0.3
61	0.0	0.2	0.2	0.3	0.4	0.5	0.7	0.6	0.4
62	0.0	0.2	0.3	0.4	0.5	0.6	0.8	0.8	0.5
63	0.0	0.2	0.3	0.5	0.6	0.7	0.9	0.9	0.7
64	0.0	0.3	0.4	0.6	0.7	0.8	1.1	1.0	0.9
65	0.0	0.4	0.5	0.7	0.9	1.0	1.2	1.2	1.1
66	0.1	0.5	0.6	0.9	1.0	1.2	1.4	1.4	1.3
67	0.2	0.6	0.8	1.1	1.3	1.5	1.7	1.7	1.6
68	0.3	0.8	1.1	1.4	1.6	1.8	2.0	2.0	2.0
69	0.5	1.1	1.4	1.7	1.9	2.1	2.3	2.4	2.4
70	0.9	1.5	1.8	2.1	2.4	2.6	2.7	2.8	2.9
71	1.6	2.1	2.4	2.7	2.9	3.1	3.3	3.4	3.4
72	2.3	2.8	3.0	3.4	3.6	3.8	3.9	4.0	4.1
73	3.2	3.6	3.8	4.1	4.3	4.5	4.6	4.7	4.8
74	4.1	4.4	4.6	4.8	5.0	5.2	5.3	5.4	5.5
75	5.0	5.2	5.4	5.7	5.8	6.0	6.1	6.2	6.3
76	6.0	6.1	6.3	6.5	6.6	6.8	6.9	7.0	7.1
77	7.0	7.0	7.2	7.4	7.5	7.6	7.7	7.8	7.9
78	8.0	8.0	8.1	8.3	8.4	8.5	8.6	8.6	8.8
79	9.0	9.0	9.0	9.2	9.3	9.4	9.4	9.5	9.6
80	10.	10.	10.	10.	10.	10.	10.	10.	10.

Average Volatility

STOCK PRICE	NUMBER OF MONTHS BEFORE THE OPTIONS EXPIRE								
	1	2	3	4	5	6	7	8	9
60	0.1	0.3	0.6	0.9	1.1	1.2	1.3	1.5	1.8
61	0.1	0.4	0.7	1.0	1.2	1.3	1.4	1.7	2.0
62	0.2	0.5	0.8	1.1	1.3	1.4	1.6	1.9	2.2
63	0.2	0.6	0.9	1.2	1.5	1.6	1.8	2.0	2.4
64	0.3	0.7	1.0	1.4	1.6	1.8	2.0	2.3	2.6
65	0.3	0.8	1.2	1.6	1.9	2.0	2.2	2.5	2.9
66	0.5	1.0	1.4	1.8	2.1	2.3	2.5	2.8	3.2
67	0.6	1.2	1.7	2.1	2.4	2.6	2.8	3.1	3.5
68	0.8	1.5	2.0	2.5	2.8	2.9	3.1	3.5	3.9
69	1.1	1.8	2.3	2.8	3.2	3.3	3.6	3.9	4.3
70	1.5	2.3	2.8	3.3	3.6	3.8	4.0	4.4	4.8
71	2.1	2.8	3.3	3.8	4.2	4.4	4.6	4.9	5.3
72	2.8	3.5	4.0	4.4	4.8	4.9	5.2	5.5	5.9
73	3.6	4.2	4.6	5.1	5.4	5.6	5.8	6.1	6.5
74	4.4	4.9	5.4	5.8	6.1	6.3	6.5	6.8	7.2
75	5.2	5.8	6.1	6.6	6.8	7.0	7.2	7.5	7.9
76	6.1	6.6	7.0	7.3	7.6	7.8	8.0	8.2	8.6
77	7.1	7.4	7.8	8.1	8.4	8.5	8.7	9.0	9.3
78	8.0	8.3	8.6	9.0	9.2	9.3	9.5	9.8	10.
79	9.0	9.2	9.5	9.8	10.	10.	10.	10.	10.
80	10.	10.	10.	10.	10.	11.	11.	11.	11.

High Volatility

STOCK PRICE	NUMBER OF MONTHS BEFORE THE OPTIONS EXPIRE								
	1	2	3	4	5	6	7	8	9
60	0.6	1.5	2.1	2.8	3.4	3.8	4.1	4.5	5.1
61	0.7	1.7	2.3	3.0	3.7	4.1	4.3	4.8	5.4
62	0.8	1.8	2.5	3.3	3.9	4.3	4.6	5.1	5.7
63	0.9	2.0	2.7	3.5	4.2	4.6	4.9	5.4	6.0
64	1.0	2.2	3.0	3.8	4.5	4.9	5.2	5.7	6.4
65	1.2	2.5	3.3	4.1	4.8	5.2	5.6	6.1	6.7
66	1.4	2.8	3.6	4.5	5.2	5.6	5.9	6.4	7.1
67	1.7	3.1	3.9	4.8	5.5	5.9	6.3	6.8	7.5
68	2.0	3.4	4.3	5.2	5.9	6.4	6.7	7.2	7.9
69	2.4	3.9	4.7	5.7	6.4	6.8	7.2	7.7	8.4
70	2.8	4.3	5.2	6.2	6.9	7.3	7.6	8.2	8.9
71	3.4	4.9	5.7	6.7	7.4	7.8	8.2	8.7	9.4
72	4.0	5.5	6.3	7.3	8.0	8.4	8.7	9.3	10.
73	4.7	6.1	6.9	7.9	8.5	9.0	9.3	9.8	10.
74	5.4	6.8	7.6	8.5	9.2	9.6	9.9	10.	11.
75	6.2	7.5	8.3	9.2	9.8	10.	10.	11.	11.
76	7.0	8.2	9.0	9.9	10.	10.	11.	11.	12.
77	7.8	8.9	9.7	10.	11.	11.	11.	12.	13.
78	8.6	9.7	10.	11.	11.	12.	12.	13.	13.
79	9.5	10.	11.	12.	12.	13.	13.	13.	14.
80	10.	11.	12.	12.	13.	13.	14.	14.	15.

COVERED OPTION
WRITING TABLE   Exercise Price is (80)

Low Volatility

STOCK PRICE	1	2	3	4	5	6	7	8	9
			NUMBER OF MONTHS BEFORE THE OPTIONS EXPIRE						
70	0.1	0.1	0.3	0.5	0.6	0.6	0.7	0.9	1.1
71	0.1	0.2	0.3	0.5	0.7	0.7	0.8	1.0	1.2
72	0.1	0.2	0.4	0.6	0.8	0.8	0.9	1.1	1.3
73	0.1	0.3	0.5	0.7	0.9	1.0	1.1	1.3	1.5
74	0.1	0.3	0.6	0.9	1.0	1.1	1.2	1.4	1.7
75	0.2	0.4	0.7	1.0	1.2	1.3	1.4	1.6	1.9
76	0.2	0.6	0.9	1.2	1.4	1.5	1.6	1.9	2.2
77	0.3	0.7	1.1	1.4	1.6	1.8	1.9	2.2	2.5
78	0.5	1.0	1.3	1.7	1.9	2.1	2.2	2.5	2.8
79	0.7	1.3	1.7	2.1	2.3	2.5	2.6	2.9	3.2
80	1.1	1.7	2.1	2.5	2.8	2.9	3.1	3.3	3.7
81	1.7	2.3	2.7	3.1	3.3	3.5	3.6	3.9	4.2
82	2.5	3.0	3.3	3.7	3.9	4.1	4.3	4.5	4.8
83	3.3	3.7	4.0	4.4	4.6	4.8	4.9	5.2	5.5
84	4.1	4.5	4.8	5.2	5.4	5.5	5.6	5.9	6.1
85	5.0	5.4	5.6	5.9	6.1	6.2	6.4	6.6	6.9
86	6.0	6.2	6.5	6.8	6.9	7.0	7.2	7.4	7.6
87	7.0	7.1	7.3	7.6	7.8	7.9	8.0	8.2	8.4
88	8.0	8.1	8.2	8.5	8.6	8.7	8.8	9.0	9.2
89	9.0	9.0	9.1	9.4	9.5	9.6	9.7	9.9	10.
90	10.	10.	10.	10.	10.	10.	10.	10.	10.

Average Volatility

STOCK PRICE	1	2	3	4	5	6	7	8	9
			NUMBER OF MONTHS BEFORE THE OPTIONS EXPIRE						
70	0.2	0.5	0.8	1.1	1.4	1.6	1.7	2.0	2.3
71	0.2	0.5	0.9	1.2	1.5	1.7	1.8	2.2	2.5
72	0.3	0.6	1.0	1.3	1.7	1.9	2.0	2.4	2.7
73	0.3	0.7	1.1	1.5	1.9	2.1	2.2	2.6	2.9
74	0.4	0.9	1.3	1.7	2.1	2.3	2.5	2.8	3.2
75	0.5	1.0	1.5	1.9	2.3	2.6	2.7	3.1	3.5
76	0.6	1.2	1.7	2.2	2.6	2.9	3.0	3.4	3.8
77	0.8	1.5	2.0	2.5	2.9	3.2	3.4	3.8	4.2
78	1.0	1.8	2.3	2.8	3.3	3.5	3.7	4.1	4.5
79	1.3	2.1	2.7	3.2	3.7	4.0	4.1	4.6	5.0
80	1.7	2.6	3.2	3.7	4.2	4.4	4.6	5.0	5.4
81	2.3	3.1	3.7	4.3	4.7	5.0	5.2	5.6	6.0
82	3.0	3.8	4.3	4.9	5.3	5.6	5.7	6.2	6.5
83	3.7	4.5	5.0	5.5	5.9	6.2	6.4	6.8	7.2
84	4.5	5.2	5.7	6.2	6.6	6.8	7.0	7.4	7.8
85	5.4	6.0	6.5	6.9	7.3	7.5	7.7	8.1	8.5
86	6.3	6.8	7.3	7.7	8.0	8.3	8.5	8.8	9.2
87	7.2	7.6	8.1	8.5	8.8	9.0	9.2	9.6	9.9
88	8.1	8.5	8.9	9.3	9.6	9.8	10.	10.	10.
89	9.0	9.4	9.7	10.	10.	10.	10.	11.	11.
90	10.	10.	10.	10.	11.	11.	11.	11.	12.

High Volatility

STOCK PRICE	1	2	3	4	5	6	7	8	9
			NUMBER OF MONTHS BEFORE THE OPTIONS EXPIRE						
70	0.8	1.9	2.8	3.5	4.2	4.5	5.1	5.7	6.3
71	0.9	2.1	3.0	3.8	4.5	4.8	5.3	6.0	6.6
72	1.1	2.3	3.2	4.0	4.7	5.1	5.6	6.3	6.9
73	1.2	2.5	3.5	4.3	5.0	5.4	6.0	6.6	7.3
74	1.4	2.8	3.7	4.6	5.4	5.7	6.3	7.0	7.6
75	1.6	3.0	4.0	5.0	5.7	6.1	6.6	7.3	8.0
76	1.8	3.3	4.4	5.3	6.1	6.4	7.0	7.7	8.4
77	2.1	3.7	4.7	5.7	6.4	6.8	7.4	8.1	8.8
78	2.4	4.0	5.1	6.1	6.9	7.3	7.8	8.5	9.2
79	2.8	4.5	5.5	6.5	7.3	7.7	8.3	9.0	9.7
80	3.2	4.9	6.0	7.0	7.8	8.2	8.8	9.5	10.
81	3.8	5.5	6.5	7.5	8.3	8.7	9.3	10.	11.
82	4.4	6.0	7.1	8.1	8.9	9.3	9.9	10.	11.
83	5.1	6.7	7.7	8.7	9.5	9.9	10.	11.	11.
84	5.8	7.3	8.3	9.3	10.	10.	11.	11.	12.
85	6.5	8.0	9.0	10.	10.	11.	11.	12.	13.
86	7.3	8.7	9.7	10.	11.	11.	12.	13.	13.
87	8.1	9.5	10.	11.	12.	12.	13.	13.	14.
88	8.9	10.	11.	12.	12.	13.	13.	14.	15.
89	9.8	11.	11.	12.	13.	13.	14.	15.	15.
90	10.	11.	12.	13.	14.	14.	15.	15.	16.

COVERED OPTION
WRITING TABLE   Exercise Price is 90

Low Volatility

STOCK PRICE	NUMBER OF MONTHS BEFORE THE OPTIONS EXPIRE								
	1	2	3	4	5	6	7	8	9
80	0.1	0.2	0.4	0.6	0.8	0.9	1.0	1.2	1.4
81	0.1	0.2	0.4	0.7	0.9	1.0	1.1	1.3	1.5
82	0.1	0.3	0.5	0.8	1.0	1.1	1.2	1.4	1.7
83	0.2	0.4	0.6	0.9	1.1	1.3	1.4	1.6	1.8
84	0.2	0.5	0.7	1.0	1.3	1.4	1.5	1.8	2.0
85	0.2	0.6	0.9	1.2	1.5	1.6	1.7	2.0	2.3
86	0.3	0.7	1.0	1.4	1.7	1.9	2.0	2.3	2.6
87	0.4	0.9	1.3	1.7	2.0	2.2	2.3	2.6	2.9
88	0.6	1.1	1.6	2.0	2.3	2.5	2.6	2.9	3.2
89	0.9	1.5	1.9	2.4	2.7	2.9	3.0	3.3	3.6
90	1.3	1.9	2.3	2.8	3.1	3.3	3.5	3.8	4.1
91	1.9	2.5	2.9	3.4	3.7	3.9	4.0	4.3	4.6
92	2.6	3.1	3.6	4.0	4.3	4.5	4.6	4.9	5.2
93	3.4	3.9	4.3	4.7	5.0	5.1	5.3	5.6	5.9
94	4.2	4.7	5.0	5.4	5.7	5.8	6.0	6.3	6.6
95	5.1	5.5	5.8	6.2	6.4	6.6	6.7	7.0	7.3
96	6.0	6.4	6.6	7.0	7.2	7.4	7.5	7.7	8.0
97	7.0	7.2	7.5	7.8	8.0	8.2	8.3	8.5	8.8
98	8.0	8.2	8.4	8.7	8.9	9.0	9.1	9.3	9.6
99	9.0	9.1	9.3	9.5	9.7	9.8	10.	10.	10.

Average Volatility

STOCK PRICE	NUMBER OF MONTHS BEFORE THE OPTIONS EXPIRE								
	1	2	3	4	5	6	7	8	9
80	0.2	0.7	1.0	1.3	1.6	1.9	2.3	2.3	2.0
81	0.1	0.8	1.1	1.4	1.8	2.1	2.5	2.5	2.2
82	0.2	0.9	1.3	1.6	2.0	2.3	2.7	2.7	2.5
83	0.3	1.0	1.4	1.8	2.2	2.5	2.9	2.9	2.8
84	0.4	1.2	1.6	2.0	2.4	2.8	3.1	3.2	3.1
85	0.5	1.4	1.8	2.3	2.7	3.0	3.4	3.5	3.4
86	0.6	1.6	2.1	2.5	3.0	3.3	3.7	3.8	3.8
87	0.8	1.8	2.4	2.9	3.3	3.7	4.1	4.2	4.1
88	1.1	2.1	2.7	3.2	3.7	4.1	4.4	4.6	4.6
89	1.4	2.5	3.1	3.6	4.1	4.5	4.8	5.0	5.0
90	1.9	3.0	3.5	4.1	4.6	5.0	5.3	5.5	5.5
91	2.5	3.5	4.1	4.7	5.1	5.5	5.8	6.0	6.1
92	3.2	4.1	4.7	5.3	5.7	6.1	6.4	6.6	6.7
93	3.9	4.8	5.3	5.9	6.3	6.7	7.0	7.2	7.3
94	4.7	5.5	6.0	6.6	7.0	7.4	7.6	7.8	7.9
95	5.5	6.3	6.8	7.3	7.7	8.0	8.3	8.5	8.6
96	6.4	7.1	7.5	8.0	8.4	8.8	9.0	9.2	9.3
97	7.2	7.9	8.3	8.8	9.2	9.5	9.7	9.9	10.
98	8.2	8.7	9.1	9.6	9.9	10.	10.	10.	10.
99	9.1	9.6	9.9	10.	10.	11.	11.	11.	11.

High Volatility

STOCK PRICE	NUMBER OF MONTHS BEFORE THE OPTIONS EXPIRE								
	1	2	3	4	5	6	7	8	9
80	1.1	2.4	3.3	4.2	5.0	5.6	6.0	6.7	7.5
81	1.2	2.6	3.5	4.5	5.3	5.9	6.3	7.0	7.9
82	1.3	2.8	3.8	4.8	5.6	6.2	6.7	7.4	8.2
83	1.5	3.1	4.0	5.1	5.9	6.5	7.0	7.7	8.5
84	1.7	3.3	4.3	5.4	6.3	6.8	7.3	8.0	8.9
85	1.9	3.6	4.7	5.8	6.6	7.2	7.7	8.4	9.3
86	2.1	4.0	5.0	6.1	7.0	7.6	8.1	8.8	9.7
87	2.4	4.3	5.4	6.5	7.4	8.0	8.5	9.2	10.
88	2.8	4.7	5.8	6.9	7.8	8.4	8.9	9.7	10.
89	3.2	5.1	6.2	7.4	8.3	8.9	9.4	10.	11.
90	3.6	5.6	6.7	7.9	8.7	9.3	9.9	10.	11.
91	4.2	6.1	7.2	8.4	9.3	9.9	10.	11.	12.
92	4.8	6.7	7.8	9.0	9.8	10.	10.	11.	12.
93	5.4	7.3	8.4	9.6	10.	11.	11.	12.	13.
94	6.1	7.9	9.0	10.	11.	11.	12.	12.	13.
95	6.9	8.6	9.7	10.	11.	12.	12.	13.	14.
96	7.6	9.3	10.	11.	12.	12.	13.	14.	14.
97	8.4	10.	11.	12.	12.	13.	14.	14.	15.
98	9.2	10.	11.	12.	13.	14.	14.	15.	16.
99	10.	11.	12.	13.	14.	14.	15.	16.	16.

COVERED OPTION
WRITING TABLE Exercise Price is (100)

Low Volatility

STOCK PRICE — NUMBER OF MONTHS BEFORE THE OPTIONS EXPIRE

STOCK PRICE	1	2	3	4	5	6	7	8	9
90	0.2	0.3	0.5	0.8	1.0	1.1	1.3	1.4	1.6
91	0.1	0.3	0.6	0.9	1.1	1.2	1.4	1.5	1.8
92	0.1	0.4	0.7	1.0	1.2	1.4	1.5	1.7	2.0
93	0.2	0.5	0.8	1.1	1.4	1.5	1.7	1.9	2.2
94	0.2	0.6	0.9	1.3	1.5	1.7	1.9	2.1	2.4
95	0.3	0.7	1.1	1.5	1.7	1.9	2.1	2.3	2.7
96	0.4	0.9	1.3	1.7	2.0	2.2	2.4	2.6	3.0
97	0.5	1.1	1.5	2.0	2.3	2.5	2.7	2.9	3.3
98	0.7	1.4	1.8	2.3	2.6	2.8	3.0	3.3	3.7
99	1.0	1.7	2.2	2.7	3.0	3.2	3.4	3.7	4.1
100	1.4	2.2	2.6	3.1	3.5	3.7	3.9	4.2	4.5
101	2.0	2.7	3.2	3.7	4.0	4.2	4.5	4.7	5.1
102	2.7	3.4	3.8	4.3	4.6	4.8	5.0	5.3	5.7
103	3.5	4.1	4.5	5.0	5.3	5.5	5.7	5.9	6.3
104	4.3	4.9	5.2	5.7	6.0	6.2	6.4	6.6	7.0
105	5.2	5.7	6.0	6.4	6.7	6.9	7.1	7.3	7.7
106	6.1	6.5	6.8	7.2	7.5	7.7	7.8	8.1	8.4
107	7.0	7.4	7.7	8.0	8.3	8.4	8.6	8.8	9.2
108	8.0	8.3	8.5	8.9	9.1	9.3	9.4	9.6	9.9
109	9.0	9.2	9.4	9.7	9.9	10.	10.	10.	10.
110	10.	10.	10.	10.	10.	10.	11.	11.	11.

Average Volatility

STOCK PRICE — NUMBER OF MONTHS BEFORE THE OPTIONS EXPIRE

STOCK PRICE	1	2	3	4	5	6	7	8	9
90	0.3	0.8	1.3	1.8	2.1	2.3	2.5	2.9	3.4
91	0.4	0.9	1.4	2.0	2.3	2.5	2.7	3.2	3.6
92	0.4	1.0	1.6	2.1	2.5	2.7	3.0	3.4	3.9
93	0.5	1.2	1.8	2.3	2.7	2.9	3.2	3.7	4.2
94	0.6	1.3	2.0	2.6	3.0	3.2	3.5	3.9	4.5
95	0.8	1.5	2.2	2.8	3.3	3.5	3.8	4.3	4.8
96	0.9	1.8	2.5	3.1	3.6	3.8	4.1	4.6	5.1
97	1.1	2.1	2.8	3.5	3.9	4.2	4.5	5.0	5.5
98	1.4	2.4	3.1	3.8	4.3	4.5	4.9	5.4	5.9
99	1.7	2.8	3.5	4.3	4.7	5.0	5.3	5.8	6.3
100	2.2	3.2	4.0	4.7	5.2	5.5	5.8	6.3	6.8
101	2.8	3.8	4.5	5.3	5.7	6.0	6.3	6.8	7.4
102	3.4	4.4	5.1	5.8	6.3	6.6	6.9	7.4	7.9
103	4.1	5.1	5.8	6.5	6.9	7.2	7.5	8.0	8.5
104	4.9	5.8	6.5	7.1	7.6	7.8	8.1	8.6	9.1
105	5.7	6.5	7.2	7.8	8.2	8.5	8.8	9.3	9.8
106	6.5	7.3	7.9	8.5	8.9	9.2	9.5	10.	10.
107	7.4	8.1	8.7	9.3	9.7	9.9	10.	10.	11.
108	8.3	8.9	9.5	10.	10.	10.	10.	11.	11.
109	9.2	9.8	10.	10.	11.	11.	11.	12.	12.
110	10.	10.	11.	11.	12.	12.	12.	12.	13.

High Volatility

STOCK PRICE — NUMBER OF MONTHS BEFORE THE OPTIONS EXPIRE

STOCK PRICE	1	2	3	4	5	6	7	8	9
90	1.3	2.8	3.9	5.2	5.8	6.5	7.1	7.9	8.6
91	1.4	3.0	4.2	5.5	6.2	6.8	7.4	8.2	8.9
92	1.6	3.3	4.5	5.8	6.5	7.1	7.7	8.5	9.3
93	1.8	3.5	4.8	6.1	6.8	7.5	8.0	8.9	9.6
94	2.0	3.8	5.1	6.4	7.1	7.8	8.4	9.2	10.
95	2.2	4.1	5.4	6.8	7.5	8.2	8.7	9.6	10.
96	2.5	4.5	5.8	7.2	7.9	8.6	9.1	10.	10.
97	2.8	4.8	6.1	7.6	8.3	9.0	9.6	10.	11.
98	3.2	5.2	6.6	8.0	8.7	9.4	10.	10.	11.
99	3.6	5.6	7.0	8.5	9.2	9.9	10.	11.	12.
100	4.0	6.1	7.5	8.9	9.7	10.	10.	11.	12.
101	4.6	6.7	8.0	9.5	10.	10.	11.	12.	13.
102	5.2	7.2	8.6	10.	10.	11.	12.	12.	13.
103	5.8	7.8	9.2	10.	11.	12.	12.	13.	14.
104	6.5	8.5	9.8	11.	11.	12.	13.	14.	14.
105	7.2	9.1	10.	11.	12.	13.	13.	14.	15.
106	8.0	9.8	11.	12.	13.	13.	14.	15.	16.
107	8.7	10.	11.	13.	13.	14.	15.	15.	16.
108	9.5	11.	12.	13.	14.	15.	15.	16.	17.
109	10.	12.	13.	14.	15.	15.	16.	17.	18.
110	11.	12.	13.	15.	15.	16.	17.	17.	18.